1977	1979	1981	1983	1984	October 1985
.9018	.8946	.8702	1.1098	1.1395	1.4225
35.843	29.319	37.129	51.132	57.784	53.602
1.0635	1.1714	1.1989	1.2324	1.2951	1.3665
6.003	5.261	7.123	9.145	10.357	9.591
4.9136	4.2544	5.4346	7.6213	8.7391	8.0675
2.3222	1.8329	2.2600	2.5533	2.8459	2.6444
882.4	830.9	1136.8	1518.8	1757.0	1785.4
268.51	219.14	220.54	237.51	237.52	214.73
2.4543	2.0060	2.4952	2.8541	3.2087	2.9820
5.3235	5.0641	5.7395	7.2964	8.1615	7.9084
75.96	67.13	92.32	143.43	160.76	161.65
4.4816	4.2871	5.0634	7.6671	8.2718	7.9550
2.4035	1.6627	1.9642	2.0991	2.3497	2.1680
1.7455	2.1216	2.0279	1.5170	1.3363	1.4230
.28657	.27637	.27879	.29148	.29606	.29517
3.5251	3.3608	3.3826	3.4547	3.5219	3.6450
.00004	.00013	.00044	.01053	.06765	.80050
14.1	26.9	93.1	577.0	1848.0	8186.5
1.8578	1.5550	1.7045	1.9757	2.3200	3.0673
.39131	.7000	.7000	.7000	.7000	.7000
.00105	.00254	.01143	.05621	.29321	1.4789
22.57	22.81	24.51	120.09	167.83	313.36
2.4394	2.1746	2.1127	2.1131	2.1331	2.1371
.8696	.8420	.8776	1.1141	1.4753	2.5947

MULTINATIONAL BUSINESS FINANCE

FOURTH EDITION

MULTINATIONAL BUSINESS FINANCE

FOURTH EDITION

David K. Eiteman
University of California, Los Angeles

Arthur I. Stonehill
Oregon State University

With a contribution by
Donald R. Lessard
Massachusetts Institute of Technology

ADDISON-WESLEY PUBLISHING COMPANY
Reading, Massachusetts □ Menlo Park, California
Don Mills, Ontario □ Wokingham, England □ Amsterdam □ Sydney
Singapore □ Tokyo □ Madrid □ Bogotá □ Santiago □ San Juan

Sponsoring Editor: Steve Dane
Production Coordinator: Marcia Strykowski
Packager: Spencer Graphics and Editorial Services
Designer: Catherine Dorin
Manufacturing Supervisor: Hugh Crawford

This book is in the Addison-Wesley Series in International Finance

Library of Congress Cataloging-in-Publication Data

Eiteman, David K.
Multinational business finance.

Includes bibliographies and indexes.
1. International business enterprises—Finance.
I. Stonehill, Arthur I. II. Title.
HG4027.5.E36 1986 658.1'599 85-22915
ISBN 0-201-11436-4

Reprinted with corrections, November 1986

ISBN 0-201-11436-4
EFGHIJ-DO-898

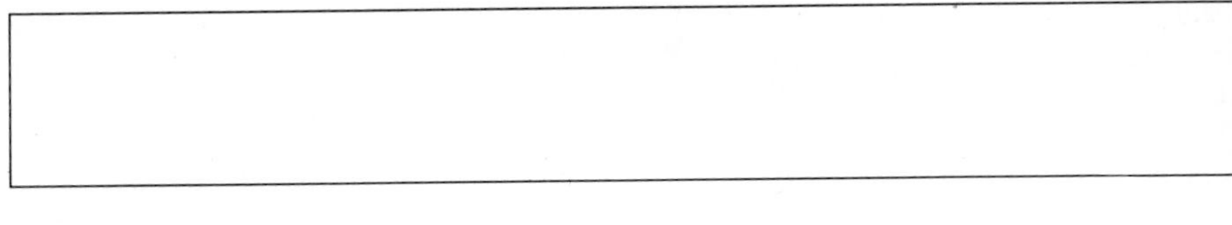

Preface

The unifying theme of this fourth edition of *Multinational Business Finance* is that financial managers of multinational firms must perceive and respond to imperfections in world product, factor, and financial markets. If these markets were at all times identical to domestic markets for the same products, factors, and financial instruments, multinational firms would have no particular reason to thrive, and the tasks of their financial managers would be indistinguishable from the tasks performed by domestic financial managers.

The unprecedented growth of multinational business activity in the past several decades came about in part because multinational firms successfully identified their comparative advantages in perceiving and reacting to the various market imperfections. *Multinational Business Finance* is concerned with developing the body of knowledge, attitudes, and skills needed by persons who are, or who will be, charged with making financial decisions for such global enterprises.

The existence of market imperfections means that many of the most important decisions in financial management of a multinational firm have no domestic counterpart but arise solely because products, factors of production, or financial resources and claims are transferred across national borders and from one economy or market to another. There is no counterpart in domestic business for the selling of securities denominated in one currency to raise funds for expenditure in another currency, for the need to protect the value of future cash flows from damage caused by unexpected exchange rate changes, or for many of the considerations that influence analysis of a firm's foreign investment decision, cost of capital, and financial structure.

The fourth edition of *Multinational Business Finance* is appropriate for the same audiences as the first three editions. Earlier editions have been widely used in international financial management courses at universities, company management development programs, and management institutes in the United States and abroad. A French edition, *La Gestion Financière des Enterprises Multinationales*, was published in Paris by the Club du Livre de Management, and two illegal pirate versions are available in Taiwan and Korea. (The latter presumably represent an imperfection in the world market for books!)

Readers will find *Multinational Business Finance* most meaningful if they have background knowledge or experience equivalent to a basic finance course using a text such as J. Fred Weston and Eugene F. Brigham's *Essentials of Managerial Finance* (Dryden Press) or James C. Van Horne's *Fundamentals of Financial Management* (Prentice-Hall). A previous course in international economics is desirable, but the text has been designed to cover sufficient economic material so that a separate background is not essential.

The fourth edition of *Multinational Business Finance* has been revised to incorporate theoretical and empirical research that has appeared in the past three years. Discussion of the international monetary system has been expanded and separated from the balance of payments and international debt problem. A revised chapter on the foreign exchange market now includes foreign currency options. Recent empirical work on exchange rate prediction has been added to the chapter on foreign exchange forecasting. Foreign exchange exposure continues to be treated both from the perspective of changes promulgated by the Financial Accounting Standards Board as Statement Number 52 and in terms of the economic or cash flow implications of exchange rate changes. Discussion of the direct foreign investment decision has been updated. New material has been added to the coverage of evaluation of performance. International banking has been heavily revised, especially with respect to country risk analysis. The accounting chapter has been revised to include international comparative ratio analysis. Obsolete material from the third edition has been deleted, and thus the overall size of the book has not increased.

The authors are grateful to the numerous professors who used earlier editions of this book and provided suggestions for changes. In particular, Lemma Senbet (University of Wisconsin) provided a valuable suggestion on reordering the chapters. Other valuable suggestions on specific topics were made by Alfred Hofflander (UCLA), Laura Smyth (Foreign Credit Insurance Association), Vinod Bavishi (University of Connecticut), Vihang Errunza (McGill University), Hany Shawky (State University of New York at Albany), Russell Taussig (University of Hawaii), Rita Maldanado-Baer (New York University), Robert Chia (National University of Singapore), James Baker (Kent State University), David Babbel (University of California, Berkeley), Alan Rugman (Dalhousie University), and Harald Vestergaard

(Copenhagen School of Economics and Business Administration). Kåre Dullum (Novo Industri A/S) made a particularly valuable contribution to the expanded treatment of segmented capital markets and cost of capital.

The authors continue to be greatly indebted to the reviewers and contributors to the earlier editions, which naturally still form the basis of the fourth edition. We are especially thankful to the three principal reviewers of the second edition: Gunter Dufey of the University of Michigan, Donald Lessard of MIT, and Alan Shapiro of the University of Southern California. In addition, a significant contribution was made by Frederick Choi of New York University. The authors would also like to recognize valuable inputs from David Bates (Omark Industries), Michael Brooke (University of Manchester, England), Robert Carlson (Wake Forest University), Payson Cha (The Cha Group, Hong Kong), Chi Ming Cha (The Cha Group, Hong Kong), Robert Cornu (Cranfield School of Management, England), Steven Dawson (University of Hawaii), Claudio de la Fuente (Security Pacific National Bank), William R. Folks, Jr. (University of South Carolina), Lewis Freitas (University of Hawaii), Ian Giddy (New York University), David Heenan (Theo Davies), David N. Hepburn, Jr. (Wells Fargo Bank), Willem Winter (First Interstate Bank of Oregon), Kenneth Knox (Tektronix, Inc.), Lee Remmers (INSEAD, France), R. J. Rummel (University of Hawaii), John Scott (Hyster Company), Norman Toy (Columbia University), and Richard Wright (McGill University).

Inevitably woven into the fabric of the book are ideas received from faculty colleagues and students at institutions where the authors have taught, including the University of California (Berkeley and Los Angeles campuses), Cranfield School of Management (England), University of Hawaii, North European Management Institute (Norway), the Copenhagen School of Economics and Business Administration (Denmark), National University of Singapore, and Oregon State University. Further ideas came from consulting assignments in Argentina, Belgium, Canada, Hong Kong, Indonesia, Japan, Malaysia, Mexico, the Netherlands, Norway, Taiwan, the United Kingdom, and Venezuela.

Finally, we would like to rededicate this book to our parents, the late Wilford Eiteman, Sylvia Eiteman, and Harold and Norma Stonehill, who gave us the motivation to become academicians and authors. We thank our immediate families, Kari, Inger, Marcia, and Naomi, for their patience through the years spent preparing the four editions of this book. Keng-Fong Pang, Carol Spencer, and Eva Hofenbredl deserve special thanks for their excellent help in producing the final manuscript.

Pacific Palisades, California D. K. E.
Corvallis, Oregon A. I. S.

Contents

PART I
The Multinational Corporation and Its International Environment

PART III
Long-Run Investment Decisions

8
The Foreign Investment Decision 245

9
Political Risk Management 288

10
Multinational Capital Budgeting 330

PART V
Working Capital Management and Control

15
Working Capital Management 549

16
Performance Evaluation and Control 595

17
Comparative Accounting and Financial Statement Analysis 621

MULTINATIONAL BUSINESS FINANCE

FOURTH EDITION

PART I

The Multinational Corporation and Its International Environment

1

The Multinational Firm: Its Rationale, Goals, and Constraints

For several centuries economists have used the classical economic theory of comparative advantage to explain trade movements between nations. Springing from the writings of Adam Smith and David Ricardo in the eighteenth and nineteenth centuries, the theory in simple terms states that everyone gains if each nation specializes in the production of those goods that it produces *relatively* most efficiently and imports those goods that other countries produce *relatively* most efficiently. The theory has supported free-trade arguments.

The doctrine of comparative advantage made an initial assumption that although the products of economic activity could move internationally, the factors of production were relatively fixed in a geographic sense. Land, labor, and capital were assumed to be internationally immobile. Although the early economists did not use the expression, by implication other such factors as managerial skills and research and development abilities were assumed to be largely attributes of particular nations.

The post–World War II wave of direct foreign investment and the growth of multinational business enterprises is perhaps the major phenomenon of the last half of the twentieth century. This development, which holds such potential for the economic betterment of the world's population, runs counter to the postulates of Smith and Ricardo in that it is based on international mobility of the most important factors of production in the twentieth century. Capital raised in London in the Eurodollar market by a Belgium-based corporation may finance the acquisition of machinery by a subsidiary located in Australia. A management team from French Renault may take over a U.S.-built automotive complex in the Argentine. Clothing for dolls, sewn in Korea on Japanese-supplied sewing machines according to U.S. specifications, may be shipped to northern

Mexico for assembly with other components into dolls being manufactured by a U.S. firm for sale in New York and London during the Christmas season. A California-manufactured air bus, the Lockheed L-1011, is powered by British Rolls-Royce engines, while a competing air bus, the Douglas DC-10, flies on Canadian wing assemblies. A Hong Kong bank originally developed with British management and capital buys control of a major upstate New York banking chain, which in turn finances the construction in Korea of ships intended for the Greek merchant marine.

RATIONALE FOR THE EXISTENCE OF MULTINATIONAL FIRMS

The theme repeated throughout this book is that the multinational firm has a strong economic and business rationale. From an economic perspective host countries welcome multinational firms because they are viewed as agents of technology transfer and host country economic development. From a business perspective multinational firms are eager for opportunities to invest in geographic locations where they can earn a rate of return high enough to compensate them for the perceived level of risk. National and international market imperfections provide these opportunities.

Although a strong economic and business rationale exists for the success of multinational firms, they must live within host country economic, political, social, and religious constraints imposed on the free implementation of their goals. Thus, maximizing the value of the multinational firms for the benefit of their stockholders, or even for the benefit of some other interest group, may conflict with the rights of national sovereignty, which nearly always override the rights of individual firms, multinational or domestic.

Rate of Return

Multinational firms strive to take advantage of imperfections in national markets for products, factors of production, and financial assets. Imperfections in the market for products translate into market opportunities for multinational firms. Large international firms are better able to exploit such competitive factors as economies of scale, managerial and technological expertise, product differentiation, and financial strength than are their local competitors. In fact, multinational firms thrive best in markets characterized by international oligopolistic competition where these factors are particularly critical. In addition, once multinational firms have established a physical presence abroad, they are in a better position than purely domestic firms to identify and implement market opportunities through their own internal information network.

Multinational firms are also well positioned to identify and exploit imperfections in the market for factors of production. For example, their own internal information network can identify countries in which labor is inexpensive relative to its productivity, because multinational firms possess comparative, realized manufacturing costs from their own affiliates. Domestic firms typically are unaware of specific opportunities to reduce costs by manufacturing in foreign locations. Once aware of this factor, though, they still must rely on costly, ad hoc field studies starting from a low base of market knowledge. Multinationals are also able to develop and utilize those raw material sources that host country firms cannot develop because of a lack of technological or managerial expertise, economies of scale, or sufficient financial strength.

In some cases the common stock of multinational firms may serve as a vehicle for investors who wish to hold internationally diversified portfolios but are prevented from achieving diversification because of perceived and real imperfections in the market for financial assets. For example, international portfolio investors can be frustrated by foreign exchange controls, withholding taxes on dividends, capital market controls, lack of full disclosure, and lack of knowledge about foreign securities markets. The multinational firms' common stock may be perceived as a convenient proxy for international diversification without the headaches involved in dealing with foreign securities markets.

Risk

Multinational firms are particularly well suited to the task of managing risk from the perspectives of all interest groups. Geographical and currency diversification allow multinational firms to minimize fluctuations in returns due to business cycles, to maintain or improve their competitive positions in the face of foreign exchange rate changes, to reduce the impact of political interference, to diversify the risk of technological obsolescence, and to minimize their cost of capital.

Geographical diversification of operations permits multinational firms to reduce fluctuations in their earnings, cash flow, and perhaps stock market value. Their financial performances are a weighted average of results from markets that are seldom perfectly correlated with each other. The lower the correlation, the better the chance for reducing bankruptcy risk and the more valuable the firms might be in a portfolio theory context if securities market imperfections exist.

Unexpected changes in foreign exchange rates can create disequilibria, which, if properly understood by firms, can lead to opportunities for increased profit. For example, a country that undervalues its currency creates a foreign exchange risk for those firms that export to that country. However, the same undervaluation creates an opportunity to increase operating profits on exports from that country, an opportunity that would be beneficial to multinational or host country firms with a manufacturing base in that country. In effect, geographical diversification by multinational firms reduces the chance that their financial performance will be overly dependent on the exchange rate policy of any single country, or that their real asset values will erode because of hyperinflation in any one country.

The risk of political interference cannot be avoided, but geographical diversification can minimize the damage caused by any single country. It also increases the bargaining power of multinational firms when they attempt to prevent interference, or, failing that, it allows them to make the best deal possible to salvage some residual benefits from a previous investment. Although purely domestic firms are not subject to political risk abroad, they are not immune to political interference and even expropriation at home. In that sense multinational firms have the advantage of being potentially stateless. Expropriation of "parent" firms may not mean the end of the multinationals as entities, because management can be relocated and continue to run surviving affiliates.

High-technology industries can remain internationally competitive only if they have continuous access to the latest research and development. Such activities are often concentrated geographically in a few centers of excellence. For example, to be at the frontier of knowledge in the electronics industry, a firm should, ideally, maintain a physical presence or strong contacts with the centers of excellence that have developed in the United States in the "Silicon Valley" south of San Francisco or in similar areas near Boston and Dallas–Fort Worth. Additional centers of excellence exist in Japan, the United Kingdom, France, the Netherlands, Sweden, and West Germany. Although one cannot predict which center of excellence or which researcher will produce the next exciting breakthrough, a firm that has diversified internationally by locating in each of these centers has a high probability of maintaining a competitive technological position in the electronics industry.

Financing risk can be considerably reduced for multinationals in comparison to domestic firms. Multinationals have access to both international and national debt and equity markets. Other things being equal, this added availability of capital reduces their cost of capital in comparison to firms that are restricted to raising funds from only one capital market. In addition, when foreign exchange markets are in disequilibrium, multinational firms have the option to finance in different currencies, some of which may offer temporarily lower required rates of return than would be justified by expected changes in exchange rates.

ORGANIZATION OF THE BOOK

In the remainder of this chapter we will examine the potential conflict between the goals of multinational firms and those of host countries. In Chapter 2 we describe the international monetary system's historical development, institutions, and current problems. Chapter 3 explains the balance of payments mechanism and international debt problems of less developed countries. Chapter 4 describes how the foreign exchange market functions.

Part II returns to the theme of the book, introduced above. The economic and business rationale for the existence of multinational firms is spotlighted in a foreign exchange risk context. Chapter 5 analyzes the variables which cause exchange rates to change. Chapter 6 covers the managerial problem of measuring what is exposed to foreign exchange rate risk. Chapter 7 shows how multinational firms can respond to foreign exchange exposure in such a way as to improve their long-run risk/return performance.

Part III expands on the theme still further. Chapter 8 examines the various economic theories that support the assertion that market imperfections create opportunities for the existence of multinational firms. Chapter 9 examines in more detail the nature of political risk constraints on the multinational firm. Chapter 10 shows how multinational firms can analyze a specific project opportunity by using a modified version of the traditional capital budgeting framework.

Part IV enlarges the theme to financing decisions. Chapter 11 presents background material on international capital markets. Chapter 12 shows how the multinational firm is best positioned to minimize its long-term worldwide cost of capital. Chapter 13 illustrates the opportunities available to multinationals for minimizing the cost of short- and intermediate-term financing through the international banking system. The peculiar problems of international banks themselves are analyzed here, because these banks are also multinational in scope and conception. Chapter 14 covers traditional export and import financing.

Part V covers working capital management and control. Working capital management is the subject of Chapter 15. Chapter 16 discusses problems of organizing the international finance function and evaluating performance. Chapter 17 examines comparative accounting and financial statement analysis. Chapter 18 describes tax planning.

FINANCIAL GOALS IN THEORY

In choosing financial goals and making the policy decisions necessary to implement those goals, financial executives of multinational firms must recognize the institutional, cultural, and political differences among host countries, which bring about different national perceptions of the "proper" goals of a business entity. Foreign affiliates operated to maximize the market value of the parent firm's common stock, the approach advocated by contemporary finance theory, often find themselves in conflict with host country aspirations and local business operating norms. Differing viewpoints on financial goals can even lead to friction within a multinational firm if local managers are citizens of the host country. Such managers are often experienced only in local business standards. Additionally they will have, quite naturally and correctly, a degree of loyalty to host country aspirations. The suitability of merger or joint-venture partners across national borders depends partly on how the importance of market value is perceived by the potential partners. Other corporate goals may be preferred by a firm located in a country where equity markets are very imperfect and market value nearly impossible to determine, and where society does not appropriately value the contribution of the stockholder.

The majority of finance theorists throughout the world today profess that a firm's financial goal should be to maximize the wealth of its stockholders. This goal first emerged in finance literature in the United States and the United Kingdom in the late 1950s and has been widely adopted by theorists and finance textbooks in other countries. Whether or not a goal of maximizing stockholder wealth should form the sole basis for a normative universal theory of finance is debatable. In this section the evolution of financial goals in the literature is described. The following section surveys practice in five countries and reveals that the stockholder wealth goal is not often used in practice outside the United States because of numerous institutional, cultural, and political differences. In the next section a variety of public policy constraints are analyzed because they too impact a firm's choice of financial goals and policies. In the last section a compromise set of goals is suggested for use by multinational firms.

Profit Maximization

Prior to World War I the field of finance was considered a subset of economics and law. Financial reporting requirements were primitive, and security markets were essentially unregulated. Finance literature was mainly concerned with describing financial instruments and markets and with the legal claims of various investors. Little attention was paid to the way in which a firm might improve its financing or investment decisions. The proper financial goal of the firm was assumed to be profit maximization, in accordance with the classical economic theories of Adam Smith, David Ricardo, and Alfred Marshall. Profit was not well defined but was accepted to mean long-run net profit.

During the stock market boom of the 1920s finance literature focused on techniques for raising capital, on how security values seemed to be determined, and on the advantages of leverage. The stock market crash and corporate bankruptcies of the 1930s led finance texts to concentrate on the dangers of too much leverage and illiquidity. Throughout the interwar period, however, the main emphasis continued to be on how financial instruments were used, how financial markets functioned, and how creditors and stockholders could protect themselves from the dangers of mismanagement, fraud, and depressed economic times. Decision making within the firm was largely unexplored, and profit maximization continued to be the assumed goal for business.

Net Present Value Maximization

During the post–World War II era finance theory gradually became concerned with efficient allocation of capital within the firm and the role of the firm in an efficient capital market context. Joel Dean's 1951 book on capital budgeting launched a flood of articles, books, and management seminars on the need to allocate the firm's financial resources to individual assets on the basis of the expected net present value of their cash flows.[1] Net present value was determined by discounting expected future cash flows by the firm's weighted average cost of capital. It followed that if a firm maximized the sum of the net present values of all individual investment projects, given its finance structure, the firm would maximize net earnings after taxes over the long run. In the short run, of course, net earnings would not necessarily be maximized because the benefits of long-run investments would not flow through the accounting statements until later. The operational goal of maximizing net present value was considered superior to simple net earnings maximization because it took into account the time value of money.

Minimizing the Cost of Capital

Later during the 1950s theoretical attention also began to focus on the financing decision. Whereas capital budgeting helps a firm allocate its funds in the most efficient way, thus maximizing operating earnings, the financing decision determines how operating earnings will be divided among creditors, stockholders, and the income tax collector. Furthermore, capital budgeting itself requires the measurement of a firm's weighted average cost of capital. Thus the investment decision and the financing decision are interdependent. Durand and others initiated the work of measuring the cost of capital with the objective of finding a firm's optimal financial structure, defined as a mix of capital sources that minimizes the firm's weighted average cost of capital.[2] If cost of capital were minimized, the total value of the firm's securities would be maximized, by definition. Thus maximizing the value of a firm's securities became the "proper" financial objective as a result of the need to minimize the cost of capital for capital budgeting purposes.

Stockholder Wealth Maximization

If the market value of a firm's securities is to be maximized, a model must be constructed that can explain how value is determined. From the 1950s to the present time numerous attempts have been made to explain market value. The market value of bonds and preferred stock can easily be explained on the basis of the discounted present value of relatively certain future cash flows. The problem of common stock valuation has been more difficult to solve.

The famous Modigliani and Miller article of 1958 initiated a long debate about whether financial structure has any effect on common stock price.[3] The main argument in support of their position that structure has no effect is that the benefits of relatively cheap debt are offset by the negative effect of increased financial risk on the common stock price. Perhaps of equal importance, Modigliani and Miller focused attention more specifically on the role of risk in determining the market value of common stock. They offered strong theoretical support to those who felt that maximizing the market value of a firm's common stock should indeed be the prime goal of financial management, rather than a secondary goal dominated by the net present value maximization goal of capital budgeting. The main advantage for the market value goal is that it takes into account all present and potential investors' perceptions of the amount and timing of a firm's earnings per share and dividends, as well as the risk characteristics of the firm itself. It should be noted that maximizing the values of debt and preferred securities is dropped from this model's maximization goal.

Since one of the keys to market value of common stock is its perceived risk, the next theoretical step was to define and introduce various measures of risk into valuation models. Initially risk was broken into two categories, business risk and financial risk. Business risk was defined as the fluctuation in operating earnings caused by economic conditions and the firm's managerial skill, regardless of how the firm was financed. Financial risk was defined as the fluctuations in earnings per share caused by the manner in which the firm was financed, i.e., by the degree of financial leverage, given the level of operating earnings.

Portfolio Theory and the Capital Asset Pricing Model

Starting with the theoretical work of Markowitz on portfolio theory in 1959, an additional dimension of risk was incorporated into valuation models.[4] Sharpe and others used the Markowitz framework for constructing the modern capital asset pricing model (CAPM).[5] Instead of concentrating on business and financial risk of a firm in isolation, the CAPM model attempts to explain how security prices would be determined in a world of risk-averse investors and efficient capital markets.

In the CAPM model individual investors are assumed to have varying preferences with respect to the risk/return trade-off, but collectively the risk/return trade-off can be represented by a capital market line. Given the capital market line and a risk-free asset, such as U.S. Treasury bills, an investor can construct a portfolio that maximizes return for a given level of risk, or minimizes risk for a given level of return. Risk is defined as the variance or standard deviation of returns on the investor's portfolio. Investor returns are defined as the sum of capital gains and dividends on a portfolio held for a specified time period.

The optimal portfolio for an investor consists of some combination of the risk-free security (or loans) and the so-called "market portfolio" of risky securities. By diversification, an efficient portfolio can eliminate "unsystematic risk," which is the variance in returns on individual securities unrelated to the securities market. "Systematic risk," the variance in returns common to the economy and thus reflected in overall security market fluctuations, cannot be eliminated. In this model the price of an individual security is a function of the risk-free rate plus a risk premium determined by the degree to which the security's return covaries with the return on the market portfolio. Securities that have returns less than perfectly correlated with the market portfolio have lower risk premiums because they do not add as much variance to an investor's portfolio as securities that are perfectly correlated with the market portfolio. Under the CAPM a firm should consider the impact of its investment, financing, and dividend decisions on its risk in a market portfolio context.

Arbitrage Pricing Theory

Arbitrage pricing theory (APT), first proposed by Ross in 1976, is the newest attempt by financial economists to construct a model which can explain security and asset prices.[6] The APT, like the CAPM, is simple enough conceptually that it might soon become operational. The APT attempts to explain security prices as a function of several underlying macroeconomic variables rather than the CAPM's single variable, i.e., the degree of covariance with a stock market index.

Empirical tests of the APT and comparisons of its predictions with those of the CAPM are promising, but the APT has not yet supplanted the CAPM in finance textbooks or in practice.[7] Tests of the APT show that security prices are sensitive to unexpected changes in such macroeconomic variables as the level of industrial production, the term structure of interest rates, inflation rates, and the difference between returns on low-rated and high-rated bonds.[8] Several other variables have explanatory values according to some of the tests so there is not yet complete agreement on the exact specifications of an operational APT model that could be used in industry.

Satisficing and Goal Conflict

Organization theorists have long questioned the validity of the economic model of the firm and, more recently, the stockholder wealth maximization model. Cyert and March are among those who have constructed a behavioral theory of the firm that questions whether either profit maximization or stockholder wealth maximization gives an accurate description of a firm's goal.[9] Instead organization theorists picture the firm as a coalition of interest groups, each of which strives to maximize its own return from the firm. The result is an uneasy bargaining situation, with each group forced to "satisfice" its goals in order for the firm to remain viable. The stockholders are a strong interest group, but there is no prediction that their goals will necessarily dominate the coalition.

Some financial theorists, such as Anthony and Donaldson, observed in the early 1960s that there was an inherent conflict between managerial and stockholder goals. They suggested that many firms behave as if they were maximizing managerial wealth and minimizing managerial risk rather than maximizing stockholder wealth.[10] A more recent study by Findlay and Whitmore observed that firms do not formulate their main financial decisions, such as capital budgeting, capital structure, or dividend decisions, in accordance with what would be optimal if stockholder wealth maximization were the goal.[11] On the contrary, their study suggests a goal of reduction of risk for the managers themselves.

Corporate Wealth Maximization

Donaldson and Lorsch have recently published a convincing empirical study of deviation from stockholder wealth maximization.[12] Their observations are consistent with the behavioral theory of the firm. They introduce a theory of "corporate wealth maximization" to explain the way managers choose a firm's overall mission, strategy, and financial goals. Their ten-year study of large, mature, U.S. industrial firms suggests that goal setting is done by top management, which identifies the corporate mission and designs a five-year strategic plan. This plan contains specific goals related not only to financial management but also to product policy, market share, and other nonfinancial variables.

Management's goal setting is constrained by the need to satisfy various important constituencies such as "the capital market of lenders and shareholders; the product market, which includes suppliers and host communities as well as customers; the organization itself, with particular emphasis on the managerial, technical, and supervisory personnel who are the key career employees; and society or the public at large."[13]

Management's choice of specific goals is strongly motivated by a desire for organizational survival. Other important motives are the need for managerial independence, organizational self-sufficiency, and managerial self-fulfillment. A key element for achieving these goals is to eliminate dependence on external capital markets, which are regarded by management as fickle and undependable. Thus management appears to be distancing itself as much as possible from reliance on stockholders or creditors, rather than managing on their behalf.

A goal of corporate wealth maximization may be consistent with economic rationality even if it deviates from accepted finance theory. After all, it is management and the other nonstockholder interest groups that suffer the consequences if a firm's earnings or cash flow are highly variable, particularly if this causes strained relations with creditors and suppliers or even the threat of bankruptcy. It does no good for management to explain that part of total risk (standard deviation of market returns, earnings, or cash flow) can be diversified away by stockholders in their efficient portfolios and that only systematic risk (correlation with the market as a whole) is worth worrying about. The risk to management, employees, suppliers, creditors, and all other nonstockholder interest groups varies directly with the riskiness of earnings and especially cash flow. It is highly unlikely that management will be fired if its choice of investment projects maintains a modest level of earnings and cash flow even if these returns are perfectly positively correlated with the relevant stock market index. On the other hand, if management makes some "defensive" investments that are perfectly negatively correlated with the relevant stock market index, thus reducing systematic risk, it can easily be fired if earnings or cash flow become negative occasionally.

Agency Theory

Agency theory is the most recent attempt by finance theorists to recognize organizational impediments to stockholder wealth maximization.[14] In this theory stockholders are regarded as principals and management as their agents. The objective is to create a contract that will motivate and bind the agents (management) to perform according to the interests of the principals (stockholders), while minimizing the cost of the agency relationship. Agency costs include the costs of structuring the contract, as well as administering and enforcing its terms. Included are the costs of monitoring management's activities and of "bonding." Bonding costs are incurred by management to guarantee that they will not act against the stockholders' interests. In addition, if the agency relationship is not optimally structured or enforced, a residual opportunity cost loss will also be incurred.[15]

Management compensation contracts can be structured to reduce agency costs while guaranteeing that the stockholders' interests are paramount. For example, if a large part of management's compensation comes from stock options, they will probably behave in the interests of stockholders without excessive monitoring or bonding costs. Even "golden parachute contracts," which are very favorable severance contracts, may be justified on the grounds that management should be more willing to pursue and accept proposals for acquisition of their firms. Stockholders of acquired firms generally benefit from acquisition, while management personnel lose their jobs. However, the golden parachute assures management that their income will continue for a long time, and they may also receive an immediate cash benefit or other increment to their personal wealth.[16]

Agency theory has been extended to include analysis of the natural conflict between creditors, particularly bondholders, and stockholders. Some actions taken by stockholders could come at the expense of bondholders while increasing the stockholders' wealth. For example, dividend payouts could be unexpectedly increased; additional debts senior to existing bonds could be created; higher risk projects could be undertaken; or lower-risk projects could be rejected even if net present values are positive. Bond covenants restricting dividend payouts, sale of assets, dilution, or other decisions that increase bondholder risk are contractual means of reducing agency costs.

In summary, agency theory is the best attempt yet by finance theorists to recognize goal conflicts as originally observed by organizational theorists. At this point in time, however, agency theory still has not been extended to include interest groups other than stockholders, management, and creditors, even though this is conceptually feasible. Until this extension takes place a considerable gap will exist between the way finance theory views stockholder wealth maximization and the way organization theory views it. In the next section we will observe how managers in five countries view the proper choice of financial goals for a firm.

FINANCIAL GOALS IN PRACTICE IN AN INTERNATIONAL PERSPECTIVE

Choice between stockholder wealth maximization and other goals of financial management is a value judgment that differs among managers in different countries. To shed some light on differing national attitudes toward corporate financial goals and toward capital structures, an international consortium of finance academicians and practitioners undertook a survey of financial executives of manufacturing firms in five industrial countries.[17] Financial executives from 87 firms in four selected industries in France, Japan, the Netherlands, Norway, and the United States were interviewed and asked to rank selected financial goals in order of importance to their firms. Results of this survey follow.

Exhibit 1.1 shows the financial goals survey question and weighted responses. The financial executives showed a clear preference for an accounting-oriented financial goal of maximizing growth in corporate earnings (6), either of total earnings (France, Japan, and the Netherlands), of earnings before interest and taxes (Norway), or per share earnings (United States).

The next two most important goals were maximizing return on equity (9) and guaranteeing that funds are always available when needed (2). The choice of return on equity is further evidence of the accounting orientation toward rate of return held by many financial executives. The importance of guaranteeing funds availability is evidence of a strong concern for cash flow, especially by non-U.S. financial executives.

Financial goals oriented toward maximizing stockholder wealth (1, 4, 7) drew only minimal support. Even in the United States financial executives overwhelmingly picked maximizing growth in earnings per share in preference to maximizing market value of common stock. Finance theorists believe this choice might be an indirect way of maximizing stockholder wealth, given the widespread belief by business executives that market value of common stock depends primarily on expected future earnings and dividends.

More important than the quantitative results of the survey are the institutional, cultural, and political reasons that motivated the executives' choices.

France

French financial executives selected growth in aftertax earnings (6) because they believed that this objective was the best measure of overall managerial success. In France, Japan, the Netherlands, and Norway the concept of "per share" is not normally used. Growth in aftertax earnings per share was interpreted to mean growth in aftertax earnings (not per share) during the interviews. They also chose a goal of guaranteeing that funds are available (2), because this feature was perceived as their own main contribution to success of the firm. Most respondents were concerned about the lack of rationality of common stock prices on the Paris Bourse (Stock Exchange) and the lack of company control over stock prices. The French executives also felt that they must not overtly favor stockholder goals in a country where 40% of the electorate votes in a "socialistic" way and does not particularly favor maintenance of the private enterprise system in its present form. Thus French financial executives often prudently limited dividends in favor of maintaining strategic liquid reserves, and they generally favored financial goals that guaranteed the growth and safety of the firm itself rather than maximizing stockholder wealth through stock price appreciation (4).

Japan

Japanese financial executives also chose growth in aftertax earnings (6) as the most important financial goal, and they ranked highly other goals that guaranteed the growth and safety of the firm itself. Goals oriented toward market value of common stock (4) received scant support because of certain institutional characteristics of the Japanese capital market and the role of the Japanese stockholder.

The Japanese capital market has not been the liquid and responsive capital market envisioned in finance theory until recent years. World War II left no accumulated financial savings. The Japanese commercial banking system, supported strongly by the Central Bank, provided most of the necessary capital to fuel Japan's spectacular postwar recovery. Equity and long-term debt markets provided a relatively small share of the capital needed. As a result, until the 1980s equity markets were thin and unresponsive. Until 1970 new issues of common stock were typically sold at par value on a preemptive basis well below market value. Dividends were usually

EXHIBIT 1.1
Financial Goals Survey
Mean of rankings of financial goals by executives from 87 manufacturing firms in five countries
Most important = 5. Least important = 0.

	1	*2*	*3*	*4*	*5*
	Maximize share price appreciation plus dividend	*Guaranteed availability of capital*	*Maximize book value*	*Maximize market value of shares*	*Maximize liquidation value*
Mean Ranking					
France	3.88	4.25	.38	2.63	.38
Japan	.10	1.90	1.10	.10	0
Netherlands	0	2.62	.92	1.62	.23
Norway	2.12	3.58	1.88	0	.19
U.S.A.	2.40	1.95	1.65	2.50	.35
Total sample size					
Standard Deviation					
France	.93	.97	.99	1.73	.99
Japan	.44	2.21	1.76	.44	0
Netherlands	0	2.24	1.54	2.06	.42
Norway	1.85	1.80	1.65	0	.96
U.S.A.	2.08	1.86	1.96	2.36	1.11

Source: Arthur Stonehill, Theo Beekhuisen, Richard Wright, Lee Remmers, Norman Toy, Antonio Parés, Alan Shapiro, Douglas Egan, and Thomas Bates, "Financial Goals and Debt Ratio Determinants: A Survey of Practice in Five Countries," *Financial Management,* Autumn 1975, pp. 27–41.

Note: Financial executives from 87 manufacturing firms in five countries were asked to rank a given set of 12 financial objectives for their firms. The weighting system was as follows: choice 1–2 = 5 points; choice 3–4 = 4

fixed in terms of par value and did not vary with company performance. Some flexibility in dividend payout was achieved through the issue of new shares to existing stockholders at prices below market value but with the same dividend per share on all shares, new and old. In recent years new common stock issues have been sold at market value. Generally speaking, however, Japanese financial executives consider stock issues to be fixed dividend obligations that are invariably much more expensive than debt. As a result, most Japanese corporations maintain as high a·debt ratio (65–80% debt) as possible.

The majority of Japanese common stock is not held by the portfolio investor of finance theory but rather by a family of closely related companies and financial institutions. This stems from the pre–World War II *Zaibatsu* tradition. The motive for holding common stock is not primarily for portfolio returns but rather for recognizing and strengthening existing cred-

6 Maximize growth of earnings per share	*7* Maximize price/ earnings ratio	*8* Maximize earnings before interest and taxes	*9* Maximize return on investment (net income divided by net worth)	*10* Maximize return on sales (net income divided by sales)	*11* Maximize cash flow per share	*12* Other	Sample size
4.63	3.13	3.25	2.25	3.63	2.63	.38	8
2.95	0	.95	1.90	2.10	.55	1.00	20
3.92	1.92	1.46	2.69	1.69	2.00	1.00	13
1.81	1.42	3.42	3.73	2.77	1.85	.54	26
4.35	2.00	1.85	2.60	2.20	1.45	1.15	20
							87
.70	.93	.97	.66	1.58	1.11	.99	
2.06	0	1.53	1.87	1.89	1.02	1.90	
1.77	2.06	1.99	2.23	2.01	2.08	1.88	
1.52	1.52	2.02	1.74	2.83	1.81	1.39	
1.24	1.76	1.85	1.85	2.04	1.43	2.03	

points; choice 5–6 = 3 points; choice 7–8 = 2 points, choice 9–10 = 1 point; blanks = 0 points. No respondent ranked more than 10 of the 12 objectives, so there were always some blanks. The best possible score would be 5 and the worst 0. The score is the mean for all firms in the country. The standard deviations are shown below the scores.

itor, supplier, or customer relationships. The expected benefits come from these operating business relationships rather than from dividends or common stock price appreciation. In fact, since these business relationships are seen as permanent, the stockholders do not expect to sell their shares within their managerial time horizon. Furthermore, even a partial sale of common stock would be considered a loss of confidence in the firm whose shares were sold, thus hurting good business relationships.

Close stockholder relationships also reduce the perceived risk to the common stockholder of the high degree of financial leverage employed. The commercial banks are very loyal to their corporate customers, often permitting them to make fixed dividend payments at the same time as they postpone loan repayments. The loyalty of commercial banks is enhanced by the willingness of the Central Bank to stand by the commercial banks during a liquidity crisis.

It should be noted that there are some exceptions. A few major Japanese firms, such as Sony Corporation and Toyota Motors, do not belong to any family group. They operate independently and look to international capital markets for some of their long-term financing. As a result, they maintain debt ratios and financial goals that are acceptable to the foreign lenders. They are also somewhat stockholder-oriented because their stock is held by a mix of institutional, individual, and foreign investors who have no other business relationships with the firms but are investing solely for capital gains and dividends.

In summary, fixed dividend policy and loyalty of bankers considerably reduce investors' risk of holding most common stock in Japan. Despite the high degree of leverage the Japanese common stockholder plays a role more closely akin to the preferred stockholder in the United States than to the risk-taking common stockholder visualized in finance theory.

The Netherlands

Like their counterparts in France and Japan, Dutch financial executives favored a financial goal of growth in aftertax earnings (6). The next most important goals were maximizing return on equity (9) and guaranteeing the availability of funds (2). Maximizing market value of common stock (4) received almost no support as an important goal. On the contrary, once again all three preferred goals referred to internal measures of success.

Norway

Norwegian financial executives showed almost equal preference for three goals: maximizing return on equity (9); guaranteeing that funds are available (2); and maximizing earnings before interest and taxes (8). Maximizing market value of common stock (4) was unimportant. Once again it is necessary to examine certain institutional, cultural, and political variables to understand the Norwegian choices.

The tax system does not particularly favor a goal of maintaining a high price for common stock on the Oslo Bourse (Stock Exchange). Many Norwegians believe that everybody should have almost equal rewards from the economic system. As a result, personal income taxes are steeply progressive, and a wealth tax of 2 to 3% is imposed on all personal assets, including common stock holdings at market value. The higher the market value, the higher is the wealth tax. The situation is analogous to that of the homeowner who wishes a house to be appraised at a low market value for property tax purposes as long as he or she owns it—but wants the market value to be higher when the house is to be sold. Since most Norwegian common stock is closely held for long-run gain by financial institutions, trust funds, and wealthy individuals such as shipowners, there is no great desire to have a high short-run market price of common stock that would be subject to the higher wealth tax. A second negative tax factor in wishing for market value appreciation is that until recently capital gains were taxed at regular income tax rates. Thus it was better to receive returns in the form of a certain dividend than an uncertain capital gain as long as the tax effect would be the same either way.

Financial reporting practice in Norway is to minimize and normalize (levelize) earnings. Since the tax books and public disclosure books must be the same, most firms prefer to minimize income for tax purposes rather than report growing earnings per share. Tax minimization is an important goal, because the corporate income tax rate is about 60%. In addition to minimizing reported income, most firms attempt to normalize income by taking advantage of a variety of tax-free reserves set up for national macroeconomic purposes, such as a reserve for investment in North Norway and other less developed regions of Norway. Minimizing reported income is further encouraged by a fear that labor unions will grab any above-average reported earnings at the next bargaining agreement.

As a result of these tax and reporting practices, Norwegian financial statements do not resemble statements in the United States or elsewhere. Instead of exuding optimism and encouragement for stockholders to hold or purchase their shares, Norwegian companies blame on luck any income they have been unable to shelter from taxes and forecast a conservative picture for future corporate earnings. Needless to say, neither the minimized and normalized reported earnings nor the text of the annual reports is a very reliable indication of future earnings or risk. It is almost impossible for an outside investor to make a rational portfolio choice, with the result that few individuals in Norway own common stock, and new stock issues have provided only a negligible proportion of the long-term funds needed in the private sector. In fact, the average debt ratio for manufacturing firms approaches 80%, and nearly all equity has been accumulated through retained earnings rather than new issues.

One further political factor is important in understanding the Norwegian choice of corporate financial goals. Industrial democracy has "arrived" in Norway. Employees have the right to choose one-third of the board of directors for firms with 50 or more employees. Most major decisions, such as investments in new plant or relocation of existing plants, require the approval of the *bedriftsforsamling* in addition to the normal board of directors. The *bedriftsforsamling* consists of representatives, one-third of whom are chosen respectively by employees, the public sector, and the stockholders. Needless to say, management finds it difficult to make policy decisions or choose financial goals, such as maximizing the market price of common stock, which appear to favor the stockholders over these other interest groups. There is general agreement, however, that common stockholders should receive a fair cash dividend return on the investment. Beyond that there is little support for extra compensation through capital gains. In summary, one prominent Norwegian financial observer, who will remain unnamed, summarized the Norwegian manager's attitude toward the common stockholder as follows: *"De er haaret i suppa,"* which means, "They are the hair in the soup!"

United States

Even in the United States financial executives overwhelmingly chose growth in earnings per share (6) in preference to any goal related to market value of common stock. Their responses can be interpreted to mean that the executives believe that stock market prices are not under the firm's control, whereas maximizing growth in earnings is an attainable objective insofar as it is determined by the choice and risk of investments and can lead indirectly to higher stock prices. On the other hand, growth in earnings is a goal consistent with many other organizational goals that do not necessarily help the stockholder. Furthermore, many of the executives interviewed were not really convinced that earnings per share was a consistent influence on common stock price within their managerial time horizon. Instead they believed that much of the movement in stock prices was either irrational or random. Therefore they preferred to be evaluated by nonmarket measures of performance such as earnings, return on equity, and growth. In fact, although asset growth and sales growth were not available in the survey as potential financial goal choices, they were in fact preferred goals of many firms. Growth in earnings was desirable because it provided a way to finance the desired growth, both directly and indirectly because of its use as a base for more leverage.

Conclusion from Survey Results

In conclusion, there is considerable doubt that the current state of the art in finance theory has been accepted by the finance practitioner in a variety of national settings. Whether financial managers should accept the gospel of maximizing stockholder wealth is a value judgment, not a law of nature or an incontrovertible rational choice. It is obvious that different national institutional, cultural, and political variables play a role in defining what is of value and also rational within a particular environment.

In the case of multinational firms the choice of financial goals for foreign affiliates can lead to some sensitive conflicts of interest. It is difficult enough to choose a rational financial goal compatible with such home country norms as described in the five-country survey above. Imagine the problem of choosing for each foreign affiliate financial goals that do not conflict with its respective host country norms and yet are contributing positively to the financial goals of a consolidated worldwide corporation!

PUBLIC POLICY CONSTRAINTS ON CORPORATE FINANCIAL GOALS

The choice of financial goals for multinational firms is further complicated by an array of host country constraints, some of which apply to all firms within their jurisdiction and some of which apply mainly to foreign firms. Needless to say, maximizing stockholders' wealth of a parent firm that happens to have an affiliate in a host country would not be a very acceptable operating guideline in that host country unless all other host country constraints were first satisfied. It is now necessary to describe the nature of these public policy constraints on the free choice of corporate financial goals and, in particular, the financial goals of foreign-owned affiliates.

The international monetary system provides the financial structure and "rules of the game" to govern countries in their financial relations with each other, but within these broad international constraints each country provides its own financial structure and rules for firms operating within its jurisdiction. The national financial structure and rules, however, are merely part of the assortment of instruments a country can use in its pursuit of national goals. Governments also employ a variety of nonfinancial instruments designed to help achieve society's economic, political, social, cultural, and ideological goals.

In some cases instruments designed to achieve economic goals have an undesirable impact on noneconomic goals. Conflict of opinion over national goals requires government policymakers and planners to set priorities, a fact that makes national planning a political art rather than a deterministic science. At any one time there is usually ambiguity as to the order of priorities, and this situation is further complicated by shifts in national priorities over time.

From the viewpoint of the multinational firm all national economic, political, social, cultural, and ideological goals—as well as the policy instruments used to accomplish these—are parameters that circumscribe the firm's activities. It is unfortunate for the multinational firm that often government policies are unclear, or that two or more policies seem to be contradictory. Nevertheless, every host government has the right to be ambiguous, because ordering and implementing national priorities are not a science. Multinational firms must learn to live with this ambiguity. The important thing to remember is that they must be able to *predict* and *adapt* to changing national priorities and the resulting changes in the policy instruments.

Even if multinational firms follow a policy of adapting to national priorities, host country governments may still feel ambivalent toward them. After all, there is no consensus as to what constitutes favorable or unfavorable performance by multinational firms with respect to national goals. For instance, several economically oriented studies have been completed that seem to show a favorable quantitative impact of foreign-owned firms on such host country economic goals as growth, employment, price stability, and balance of payments. There are also some studies that demonstrate the contrary.[18] Whether or not the economic effect is favorable, the methodology of the social sciences has not been developed to the extent that it has been possible to quantify the kind of impact foreign-owned firms have had on the host country's less tangible national political, social, cultural, and ideological goals. Therefore it is on noneconomic grounds that foreign-owned firms are most vulnerable to attack.

ECONOMIC CONSTRAINTS

Although national economic priorities vary, most countries wish to have a sustainable rate of growth in GNP and income, full employment, price stability, balance in their external economy, and a fair distribution of income. Policy instruments designed to achieve these goals usually constrain and direct the operations of both domestic and multinational firms, but sometimes the operations of multinational firms interfere with the smooth functioning of these policy instruments.

Monetary Policy

Nearly every country attempts to control the cost and availability of credit and long-term capital as a means of influencing growth, employment, prices, balance of payments, and income distribution. However, few countries have a money or capital market that is sufficiently developed and responsive to make a decisive impact on these economic variables. The United States and the United Kingdom have typically been able to use monetary policy more effectively than most other industrialized countries because of the breadth and sophistication of their money and capital markets and institutions. The less developed countries as a whole have not been successful in influencing economic variables through general monetary policy (interest rates and overall supply of money), although they have scored some successes with direct controls such as credit rationing, forced saving, and specialized lending by development banks or funds.

Multinational firms are subject to the same monetary and credit constraints as local firms; however, they are periodically criticized for circumventing the spirit of monetary and credit restraint, even when complying with the letter of the law. If credit becomes too expensive or unavailable because of purposeful national monetary restraint, an affiliate of a multinational firm would probably still have access to capital from its parent, its sister affiliates, or the Eurodollar market. Thus the multinational affiliate would be able to implement its spending plans, while smaller local competitors would be restricted because of lack of access to external capital. Of course, host countries can and do have the option of limiting spending through direct rationing controls rather than relying on indirect monetary controls.

Another frustration of national monetary policy has occurred when multinational firms have suddenly converted large amounts of foreign exchange into local currency to buy out a local company, carry out a large new investment, or simply to hold excess working capital or speculative funds temporarily while riding out a foreign exchange crisis in one or more other countries (so-called hot money flows). The United Kingdom, the United States, West Germany, France, Italy, and Switzerland have been the frequent victims of such temporary distortions of their money supply. In most cases conversion of the foreign exchange into local currency creates an instant increase in the local money supply, which has to be offset by central bank action (open-market operations, etc.). Usually there are time lags, depending on the depth of the particular money market, during which national monetary policy is not effective.

Before the advent of floating exchange rates the United States encouraged central banks of other countries to hold their monetary reserves in dollars rather than gold as a means of protecting the international monetary system. President de Gaulle of France was accused of being cantankerous when he advocated that France exchange its excess reserve dollars for gold during the 1960s. From de Gaulle's point of view the Bank of France was willingly accepting unnecessary dollars and supplying the francs that U.S. companies were using to buy French firms. Examples cited were General Electric's purchase of Machines Bull and Chrysler's purchase of Simca. De Gaulle saw no reason for the Bank of France to finance the takeover of French firms. Furthermore, he argued that exchanging francs for the unwanted dollars expanded the franc money supply and led to inflation when the ex-stockholders spent or invested their receipts.

The opposite argument, however, was that when the price of francs approached the upper limit of the allowable trading band vis-à-vis the dollar, the Bank of France was not necessarily forced to buy the undesired dollars. Moreover, the Bank of France could have neutralized the influx of dollars by a corresponding restriction in the supply of francs or by spending those dollars.

Even though most of the conflicts between the financial policies of multinational firms and the monetary policies of host countries have been inadvertent, with the multinational firms scrupulously following all local regulations, multinational firms may have to practice "financial diplomacy" above and beyond the call of duty. For example, several times during the 1960s, before eventual devaluation of the pound in 1967, the pound sterling was under attack by speculators and in serious danger of being devalued. A handful of multinational oil companies, including several that were U.S.-owned, were reported to have had pound balances that were large enough to determine the outcome. If they converted to dollars, they would minimize their own foreign exchange exposure and probable loss to their stockholders. If they held their pounds, they would help the Bank of England in its fight to retain the par value of the pound. They chose the latter course. Whether this was correct depends on balancing the potential long-run payoff of "financial diplomacy," in terms of better relationships with the host country monetary authorities, against the potential short-run loss due to devaluation. In this particular case there was, in fact, a quid pro quo. The Bank of England exempted the cooperating foreign firms from the general restraint placed on British firms to keep them from borrowing abroad.

Fiscal Policy

The operations of multinational firms may conflict with host country fiscal policy instruments. On the tax side of the government budget a multinational firm may operate with favorable tax concessions both as to tax rates and a tax base. This is the fault of the host government's eagerness to attract a particular foreign investment, but a later government may regret the tax concessions made by its predecessors. Even if no favorable tax concessions exist, the multinational firm may be able to reduce its tax base in one country in favor of a larger tax base in another country through the medium of transfer pricing. This opportunity arises when an affiliate in one country imports (or exports) raw materials, components, or services (financing, license fees, sales commissions, management fees, etc.) from (or to) a related affiliate or parent firm. The price of the transfer of goods or services might be set so high that all profit from the transaction is earned in the country with the most favorable tax base. The transfer-pricing problem is discussed in detail in Chapter 15. There are also a number of other potential sources of conflict over the size of the tax base.

On the government spending side of the budget, multinational firms may create the need for economic and social overhead facilities. For example, many mining, oil, and plantation investments have been located in geographically isolated areas. Transportation and public utility facilities, housing, educational and health facilities, and many other indirect support requirements are often needed. The host government may not be able to provide the overhead services. If the investing firm provides them, a dependency relationship is established, and the foreign firm may be accused of paternalism or economic imperialism.

Balance of Payments and Exchange Rate Policies

In response to balance of payment and exchange rate difficulties, governments are forced to promulgate regulations that can severely hamper the operations of multinational firms. It is critical for the management of multinational firms to understand both the causes and likely policy reactions to a balance of payments deficit or strong pressure on a national currency.

The United Kingdom, for example, has typically relied on the classical method of restrictive policy to slow its rate of growth and inflation. Tight monetary policy supposedly should reduce imports, release goods for export, and attract capital imports to London via higher interest rates on savings. The British have also at times limited tourist expenditures abroad, restricted the convertibility of one type of sterling ("investment" sterling), conducted an active "income policy" (limits on wage and price increases), and imposed a temporary import surcharge along with an import deposit requirement.

Many Latin American countries have resorted to frequent devaluations, the use of multiple exchange rates for different categories of imports and exports, licensing imports, import deposit requirements, demanding extended credit terms to finance imports, and refinancing outstanding debt with loans from international and national agencies whenever possible. The use of exchange controls, including inconvertibility of currency, can be particularly damaging to multinational business because local inflation typically diminishes the value of the blocked currency. Thus, although a subsidiary may be making large paper profits in terms of local currency, none of these profits can be repatriated, although there are ways to transfer the risk of inconvertibility to insuring agencies (Chapter 9).

Prior to 1971 the United States was not willing to respond to balance of payments deficits by sacrificing domestic growth and employment; nor was it willing to impose direct controls on foreign exchange transactions, use devaluations or multiple exchange rates, severely limit tourist expenditures, or even significantly increase domestic interest rates to attract capital import. Instead until 1971 the United States relied on selective "hunt-and-peck" policies, which tried to make marginal improvements in each balance of payment account. For instance, during the period 1963–1974 it imposed an "interest equalization tax" on issues of foreign securities floated in U.S. capital markets, making such lending more expensive for foreign borrowers. AID and overseas military purchases were tied wherever possible to U.S. sourcing. Through changes in the U.S. tax laws in 1962 and 1975, foreign tax havens were made less attractive. NATO member countries, particularly West Germany, were pressured into buying their military armaments in the United States as an offset to the presence and spending of the U.S. military forces in Europe and other overseas areas. Export promotion activities of the U.S. government, such as trade fairs, export credit insurance, and Export-Import Bank lending, were improved. A "voluntary" program of restraint on direct foreign investment was imposed on the business community in February 1965, with an implied threat of mandatory controls to follow if the "voluntary" system's goals were not achieved. Otherwise the U.S. government concentrated on financing its deficit by special long-term U.S. government security sales to foreign central banks, moral suasion on foreign central banks not to convert dollars to gold, arrangement of standby swap agreements, and a general attempt to maintain the facade of confidence that the balance of payments deficits were transitory rather than structural.

During the period 1968–1974 the United States had a program of "mandatory" controls on direct overseas investments by U.S. investors. The purpose of the mandatory program was to limit direct foreign investment including reinvestment of foreign earnings. During the same 1968–1974 period the Board of Governors of the Federal Reserve System employed a companion set of restrictive guidelines for foreign lending by U.S. commercial banks. Larger commercial banks were limited to extending foreign credits of no more than 103% of the foreign credits outstanding on December 31, 1964. On August 15, 1971, President Nixon placed a 10% surcharge on imports, ceased official purchases or sales of gold for dollars, and imposed an immediate wage-price freeze on nearly all goods and services. He also asked Congress for tax relief for business (investment credit) and consumers (speedup of increase in exemptions). The import surcharge, floating the dollar, and the wage-price freeze were all major breaks with the U.S. tradition of selective policies. Although the import surcharge was removed in December 1971 and the wage-price freeze was replaced by modified wage-price controls, and later abandoned, it was obvious that even the United States would revert to direct controls if necessary to cure its balance of payments deficits.

Economic Protectionism

Several national economic policy constraints are motivated mainly by protectionism but partly by balance of payments and national economic development. Both tariff and nontariff barriers to trade fall in this category. Since negotiations under the General Agreement on Tariffs and Trade (GATT) have succeeded in reducing the general level of tariffs during the past three decades, nontariff barriers to trade have become more important.

Nontariff barriers are measures other than conventional tariffs that restrict imports or artificially stimulate exports. A list of the major types and subcategories of nontariff barriers is shown in Exhibit 1.2.

Nontariff barriers are frequently difficult to identify as clearly protectionistic, as when they are indistinguishable from stringent health, safety, sanitation, or certification requirements. The United States has long excluded fresh Argentine beef because of hoof-and-mouth disease in that country, although most European countries have not found a similar exclusion necessary. The French regard their ban on whiskey advertisements as a social regulation, while American whiskey exporters consider it a barrier. Germany demands that imports of meal used to feed poultry and swine contain no more than 5% fat, thus excluding certain U.S. feeds that contain 10%. U.S. feed-meal manufacturers do not believe that the difference between 5 and 10% fat influences the well-being of the animals, but nevertheless they do not wish to incur the capital costs necessary to re-equip for the German market.

EXHIBIT 1.2
Types of Nontariff Barriers

1. Specific limitations on trade, which either limit the amount of imports directly or establish import procedures that make importing more difficult.
   a. Quotas, which limit the quantity or value allowed for specific imported products for specific time periods.
   b. Licensing requirements that must be met before trading.
   c. Proportion restrictions of foreign to domestic goods or content.
   d. Minimum import price limits set equal to or above domestic prices.
   e. Embargoes prohibiting products originating in specific countries.
2. Customs and administrative entry procedures, which include inconsistent procedures for valuation, classification of documents, or assessing fees.
   a. Valuation of imports on an arbitrary basis at the discretion of customs officials.
   b. Antidumping countermeasures against imported goods sold below prices in the home market of the exporter.
   c. Tariff classifications that are inconsistent.
   d. Documentation requirements that are overburdensome.
   e. Fees charged to cover costs of entry procedures.
3. Unduly stringent or discriminating standards imposed in the name of protecting health, safety, and quality.
   a. Disparities between quality standards required by different countries.
   b. Differing intergovernmental acceptance standards or testing methods.
   c. Application of packaging and labeling standards in unduly stringent or discriminating ways.
4. Governmental participation in trade.
   a. Government procurement policies that favor domestic over imported products without regard to relative price and quality.
   b. Export subsidies, either directly or via taxes or export credit terms, provided by government.
   c. Countervailing duties charged by importing country to offset export subsidies granted by exporting country.
   d. Domestic assistance programs granted all domestic producers, both exporters and those producing for domestic consumption.
5. Charges on imports.
   a. Prior import deposit requirements, requiring a non-interest-bearing deposit equal to some percentage of import value (sometimes up to 100%) to be deposited prior to time of import and refunded at a later date. The "cost" is equal to the cost of capital on the funds so tied up.
   b. Border tax adjustments, in which border taxes are levied on imports to tax them in the same manner as domestic goods and are rebated on exports. Countries relying on indirect taxes (such as the value-added taxes used in

EXHIBIT 1.2 (Cont.)

Europe) are given an advantage over countries relying on direct taxes (such as corporate income taxes), since indirect taxes can be rebated but direct taxes cannot be rebated.

c. Administrative fees levied.

d. Special supplementary duties levied.

e. Import credit discrimination.

f. Variable levies.

6. Other nontariff barriers.

a. Voluntary export restraints by exporting country, often at the request (with or without political pressure) of the importing country.

b. Orderly marketing agreements, wherein countries agree formally to restrict trade.

Source: Adapted from material in A. D. Cao, "Non-tariff Barriers to U.S. Manufactured Exports," *Columbia Journal of World Business*, Summer 1980, pp. 93–102.

Japan ruled certain imports of canned goods unacceptable under the applicable agricultural standard because the figures for the day, month, and year of canning were spaced too far apart on the labels. Japan's complex distribution system makes it difficult for foreigners to get direct access to consumers.

France turned the tables on Japan in 1982 when it ordered all foreign-made video recorders to clear a tiny customs office in the inland city of Poitiers, where they were subject to very zealous inspection. As a result, imports of video recorders, mostly Japanese, fell from 64,000 per month to 10,000 per month.

Examples of nontariff barriers used by the U.S. government include "persuasion" of foreign countries to "voluntarily" impose quotas on their exports to the United States of such items as cotton shirts, steel, television sets, shoes, and automobiles. The same types of quotas exist in Western Europe. Japan, Hong Kong, Korea, and Taiwan have been particularly affected by the quota system. Like many other countries that officially encourage buying domestically, the United States has a "buy American" executive order that results in governmental agencies giving a percentage preference to U.S. goods even when imported goods would be cheaper or more efficient. Japanese steel has been particularly victimized by exclusion from state or local government purchase in California because of a "buy California" executive order. The U.S. antidumping law (as well as the GATT provision against dumping) may also be a hidden barrier to imports if enforced in a pernicious manner.

Tax rebate and other subsidies are often used for economic protection or favoritism. The General Agreement on Tariffs and Trade, the international organization which oversees most of the foreign trade rules of the world, allows governments to rebate to exporters such "indirect" taxes as sales taxes and franchise taxes but does not allow the rebating of "direct" taxes such as income taxes. Because European governments rely relatively more heavily on indirect taxes, the export prices of European goods need not bear the tax assessments of local governments. The value-added tax (VAT) adopted by many European countries is an example of an indirect tax favoring domestic goods over goods imported from a country that uses an income tax. Price of U.S. exports must be high enough to cover the income tax component to be assessed upon the profit, since the income tax is direct and thus not rebatable. Some countries provide low-cost export loans, very favorable foreign credit insurance, and tied economic development aid as other indirect ways to subsidize exports.

The impetus for nontariff barriers, like the impetus for regular tariff protection, usually comes from producers who can expect to be hurt by the changes in relative efficiency inherent in a changing world; such barriers are most frequently adopted to protect a particularly influential industry rather than for the more general reasons of influencing a country's balance of payments or economic development. These forces are not entirely separate, for a country with particular balance of payments problems or a low level of economic development is more likely to be receptive to protection pleas from its less efficient industries than is an economically advanced country whose balance of payments has been favorable.

Economic Development Policies

Protection of "infant industries" has often been advanced as the only defensible argument for a protective tariff. Unfortunately, too many industries have been granted protection for too long after they have matured. Some of the less developed countries have stretched the interpretation to include "infant countries," meaning that they seek to protect all their industries even though some are unlikely ever to develop a comparative advantage. Regardless of whether this position is intellectually defensible, most less developed countries have adopted policies to stimulate economic integration of their own industries. These are often in conflict with the multinational firm's attempt to rationalize production on a worldwide basis, taking advantage of comparative advantage wherever it occurs. For example, India, Mexico, Brazil, Argentina, and numerous other less developed countries require multinational firms to manufacture an increasing proportion of components locally rather than assemble imported components with a minimum of local manufacture. Automobile firms and other manufacturers who use large numbers of component parts have been particularly pressed for local manufacture. In fact, General Motors withdrew its assembly operation from India in the 1950s over just such a conflict.

Host country demands for a local share in ownership of foreign subsidiaries is another example of potential conflict caused by economic development policy. In this case other motives are also involved, such as a goal of "fair distribution of income," national pride, and chauvinism. India's insistence on local ownership caused IBM to remove its operations from there in 1977.

Although direct foreign investment has often been heralded as contributing to economic development and is eagerly sought by many developing countries, the very fulfillment of its promise has often unintentionally created a "dual economy." Local citizens associated with the foreign firms, either as employees or suppliers, have prospered and advanced economically to become an elite class. Other citizens untouched by the foreign firms or industry sector being developed are left in their original state of poverty. Thus a two-class society is created, causing its own problems of internal dissension, jealousy, greed, and graft. The early plantation, oil, and mining investments were often the inadvertent victims of their own success, having been blamed for creating these dual economies.

Regional common markets and free-trade areas, which are a partial response to economic development goals, create both opportunities and constraints for multinational firms. On the one hand, there is a "trade creation" effect as tariff barriers are removed internally among member countries. This creates an opportunity for the multinational firm to invest in local manufacture in a market large enough to achieve economies of scale. On the other hand, there is a "trade diversion" effect. Firms that were previously exporting to the member countries are forced to overcome a common external tariff in the case of common markets, or individual-country tariffs in the case of free-trade areas, in order to compete with firms located within the protected markets.

The formation of the European Common Market (1957) and the European Free Trade Association (1958) stimulated rapid growth in foreign direct investment, as multinational firms, particularly U.S.-based ones, acted to save their former export markets, or seized the opportunity to enter a large protected market comparable with the United States in growth prospects. Most observers believe that this influx had a favorable impact on economic development. For the less developed countries, however, the formation of the Latin American Free Trade Area, the Central American Common Market, and various African and Asian regional groupings has not evoked a similar large influx of foreign direct investment, perhaps because of restrictions or perceived political risk. There has been some foreign response and some increase in indigenous private investment, but it is still unclear whether the "trade creation" effect has outweighed the "trade diversion" effect on balance.

NONECONOMIC CONSTRAINTS

Even when all political parties within a host country agree that foreign direct investment would have a favorable impact on their economic goals, they may oppose it on noneconomic grounds. The most common arguments against multinational firms are the following:

1. economic imperialism;

2. national security;

3. private enterprise inconsistent with a socialist form of government;

4. incompatibility with host country religion or cultural heritage;

5. political expediency.

Economic Imperialism

In the ex-colonial countries a widespread suspicion exists that multinational firms represent another invidious form of imperialism, albeit economic rather than political or military. These countries often fail to differentiate between profit-motivated private foreign enterprises and the home governments of the parent enterprise. After all, the Dutch and British East India companies, the Hudson's Bay Company, the international petroleum and mining companies, and most of the other early multinational companies arrived on the local scene hand in hand with military and political domination. These early multinational firms thus contributed to our present-day colonial legacy.

Even today some governments remain active in support and control of their own multinational firms. "Japan Incorporated" has been heard more and more frequently from American sources as Toyota, Nissan Motors, Mitsubishi, Mitsui, Sony, and others invade the U.S. market and establish large subsidiaries. The Japanese government and business community cooperate closely, but it is probably unfair to conclude that Japanese business is an instrument of economic imperialism sponsored by the Japanese government.

It is obvious to most Americans that the U.S. government and business do not cooperate closely on direct foreign investment. In fact, most political regulation seems predicated on U.S. government distrust of business and so suggests the opposite. Furthermore, the United States does not have a large colonial heritage to live down, having once been a colony itself. Nevertheless, U.S. multinational firms are still perceived by many foreigners as instruments of U.S. foreign policy. The fact that the former direct investment controls and the present investment guarantee program favor U.S. investments in less developed countries is misinterpreted to mean that the U.S. government wants to use U.S. multinational firms to secure economic control of these host countries.

National Security

Some host countries have become alarmed that foreign control of key industry sectors is inimical to national security. One need only read Servan-Schreiber, *The American Challenge,* to perceive the French attitude of the 1960s toward U.S. control of the computer, electronics, and other defense-related French industries.[19] Indeed, de Gaulle's *"force de frappe"* had a rather empty ring, as long as a significant portion of French military hardware was U.S.-made. The national security fear may also have had a part in Japan's former policy of severe restriction on foreign investment within its borders.

Canada has established a commission to screen and control new direct foreign investments, most of which are from the United States. Their concern is that more than half of Canadian manufacturing and mining is U.S.-owned, including most of the growth sectors and those related to national security. This situation could make it virtually impossible for Canada to follow an independent foreign policy. Often cited is the well-publicized conflict during the 1960s that stemmed from U.S. Ford's insistence that Canadian Ford not export trucks to the People's Republic of China. Such an export would have been allowable and even encouraged under Canadian law and foreign policy (Canada recognized the People's Republic of China) but was contrary to U.S. foreign policy at that time.

Scandinavian critics have sometimes questioned whether foreign direct investments in their countries have not compromised their historical efforts to maintain neutrality during continental wars. For example, in Norway during World War I, attempts by foreign-owned enterprises to maintain normal business relationships with their foreign investors and customers threatened to compromise the official Norwegian policy of neutrality. In both world wars the transit of Swedish iron ore from the Luossavaara Kiirunavaara mines through the Norwegian port of Narvik was of prime concern to the belligerent powers. Approximately a quarter of Germany's iron ore requirements came from this source. For this reason Narvik was the scene of bitter fighting between the British-French-Norwegian forces and the invading German forces in 1940. During the German occupation in World War II Norwegian factories and mines, which were important suppliers of the German steel industry and its potential nuclear capability (heavy-water supplies), were bombed or sabotaged by the Allies, with numerous civilian casualties resulting. Nearly all these military targets were foreign-owned enterprises (British, French, Swedish, and German, primarily) which would probably not have existed without the original foreign investment.[20]

Socialism

The most dramatic conflicts between foreign investors and host governments have occurred during periods of social transition within the host country.

Russia after World War I, the East European countries and China after World War II, Cuba in 1959, Libya in 1969, Chile in 1971, and Iran in 1979 are examples. In most cases, however, the fact that a private enterprise was foreign was not as important as the fact that it was private. The public policy constraints applied to all private enterprises and included everything from modest regulation to outright expropriation without compensation.

Religious and Cultural Heritage

In some cases the Judeo-Christian religious and cultural heritages of many multinational firms conflict with the traditions of the host countries. For example, in the Middle East, oil company executives and technicians bring with them a liberal outlook toward alcohol and women that is in direct contrast to the teachings of Islam. In some Arab countries, drinking of alcoholic beverages by foreign nationals is restricted to their own living quarters or enclave, but their example creates tension within the Moslem community. Western acceptance of women as executives and their assignment to positions of responsibility involving negotiation and decision making in the Middle East, Asia, and Africa often conflict with established local mores. Even proper dress codes for women executives or the wives of male executives may cause problems. As multinational firms adjust to changing standards in the Western world, they are often perceived as imposing "cultural imperialism" on their more traditional host countries through transfer of managerial values, work ethics, and social conscience.

Political Expediency

Sometimes a host government officially approves of the overall economic and noneconomic performance of the foreign-owned firms, but a minority political party is critical of it—ostensibly on some rational grounds, but pragmatically on the basis of being out of office and needing an issue.

Another type of political expediency occurs when host country governments try to use foreign affiliates located within their boundaries as hostages to influence the behavior of the countries in which their parents are based. The Arab boycott of foreign firms dealing with Israel is an example of the hostage strategy.

CONCLUSION—A COMPROMISE VIEWPOINT

The interface between affiliates of multinational firms and host countries complicates the choice of financial goals for the foreign affiliates, and thereby indirectly for the parent as well. Modern finance theory is built on the presumption that a firm should be operated for the ultimate benefit of its stockholders, but if a foreign affiliate is operated with this goal, it will often conflict with host country business norms, the value systems of its own management who are host country citizens, and host country economic, political, and cultural aspirations.

It has been shown that a variety of institutional, cultural, political, and tax factors often cause financial executives of business firms domiciled outside the United States to choose financial goals that treat stockholders as just one of the many important interest groups with a stake in the firm. The value of the stockholders' contribution in terms of providing new sources of funds to business may be minimal, such as in Norway and Japan. The risk borne by stockholders also varies, depending on institutional factors such as those found in Japan. The role of private ownership and control of firms may be under scrutiny, such as in France and Norway. In short, whether financial managers should accept stockholder wealth maximization as the most important goal is a value judgment that must be based on a particular society's value system. The fact that modern finance theory has had mostly U.S. and U.K. origins, and is based on assumptions about capital markets and investor preferences found in those countries, does not make the theory easily transferable to other countries.

In addition to local business norms, public policy constraints limit what foreign affiliates are able to accomplish with respect to maximizing their stockholders' wealth. Economic constraints on multinational firms are imposed through the usual instruments of monetary, fiscal, and balance of payments policies. Furthermore, the multinationals are subject to barriers caused by economic protectionism and national development priorities. Noneconomic constraints sometimes include policies that are motivated by resistance to perceived economic imperialism, national security needs, a shift to a socialistic form of government, religious and cultural beliefs, or sometimes just plain political expediency.

Should multinational firms forget about finance theory's stockholder wealth maximization goal because of the conflict with host countries' business norms and public policy constraints? The answer is probably no, but they must recognize serious limitations on their ability to implement this goal when dealing with foreign affiliates. In particular, they will need to satisfy constraints set by local business norms and public policy. This does not mean that all local norms must be followed exactly, but where significant deviations occur, the multinational firm should be prepared to justify them not only to host country government officials but to their own local management, employees, creditors, and other interest groups.

Since the survey showed that no single financial goal is acceptable to both theorists and financial practitioners, either within the same country or between countries, we will adopt a compromise viewpoint throughout the remainder of this book. Wherever appropriate we will analyze financial decisions from three different perspectives:

1. impact on the firm's long-run consolidated earnings (per share);
2. impact on the firm's cash flow;
3. impact on the firm's market value.

Analysis of the impact of financial decisions on growth and stability of a firm's long-run consolidated net earnings (per share) reflects the survey preference of financial executives for the earnings measure of performance. Many finance theorists and practitioners also believe that the market value of a firm's common stock is primarily a function of expected earnings and dividends, adjusted for total risk (standard deviation) but not for portfolio risk. In trying to maximize consolidated earnings, one should remember that operating earnings in each foreign affiliate will be constrained by the need to maintain a level sufficient to pay competitive wages, reduce financial risk for local creditors and suppliers, and provide a reasonable share of the tax burden. If a foreign affiliate's earnings are obviously depressed in order to minimize a firm's worldwide taxes, the multinational will be accused of "milking" the host country.

Analysis of the impact of financial decisions on the firm's cash flow reflects the survey preference for guaranteeing funds availability. Once again the multinational should be concerned not only about its consolidated cash flow but also about the cash flow in each foreign affiliate. If a foreign affiliate's financial structure is highly leveraged locally (e.g., for foreign exchange risk protection or ease of repatriating funds), it behooves a multinational to ensure that cash coverage is sufficient to cover the financial risk to local creditors and suppliers. A binding parent guarantee of loans by a foreign affiliate would usually be an acceptable alternative from the local viewpoint. There have been very few cases in which a parent has abandoned a failing unguaranteed foreign affiliate. This type of undiplomatic action can lead to future host country interference with the choice of financial structure and sourcing of funds for affiliates of other multinationals. Fortunately, the overwhelming majority of multinationals consider even unguaranteed loans by affiliates as an obligation of the parent.

Analysis of the impact of financial decisions on a firm's market value reflects the preferred goal of finance theory. In particular, we will examine whether multinational operations appear to have a favorable effect on a firm's market value either through a financial portfolio effect or through an ability to capitalize on imperfections in national markets for real assets and factors of production.

In conclusion, all three financial goals are not necessarily mutually exclusive. Quite the contrary; all interest groups in the coalition that make up a firm in the organization theory model could benefit if the "size of the pot" to be divided were maximized. Thus everyone could conceivably benefit if a firm had the highest and most stable possible operating earnings, cash flow, and market value. The problem comes in the bargain for distribution of benefits. A high market value of common stock does not appear to employees as an important benefit unless they own it. Higher corporate earnings and cash flow may or may not be shared with the employees in terms of higher wages and job security or used to reduce the financial risk borne by creditors and suppliers. On the other hand, it can be shown in a Pareto sense that operating with these three financial goals does not necessarily harm any of the interest groups and may benefit some of them to a greater or lesser extent. It is only when exclusive and excessive attention is paid to one of the goals to the detriment of the others that benefits may be significantly biased in the direction of one of the interest groups, with little benefit for the other interest groups.

NOTES

1. Joel Dean, *Capital Budgeting,* New York: Columbia University Press, 1951.

2. David Durand, "Costs of Debt and Equity Funds for Business: Trends and Problems of Measurement," in Ezra Solomon, ed., *The Management of Corporate Capital,* Chicago: University of Chicago Press, 1959, pp. 91–121.

3. Franco Modigliani and Merton Miller, "The Cost of Capital, Corporation Finance and the Theory of Investment," *American Economic Review,* June 1958, pp. 261–297.

4. Harry M. Markowitz, *Portfolio Selection: Efficient Diversification of Investments,* New York: Wiley, 1959.

5. William F. Sharpe, "A Simplified Model for Portfolio Analysis," *Management Science,* January 1963, pp. 277–293. Also see William F. Sharpe, "Capital Asset Prices: A Theory of Market Equilibrium under Conditions of Risk," *Journal of Finance,* September 1964, pp. 425–442.

6. Stephen A. Ross, "The Arbitrage Theory of Capital Asset Pricing," *Journal of Economic Theory,* December 1976, pp. 341–360.

7. Richard Roll and Stephen A. Ross, "An Empirical Investigation of the Arbitrage Pricing Theory," *Journal of Finance,* December 1980, pp. 1073–1103. Also see Nai-Fu Chen, "Some Empirical Tests of the Theory of Arbitrage Pricing," *Journal of Finance,* December 1983, pp. 1393–1414.

8. A good summary of APT and its tests expressed in lay terms can be found in Dorothy H. Bower, Richard S. Bower, and Dennis E. Logue, "A Primer on Arbitrage Pricing Theory," *Midland Corporate Finance Journal,* Fall 1984, pp. 31–40.

9. Richard Cyert and James March, *A Behavioral Theory of the Firm,* Englewood Cliffs, N.J.: Prentice-Hall, 1963.

10. Robert Anthony, "The Trouble with Profit Maximization," *Harvard Business Review,* November/December 1960, pp. 126–134. Also see Gordon Donaldson, "Financial Goals: Management vs. Stockholders," *Harvard Business Review,* May/June 1963, pp. 116–129.

11. M. Chapman Findlay III and G.A. Whitmore, "Beyond Shareholder Wealth Maximization," *Financial Management,* Winter 1974, pp. 25–35.

12. Gordon Donaldson and Jay W. Lorsch, *Decision Making at the Top: The Shaping of Strategic Direction,* New York: Basic Books, 1983. Also see Gordon Donaldson, *Managing Corporate Wealth: The Operation of a Comprehensive Financial Goals System,* New York: Praeger, 1984.

13. Donaldson, *Managing Corporate Wealth,* p. 25.

14. A good summary of agency theory can be found in Michael C. Jensen and Clifford W. Smith, Jr., "Stockholder, Manager, and Creditor Interests: Applications of Agency Theory," in Edward I. Altman and Marti G. Subrahmanyam, eds., *Recent Advances in Corporate Finance,* Homewood, Ill.: Irwin, 1985, pp. 93–131. Two frequently cited contributions to agency theory are Stephen A. Ross, "The Economic Theory of Agency: The Principal's Problem," *American Economic Review,* May 1973, pp. 134–139; and Michael C. Jensen and William H. Meckling, "Theory of the Firm: Management Behavior, Agency Costs and Ownership Structure," *Journal of Financial Economics,* October 1976, pp. 305–360.

15. Jensen and Meckling, "Theory of the Firm."

16. Michael C. Jensen and Richard S. Ruback, "The Market for Corporate Control: The Scientific Evidence," *Journal of Financial Economics,* April 1983, pp. 5–50.

17. Arthur Stonehill, Theo Beekhuisen, Richard Wright, Lee Remmers, Norman Toy, Antonio Parés, Alan Shapiro, Douglas Egan, and Thomas Bates, "Financial Goals and Debt Ratio Determinants: A Survey of Practice in Five Countries," *Financial Management,* Autumn 1975, pp. 27–41.

18. For summaries of the foreign investment literature see the bibliography for Chapter 8.

19. J. J. Servan-Schreiber, *The American Challenge,* London: Hamish Hamilton, 1968.

20. Arthur Stonehill, *Foreign Ownership in Norwegian Enterprises,* Oslo, Norway: Central Bureau of Statistics, 1965, p. 153.

BIBLIOGRAPHY

Aggarwal, Raj, *Financial Policies for the Multinational Company,* New York: Praeger, 1976.

———, "Investment Performance of U.S.-Based Multinational Companies: Comments and a Perspective of International Diversification of Real Assets," *Journal of International Business Studies,* Spring–Summer 1980, pp. 98–104.

———, *The Literature of International Business Finance: A Bibliography,* New York: Praeger, 1984.

Agmon, Tamir, and Charles P. Kindleberger, *Multinationals from Small Countries,* Cambridge: MIT Press, 1977.

Ajami, Riad A., and David A. Ricks, "Motives of Non-American Firms Investing in the United States," *Journal of International Business Studies,* Winter 1981, pp. 24–34.

Bergendahl, Goran, "Overview of International Financial Management," in Goran Bergendahl, ed., *International Financial Management,* Stockholm: P. A. Norstedt & Soners forlag, 1982, pp. 14–28.

Bower, Dorothy H., Richard S. Bower, and Dennis E. Logue, "A Primer on Arbitrage Pricing Theory," *Midland Corporate Finance Journal,* Fall 1984, pp. 31–40.

Brooke, Michael Z., and H. Lee Remmers, eds., *The Multinational Company in Europe,* Ann Arbor: University of Michigan Press, 1974.

Chen, Nai-Fu, "Some Empirical Tests of the Theory of Arbitrage Pricing," *Journal of Finance,* December 1983, pp. 1393–1414.

Curhan, J. P., W. H. Davidson, and R. Suri, *Tracing the Multinationals,* Cambridge, Mass.: Ballinger, 1977.

Donaldson, Gordon, *Managing Corporate Wealth: The Operation of a Comprehensive Financial Goals System,* New York: Praeger, 1984.

Donaldson, Gordon, and Jay W. Lorsch, *Decision Making at the Top: The Shaping of Strategic Direction,* New York: Basic Books, 1983.

Dunning, John H., ed., *Economic Analysis and the Multinational Enterprise,* New York: Praeger, 1974.

England, George W., "Managers and Their Value Systems: A Five-Country Comparative Study," *Columbia Journal of World Business,* Summer 1978, pp. 35–44.

Fayerweather, John, "Canadian Foreign Investment Policy," *California Management Review,* Spring 1975, pp. 74–83.

Fayerweather, John, ed., *Host National Attitudes toward Multinational Corporations,* New York: Praeger, 1982.

Feiger, George, and Bertrand Jacquillat, *International Finance, Text and Cases,* Boston, Mass.: Allyn & Bacon, 1982.

Findlay, M. Chapman, III, and G. A. Whitmore, "Beyond Shareholder Wealth Maximization," *Financial Management,* Winter 1974, pp. 25–35.

Franko, Lawrence G., "Foreign Direct Investment in Less Developed Countries: Impact on Home Countries," *Journal of International Business Studies,* Winter 1978, pp. 55–65.

Gay, Gerald D., and Robert W. Kolb, ed., *International Finance: Concepts and Issues,* Richmond, Va.: Robert F. Dame, 1983.

George, Abraham, and Ian H. Giddy, *International Finance Handbook,* Vols. 1 and 2, New York: Wiley, 1983.

Investing, Licensing and Trading Conditions Abroad, New York: Business International, a reference service that is continually updated.

Jensen, Michael C., and William H. Meckling, "Theory of the Firm: Management Behavior, Agency Costs and Ownership Structure," *Journal of Financial Economics,* October 1976, pp. 305–360.

Jensen, Michael C., and Clifford W. Smith, Jr., "Stockholder, Manager, and Creditor Interests: Applications of Agency Theory," in Edward I. Altman and Marti G. Subrahmanyam, eds., *Recent Advances in Corporate Finance,* Homewood, Ill.: Irwin, 1985, pp. 93–131.

Jensen, Michael C., and Richard S. Ruback, "The Market for Corporate Control: The Scientific Evidence," *Journal of Financial Economics,* April 1983, pp. 5–50.

Lessard, Donald R., ed., *International Financial Management, Theory and Application,* New York: Wiley, 1985.

Levi, Maurice, *International Finance: Financial Management and the International Economy,* New York: McGraw-Hill, 1983.

Lozoya, Jorge, and A. K. Bhattacharya, eds., *The Financial Issues of the New International Economic Order,* New York: Pergamon Press, 1980.

Mikhail, Azmi D., and Hany A. Shawky, "Investment Performance of U.S.-Based MNCs," *Journal of International Business Studies,* Spring–Summer 1979, pp. 53–66.

Robbins, Sidney M., and Robert B. Stobaugh, *Money in the Multinational Enterprise,* New York: Basic Books, 1973.

Robock, Stefan H., and Kenneth Simmonds, *International Business and Multinational Enterprises,* 3rd ed., Homewood, Ill.: Irwin, 1983.

Rodriguez, Rita M., and Eugene E. Carter, *International Financial Management,* 3rd ed., Englewood Cliffs, N.J.: Prentice-Hall, 1984.

Roll, Richard, and Stephen A. Ross, "An Empirical Investigation of the Arbitrage Pricing Theory," *Journal of Finance,* December 1980, pp. 1073–1103.

Root, Franklin R., *International Trade and Investment,* 5th ed., Cincinnati: Southwestern, 1984.

Ross, Stephen A., "The Economic Theory of Agency: The Principal's Problem," *American Economic Review,* May 1973, pp. 134–139.

———, "The Arbitrage Theory of Capital Asset Pricing," *Journal of Economic Theory,* December 1976, pp. 341–360.

Shapiro, Alan C., *Multinational Financial Management,* Boston: Allyn & Bacon, 1982.

Sigmund, Paul E., *Multinationals in Latin America: The Politics of Nationalism,* Madison: University of Wisconsin Press, 1980.

Solomon, Lewis D., *Multinational Corporations and the Emerging World Order,* New York: Kennikat Press, 1978.

Stonehill, Arthur, Theo Beekhuisen, Richard Wright, Lee Remmers, Norman Toy, Antonio Parés, Alan Shapiro, Douglas Egan, and Thomas Bates, "Financial Goals and Debt Ratio Determinants: A Survey of Practice in Five Countries," *Financial Management,* Autumn 1975, pp. 27–41.

Stopford, J. M., J. H. Dunning, and K. D. Haberick, *The World Directory of Multinational Enterprises,* New York: Facts on File, 1981.

Turner, William D., and Stephen K. Green, "Global Challenge to Corporate Treasurers," *McKinsey Quarterly,* Spring 1982, pp. 53–61.

Vaupel, James W., and Joan P. Curham, *The World's Multinational Enterprises,* Boston: Harvard Business School Division of Research, 1973.

Vernon, Raymond, *Sovereignty at Bay: The Multinational Spread of U.S. Enterprises,* New York: Basic Books, 1971.

———, *Storm over the Multinationals,* Cambridge, Mass.: Harvard University Press, 1977.

Vernon, Raymond R., and Louis T. Wells, Jr., *Manager in the International Economy,* 4th ed., Englewood Cliffs, N.J.: Prentice-Hall, 1981.

Waldemann, Raymond J., *Regulating International Business through Codes of Conduct,* Washington, D.C.: American Enterprise Institute for Public Policy Research, 1980.

Wilkins, Mira, *The Maturing of Multinational Enterprise,* Cambridge, Mass.: Harvard University Press, 1974.

DIRECTORIES OF MULTINATIONAL FIRMS

American Export Register, New York: Thomas International Publishing, Annual.

American Register of Exporters and Importers, New York: American Register of Exporters and Importers Corporation, Annual.

Angel, Juvenal L., *Directory of American Firms Operating in Foreign Countries,* periodic editions, New York: Uniworld Business Publications.

Directory of United States Importers, New York: The Journal of Commerce, Biannual.

International Directory of Corporate Affiliations, subtitled "Who Owns Whom Worldwide—The Family Tree of Major Corporations of the World," Skokie, Ill.: National Register Publishing Company, 1983/84.

2

International Monetary System

Foreign exchange risk is currently an area of great concern to financial managers of multinational firms, international bankers, and international portfolio investors. Under the current system of partly floating and partly fixed exchange rates, multinational firms, banks, and individual investors have experienced significant real and paper fluctuations in earnings due to changes in relative exchange rates. Policies to forecast and react to exchange rate fluctuations are still evolving as understanding of the functioning of the international monetary system grows, as accounting rules for foreign exchange gains and losses become clarified, and as the economic effect of exchange rate changes on future cash flows and market values becomes recognized.

In order to manage foreign exchange risk, management must first understand how the international monetary system has evolved over time and how it functions today.[1] The international monetary system is defined in this book as the structure within which foreign exchange rates are determined, international trade and capital flows accommodated, and balance of payments adjustments made.

INTERNATIONAL MONETARY SYSTEM BEFORE 1971

Gold Standard

From the days of the Pharaohs (about 3000 B.C.) gold was used as a medium of exchange and a store of value. The Greeks and Romans used gold coins and passed on this tradition through the mercantile era to the nineteenth century. The great increase in trade during the free-trade period of the late nineteenth century led to a need for a more formalized system for settling international trade balances. Although there were no multilateral agreements such as exist today, one country after another declared a par value for its currency in terms of gold and then tried to adhere to the so-called rules of the game of what came to be known later as the classical gold standard. The United States was a latecomer to the game and did not go on the gold standard until 1879. The gold standard worked adequately until World War I interrupted trade patterns and caused the main trading countries to suspend its operation.

Fluctuating Exchange Rates

During World War I and the early 1920s, currencies were allowed to fluctuate over fairly wide ranges in terms of gold and each other. Theoretically it was expected that supply and demand for a country's exports and imports would cause moderate changes in its exchange rate about a central equilibrium value. This was the same function that the gold flow performed under the previous gold standard. Unfortunately, flexible exchange rates did not work in an equilibrating manner. On the contrary, international speculators sold the weak currencies short, causing them to fall further in value than warranted by the real economic factors. The reverse happened with strong currencies. Fluctuations in currency values could not be offset by the relatively thin forward exchange market except at exorbitant cost. The net result was that the volume of world trade did not grow in the 1920s in proportion to world gross national product (GNP) and declined to a very low level with the advent of the Depression in the 1930s.

Several attempts were made to get back on the gold standard. The United States returned to it in 1919, the United Kingdom in 1925, and France in 1928. The problem of finding reasonably stable new parity values for gold was never really solved before the collapse of the Austrian banking system in 1931 caused most trading nations to abandon the gold standard again. The United States returned to a modified gold standard in 1934. Gold was priced at $35 per ounce but was traded only with foreign central banks, not private citizens. From 1934 to the end of World War II exchange rates were theoretically determined by each currency's value in terms of gold, but only the dollar was convertible into gold. During World War II and its immediate aftermath many of the main trading currencies lost their convertibility into other currencies. The dollar was the only major trading currency that could be freely converted.

Gold Exchange Standard, 1944–1971

Bretton Woods Conference A so-called gold exchange standard was adopted by the Allied Powers as a result of negotiations at Bretton Woods, New Hampshire, in 1944. The International Monetary Fund (IMF) and the

International Bank for Reconstruction and Development (World Bank) were created at this conference.[2]

Under the provisions of the Bretton Woods Agreement, all countries were to fix the value of their currencies in terms of gold but were not required to exchange their currencies for gold. Only the dollar remained convertible into gold (at $35 per ounce). Therefore all countries decided what they wished their exchange rates to be vis-à-vis the dollar, then calculated what the gold par value of their currencies should be to give the desired dollar exchange rate. All participating countries agreed to try to maintain the value of their currencies within 1% of par by buying or selling foreign exchange or gold as needed. Devaluation was not to be used as a competitive trade policy, but if a currency became too weak to defend, a devaluation of up to 10% would be allowed without formal approval by the IMF. Larger devaluations required the IMF's approval.

International Monetary Fund The International Monetary Fund was established to render temporary assistance to countries trying to defend their currencies against cyclical, seasonal, or random occurrences. The IMF can also assist a country having structural trade problems if the country is taking adequate steps to correct its problems. However, if persistent deficits occur, the IMF cannot save a country from eventual devaluation. The Soviet Union participated in the Bretton Woods meeting, as one of the Allied Powers, but eventually it chose not to join either the International Monetary Fund or the World Bank.

To carry out its task, the IMF was originally funded by each member subscribing to a quota based on expected post–World War II trade patterns.[3] The quotas have since been expanded and the distribution revised a number of times, most recently in 1983, to accommodate the growth in overall world trade, new additions to IMF membership, and growth in importance of the exporting countries. In August 1985 the quotas were equivalent to $92.5 billion.

The original quotas were paid 25% in gold or dollars and 75% in local currencies. Any member could borrow back up to its original 25% gold or convertible-currency payment, called the "gold tranche," in any 12-month period, plus 100% of its total quota. Thus a member was able to borrow 125% of its quota in convertible currencies or gold even though it only paid in 25% in convertible currencies or gold. The IMF imposed restrictions on borrowing beyond the first 25% of quota to ensure that steps were being taken to correct the borrower's currency problems.

Over the years access to IMF loans has been gradually liberalized. Under the guidelines presently in effect each of the 146 member countries could borrow annually up to 150% of its quota, or up to 450% during a three-year period. Cumulative access, net of scheduled repayments, could be up to 600% of a member's quota.[4]

Relative distribution of quotas is important as a determinant of the relative distribution of voting power. The industrialized countries have always maintained voting control, since they have subscribed to a majority of the quotas. At the present time the United States holds a little over 21% of voting control. Other large voting rights are held by the United Kingdom (7.4%), West Germany (5.4%), France (4.8%), Japan (4.2%), Saudi Arabia (3.5%), and Canada (3.4%).[5]

In addition to its quota resources, the IMF currently has access under certain circumstances to about $19 billion which it can borrow from the major industrialized countries. Under the General Arrangements to Borrow (GAB) and associated agreements, most recently renewed and expanded in 1983, the IMF can use the borrowed funds not only to help the GAB members over temporary exchange problems but also to assist nonmembers, such as countries with heavy external debt burdens.

Adequacy of international monetary reserves prior to the crisis of 1971 During the post–World War II era the various central banks held gold, dollars, pounds sterling, other convertible trading currencies, and "special drawing rights" (to be explained shortly) as reserves to help them maintain their currency value. Since a country's gold tranche could be withdrawn automatically from the IMF, countries considered it part of their reserves. Exhibit 2.1 shows the composition of world monetary reserves as they stood on October 31, 1971. Exhibit 2.2 shows a breakdown of reserves by area and compares the reserves of 1971 to those of 1949. Since the supply of monetary gold and the gold tranche remained virtually constant after 1949, nearly all the growth in world monetary reserves from $46 billion in 1949 to $117 billion in 1971 was due to increased holdings of foreign exchange (mainly dollars) and "special drawing rights."

Return of the major trading nations to full convertibility of their currencies in 1959 and the concurrent development of common markets and free-trade areas caused a rapid increase in trade and foreign direct invest-

EXHIBIT 2.1
Composition of World Monetary Reserves as of October 31, 1971 (rounded to nearest billions of dollars

Gold	36
Gold tranche in IMF	6
Special drawing rights	6
Foreign exchange	69
Total	117

Source: IMF, *International Financial Statistics,* February 1972, p. 18.

EXHIBIT 2.2
International Reserves, 1949 and 1971 (rounded to nearest billions of dollars)

Area and country	*December 1949*	*October 1971*
All Countries	46	117
Developed areas:	37	96
United States	26	12
Western Europe	8	54
Canada	1	5
Japan	0	13
Australia, New Zealand, and South Africa	2	4
Less developed areas:	10	21
Latin America	3	6
Middle East	1	4
Other Asia	3	5
Other Africa	3	5

Source: IMF, *International Financial Statistics*, February 1972, p. 18.

ment. The year 1959 also marked the beginning of large deficits in the U.S. balance of payments, but it was not until the early 1960s that an international monetary reserve dilemma was recognized.[6] Virtually all the newly mined gold (about $1 billion per year) was being absorbed by commercial users or lost to hoarders. The only way that international monetary reserves could increase in step with the increase in trade and foreign investment was for the reserve-currency countries to run deficits in their balance of payments so that other countries received more reserve currencies than they paid out.

Unfortunately, as some of the reserve-currency countries ran deficits, especially the United States, the United Kingdom, and France, a credibility gap developed. Monetary speculators and central bankers began to doubt the ability of these reserve-currency countries to continue to convert their currency into gold (in the case of dollars) and dollars (in the case of non-dollar reserve currencies). Evidence of this distrust manifested itself on the London free market in wide fluctuations in the price of gold above the $35 per ounce official rate and in the drain of gold and foreign exchange from the deficit countries. The United Kingdom was forced to devalue the pound in 1967 after several years of crisis and rumored devaluation. France devalued the franc in 1969. The United States reacted to its continuing balance of payments deficits in 1963 by levying an interest equalization tax on foreign borrowing in U.S. capital markets. This tax effectively forced foreign borrowers to raise long-term capital elsewhere and hastened the development of the Eurobond market. As U.S. balance of payments deficits continued, voluntary controls on new dollar capital outflows from U.S. firms were imposed in 1965. These controls were followed in 1968 by mandatory controls on direct foreign investment by U.S. firms and credit restraint on foreign lending by U.S. banks. In both cases the controls limited new dollar outflows to developed countries to a given percentage of a base-year figure. New direct investment and lending to less developed countries were controlled on a much more liberal basis. Despite these precautions the U.S. balance of payments position continued to worsen and credibility deteriorated until the crisis of 1971.

Modification of the Gold Exchange Standard

Official currency swaps Official currency swaps provided a temporary supplement to international monetary reserves during the 1960s.[7] Swap agreements were negotiated among the central banks of the "Group of Ten" most industrialized countries. Instant reserves were created by a swap of credit lines between central banks. For example, if the United Kingdom were losing gold to West Germany, the Bank of England could create a pound sterling credit in favor of the Bundesbank (Germany's Central Bank) and the Bundesbank in turn would create a Deutschemark credit in favor of the Bank of England. The Bank of England would then use the Deutschemarks to buy pounds, but the Bundesbank would not draw on its pound line of credit. Thus there would be an upward buying pressure on the pound and an excess supply of Deutschemarks, causing, it was hoped, a return flow of gold or dollars to the United Kingdom. When this return flow occurred, the Deutschemarks were repaid to the Bundesbank and the swap retired. The problem of a need for growth in permanent reserves to maintain the ratio of reserves to world trade was not solved, however. The early reciprocal swap lines totaled $6.25 billion, but these were increased in 1973 to $18 billion and then gradually to $30 billion by 1985.

Special drawing rights A more lasting solution to the need for growth in world monetary reserves was started with the creation of "special drawing rights" on the IMF. In late 1967, at Rio de Janeiro, agreement was reached in principle on a system whereby the IMF would create new reserves called special drawing rights (SDRs) and distribute them to each member country in proportion to that member's quota. Creation of these reserves would be in an amount sufficient to maintain the proportion of reserves to world trade. SDRs would be exchanged only among central banks, and would be convertible into other currency but not directly into gold. The IMF issued the first SDRs in 1970, and by early 1985 a total of a little more than SDR 14 billion (U.S. $15 billion) were outstanding, representing about 4% of world international reserves other than gold.

The SDR's value was originally based on the average value of a basket of 16 major trading currencies weighted according to their importance in

EXHIBIT 2.3
SDR Valuation on January 2, 1981

Currency	*Currency amount*	*Exchange rate on January 2, 1981*	*U.S. dollar equivalent*	*Currency weight (%)*
U.S. dollar	.5400	1.00000	.540000	42.5
Deutschemark	.4600	1.97400	.233029	18.3
French franc	.7400	4.56000	.162281	12.8
Japanese yen	34.0000	202.87000	.167595	13.2
Pound sterling	.0710	2.37800	.168838	13.3
				100.0

SDR value of U.S. $1.00 = .786322
U.S. dollar value of SDR = 1.27174

Source: IMF, *IMF Survey,* January 12, 1981, p. 6. (Percentage weight calculations added.)
Note: Currency amount is the currency components of the basket. Exchange rate is given in terms of currency units per U.S. dollar, except for the pound sterling, which is expressed as U.S. dollars per pound sterling. All rates are at noon in the London foreign exchange market. U.S. dollar equivalents are the U.S. dollar equivalents of the currency amounts in the first column at the exchange rates in the second column—that is, column 1 divided by column 2, except for the pound sterling, for which the amounts in the two columns are multiplied.

world trade. The first SDR unit was equal to one U.S. dollar, but the SDR fluctuates in value relative to the U.S. dollar, depending on the relative performance of the individual currencies.

On January 1, 1981, the basket of currencies was officially reduced from 16 to 5. Exhibit 2.3 shows the new method of valuation. One SDR unit equaled $1.27174 both before and after conversion to the new valuation system. Once the U.S. dollar/SDR exchange rate is established, the value of any other currency in terms of the SDR can be determined by using its market rate vis-à-vis the dollar and then converting it to SDRs using the U.S. dollar/SDR rate. SDR rates for more than 40 currencies are calculated and announced daily by the IMF. As of November 1985 one SDR was worth a little over $1.07.

INTERNATIONAL MONETARY CRISIS OF 1971–1973

Crisis of August 1971

Lack of confidence in the international monetary system, and the dollar in particular, reached a peak in August 1971, when it became obvious that the United States was heading toward an all-time high balance of payments deficit, which ultimately reached $29.6 billion for 1971 on a reserve transactions basis. On August 15, 1971, President Nixon suspended official purchases or sales of gold by the U.S. Treasury. Furthermore, in what was termed "Phase I" of a series of policy changes, the United States temporarily imposed a 10% surcharge on all imports, and all domestic U.S. prices were frozen at existing rates.

Because the price of gold at $35 per ounce was theoretically left unchanged, there was no immediate impact on the amount of international monetary reserves. Nevertheless, the United States served notice to the world that the dollar could no longer be used as the basis for the gold exchange standard.

In the meantime, exchange rates of most of the leading trading countries were allowed to float in relation to the dollar and thus indirectly in relation to gold. By the end of 1971 most of the major trading currencies had appreciated vis-à-vis the dollar. This amounted to a *de facto* devaluation of the dollar.[8]

Meanwhile, bargaining was taking place among the major trading nations with the object of restoring confidence in the international monetary system. U.S. Treasury Secretary John Connally, the leader of the U.S. bargaining team, insisted that part of the problem with the U.S. balance of payments, and thus indirectly the international monetary system, was that trade barriers erected by other countries against the dollar after World War II during a period of severe dollar shortages had not been removed when a dollar glut eventually developed. Furthermore, certain currencies, notably the Deutschemark and the yen, were greatly undervalued, thus causing a severe price handicap for U.S. exporters competing in third markets. This situation also encouraged large imports into the United States of German and Japanese goods. Therefore Connally insisted that trade barriers against the United States be dropped and that the undervalued currencies be revalued upward as a condition for the United States to return to convertibility and to drop the import surcharge.

The non-U.S. delegates argued that dropping trade barriers was a long-term project and that something needed to be done immediately. The easiest solution would be for the United States to devalue the dollar relative to gold.

Devaluation of the dollar had been proposed periodically during the late 1960s and early 1970s as a solution to the shortage of international monetary reserves and the U.S. balance of payments problem. If the price of gold were doubled, for example, world gold reserves would be doubled, at least in terms of dollars. Devaluation would also encourage more mining of gold. The United States had always opposed devaluation on the grounds that virtually all other countries would devalue their currencies to maintain their same official exchange rate vis-à-vis the dollar. After all, that is how they determined their par value initially. If such a worldwide devaluation occurred, the United States would still have the same balance of payments problem and the day of reckoning would simply be postponed. Furthermore, the main beneficiaries would be the gold-mining countries, the Soviet Union and South Africa, neither of which were admired politically in the United States. The main losers would be Germany and Japan, countries that had cooperated the most by maintaining their reserves in dollars.

Smithsonian Agreement of December 1971

Multilateral bargaining sessions among the world's leading trading nations, namely the Group of Ten, reached a compromise agreement at the Washington, D.C., meeting of December 17–18, 1971, later known as the Smithsonian Agreement. The United States agreed to devalue the dollar to \$38 per ounce of gold (an 8.57% devaluation), subject to ratification by Congress. In return, each of the other members of the Group of Ten agreed to revalue their own currencies upward in relation to the dollar by specified amounts. Actual revaluations ranged from 7.4% by Canada to 16.9% by Japan. Furthermore, the trading band around par value was expanded from the existing 1% band to plus or minus 2.25%, which meant a maximum movement of 4.5% with respect to the U.S. dollar.

The "Snake"

Starting in April/May 1972, members of the European Economic Community (EEC), plus prospective members Denmark, Ireland, Norway, and the United Kingdom, entered into the European Joint Float Agreement. This agreement became known as "the snake." Under this arrangement values of members' currencies were to be held within a 2.25% trading band with respect to each other. Jointly they were allowed to float within a 4.5% band with respect to the U.S. dollar, as permitted under the Smithsonian Agreement. This float within a float earned the name "the snake within the tunnel." To top it off, the Dutch and Belgians agreed to maintain a still narrower 1% trading band with respect to each other. Naturally this arrangement achieved the ultimate distinction of being known as "the worm within the snake within the tunnel." Within two months, however, market pressures forced the United Kingdom to withdraw from the snake, followed quickly by Denmark. Although Denmark rejoined the snake in October 1972, Italy withdrew in February 1973.

FLOATING EXCHANGE RATES, 1973–1979

International Monetary Crisis of February 1973

By the second half of 1972, new currency alignments were already being tested. The dollar was weak because of the continued U.S. balance of payments deficit. Moreover, convertibility of the dollar into gold was still suspended, with little prospect for a return to convertibility in the near future. In fact, the price of gold on the London free market in August 1972 was $70 per ounce rather than $38 per ounce.

The Smithsonian Agreement was less than a year old before market pressures forced changes in the new rates. The U.K. pound was floated in June 1972 and the Swiss franc in January 1973. In early 1973 the U.S. dollar came under attack once again, thereby forcing a second devaluation on February 12, 1973, this time by 10% to $42.22 per ounce. By late February 1973 a fixed-rate system appeared no longer feasible given the extreme surges of speculative flows of currencies. The major foreign exchange markets were actually closed for several weeks in March 1973, and when they reopened, most currencies were allowed to float temporarily to levels determined by market forces. Par values were left unchanged.

With the advent of floating exchange rates in March 1973, countries with strong balance of payments positions watched their currencies shoot up in value relative to countries with large balance of payments deficits. In particular, West Germany, the Netherlands, Switzerland, Japan, and the Scandinavian countries were shown to have the strong currencies, whereas the United States and the United Kingdom had the weak currencies. By June 1973 the U.S. dollar had lost an additional 10% in value relative to its major trading partners. Even within the snake, Germany, the Netherlands, and Norway were all forced to revalue their currencies upward with respect to the snake's other members. Nevertheless, members of the snake tried to maintain their own 2.25% trading band while abandoning the tunnel, since the 4.5% trading band vis-à-vis the U.S. dollar was no longer a constraint.

Oil Crisis of 1973–1974 and Its Aftermath

Starting in October 1973 oil prices began to rise precipitously, followed by the oil embargo and its aftermath, the quadrupling of oil prices by 1974. These events cast a new light on the long-run balance of payments strength of the industrial countries. It appeared that the United States, being more self-reliant in energy sources, would fare better in making the adjustment to higher energy costs and lower energy availability than most European countries and Japan. North Sea oil and gas discoveries also placed the United Kingdom, Norway, and the Netherlands in a more favorable energy position than the other European countries. In fact, by the end of 1973 the U.S. dollar had recovered its summer losses and the U.S. balance of payments position was strengthening because of the increased competitiveness of U.S. goods and services at the lower value for the dollar.

On January 29, 1974, the United States removed all controls on capital flows, including the interest equalization tax, foreign direct investment program, and the Federal Reserve's foreign credit restraint program. This was done partly to reflect improvement in the U.S. balance of payments and subsequent strengthening of the U.S. dollar but also in anticipation of the growth of U.S. dollars held by petroleum-exporting countries, the so-called petrodollars. By removing capital controls, the United States hoped to encourage petrodollar holders to maintain their newfound wealth in dollars and to recycle these dollars through the U.S. capital market. This policy was modestly successful, except that most of the petrodollars were recycled through the Eurodollar and Eurobond markets.

Most of the non-OPEC world suffered a severe slowdown in economic growth rates during 1974 and 1975 before it absorbed the impact of the oil shock. Although growth rates picked up in 1976 and 1977, so did rates of inflation. This combination resulted in restrictive monetary and fiscal policies, particularly in Europe and Japan but also to a lesser degree in the United States. The Carter administration continued to give full employment priority over inflation. As a result, the U.S. balance of payments began to deteriorate in 1976, with the situation worsening in 1977.

Reform of the International Monetary System

Members who signed the Smithsonian Agreement in December 1971 recognized that the time was ripe for some major changes in the international monetary system devised at Bretton Woods in 1944, but no agreement existed on what changes would be desirable. Some felt a return to fixed rates was imperative, but the majority believed that some sort of managed float would be needed to manage the huge increase in potential "hot money," particularly the immense "dollar overhang" held by central banks, the commercial banking systems of the world, and individuals. In September 1972 the IMF appointed the so-called Committee of 20, an expanded version of the Group of Ten, to suggest revisions to the international monetary system by July 1974. The reality of the oil crisis that immediately followed and sharp differences within the committee caused it to fail in its mission, but it laid the groundwork for the IMF meeting at Jamaica in January 1976.

At Jamaica an agreement was reached that provides the rules of the game for today's system. Highlights of the Jamaica Agreement are as follows:

- Floating rates were declared acceptable, although member countries are permitted to interfere to even out unwarranted fluctuations caused by sheer speculation. In other words, member countries are no longer expected to maintain a band around par value.
- Gold was demonetized as a reserve asset. The IMF agreed to return 25 million ounces to its members and to sell another 25 million ounces at the going market price (around $2 billion). The proceeds of the sale were to be placed in a trust fund to help the poorer nations. Members could also sell their own gold reserves at market price rather than at the previous par value price.

- IMF quotas were increased to $41 billion. Subsequently they were increased to the present equivalent of $92.5 billion. The non–oil-exporting less developed countries were given improved access to borrowing at the IMF. Voting rights were adjusted to reflect the new distribution of trade and reserves, including a total of 10% of voting power to OPEC countries.
- A special $9 billion fund managed by the IMF for use by countries with balance of payments problems due to increased oil prices was confirmed. This "oil facility" was actually started in 1974, was expanded since then, and expired in 1983.

Petrodollars

OPEC's success at raising oil prices led to a rapid shift in wealth from the industrialized countries to the oil-exporting countries. Although a large proportion of the incremental oil revenues were recycled by the exporters through increased imports of goods and services for ambitious development plans (Iran, Indonesia, Venezuela, and Nigeria), very large dollar reserves were accumulated by Saudi Arabia and Kuwait because they did not have the population base to justify huge increases in imports. These surplus dollars were by and large reinvested in U.S. dollar and Eurocurrency bank deposits and government securities. To give an idea of the shift in wealth, and particularly in international reserves, Exhibit 2.4 presents an update of Exhibit 2.2 but with the oil-exporting countries separated out. Note the tremendous increase in reserves of the oil exporters from $8 billion in 1971 to $71 billion in 1977. In particular, Saudi Arabia's reserves had grown from $1 billion in 1971 to $28 billion in 1977. Other exceptionally large increases in reserves were recorded by Germany, the United Kingdom, Japan, and the less developed areas. Since the supply of gold, gold tranche in the IMF, and SDRs held by central banks increased by only a little over $2 billion from 1971 to 1977, almost the entire growth in international reserves of $163 billion was in foreign-currency holdings of central banks, particularly dollars.

Triggered mainly by the oil price shock, foreign exchange rates fluctuated rather severely during the period 1974–1977 in response to differential national rates of inflation, interest rates, structural shifts in the balance of payments, and outright speculation. In the face of these pressures the snake did not hold together as planned. France withdrew in 1974, rejoined in 1975, and withdrew again in 1976. During 1976 and 1977 the three Scandinavian members devalued their currencies as the strength of the Deutschemark threatened their international price competitiveness. Sweden withdrew from the snake in 1977, and Norway withdrew in 1978. Although this attempt at close European monetary collaboration failed, lessons were learned, which paved the way for later cooperation.

EXHIBIT 2.4
International Reserves, October 1971 and July 1977 (rounded to nearest billions of dollars)

Area and country	*October 1971*	*July 1977*
All Countries	117	280
Developed areas:	96	161
United States	12	19
Western Europe	54	116
Canada	5	5
Japan	13	19
Australia, New Zealand, and South Africa	4	3
Oil-exporting countries	8	71
Less developed areas (excludes oil exporters):	13	48
Other Latin America	5	16
Other Middle East	1	7
Other Asia	5	21
Other Africa	2	4

Source: IMF, *International Financial Statistics,* October 1977, p. 25.
Note: The source provided data in terms of SDRs. These have been converted to U.S. dollars at the rates of \$1.00 = SDR1 in 1971 and \$1.16 = SDR1 in 1977.

To illustrate the magnitude of currency fluctuations since 1971, Exhibit 2.5 shows exchange rates for major currencies. Exhibit 2.6 shows percentage changes in the dollar value of these currencies for the decade 1971–1981 and for three two-year periods from 1971 to 1977. Note in Exhibit 2.6 that during the 1971–1973 period and again during the 1973–1975 period almost all currencies strengthened relative to the dollar. However, between 1975 and 1977 only two currencies, the Swiss franc and the Japanese yen, strengthened relative to the dollar.

U.S. Dollar Crisis of 1977–1978

During the period 1977–1978 expansionary policies of the Carter administration led to a substantial rate of growth in GNP and a reduction in unemployment in the United States but also to an increased rate of inflation and a deterioration of the U.S. balance of payments. Germany, Japan, Switzerland, and the Netherlands, which were pursuing a more conservative growth policy with lower rates of inflation, ran rather large surpluses in their balance of payments. As a result, their currencies appreciated vis-à-vis the U.S. dollar. The situation worsened throughout 1978 as the U.S. government followed a policy of "benign neglect." This meant ignoring the depreciation of the dollar because domestic economic goals were accorded

EXHIBIT 2.5
Exchange Rates for Selected Countries (units of foreign currency per U.S. dollar; average exchange rates for the first quarter of each calendar year)

Country	*Currency*	*Symbol*	*1971*	*1972*	*1973*
Argentina	Peso	$a	4.000	5.000	5.000
Australia	Dollar	$A	0.887	.840	.706
Belgium	Franc	BF	49.620	44.057	41.852
Brazil	Cruzeiro	Cr$	5.110	5.845	6.030
Canada	Dollar	Can$	1.008	.997	1.003
Denmark	Krone	DKr	7.498	6.975	6.208
France	Franc	FF	5.514	5.028	4.541
Germany	Deutschemark	DM	3.630	3.168	2.838
India	Rupee	Rs	7.502	7.214	7.589
Iran	Rial	R1	76.380	76.380	68.720
Italy	Lira	Lit	621.900	582.50	582.50
Japan	Yen	¥	357.400	304.20	265.83
Kuwait	Dinar	KD	.357	.329	.294
Mexico	Peso	Ps	12.500	12.500	12.500
Netherlands	Guilder	fl	3.595	3.193	3.048
Norway	Krone	NKr	7.140	6.595	5.900
Saudi Arabia	Riyal	SR	4.500	4.150	3.730
South Africa	Rand	R	.712	.747	.705
Spain	Peseta	Pts	69.700	64.582	58.273
Sweden	Krona	SKr	5.165	4.776	4.493
Switzerland	Franc	S.Fcs	4.295	3.840	3.237
United Kingdom[a]	Pound	£	2.417	2.616	2.478

Source: IMF, *International Financial Statistics*, monthly issues.

[a]U.S. dollars per U.K. pound. Traditionally the U.K. pound has been quoted in units of foreign currency (such as the U.S. dollar) per pound because until 1974 the pound was not a decimal currency.

a higher priority. Such a policy led to worldwide loss of confidence in the dollar. Central bankers who had previously absorbed excess dollars in the marketplace in order to cushion its fall began to shift their official reserves out of dollars into Deutschemarks and Swiss francs. They were joined by wealthy investors, particularly the Saudi Arabians. The market for dollar-denominated Eurobonds dried up as investors demanded issues denominated in other currencies.

By October 1978 the dollar had depreciated about 20% on a trade-weighted basis compared to early 1977. This depreciation was well beyond what could be predicted by economic analysis of inflation and interest rate differentials (a subject to be covered in Chapter 5). The dollar's decline worsened domestic U.S. inflation as the prices of imports rose. OPEC members considered switching the pricing of oil from dollars to a more stable

1974	*1975*	*1976*	*1977*	*1978*	*1979*	*1980*	*1981*
5.000	10.000	93.39	313.83	721.000	1316.500	1747.500	2368.000
.672	.739	.796	.915	.875	.894	.923	.856
38.950	34.663	39.216	36.757	31.480	29.540	31.170	34.448
6.455	7.735	9.533	12.657	16.945	23.130	46.800	76.530
1.028	.997	.995	1.030	1.132	1.161	1.191	1.187
6.055	5.440	6.147	5.890	5.564	5.191	6.026	6.621
4.764	4.215	4.523	4.977	4.580	4.297	4.478	4.958
2.523	2.345	2.574	2.395	2.023	1.868	1.942	2.102
7.767	7.794	8.931	8.843	8.433	8.150	8.193	8.196
67.625	66.641	69.373	70.625	70.475	70.475	70.475	75.399
622.250	632.03	765.16	882.62	852.500	839.900	898.250	1047.950
276.00	293.80	302.39	285.57	222.400	209.300	249.700	211.000
.294	.286	.294	.289	.276	.276	.276	.274
12.500	12.500	12.500	22.026	22.743	22.827	22.851	23.762
2.685	2.394	2.675	2.503	2.163	2.014	2.127	2.328
5.475	4.915	5.542	5.270	5.308	5.108	5.170	5.372
3.550	3.475	3.530	3.530	3.455	3.355	3.325	3.345
.671	.671	.870	.870	.870	.846	.810	.798
59.122	55.978	63.802	68.789	80.023	68.198	72.300	85.305
4.392	3.942	4.385	4.224	4.589	4.371	4.457	4.592
3.000	2.527	2.579	2.520	1.868	1.691	1.832	1.912
2.394	2.409	2.000	1.714	1.856	2.067	2.167	2.244

currency, such as the SDR, in response to the decline in the real value of their oil exports and monetary reserves.

The Carter administration finally reacted on November 1, 1978, with a program designed to restore confidence in the dollar. The program included a sharp increase in interest rates, a promised reduction in the federal budget deficit, and creation of a $30 billion fund of foreign currencies to be used to support the dollar in foreign exchange markets. The latter was to be raised by sales of foreign-currency-denominated bonds, borrowing from the IMF, and expanding the existing swap agreements with foreign central banks.

The Carter program worked temporarily. Its shock value changed short-term expectations and signaled a switch in U.S. policy to one of concern rather than neglect for the dollar's international value.

EXHIBIT 2.6
Percent Change in Dollar Value for Selected Currencies (first quarter 1971 to first quarter 1981 and selected subperiods

Currency	*1971–1981 (decade)*	*1971–1973 (two years)*	*1973–1975 (two years)*	*1975–1977 (two years)*
Swiss franc	+124.6	+32.7	+28.1	+2.8
Deutschemark	+72.7	+27.9	+21.0	−2.1
Japanese yen	+69.4	+34.4	−9.5	+2.9
Netherlands guilder	+54.4	+17.9	+27.3	−4.4
Belgian franc	+44.0	+18.6	+20.7	−5.7
Saudi Arabian riyal	+34.5	+20.6	+7.3	−1.6
Norwegian krone	+32.9	+21.0	+20.0	−6.7
Kuwait dinar	+30.3	+21.4	+2.8	−1.0
Danish krone	+13.2	+20.8	+14.1	−7.6
Swedish krona	+12.5	+15.0	+14.0	−6.7
French franc	+11.2	+21.4	+7.7	−15.3
United Kingdom pound	+7.2	+2.5	−2.9	−28.9
Australian dollar	+3.6	+25.6	−4.5	−19.2
Iranian rial	−1.9	+11.1	+3.1	−5.0
Indian rupee	−8.5	−1.1	−2.6	−11.9
South African rand	−10.8	+1.0	+5.1	−22.9
Canadian dollar	−15.1	+.5	−.6	−3.2
Spanish peseta	−18.3	+19.6	+4.1	−18.6
Italian lira	−40.7	+6.8	−7.8	−28.4
Mexican peso	−47.4	0	0	−43.2
Brazilian cruzeiro	−93.3	−15.3	−22.0	−38.9
Argentine peso	−99.8	−20.0	−50.0	−96.8

FLOATING CURRENCY BLOCS, 1979 TO THE PRESENT

By February 1979 the dollar was again under pressure because of turmoil in Iran, low U.S. interest rates relative to inflation, and an ominous trend toward central bankers' diversifying their foreign currency reserves into Deutschemarks, Japanese yen, and Swiss francs. This trend was aided by a newfound willingness on the part of Germany, Japan, and Switzerland to issue the appropriate interest-bearing securities to Saudi Arabia and other OPEC surplus countries as a means of financing their dramatically increasing oil import bills.

Oil Crisis of 1979

In addition to diversifying their reserves, OPEC members reacted to the dollar's weakness by enforcing a doubling of oil prices during 1979. As a result, the industrial countries once again slipped into recession, just as they had in 1974–1975. This recession fostered rapid swings in both interest and exchange rates. For example, a credit crunch in the United States caused historically high interest rates toward the end of 1979, followed by a precipitous decline in the middle of 1980, when Treasury bills fell below 8%. Still another credit crunch occurred at the end of 1980, when Treasury bills climbed to 15%. Treasury bills climbed even slightly higher during 1981.

Iranian Freeze of November 1979

Foreign exchange market conditions became more unsettled in November 1979 when President Carter froze all Iranian assets in the United States as well as in U.S. banks abroad. Other OPEC members, especially Saudi Arabia, were naturally alarmed at this action because they could visualize the same thing happening to their assets under the wrong circumstances in the future. As a result, dollar funds were discretely moved out of U.S. banks into non-U.S. banks in the Eurodollar market. In addition, some dollars were converted into other reserve currencies in order to keep assets safe from any potential future U.S. unilateral actions.

Despite these transfers the U.S. dollar held its own in 1980, because the U.S. was perceived to be able to weather the doubling of oil prices better than its main rival currency countries, Germany and Japan. In fact, in late 1980 and throughout 1981 the U.S. dollar showed unexpected strength and the Deutschemark unexpected weakness. The dollar's strength came from a change in market expectations about future inflation in the United States as a result of the election of Ronald Reagan as president. Furthermore, partly as a result of reduced energy demand, the U.S. balance of payments finally changed to a current account surplus in 1980. Finally, U.S. interest rates were relatively high compared to expected inflation and comparable rates in Germany. The weakness of the Deutschemark was mainly due to a large German balance of payments deficit on current account in 1980 and relatively low interest rates designed to pull Germany out of recession.

European Monetary System (EMS), 1979

Chaotic conditions in foreign exchange markets in 1978 hastened the need to create mechanisms that would foster more stability. One of these mechanisms arose from the ashes of the all-but-defunct snake cooperation. In March 1979 the nine members of the EEC established the European Monetary System (EMS).

Under the EMS arrangement, a new composite currency called the European currency unit (ECU) was created. It is similar to the SDR in that it exists only on the books of the members of the EMS, not as a circulating currency. It is used as a monetary asset that members hold as a reserve currency to lend, borrow, and settle accounts with each other. Its value is based on the weighted value of the member currencies, with the weights based on each member's share of intra-European trade and the relative size of its GNP. The ECU was originally worth $1.40, but its value varies over time as the members' currencies float jointly with respect to the U.S. dollar and other nonmember currencies. In November 1985 the ECU was worth about $0.84.

Each of the member countries values its currency in terms of the ECU, thus forming a bilateral grid. If a member's currency deviates by more than 2.25% (6% for the Italian lira) from the central rate of another member's currency, both members are required to take action in the foreign exchange markets to force the rate back within the 2.25% trading band. However, if a member's currency should deviate by more than 1.69% (4.5% for the Italian lira) from its central rate within the bilateral grid, the "threshold of divergence" is reached. The deviating member must then take steps to correct the problem, or, failing that, either devalue or revalue its currency's ECU value within the bilateral grid.[9]

Members intervene in the foreign exchange markets through the system of mutual credit facilities. Each member can borrow almost unlimited amounts of foreign currency from other members for periods that can be extended up to three months. A second line of defense includes loans that can be extended to nine months, but the total amount available is limited to a pool of credit, originally about 14 billion ECUs, and the size of the member's quota in the pool. Additional funds are available for maturities of from two to five years from a second pool, originally about 11 billion ECUs, but to use these funds, the borrowing member must correct domestic economic policies that are causing its currency to deviate.

The European Monetary Cooperation Fund (EMCF) was established in 1982 as an institution to administer the various credit facilities and issue an initial supply of ECUs to the member countries similar to the way the IMF issues SDRs. The members deposit 20% of their gold and dollar reserves with it in return for a corresponding amount of ECUs.

The EMS got off to a rocky start. The events of 1979 and 1980 forced a 1981 revaluation of the Deutschemark and Dutch guilder and devaluations of the French franc, Danish krone, and Italian lira. The British have not participated in the joint float so far.

Multicurrency Reserve System

With the joint float of the EMS, the continued strength of the Japanese yen, and the reemergence of gold as a key reserve asset, the international monetary system gradually evolved into a series of currency blocs. Within each currency bloc currencies float within a narrow band. The currency blocs themselves float with respect to each other, typically pulled by the strongest currency in each bloc. The main blocs are anchored by the Deutschemark (EMS), the U.S. dollar, the Japanese yen, and the British pound.

To reduce exchange risk, the world's central bankers diversified their portfolios of reserve assets to include one or more key currencies from each currency bloc, as well as Swiss francs, gold, ECUs, and SDRs. By the end of 1983 the foreign exchange component of central bank reserves was composed as follows: U.S. dollars, 74%; Deutschemarks, 13%; Japanese yen, 5%; U.K. pound sterling, 3%; Swiss francs, 1%; and Dutch guilders, 1%.[10] Exhibit 2.7 presents estimates prepared by the Basle-based Bank for International Settlements of the size and type of reserve assets held at the end of 1984. Note that the OPEC countries held reserve assets, including gold, valued at $81.7 billion, which is almost 12% of the global total reserve assets of $685.1 billion. Another interesting highlight is the inclusion of ECUs as a reserve asset. At $37.7 billion, they represented 5.5% of the global total and were nearly as large as the reserve positions held in the IMF.

A tremendous increase in the value of gold holdings during the 1977–1984 period can be attributed solely to a rise in the price of gold, despite an actual decline in the number of ounces held in official reserves. During this period the demand for gold by private institutions, individuals, central banks, and speculators was fueled by fear of worldwide recession, increasing inflation, and political insecurity from the events in Iran. As a result, the market price of gold rose from a plateau of around $150 per ounce in the 1974–1977 period to $525 per ounce in late 1979. It ultimately reached a high of over $800 per ounce in 1980 before falling back below $400 per ounce in 1981. Because central banks in recent years have used market prices for valuing their gold, the gold reserves at the end of 1984 were valued at $290.6 billion, compared to $36 billion in 1971 (Exhibit 2.1) for a slightly larger number of ounces valued at $35 per ounce.

In the long run the use of a multicurrency reserve system may stabilize the value of each individual central bank's portfolio of reserve assets. On the other hand, decisions by central bankers and a few OPEC countries to switch the composition of portfolios could be very destabilizing for individual currencies. Under these circumstances the burden of domestic adjustment to international monetary pressures will be shared by the United States, Germany, Japan, and Switzerland rather than fall on the United States alone, which was the case up until 1978. All these countries, except the United States, have previously tried to avoid having their currencies used as reserve assets because of the fear that it would limit their ability to conduct independent economic policies. The fact is that it will be increasingly difficult for all major industrial countries to conduct independent monetary and fiscal policies without regard to international consequences. As we will see

EXHIBIT 2.7
Changes in Global Reserves, 1982–1984 (unless otherwise indicated, in billions of U.S. dollars at current prices)

Areas and periods	*Gold (in millions of ounces)*	*Gold (in billions of U.S. dollars)*[a]	*Foreign exchange*	*IMF reserve positions*	*SDRs*	*ECUs*	*Nongold total*	*Total*
Group of Ten Countries								
1982	−0.3	35.4	−10.8	3.3	1.8	−8.4	−14.1	
1983	−0.8	−49.5	2.7	7.2	−3.1	3.2	10.0	
1984	−0.6	−53.7	4.2	−0.1	0.7	−6.9	− 2.1	
Amounts outstanding at end-1984	737.8	228.0	103.5	24.8	11.9	37.3	177.5	405.5
Other Developed Countries[b]								
1982	−1.7	3.5	0.8	−0.3	−0.2	—	0.3	
1983	−1.3	− 6.3	2.6	0.9	−0.5	0.4	3.4	
1984	−0.3	− 6.4	6.9	—	0.3	−0.4	6.8	
Amounts outstanding at end-1984	86.6	26.8	44.9	2.2	1.2	0.4	48.7	75.0
OPEC Member Countries								
1982	0.3	2.2	−11.4	0.7	0.2		−10.5	
1983	0.1	− 2.9	− 8.2	4.4	−0.7		− 4.5	
1984	0.1	− 3.1	− 2.8	0.5	0.1		− 2.2	
Amounts outstanding at end-1984	44.0	13.6	54.1	12.3	1.7		68.1	81.7

***Other Developing Countries*[c]**								
1982	−1.8	2.8	− 0.7	−0.4	−1.3		− 2.4	
1983	−0.4	− 5.0	7.4	0.3	−0.2		7.5	
1984	−1.0	− 5.6	14.4	−0.6	−0.1		13.7	
Amounts outstanding at end-1984	71.9	22.2	97.5	1.4	1.3		100.2	122.4
Total of Above Countries								
1982	−3.5	43.9	−22.1	3.3	0.5	−8.4	−26.7	
1983	−2.4	−63.7	4.5	12.8	−4.5	3.6	16.4	
1984	−1.8	−68.8	22.7	−0.2	1.0	−7.3	16.2	
Amounts outstanding at end-1984	940.3	290.6	300.0	40.7	16.1	37.7	394.5	685.1

Source: Bank for International Settlements, *Fifty-fifth Annual Report,* Basle, Switzerland, June 10, 1985, p. 158.

[a]Gold reserves valued at market prices.

[b]Excluding eastern European countries.

[c]Including Israel and the offshore financial centers.

in Chapter 5, the world's economies are inexorably linked through a strong interrelationship among exchange rates, interest rates, and inflation rates. The strength of the U.S. dollar alone can no longer shelter other economies from the discipline of the international marketplace.

Exchange Rate Developments, 1980–1985

The period 1980–1985 was characterized by unexpected strength of the U.S. dollar and its counterpart, unexpected weakness of the EMS currencies and the U.K. pound. The strength of the U.S. dollar was due to a combination of favorable factors that overcame the unfavorable effect of a large and growing U.S. balance of payments deficit on current account. Strong growth in the United States attracted heavy inflows on capital account from investors seeking higher returns on real asset investments. High real returns (adjusted for inflation) on financial assets also attracted foreign inflows to purchase debt securities. Political turmoil in other parts of the world reinforced the common perception of the United States as a safe political haven for personal wealth. U.S. banks sharply curtailed their lending to less developed countries, which were overburdened with external debt. More attractive opportunities caused by growth with low inflation in the United States also motivated U.S. banks and international portfolio investors to divert funds from other markets back to the U.S. market.

The U.S. rate of inflation was kept under control despite the huge U.S. government budget deficit because a growing stream of imports, motivated by the relatively high price of the U.S. dollar, provided stiff price competition for U.S.-made goods. In addition, a worldwide glut of oil and other basic commodities reduced the U.S.-dollar costs of these necessary imports.

Exhibit 2.8 shows how the nominal effective exchange rates of major trading countries fared with respect to each other during the period 1980–1985 (June). In contrast to Exhibit 2.5, this exhibit shows exchange rate fluctuations on a trade-weighted basis rather than on a bilateral basis with the U.S. dollar. This is consistent with the trend toward currencies being managed with reference to a bloc, such as the EMS, rather than to the U.S. dollar. The index numbers in Exhibit 2.8, with the average for the years 1980–1982 fixed at 100, show how each country's exchange rate changed with respect to the exchange rate of its trading partners, weighted by the size of its bilateral trade in manufactures with these partners in 1980.

It is obvious from Exhibit 2.8 that the U.S. dollar made a spectacular recovery from its earlier lows in the late 1970s. The index for the U.S. dollar rose from 90.7 in 1980 to a high of 136.9 in March 1985, receding to 130.4 in June 1985. Note that this level is considerably above its level of 114.6 prior to June 1970, when exchange rates were still fixed. In contrast, the U.K. pound tumbled from an index of 99.8 in 1980 to 81.0 in January 1985 before recovering to 90.5 in June 1985. This level is considerably below the level of 147.5 existing during fixed exchange rates in 1970. The Deutschemark showed some strength relative to the EMS currencies and the U.K. pound but still weakened relative to the U.S. dollar. The Japanese yen strengthened from an index of 95.5 in 1980 to 112.1 in 1985.

The increase in value of the U.S. dollar raised havoc with the U.S. balance of trade, as will be discussed in Chapter 3, and led to increased talk in the United States of protectionist measures to counter an "overvalued dollar" and "undervalued yen." What do these terms really mean?

Exchange rates are partly determined in the long run by relative national rates of inflation, just as nominal interest rates are a function of expected inflation and a real return to saving. These theories, known as "purchasing power parity" and the "Fisher Effect," respectively, are discussed formally in Chapter 5. Economists have devised an index that attempts to measure changes in exchange rates after adjusting for differential national rates of inflation. Several versions of such an index exist, each using a different price index for the adjustment. Exhibit 2.9 presents an easily available and useful index produced monthly by Morgan Guaranty Trust Company of New York. It measures the "real effective exchange rates" of the same countries shown in Exhibit 2.8. The only difference is that the nominal effective exchange rates in Exhibit 2.8 have been adjusted for differential inflation in wholesale prices of nonfood manufactures. If changes in exchange rates just offset differential inflation rates, all the index values would stay at 100. If an exchange rate strengthened more than justified by differential inflation, its index would rise above 100, and vice versa.

Note in Exhibit 2.9 that the U.S. dollar index was at 123.5 in June 1985. This can be interpreted to mean that the U.S. dollar was overvalued by 23.5% compared with the other 15 countries included in the index, using 1980–1982 as the base year. In contrast, the Japanese yen was at 93.6 in June 1985. It was slightly undervalued compared with the other 15 countries but almost 30% undervalued compared with the U.S. dollar (123.5 − 93.6 = 29.9). Critics are quick to point out that in the short run this would give Japanese goods a 30% price advantage over comparable U.S. goods due to the foreign exchange effect. Although this is an oversimplification, as we will see later, it is an appealing argument for protectionism.

Exchange Rate Variability

To what extent have floating rates increased the actual variability of exchange rates? Under the floating rate system, exchange rates adjust a little every day instead of the large one-time adjustments characteristic of the prior fixed exchange rate period. If the balance of payments adjustment mechanism is working correctly, exchange rates should eventually tend toward the same level under either floating or fixed rates, but the path

EXHIBIT 2.8
Nominal Effective Exchange Rates

	United States	*Canada*	*Japan*	*Australia*	*France*	*Germany*	*Italy*	*United Kingdom*
Pre-June 1970 parities	114.6	114.4	69.0	116.4	111.1	66.2	226.2	147.5
Smithsonian central rates	103.1	121.9	77.2	116.7	109.8	68.9	220.9	146.7
1980	90.7	100.4	95.5	96.0	106.5	100.0	108.4	99.8
1981	99.5	100.2	105.8	104.0	100.4	97.2	98.8	102.1
1982	109.8	99.4	98.6	100.1	93.1	102.8	92.8	98.1
1983	114.2	100.8	107.8	92.0	87.3	107.6	90.3	91.6
1984	122.4	97.3	113.0	94.2	84.4	107.4	86.7	88.1
1984								
July	124.2	95.4	110.8	90.3	84.6	107.7	87.3	87.7
August	124.0	97.0	111.4	91.9	84.3	107.3	86.6	87.9
September	127.3	96.7	112.0	92.1	83.6	106.2	85.9	87.1
October	128.5	96.6	112.0	93.6	83.7	106.3	85.7	85.3
November	126.8	96.5	112.5	95.0	84.0	106.7	85.6	85.2
December	129.5	96.7	112.0	94.8	83.6	106.1	86.0	83.7
1985								
January	132.0	96.9	110.5	93.8	83.7	106.2	86.3	81.0
February	136.4	95.3	110.0	86.8	83.5	105.8	85.4	81.4
March	136.9	93.2	111.3	81.5	83.7	105.9	83.7	84.0
April	131.7	93.6	111.5	74.2	84.5	106.7	83.0	88.1
May	132.0	92.9	111.5	76.3	84.4	106.5	82.9	89.2
June	130.4	93.2	112.1	74.3	84.5	106.5	83.0	90.5

Source: Morgan Guaranty Trust Company of New York, *World Financial Markets,* July 1985, p. 12.

Note: Index numbers, 1980–1982 average = 100. Each index shows a currency's trade-weighted appreciation or depreciation measured against 15 other major currencies, using averages of daily noon spot exchange rates in New York and bilateral trade weights based on 1980 trade in manufactures. Annual figures are calendar year averages.

taken creates different challenges for managers who must forecast exchange rates and for government officials who must manage the economy.

John Williamson has identified the problem of assessing exchange rate variability as follows: "It is important to distinguish between short-term *volatility* and persistent *misalignments.* By volatility is meant the amount of short-run variability in the exchange rate from hour to hour, day to day, week to week, or month to month. By misalignment is meant a persistent departure of the exchange rate from its long run equilibrium level."[11]

Exhibit 2.10 compares exchange rate volatility during selected fixed and floating rate years. It shows the coefficient of variation of daily nom-

Austria	Belgium	Netherlands	Spain	Switzerland	Denmark	Norway	Sweden
80.6	91.1	82.1	143.2	51.3	113.0	92.3	119.6
80.6	92.3	82.9	142.7	53.2	110.8	90.9	117.6
99.4	105.9	100.2	106.5	95.4	105.1	98.2	103.9
98.9	101.8	97.1	99.4	98.3	99.2	100.1	103.3
101.7	92.3	102.7	94.1	106.3	95.7	101.7	92.8
103.6	90.0	105.0	78.4	111.5	96.4	99.4	82.2
103.6	88.9	104.0	77.4	110.5	93.9	97.8	84.3
104.1	89.3	104.0	77.3	107.9	93.7	97.4	84.4
103.8	89.3	103.8	76.6	108.8	93.6	97.1	84.6
103.2	88.9	103.1	76.9	109.3	93.2	96.9	85.6
103.2	88.7	103.2	77.0	109.8	93.4	97.1	85.6
103.4	89.3	103.5	77.4	110.2	94.2	95.5	85.1
103.2	89.3	103.0	77.8	109.5	94.5	95.5	85.0
103.4	89.9	103.0	78.1	107.8	95.0	95.7	85.0
103.3	89.3	102.5	77.6	105.9	94.4	95.8	85.5
103.0	89.0	102.5	77.2	105.8	94.3	95.7	84.6
103.8	89.2	102.9	77.5	108.0	94.5	96.0	83.6
103.5	89.0	102.9	76.5	107.4	93.7	96.0	83.8
103.5	88.9	103.1	75.8	107.7	94.2	95.8	83.8

inal exchange rates against a six-month moving average of the U.S. dollar. Williamson concludes:

> It can be seen that exchange rate volatility in the Bretton Woods period was very sensitive to par value changes. In 1969 the French franc was devalued and the DM was revalued, and in consequence volatility was substantial. Similarly, the measure of sterling volatility in 1968 reflects the sterling devaluation of late 1967. In years when there was no par value change, volatility was small, an average of 0.2 percent. Under floating, volatility is regularly as large as it used to be in the years of par value changes under the Bretton Woods system, an average of close to 2 percent. Since par value changes were infrequent occurrences, it is clear that volatility on this measure has increased greatly since the advent of floating, by a factor of between 5 and 10, just as on the IMF measure. Moreover, volatility has, if anything, increased since the early years of floating, rather than diminishing as the markets gained experience.[12]

EXHIBIT 2.9
Real Effective Exchange Rates

	United States	*Canada*	*Japan*	*Australia*	*France*	*Germany*	*Italy*	*United Kingdom*
1980	89.4	99.6	103.0	93.0	102.1	103.5	103.5	99.9
1981	100.6	100.0	104.6	102.7	100.1	97.3	98.7	102.3
1982	109.9	100.4	92.3	104.3	97.8	99.2	97.8	97.9
1983	112.7	103.1	96.6	100.0	96.1	99.3	100.1	92.0
1984	118.2	101.2	97.6	105.1	96.8	96.5	101.1	89.3
1984								
July	120.0	99.5	95.4	101.1	97.9	96.6	101.7	89.0
August	119.5	101.2	96.0	103.3	97.2	96.1	101.5	89.4
September	121.5	101.4	96.8	103.7	96.3	95.2	101.0	88.8
October	123.6	100.4	96.0	105.0	96.5	95.2	100.8	86.8
November	122.0	100.4	96.2	106.4	97.0	95.3	101.2	86.9
December	123.9	101.1	95.7	106.6	98.0	94.5	101.4	85.4
1985								
January	126.2	101.4	94.1	105.4	97.0	94.9	102.6	83.1
February	129.7	100.0	93.5	97.4	97.1	94.6	101.6	83.9
March	129.8	98.0	94.1	91.5	97.3	94.2	100.8	86.6
April	125.2	98.2	93.7	83.3	98.3	94.8	100.5	91.3
May	125.2	97.7	93.5	85.7	98.3	94.6	101.0	92.2
June	123.5	98.1	93.6	83.5	98.5	94.5	101.9	93.8

Source: Morgan Guaranty Trust Company of New York, *World Financial Markets,* July 1985, p. 12.

Note: Index numbers, 1980–1982 average = 100. Each index is the corresponding nominal effective exchange rate adjusted for differential inflation in wholesale prices of nonfood manufactures. Underlying price data are partly estimated. Index revisions reflect revised price information or, less frequently, adoption of new price indices to measure inflation in one or more countries.

Exhibit 2.11 is an attempt to measure the degree of misalignment of exchange rates during fixed and floating rate periods. It shows maximum swings in the real effective exchange rates of five major currencies for the fixed exchange rate period of 1963–1972 and the floating rate period of 1973–1982. It is clear that maximum swings in the floating rate period were much larger for the Deutschemark, yen, pound sterling, and dollar. The French franc swing was greater in the fixed rate period thanks to several large devaluations. It should also be noted that the French franc and Deutschemark have attempted to maintain relatively fixed bilateral rates with each other, even during the floating period, as part of the European effort to promote exchange rate stability under the snake and EMS systems.

Austria	Belgium	Netherlands	Spain	Switzerland	Denmark	Norway	Sweden
100.2	107.5	99.9	100.9	96.7	103.5	96.6	101.2
99.1	100.3	97.6	99.4	98.7	99.2	100.9	102.1
100.7	92.3	102.5	99.8	102.6	97.3	102.5	96.7
101.7	92.0	101.8	90.6	104.4	98.8	101.3	91.5
102.7	90.9	100.1	95.0	99.4	96.5	100.1	96.9
103.0	90.8	100.3	95.1	96.7	95.3	99.1	97.0
103.0	91.3	99.9	94.3	97.3	95.8	98.5	97.8
102.0	90.8	99.2	95.6	97.9	97.2	99.5	98.9
101.8	90.6	98.8	96.0	98.8	96.6	100.1	99.1
102.5	91.7	98.7	96.9	98.7	98.0	98.3	98.3
102.3	91.2	98.0	97.6	98.0	98.1	98.0	98.7
102.3	92.1	97.4	98.6	96.4	97.8	97.4	99.4
102.0	91.5	96.4	98.5	95.0	96.3	98.1	100.2
101.6	91.2	95.9	98.1	95.6	97.5	98.4	99.7
102.4	91.5	95.9	98.9	96.4	98.3	98.5	98.6
101.9	91.4	95.5	98.2	96.0	97.7	98.3	99.4
101.8	91.3	95.2	97.6	96.3	98.5	98.3	99.8

EXHIBIT 2.10
Exchange Rate Volatility under Pegged and Floating Exchange Rates

	1968	*1969*	*1975*	*1982*
Deutschemark	0.3	1.2[a]	1.7	1.6
French franc	0.1	2.3[a]	1.6	2.2
Japanese yen	n.a.	n.a.	0.7	2.5
Pound sterling	0.7[a]	0.2	1.0	1.1

Source: IMF *International Financial Statistics.* From John Williamson, *The Exchange Rate System,* Second Edition, Washington, D.C.: Institute for International Economics, June 1985.

Note: Coefficient of variation of daily nominal exchange rate against dollar around six-month moving average, expressed as percentage.

n.a. Not available.

[a]Figure was influenced by a par value change.

EXHIBIT 2.11
Maximum Swings in Real Effective Exchange Rates of Five Major Currencies, 1963–1972 and 1973–1982 (percentages)

	1963–1972	*1973–1982*
Deutschemark	13	22
French franc	27	19
Japanese yen	14	35
Pound sterling	17	60
U.S. dollar	14	32
Average	17	34

Source: IMF statistics for relative wholesale prices vis-à-vis other industrial countries. From John Williamson, *The Exchange Rate System,* Second Edition, Washington, D.C.: Institute for International Economics, June 1985.

Note: The results presented in the table cannot be dismissed as a reflection of wild swings in the first couple of years after floating was adopted, when the market was still undergoing a learning process. Elimination of the period 1973–1975 would alter the figures only for the DM and French franc, reducing them marginally to 18 percent and 17 percent, respectively. (Deletion of the years 1963–1965 would have a rather similar effect, reducing the figures for the French franc and yen to 24 percent and 10 percent, respectively.)

SUMMARY

We have traced the historical evolution of the international monetary system with emphasis on the period from World War II to the present. The gold exchange standard, buttressed by the International Monetary Fund, SDRs, swap agreements among central banks, and a considerable spirit of cooperation, managed to hold together during the period 1944–1971. However, continuing U.S. balance of payments deficits during the 1960s weakened the ability of the U.S. dollar to function as the world's main reserve currency. A final loss of confidence in the dollar in 1971 caused it to be devalued. A further devaluation followed in 1973, at which time the United States abandoned any attempt to retain the dollar's tie to gold. Thus began the period of floating exchange rates, which still exist today.

The first oil price crisis of 1973–1974 removed any hope of quickly returning to a fixed exchange rate system. This oil crisis also caused the non-oil less developed countries to suffer increasing balance of payments deficits on current account. The newly rich OPEC countries recycled their surplus funds in the Eurocurrency market, which grew immensely. Portfolio currency decisions by OPEC central bankers became a key to stability in foreign exchange markets.

Freely floating exchange rates were made official by the Jamaica Agreement of 1976, which also initiated other reforms in the international monetary system to recognize the realities of the new order. The IMF was strengthened, gold was demonetized, and modest balance of payments support was offered to the less developed countries by both the developed countries and OPEC.

Another loss of confidence in the dollar in 1977–1978 caused further instability in foreign exchange markets. Other countries reacted to this loss of confidence by attempting to tie their currencies to their most important trading partners. For example, the European Monetary System (EMS) was formed as a major currency bloc. Thus floating individual currencies evolved into a system of floating currency blocs, including the EMS, dollar, pound sterling, and yen blocs. Central banks diversified their international reserves.

The second oil crisis and Iranian freeze, which occurred in 1979, once again caused turmoil in the foreign exchange markets. This time the dollar was strong and the European currencies were weak. In fact, from 1980 to the present the dollar strengthened relative to all trading currencies on both a nominal and real effective basis. Overvaluation of the dollar relative to the yen, EMS currencies, and U.K. pound has been a factor in the deteriorating U.S. balance of payments and evoked considerable protectionist sentiment in the United States. The balance of payments problems of the United States and the non-OPEC less developed countries is the subject of the next chapter.

NOTES

1. For more complete background material on the international monetary system, see the latest edition of any of the standard international economics textbooks.

2. For a detailed analysis of the immediate post–World War II international monetary system, see Robert Triffin, *Europe and the Money Muddle,* New Haven, Conn.: Yale University Press, 1957.

3. Current international financial statistics covering the IMF and member countries appear in the current month's issue of IMF, *International Financial Statistics,* Washington, D.C.

4. International Monetary Fund, *Annual Report,* Washington, D.C.: International Monetary Fund, 1984, pp. 74–75.

5. *Ibid.,* pp. 106–108.

6. A widely read pioneering analysis of the adequacy of international reserves appears in Robert Triffin, *Gold and the Dollar Crisis,* New Haven, Conn.: Yale University Press, 1961.

7. Current reports on official currency swaps and other operations of central banks in the foreign exchange markets are published several times a year in the monthly *Federal Reserve Bulletin,* Board of Governors of the Federal Reserve System, Washington, D.C.

8. A discussion of terms used in reporting changes in exchange rates is appropriate, if for no other reason than that newspaper accounts often use the word *devaluation* incorrectly. The term *devaluation* in a narrow and semantically correct sense refers only to a drop in foreign exchange value of a currency that is pegged to gold or to another currency. The opposite of devaluation is *revaluation,* or occasionally *upvaluation.* The terms *weakening, deterioration,* or *depreciation* refer to a drop in the foreign exchange value of a floating currency. The opposite of weakening is *appreciating* or *strengthening,* which refers to a gain in the exchange value of a floating currency. A currency is considered "soft" if it is expected to be devalued or to depreciate relative to major currencies, or if its exchange value is being artificially sustained by its government. A currency is considered "hard" if it is expected to revalue or appreciate relative to major trading currencies.

9. Professor H. Lee Remmers of INSEAD (Fontainebleau, France) has sent us the following clarification: "The divergence is measured as the difference between the ECU market value of each currency and its ECU parity. The point at which a currency reaches its threshold is 75% of the maximum divergence possible. This maximum will be different for each currency in the ECU in proportion to its weight. Therefore, the DM will have the lowest threshold (about 1.06%) since it is the most important component of the ECU, and the Irish punt will have the highest (1.67%) since it accounts for the smallest weight. There is at least one currency advisory service (as well as the *Financial Times*) that publishes the 'divergence indicator' on a regular basis—this indicator being a sort of early warning signal that pressure is building on a currency foreshadowing a possible realignment."

10. Derived from International Monetary Fund, *Annual Report,* 1984, p. 62.

11. John Williamson, *The Exchange Rate System,* Second Edition, Washington, D.C.: Institute for International Economics, June 1985.

12. Ibid.

BIBLIOGRAPHY

Agmon, Tamir, Robert G. Hawkins, and Richard M. Levich, eds., *The Future of the International Monetary System,* Lexington, Mass.: Lexington Books, 1984.

Anderson, Birgitta, "Currency-Basket Loans: A Means for Reducing Foreign Exchange Risks," in Goran Bergendahl, ed., *International Financial Management,* Stockholm: P. A. Norstedt & Soners forlag, 1982, pp. 54–70.

Archeim, J., and Y. S. Park, "Artificial Currency Units: The Functional Currency Areas," *Essays in International Finance, No. 114,* Princeton, N.J.: International Finance Section, Princeton University, April 1976.

Canterbery, E. Ray, and Jeff Madura, "Commercial Use of the SDR," *Columbia Journal of World Business,* Winter 1982, pp. 11–16.

Coes, Donald V., "The Crawling Peg and Exchange Rate Uncertainty," in John Williamson, ed., *Exchange Rate Rules,* London: Macmillan, and New York: St. Martin's Press, 1981.

Dornbusch, Rudiger, "The Theory of Flexible Exchange Rate Regimes and Macroeconomic Policy," *Scandinavian Journal of Economics,* May 1976, pp. 255–275; reprinted in Jacob A. Frenkel and Harry G. Johnson, eds., *The Economics of Exchange Rates,* Reading, Mass.: Addison-Wesley, 1978, pp. 27–46.

Epstein, Edward J., "Ruling the World of Money" (Bank for International Settlements), *Harper's,* November 1983, pp. 43–48.

Fleming, J. Marcus, "Floating Exchange Rates, Asymmetrical Intervention, and the Management of International Liquidity," *IMF Staff Papers,* July 1975, pp. 263–283.

Haberler, Gottfried, "The International Monetary System in the World Recession," in William J. Fellner, ed., *Contemporary Economic Problems, 1983–84,* Washington, D.C.: American Enterprise Institute, 1983.

Korteweg, Pieter, "Exchange-Rate Policy, Monetary Policy, and Real Exchange-Rate Variability," *Essays in International Finance, No. 140,* Princeton, N.J.: International Finance Section, Princeton University, December 1980.

Levi, Maurice, *International Finance,* New York: McGraw-Hill, 1983.

Lewellen, Wilbur G., and James S. Ang, "Inflation, Currency Exchange Rates, and the International Securities Markets," *Journal of Business Research,* March 1984, pp. 97–114.

Lomax, David F., "Prospects for the European Monetary System," *National Westminster Bank Quarterly Review,* May 1983, pp. 33–50.

McKinnon, Ronald I., *Money in International Exchanges (The Convertible Currency System),* New York and Oxford: Oxford University Press, 1979.

Makin, John H., "Fixed versus Floating: A Red Herring," *Columbia Journal of World Business,* Winter 1979, pp. 7–14.

Mayer, Helmut, and Hiroo Taguchi, *Official Intervention in the Exchange Markets: Stabilising or Destabilising?* Basle, Switzerland: Bank for International Settlements, 1983.

Pippenger, John E., *Fundamentals of International Finance,* Englewood Cliffs, N.J.: Prentice-Hall, 1984.

Rodriguez, Rita, "The Increasing Attraction of the SDR to Business Corporations," *Euromoney,* December 1981, pp. 169–179.

Shafer, Jeffrey R., and Bonnie E. Loopesko, "Floating Exchange Rates after Ten Years," *Brookings Papers on Economic Activity,* Washington, D.C.: Brookings Institution, 1983.

Taylor, Dean, "Official Intervention in the Foreign Exchange Market, or Bet against the Central Bank," *Journal of Political Economy,* April 1982, pp. 356–368.

Tinbergen, Jan, coordinator, *Reshaping the International Order: A Report to the Club of Rome,* New York: Dutton, 1976.

Weil, Gordon, "Exchange-Rate Regime Selection in Theory and Practice," New York University Monograph Series in Finance and Economics, 1983.

Westerfield, Janice M., "Empirical Properties of Foreign Exchange Rates under Fixed and Floating Rate Regimes," *Journal of International Economics,* June 1977, pp. 181–200.

Whitman, Marina, "The Payments Adjustment Process and the Exchange Rate Regime: What Have We Learned?" *American Economic Review,* May 1975, pp. 133–146.

Wihlborg, Clas, "The Effectiveness of Exchange Controls on Financial Capital Flows," *Columbia Journal of World Business,* Winter 1982, pp. 3–10.

Williamson, John, "A Survey of the Literature on the Optimal Peg," *Journal of Development Economics,* September 1982.

———, *The Open Economy and the World Economy,* New York: Basic Books, 1983.

———, *The Exchange Rate System,* Washington, D.C.: Institute for International Economics, September 1983.

Zis, George, "Exchange-Rate Fluctuations: 1973–82," *National Westminster Bank Quarterly Review,* August 1983, pp. 2–13.

3

Balance of Payments and the International Debt Problem

Transactions between nations are measured by an accounting system called the *balance of payments*, which reveals whether countries are in surplus or deficit on trade and capital transactions with the rest of the world. This information is useful to business managers for two main reasons:

- The balance of payments helps to forecast a country's market potential, especially in the short run. A country experiencing a serious balance of payments deficit is not likely to import as much as it would if it were running a surplus.

- The balance of payments is an important indicator of pressure on a country's foreign exchange rate, and thus on the potential for a firm trading with or investing in that country to experience exchange gains or losses.

The balance of payments is also important to government officials because it influences a nation's gross national product, employment, prices, exchange rates, and interest rates. The study of how countries adjust to a balance of payments deficit or surplus is in the domain of international economics and will therefore not be covered formally in this book. However, we will discuss in this chapter how the balance of payments is measured and the problems experienced by countries during recent years. This is important background information for our later use in forecasting foreign exchange rates (Chapter 5) and in analyzing the problems of international banks (Chapter 13).

MEASURING THE BALANCE OF PAYMENTS

Balance of payments accounts are a systematized procedure for measuring, summarizing, and stating the effect of all financial and economic transactions between residents of one country and residents of the remainder of the world during a particular time period. If expenditures abroad by residents of one nation exceed what the residents of that nation can earn or otherwise receive from abroad, that nation is generally deemed to have a "deficit" in its balance of payments. However, if a nation earns more abroad than it spends, that nation incurs a "surplus." Balance of payments accounts are intended to show the size of any deficit or surplus and to indicate the manner in which it was financed.

Debits and Credits

In dealing with the rest of the world, a country earns foreign exchange on some transactions and expends foreign exchange on others. Transactions that earn foreign exchange are recorded in the balance of payments statistics as a "credit" and are marked by a plus (+) sign. As a general matter, credits are obtained by selling to nonresidents either real or financial assets or services. For example, the export of U.S.-made machinery earns foreign exchange and is therefore a credit. The sale to a foreigner of a service, such as an airline trip on a U.S. carrier, also earns foreign exchange and is a credit. Conceptually the sale of the trip to the foreigner is an export of a U.S. service to a nonresident of the United States—even though the trip may have taken place between New York and San Francisco, or between Bombay and Cairo, rather than between a U.S. and a foreign city.

Borrowing abroad earns foreign exchange and is therefore recorded as a credit. This type of transaction may be viewed as though it were the export of U.S. securities (shares of stock, bonds, promissory notes, etc.) to foreigners; thus it generates foreign exchange in a manner analogous to the export of such tangible merchandise as machines.

Transactions that expend foreign exchange are recorded as debits and are marked with a minus (−) sign. The foremost example is the import of goods from foreign countries. When U.S. residents buy coffee from Latin America, foreign exchange is expended and the import is recorded as a debit. Similarly, when U.S. residents purchase foreign services, such as insurance policies taken out with Lloyds of London or the shipping of merchandise in a vessel owned by a Korean shipping company, foreign exchange is used. Lending to foreigners also uses foreign exchange and is recorded as a debit; foreign lending may be considered as equivalent to the importing of foreign securities.

A useful format for balance of payments data appears in Exhibit 3.1, which is taken from the IMF's monthly publication, *Balance of Payments*

EXHIBIT 3.1
Balance of Payments of the United States 1977–1984: Aggregated Presentation (in billions of SDRs)

	1977	*1978*	*1979*	*1980*	*1981*	*1982*	*1983*	*1984*
A. Current Account, excl. Group F	−12.39	−12.52	−.72	1.46	5.48	−8.58	−39.21	−99.44
Merchandise: exports f.o.b.	103.48	113.29	142.74	172.38	201.02	191.12	187.37	215.05
Merchandise: imports f.o.b.	−130.09	−140.55	−164.04	−191.95	−224.89	−224.36	−244.74	−319.94
Trade balance	−26.61	−27.25	−21.31	−19.57	−23.87	−33.24	−57.37	−104.89
Other goods, services, and income: credit	54.37	62.15	79.16	90.79	117.75	125.24	123.50	138.62
Reinvested earnings	*5.49*	*9.02*	*14.68*	*13.06*	*11.42*	*5.72*	*8.49*	*12.39*
Other investment income	*22.08*	*24.63*	*34.93*	*42.61*	*61.96*	*70.25*	*63.60*	*73.13*
Other	*26.80*	*28.49*	*29.55*	*35.12*	*44.37*	*49.27*	*51.40*	*53.10*
Other goods, services, and income: debit	−35.87	−42.94	−53.85	−63.93	−82.09	−92.56	−96.62	−121.51
Reinvested earnings	*−1.36*	*−2.06*	*−3.07*	*−3.96*	*−2.34*	*1.18*	*−1.29*	*−4.44*
Other investment income	*−10.81*	*−15.20*	*−22.40*	*−28.35*	*−41.86*	*−51.96*	*−48.81*	*−63.46*
Other	*−23.69*	*−25.67*	*−28.38*	*−31.62*	*−37.88*	*−41.78*	*−46.52*	*−53.61*
Total: goods, services, and income	−8.11	−8.05	4.00	7.30	11.80	−.55	−30.49	−87.78
Private unrequited transfers	−.70	−.69	−.70	−.79	−.78	−1.06	−.95	−1.35
Total, excl. official unrequited transfers	−8.81	−8.74	3.30	6.50	11.01	−1.61	−31.44	−89.13
Official unrequited transfers	−3.57	−3.78	−4.02	−5.04	−5.54	−6.97	−7.77	−10.31
Grants (excluding military)	*−2.39*	*−2.54*	*−2.74*	*−3.63*	*−3.80*	*−4.92*	*−5.70*	*−8.11*
Other	*−1.18*	*−1.24*	*−1.28*	*−1.41*	*−1.74*	*−2.05*	*−2.06*	*−2.20*
B. Direct Investment and Other Long-Term Capital, excl. Groups F through H	−10.61	−9.37	−18.30	−6.61	1.25	−3.54	−6.75	29.86
Direct investment	−7.00	−6.53	−10.35	−1.88	15.25	17.92	5.97	14.68
In United States	*3.19*	*6.31*	*9.18*	*12.99*	*20.88*	*13.51*	*10.58*	*20.65*
Abroad	*−10.19*	*−12.84*	*−19.54*	*−14.87*	*−5.63*	*4.40*	*−4.61*	*−5.97*
Portfolio investment	−.44	−.29	−1.68	2.20	2.28	−.77	4.00	29.02
Other long-term capital								
Resident official sector	−2.45	−2.31	−2.57	−4.50	−4.31	−6.25	−4.72	−4.51
Disbursements on loans extended	*−4.76*	*−5.28*	*−5.48*	*−6.69*	*−6.85*	*−7.81*	*−7.61*	*−7.46*
Repayments on loans extended	*2.29*	*2.32*	*2.92*	*3.11*	*3.37*	*3.45*	*4.28*	*3.93*
Other	*.03*	*.64*	*−.01*	*−.92*	*−.83*	*−1.89*	*−1.39*	*−.98*

Deposit money banks	−.34	−.05	−4.44	−2.42	−11.97	−14.45	−12.00	−9.33
Other sectors	−.38	−.19	.75	—	—	—	—	—
Total, Groups A plus B	**−23.00**	**−21.89**	**−19.02**	**−5.14**	**6.72**	**−12.12**	**−45.95**	**−69.58**
C. *Other Short-Term Capital, excl. Groups F through H*	**−5.16**	**−14.77**	**7.18**	**−21.07**	**−22.32**	**−16.28**	**33.74**	**40.35**
Resident official sector	−1.16	.22	−.27	1.35	1.00	6.50	5.23	.85
Deposit money banks	−3.64	−13.64	15.96	−21.02	−18.30	−23.87	29.25	24.24
Other sectors	−.36	−1.36	−8.51	−1.41	−5.02	1.09	−.74	15.26
D. *Net Errors and Omissions*	**−1.73**	**10.22**	**19.72**	**19.25**	**14.70**	**30.09**	**8.47**	**29.41**
Total, Groups A through D	**−29.89**	**−26.44**	**7.87**	**−6.96**	**−.90**	**1.69**	**−3.75**	**.18**
E. *Counterpart Items*	−.12	−.66	−2.22	.80	.63	−.13	−.43	−.59
Monetization/demonetization of gold	—	−.40	−2.81	−.14	−.09	−.03	−.26	−.23
Allocation/cancellation of SDRs	—	—	.87	.87	.86	—	—	—
Valuation changes in reserves	−.12	−.26	−.29	.07	−.13	−.11	−.17	−.36
Total, Groups A through E	**−30.01**	**−27.10**	**5.65**	**−6.16**	**−.27**	**1.56**	**−4.18**	**−.41**
F. *Exceptional Financing*	—	1.23	2.85	.90	—	—	—	—
Security issues in foreign currencies	—	1.23	2.85	.90	—	—	—	—
Total, Groups A through F	**−30.01**	**−25.87**	**8.50**	**−5.26**	**−.27**	**1.56**	**−4.18**	**−.41**
G. *Liabilities Constituting Foreign Authorities' Reserves*	30.21	24.62	−10.70	11.45	4.20	2.84	4.86	2.89
Total, Groups A through G	.20	−1.25	−2.21	6.19	3.93	4.39	.68	2.48
H. *Total Change in Reserves*	−.20	1.25	2.21	−6.19	−3.93	−4.39	−.68	−2.48
Monetary gold	−.10	.35	2.76	.13	.10	.03	.25	.23
SDRs	−.10	.97	−.87	.02	−1.47	−1.24	−.04	−.95
Reserve position in the Fund	−.26	3.27	−.15	−1.29	−2.11	−2.32	−4.14	−.97
Foreign exchange assets	.26	−3.34	.47	−5.06	−.45	−.86	3.25	−.78
Other claims	—	—	—	—	—	—	—	—
Use of Fund credit	—	—	—	—	—	—	—	—
Conversion Rates: U.S. dollars per SDR	**1.1675**	**1.2520**	**1.2920**	**1.3015**	**1.1792**	**1.1040**	**1.0690**	**1.0250**

Source: IMF, *Balance of Payments Statistics,* May 1985, p. 25.

Statistics. This source is valuable for comparing various countries, because a comparable format is used for the balance of payments statistics of each nation. Exhibit 3.1 is based on the IMF's presentation of the balance of payments of the United States for the period 1977–1984. Note that the amounts are stated in terms of SDRs, with the U.S. dollar price of an SDR given at the bottom of the exhibit.

Analytical Arrangement

In any balance of payments presentation all transactions between residents and nonresidents are conceptually divided into two analytical categories, the sum of which is zero. Thus in one sense the balance of payments always balances. One can visualize the statement as having an imaginary horizontal line drawn across the list of accounts such that all transactions "above the line" are financed by all transactions "below the line." This imaginary line may be drawn higher or lower, depending on the analytical need of the person evaluating the accounts.

The IMF presentation in Exhibit 3.1 is intended to facilitate a variety of analytical perspectives, with a user able to regard as "above the line" any cumulative partial balance from Group A down through Group G. Most of the partial balances from Group A down have a name and particular analytical use, as will be discussed below.

Trade Balance

The *trade balance* is defined as the net balance on merchandise trade. The first two lines under Group A of Exhibit 3.1 show exports and imports of merchandise such as wheat, machinery, automobiles, bananas, aircraft, and oil. In each year the United States ran a deficit on its trade balance, as shown on the third line under Group A.

Balance on Current Account

The concept of *current account* expands the trade balance concept to include earnings and expenditures for services and "invisible" trade items, such as transportation, tourism, investment income including earnings from foreign affiliates, and military expenditures. When the net effect of these items is added to the merchandise trade balance, the resultant "balance on goods, services, and income" measures the net transfer of real resources between the United States and the rest of the world. As shown in Exhibit 3.1 on the twelfth line under Group A, this balance deteriorated badly in 1983 and 1984 due to the exceptional strength of the dollar. Analysis of the balance of payments presumes that the balance down through "balance of goods, services, and income" is determined autonomously because of pricing, quality, or similar factors.

The remaining items in Group A, private and official unrequited transfers, measure unilateral transfers not matched by a quid pro quo transaction. Unrequited transfers include sums sent home by migrant workers, parental payments to students studying abroad, private gifts, pension payments to retirees living abroad, and governmental gifts or grants.

The net sum of all merchandise, service, income, and unrequited transfers is the "balance on current account," shown at the top of Group A. The balance on current account is the measure most frequently used in economic policy analysis since it comes closest to measuring the effect of the international sector on a nation's GNP. It is also the measure most often cited in the news media when reporting the balance of payments results.

Basic Balance

The *basic balance* is the net result of activities in Groups A and B. Group B measures long-term capital flows, including direct foreign investments. Long-term capital flows are presumed to be autonomous because of fundamental desires to invest for the long run. The basic balance is useful in evaluating long-term trends in the balance of payments, since it does not include the volatile, easily reversible, short-term capital flows. With the exception of 1981 the United States had a deficit on its basic balance account.

Overall Balance, or Official Settlements Balance

The *overall balance,* sometimes called the *official settlements balance,* is the net result of activities in Groups A, B, C, and D.

Group C measures short-term capital movements, such as transactions in money market instruments and bank deposits. In one sense these are autonomous in that they occur for their own sake. From another perspective, however, they are often induced by the monetary policies of various countries. For this reason short-term capital movements are sometimes regarded as volatile and readily reversible rather than as fundamental and stable in nature.

Group D measures errors and omissions. This account is comprised of transactions that are known to have occurred but for which no specific measure was made. The account arises because balance of payments statistics are gathered on a single-entry basis, rather than on a double-entry basis as in corporate accounting, from statistics collected when goods move through customshouses or funds flow through the banking system. Many transactions are not recorded but are known to have occurred because other components of the statistical series reveal an imbalance. Because most errors and omissions are in current account or capital items, the errors and omissions balance is placed before striking the balance labeled "Total, Groups A through D," which is the overall balance.

The overall balance is one of the most frequently used measures because it represents the sum of all autonomous transactions that must be financed by the use of official reserves or of other nonreserve official transactions that are often viewed as being a substitute for reserve transactions. It is a comprehensive balance often used to judge a country's overall competitive position in terms of all private transactions with the rest of the world. Deficits or surpluses in the overall balance are frequently used to judge pressure for exchange rate changes. The overall balance of the United States has been nearly zero during the last four years.

Other Adjustments

Groups E, F, and G in Exhibit 3.1 constitute transactions that have official attributes but are not counted in official reserves. Counterpart items are transactions that create or destroy official reserves. The monetization or demonetization of gold arises because gold is a commodity when held by private parties but a monetary reserve item when held by the central authorities. Monetization of gold means gold has moved from private hands to official accounts. Allocation or cancellation of SDRs represents a change in official holdings. Exceptional financing refers to financing mobilized by authorities outside of reserve transactions. Typical examples are postponing debt repayments or drawing on loans to finance transactions that would otherwise have depleted the country's reserve assets.

Changes in Reserves

The net result of activities in Groups A through G in Exhibit 3.1 must be financed by changes in official monetary reserves. Group H shows changes in the reserve holdings of the United States. These consist of monetary gold, SDRs, the U.S. reserve position with the IMF, and U.S. holdings of foreign exchange assets.

Meaning of a Deficit or Surplus

The meaning of a deficit or surplus in the balance of payments has changed since the advent of floating exchange rates. Traditionally, these terms were used as evidence of pressure on a country's foreign exchange rate. Pressure was measured by transactions that were compensatory in nature, i.e., forced on the government to "settle" the deficit.

In a floating rate world the traditional measures no longer necessarily indicate pressure on exchange rates, since the rates are changing all the time and often the causal relationship is reversed. A change in exchange rates could induce a balance of payments deficit or surplus. For example, the overvalued dollar of recent years has been cited as one reason for the increasing U.S. balance of payments deficits. In fact, based on the recommendation of a blue-ribbon U.S. government advisory committee, the U.S. balance of payments data are published without an attempt to call any particular grouping of accounts "the deficit."[1]

Apart from implications for pressure on foreign exchange rates, the balance of payments has also been used for economic development analysis. In that context a deficit or surplus in the current account is not necessarily good or bad for a country. From a *national income* viewpoint, a deficit on current account could have a negative effect on GNP and employment if underemployment exists, whereas a surplus could have a positive effect. However, if full employment exists, a current account deficit that can be financed abroad would allow the import of investment goods that would not have been possible otherwise.

From a *program* viewpoint, economic development usually requires a net import of goods and services (deficit in the current account) financed by foreign savings. Less developed countries find it nearly impossible to generate sufficient domestic savings or technical and managerial know-how to reach the "takeoff" point without external aid.

Finally, from a *liquidity* viewpoint, a deficit could mean that a country is building up a net long-term creditor position vis-à-vis the rest of the world through foreign direct investments and long-term loans while simultaneously building up its short-term liabilities to the rest of the world.

BALANCE OF PAYMENTS ADJUSTMENT AND THE INTERNATIONAL DEBT PROBLEM

During the past 15 years the international economy experienced numerous external shocks that evoked the need for individual countries to adjust to balance of payments problems. The first big adjustment was by the United States in 1971–1973 when it was forced to abandon the gold exchange standard because of persistent and growing balance of payments deficits. Oil price increases in 1974 and 1979 caused temporary balance of payments problems for the industrial countries, but lasting problems for the non-OPEC developing countries. In the late 1970s the Eastern Bloc countries overcommitted themselves to economic development programs. They developed balance of payments deficits on current account due to a rapid growth in imports, financed primarily by private-sector banks in Western Europe. In the 1980s, the United States experienced a large balance of payments deficit on current account caused in part by an overvalued dollar, but financed very willingly by the rest of the world. Japan developed a large surplus on current account, due in part to an undervalued yen, but also to rapid increases in productivity. As a result Japan became a major supplier of financial capital through international portfolio investments and increased foreign direct investment.

The Non-OPEC Developing Countries

Adjusting to energy price increases has been a worldwide problem since 1974. These increases have led to an immense transfer of wealth to OPEC countries and have had serious repercussions for the potential stability of the international monetary system as it attempts to recycle the OPEC funds. The major industrial nations have on the whole been able to adjust to higher energy prices, albeit at the expense of low growth, unemployment, and inflation. However, many less developed countries have been driven to the brink of international bankruptcy. They have had to increase their debt to both private and government banking sources to an extent that endangers the credibility of the entire international banking system. Country defaults on external debt to banks and governments have become commonplace.

To illustrate the dimensions of the problem, Exhibit 3.2 shows for the period 1974–1984 the current account deficits of non-OPEC developing countries, their terms of trade, net borrowing from banks, and net interest payments. The Latin American countries are shown on the left diagram and all other non-OPEC developing countries on the right diagram.

The problem has been particularly severe for Latin American countries. Exhibit 3.2 shows that their composite deficit on current account, represented by the white and shaded bars, rose from somewhat over $10 billion in 1974 to over $40 billion in 1981 before falling to about $30 billion in 1984. During the period 1977–1981 their terms of trade, measured by an index of export prices divided by an index of import prices (the broken line), fell sharply from being 20% more favorable in 1977 than the base year of 1974 to being 20% less favorable in 1981. This means they were paying relatively more for their imports and receiving lower prices for their exports in 1981 than in 1977.

In order to finance the deficit, Latin American countries were forced to borrow heavily from banks, as shown by the dark bars. After stringent deflationary policies, they finally showed some net repayments of bank loans in 1984.

The net interest/export ratio, shown by the solid line, rose to over 40% in 1982 before falling to about 35% in 1984. This ratio indicates what percent of export receipts must be used to keep interest on the bank debt current.

Exhibit 3.3 shows in more detail the seriousness of the international debt problem for both Latin American and other non-OPEC developing countries. Total composite international indebtedness of Latin American countries, shown by the bars, exceeded $300 billion by 1984, equal to over

EXHIBIT 3.2
Factors Influencing the Borrowing Needs and Recourse to International Bank Finance of Non-OPEC Developing Countries, 1974–1984

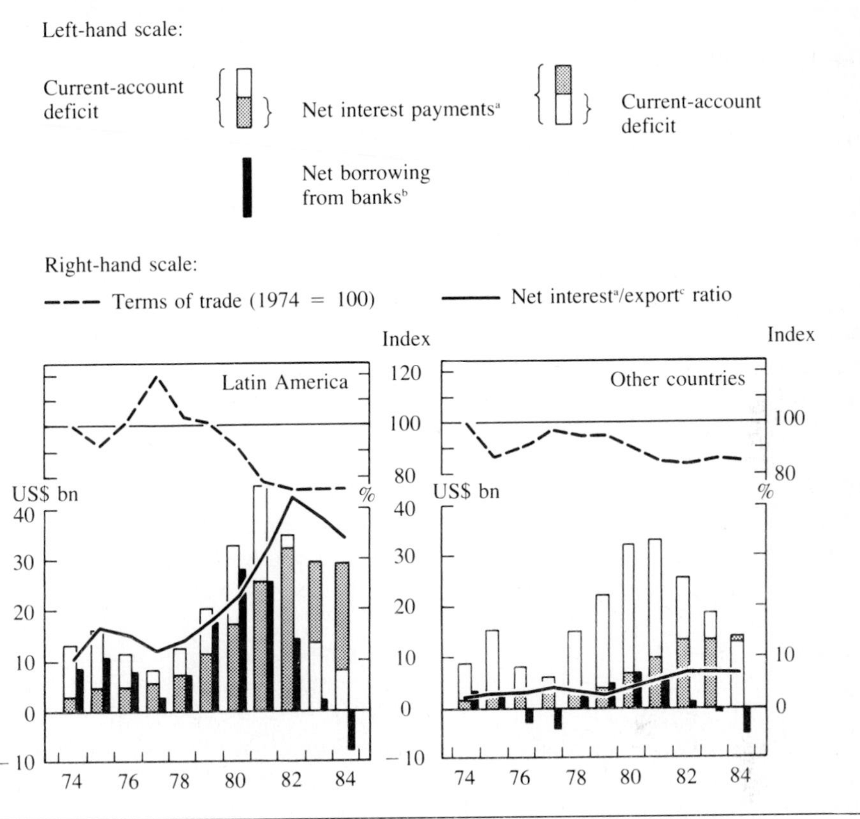

Source: Bank for International Settlements, *Fifty-fifth Annual Report,* Basle, Switzerland, June 10, 1985, p. 134.

[a]Estimated.

[b]Calculated in constant dollars.

[c]Exports of goods and services.

350% of exports (the broken line). Private-sector bank debt alone represented about 250% of export receipts (the solid line). The problems of other non-OPEC developing countries were also serious, as shown on the right-hand diagram, but not as desperate as the plight of the Latin American countries.

It is small wonder that the non-OPEC developing countries need to reschedule their external debts and slow down their rates of growth. The problem of how the banks got into this mess and how they plan to get out of it is covered in Chapter 13 ("International Banking").

EXHIBIT 3.3
Evolution of Non-OPEC Developing Countries' International Indebtedness, 1973–1984

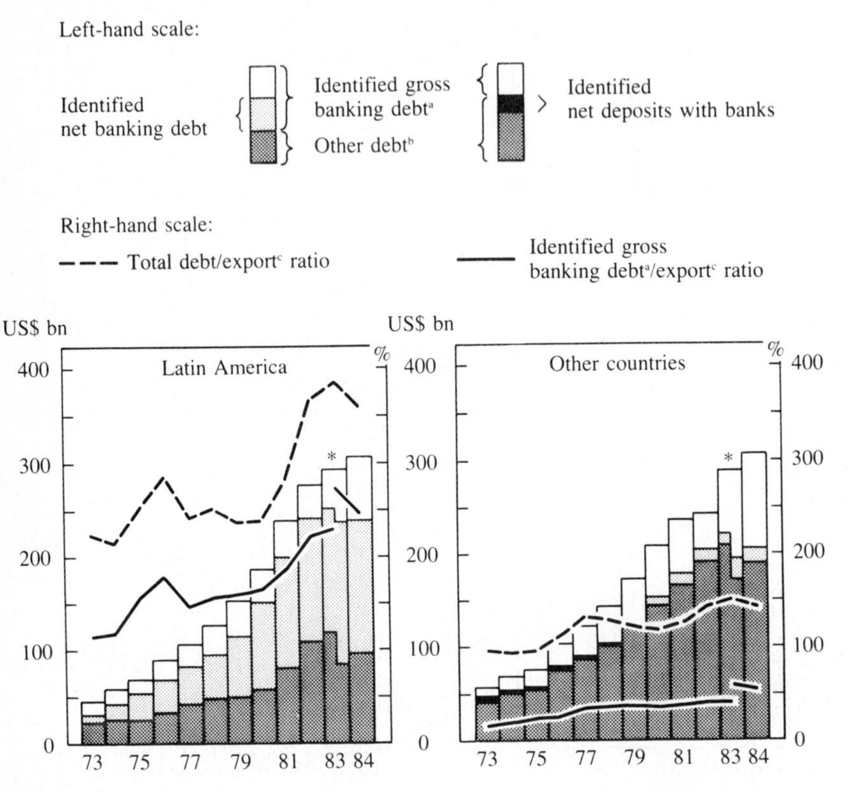

Source: Bank for International Settlements, *Fifty-fifth Annual Report,* Basle, Switzerland, June 10, 1985, p. 135.

*Break in series due to the broadening of the coverage of the BIS international banking statistics.

[a]Vis-à-vis banks located in BIS reporting countries.

[b]Estimated.

[c]Exports of goods and services.

Eastern Bloc Countries

The balance of payments and external debt problems of the Eastern Bloc countries first surfaced in the late 1970s, when Poland defaulted on its external debt. Exhibit 3.4 shows the growth in hard currency debt for the East European (Comecon) countries during the period 1976–1979. Poland

EXHIBIT 3.4
Hard Currency Debt of Comecon Countries (in billions of dollars at year end)

	1976	*1977*	*1978*	*1979*
Gross Amounts				
Bulgaria	3.2	3.7	4.3	4.5
Czechoslovakia	1.9	2.6	3.2	4.0
German Democratic Republic	5.8	7.1	8.9	10.1
Hungary	4.0	5.7	7.5	8.0
Poland	11.5	14.0	17.8	21.1
Rumania	2.9	3.6	5.2	7.0
Soviet Union	14.8	15.7	17.2	17.2
Comecon banks[a]	3.5	4.2	4.8	5.2
Total	47.6	56.6	68.9	77.1
Net Amounts				
Bulgaria	2.8	3.2	3.7	3.7
Czechoslovakia	1.4	2.1	2.5	3.1
German Democratic Republic	5.0	6.1	7.6	8.5
Hungary	2.9	4.5	6.5	7.3
Poland	10.7	13.5	17.0	20.0
Rumania	2.5	3.4	5.0	6.7
Soviet Union	10.1	11.2	11.2	10.2
Comecon banks[a]	3.5	4.2	4.8	5.2
Total	38.9	48.2	58.3	64.7

Source: Organization for Economic Cooperation and Development, *Financial Market Statistics 1981,* p. 8.
[a]International Investment Bank and International Bank for Economic Co-operation; no separate estimates of gross and net debt for the Comecon banks are available; figures refer to estimated net indebtedness to Western banks.

doubled its debt during this period and accounted for almost one-third of Comecon debt by 1979.

The debt/export and debt-servicing ratios for Comecon countries in 1979 are shown in Exhibit 3.5. Poland would have needed to use 113% of receipts from exports of goods and services just to meet current interest and principal payments on its external debt!

The United States and Japan

During the past few years the United States has been running a large and growing deficit on current account, while Japan has a large and growing surplus. Exhibit 3.6 presents international current account balances for all

EXHIBIT 3.5
Selected Debt Ratios of Comecon Countries, 1979

	Debt/export ratio	*Debt-servicing ratio*
Bulgaria	3.8	.90
Czechoslovakia	1.0	.26
German Democratic Republic	2.0	.58
Hungary	2.8	.47
Poland	3.9	1.13
Rumania	2.0	.36
Soviet Union	.5	.23
Total Comecon	1.4	.40

Source: Organization for Economic Cooperation and Development, *Financial Market Statistics 1981*, p. 11.

Note: *Debt/export ratio:* relationship between total net hard currency debt at the end of 1979 and total exports (FOB) to the industrial market economies in 1979, as derived from Western sources, published in the *United Nations Economic Bulletin for Europe*, Vol. 32, No. 1; total Comecon excludes debt of Comecon banks. *Debt-servicing ratio:* relationship between payments of interest and principal on medium- and long-term outstanding debt and total exports to the West.

countries for the period 1982–1984. The U.S. deficit on current account grew from $7.1 billion to $101.7 billion during this period, while Japan's surplus grew from $6.9 billion to $35.0 billion. Although these results appear to have had minimal impact on foreign exchange rates because of other offsetting factors, they have led to a surge of protectionist sentiment in the United States and worldwide pressure on Japan to open its markets and increase imports.

SUMMARY

In this chapter we have shown how the balance of payments is measured by a system of debits and credits arranged in a manner that highlights various measures of balance. These include the trade balance, balance on current account, basic balance, and official settlements balance. The meaning of a deficit or surplus was explained. Balance of payments adjustment problems were described with particular emphasis on the continuing problems of the non-OPEC developing countries. Eastern bloc problems, highlighted by Poland's default, were also covered. This chapter concluded with reference to the current U.S. deficit and Japanese surplus in their balance of payments current accounts.

EXHIBIT 3.6
International Current-Account Balances, 1982–1984 (in billions of U.S. dollars)

	TRADE BALANCE (F.O.B.)			*INVISIBLES BALANCE*			*CURRENT BALANCE*		
Countries and areas	*1982*	*1983*	*1984*	*1982*	*1983*	*1984*	*1982*	*1983*	*1984*
Belgium/Luxembourg	−3.6	−1.9	−1.2	0.9	1.5	1.5	−2.7	−0.4	0.3
Canada	14.4	14.4	16.1	−12.3	−13.0	−14.6	2.1	1.4	1.5
France	−15.5	−8.4	−4.1	3.4	4.0	4.0	−12.1	−4.4	−0.1
Germany	24.5	21.5	21.4	−21.2	−17.3	−15.4	3.3	4.2	6.0
Italy	−8.0	−3.1	−6.1	2.5	3.7	3.0	−5.5	0.6	−3.1
Japan	18.1	31.5	44.4	−11.2	−10.7	−9.4	6.9	20.8	35.0
Netherlands	4.6	4.3	5.3	−0.9	−0.5	−0.5	3.7	3.8	4.8
Sweden	0.8	3.1	4.7	−4.3	−4.0	−4.6	−3.5	−0.9	0.1
Switzerland	−2.8	−3.8	−3.9	6.8	7.3	7.6	4.0	3.5	3.7
United Kingdom	3.5	−1.8	−5.5	5.1	5.7	5.5	8.6	3.9	0.0
United States	−36.5	−61.1	−107.4	29.4	19.5	5.7	−7.1	−41.6	−101.7
Group of Ten countries	−0.5	−5.3	−36.3	−1.8	−3.8	−17.2	−2.3	−9.1	−53.5
Australia	−2.6	0.0	−0.8	−5.5	−5.8	−7.2	−8.1	−5.8	−8.0
Austria	−3.3	−3.4	−3.5	3.9	3.6	2.9	0.6	0.2	−0.6
Denmark	−0.8	0.2	−0.2	−1.5	−1.4	−1.5	−2.3	−1.2	−1.7
Finland	0.3	0.2	1.7	−1.1	−1.1	−1.7	−0.8	−0.9	0.0
Greece	−4.8	−4.3	−4.3	2.9	2.4	2.1	−1.9	−1.9	−2.2
Ireland	−1.1	−0.2	−0.2	−0.8	−0.9	−0.7	−1.9	−1.1	−0.9
New Zealand	−0.1	0.2	0.0	−1.4	−1.3	−1.2	−1.5	−1.1	−1.2
Norway	2.4	4.3	5.3	−1.7	−2.1	−1.8	0.7	2.2	3.5
Portugal	−4.9	−2.4	−1.4	1.6	1.4	0.9	−3.3	−1.0	−0.5
South Africa	0.7	4.0	1.9	−3.8	−3.7	−2.6	−3.1	0.3	−0.7
Spain	−9.3	−7.4	−4.0	5.1	4.9	6.0	−4.2	−2.5	2.0

EXHIBIT 3.6 (Cont.)

	TRADE BALANCE (F.O.B.)			*INVISIBLES BALANCE*			*CURRENT BALANCE*		
Countries and areas	*1982*	*1983*	*1984*	*1982*	*1983*	*1984*	*1982*	*1983*	*1984*
Turkey	−2.7	−3.0	−3.0	1.8	1.2	1.6	−0.9	−1.8	−1.4
Yugoslavia	−2.0	−1.2	−0.7	1.5	1.5	1.2	−0.5	0.3	0.5
Other developed countries	−28.2	−13.0	−9.2	1.0	−1.3	−2.0	−27.2	−14.3	−11.2
Total developed countries	−29	−18	−46	−1	−5	−19	−30	−23	−65
OPEC countries	62	44	55	−79	−65	−65	−17	−21	−10
Non-OPEC developing countries	−43	−20	−3	−20	−15	−19	−63	−35	−22
Total developing countries	19	24	52	−99	−80	−84	−80	−56	−32
Eastern European countries[a]	13	13	15	−6	−5	−5	7	8	10
Total	3	19	21	−106	−90	−108	−103	−71	−87

Sources: IMF, OECD, national sources and own estimates. From Bank for International Settlements, *Fifty-fifth Annual Report,* Basle, Switzerland, June 10, 1985, p. 90.

Note: Balances are given on a transactions basis.

[a]Bulgaria, Czechoslovakia, German Democratic Republic, Hungary, Poland, Rumania, and the USSR.

NOTE

1. See Patricia Hagen Kuwayama, "Measuring the United States Balance of Payments," *Monthly Review, Federal Reserve Bank of New York,* August 1975, pp. 183–194. Also see Charles N. Stabler, " 'Bottom Line' Data on Payments Balance Held Meaningless by U.S. Advisory Board," *Wall Street Journal,* December 10, 1975, p. 6.

BIBLIOGRAPHY

Bergsten, C. Fred, "What to Do about the U.S.-Japan Economic Conflict," *Foreign Affairs,* Summer 1982, pp. 1059–1075.

———, *Trade Policy in the 1980s,* Washington, D.C.: Institute for International Economics, November 1982.

Cline, William R., *International Debt and the Stability of the World Economy.* Washington, D.C.: Institute for International Economics, September 1983.

Dale, Richard S., and Richard P. Mattione, *Managing Global Debt,* Washington, D.C.: The Brookings Institution, 1983.

Ensor, Richard, ed., *Assessing Country Risk,* London: Euromoney Publications, 1981.

Feder, Gershon, and Richard Just, "A Study of Debt Servicing Capacity of Developing Countries," *Journal of Development Studies,* April 1980, pp. 25–38.

Garg, Ramesh C., "Loans to LDCs and Massive Defaults," *Intereconomics,* January/February 1981, pp. 19–25.

———, "Will Argentina Default?" *The Bankers Magazine,* January–February 1983, pp. 13–17.

Hutchinson, Michael, and Charles Piggott, "Budget Deficits, Exchange Rates and the Current Account: Theory and U.S. Evidence," Federal Reserve Bank of San Francisco, *Economic Review,* Fall 1984, pp. 5–25.

Khoury, Sarkis J., "Sovereign Debt: A Critical Look at the Causes and the Nature of the Problem," *Essays in International Business,* No. 5, July 1985.

McDonald, Donogh C., "Debt Capacity and Developing Country Borrowings: A Survey of the Literature," *IMF Staff Papers,* December 1982, pp. 603–646.

Morgan Guaranty Trust Company of New York, "Global Debt: Assessment and Long-term Strategy," *World Financial Markets,* June 1983, pp. 1–15.

———, "International Debt: Progress Report and the Task Ahead," *World Financial Markets,* September 1983, pp. 1–13.

———, "Strengthening U.S. Competitiveness," *World Financial Markets,* September 1984, pp. 1–13.

———, "The LDC Debt Problem—At the Midpoint," *World Financial Markets,* October/November 1984, pp. 1–11.

———, "The Bonn Summit and the U.S. Trade Deficit," *World Financial Markets,* March/April 1985, pp. 1–13.

Walter, Ingo, "Country Risk, Portfolio Decisions and Regulation in International Bank Lending," *Journal of Banking and Finance,* May 1981, pp. 77–92.

4

Foreign Exchange Market

Geographically the foreign exchange market spans the globe, with prices moving and currencies traded somewhere every hour of every business day. Major world trading starts each morning in Wellington and Sydney, moves west to Tokyo, Hong Kong, and Singapore, passes on to Bahrain, shifts to the main European markets of Frankfurt, Zurich, and London, jumps the Atlantic to New York, and ends up in San Francisco and Los Angeles. The market is deepest, or most liquid, early in the European afternoon, when both European and U.S. East Coast markets are open. This period is regarded as the best time to ensure the smooth execution of a very large order.

At the end of the day in California, when traders in Tokyo and Hong Kong are just getting up for the next day, the market is thinnest. During these hours, when the U.S. West Coast is awake and Europe sleeps, aggressive speculators or central banks sometimes try to move prices by trading large blocks, and thus influence attitudes in Europe the following morning about particular currencies. Many of the largest international banks operate foreign exchange trading rooms in each major geographic trading center in order to serve important commercial accounts on a 24-hour-a-day basis.

In some countries, such as France, a portion of the foreign exchange trading is conducted on an official trading floor by open bidding. Closing prices are published as the official price, or "fixing," for the day, and certain commercial and investment transactions are based on this officially published price. In some countries local firms, including affiliates of multinational corporations, that earn foreign exchange from exports surrender that foreign exchange to the central bank at the daily fixing price.

Banks engaged in foreign exchange trading are connected by a highly sophisticated telecommunications network. Professional dealers and brokers obtain exchange rate quotes on desktop video monitors and communicate with one another by telephone and telex. In fact, a foreign exchange trading room physically resembles a stock brokerage office. The foreign exchange departments of many nonbank business firms also have video monitors that they use to keep in touch with the market and to decide which banks are making the best quotations. The two leading suppliers of foreign exchange information systems are Telerate, which started in 1969, and Reuters, which began its service in 1973.

FUNCTIONS OF THE FOREIGN EXCHANGE MARKET

The foreign exchange market is the mechanism by which one may transfer purchasing power between countries, obtain or provide credit for international trade transactions, and minimize exposure to the risks of exchange rate fluctuations.

Transfer of Purchasing Power

Transfer of purchasing power is necessary because international trade and capital transactions usually involve parties living in countries with different national currencies. Usually each party wants to hold its own currency, although the trade or capital transaction can be invoiced in any convenient currency. For example, a Japanese exporter may sell Toyota automobiles to an Australian importer. The exporter could invoice the Australian importer in Japanese yen, Australian dollars, or a third-country currency such as U.S. dollars. The currency would be agreed on beforehand.

Whichever currency is used, one or more of the parties needs to transfer purchasing power to or from its own national currency. If the transaction is in yen, the Australian importer must exchange Australian dollars for yen to make payment. If Australian dollars are used, the Japanese exporter must exchange Australian dollars for yen. If U.S. dollars are used, the Australian importer must first exchange Australian dollars for U.S. dollars, and the Japanese exporter must then exchange U.S. dollars for yen. The foreign exchange market provides the mechanism for carrying out these purchasing power transfers.

Provision of Credit

Since the movement of goods between countries takes time, a means must be devised to finance inventory in transit. In the case of the Toyota automobile transaction, somebody would need to finance the automobiles while they are being shipped to Australia and also while they are "floored" with the Toyota dealers in Australia before final sale to a customer. The elapsed time typically might be anywhere from a few weeks to six months, depending on the kind of shipment.

In the case of automobiles, the Japanese exporter may agree to provide credit by carrying the accounts receivable of the Australian importer, with or without interest. Alternatively, the Australian importer may pay cash on shipment from Japan and finance the automobiles under its normal inventory financing arrangement. The foreign exchange market provides a third source of credit. Specialized instruments, such as bankers' acceptances and letters of credit, are available to finance trade. (These documents are explained in Chapter 14, "Import and Export Financing.")

Minimizing Foreign Exchange Risk

Neither the Australian importer nor the Japanese exporter may wish to carry the risk of exchange rate fluctuations. Each may prefer to earn a normal business profit on the automobile transaction rather than risk an unexpected change in anticipated profit should exchange rates suddenly change. The foreign exchange market provides "hedging" facilities for transferring the foreign exchange risk to someone else. (These facilities are explained later in this chapter and in Chapter 7, "Managing Foreign Exchange Exposure.")

MARKET PARTICIPANTS

The foreign exchange market consists of two tiers, the *interbank* or *wholesale* market, and the *client* or *retail* market. Individual transactions in the interbank market are usually for large sums that are multiples of a million U.S. dollars or the equivalent value in other currencies. By contrast, contracts between a bank and its clients are usually for specific amounts, sometimes down to the last penny.

Four broad categories of participants operate within these two tiers: bank and nonbank foreign exchange dealers; individuals and firms conducting commercial or investment transactions; speculators and arbitragers; and central banks and treasuries.

Bank and Nonbank Foreign Exchange Dealers

Banks, and a few nonbank foreign exchange dealers, operate in both the interbank and client markets. They profit from buying foreign exchange at a "bid" price and reselling it at a slightly higher "offer" (also called "ask") price. Competition among dealers worldwide keeps the spread between bid and offer thin and so contributes to making the foreign exchange market "efficient" in the same sense as the securities markets.

Dealers in the foreign exchange departments of large international banks often function as "market makers." They stand willing at all times to buy and sell those currencies in which they specialize. Market-making dealers usually maintain an "inventory" position in such currencies. They trade with other banks in their own monetary centers and in other centers around the world in order to maintain inventories within the trading limits set by bank policies. Trading limits are important because foreign exchange departments of many banks operate as profit centers, and individual dealers are compensated on a profit incentive basis. Unauthorized violations of trading limits by dealers under profit pressure have occasionally caused embarrassing losses to major banks.

Small to medium-sized banks are likely to participate but not be market makers in the interbank market. Instead of maintaining significant inventory positions, they buy from and sell to larger banks to offset retail transactions with their own customers. Of course, even market-making banks do not make markets in every currency. They trade for their own account in those currencies of most interest to their customers and become participants when filling customer needs in less important currencies.

A certain portion of interbank trading is conducted through foreign exchange brokers, who bring buyer and seller together for a fee but are not themselves principals in the transaction. The use of independent foreign exchange brokers permits banks to trade without revealing their name to the opposite party until an agreement is reached. Thus the name of the party cannot influence the price quoted. The Federal Reserve Bank of New York surveyed 119 banking institutions and 10 foreign exchange brokers throughout the United States on their foreign exchange transactions during April 1983.[1] The survey revealed that 56% of interbank transactions in foreign currencies for immediate delivery were intermediated by foreign exchange brokers.

Individuals and Firms Conducting Commercial and Investment Transactions

Individuals and firms use the foreign exchange market to facilitate execution of commercial or investment transactions. This group consists of importers and exporters, international portfolio investors, multinational firms, and tourists. Their use of the foreign exchange market is necessary but nevertheless incidental to the underlying commercial or investment purpose. Some of these participants use the market to "hedge" foreign exchange risk, a process to be explained in Chapter 7.

Speculators and Arbitragers

Speculators and arbitragers profit from trading within the market itself. Their motive differs from that of dealers in that speculators and arbitragers are operating only in their own interest without a need or obligation to serve clients or to ensure a continuous market. Whereas dealers seek profit from the spread between bid and offer and only incidentally seek to profit from general price changes, speculators seek all of their profit from a change in general price levels. Arbitragers seek to profit from simultaneous price differences in different markets.

A large proportion of speculation and arbitrage is conducted by traders in the foreign exchange departments of banks, on behalf of the bank. Thus banks act both as exchange dealers and as speculators and arbitragers. (Banks seldom admit to speculating; instead they see themselves as "taking an aggressive position"!)

Central Banks and Treasuries

Central banks and treasuries use the market to acquire or dispose of foreign exchange reserves as well as to influence the price at which their own currency is traded. They may act to support the value of their own currency because of policies adopted at the national level or because of commitments entered into through membership in such joint float agreements as the European Monetary System. Consequently their motive is not to earn a profit as such, but rather to influence the foreign exchange value of their currency in a manner that will be beneficial to the interests of their citizens. In many instances they will be doing their job best when they willingly take a loss on their foreign exchange transactions.

SIZE OF THE MARKET

The daily volume of foreign exchange trading worldwide is immense but impossible to measure. A 1983 survey of U.S. banks and brokers by the Federal Reserve Bank of New York gives a clue as to the size of the market in the United States but does not estimate the volume transacted in the many other markets worldwide. In fact, London, Frankfurt, and Zurich are widely believed to enjoy larger foreign exchange trading volumes than New York. According to the 1983 survey, the average volume of foreign exchange trading by the sample U.S. banks and brokers each business day during April 1983 was $48 billion. For April 1983 as a whole the sample bank and broker volume was $998.4 billion.[2]

If April 1983 were a typical month, the annual trading volume in the U.S. portion of the worldwide foreign exchange market would be close to $12 trillion. To put this in perspective, during 1983 the U.S. money supply measured by M1 (demand deposits) averaged $0.5 trillion, and by M2 (includes time deposits) averaged $2.2 trillion. The U.S. federal government debt averaged $1.3 trillion; the U.S. gross national product was $3.3 trillion; U.S. exports were $0.2 trillion; and imports were $0.25 trillion. Trading volume in 1984 on the New York Stock Exchange was almost $0.8 trillion.[3]

According to the Federal Reserve Bank of New York's 1983 survey, the relative importance of foreign currencies traded in the United States is as

EXHIBIT 4.1
Foreign Currencies Traded by Banks in the U.S. Foreign Exchange Market, April 1983

	Amount (in billions of U.S. dollars)	*Percentage*
Deutschemarks	228.6	32.5
Japanese yen	154.7	22.0
British pounds	117.0	16.6
Swiss francs	86.0	12.2
Canadian dollars	52.6	7.5
French francs	30.8	4.4
Dutch guilders	11.2	1.6
Italian lira	5.6	0.8
Belgian francs	2.8	0.4
All other	14.6	2.1
	703.9	100.0

Source: Federal Reserve Bank of Chicago, *International Letter,* October 7, 1983.

shown in Exhibit 4.1. The Deutschemark is the most actively traded currency, followed in order by the Japanese yen, the U.K. pound sterling, the Swiss franc, the Canadian dollar, and the French franc.

TYPES OF TRANSACTIONS

Transactions in the foreign exchange market are executed on a "spot," "forward," or "swap" basis. A spot transaction requires almost immediate delivery of foreign exchange. A forward transaction requires delivery of foreign exchange at some future date. A swap transaction is a simultaneous purchase and sale of a foreign currency.

Because of the great depth of the market for U.S. dollars compared with other currencies, most foreign exchange trading in the interbank market is between the U.S. dollar and other currencies. Thus a transaction involving the exchange of, say, yen for Deutschemarks will usually be carried out by exchanging yen for dollars and dollars for Deutschemarks.

Spot Transactions

A spot transaction in the interbank market is the purchase of foreign exchange, with delivery and payment between banks to be completed, normally, on the second following business day. One-day settlement is normal between the U.S. and Canadian dollars. The date of settlement is referred to as the "value date." On the value date, most dollar transactions in the world are settled through the computerized Clearing House Interbank Payments System (CHIPS) in New York, which provides for calculation of net balances owed by any one bank to another and for payment by 6:00 P.M. that same day in Federal Reserve Bank of New York funds.

A typical spot transaction in the interbank market might involve a U.S. bank contracting on a Monday for the transfer of £10,000,000 to the account of a London bank. If the spot exchange rate were $1.4984/£, the U.S. bank would transfer £10,000,000 to the London bank on Wednesday, and the London bank would transfer $14,984,000 to the U.S. bank at the same time. A spot transaction between a bank and its commercial customer would not necessarily involve a wait of two days for settlement.

Spot transactions dominate the interbank market. They represented 63% of the transactions undertaken by U.S. banks in April 1983, according to the survey by the Federal Reserve Bank of New York.[4]

Forward Transactions

A forward transaction (also called "outright forward") requires delivery at a future value date of a specified amount of one currency for a specified amount of another currency. The exchange rate is established at the time the contract is agreed on, but payment and delivery are not required until maturity. Forward exchange rates are normally quoted for value dates of one, two, three, six, and twelve months, but actual contracts can be arranged for other numbers of months or, on occasion, for periods of more than one year. Payment is on the second business day after the even-month anniversary of the trade. Thus a two-month forward transaction entered into on March 18 will be for a value date of May 20, or the next business day if May 20 falls on a weekend or holiday.

Although most forward contracts have specific maturity dates, "forward option" contracts that permit delivery at the beginning of a month (first to tenth day of the month), at the middle (eleventh to twentieth), or at the end (twenty-first to thirty-first) can be arranged. Such contracts cost more, but are preferred when a business firm does not know the exact date of receipt of foreign funds.

Note that as a matter of terminology one can speak of "buying forward" or "selling forward" to describe the same transaction. A contract to deliver dollars for guilders in six months might be referred to as "buying guilders forward for dollars" or "selling dollars forward for guilders."

Outright forward transactions in the interbank market are normally entered into by banks to offset forward exchange contracts with nonbank customers such as business firms and individuals. These customers usually make an outright forward transaction with the bank to protect themselves against a change in home currency value of foreign funds to be received or delivered in a business transaction.

Although outright forward contracts are quite important for multinational firms, they represent a relatively small proportion of the volume of trading by banks. According to the survey by the Federal Reserve Bank of New York, outright forward contracts accounted for only 6% of foreign exchange transactions undertaken by the sample U.S. banks in April 1983.[5]

Swap Transactions

A swap transaction in the interbank market is the simultaneous purchase and sale of a given amount of foreign exchange for two different value dates. Both purchase and sale are with the same other bank. A common type of swap is a "spot against forward." The dealer buys a currency in the spot market and simultaneously sells the same amount back to the same bank in the forward market. Since this is executed as a single transaction with one other bank, the dealer incurs no unexpected foreign exchange risk. The difference between the spot and forward rates is known and fixed.

A more sophisticated transaction is called a "forward-forward" swap. For example, a dealer could sell £20,000,000 forward for dollars for delivery in two months at $1.4870/£ and simultaneously purchase back £20,000,000 forward for delivery in three months at $1.4820/£. The difference between the buying price and the selling price is equivalent to the interest rate differential between borrowing costs of the two currencies. A swap can be viewed as a technique for borrowing one currency on a fully collateralized basis. (Swap quotations will be discussed in the section that follows.)

Swap transactions are very important in the interbank market. They represented 33% of foreign exchange transactions in April 1983 for the sample U.S. banks.[6]

FOREIGN EXCHANGE RATES AND QUOTATIONS

A foreign exchange rate is the price of one currency expressed in terms of another currency. A foreign exchange quotation is a statement of willingness to trade at an announced rate. Foreign exchange quotations are either direct or indirect. A *direct* quote is the home currency price of a unit of foreign currency. In the United States, $0.1265/FF is a direct quote for the French franc. An *indirect* quote is the price of one unit of the home currency in terms of the foreign currency. In the United States a quotation of FF7.9045/$ is an indirect quote for the French franc. Direct and indirect quotations are reciprocals: 1 divided by 7.9045 equals 0.1265. Since France is the home country of the franc, the quote of FF7.9045/$, which is an indirect quote in New York, is a direct quote in Paris.

European and American Terms

Most quotations in the interbank market are made in "European terms," which means the foreign currency price of a U.S. dollar. The normal way throughout the world of quoting the relationship between the franc and the dollar is thus FF7.9045/$; this may also be called "French terms." A quote for the Japanese yen of ¥233.09/$ may be called "Japanese terms." Outside the United States, then, most quotations are given on a direct basis, i.e., the local currency price of the U.S. dollar. This same quotation in the United States becomes an indirect quotation. This universal way of expressing foreign exchange quotations was adopted in 1978 to facilitate worldwide trading through telecommunications.

The alternative way of expressing exchange rates, the dollar price of a unit of foreign currency, is referred to as "American terms." American terms are normally used for quotations of the U.K. pound sterling, Australian dollar, New Zealand dollar, and Irish punt, but are otherwise not used in the interbank market. Sterling is quoted as the foreign currency price of a pound for historical reasons: For many centuries a pound sterling was divided into 20 shillings, each of which had 12 pence. Multiplication and division with this nondecimal currency was difficult, so the custom was for foreign exchange prices in London, then the undisputed financial capital of the world, to be stated in foreign currency units per pound. This practice remained even after sterling changed to a decimal basis in 1971. The other three currencies are quoted on American terms because of their close historical ties to Great Britain.

American terms are still used in many retail markets, and are normally used to express quotations on the foreign currency futures market in Chicago and on the foreign exchange options market in Philadelphia. (These special markets are discussed at the end of this chapter.)

Bid and Offer Quotations

Actual quotations are made in terms of a "bid" and an "offer" (also referred to as "ask") price. Additionally they are made without use of the currency signs, which are implicit from the context or the headings on a trader's screen. The franc/dollar quotation used earlier was a middle rate between the bid and offer. The actual quote appeared: 7.9030 to 7.9060, meaning that the dealer is willing to buy dollars at FF7.9030/$ and is willing to offer or sell dollars at FF7.9060/$. Tradition dictates that the bid be given before the offer. The dealers' profit comes from the difference between buying and selling prices, rather than from charging a commission.

Assume that a bank makes the quotations shown in the top half of Exhibit 4.2. The spot quotations indicate that the bank's foreign exchange trader will buy dollars (i.e., sell marks) at the bid price of DM2.5875 per

EXHIBIT 4.2
Foreign Exchange Quotations

	DEUTSCHEMARKS (DM/$)		*FRENCH FRANCS (FF/$)*	
	Bid	*Offer*	*Bid*	*Offer*
Outright Quotations				
Spot	2.5875	2.5885	7.9030	7.9060
One month forward	2.5781	2.5795	7.9255	7.9310
Two months forward	2.5701	2.5714	7.9550	7.9600
Three months forward	2.5625	2.5639	8.0005	8.0095
Six months forward	2.5382	2.5400	8.1430	8.1510
Points Quotations				
One month forward	94–90		225–250	
Two months forward	174–171		520–540	
Three months forward	250–246		975–1035	
Six months forward	492–485		2400–2450	

dollar. The trader will sell dollars (i.e., buy marks) at the offer price of DM2.5885 per dollar.

Traders tend to abbreviate, whether talking on the phone or putting quotations on a video screen. The first term, the bid, of a spot quotation may be given in full; i.e., "2.5875." However, the second term, the offer, will probably be expressed only as the digits that differ from the bid. Hence the bid and ask for spot Deutschemarks would be printed: *2.5875–85* on a video screen or spoken as "2.5875 (pause) 85" or "2.5875 to 85" on the telephone. On the phone the first digits may be assumed to be known, and the dealer may simply say "75 (pause) 85" or "75 to 85."

Premiums and Discounts

Forward quotations are at either a premium or a discount from the spot rate. A premium means that the direct price in the forward market is higher than the direct price in the spot market, while a discount means that the direct forward price is less than the direct spot price. On rare occasions when the spot and forward are the same, traders say the forward price is "flat." In Exhibit 4.2 above, the three-month forward dollar is offered at 2.5639, which is less than the spot offer of 2.5885. Since these quotations are direct in Germany, the lower price for a forward dollar in Germany means that the forward dollar is at a discount in Germany.

If one were in the United States, the forward mark would be regarded as at a premium. This can be verified by taking the reciprocals of the quotes in the table. The spot mark would be 1/2.5885 = $0.3863. The forward mark would be 1/2.5639 = $0.3900. The price of a forward mark when expressed in dollars is above the price of a spot mark, so the forward mark is at a premium in the United States. It is important to remember that an exchange rate that is a premium in one country becomes a discount when viewed from the opposite country.

Outright Forward and Swap Quotations

An outright forward quotation means the full price is stated. Outright forward quotations in the top half of Exhibit 4.2 show the six-month forward French franc quoted as "FF8.1430/$ bid, FF8.1510/$ offer." Outright quotations are usually reported in newspapers and used by banks in dealing with retail customers.

Point quotations Among themselves foreign exchange traders more frequently express forward rates in terms of "points," also referred to as "swap rates." The bottom half of Exhibit 4.2 shows the forward quotations as they would be given on a points basis. A quotation in points is not a foreign exchange rate as such. Rather it is the differential between the forward rate and the spot rate. Consequently, the spot rate cannot be given on a points basis.

A "point" is the last digit of a quotation, and convention dictates the number of decimal points in each quotation. Deutschemark and French franc quotations for the U.S. dollar are made to four decimal points. Hence a point is equal to 0.0001 of the currency. The point is used in foreign exchange quotations, however, without the decimal point or the leading zeros. A *point quotation* refers to the number of points away from the outright spot rate, with the first number referring to points away from the spot bid and the second number to points away from the spot offer. A slash (/) or a dash (–) is often used to separate the bid and offer point quotations on video screens or in print. A pause or the word "to" is used in voice communication.

In the franc/dollar quotations in Exhibit 4.2, forward prices for the dollars are more expensive than spot prices, meaning that the forward dollar is at a premium relative to the franc. Hence points must be added to the spot quotation to obtain the higher forward quotation. The six-month forward franc/dollar quotation is derived as follows:

	Bid	*Offer*
Spot	7.9030	7.9060
Add points for premium	+ 2400	+ 2450
Forward (six months)	8.1430	8.1510

Forward dollars are at a discount relative to the Deutschemark, so the points are subtracted. The three-month forward mark/dollar quotation is derived as follows:

	Bid	*Ask*
Spot	2.5875	2.5885
Subtract points for discount	– 250	– 246
Forward (three months)	2.5625	2.5639

In the above Deutschemark example, a trader might say that the three-month forward dollar is at a "discount of 250 to 246 points," indicating that the points should be subtracted from the spot rate. Most often, however, traders follow an operational rule that indicates whether the forward quote is at a premium or a discount without having to say "premium" or "discount." When the bid *in points* is smaller than the ask *in points,* as in the French franc example above, the trader knows that the points should be added and that the forward quotation is at a premium. When the bid *in points* is larger than the ask *in points,* as in the Deutschemark example, the trader knows that the points should be subtracted and the forward quotation is at a discount. Another simple rule of thumb, if one knows interest rates in the two countries, is to remember the currency with higher interest rates will be at a discount from the currency with lower interest rates.

The expression "swap rate" is used to indicate a bid and ask quotation expressed in points away from the spot rate. Many forward exchange transactions in the interbank market involve a simultaneous purchase for one date and sale (reversing the purchase) for another date. The swap is a way to borrow one currency for a limited time while giving up the use of another currency for the same time; i.e., it is a short-term borrowing of one currency combined with a short-term loan of an equivalent amount in another currency. The two parties could, if they wanted, charge each other interest at the going rate for each of the currencies. A simpler approach would be for the party acquiring the more expensive currency to pay the interest differential to the party acquiring the less expensive currency—in effect netting out a constant amount.

The swap rate simply expresses this net interest differential on a points basis rather than as an interest rate. A points quotation and an interest rate differential are equivalent, as will be explained in the following section.

Swap quotations in percentage terms Swap quotations are sometimes expressed in terms of a percent-per-annum deviation from the spot rate. This method of quotation facilitates comparison of premiums or discounts in the forward foreign exchange market with interest rate differentials. When quotations are on an indirect basis, an approximate formula for the percent-per-annum premium or discount is as follows:

$$\text{Forward premium or discount as a percent per annum (indirect basis)} = \frac{\text{spot rate} - \text{forward rate}}{\text{forward rate}} \times \frac{12}{n} \times 100 \qquad (1)$$

where n = the number of months in the contract. Using the spot and three-month forward offer mark/dollar quotation from Exhibit 4.2, we obtain

$$\text{Forward premium or discount as a percent per annum (indirect basis)} = \frac{2.5885 - 2.5639}{2.5639} \times \frac{12}{3} \times 100 = +3.8379\%.$$

Relative to the dollar, the three-month forward mark is quoted at a premium of 3.8379% per annum.

If quotations are on a direct basis, the formula is as follows:

$$\text{Forward premium or discount as a percent per annum (direct basis)} = \frac{\text{forward rate} - \text{spot rate}}{\text{spot rate}} \times \frac{12}{n} \times 100 \qquad (2)$$

Reciprocals of the mark/dollar quotations in Exhibit 4.2 are dollar/mark quotations, which are direct quotes in the United States. Applying these dollar/mark quotations in equation (2) above gives:

$$\text{Forward premium or discount as a percent per annum (direct basis)} = \frac{0.3900 - 0.3863}{0.3863} \times \frac{12}{3} \times 100 = +3.8312\%.$$

The three-month forward mark is quoted at a premium of 3.8312% per annum over the dollar. The slight difference of .0067 of a percentage point is caused by rounding.

Cross Rates

On occasion a person dealing in foreign exchange will want to obtain an exchange rate between two currencies from their common relationship with a third currency. Suppose, for example, that an Amsterdam merchant about to visit Copenhagen cannot find a Dutch guilder (symbol *fl*) quote for the Danish krone (symbol *DKr*). However, U.S. dollars are quoted in both currencies as follows:

Dutch guilder:	*fl* 3.0245/$
Danish krone:	*DKr*9.7215/$

The Amsterdam merchant can exchange 3.0245 guilders for one U.S. dollar, and with that dollar buy 9.7215 krone. The exchange rate calculation would be:

$$\frac{\text{Dutch guilders/dollar}}{\text{Danish kroner/dollar}} = \frac{fl\ 3.0245/\$}{DKr9.7215/\$} = fl\ 0.3111/DKr$$

In Europe and Asia many nondollar quotations are in terms of the home currency price of 100 units of the foreign currency, expressed to four decimal points. Thus a posted rate in Amsterdam for Danish kroner would probably read "*fl* 31.1114 per 100 Danish kroner."

Cross rates also are used to check the internal consistency of two separate foreign exchange forecasts. The mark/dollar exchange rate for next year may be forecast by a firm's staff in Germany, and the franc/dollar exchange rate for next year may be forecast separately by the firm's staff in France. The home treasury office should calculate the implied cross rate between marks and francs to see if it is reasonable. If, for example, the implied cross rate is outside of the bounds set by the European Monetary System, the original forecasts are likely to be in error—unless the forecaster believes that parities in the European Monetary System will be changed.

Percent Change in Exchange Rates

The amount of depreciation or appreciation caused by a change in exchange rates and expressed as a percentage can be determined from the following formulas. Assume that the pound sterling is quoted on a direct basis at $1.5000 before it drops in value, and at $1.2000 after.

$$\text{Percent change (direct)} = \frac{\text{ending rate} - \text{beginning rate}}{\text{beginning rate}} \times 100 \quad (3)$$

$$= \frac{1.2000 - 1.5000}{1.5000} \times 100 = -20.00\%$$

If the exchange rate is given on an indirect basis, the formula is different. The indirect quote for the pound sterling before depreciation is the reciprocal of $1.5000, or £0.6667/$. After depreciation the indirect quote is £0.8333/$. The formula is:

$$\text{Percent change (indirect)} = \frac{\text{beginning rate} - \text{ending rate}}{\text{ending rate}} \times 100 \quad (4)$$

$$= \frac{0.6667 - 0.8333}{0.8333} \times 100 = -20.00\%$$

INTEREST RATE PARITY

Prices in the spot and forward markets are considerably influenced by national monetary policies. Changes in differential national interest rates generate large movements of profit-seeking short-term funds between national money markets. The theory of interest rate parity links various national money market rates to foreign exchange rates.

The theory of interest rate parity states that except for transaction costs the difference in national interest rates for securities of similar risk and maturity should be equal but opposite in sign to the forward exchange rate discount or premium for the foreign currency.[7]

Covered Interest Arbitrage

The rationale for interest rate parity stems from use of a technique called "covered interest arbitrage." Understanding this technique is important because it is widely used by arbitragers to improve their return on short-term liquid funds without an increase in risk. The covered interest arbitrage incentive causes capital flows that tend to enforce interest rate parity.

To illustrate, assume that the following relationship exists between the U.K. pound and the U.S. dollar:

Pound spot rate: \$1.4000/£

Pound three-month forward rate: \$1.3860/£

Forward discount on the pound:

$$\frac{\$1.3860 - \$1.4000}{\$1.4000} \times \frac{12}{3} \times 100 = -4.00\% \text{ per annum}$$

U.K. three-month interest rate: 12.00% per annum

U.S. three-month interest rate: 7.00% per annum

Transaction costs: 0.15%; i.e., 15/100 of 1%

Transaction size: \$2,800,000 or £2,000,000

In this situation, U.K. three-month interest rates are 5% per annum above comparable U.S. rates, but the three-month forward exchange rate is only 4% per annum below the spot rate. According to the theory of interest rate parity, the market is not in equilibrium; hence an arbitrager should be able to make a profit and in the process nudge the market toward equilibrium.

Since the gain to be made on the interest rate differential is greater than the loss to be suffered on the exchange rate differential, the arbitrager would move funds to the market with the higher interest rate. If the differences were reversed, the arbitrager would move funds toward the market with the lower interest rate. In this example the arbitrager would take the following steps:

Today:

Step 1. Borrow \$2,800,000 at 1.75% per quarter (7.00% per annum) for three months. This step might also be accomplished by selling existing U.S. Treasury bills and thus sacrificing a three-month yield of 7.00% per annum.

Step 2. Exchange the \$2,800,000 for pounds at the spot rate of \$1.4000/£, receiving £2,000,000.

Step 3. Invest the £2,000,000 for three months in U.K. government bills, yielding 3.00% per quarter (12.00% per annum).

Step 4. Sell £2,060,000 forward three months at $1.3860/£. The amount to be sold forward includes both the principal of £2,000,000 and three months' interest of £60,000.

Step 5. Pay transaction costs of $2,800,000 × 0.0015 = $4,200.

Three months from today:

Step 6. Redeem U.K. government bills for £2,060,000.

Step 7. Fulfill the forward contract by delivering £2,060,000 at $1.3860/£, receiving $2,855,160.

Step 8. Repay the dollar loan of $2,800,000 plus three months' interest at 1.75% per quarter, equal to $49,000, or a total of $2,849,000.

The profit on this covered interest arbitrage is:

Proceeds from forward contract (Step 7)	$2,855,160
Less repayment of dollar loan (Step 8)	−2,849,000
Less transaction costs (Step 5)	− 4,200
Net profit before taxes	$ 1,960

The tax on this profit depends on where the contracts are executed and where the arbitragers are domiciled. The United States and the United Kingdom treat foreign exchange gains and losses differently, depending on the motive for the transaction.

Equilibrium

Exhibit 4.3 shows the conditions necessary for equilibrium. The vertical axis shows the difference in interest rates in favor of the foreign currency, and the horizontal axis shows the forward premium or discount on that currency. The interest rate parity line shows the equilibrium state, but transaction costs cause the line to be a band rather than a thin line. Transaction costs arise from foreign exchange and investment brokerage costs on buying and selling securities. Transaction costs have been estimated to be as low as 0.13% during tranquil periods in the foreign exchange market to as high as 1.03% during turbulent periods.[8] Typical transaction costs in recent years have been in the range of 0.18% to 0.25% on an annual basis. Point *X* shows an equilibrium position where a 5% higher rate of interest in the United Kingdom should be offset by a 5% discount on the forward pound.

The disequilibrium situation, which encouraged the interest rate arbitrage in the previous example, is illustrated by point *Y*. It is located off the interest parity line because the interest differential in favor of the United Kingdom is 5% (annual basis), whereas the forward discount on the pound is only 4% (annual basis).

EXHIBIT 4.3
Interest Rate Parity

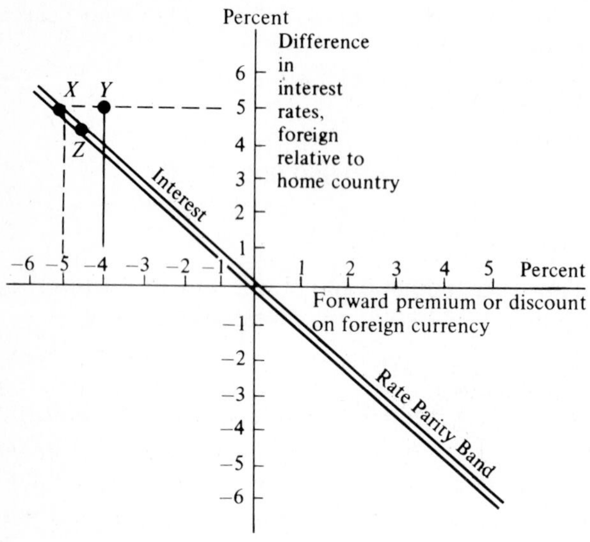

The situation depicted by point *Y* is unstable because all investors have an incentive to execute the same covered interest arbitrage. After all, except for a remote political risk, the arbitrage gain is virtually risk-free. U.S. and U.K. government bills are essentially risk-free since they are prime obligations of two sovereign governments that can always print more money to redeem their debts. If forward contracts are with reputable banks that can deliver as promised, virtually no risk exists.

Some observers have suggested that political risk does exist, since one of the governments might apply capital controls that would prevent execution of the forward contracts.[9] This risk is fairly remote in the U.S.–U.K. example, particularly since a large portion of the funds used for arbitrage comes from dollars and pounds deposited in other countries (i.e., Eurocurrencies), and these markets are very difficult for governments to control. The concern may be valid, however, with other country pairings.

If everybody takes advantage of the covered interest arbitrage opportunity, funds will flow out of U.S. dollars and into spot pounds to purchase U.K. government bills. This activity should raise the value of spot pounds relative to spot dollars, since demand for pounds increases and that for dollars decreases. It should also reduce the yield on U.K. government bills because the demand for them has increased, and this in turn should push their price up.

Simultaneously an increased demand to sell pounds forward three months for dollars develops. This activity should increase the discount on the pound in the forward market, since the supply of pounds for three-month delivery is now greater than the demand for them.

The net result of these pressures in the money and foreign exchange markets is to narrow the interest spread between the United States and United Kingdom and increase the forward discount on the pound. In other words, these pressures move point *Y* in Exhibit 4.3 toward point *Z* on the interest rate parity line, ignoring transaction costs to keep the example simple. Thus interest rate parity tends to be enforced by the play of free market forces seeking an essentially riskless profit.

In reality periodic opportunities do exist for covered interest arbitrage. Sometimes these are illusory because of temporarily increased transaction costs or government interference. Often they are fleeting, i.e., available only to the market makers themselves (banks) and only for a few minutes.

Covered interest arbitrage also takes place between other major trading currencies. Canada–United States, Germany–United States, Switzerland–United States, and Japan–United States have presented opportunities from time to time. Since most of the less developed countries have neither forward markets nor the safe government securities necessary to ensure a nearly riskless investment, little opportunity exists for covered interest arbitrage involving those countries.

SPECULATING IN THE FOREIGN EXCHANGE MARKET

To speculate in the foreign exchange market is to enter into a transaction for the purpose of making a profit from anticipated but uncertain changes in foreign exchange rates. A speculative transaction does not arise from the normal course of business or trade. Rather it is a risky operation undertaken for its own sake.

To illustrate the techniques involved, assume that the Dutch guilder is quoted as follows:

Spot rate:	*fl* 2.9000/$
Six-month forward rate:	*fl* 2.8000/$

A speculator believes that in six months the spot rate for the guilder will strengthen to *fl* 2.7000/$, and this speculator has $40,000. The speculator may try to profit in either the spot or forward market.

Speculating in the Spot Market

With $40,000 the speculator could buy $40,000 × *fl* 2.9000/$ = *fl* 116,000 in the spot market. If the speculator's expectations prove correct, the *fl* 116,000 can be sold at *fl* 2.7000/$ in six months, grossing $42,963 for a net profit of $2,963, or 7.41% for six months (14.82% per annum) on the original $40,000 of capital. Depending on changes in expectations after the spot purchase, the speculator could close out the position before six months or hold it longer than six months. The speculator is not bound by the six-month target but may simply hold until a sale would be profitable. An added variable, which we will not consider at this moment, is that the guilders could be invested in the Netherlands for six months to earn interest. Alternatively, if the speculation were not attempted, the speculator could earn interest on the dollars held in the United States.

Spot speculation is risky. Should the spot guilder weaken to, say, *fl* 3.000/$, the *fl* 116,000 would have an ending value of $38,667 and the speculator would lose $1,333. In theory there is no limit to the potential profit, but the maximum loss would be $40,000, the amount invested. In some situations a bank or other foreign exchange dealer might permit a customer to buy spot foreign exchange on margin, depositing, say, 25% of the purchase price and borrowing the remainder. In such a situation the capital of $40,000 might be used to buy $160,000 worth of guilders, or *fl* 464,000. Such a margin transaction would lever profits up or losses down, depending on the ending spot rate.

Speculating in the Forward Market

A person can speculate in the forward market by buying (or selling) in the forward market and then closing out (i.e., "covering") that forward position at a later date. The forward contract can be covered by waiting until maturity and selling (or buying) the currency spot, or by entering into an opposite forward contract before the first contract matures. The offsetting contract would have the same maturity date as the original contract.

Continuing with the guilder example, one speculative alternative is to buy guilders forward for dollars at the present time, wait until the date at which the contract matures, deliver dollars for guilders at that time, and sell the guilders in the spot market for whatever they will bring. Given the expectations stated earlier, the speculator should buy *fl* 112,000 forward at a forward price of *fl* 2.8000/$, thus agreeing to deliver $40,000 and receive *fl* 112,000 in six months. If the speculator's expectation for the future spot price is correct, the *fl* 112,000 received in six months can be sold at *fl* 2.7000/$ for $41,481. The profit would be $1,481.

In this speculation the maximum loss is $40,000, a loss that will be realized if the currency acquired (guilders) has no value in six months. The maximum gain in dollars is unlimited, since the acquired guilders can in theory rise to an infinite value in dollars.

An alternate speculation is to sell guilders forward. This will be profitable only when the spot value of the guilder in dollar terms weakens. Suppose that the forward rate is *fl* 2.8000/$, as before, but the speculator instead expects the spot price in six months to weaken to *fl* 3.1000/$. The speculator would then sell guilders for dollars in the forward market, wait until the date at which the contract matures, buy guilders in the spot market, deliver them against the forward contract, and receive dollars. Using the speculator's expectations, the speculator would sell *fl* 112,000 forward six months for dollars. In six months the speculator would buy *fl* 112,000 in the spot market at *fl* 3.1000/$ for a total cost of $36,129, deliver the guilders against the forward contract, and receive $40,000, for a profit of $3,871.

Under this second alternative, the maximum loss can be infinite, a loss that will be realized if the guilder rises to an infinite value in six months and the speculator is forced to buy guilders spot at this infinite price. The maximum gain is $40,000, an amount that will be realized if guilders fall in value to zero.

Structural Differences

Forward market speculation has several structural differences from spot speculation. Because the contract is for six months, it cannot be held longer than that date. As was mentioned, it can be closed prior to maturity by buying an opposite forward contract with a maturity equal to the remaining number of days in the original contract, and then using one contract to offset the other.

The profit of $1,481 in the forward example above cannot be related to any investment base to determine a rate of return. No capital is actually invested at the time a forward contract is purchased. The profit is thus a reward for taking a speculative risk, not a return on an invested sum as that term is usually understood. Some dealers may require a deposit (or "margin"), depending on the credit standing of the potential speculator. The purpose of the margin is to provide cash protection for the dealer in case the speculation turns into a loss and the speculator turns out not to have sufficient funds to deliver on the contract.

A number of more sophisticated ways to speculate in the forward market are possible. One of these is to speculate on cross rates getting out of alignment. Another is to speculate on a change over time in the spread between spot and forward rates. Yet a third is to speculate on a change over time in the spread between forward rates of two different maturities. An example of speculating on a change in the spread between two forward rates is presented in the appendix to this chapter.

FOREIGN CURRENCY FUTURES

A foreign currency futures contract is similar to other commodity futures contracts. It promises future delivery of a standard amount of a foreign currency at a specified time, place, and price.[10]

The International Monetary Market of Chicago

The most important marketplace for foreign currency futures is the International Monetary Market (IMM) of Chicago, organized in 1972 as a division of the Chicago Mercantile Exchange. The IMM has experienced spectacular growth in the dollar volume of contracts traded, but is still small compared with the interbank foreign exchange market.

In 1984 the Chicago Mercantile Exchange entered into partnership with the Singapore International Monetary Exchange (SIMEX) to provide standardized trading in futures contracts in gold, Eurodollar deposits, Deutschemarks, and Japanese yen. Contracts on the IMM and SIMEX are interchangeable, so contracts opened on one exchange may be liquidated on the other. Because Singapore is 14 hours ahead of Chicago time, the mutual offset facility is an initial step toward round-the-clock trading in currency futures.

The success of the IMM has encouraged the opening of other currency futures markets in New York (New York Futures Exchange, a subsidiary of the New York Stock Exchange), London (London International Financial Futures Exchange), Canada, and Australia. So far none of these rivals have come close to the trading volume of the IMM.

IMM Contracts

On the IMM, contracts are available in the eight currencies shown in Exhibit 4.4, as well as in gold, 90-day U.S. Treasury bills, domestic certificates of deposit, and Eurodollar time deposits. The IMM has its own standardized two-letter currency symbols, intended for transmission over its telegraphic ticker tape. The symbols are also shown in Exhibit 4.4.

An IMM contract has a number of standardized attributes, some of which are shown in Exhibit 4.4. Contract size is specified as a fixed amount of foreign currency, and prices are quoted in U.S. dollar terms. Allowable price gradients for specific quotations and for maximum daily trading ranges are established. For example, Exhibit 4.4 shows that a contract for £25,000 sterling is quoted to four decimal points with a minimum price fluctuation of $.0005, or 5 points.

A maximum daily price range is set for every currency each day, so that a participant is not exposed to more than a limited amount of daily price changes. The "normal limit" for the pound sterling is $.0500, or 500 points, which means that no single contract can vary in price by more than 500 points ($1,250) from the previous day. However if prices move to this maximum for two days in succession, an "expanded limit" provision allows the third-day price to move by 150% of the normal limit, the fourth-day price to move by 200%, and the fifth-day price to move in an unlimited amount. On the sixth trading day normal limits again apply.

EXHIBIT 4.4
International Monetary Market Contract Specifications

	Contract size	Minimum price fluctuation	Normal daily price limit	MARGIN REQUIREMENTS	
				Initial	Maintenance
Currency and IMM Ticker Symbol					
Pound sterling (BP)	BP 25,000	$ .0005 = 5 points	$.0500	$1,500	$1,000
Canadian dollar (CD)	CD 100,000	.0001 = 1 point	.0075	900	700
Dutch guilder (DG)	DG 125,000	.0001 = 1 point	.0100	1,200	900
Deutschemark (DM)	DM 125,000	.0001 = 1 point	.0100	1,500	1,000
Japanese yen (JY)	JY 12,500,000	.000001 = 1 point	.000100	1,500	1,000
Mexican peso (MP)	MP 1,000,000	.00001 = 1 point	.00150	3,000	2,500
Swiss franc (SF)	SF 125,000	.0001 = 1 point	.0150	2,000	1,500
French franc (FR)	FR 250,000	.00005 = 5 points	.00500	1,200	900
Other Contracts and IMM Ticker Symbol					
Gold (GD)	100 troy ounces	.10 = 10 points	$50/oz	Varies with purpose	
90-day U.S. Treasury bill (TB)	$1,000,000	.01 = 1 basis point	60 points	$1,500	$1,200
Domestic certificate of deposit (DC)	$1,000,000	.01 = 1 basis point	80 points	1,500	1,200
Eurodollar time deposit (ED)	$1,000,000	.01 = 1 basis point	100 points	1,500	1,200

Source: International Monetary Market, *Contract Specifications,* August 15, 1983.

All currency futures contracts mature, i.e., have a delivery date, on the third Wednesday of January, March, April, June, July, September, October, or December. A buyer on, say, February 1 would thus have available eight contract maturities, maturing from the third Wednesday of the following month (March) to the third Wednesday of January of the following year. Spot contracts mature on the third Wednesday of every month, and all contracts (futures and spot) are settled (i.e., delivered and paid for) on the third Wednesday of the appropriate month. The last trading day for any contract is the second business day prior to the Wednesday on which it matures.

Foreign Currency Futures vs. Bank Trading for Clients

IMM contracts differ from client contracts arranged with banks. Public customers place orders for execution through a broker on the trading floor of the IMM. The public buys or sells foreign exchange directly with a bank.

IMM trading is conducted by floor brokers who execute orders for customers of member firms at prices determined by competition on the floor. Trading is by voice at a designated location on the floor. Commercial banks make quotes to clients that are determined by prices set in the interbank market.

IMM trading is conducted only during trading hours, although extended trading is possible because of the link with SIMEX in Singapore. Interbank trading is conducted 24 hours a day around the world, and business clients of major banks can arrange for round-the-clock access to a bank trading room.

Public participants buying through the IMM are unknown to each other, and the opposite party to every trade is the Exchange Clearing House. Public clients deal with their bank, and that bank is the opposite party to every client trade.

IMM trading is open to anyone who can deposit the requisite margin, and consequently individual investors and speculators have easy access to the market. Spot and forward trading with a bank is generally open to anyone with cash or a line of credit.

Transactions on the IMM are for multiples of standard-sized contracts, where the value of a single contract, depending on the currency, is most often between $30,000 and $75,000. Larger transactions require multiple contracts, which is not a problem for individuals or smaller corporations. Large firms prefer banks because the interbank market is more liquid. In addition, most large firms regard foreign exchange trading as part of their total banking relationship, and foreign exchange trading compensates their bank for other services received.

IMM contracts are available only for a set of fixed maturities, the longest of which is nine months. Banks will write contracts for their customers for any maturity up to a year, and will occasionally write contracts for longer than one year.

IMM member brokers charge a single commission to customers to cover both the purchase and the later sale of a contract. Bank clients pay a net price with no commission because banks make their profit from the spread between their bid and ask.

The IMM enforces limits on the maximum daily price movement on a contract, while the interbank market is a free market in which prices may change by as much as is needed to match buyers and sellers.

FOREIGN CURRENCY OPTIONS

In the last three years the use of foreign currency options as a hedging tool and for speculative purposes has blossomed into a major foreign exchange activity. A number of banks in the United States and other capital markets offer flexible foreign currency options on transactions of $1 million or more. The bank market, or over-the-counter market, as it is called, offers custom-tailored options on all major trading currencies for any time period up to one year. These options provide a useful alternative to forward and future contracts for firms interested in hedging foreign exchange risk.

In December 1982, the Philadelphia Stock Exchange introduced trading in standardized foreign currency option contracts in the United States. The Chicago Mercantile Exchange and other exchanges in the United States and abroad have followed suit. Exchange-traded contracts are particularly appealing to speculators and individuals who would not normally have access to the over-the-counter market. Banks and business firms also trade on the exchanges because this is one of several alternative ways they can offset the risk of options they have transacted with clients or other banks.

Currency Option Definitions

- A foreign currency option is a contract giving the buyer the right to buy or sell a given amount of foreign exchange at a fixed price per unit for a specified time period from the seller.
- An "American option" gives the buyer the right to exercise the option on any day before the expiration date of the contract. A "European option" allows the buyer to exercise the option only on the expiration date.
- An option to purchase foreign currency is a "call" and an option to sell is a "put."
- The "exercise" or "strike" price is the specified exchange rate at which the option can be exercised. A strike price can be set (1) "at-the-money," which is usually the spot exchange rate, (2) "out-of-the-money," a price

which if immediately exercised would cause a loss, and (3) "in-the-money," a price which if immediately exercised would cause a gain.

- A "premium" is the price of an option, usually paid in advance to the seller. The premium is determined by (1) the strike price relative to the spot exchange rate, (2) relative interest rates, (3) maturity, (4) currency volatility, and (5) supply and demand for specific options.[11] In the over-the-counter (bank) market premiums are quoted as a percentage of the transaction amount. For exchange-traded options, premiums are quoted in cents per unit of foreign currency.

Foreign Currency Options on the Philadelphia Stock Exchange

Foreign currency options on five major currencies are traded on the Philadelphia Stock Exchange. Contract sizes are half the size of futures contracts on the IMM for the same currencies:

Deutschemarks	DM	62,500 per contract
Swiss francs	SF	62,500 per contract
British pounds	£	12,500 per contract
Canadian dollars	C$	50,000 per contract
Japanese yen	¥	6,250,000 per contract

If, for example, a person wants to buy an option on DM1,000,000, that person will purchase sixteen contracts: DM1,000,000/DM62,500 per contract = 16 contracts.

Quotes in the *Wall Street Journal* for options on the U.K. pound might appear as follows, where prices and premiums are stated in cents per unit of foreign currency:

		CALLS			*PUTS*		
Current spot price	*Strike price*	*Dec.*	*March*	*June*	*Dec.*	*March*	*June*
142.01	140	—	3.85	—	—	—	—
142.01	145	—	2.00	2.35	—	3.50	—
142.01	150	—	—	—	7.65	8.00	—
142.01	155	—	0.05	—	—	—	—

The near maturities, such as December, usually trade more frequently than the more remote maturities. The dash means that particular contract was not traded the previous day. Quotations are usually available for more combinations of strike price and expiration date than are actually traded and thus reported in the newspaper.

Each currency option expires on the Saturday preceding the third Wednesday of the expiration month; expiration months are March, June, September, and December. However, only the three nearest expiration months trade at any one time. Thus in November, trading would occur in December, March, and June contracts as shown above. December contracts would expire on the Saturday preceding the third Wednesday of December, after which trading in September contracts would be opened. The longest option available at any one time is thus nine months.

In the table above, "Current spot price" means that \$1.4201 is the current spot dollar price of one U.K. pound. "Strike price" means the price per pound that must be paid if the option is exercised. On the above date, options with four separate strike prices, ranging from \$1.40 per pound to \$1.55 per pound, were available. Options are available at striking prices that are rounded from the spot price in the market when these options were first offered.

The body of the table contains the purchase price or premium for each option, expressed in U.S. cents per unit of foreign currency. In the table, a March 145 call option premium is two cents per pound. Since one option contract consists of a call on £12,500, the premium for the option would be £12,500 × \$0.02/£ = \$250.00. A March 150 put could be purchased for \$0.08 per pound, or \$1,000.

Speculating with Foreign Currency Options

A speculator buying a March 145 call would pay \$0.02 per pound for the option to purchase £12,500 at \$1.4500 per pound, with the option good until the following March. Should the pound rise in the spot market to a price above \$1.4500, say \$1.5100, the speculator could purchase the pounds through the option for \$1.4500 and resell them for \$1.5100 in the spot market, making a gross profit of \$0.06 per pound or \$750 on a single contract. Subtracting the premium (i.e., purchase price) of \$250 from the gross profit of \$750 leaves a profit before brokerage costs of \$500 on an investment of \$250. Usually the speculator does not exercise the option and sell the pounds on the spot market; rather the option contract is sold back to the writer at a price that reflects the appreciation in value of the underlying currency, the length of time to maturity, expected currency volatility, interest rates, and other variables that affect the value of a traded option.

In the above example the speculator also has the opportunity to offset the option by a forward market transaction. Suppose on the day that the pound rose in value to \$1.5100 in the spot market the forward rate on the pound rose to \$1.5700 for March delivery. Now the speculator could sell £12,500 forward for March delivery, at which time the option would be exercised to purchase £12,500 at \$1.4500 per pound. The speculator could lock in a certain $0.12 per pound gross profit before deducting premium and brokerage costs. This strategy would dominate the other one of selling the pounds in the spot market at $1.5100 per pound today if the present value of $1.5700 received in March discounted to today is greater than $1.5100.

In fact, the speculator need not wait until March but could sell forward for any date before then and exercise the option when that date arrived. Whether this would be profitable depends again on whether the present value of the difference between the relevant forward rate and the exercise price of the option discounted to today is greater than $1.5100.

SUMMARY

In this chapter we have discussed the three functions of the foreign exchange market: (1) transfer of purchasing power, (2) provision of credit, and (3) minimizing foreign exchange risk.

The foreign exchange market is comprised of two tiers: the interbank market and the client market. Within these tiers participants include: (1) foreign exchange dealers, (2) individuals and firms conducting commercial or investment transactions, (3) speculators and arbitragers, and (4) central banks and treasuries.

Transactions are executed on a spot, forward, or swap basis. Rates are quoted on a direct or indirect basis. Each quote contains a bid and offer price. Forward rates are often quoted as a percentage discount or premium from the spot rate.

Interest rate parity is a theory that equates differences in national interest rates with the forward discount or premium on foreign currency. Covered interest arbitrage is a riskless technique used to profit from deviations in interest rate parity.

A more risky way to play the foreign exchange market is to speculate in the spot or forward markets. This can be done in the interbank market only by large creditworthy institutions and firms. Individual speculators are served by foreign currency futures markets, such as the IMM in Chicago, and by the popular options markets, such as the one on the Philadelphia Stock Exchange.

NOTES

1. Earlier surveys were conducted by the Federal Reserve Bank of New York in 1977 and 1980. The results of the 1983 survey are summarized in at least two sources: Julian Walmsley, "The New York Foreign Exchange Market," *The Bankers Magazine,* January–February 1984, pp. 67–69; and *International Letter,* Federal Reserve Bank of Chicago, October 7, 1983.

2. *International Letter,* Federal Reserve Bank of Chicago, October 1983, p. 1.

3. Federal Reserve Bulletin, March 1984, pp. A13, A31, A50, A53; *New York Stock Exchange Fact Book,* 1985, p. 6.

4. Federal Reserve Bulletin, March 1984, p. 2.

5. Ibid.

6. Ibid.

7. The theory is usually applicable only to short-term securities with a maturity of one year or less, since forward quotes are not routinely available for periods longer than one year.

8. William J. Branson, "The Minimum Covered Interest Differential Needed for International Arbitrage Activity," *Journal of Political Economy,* November–December 1969, pp. 1028–1035. Also see Jacob A. Frenkel and Richard M. Levich, "Transaction Costs and Interest Arbitrage: Tranquil versus Turbulent Periods," *Journal of Political Economy,* December 1977, pp. 1209–1226.

9. Robert Z. Aliber, "The Interest Rate Parity Theorem: A Reinterpretation," *Journal of Political Economy,* December 1973, pp. 1451–1459.

10. Two good sources of information on foreign currency futures are Karl V. Chalupa, "Foreign Currency Futures: Reducing Foreign Exchange Risk," *Economic Perspectives,* Federal Reserve Bank of Chicago, Winter 1982; and Henry N. Goldstein, "Foreign Currency Futures: Some Further Aspects," *Economic Perspectives,* Federal Reserve Bank of Chicago, November/December 1983, pp. 3–13.

11. The value of foreign currency options is based on a modified version of the Black and Scholes model for domestic options. The original Black and Scholes model is described in Fisher Black and Myron Scholes, "The Pricing of Options and Corporate Liabilities," *Journal of Political Economy,* May/June 1973, pp. 637–659. Foreign currency option valuation models can be found in Mark Garman and Steven Kohlhagen, "Foreign Currency Option Values," *Journal of International Money and Finance,* December 1983, pp. 231–237; J. Orlin Grabbe, "The Pricing of Call and Put Options on Foreign Exchange," *Journal of International Money and Finance,* December 1983, pp. 239–253; and Nahum Biger and John Hull, "The Valuation of Currency Options," *Financial Management,* Spring 1983, pp. 24–28.

Chapter 4: Appendix
Speculating on a Change in Spreads

Occasionally a person will speculate on a change in the spread between spot and forward quotations. This speculation is carried out by simultaneously buying and selling in the forward market for different maturities and subsequently closing out both positions at a later date. The operation may be visualized as follows:

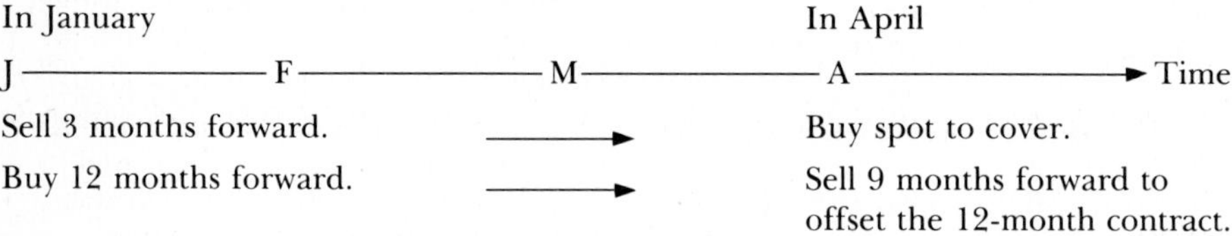

Such a speculation has the advantage that the trading position of the speculator is at all times balanced, or in a "square" position, with forward purchases equal to forward sales. The speculator's profit will be determined by changes in the spread between the spot and forward rates of the first pair of transactions (January above) and the second pair (April above). Changes in the spread are, in turn, the results of changing interest rate differentials between two countries. Thus the speculator in an operation such as this is betting that the interest differential will change.

To illustrate, assume actual and expected interest rates in January are as follows, expressed as an annual percentage:

	Actual January interest rate for 3-month (i.e., April) maturities	*Actual January interest rate for 12-month (i.e., next January) maturities*	*Expected interest rate for April for 9-month (i.e., next January) maturities*
United States	14.00%	15.00%	16.00%
Netherlands	8.00	9.00	9.00
Differential	6.00%	6.00%	7.00%

If the present spot rate is *fl* 2.9000/$ and forward quotations reflect the interest rate differential, the above interest rates may be used to calculate current quotations in the forward market. Equation 1 on page 100 can be transformed to the following equations:

$$\text{January 3-month forward quote} = \frac{2.9000}{1 + (6.00/100 \times 3/12)} = 2.8571$$

$$\text{January 12-month forward quote} = \frac{2.9000}{1 + (6.00/100 \times 12/12)} = 2.7358$$

Assume that the speculator has no particular opinion about the direction in which the spot market will move, but believes that by April the interest rate differential will be 7.00% per annum. If the spot rate in April were to be the same is it was in January—i.e., *fl* 2.9000/$—the April quotation for 9 months forward would be as follows:

$$\text{April 9-month forward quote} = \frac{2.9000}{1 + (7.00/100 \times 9/12)} = 2.7553$$

The speculator should buy and sell dollars as follows:

In January:

Buy $ 3 months forward	@ 2.8571	Sell $ 12 months forward	@ 2.7358
In April:			
Sell $ spot	@ 2.9000	Buy $ 9 months forward	@ 2.7553
Profit	429	Loss	(195)

Net profit on the operation per dollar traded would be:

Profit on the 3-month contract:	*fl* 0.0429
Loss on the 12-month contract:	−0.0195
Net profit:	*fl* 0.0234 or 234 points

This type of speculation is safe for small changes in the spot rate, as can be illustrated with similar calculations based on both an increase and a decrease in the April spot rate.

	Spot rate increase	*Spot rate decrease*
Assumed April spot rate	3.2000	2.7000
April 9-month forward quote at a 7.00% interest rate differential	3.0404	2.5653
First transaction		
In January buy dollars 3 months forward	2.8571	2.8571
In April sell dollars spot	3.2000	2.7000
Profit or (loss)	0.3429	(0.1571)

	Spot rate increase	*Spot rate decrease*
Second transaction		
In January sell dollars 12 months forward	2.7358	2.7358
In April buy dollars 9 months forward	3.0404	2.5653
Profit or (loss)	(0.3046)	0.1705
Net profit on both transactions	0.0383	0.0134

The above example indicates that a profit is made when the spot rate rises or falls by a small amount. If the change in the spot rate is sufficiently large, however, the operation may produce a loss. Success in this type of speculation depends on accurately forecasting the change in interest rate differentials or the change in spreads between spot and forward quotations. The above example was in terms of an increase in the interest rate differential. If instead one expected the interest rate differential to decline, one could speculate successfully by reversing the direction of the trades, selling 3 months forward and buying 12 months forward in January and reversing these trades in April.

BIBLIOGRAPHY

Adler, Michael, and Bernard Dumas, "Portfolio Choice and the Demand for Forward Exchange," *American Economic Review,* May 1976, pp. 332–339.

Agmon, Tamir, and Rafael Eldor, "Currency Options Cope with Uncertainty," *Euromoney,* May 1983, pp. 227–228.

Aliber, Robert Z., "The Interest Rate Parity Theorem: A Reinterpretation," *Journal of Political Economy,* December 1973, pp. 1451–1459.

Askari, Hossein, and Franco Modigliani, "A Note on Capital Movements and the Relation of Spread in Spot and Forward Rates to Variations in the Short-Term Interest Differential," *Kyklos,* No. 1, 1977, pp. 38–50.

Biger, Nahum, and John Hull, "The Valuation of Currency Options," *Financial Management,* Spring 1983, pp. 24–28.

Black, Fischer, and Myron Scholes, "The Pricing of Options and Corporate Liabilities," *Journal of Political Economy,* May/June 1973, pp. 637–659.

Byler, Ezra U., and James C. Baker, "S.W.I.F.T.: A Fast Method to Facilitate International Financial Transactions," *Journal of World Trade Law,* September–October 1983, pp. 458–465.

Callier, Philippe, "Speculation and the Forward Foreign Exchange Rate: A Note," *Journal of Finance,* March 1980, pp. 173–176.

Chalupa, Karl V., "Foreign Currency Futures: Reducing Foreign Exchange Risk," *Economic Perspectives,* Federal Reserve Bank of Chicago, Winter 1982, pp. 3–11.

Christofides, N., R. D. Hewins, and G. R. Salkin, "Graph Theoretic Approaches to Foreign Exchange Operations," *Journal of Financial and Quantitative Analysis,* September 1979, pp. 481–500.

Cornell, Bradford W., "Determinants of the Bid-Ask Spread on Forward Exchange Contracts under Floating Exchange Rates," *Journal of International Business Studies,* Fall 1978, pp. 33–41.

Cornell, Bradford, and Marc R. Reinganum, "Forward and Future Prices," *Journal of Finance,* December 1981, pp. 1035–1045.

Deardorff, Alan, "One-Way Arbitrage and Its Implications for Foreign Exchange Markets," *Journal of Political Economy,* April 1979, pp. 351–364.

"Foreign Exchange Transactions in the U.S. Foreign Exchange Market," *International Letter,* Federal Reserve Bank of Chicago, October 7, 1983.

Feiger, George, and Bertrand Jacquillat, "Currency Option Bonds, Puts and Calls on Spot Exchange and the Hedging of Contingent Foreign Earnings," *Journal of Finance,* December 1979, pp. 1129–1139.

Frenkel, Jacob A., and Richard M. Levich, "Covered Interest Arbitrage: Unexploited Profits?" *Journal of Political Economy,* April 1975, pp. 325–338.

———, "Transaction Costs and Interest Arbitrage: Tranquil versus Turbulent Periods," *Journal of Political Economy,* November–December 1977, pp. 1209–1226.

Gadkari, Vilas, *Relative Pricing of Currency Options,* New York: Salomon Brothers, May 1984.

Garman, Mark B., and Steven W. Kohlhagen, "Foreign Currency Option Values," *Journal of International Money and Finance,* December 1983, pp. 231–237.

Giddy, Ian H., "Measuring the World Foreign Exchange Market," *Columbia Journal of World Business,* Winter 1979, pp. 36–48.

———, "Foreign Exchange Options," *Journal of Futures Markets,* Summer 1983, pp. 143–166.

———, "The Foreign Exchange Option as a Hedging Tool," *Midland Corporate Finance Journal,* Fall 1983, pp. 32–42.

Goldstein, Henry, "Foreign Currency Futures: Some Further Aspects," *Economic Perspectives,* Federal Reserve Bank of Chicago, November–December 1983, pp. 3–13.

Grabbe, J. Orlin, "The Pricing of Call and Put Options on Foreign Exchange," *Journal of International Money and Finance,* December 1983, pp. 239–253.

Grammatikos, Theoharry, and Anthony Saunders, "Stability and the Hedging Performance of Foreign Currency Futures," *Journal of Futures Markets,* Fall 1983, pp. 295–305.

Gupta, Sanjeev, "A Note on the Efficiency of Black Markets in Foreign Currencies," *Journal of Finance,* June 1981, pp. 705–710.

Hilley, John L., Carl R. Beidleman, and James A. Greenleaf, "Does Covered Interest Arbitrage Dominate in Foreign Exchange Markets?" *Columbia Journal of World Business,* Winter 1979, pp. 99–107.

———, "Why There Is No Long Forward Market in Foreign Exchange," *Euromoney,* January 1981, pp. 94–103.

Hull, John, "The Valuation of Currency Options: Reply," *Financial Management,* Summer 1984, p. 53.

Kubarych, Roger M., *Foreign Exchange Markets in the United States,* rev. ed., New York: Federal Reserve Bank of New York, 1983.

Levi, Maurice, *International Finance: Financial Management and the International Economy,* New York: McGraw-Hill, 1983, Chapters 2–3.

Loosigian, Allen M., *Foreign Exchange Futures,* Homewood, Ill.: Dow Jones–Irwin, 1981.

Panton, Don B., and O. Maurice Joy, "Empirical Evidence on International Monetary Market Currency Futures," *Journal of International Business Studies,* Fall 1978, pp. 59–68.

Philadelphia Stock Exchange, "Controlling Risk with Foreign Currency Options," *Euromoney,* February 1985. (Supplementary issue; the entire issue is devoted to foreign currency options.)

Pitts, Mark, "The Valuation of Currency Options: Comment," *Financial Management,* Summer 1984, pp. 51–52.

Revey, Patricia A., "Evolution and Growth of the United States Foreign Exchange Market," *Quarterly Review,* Federal Reserve Bank of New York, Autumn 1981.

Riehl, Heinz, and Rita Rodriguez, *Foreign Exchange and Money Markets,* New York: McGraw-Hill, 1983.

Ruck, Adam, "Understanding Foreign Exchange Trading," *Euromoney,* April 1981, pp. 117–124.

Stokes, Houston H., and Hugh Neuburger, "Interest Arbitrage, Forward Speculation and the Determination of the Forward Exchange Rate," *Columbia Journal of World Business,* Winter 1979, pp. 86–98.

Walker, Townsend, *A Guide for Using the Foreign Exchange Market,* New York: Ronald Press/John Wiley & Sons, 1981.

Walmsley, Julian, "The New York Foreign Exchange Market," *Bankers Magazine* (US), January–February 1984, pp. 67–69.

Weisweiller, Rudi, *Introduction to Foreign Exchange,* Cambridge, England: Woodhead-Faulkner, Ltd., 1983.

Problems for Part I

1. The following outright foreign exchange quotations are given for the Swiss franc:

	Bid	*Ask*
Spot rate	SF2.4180/$	SF2.4200/$
One month forward	2.4026	2.4051
Three months forward	2.3716	2.3746
Six months forward	2.3245	2.3285

a. Calculate forward quotes for both bid and ask in terms of points.

b. Assume you are in the United States. Calculate forward quotes for the Swiss franc as an annual percentage premium or discount. Would a foreign exchange trader in Switzerland get a different answer if asked to calculate the annual percentage premium or discount for each forward rate on the U.S. dollar? Why?

2. The spot rate and forward swap rates for the Canadian dollar are shown below:

	Bid	*Ask*
Spot rate	C$1.3274/US$	C$1.3290/US$
One month forward	2	10
Three months forward	16	30
Six months forward	44	64

a. Calculate outright forward quotes for both bid and ask.

b. Assume you are in the United States. Calculate forward quotes for the Canadian dollar as an annual percentage premium or discount. Would a foreign exchange trader in Canada get a different answer if asked to calculate the annual percentage premium or discount on the U.S. dollar? Why?

3. Given that the following currencies change in value relative to the dollar as indicated, calculate the ending exchange rate in terms of local currency units per dollar.

Currency	*Initial exchange rate*	*Change relative to dollar*
Argentine austral	₳0.80/US$	devalues 30%
Saudi rial	SR3.50/US$	appreciates 20%

4. A foreign exchange dealer in Singapore normally provides quotes for spot, one month, three months, and six months. When you ask over the telephone for current quotations for the Deutschemark against the U.S. dollar, the dealer replies:

   "2.8600 to 15, 154 to 149, 474 to 459, 916 to 891."

   The following questions are based on this set of quotations.

   a. If you want to sell DM1,000,000 spot, what would you receive in dollars?

   b. If you want to buy DM16,000,000 forward three months for dollars, what would your cost be? When would you make payment?

   c. In New York, three-month Treasury bills yield 12% per annum. Using mid-rates (halfway between the bid and ask), what should be the yield on German three-month bills?

   d. Verify your answer to part *c* with a hypothetical investment of $10,000,000 for three months in both countries. Use mid-rates, and ignore charges and taxes.

5. You have the following quotations and expectations for the British pound:

Present spot rate:	$1.3200/£
Six-month forward rate:	$1.3500/£
Six-month call option on pounds at a strike price of $1.32 and a premium of 4 cents per pound on the Philadelphia Stock Exchange	
Your expectation for the spot rate in six months:	$1.3700/£

   Assume you have $5,000,000 with which to speculate. Ignore transaction costs, taxes, and interest that might be earned on idle cash balances.

   a. If your expectations prove correct, what would be your dollar profit from speculating in the spot market?

      i. What risks are associated with this operation?

      ii. How much capital must be committed?

b. If your expectations prove correct, what would be your dollar profit from speculating via the forward market?

i. What risks are associated with this operation?

ii. How much capital must be committed?

c. If your expectations prove correct, what would be your dollar profit from speculating via the option market?

i. What risks are associated with this operation?

ii. How much capital must be committed?

d. What are the consequences of the three alternatives if interest can be earned on idle cash balances?

6. Your corporation must make a $25 million domestic payment in New York in three months. The dollars are available now, and you decide to invest them for three months. The U.S. three-month Treasury bill rate is 15% per annum, and the Swiss three-month bank rate is 8% per annum. The spot exchange rate is SF2.4190/$, and the three-month forward rate is SF2.4038/$.

a. Where should you invest for maximum yield with no risk?

b. Given the stated interest rates, what forward quotation would create equilibrium, with no advantage or disadvantage associated with investing in one country or the other? Ignore transaction costs.

c. Would you change your decision about where to invest if the Swiss interest rate were 14% per annum?

d. Given the stated spot and forward exchange rates and the U.S. interest rate, what is the equilibrium or break-even Swiss interest rate?

7. You are the international treasurer of Great Sugar & Molasses Corporation (GSM), and you must transfer DM1,000,000 from GSM's German affiliate to its Italian affiliate. The transfer: (1) is permanent; i.e., will not be returned to Germany or the United States, and (2) has no tax consequences. GSM has the marks available in Germany right now, and does not need lira in Italy until six months from today. The following additional information is available:

DM/$ spot rate:	DM2.5880/$
DM/$ six-month forward rate:	DM2.5391/$
Lit/$ spot rate:	Lit1,573.25/$
Lit/$ six-month forward rate:	Lit1,642.12/$
Six-month German CD rate:	8% per annum
Six-month Italian CD rate:	12% per annum

a. Should you transfer the funds now or in six months? What is the monetary amount gained from the best alternative, relative to the second alternative?

b. If everything were to remain the same except Italian interest rates, what would be the new rate of interest in Italy that would create equilibrium?

c. If everything were to remain the same except the six-month forward exchange rate, what new Lit/DM forward rate would create equilibrium?

8. In August the following quotations are given for the British pound:

Spot rate (in August):	\$1.4000/£
3-month forward rate (for November):	\$1.3850/£
12-month forward rate (for following August):	\$1.3400/£

In August a speculator has the following expectations for rates in November:

Expected spot rate (for November):	\$1.4200/£
Expected 9-month forward rate (for following August):	\$1.3795/£

In August the discounts on the 3-month and 12-month forward quotations amount to 50 points per month, and in November the expectation is for the spread to diminish to 45 points per month. How could the speculator benefit from the expected drop in the amount of discount? If the expectations prove correct, how much profit per British pound could be earned?

9. The ¥/\$ spot rate is ¥202.00/\$. The six-month forward rate is ¥200.27/\$. Six-month government bills yield 5% per annum in Japan and 8% per annum in the United States. Assuming you can borrow \$1 million or its yen equivalent, show how you can make a "risk-free" profit. Assume transaction costs are \$500 or its yen equivalent, paid at the start. Ignore income taxes.

10. The DM/\$ spot rate is DM2.5200/\$. The three-month forward rate is DM2.4900/\$. Interest rates for three-month money market instruments and interbank loans are 5% in Germany and 9% in the United States on an annualized basis. How could a U.S. bank make a risk-free profit given the opportunity to borrow or invest at these rates in either country? Assume the bank's foreign exchange trader is authorized to use \$3 million or its DM equivalent. Assume transaction costs are \$2,000 or its DM equivalent paid at the start of the transactions.

PART II

Foreign Exchange Risk Management

5

Forecasting Foreign Exchange Rates

Are changes in exchange rates predictable? Because changes in exchange rates are one of the major causes of financial uncertainty for a multinational firm, the answer to this question is critical to an understanding of what multinational financial managers can or should do about their exposure to foreign exchange rate changes.

The present international monetary system is characterized by a mix of freely floating, managed floating, and fixed exchange rates. Therefore no single general theory is available that is suitable for forecasting exchange rate changes under all conditions. Nevertheless, a very useful economic theory does exist that explains how foreign exchange rates should behave under freely floating conditions, i.e., without any government interference. Out of this theory come several of the most popular forecasting variables. In addition forecasters recognize certain other economic variables that influence exchange rates under managed floating and fixed rate systems. The biggest problem comes in finding suitable variables to predict the politics of devaluation under a managed floating or fixed rate system. Under a fixed rate system government intervention is sometimes predictable because the rules of the game are clearly understood by all participants. However, under a managed floating system, sometimes called a "dirty float," the rules for government interference are not known to the private sector participants, and it is hard to discover which economic and political variables will ultimately move a government to change its exchange rate.

Our approach to forecasting will be first to explain the basic economic theory that applies to exchange rate determination under a freely floating system. Next we analyze other economic and political variables that are important forecasting indicators under managed and fixed rate systems.

FORECASTING UNDER A FLOATING EXCHANGE RATE SYSTEM

Under a freely floating system spot exchange rates are theoretically determined by the interplay of differing national rates of inflation, interest rates, and the forward premium or discount. Exhibit 5.1 illustrates these relationships, using a simplified two-country example of the United States and United Kingdom. The diagram shows that if the forecast rate of inflation for one year ahead is 4% higher in the United Kingdom than in the United States, the pound sterling can be forecast to decline in value by 4% relative to the U.S. dollar. Furthermore, under these inflation conditions interest rates for one-year maturities of comparable risk can be expected to be 4%

EXHIBIT 5.1
Theoretical Relationship among Spot Exchange Rates, Forward Rates, Interest Rates, and Inflation Rates

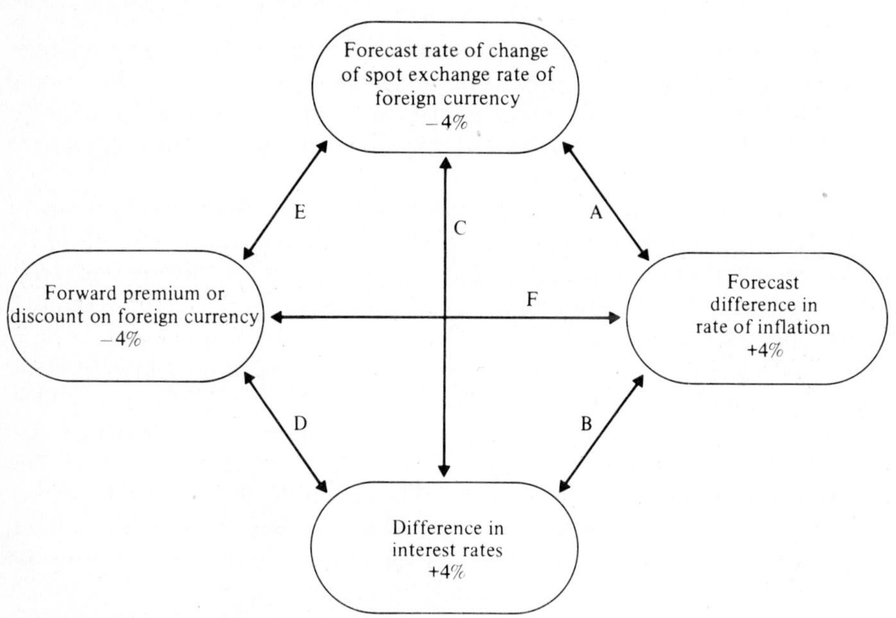

Assumptions:

1. Spot exchange rate today: £1.00 = $1.4000.
2. Forward exchange rate (one year): £1.00 = $1.3440.
3. Forward discount on pound = [(1.3440 − 1.4000)/1.4000] × 100 = −4%.
4. Forecast spot exchange rate in one year: £1.00 = $1.3440.
5. Forecast rate of change of spot exchange rate for pound: −4%.
6. Forecast rate of inflation for one year: U.S. = 4%; U.K. = 8%.
7. Forecast difference in rate of inflation: +4%.
8. Interest rates on one-year government maturities: U.S. = 7%; U.K. = 11%.
9. Difference in interest rates: +4%.

higher on U.K. pound securities than on U.S. dollar securities. We would also expect the one-year forward rate on the U.K. pound to be at a 4% discount relative to the dollar.

Five theories underlie the relationships illustrated in Exhibit 5.1:[1]

1. the Theory of Purchasing Power Parity (Relationship A);
2. the Fisher Effect (Relationship B);
3. the International Fisher Effect (Relationship C);
4. the Theory of Interest Rate Parity (Relationship D);
5. the forward rate as an unbiased predictor of the future spot rate (Relationship E).

Theory of Purchasing Power Parity

The theory of purchasing power parity holds that if the spot exchange rate between two countries starts in equilibrium, any change in the differential rate of inflation between them tends to be offset over the long run by an equal but opposite change in the spot exchange rate. In Exhibit 5.1 (Relationship A) a 4% higher rate of inflation in the United Kingdom is offset by a 4% depreciation in the spot exchange rate of U.K. pounds for U.S. dollars.

Exhibit 5.2 shows a more general case of purchasing power parity. The vertical axis shows the percentage appreciation of the foreign currency relative to the home currency, and the horizontal axis shows the percentage higher or lower rate of inflation in the foreign country relative to the home country. The diagonal parity line shows the equilibrium position between a change in the exchange rate and relative inflation rates. For instance, point *P* represents the equilibrium in our previous example, where inflation in the United Kingdom is 4% higher than in the United States.

The theory of purchasing power parity was first popularized by the economist Gustav Cassel after World War I to answer the question of what the new exchange rate parities should be after World War I interrupted the fixed exchange rate system.

A justification for purchasing power parity is that if a country experiences inflation rates higher than those of its main trading partners, its exports of goods and services will become less competitive with comparable products produced elsewhere. Imports from abroad will also become more price competitive with higher-priced domestic products.

Price elasticity of demand The balance on current account is especially sensitive to changes in national price levels in both relative and absolute terms. If a country's exports increase in price faster than the same goods in competing countries, and exchange rates remain unchanged, the exports

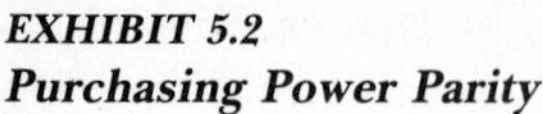

EXHIBIT 5.2
Purchasing Power Parity

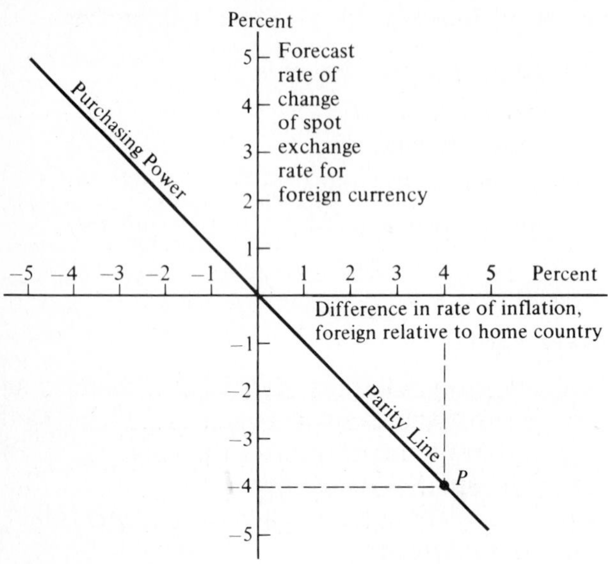

from the inflating country will probably be reduced in volume. The reverse is true of imports as relatively cheaper imports replace similar higher-priced domestic goods. The economic concept of *price elasticity of demand* is a relevant measure of this effect. Price elasticity of demand is a measure of the relative change in quantity sold for a given percentage change in price. More specifically,

$$E = \frac{\Delta Q}{Q} \div \frac{\Delta P}{P},$$

where

E is the price elasticity of demand,
ΔQ is the change in quantity sold,
Q is the original quantity sold,
ΔP is the change in price, and
P is the original price.

For example, suppose the delivered price of British sweaters in the United States increases by 10% in dollar terms, resulting in a 20% loss in number of sweaters sold. In this case price elasticity of demand would equal 20%/10% = 2. The British sweater exporter would end up with less total dollar revenue because the loss in volume would more than offset the higher dollar price. In fact, there will always be a loss in total sales revenue if price elasticity of demand is greater than one. Products of this type are price elastic.

If price elasticity of demand is less than one, a gain in total sales revenue will result from an increase in price. In this case the product is price inelastic. The point where price elasticity of demand is equal to one is called unitary elasticity. Around this point there would be no net change in sales revenue for a small change in price.

Most products in mature industries (such as textiles, machine tools, and electrical appliances) tend to be price elastic, whereas necessary products in short supply are usually price inelastic. The U.S. International Trade Committee published a study in August 1975 that estimated the relative price elasticity of imports compared to domestic substitutes.[2] The commission studied 20 products that were being considered for U.S. tariff reductions. A tariff reduction would lower the relative price of an imported product compared to its U.S. domestic substitute. Among products with the highest import price sensitivity (all much greater than one) were footwear (leather and rubber), synthetic fibers, leather gloves, toys and games, passenger cars, and silverware. The lowest price elasticities (all less than one) were attributed to watches and clocks, veneer and plywood, fabric dress and work gloves, cutlery, and typewriters.

If a country's exports are predominantly price elastic, as is the case for the United Kingdom, a relatively high rate of inflation will cause a large negative impact on the balance of goods and services, unless offset by devaluation of the currency. Devaluation of the pound, in the U.K. example, could lower prices of U.K. exports in foreign currency terms if the prices of its exports are unchanged in pounds. On the other hand, if U.K. exporters maintain fixed foreign currency prices despite the devaluation, there would probably be no change in volume or sales revenue in foreign currency terms. Sales revenue in pounds would increase because of the more favorable exchange rate, but the pounds received would be worth less in real purchasing power because of domestic British inflation.

The same reasoning can be applied to imports. If a country's imports are price elastic, relatively high domestic inflation will cause a disproportionately large increase in imports because of the lower prices of imports in pound terms. An overvalued exchange rate, such as experienced by the United States in recent years, should have the same kind of impact on imports. They would appear to be low priced compared to competing domestically produced goods.

Empirical tests of purchasing power parity There have been many empirical tests of the theory of purchasing power parity over the years, including several encompassing recent time periods.[3] The general conclusion has been that the theory holds up well over the very long run but not as well for shorter time periods. On the other hand, there are several problems with the tests.

One problem is that most of the tests use an index of prices such as the wholesale price index. This index may be misleading since only goods that are traded directly affect the balance on goods and services. Nevertheless, even such nontraded goods as housing and medical costs indirectly affect the price of traded goods through their influence on the overall cost of living and thus on wage demands.

A second problem is that the tests should be based on comparing a similar market basket of goods in each country with all its trading partners. If purchasing power parity is working, and there are no government interferences, the effective prices for a similar basket of goods should be the same in every country once exchange rates and prices have adjusted to worldwide purchasing power parity. This is known as the "law of one price."

A third problem is that purchasing power parity theory requires a knowledge of what the market is forecasting for differential inflation rates, but the data that are available are either realized inflation rates or existing differential interest rates used as a proxy for expected inflation.

A fourth problem is that there has hardly been a time period to test in which at least some government interference in the trade process did not exist.

A fifth problem is that many other factors besides relative prices influence the balance on current account. For example, changes in the level of national income may be important. In a fashion similar to price elasticity, *income elasticity of demand* measures the relative change in quantity sold for a given percentage change in income. More specifically,

$$I = \frac{\Delta Q}{Q} \div \frac{\Delta Y}{Y},$$

where

I is the income elasticity of demand,

ΔQ is the change in quantity sold,

Q is the original quantity sold,

ΔY is the change in income, and

Y is the original income.

For example, suppose that personal disposable income in the United States increased in real terms by 5%, and this situation caused a 10% increase in sweaters purchased. Income elasticity of demand is therefore 2, and we say that sales of sweaters are income elastic. In our example of the British sweater exporter, British exporters might increase sales revenue because of the income elasticity of sales of sweaters in general. Of course, if the British sweater exporter does not raise the price, it might receive the full benefit of the income effect.

Because not all countries follow the same business cycle, the income effect on balance of payments is received in different countries at different times. For example, many analysts believe that part of the present problem with the U.S. balance of payments on current account is due to increased imports stemming from a faster U.S. rate of growth and recovery from a worldwide recession.

In addition to the level of national income, other factors that influence a country's balance on current account include barriers to trade such as tariffs, quotas, and other "invisible" barriers. These can protect some countries from imports at the expense of others. Changes in relative productivity over the long run might change the relative price situation and through price elasticity of demand influence trade volume. New discoveries of scarce raw materials, such as oil, can have a profound effect. This was the case for the United Kingdom, the Netherlands, and Norway, which were the prime beneficiaries of North Sea oil and gas discoveries. Technology gaps develop periodically to give some country a temporary advantage, such as the semiconductor industry in the United States or shipbuilding in Japan. Government subsidies, or tied development aid, can create exports that would otherwise not occur. Crop failures have occasionally given food exporters such as the United States, Canada, Australia, New Zealand, Brazil, and Argentina temporary bonanzas on exports.[4]

Despite these limitations the empirical studies of purchasing power parity still show the postulated proportional relationship over the long run between spot exchange rates and relative rates of inflation. That fact exists regardless of whether it is caused by purchasing power parity alone or by a combination of other factors. Therefore for purposes of long-run exchange rate forecasting, most forecasters and forecasting models include variables to capture long-run trends in relative price levels.

Since most empirical studies of purchasing power parity are somewhat dated by the time they are published—and often analyze only a few key currencies—business forecasters utilize services that continuously update relative price and exchange rate changes for a large number of countries. One of the best of these services is published monthly by Morgan Guaranty Trust Company of New York in its *World Financial Markets.* An example covering the period 1980–1984 was presented in Exhibit 2.9.

With reference to Exhibit 2.9, if purchasing power parity were working perfectly the index showing a country's real effective exchange rate should stay at 100. If the index numbers for 1980 are compared to those for December 1984, purchasing power parity seems to be holding reasonably well for most countries, with the notable exceptions of the United States and United Kingdom. However, considerable deviations from 100 occur not only for extended periods of time but also within a single year. For example, the index for the United Kingdom rose from 83.1 in January 1985 to 93.2 in June 1985.

Fisher Effect

The Fisher Effect, named after economist Irving Fisher, states that nominal interest rates in each country are equal to the required real rate of return to the investor plus the expected rate of inflation. In a world where investors can buy any interest-bearing securities, real rates of return should tend toward equality everywhere, but nominal rates of interest will vary by the difference in expected rates of inflation.

In Exhibit 5.1 (Relationship B) nominal interest rates in the United Kingdom on one-year maturities are 11%, or four percentage points higher than the 7% available in the United States. This difference is consistent with the four-percentage-point difference in expected rates of inflation of 8% in the United Kingdom and 4% in the United States. In both countries the real (inflation-adjusted) rate of return to investors is 3% (nominal return minus inflation rate).

Exhibit 5.3 shows a more general case of the Fisher Effect. The vertical axis shows the percentage higher or lower forecast rate of inflation in the foreign country relative to the home country, and the horizontal axis shows the percentage difference in interest rates for the same time period. The parity line shows the Fisher Effect. For example, point *I* shows the position in our previous example where the 4% higher forecast rate of inflation in the United Kingdom is consistent with a 4% higher rate of interest in the United Kingdom. The main importance of the Fisher Effect in forecasting

EXHIBIT 5.3
Fisher Effect

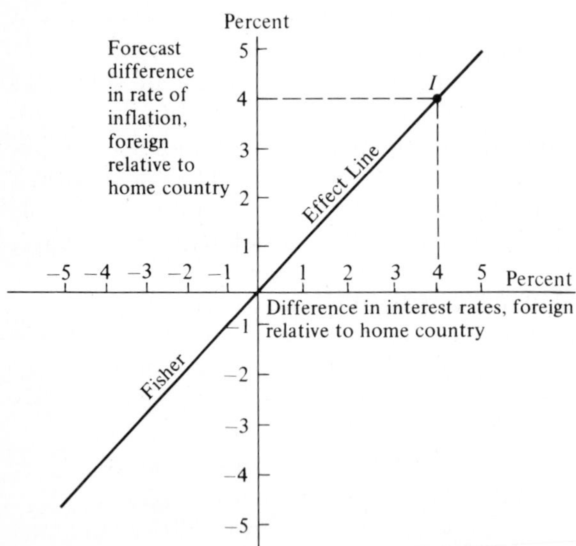

exchange rate changes is its corollary, the International Fisher Effect, which is described in the next section.

Empirical tests using ex-post national inflation rates have shown the Fisher Effect to exist particularly for short-maturity government securities such as Treasury bills and notes. Comparisons based on longer maturities suffer from the increased financial risk inherent in fluctuations of the market value of the bonds prior to maturity. Comparisons of private sector securities are influenced by unequal credit-worthiness of the issuers. All the tests are inconclusive to the extent that the ex-post rate of inflation does not correctly measure the ex-ante expected rate of inflation.

International Fisher Effect

The International Fisher Effect (also called Fisher Open) holds that the spot exchange rate should change in an equal but opposite direction to the difference in interest rates between two countries. Exhibit 5.1 (Relationship C) shows that the U.K. pound should depreciate by 4% relative to the U.S. dollar to be consistent with a 4% higher rate of interest in the United Kingdom.

Exhibit 5.4 shows a more general case of the International Fisher Effect. The vertical axis shows the forecast rate of change in the spot exchange rate and the horizontal axis shows the difference in interest rates. The

EXHIBIT 5.4
International Fisher Effect

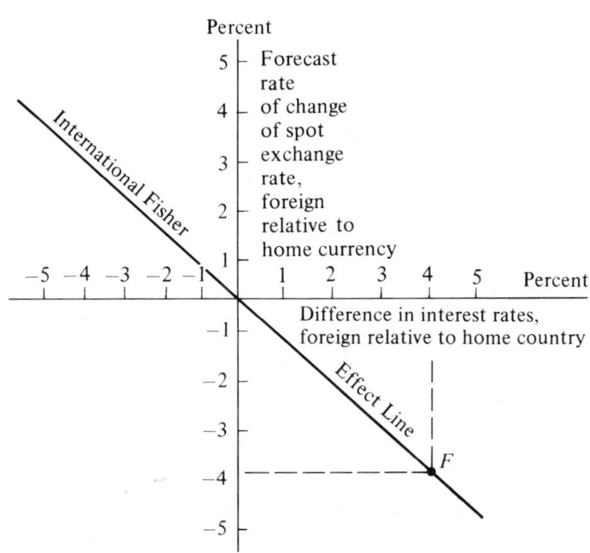

parity line shows the International Fisher Effect. For instance, point *F* shows the position in our previous example where the 4% forecast depreciation in the U.K. pound relative to the U.S. dollar is equal to the 4% higher rate of interest in the United Kingdom.

The justification for the International Fisher Effect is that U.S. dollar investors in U.K. securities must be rewarded with a higher interest rate to offset the expected rate of depreciation of the U.K. pound when they attempt to convert the principal and interest back into U.S. dollars. The U.K. pound investors in U.S. dollar securities are willing to receive a lower interest rate because they can compensate for this when converting dollars back to pounds.

Empirical tests lend some support to the relationship postulated by the International Fisher Effect, although considerable short-run deviations occur.[5] However, a more serious criticism has been posed by recent studies that suggest the existence of a foreign exchange risk premium for most major currencies. Thus the expected change in exchange rates might be consistently more than the difference in interest rates.[6]

As a result of the International Fisher Effect, forecasters and forecasting models almost always include a variable that captures relative interest rates when forecasting changes in a country's spot exchange rate.

Theory of Interest Rate Parity

As we explained in Chapter 4, the theory of interest rate parity states that except for transaction cost a difference in national interest rates for securities of similar risk and maturity should be equal but opposite in sign to the forward exchange rate discount or premium for the foreign currency. Exhibit 5.1 (Relationship D) shows the 4% higher annual interest rate in the United Kingdom to be offset by a 4% discount on the U.K. pound for delivery one year forward.

Forward Rate as an Unbiased Predictor of the Future Spot Rate

Some forecasters believe that for the major freely floating currencies, foreign exchange markets are "efficient" and forward exchange rates are unbiased predictors of future spot exchange rates.[7] In the example in Exhibit 5.1 (Relationship E) this theory means that the 4% one-year forward discount on the U.K. pound is an unbiased predictor that the pound will depreciate by 4% over the next year.

Exhibit 5.5 shows the general case. The vertical axis shows the forecast rate of change of the spot exchange rate and the horizontal axis shows the forward premium or discount. The diagonal line represents the equality of forward rates with forecast future spot rates of the same maturity. Point *U*

EXHIBIT 5.5
Forward Rate as an Unbiased Predictor of the Future Spot Rate

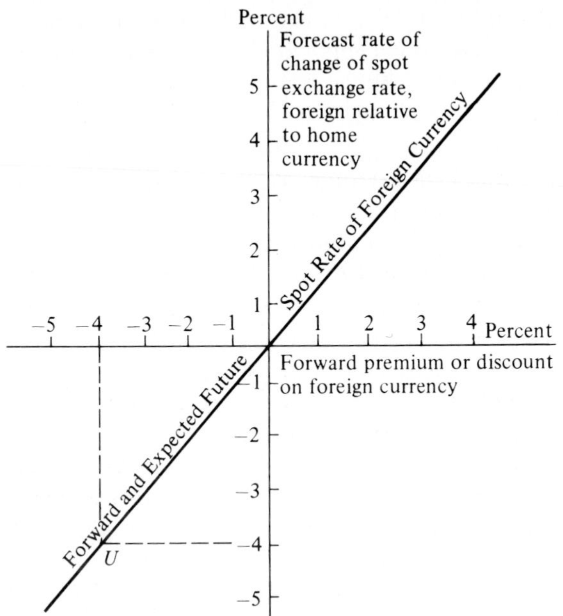

shows the relationship in our previous example where the 4% discount on one-year forward pounds is an unbiased predictor of the 4% depreciation in the rate for spot pounds delivered one year from now.

The rationale for this relationship is based on a belief that the foreign exchange market is reasonably "efficient." This assumes that all relevant information is quickly reflected in both the spot and forward exchange markets, transaction costs are low, and instruments denominated in different currencies are perfect substitutes for one another.

In our example, if the spot rate for the pound one year from now is actually 5% lower than it is today instead of the forecasted 4%, those who purchased the pounds forward one year at today's 4% discount would have been better off to wait for a year and purchase the pounds spot at a 5% discount from today's price. The reverse is true for those lucky enough to sell their pounds today for one-year forward delivery at the 4% discount rate. Since the market is efficient, there is no reason to believe that either the sellers or the buyers are consistently going to forecast the actual exchange rate. In fact, unless somebody has inside information—i.e., an inefficient market—an equal chance exists of being above or below forecast.

Empirical studies of the efficient foreign exchange market hypothesis have yielded conflicting results. This may be partly due to the short time period during which rates have floated, which makes it difficult to obtain enough observations to attain statistical significance. Nevertheless a consensus is developing that rejects the efficient market hypothesis. It appears that the forward rate is not an unbiased predictor of the future spot rate and it does pay to use resources to attempt to forecast exchange rates.

Early studies seemed to favor the efficient market hypothesis.[8] For example, Giddy and Dufey tested five different forecasting methods against foreign exchange quotations for the Canadian dollar, British pound, and French franc for the 1973–1974 period of floating exchange rates and found results consistent with the notion that the foreign exchange market is efficient and exchange rate forecasting is not profitable. Their major tests were on the so-called weak form of the random walk hypothesis, which asserts that successive changes in prices are independent of the sequence of past prices, and their conclusion was that "for short periods, one *is* able to detect a low degree of market inefficiency in the foreign exchange market. But the longer the forecasting horizon, the more evident is the inaccuracy of the time series forecasting of exchange rate changes."[9]

Kohlhagen, in an attempt to determine whether the forward exchange market is a low-cost means of hedging exchange risks, examined 90-day forward rates and subsequent spot rates for six countries (Canada, Denmark, France, West Germany, Switzerland, the United Kingdom) for the period of floating rates from April 1973 through December 1974, as well as for an earlier period of fixed exchange rates.[10] Among his findings was the observation that any difference between the forward rate and subsequent spot rate at the maturity of the forward contract could be attributed to random variations. Stated differently, any profit or loss from taking a consistently long or short position in the forward market was due to random forces, and the forward rates themselves were unbiased predictors of future spot rates.

Fama, who also studied the early floating rate period, concluded:

> When adjusted for variation through time in expected premiums, the forward rates of interest that are implicit in Treasury Bill prices contain assessments of expected future spot rates of interest that are about as good as those that can be obtained from the information in past spot rates. Moreover, in setting bill prices and forward rates, the market reacts appropriately to the negative autocorrelation in monthly changes in the spot rate and to changes through time in the degree of this autocorrelation. This evidence is consistent with the market efficiency proposition that in setting bill prices, the market correctly uses the information in past spot rates.[11]

If these conclusions are correct, a financial executive cannot expect to profit in any consistent manner from forecasting future exchange rates, because current quotations in the forward market reflect all that is presently known about likely future rates. While future exchange rates may well differ from the expectation implicit in the present forward market quotation, one cannot know today which way actual future quotations will differ from today's forward rate. The expected mean value of deviations is zero. The forward rate is therefore an "unbiased" estimator of the future spot rate. Note that "unbiased" does not mean "accurate" in any specific situation; it simply means that over many situations one cannot consistently forecast the inaccuracies.

More recent tests of foreign exchange market efficiency, using longer time periods of analysis, challenge the earlier findings and conclude that either exchange market efficiency is untestable or, if it is testable, the market is not efficient. Furthermore, the existence and success of foreign exchange forecasting services suggest that managers are willing to pay a price for forecast information even though they can use the forward rate as a forecast at no cost.[12]

One of the most comprehensive tests was undertaken by the Working Group on Exchange Market Intervention, which produced the so-called Jurgensen Report. They reported as follows:

> The tests provided clear evidence that consideration of readily accessible information on inflation and interest rate differentials yielded a better prediction of the future spot rate than that implied by the forward rate. Moreover, the repeated application of certain foreign exchange trading rules indicated a high probability of making some profit. However, some members thought that the results for some currencies may have been affected by the existence of capital controls, although the results were similar for the six bilateral US dollar rates tested. Other time series studies performed by the Group confirmed the existence of better predictors of the future spot rate than the forward rate.[13]

If the exchange market is not efficient, it would pay for a firm to spend resources on forecasting exchange rates. This is the opposite conclusion to the one in which exchange markets are efficient.

Forward Rates and Differential Inflation

Although there is no particular theory involved, it follows that if Relationships A–E in Exhibit 5.1 are all true, Relationship F has to be true by definition. That is, the forward premium or discount is equal but opposite in sign to the difference in rate of inflation between two countries.

Conclusion

In conclusion, under conditions of freely floating rates the expected rate of change in the spot exchange rate, differential rates of national inflation and interest, and the forward discount or premium are all directly proportional to each other and mutually determined. A change in one of these variables has a tendency to change all of them with a feedback on the variable that changes first. If the foreign exchange and money markets are efficient, all the variables adjust very quickly to changes in any one of them. The result is that forecasting success depends primarily on having prior information that one of the relevant variables is going to change. Possession of such information is unlikely in the competitive foreign exchange and money markets, but such information might perhaps be obtained by superior forecasting of differential rates of inflation. For this reason forecasters spend a lot of energy on analyzing factors that might cause inflation rates to change, such as growth in the money supply, the business cycle, productivity rates, and capacity utilization.

FORECASTING UNDER A MANAGED EXCHANGE RATE SYSTEM

When foreign exchange rates are managed, the movement toward equilibrium in spot and forward exchange rates, interest rates, and inflation rates, which occurs under freely floating rates, is artificially prevented from happening. The tendency toward equilibrium is still there, but government central banks are willing to absorb and counter the market pressures up to a point. This situation usually means that the central banks are willing to accept foreign exchange losses as the cost of stabilizing exchange rates.

Under a fixed rate system government foreign exchange losses can be immense, since all the other market participants can depend on government intervention to maintain parity. At some point, however, even governments must resign themselves to market pressure and allow the exchange rate to change. The tricky part of forecasting is to guess when this change will occur, since the timing and amount of exchange rate change is primarily a political decision.

It is not always obvious to a forecaster whether a country's exchange rate is managed, fixed, floating, or some combination of these. Exhibit 5.6 presents the IMF's version of which countries fall into each category. A country's preference for a particular exchange rate regime depends on its view of the traditional economic theory arguments for and against fixed exchange rates.

Fixed vs. Flexible Exchange Rates

Most foreign exchange forecasters thought that economists had finally resolved their disagreements about exchange rate flexibility when freely floating rates were adopted by many countries in 1973. The fact that some countries have chosen to maintain fixed rates, others use adjustable pegs, and still others manage floating rates certainly clouds the issue and complicates the task of forecasting.

The traditional arguments for and against flexible rates, and vice versa for fixed rates, are as follows:

For flexible rates:

- Flexible exchange rates permit a smoother adjustment to external shocks. No need exists to inflate or deflate the whole economy as might occur under fixed rates.
- Central banks do not need to maintain large, sterile international reserves to defend a fixed rate.
- Central banks do not need to lose money trying to defend an inappropriate rate for too long a period.
- Countries can maintain independent monetary and fiscal policies without being overly worried about their effect on the exchange rate.
- Forward markets provide an efficient and inexpensive means to eliminate foreign exchange risk for those who choose to buy such insurance.

Against flexible rates:

- Increased volatility under flexible exchange rates increases price uncertainty. This might lead to a reduction in international trade, with a corresponding lowering of the world's living standard.
- Flexible rates are inherently inflationary because they remove the external discipline imposed on a government's monetary and fiscal policy. This is particularly important to monetarists who are presently advocating a return to fixed rates.
- Flexible rates lead to destabilizing speculation that causes the exchange rate to "overshoot" its natural equilibrium level.
- Small open economies do not have efficient forward markets to enable a firm to offset exchange risk. This creates a bias against trade and an incentive for foreign direct investment in such economies.
- Temporarily misaligned rates can cause faulty decisions on resource allocation. Some industries expand or contract when they should not because they misinterpret the duration of exchange rate levels. This might create unnecessary temporary unemployment, wasted production capacity, and a call for protectionism, which is the bane of all who believe in free trade.

Politics of Devaluation

Forecasting a change in exchange rates under a managed or "dirty" float system is difficult because government policy is usually not published and specific commitments are not typically made to maintain any particular level of rates.

EXHIBIT 5.6
Exchange Arrangements as of June 30, 1985[a]

PEGGED TO				
Single currency			*Currency composite*	
U.S. dollar	*French franc*	*Other*	*SDR*	*Other*
Antigua and Barbuda	Benin	Bhutan (Indian rupee)	Burma	Algeria[c]
	Burkina Faso		Burundi	Austria
Bahamas[c]	Cameroon	The Gambia (pound sterling)	Guinea[c]	Bangladesh[c]
Barbados	Central African Republic		Iran, Islamic Republic of	Botswana
Belize				Cape Verde
Bolivia			Jordan	China
	Chad	Lesotho (South African rand)		
Djibouti	Comoros			
Dominica	Congo	Swaziland (South African rand)	Kenya[h]	Cyprus
Egypt[c]	Equatorial Guinea		Rwanda	Fiji
Ethiopia			São Tomé and Principe	Finland[h]
Ghana	Gabon			Guyana
Grenada	Ivory Coast		Seychelles	Hungary
Guatemala[c]			Sierra Leone[c]	Kuwait
	Mali			
Haiti	Niger		Vanuatu	Madagascar
Honduras[c]	Senegal		Viet Nam	Malawi
Iraq	Togo			Malaysia
				Maldives
Lao People's Democratic Republic[c]				Malta
				Mauritania
				Mauritius
Liberia				
Libyan Arab Jamahiriya				Mozambique[c]
				Nepal
Nicaragua[c]				Norway
Oman				Papua New Guinea
				Romania
Panama				
Paraguay[c]				Singapore
St. Christopher and Nevis				Solomon Islands
				Sweden
St. Lucia				Tanzania
St. Vincent and the Grenadines				Thailand
				Tunisia
Sudan[c]				Zambia
Suriname				Zimbabwe
Syrian Arab Republic[c]				
Trinidad and Tobago				
Venezuela[c]				
Yemen Arab Republic				
Yemen, People's Democratic Republic				

FLEXIBILITY LIMITED VIS-A-VIS A SINGLE CURRENCY OR GROUP OF CURRENCIES		*MORE FLEXIBLE*		
Single currency[b]	*Cooperative arrangements*	*Adjusted according to a set of indicators*	*Managed floating*	*Independently floating*
Afghanistan[c]	Belgium[c]	Brazil[d]	Argentina	Australia
Bahrain[d]	Denmark	Chile[c,d]	Costa Rica[c]	Canada
Qatar[d]	France	Colombia	Ecuador[c]	Dominican Republic
Saudi Arabia[e]	Germany, Federal Republic of	Peru[c]	El Salvador[c]	Jamaica
United Arab Emirates[e]	Ireland	Portugal	Greece	Japan
	Italy[f]	Somalia[c,g]	GuineaBissau	Lebanon
	Luxembourg[c]		Iceland	New Zealand
	Netherlands		India[i]	Philippines
			Indonesia	South Africa
			Israel	Uganda
			Korea	United Kingdom
			Mexico[c]	United States
			Morocco	Uruguay
			Nigeria	Zaïre
			Pakistan	
			Spain	
			Sri Lanka	
			Turkey	
			Western Samoa	
			Yugoslavia	

Source: International Monetary Fund, *Annual Report 1985,* Washington, D.C., 1985, p. 48.

[a]No current information is available relating to Democratic Kampuchea.

[b]All exchange rates have shown limited flexibility vis-à-vis the U.S. dollar.

[c]Member maintains dual exchange markets involving multiple exchange arrangements. The arrangement shown is that maintained in the major market.

[d]Member maintains a system of advance announcement of exchange rates.

[e]Exchange rates are determined on the basis of a fixed relationship to the SDR, within margins of up to ± 7.25 percent. However, because of the maintenance of a relatively stable relationship with the U.S. dollar, these margins are not always observed.

[f]Margins of ± 6 percent are maintained with respect to the currencies of other countries participating in the exchange rate mechanism of the European Monetary System.

[g]The exchange rate is maintained within overall margins of ± 7.5 percent about the fixed shilling/SDR relationship; the exchange rate is re-evaluated when indicative margins of ± 2.25 percent are exceeded.

[h]The exchange rate is maintained within margins of ± 2.25 percent.

[i]The exchange rate is maintained within margins of ± 5 percent on either side of a weighted composite of the currencies of the main trading partners.

Political leaders in countries whose currencies are pegged rather than floating must respond to developing economic pressure to devalue, even though the response may be to avoid the problem for as long as possible. Analysis of probable responses by a government is especially difficult, because those in authority must usually avoid revealing that devaluation is under consideration. Otherwise speculators or others in a position to sell the local currency for foreign funds would rush to do so before the devaluation, thus creating a speculative run, which adds to existing devaluation pressures. Hence devaluation most often comes hard on the heels of official denials. The executive in charge of international finance of a large West Coast company in the United States suggested to one of the authors that when the finance minister of a country finds it necessary to go on national television to assert that nothing will happen, something is certain to happen within the very near future!

To illustrate the point, one week before the British devaluation of November 1967, the prestigious London *Economist* said, "The signs in London still suggest that the policy of borrowing extensively instead of devaluing will continue." Discussing a rumored international loan to the British government in the same issue, the *Economist* said: ". . . obviously this loan, if it materializes, should help boost the pound and temporarily slays—once more—the ghost of devaluation." The pound was devalued on the day of publication! In its postmortem on the devaluation the following week, the *Economist* observed that ". . . 24 hours after [the British] cabinet had unitedly decided on devaluation, Lord Chalfont (who admittedly is a minister outside the cabinet) stood up in Paris to say that 'there is no plan to alter the exchange rate.' "

Analysis of probable political responses to devaluation pressures is usually developed by a feel for the environment rather than by quantitative techniques. A permanent resident undoubtedly would have a better understanding of the tempo and pressures of the time than would a foreigner, especially if the foreigner is new to the land and not fluent in the local language. Campaign promises of recent elections can prevent or delay an otherwise logical devaluation, as can an impending political campaign in which devaluation becomes associated with degrading of the national honor. On the other hand, a devaluation immediately after a change of administrations is often feasible because the new incumbent can blame the act on the ill-advised actions of predecessors from a different (and "less competent") political party.

Despite the political vagaries of managed and fixed rate systems there are still certain economic indicators that are useful forecasting variables. Exchange rates are almost never changed unless the market economic pressures are present. It is only the timing and size of change that are political decisions. The traditional economic variables used in forecasting exchange rate changes follow.

Balance of Payments and Interest Rate Parity

If a country spends more abroad in combined purchases and investments than it earns or otherwise acquires from abroad over a sustained period of time, the probability of devaluation increases. Foreigners will be building up, on balance, monetary claims against the country. If foreigners are willing to hold these claims in monetary form or in money market instruments, the local currency need not devalue. However, such investment depends partly upon interest rate parity. As explained earlier, if there are no artificial constraints on the operation of foreign exchange markets, interest rates and the cost of forward cover would adjust to the expected new exchange rates—or, stated alternatively, the cost of forward cover would adjust to the interest rate differential as well as to the expected new exchange rates. This market would be an efficient market. On the other hand, where markets are imperfect because of governmental interference with interest rates or intervention in the foreign exchange market, foreigners might not find it to their advantage to hold and invest locally the net funds received because of the country's balance of payments deficit. They might sell the currency at the same time that continued deficits in the country's balance of payments will act to preclude the country from earning sufficient foreign exchange to support its weakened currency. If foreigners rush to sell their accumulating balances of the foreign currency, the likelihood of devaluation or depreciation increases.

Differential Rates of Inflation

The aforementioned theory of purchasing power parity suggests that, if exchange rates are in equilibrium, an increase in prices in one country relative to another country should be matched by a corresponding change in exchange rates such that the purchasing power of the two currencies remains the same. If this adjustment does not take place, goods produced in the country with the lesser inflation would become cheaper and dominate both markets, while goods produced in the country with the greater inflation would be priced out of both markets. These two trends would lead to a balance of payments surplus in the country of lesser inflation and to a deficit in the country of greater inflation, with a corresponding tendency for exchange rates to change.

As economic indicators differential rates of inflation do little to predict the timing of a devaluation, although if exchange rates are free, the drop in value would presumably occur in a steady and consistent pattern. In a world of political intervention a country experiencing relative inflation may adopt tariffs, export subsidies, and import quotas to forestall deterioration of the balance of payments. However, unless the internal inflation rate can be slowed, such policies are likely to be no more than stopgap measures.

The probability of a devaluation increases with relatively greater internal inflation, even if the government is, for the time being, successful in forestalling actual devaluation.

It should be noted that the relationship between inflation and devaluation is not necessarily causal but one of partial correlation. In some instances inflation and devaluation alike result from a change in the cost of some other factor, such as the cost of imported petroleum. In other instances the relationship between the two is circular. Domestic inflation leads to a rise in the price of exported goods and a price advantage for imported goods, causing balance of payments or local employment problems, which in turn lead to devaluation. However, devaluation, in its turn, causes essential imports such as raw material or foodstuffs to rise in price, creating another round of domestic inflation.

Growth in the Money Supply

Since many of the economic indicators described so far are moving "coincident" with changes in exchange rates, forecasters have tried to identify indicators that "lead" changes in exchange rates. Monetarists believe that inflation occurs if a country's money supply grows faster than is warranted by real economic growth. Since there is considerable evidence that this factor may at least be a contributory one, some foreign exchange forecasters use the money supply as a timely surrogate for relative changes in prices and thus exchange rates.

Business Cycles

The phase of a country's business cycle relative to its trading partners might also put pressure on exchange rates through the effect on trade in goods and services. This pressure depends on the aforementioned income elasticity of demand for imports and exports.

Decline in International Monetary Reserves

Continued balance of payments deficits are likely to lead to a decline in the international monetary reserves of a country maintaining fixed rates, unless the deficits are matched by increased short-term foreign investment. As monetary reserves disappear, a run on the currency may occur.

Increased Spread Between Official and "Free" Rates of Exchange

Where currencies are pegged and exchange controls are imposed on the convertibility of local cash balances, falling confidence in a local currency may be measured by the rise in the spread between the unofficial free rate, the black market rate, or the parallel rate of exchange relative to the official (pegged) exchange rate. Even though exchange controls exist, some countries have a free rate for certain types of transactions. For example, remittances for imports or for dividends to foreign parent corporations may be controlled or may be required to be remitted at an official exchange rate, while at the same time other remittances, say for local residents going abroad or for foreign tourists entering the country, may be allowed at the free rate. When the free rate is technically not allowed but nevertheless tolerated, it is sometimes called the "parallel" market rate. In instances where use of the free rate is illegal and heavily punished, the term "black market" rate is used. Even when free rates are not quoted within a country, they are sometimes available in nearby countries. It may be illegal within Italy to exchange lira for other currencies. However, Switzerland has no law preventing a free market for lira within Switzerland. Thus free quotations from Switzerland may be used to judge the strength of the Italian lira. A change in the percentage discount of an official exchange rate relative to a free rate quoted in some other market is a valuable piece of evidence in measuring the pressure on a country to bring its official rate into line with reality via a devaluation.[14]

Government Policies That Treat Symptoms Rather Than Causes

In response to diminishing foreign exchange reserves, governments may treat symptoms rather than correct fundamental underlying weaknesses, thus increasing the probability of eventual devaluation. As occurs in many areas of human activity, stopgap measures in financial matters tend not only to fail in the long run but also to indicate a lack of sufficient political courage or strength to carry out fundamental reforms. Examples of symptom-treating measures are the imposition of new exchange controls or the tightening of existing controls. Ceilings on interest rates, higher import duties to protect inefficient local producers from cheaper imports, adoption of export subsidies, and restrictions on direct investments abroad (as imposed by President Lyndon Johnson in the United States in 1968) are all indicators of fundamental weakness that may be a prelude to devaluation.

Excessive Government Spending

Loss of exchange value can accompany or follow government policies that overextend the domestic or international resources of a nation. Ambitious foreign commitments—such as that of the United States in Vietnam in the late 1960s and early 1970s—can weaken the domestic economy and so lead to devaluation. A domestic welfare and social benefit program generous beyond the productivity of the local economy—such as that adopted in Uruguay after World War II—can eventually erode domestic economic strength. Tolerance by government or by society as a whole of exceedingly strong labor unions bent on maximizing their own well-being at the expense of the nation can cripple segments of the economy for a period of time and increase the likelihood of devaluation. The British have been plagued over many years by such a situation, although oil discoveries have reduced the impact on exchange rates.

SUMMARY

In this chapter we explained how foreign exchange rates might be forecast under conditions of either freely floating, managed, or fixed rates. Especially important are the theories of purchasing power parity, the Fisher Effect, the International Fisher Effect, interest rate parity, and the forward rate as an unbiased predictor of future spot rates. In addition, under managed or fixed exchange rate systems, forecasters must consider the politics of devaluation, as well as various economic indicators of pressure being placed on the exchange rate position that is being defended. These indicators include the following:

- the balance of payments deficit,
- differential national rates of inflation,
- growth in the money supply,
- lack of synchronization of national business cycles,
- a decline in international monetary reserves,
- increased spread between official and "free" rates of exchange,
- governmental policies that treat symptoms rather than causes, and
- excessive government spending.

NOTES

1. For a clear explanation of these theories see Ian H. Giddy, "An Integrated Theory of Exchange Rate Equilibrium," *Journal of Financial and Quantitative Analysis,* December 1976, pp. 863–892.

2. U.S. International Trade Commission, *Foreign Trade Elasticities for Twenty Industries,* Washington, D.C.: USITC Publication 738, August 1975.

3. See, for example, Lawrence H. Officer, "The Purchasing-Power-Parity Theory of Exchange Rates: A Review Article," *IMF Staff Papers,* March 1976, pp. 1–60. Also see Richard J. Rogalski and Joseph D. Vinso, "Price Level Variations as Predictors of Flexible Exchange Rates," *Journal of International Business Studies,* Spring–Summer 1977, pp. 71–81; Stephen P. Magee, "Contracting and Spurious Deviations from Purchasing Power Parity," in Jacob A. Frenkel and Harry G. Johnson, eds., *The Economics of Exchange Rates,* Reading, Mass.: Addison-Wesley, 1978, pp. 67–74; Lawrence Officer, Edward I. Altman, and Ingo Walter, eds., *Purchasing Power Parity and Exchange Rates: Theory, Evidence, and Relevance,* Contemporary Studies in Economic and Financial Analysis, Vol. 35., London, JAI Press, 1982.

4. For a clear explanation of noninflation factors see Pieter Korteweg, "Exchange Rate Policy, Monetary Policy, and Real Exchange Rate Variability," *Essays in International Finance No. 140,* Princeton, N.J.: Princeton University, 1980.

5. See Giddy, "Exchange Rate Equilibrium."

6. Some interesting recent studies of the Fisher Effect, the International Fisher Effect, and interest rate parity are Robert E. Cumby and Maurice Obstfeld, "A Note on Exchange-Rate Expectations and Nominal Interest Differentials: A Test of the Fisher Hypothesis," *Journal of Finance,* June 1981, pp. 697–703; Frederick S. Mishkin, "Are Real Interest Rates Equal across Countries? An Empirical Investigation of International Parity Conditions," *Journal of Finance,* December 1984, pp. 1345–1357; and Fred R. Kaen, Evangelos O. Simos, and George A. Hachey, "The Response of Forward Exchange Rates to Interest Rate Forecasting Errors," *Journal of Financial Research,* Winter 1984, pp. 281–290.

7. For example, see Ian H. Giddy and Gunter Dufey, "The Random Behavior of Flexible Exchange Rates," *Journal of International Business Studies,* Spring 1975, pp. 1–32. Also see Dennis E. Logue, Richard J. Sweeney, and Thomas D. Willett, "The Speculative Behavior of Foreign Exchange Rates during the Current Float," *Journal of Business Research,* Vol. 6, No. 2, 1978, pp. 159–173; Richard M. Levich, "Tests of Forecasting Models and Market Efficiency in the International Money Market," Frenkel and Johnson, *Economics of Exchange Rates,* pp. 129–158.

8. A good review of early foreign exchange market efficiency studies is in Stephen W. Kohlhagen, *The Behavior of Foreign Exchange Markets—A Critical Survey of the Empirical Literature,* New York: New York University Monograph Series in Finance and Economics, No. 3, 1978. An excellent summary of all the foreign exchange forecasting and management literature is in Laurent L. Jacque, "Management of Foreign Exchange Risk: A Review Article," *Journal of International Business Studies,* Spring–Summer 1981, pp. 81–101.

9. Giddy and Dufey, "Random Behavior of Flexible Exchange Rates," p. 27.

10. Steven W. Kohlhagen, "The Performance of the Foreign Exchange Markets: 1971–1974," *Journal of International Business Studies,* Fall 1975, pp. 33–39.

11. Eugene F. Fama, "Forward Rates as Predictors of Future Spot Rates," *Journal of Financial Economics,* October 1976, pp. 361–377.

12. Three such studies are reported in the following articles: Stephen Goodman, "Foreign Exchange Forecasting Techniques: Implications for Business and Policy," *Journal of Finance,* May 1979, pp. 415–427; Richard M. Levich, "Analyzing the Accuracy of Foreign Exchange Forecasting Services: Theory and Evidence," in Clas Wihlborg and Richard Levich, eds., *Exchange Risk and Exposure: Current Development in International Financial Development,* Lexington, Mass.: Heath, 1980; John F. O. Bilson, "The Evaluation and Use of Foreign Exchange Rate Forecasting Services," in R. J. Herring, ed., *Management of Foreign Exchange Risk,* Cambridge, England: Cambridge University Press, 1983, pp. 149–179.

13. The original source is a quote from the Jurgensen Report, *Report of the Working Group on Exchange Market Intervention,* Washington, D.C.: U.S. Treasury, 1983. This particular citation was from John Williamson, *The Exchange Rate System,* Washington, D.C.: Institute for International Economics, September 1983, p. 50.

14. The use of black market exchange rates to forecast changes in official rates has been tested by Sanjeev Gupta, "A Note on the Efficiency of Black Markets in Foreign Currencies," *Journal of Finance,* June 1981, pp. 705–710. He found that black markets in South Korea, Taiwan, and India were reasonably efficient in the weak form sense. Black market exchange rates anticipated changes in official rates in South Korea and Taiwan and therefore might be useful in forecasting.

BIBLIOGRAPHY

Adler, Michael, and Bernard Dumas, "Portfolio Choice and the Demand for Forward Exchange," *American Economic Review,* May 1976, pp. 332–339.

Bilson, John F. O., "Rational Expectations and the Exchange Rate," in Jacob A. Frenkel and Harry G. Johnson, eds., *The Economics of Exchange Rates,* Reading, Mass.: Addison-Wesley, 1978, pp. 75–96.

———, "Leading Indicators of Currency Devaluation," *Columbia Journal of World Business,* Winter 1979, pp. 62–76.

Calderon-Rossell, Jorge R., and Moshe Ben-Horim, "The Behavior of Foreign Exchange Rates," *Journal of International Business Studies,* Fall 1982, pp. 99–111.

Cornell, Bradford, "Spot Rates, Forward Rates, and Exchange Market Efficiency," *Journal of Financial Economics,* August 1977, pp. 55–65.

———, "Relative Price Changes and Deviations from Purchasing Power Parity," *Journal of Banking and Finance,* September 1979, pp. 263–279.

———, "Inflation, Relative Price Changes, and Exchange Risk," *Financial Management,* Autumn 1980, pp. 30–34.

Cornell, Bradford, and J. K. Dietrich, "The Efficiency of the Foreign Exchange Market under Floating Exchange Rates," *Review of Economics and Statistics,* February 1978, pp. 111–120.

Cosset, Jean-Claude, "Forward Rates as Predictors of Future Interest Rates in the Eurocurrency Market," *Journal of International Business Studies,* Winter 1982, pp. 71–83.

Cumby, Robert E., and Maurice Obstfeld, "A Note on Exchange-Rate Expectations and Nominal Interest Differentials: A Test of the Fisher Hypothesis," *Journal of Finance,* June 1981, pp. 697–703.

Dornbusch, Rudiger, "Expectations and Exchange Rate Dynamics," *Journal of Political Economy,* December 1976, pp. 1161–1176.

———, "Flexible Exchange Rates and Interdependence," *IMF Staff Papers,* March 1983, pp. 3–30.

Dufey, Gunter, and Ian Giddy, "Forecasting Exchange Rates in a Floating World," *Euromoney,* November 1975, pp. 28–35.

———, "International Financial Planning: The Use of Market-Based Forecasts," *California Management Review,* Fall 1978, pp. 69–81.

———, "Forecasting Foreign Exchange Rates: A Pedagogical Note," *Columbia Journal of World Business,* Summer 1981, pp. 53–61.

Eun, Cheol S., "Global Purchasing Power View of Exchange Risk," *Journal of Financial and Quantitative Analysis,* December 1981, pp. 639–650.

Everett, Robert M., Abraham M. George, and Aryeh Blumberg, "Appraising Currency Strengths and Weaknesses: An Operational Model for Calculating Parity Exchange Rates," *Journal of International Business Studies,* Fall 1980, pp. 80–91.

Fama, Eugene F., "Forward Rates as Predictors of Future Spot Rates," *Journal of Financial Economics,* October 1976, pp. 361–377.

Fama, E. F., and A. Farber, "Money, Bonds, and Foreign Exchange," *American Economic Review,* September 1979, pp. 639–649.

Folks, William R., and Stanley R. Stansell, "The Use of Discriminant Analysis in Forecasting Exchange Risk Movements," *Journal of International Business Studies,* Spring 1975, pp. 33–50.

Frenkel, Jacob A., "A Monetary Approach to the Exchange Rate: Doctrinal Aspects and Empirical Evidence," *Scandinavian Journal of Economics,* May 1976, pp. 200–224; reprinted in Jacob A. Frenkel and Harry G. Johnson, eds., *The Economics of Exchange Rates,* Reading, Mass.: Addison-Wesley, 1978, pp. 1–25.

———, "Flexible Exchange Rates, Prices, and the Role of 'News': Lessons from the 1970s," *Journal of Political Economy,* August 1981, pp. 665–705.

Gailliot, Henry, "Purchasing Power Parity as an Explanation of Long Term Changes in Exchange Rates," *Journal of Money, Credit, and Banking,* August 1970, pp. 348–357.

Giddy, Ian H., "An Integrated Theory of Exchange Rate Equilibrium," *Journal of Financial and Quantitative Analysis,* December 1976, pp. 863–892.

Giddy, Ian H., and Gunter Dufey, "The Random Behavior of Flexible Exchange Rates: Implications for Forecasting," *Journal of International Business Studies,* Spring 1975, pp. 1–32.

Goodman, Stephen, "Foreign Exchange Forecasting Techniques: Implications for Business and Policy," *Journal of Finance,* May 1979, pp. 415–427.

Gupta, Sanjeev, "A Note on the Efficiency of Black Markets in Foreign Currencies," *Journal of Finance,* June 1981, pp. 705–710.

Hall, Thomas W., "Inflation and Rates of Exchange: Support for SFAS No. 52," *Journal of Accounting, Auditing and Finance,* Summer 1983, pp. 299–312.

Hansen, Lars Peter, and Robert J. Hodrick, "Forward Exchange Rates as Optimal Predictors of Future Spot Rates: An Econometric Analysis," *Journal of Political Economy,* October 1980, pp. 829–853.

Hill, Joanne, and Thomas Schneeweis, "Forecasting and Hedging Effectiveness of Pound and Mark Forward and Futures Markets," *Management International Review,* Vol. 22, No. 1, 1982, pp. 43–52.

Hooper, Peter, and Steven W. Kohlhagen, "The Effect of Exchange Rate Uncertainty on the Prices and Volume of International Trade," *Journal of International Economics,* November 1978, pp. 483–511.

Isard, Peter, "How Far Can We Push the Law of One Price?" *American Economic Review,* December 1977, pp. 942–948.

Jurgensen Report, *Report of the Working Group on Exchange Market Intervention,* Washington, D.C.: U.S. Treasury, 1983.

Kaen, Fred R., Evangelos O. Simos, and George A. Hachey, "The Response of Forward Exchange Rates to Interest Rate Forecasting Errors," *Journal of Financial Research,* Winter 1984, pp. 281–290.

Kohlhagen, Steven W., "The Performance of the Foreign Exchange Markets: 1971–1974," *Journal of International Business Studies,* Fall 1975, pp. 33–39.

———, *The Behavior of Foreign Exchange Markets—A Critical Survey of the Empirical Literature,* New York: New York University Monograph Series in Finance and Economics, No. 3, 1978.

———, "The Forward Rate as an Unbiased Predictor of the Future Spot Rate," *Columbia Journal of World Business,* Winter 1979, pp. 77–85.

Korteweg, Pieter, "Exchange-Rate Policy, Monetary Policy, and Real Exchange-Rate Variability," *Essays in International Finance, No. 140,* Princeton, N.J.: Princeton University, December 1980.

Koveos, Peter, and Bruce Seifert, "Purchasing Power Parity and Black Markets," *Financial Management,* Autumn 1985, pp. 40–46.

Levich, Richard M., "On the Efficiency of Markets for Foreign Exchange," in J. Frenkel and R. Dornbusch, eds., *International Economic Policy: An Assessment of Theory and Evidence,* Baltimore: Johns Hopkins Press, 1978.

———, "Tests of Forecasting Models and Market Efficiency in the International Money Market," in Jacob A. Frenkel and Harry G. Johnson, eds., *The Economics of Exchange Rates,* Reading, Mass.: Addison-Wesley, 1978, pp. 129–158.

———, "Are Forward Exchange Rates Unbiased Predictors of Future Spot Rates?" *Columbia Journal of World Business,* Winter 1979, pp. 49–61.

———, *The International Monetary Market: An Assessment of Forecasting Techniques and Market Efficiency,* Greenwich, Conn.: JAI Press, 1979.

———, "Analyzing the Accuracy of Foreign Exchange Forecasting Services: Theory and Evidence," in Clas Wihlborg and Richard Levich, eds., *Exchange Risk and Exposure: Current Development in International Financial Development,* Lexington, Mass.: Heath, 1980.

Levich, Richard M., R. Hawkins, and Clas Wihlborg, eds., *Internationalization of Financial Markets and National Economic Policy,* Greenwich, Conn.: JAI Press, 1981.

Logue, Dennis E., Richard Sweeney, and Thomas Willett, "The Speculative Behavior of Foreign Exchange Rates during the Current Float," *Journal of Business Research,* Vol. 6, No. 2, 1978, pp. 159–173.

Longworth, David, "Testing the Efficiency of the Canadian–U.S. Exchange Market under the Assumption of No Risk Premium," *Journal of Finance,* March 1981, pp. 43–49.

Magee, Stephen P., "Contracting and Spurious Deviations from Purchasing-Power Parity," in Jacob A. Frenkel and Harry G. Johnson, eds., *The Economics of Exchange Rates,* Reading, Mass.: Addison-Wesley, 1978, pp. 67–74.

Maldonado, Rita, and Anthony Saunders, "Foreign Exchange Restrictions and the Law of One Price," *Financial Management,* Spring 1983, pp. 19–23.

Mishkin, Frederick S., "Are Real Interest Rates Equal across Countries? An Empirical Investigation of International Parity Conditions," *Journal of Finance,* December 1984, pp. 1345–1357.

Officer, Lawrence H., "The Purchasing-Power-Parity Theory of Exchange Rates: A Review Article," *IMF Staff Papers,* March 1976, pp. 1–60.

———, "The Productivity Bias for Purchasing Power Parity," *IMF Staff Papers,* November 1976, pp. 545–579.

Officer, Lawrence H., Edward I. Altman, and Ingo Walter, eds., *Purchasing Power Parity and Exchange Rates: Theory, Evidence, and Relevance,* Contemporary Studies in Economic and Financial Analysis, Vol. 35, London: JAI Press, 1982.

Papadia, Francesco, "Forward Exchange Rates as Predictors of Future Spot Rates and the Efficiency of the Foreign Exchange Market," *Journal of Banking and Finance,* June 1981, pp. 219–240.

Rogalski, Richard J., and Joseph D. Vinso, "Price Level Variations as Predictors of Flexible Exchange Rates," *Journal of International Business Studies,* Spring–Summer 1977, pp. 71–81.

———, "Empirical Properties of Foreign Exchange Rates," *Journal of International Business Studies,* Fall 1978, pp. 69–79.

Roll, Richard W., and Bruno H. Solnik, "A Pure Foreign Exchange Asset Pricing Model," *Journal of International Economics,* May 1977, pp. 161–179.

Solnik, B., "International Parity Conditions and Exchange Risk," *Journal of Banking and Finance,* August 1981, pp. 281–293.

Somanath, V. S., "Exchange Rate Expectations and the Current Exchange Rate: A Test of the Monetarist Approach," *Journal of International Business Studies,* Spring/Summer 1984, pp. 131–140.

Taylor, Dean, "Official Intervention in the Foreign Exchange Market, or Bet against the Central Bank," *Journal of Political Economy,* April 1982, pp. 356–368.

Wihlborg, Clas, "Interest Rates, Exchange Rate Adjustments, and Currency Risks: An Empirical Study, 1967–1975," *Journal of Money, Credit and Banking,* February 1982, pp. 58–75.

6

Measuring Foreign Exchange Exposure

Foreign exchange exposure is a measure of the potential for a firm's profitability, net cash flow, and market value to change because of a change in exchange rates. An important task of the financial manager is to measure foreign exchange exposure and to manage it in such a way as to maximize the net cash flow, profitability, and market value of the firm.

TYPES OF FOREIGN EXCHANGE EXPOSURE

What happens to a firm when foreign exchange rates change? The effect can be measured in several ways. Exhibit 6.1 shows schematically the three main types of foreign exchange exposure: *translation, transaction,* and *economic.*

Translation exposure measures potential accounting-based changes in a firm's consolidated financial statements that result from a change in exchange rates. Transaction exposure measures changes in the value of outstanding obligations incurred prior to a change in exchange rates but not expected to be settled until after exchange rates change. Economic exposure measures the change in expected cash flows due to an *unexpected* change in exchange rates.

Translation Exposure

Translation exposure, sometimes called accounting exposure, arises from the need to report consolidated worldwide operations according to predetermined accounting rules. Assets, liabilities, revenues, and expenses originally measured in a foreign currency must be restated in terms of a home currency in order to be consolidated with home currency accounts.

EXHIBIT 6.1
Conceptual Comparison of Difference between Translation, Transaction, and Economic Foreign Exchange Exposure

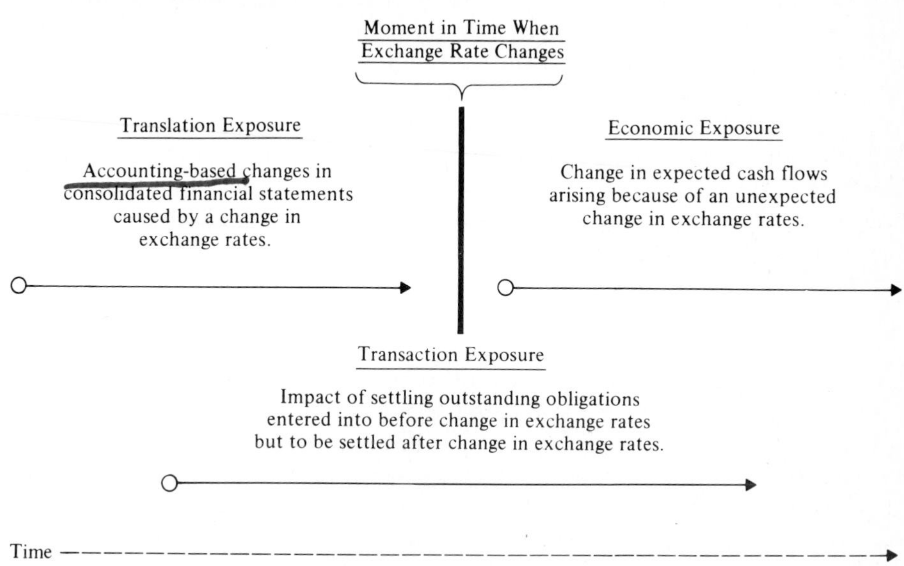

This restatement, termed "translation," follows rules set up by a parent firm's government, an accounting association, or by the firm itself.

The simplest example of translation exposure would be the loss in dollar value of a bank balance of £500,000 maintained in a British bank by a U.S. firm. If the pound were initially worth \$2.20, the bank balance would be reported on the U.S. parent firm's books at a dollar value of \$1,100,000 (i.e., £500,000 × \$2.20). If the pound should subsequently drop in value to \$1.50, the U.S. parent would then report on its own books the British bank balance as being worth \$750,000 (i.e., £500,000 × \$1.50), a loss of \$350,000. Depending on the particular accounting rules in effect, this loss might be reported in the parent's net income or the loss might be written off directly against stockholders' equity through a reserve account. The specifics of U.S. accounting rules will be discussed later in this chapter.

The example above illustrates an important distinction between the currency in which an account is *denominated* and the currency in which it is *measured.* An asset or liability is denominated in a foreign currency if the amount is fixed in terms of units of that foreign currency, regardless of any exchange rate. The British bank balance was denominated in pounds sterling; the balance would always be £500,000 no matter what the exchange rate might be. Monetary assets, such as cash and accounts receivable, and monetary liabilities, such as accounts payable and debt, are usually denominated only in a single currency.

An asset or liability may be measured in any currency, including the currency of denomination. In the above example the bank balance of £500,000 was measured (as well as denominated) in pounds sterling. At one time it was also measured in dollars as $1,100,000, and later it was again measured in dollars as $750,000. At the same dates it could also have been measured in French francs or Japanese yen. In general, monetary assets and liabilities, which are by definition denominated in a single currency, may be measured in that currency as well as in any other currency. Fixed assets (such as land, buildings, and equipment) are not denominated in any currency. However, they may be measured in any currency.

Transaction Exposure

Transaction exposure refers to gains or losses that arise from the settlement of transactions whose terms are stated in a foreign currency. Transactions include (1) purchasing or selling on credit goods or services whose prices are stated in foreign currencies, (2) borrowing or lending funds denominated in foreign currencies, (3) being a party to an unperformed forward foreign exchange contract, and (4) otherwise acquiring assets or incurring liabilities denominated in foreign currencies.

The most common example of transaction exposure arises when an enterprise has a receivable or payable denominated in a foreign currency. Suppose that a U.S. firm sells merchandise on open account to a Belgian buyer for BF400,000, payment to be made in 60 days. The exchange rate is BF40/$, and the U.S. seller expects to exchange the BF400,000 for $10,000 when payment is received. Exposure arises because of the risk that the U.S. seller will receive something other than $10,000 after the Belgian franc receipts are exchanged for dollars. For example, if the exchange rate were BF42/$ when payment was received, the U.S. seller would receive only BF400,000 ÷ BF42 = $9,524, some $476 less than was anticipated. If the exchange rate had gone to BF38/$, however, the seller would have received $10,526, an increase of $526 over the amount expected. As we stated before, exposure is the chance of *either* a loss or a gain. Note that if the U.S. seller had invoiced in dollars, the transaction exposure would have been shifted to the Belgian buyer.

A second example of transaction exposure arises when funds are borrowed or loaned and the amount involved is denominated in a foreign currency. For example, Britain's Beecham Group borrowed 100 million Swiss francs in 1971, at a time when 100 million Swiss francs were worth £10.13 million. In 1976, when the loan came due, the cost of repayment of principal was £22.73 million. The London *Sunday Times,* August 22, 1976, termed this transaction loss "an expensive lump of lolly!"

Economic Exposure

Foreign exchange economic exposure is defined as the possibility that the net present value of a firm's expected cash flows will change due to an *unexpected* change in foreign exchange rates. The change in value could be up or down, depending on the effect of the exchange rate change on sales volume, prices, and costs.

Economic exposure is far more important for the long-run health of a business entity than changes caused by translation or even transaction exposure. However, economic exposure is inevitably subjective because it depends on estimating future cash flows over an arbitrary time horizon. Thus economic exposure does not spring from the accounting process but rather derives from economic analysis. Planning for economic exposure is a total management responsibility because it involves the interaction of strategies in finance, marketing, sourcing, and production.

An *expected* change in foreign exchange rates is not included in the definition of economic exposure, because both management and investors have factored this information into their evaluation of expected operating results and market value.

From a management perspective budgeted financial statements already reflect information about the effect of an expected change in exchange rates. For example, under equilibrium conditions the forward rate might be used as an unbiased predictor of the future spot rate. In such a case management would use the forward rate when preparing the operating budgets rather than assume the spot rate would remain unchanged. Another example is that expected cash flow to amortize debt would already reflect the International Fisher Effect. The level of expected interest and principal payments would be a function of expected exchange rates rather than the existing spot rate.

From an investor's perspective, if the foreign exchange market is efficient, information about expected changes in exchange rates would be widely known and thus reflected in a firm's market value. Only unexpected changes in exchange rates, or an inefficient foreign exchange market, would cause market values to change.

Tax Exposure

Tax exposure due to a change in exchange rates varies by country, but as a general matter only *realized* foreign exchange losses are deductible for purposes of calculating income taxes. Similarly, only realized gains create taxable income. Most translation losses are not realized and so are not deductible. Some steps taken to minimize exposure, say, entering into a forward exchange contract, create taxable income or loss; other steps taken to obtain the same protection have no income tax implications. Since tax exposure is determined by the country of domicile of each affiliate, a multinational firm must plan its foreign exchange management policies, other things being equal, to maximize the worldwide tax benefit of foreign exchange losses and minimize the tax on gains.

We will now analyze in more detail the concepts of economic and translation exposure. These have proven to be difficult to comprehend and typically create the most concern for financial managers.

ECONOMIC EXPOSURE

An unexpected change in exchange rates impacts on a firm's expected cash flows at four levels, depending on the time horizon used.[1]

Short Run

The first-level impact is on expected cash flows in the one-year operating budget. The gain or loss depends on the currency of denomination of expected cash flows. The currency of denomination cannot be changed for existing obligations, such as those defined by transaction exposure, or even for implied obligations such as purchase or sales commitments. Apart from real or implied obligations, in the short run it is difficult to change sales prices or renegotiate factor costs. Therefore realized cash flows will differ from those expected in the budget. However, as time passes, prices and costs can be changed to reflect the new competitive realities caused by a change in exchange rates.

Medium Run: Equilibrium Case

The second-level impact is on expected medium-run cash flows, such as those expressed in two- to five-year budgets, assuming equilibrium conditions among foreign exchange rates, national inflation rates, and national interest rates. Under equilibrium conditions the firm should be able to adjust prices and factor costs over time to maintain the expected level of cash flows. In this case the currency of denomination of expected cash flows is not as important as the countries in which cash flows originate. National monetary, fiscal, and balance of payments policies determine whether equilibrium conditions will exist and whether firms will be allowed to adjust prices and costs.

If equilibrium exists continuously, and a firm is free to adjust its prices and costs to maintain its expected competitive position, its economic exposure may be zero. Its expected cash flows would be realized and therefore its market value unchanged since the exchange rate change was anticipated. However, it is also possible that equilibrium conditions exist but the firm is unwilling or unable to adjust operations to the new competitive environment. In such a case the firm would experience economic exposure, because its realized cash flows would differ from expected cash flows. As a result, its market value might also be altered.

Medium Run: Disequilibrium Case

The third-level impact is on expected medium-run cash flows assuming disequilibrium conditions. In this case the firm may not be able to adjust prices and costs to reflect the new competitive realities caused by a change in exchange rates. The firm's realized cash flows will differ from its expected cash flows. The firm's market value may change because of the unanticipated results.

Long Run

The fourth-level impact is on expected long-run cash flows beyond five years. At this strategic level a firm's cash flows will be influenced by the reactions of existing and potential competitors to exchange rate changes under disequilibrium conditions. In fact, all firms that are subject to international competition, whether they are purely domestic or multinational, are exposed to foreign exchange economic exposure in the long run whenever foreign exchange markets are not continuously in equilibrium. This important insight will be elaborated in Chapter 7.

ILLUSTRATION OF ECONOMIC EXPOSURE

To illustrate the consequences of economic exposure, we will develop a hypothetical example based on Instruments Napoleon, S.A., the wholly owned French affiliate of Washington Controls, Inc., a U.S.-based multinational firm. From the perspective of Washington Controls, dollars invested in Instruments Napoleon have a 20% required rate of return after taxes.

Instruments Napoleon manufactures in France from French material and labor. Half of production is sold within France and half is exported to other Common Market countries. All sales are invoiced in French francs, and accounts receivable are equal to one-fourth of annual sales. In other words, the average collection period is 90 days. Inventory is also equal to one-fourth of annual sales and is carried at direct cost, which equals 75% of sales price. Instruments Napoleon can expand or contract production volume without any significant change in unit direct costs or in overall general and administrative expenses. Depreciation on plant and equipment is FF240,000 per year, and the corporate income tax rate in France is 50%. The December 31, 1985, balance sheet is as follows:

Instruments Napoleon, S.A., Balance Sheet, December 31, 1985

Cash	FF 1,600,000	Accounts payable	FF 800,000
Accounts receivable	3,200,000	Short-term bank loan	1,600,000
Inventory	2,400,000	Long-term debt	1,600,000
Net plant and		Common stock	1,800,000
equipment	4,800,000	Retained earnings	6,200,000
	FF12,000,000		FF12,000,000

In the examples that follow, we assume that on January 1, 1986, before any commercial activity begins, the French franc unexpectedly drops 20% in value, from FF8.00/$ to FF10.00/$. If no devaluation had occurred, Instruments Napoleon was expected to perform in 1986 as follows:

Instruments Napoleon, S.A.
Expected Income and Cash Flow Statement, No Devaluation

Sales (1,000,000 units @ FF12.8/unit)	FF12,800,000
Direct costs (1,000,000 units @ FF9.6/unit)	9,600,000
Cash operating expenses (fixed)	1,200,000
Depreciation	240,000
Pretax profit	FF 1,760,000
Income tax expense (50%)	880,000
Profit after tax	FF 880,000
Add back depreciation	240,000
Cash flow from operations—in francs	FF 1,120,000
Existing exchange rate: FF8.00 = $1.00	
Cash flow from operations—in dollars	$ 140,000

Economic exposure depends on whether an unexpected change in exchange rates causes unanticipated changes in sales volume, sales prices, or operating costs. In Chapter 5 we discussed the concepts of price and income elasticity of demand for a country's exports and imports. The same principles apply to a single firm, such as Instruments Napoleon. Following a devaluation of the French franc, Instruments Napoleon might choose to maintain its domestic sales prices constant in terms of French francs or try to increase domestic prices because competing imports might now be priced higher. The firm might choose to maintain export prices constant in terms of foreign currencies, or in terms of francs, or somewhere in between. The strategy followed depends to a large measure on price elasticity of demand.

On the cost side, Instruments Napoleon's costs might rise because of more expensive imported raw materials or components, or simply because all domestic prices in France have risen and labor is now demanding higher wages to compensate for domestic inflation.

Instruments Napoleon's domestic sales and costs might also be partly determined by the effect of a French devaluation on the income elasticity of demand. To the extent that the devaluation stimulates purchases of French goods in import-competing sectors of the economy as well as greater exports of French goods, both caused by initially more competitive prices of French goods, French national income should increase. This statement assumes that the favorable effect of a French devaluation on comparative prices is not immediately offset by higher French inflation. Thus Instruments Napoleon might be able to sell more goods domestically because of price and income effects and internationally because of price effects.

To illustrate the effect of various postdevaluation scenarios on Instruments Napoleon's economic exposure, we will consider five simple cases:

1. no change in any variable;
2. increase in sales volume, other variables remain constant;
3. increase in sales price, other variables remain constant;
4. partial sales price increase, other variables remain constant; and
5. sales price increase matched by an increase in all cash costs.

To calculate the net change in present value under each of these scenarios, we will assume a five-year time horizon for any change in cash flow induced by the change in the franc/dollar exchange rate.

Case 1: No Change in Any Variable

Assume that in the five years ahead no changes occur in sales volume, sales price, or operating costs. Profits for the coming year in francs will be as expected, and cash flow from operations will be FF1,120,000. With a new exchange rate of FF10.00 per dollar, next year's cash flow measured in dollars will be FF1,120,000/10 = $112,000. The difference in first-year cash flow if a devaluation occurs at once will be:

Realized first-year cash flow, with devaluation	\$112,000
Expected first-year cash flow, no devaluation	140,000
Change in first-year cash flow	\$ 28,000

Instruments Napoleon experiences a drop in the dollar value of its French franc cash flow equal to \$28,000, and if this drop continues over the five-year time horizon, the total reduction in net cash flow will be \$28,000 × 5 = \$140,000. The discounted present value of this series of diminished dollar value cash flows will be considered later in this example.

Case 2: Volume Increases, Other Variables Remain Constant

Assume that sales within France double following the devaluation because French-made instruments are now more competitive with imports. Additionally, export volume doubles because French-made instruments are now cheaper in countries whose currencies have not weakened. The sales price is kept constant in French franc terms because management of Instruments Napoleon has not observed any change in local French operating costs.

Income and cash flow for the following year would be as follows:

Instruments Napoleon, S.A.
Income and Cash Flow Statement, Volume Increases (Case 2)

Sales (2,000,000 units @ FF12.8/unit)	FF25,600,000
Direct costs (2,000,000 units @ FF9.6/unit)	19,200,000
Cash operating expenses (fixed)	1,200,000
Depreciation	240,000
Pretax profit	FF 4,960,000
Income tax expense (50%)	2,480,000
Profit after tax	FF 2,480,000
Add back depreciation	240,000
Cash flow from operations—in francs	FF 2,720,000
New exchange rate: FF10.00 = \$1.00	
Cash flow from operations—in dollars	\$ 272,000

The cash flow shown above is not available in the first year, however, for a doubling of sales volume will require additional investment in accounts receivable and in inventory. Although a portion of this additional investment might be financed by increasing accounts payable, we will assume additional working capital is financed by cash flow from operations.

At the end of the first year accounts receivable would be equal to one-fourth of annual sales, or FF6,400,000. This amount is twice receivables of FF3,200,000 at the end of the prior year, and the incremental increase of FF3,200,000 must be financed from available cash. Year-end inventory would be equal to one-fourth of annual direct costs, or FF4,800,000, an increase of FF2,400,000 over the year-beginning level. At the end of five years these incremental cash outflows will be recaptured because any investment in current assets eventually rolls over into cash. Assuming no further change in volume, price, or costs, cash inflows for the five years would be as follows:

Year	*Item*		*Francs*	*Dollars*
1	Cash flow from operations	FF2,720,000		
	Less additional investment required in working capital	−5,600,000		
			−FF2,880,000	−$288,000
2	Cash flow from operations		2,720,000	272,000
3	Cash flow from operations		2,720,000	272,000
4	Cash flow from operations		2,720,000	272,000
5	Cash flow from operations		2,720,000	272,000
5	Incremental working capital recapture in last year		5,600,000	560,000

In this instance the devaluation causes a change in first-year cash flow from the $140,000 anticipated in the first year without devaluation to a negative flow of $288,000. However, in the remaining four years cash flow is substantially enhanced by the economic effects of the devaluation. Over time Instruments Napoleon generates significantly more cash for its owners. The devaluation produced an economic *gain* over time, rather than an economic *loss*.

The reason Instruments Napoleon is better off in Case 2 following the devaluation is that sales volume doubled while the per-unit dollar-equivalent sales price fell only 20%. In other words, the product faced a price elasticity of demand greater than one.

Case 3: Sales Price Increases, Other Variables Remain Constant

Assume that the franc sales price is raised 25%, from FF12.8 to FF16 per unit, in order to preserve the original dollar-equivalent unit sales price of $1.60/unit. Assume further that volume remains constant in spite of this price increase; i.e., customers expect to pay the same dollar-equivalent price, and local costs do not change. The situation would be as follows:

Instruments Napoleon, S.A.
Income and Cash Flow Statement, Sales Price Increase (Case 3)

Sales (1,000,000 units @ FF16.0/unit)	FF16,000,000
Direct costs (1,000,000 units @ FF9.6/unit)	9,600,000
Cash operating expenses (fixed)	1,200,000
Depreciation	240,000
Pretax profit	FF 4,960,000
Income tax expense (50%)	2,480,000
Profit after tax	FF 2,480,000
Add back depreciation	240,000
Cash flow from operations—in francs	FF 2,720,000
New exchange rate: FF10.00 = $1.00	
Cash flow from operations—in dollars	$ 272,000

In this instance Instruments Napoleon is better off following the devaluation than it was before. This is because the sales price, pegged to the international price level, increased but volume did not drop. In Case 3 the new level of accounts receivable would be one-fourth of the new sales level of FF16,000,000, or FF4,000,000, an increase of FF800,000. No additional investment in inventory would be necessary. Hence cash flow for the first five years would be as follows:

Year	*Item*		*Francs*	*Dollars*
1	Cash flow from operations	FF2,720,000		
	Less additional investment required in working capital	−800,000		
			FF1,920,000	$192,000
2	Cash flow from operations		2,720,000	272,000
3	Cash flow from operations		2,720,000	272,000
4	Cash flow from operations		2,720,000	272,000
5	Cash flow from operations		2,720,000	272,000
5	Incremental working capital recapture in last year		800,000	80,000

Expected cash flow in every year exceeds the cash flow of $140,000 that had been anticipated with no devaluation. The increase in working capital causes net cash flow to be only $192,000 in the first year, but thereafter the cash flow is $272,000 per year.

The key to this improvement is in operating leverage. If costs are incurred in francs and do not increase after a devaluation, an increase in the sales price by the amount of devaluation will lead to sharply higher profits. Nevertheless, if any portion of costs were incurred in other currencies, as would be the case if raw materials or components were imported, the situation would be different. The situation would also be different if local franc costs rose after a devaluation. One cannot generalize for all countries of the world; nevertheless, local costs usually rise to some lesser degree and with some time lag following a devaluation. In each individual country, therefore, management must have some idea of how devaluation will affect the firm's local costs over a period of time.

Case 4: Partial Sales Price Increase, Other Variables Stay Constant

One reasonable assumption might be that the domestic sales price remains the same, either because of local price controls or competition in France, but the export price rises (in francs) by the amount of the devaluation because it is determined by the local currency price in importing countries. If volume in both markets remains the same, because no buyer perceives that the price has changed, the situation would be as follows:

Instruments Napoleon, S.A.
Income and Cash Flow Statement, Partial Sales Price Increase (Case 4)

Domestic sales (500,000 units @ FF12.8/unit)	FF 6,400,000
Export sales (500,000 units @ FF16.0/unit)	8,000,000
Total sales	FF14,400,000
Direct costs (1,000,000 units @ FF9.6/unit)	9,600,000
Cash operating expenses (fixed)	1,200,000
Depreciation	240,000
Pretax profit	FF 3,360,000
Income tax expense (50%)	1,680,000
Profit after tax	FF 1,680,000
Add back depreciation	240,000
Cash flow from operations—in francs	FF 1,920,000
New exchange rate: FF10.00 = $1.00	
Cash flow from operations—in dollars	$ 192,000

Year-end accounts receivable would be FF3,600,000, an increase of FF400,000 from the level at the beginning of the year. No additional investment in inventory is necessary, so cash flow for the first five years would be as follows:

Year	*Item*		*Francs*	*Dollars*
1	Cash flow from operations	FF1,920,000		
	Less additional investment required in working capital	−400,000		
			FF1,520,000	$152,000
2	Cash flow from operations		1,920,000	192,000
3	Cash flow from operations		1,920,000	192,000
4	Cash flow from operations		1,920,000	192,000
5	Cash flow from operations		1,920,000	192,000
5	Incremental working capital recapture in last year		400,000	40,000

Cash flow in every year is larger than the $140,000 expected with no devaluation.

Case 5: Price Increase Matched by Increased Costs, No Volume Change

One last combination involves an immediate 25% increase in sales price, direct costs, and cash operating costs. Costs might rise because of local inflation, or because imported raw materials and components rise in franc cost due to devaluation. Cash flow from operations for the first year would be as follows:

Instruments Napoleon, S.A.
Income and Cash Flow Statement, Price and Costs Increase (Case 5)

Sales (1,000,000 units @ FF16.0/unit)	FF16,000,000
Direct costs (1,000,000 units @ FF12.0/unit)	12,000,000
Cash operating expenses (no longer fixed)	1,500,000
Depreciation (no change)	240,000
Pretax profit	FF 2,260,000
Income tax expense (50%)	1,130,000
Profit after tax	FF 1,130,000
Add back depreciation	240,000
Cash flow from operations—in francs	FF 1,370,000

New exchange rate: FF10.00 = $1.00

Cash flow from operations—in dollars	$ 137,000

In this situation accounts receivable will increase to FF4,000,000, an increase of FF800,000. Year-end inventory would be FF3,000,000, an increase of FF600,000. Cash flow for the first five years would be:

Year	*Item*		*Francs*	*Dollars*
1	Cash flow from operations	FF1,370,000		
	Less additional investment required in working capital	−1,400,000		
			−FF 30,000	−$ 3,000
2	Cash flow from operations		1,370,000	137,000
3	Cash flow from operations		1,370,000	137,000
4	Cash flow from operations		1,370,000	137,000
5	Cash flow from operations		1,370,000	137,000
5	Incremental working capital recapture in last year		1,400,000	140,000

In Case 5, cash flow in the first year is negative. Thereafter it is slightly less than it was under the original no-devaluation alternative.

Measurement of Loss

These five examples illustrate that an exchange rate change may influence cash flows in a variety of ways, depending on how sales, expenses, and unit volume of the firm respond to a change in exchange rates. In Exhibit 6.2 the change in expected cash flows for the five cases is summarized and compared with the cash flow expected should no devaluation occur.

The top portion of Exhibit 6.2 restates the expected cash flows for the five cases. The center portion of the exhibit shows the change in cash flow compared to the nondevaluation situation. The loss today from these changes in future cash flows is determined by their present value.

Since dollars invested in Instruments Napoleon by Washington Controls have a required rate of return after tax of 20%, the net present value economic loss caused by the devaluation is shown in the lower portion of Exhibit 6.2. In Cases 1 and 5, the net present value economic losses are $83,700 and $69,200, respectively. In the remaining three cases, devaluation leads to a net present value *gain,* ranging up to $360,200 in Case 3. An almost infinite number of combinations of volume, price, and cost could follow a devaluation, and any or all of them might become effective sooner or later.

The change in value caused by economic exposure is derived from changes in future cash flows. By comparison, translation loss as determined

EXHIBIT 6.2
Summary of Economic Loss following Devaluation for Instruments Napoleon, S.A.
Five separate cases (in thousands of U.S. dollars)

		EXPECTED CASH FLOW FOR FIRST FIVE YEARS				
Year	*No devaluation*	*Case 1*	*Case 2*	*Case 3*	*Case 4*	*Case 5*
1	140	112	−288	192	152	− 3
2	140	112	272	272	192	137
3	140	112	272	272	192	137
4	140	112	272	272	192	137
5	140	112	272	272	192	137
5 (w.c.)	0	0	560	80	40	140
		INCREASE OR DECREASE (−) IN EXPECTED CASH FLOW				
Year		*Case 1*	*Case 2*	*Case 3*	*Case 4*	*Case 5*
1		−28	−428	52	12	−143
2		−28	132	132	52	−3
3		−28	132	132	52	−3
4		−28	132	132	52	−3
5		−28	132	132	52	−3
5 (w.c.)		0	560	80	40	140
		PRESENT VALUE OF CHANGE IN EXPECTED CASH FLOW				
Year	*P.V. factor @ 20%*	*Case 1*	*Case 2*	*Case 3*	*Case 4*	*Case 5*
1	.833	−23.3	−356.5	43.3	10.0	−119.1
2	.694	−19.4	91.6	91.6	36.1	−2.1
3	.579	−16.2	76.4	76.4	30.1	−1.7
4	.482	−13.5	63.6	63.6	25.1	−1.4
5	.402	−11.3	53.1	53.1	20.9	−1.2
5 (w.c.)	.402	0	225.1	32.2	16.1	56.3
Incremental present value		−83.7	+153.3	+360.2	+138.3	−69.2

by financial accounting is derived from balance sheets and income statements. To compare economic valuation changes with translation valuation changes for Instruments Napoleon, we must first explain in detail current accounting procedures.

TRANSLATION EXPOSURE

National accounting professions have developed different conventions for translating foreign currency accounts into the reporting currency for parent company use. Three basic translation methods predominate:

1. current rate method,
2. monetary/nonmonetary method, also referred to as the temporal method in the United States since 1975, and
3. current/noncurrent method.

Hybrids among these basic methods have also been used at times.

Methods of Translation

The *current rate method* became official U.S. practice with the December 1981 issuance of *Statement of Financial Accounting Standards Number 52* (FAS #52, also referred to as SFAS #52 and FASB #52) by the Financial Accounting Standards Board, the authority in the United States that determines accounting policy for U.S. firms and certified public accountants. FAS #52 replaced FAS #8. FAS #52 requires current rate translation for all fiscal years beginning on or after December 15, 1982. The current rate method, the most prevalent practice worldwide, is used in Europe (Denmark, France, Greece, Ireland, the Netherlands, Norway, and the United Kingdom), the Far East (Australia, Hong Kong, India, Malaysia, and Singapore), Africa (Botswana, Kenya, Ivory Coast, and Senegal), and Latin America (Colombia).[2]

Details of how the current rate method is applied vary from country to country. As defined by FAS #52 for the United States, all assets and liabilities are translated at the current rate of exchange, i.e., at the rate of exchange in effect on the balance sheet date. Income statement items, including depreciation and cost of goods sold, are translated at either the actual exchange rate on the dates the various revenues, expenses, gains, and losses are incurred or at an appropriately weighted average exchange rate for the period. Dividends paid are translated at the exchange rate in effect on the date of payment.

Existing equity accounts, such as common stock and paid-in capital, are translated at historical rates. Year-end retained earnings consists of the original year-beginning retained earnings plus or minus any income or loss for the year. However, gains or losses caused by translation adjustments are *not* included in the calculation of net income, and thus the change in retained earnings does not reflect translation gains or losses. Rather translation gains or losses are reported separately and accumulated in a separate equity account with a title such as "cumulative translation adjustment" (CTA).

When the investment in the foreign affiliate is sold or liquidated, the translation gains or losses of past years accumulated in the "cumulative translation adjustment" account are removed from that account and reported as part of the gain or loss on sale or liquidation. This gain or loss is reported as net income or loss for the time period in which the sale or liquidation occurs.

Under the *monetary/nonmonetary method* monetary assets (consisting of cash, marketable securities, accounts receivable, and long-term receivables) and monetary liabilities (current liabilities and long-term debt) are translated at current exchange rates, while all other assets and liabilities are translated at historical rates. Income statement items are translated at the average exchange rate for the period, except for those items such as depreciation and cost of goods sold that are directly associated with nonmonetary assets or liabilities. These items are translated at their historic rate. The monetary/nonmonetary method is used by firms in Sweden, Taiwan, Korea, the Philippines, and a number of Central American countries.[3]

The monetary/nonmonetary method was given a precise set of rules and renamed the *temporal method* in the United States with the issuance of *Statement of Financial Accounting Standards Number 8* (FAS #8) in October 1975. FAS #8 was controversial in the United States and was replaced by FAS #52 in December 1981.

The *current/noncurrent* method is perhaps the oldest approach. No longer allowable under generally accepted accounting practices in the United States, it was nevertheless widely used prior to 1976 and is still used by many non-U.S. firms, including those in West Germany, New Zealand, and South Africa.[4] Its popularity is gradually waning as other methods are found to give more meaningful results.

Under the current/noncurrent method all current assets and current liabilities of foreign affiliates are translated into the home currency at the current exchange rate—i.e., at the exchange rate in effect on the date of the statement. Noncurrent assets and noncurrent liabilities are translated at historic rates—i.e., at the rates that were in existence on the date the assets were acquired or the liabilities incurred.

In the balance sheet, exposure to gains or losses from fluctuating currency values is determined by the net of current assets less current liabilities. Gains or losses on long-term assets and liabilities are not shown currently. Items in the income statement are generally translated at the average exchange rate for the period covered. However, those items that relate to revenue or expense items associated with noncurrent assets (such as depreciation charges) or long-term liabilities (amortization of debt discount) are translated at the same rate as the corresponding balance sheet items.

In addition to the three methods described above, hybrid methods have been used from time to time. Before January 1, 1976, U.S. firms were free to select their own method, and many combined attributes of the current/

noncurrent method and the monetary/nonmonetary method. Such individual variations most often centered around the treatment of inventory and long-term debt.

Time of Recognizing Gains or Losses

Translation by any of the methods, or by a hybrid method, usually produces a foreign exchange gain or loss when exchange rates change. This translation gain or loss reflects a change in the way values are measured by the accounting process; it does *not* reflect a cash out-of-pocket gain or loss. A remaining accounting question is whether such gain or loss should be recognized in the current time period, deferred to a later reporting period, or closed directly into retained earnings or an equity reserve account without ever having to pass through the income statement.

Prior to 1976 U.S. practice was to record net foreign exchange gains for any year in an equity reserve account, with a title such as "reserve for future foreign exchange losses," and not report the gains in current income. Net foreign exchange losses for any year were first subtracted from any existing reserve created from net gains of prior years, with any net loss after exhausting the reserve subtracted from annual income for that year.

Starting in 1976, when the provisions of FAS #8 became effective, gains and losses were required to be passed through the quarterly income statement, thus influencing quarterly as well as annual net income and earnings per share. No reserves were permitted. This "flow through" requirement existed during the late 1970s when the value of the U.S. dollar was fluctuating widely. This situation created a whipsaw effect on reported quarterly earnings, which made the provisions of FAS #8 very unpopular with business. In many multinational firms foreign exchange risk management policies were dominated by the desire to manage quarterly earnings so that they appeared to be stable—and rising. Many firms engaged in costly efforts to hedge foreign activities so that quarterly earnings would not fluctuate unduly because of noncash translation gains or losses.

Under the change in methods required under FAS #52, translation gains or losses do not influence net income for any given time period but are instead accumulated in a cumulative translation adjustment account under consolidated stockholders' equity until substantial or complete liquidation of the firm occurs. In other words, an unrealized translation gain or loss is held in an equity reserve account until the gain or loss is actually realized. In the case of fixed assets this realization might well be decades into the future. When realized, the gain or loss is reported as net income or loss for that period. Note, however, that *transaction* gains or losses, as distinguished from *translation* gains or losses, are reflected in income for the current period.

Balance Sheet Impact

Unfortunately for many U.S. firms, these cumulative translation adjustment (CTA) accounts are developing large negative (debit) balances. This occurs when foreign currency assets exceed foreign currency liabilities; i.e., when the firms have a long position in net exposed foreign assets, and the U.S. dollar appreciates. This combination has in fact existed for many U.S. firms since FAS #52 was implemented. Although these large negative CTA balances do not affect the income statement, they do increase balance sheet debt/equity ratios because they reduce net worth. A larger debt/equity ratio may be perceived as increasing financial risk by bankers, securities rating agencies, security analysts, and stockholders. This in turn could negatively affect a firm's stock market valuation in the same way as would the alternative negative impact on earnings under FAS #8. In both cases it is unclear whether or not investors factor the accounting impact of foreign exchange fluctuations on earnings and balance sheets into their perception of market value.

Functional vs. Reporting Currency

FAS #52 differentiates between a foreign affiliate's "functional" and "reporting" currency. *Functional currency* is defined as the currency of the primary economic environment in which the affiliate operates and in which it generates cash flows. The *reporting currency* is the currency in which the parent firm prepares its own financial statement, normally the home country currency.

Management must evaluate the nature and purpose of its foreign operations to decide on the appropriate functional currency. Some of the economic factors that enter into such decisions are listed in Exhibit 6.3.

In general, if the foreign affiliate's operations are relatively self-contained and integrated within a particular country, its functional currency will be the local currency of that country. Thus, for example, the German affiliate of a U.S. parent doing most of its manufacturing in Germany and selling most of its output for Deutschemarks would normally use the Deutschemark as its functional currency. If the foreign affiliate's operations are an extension of the U.S. parent's operations, the functional currency could be the U.S. dollar. An example would be an offshore manufacturing plant that receives all its raw material from the United States and resells all its production back to the United States.

If the foreign affiliate's functional currency is deemed to be the parent's currency, translation of the affiliate's statements employs the monetary/nonmonetary method of FAS #8. Thus, many U.S. multinationals continue to use the monetary/nonmonetary method for those foreign affiliates that use

EXHIBIT 6.3
Economic Factors to Consider in Determining Functional Currency

	FUNCTIONAL CURRENCY INDICATORS	
Foreign entity's	*Foreign currency*	*Parent currency*
Cash flows	Primarily in the foreign currency; no direct impact on parent cash flow	Direct impact on parent cash flow; readily available for remittance to parent
Sales price	Determined by local competition; not responsive in short-run to exchange rate changes	Determined by worldwide competition or prices; responsive in short-run to exchange rate changes
Sales markets	Active local market for affiliate's products	Sales markets mostly in parent's country or denominated in parent's currency
Expenses	Primarily incurred in local currency	Primarily for components obtained from parent's country
Financing	Primarily in foreign currency, with debt service generated by foreign operations	Primarily from parent or in parent's currency, with parent funds needed for debt service
Intercompany transactions	Few intercompany transactions, with foreign entity quite independent	Many intercompany transactions, with extensive interrelationship with parent's operations

Source: Financial Accounting Standards Board, *Statement of Financial Accounting Standards No. 52.* Stamford, Connecticut: Financial Accounting Standards Board, December 1981, derived from material on pp. 26–27.

the dollar as their functional currency, while using the current rate method for their other affiliates. Even under FAS #52, if the monetary/nonmonetary method is used any translation gains or losses are flowed through the income statement, as they were under FAS #8, rather than charged to the CTA account.

In summary, foreign currency translation can now be defined as the measurement, in a reporting currency, of assets, liabilities, revenues, and expenses of a foreign operation where the foreign accounts are originally denominated and/or measured in a functional currency that is also a foreign currency. Translation exposure is the possibility that a change in exchange rates will cause a loss or gain when the foreign operations are measured in the parent's own reporting currency.

Hyperinflation Countries

FAS #52 includes a special provision for translating statements of affiliates of U.S. firms in countries where cumulative inflation has been approximately 100% or more over a three-year period. Financial statements of these affiliates must be translated into the reporting currency using the monetary/nonmonetary method of FAS #8.

The rationale for special treatment of hyperinflation countries is to correct the distortion that occurs when depreciation at historical cost is matched against revenue at current prices. Translating depreciation, plant, and equipment at the historical exchange rate yields a higher reporting currency value than would the use of the current (depreciated) exchange rate. This should lead to a less distorted income statement and balance sheet. If the current rate were used, depreciation would be quite understated relative to replacement costs, and the book value of plant and equipment would eventually nearly disappear from the balance sheet as it becomes worth less and less in reporting currency terms. In effect, FAS #52 has declared that the functional currency of affiliates in hyperinflation countries is the reporting currency (U.S. dollars for U.S. firms).

Although the hyperinflation standard is somewhat controversial, it has some precedence in business practice. Russell Taussig has stated it very well:

> When a country is plagued with hyperinflation, it often uses the U.S. dollar or other hard currency as its de facto functional currency for actual transactions regardless of accounting standards. For example, most Israeli retailers in 1982 price their merchandise in U.S. dollars, not shekels. In the face of triple-digit inflation, they cannot change their prices every other day. The U.S. dollar becomes the unit of account. Also, when an Israeli holds U.S. dollars and the shekel is devalued, his holding in dollars remains the same, whereas if he holds currency in shekels and the shekel is devalued, his holding declines in purchasing power. The U.S. dollar becomes the storehouse of value. Consistent with the mercantile practice of businessmen in highly inflationary economies, the FASB promulgates the accounting standard that the home currency becomes the functional currency when inflation is rampant; otherwise the local currency is the functional currency. Accounting standards-setting simply is patterned after accepted business practice.[5]

ILLUSTRATION OF TRANSLATION METHODS

The difference that may result from use of one or another of the three prevalent translation methods is illustrated in the following sections, which draw on the basic example of Instruments Napoleon, S.A., used earlier to illustrate economic exposure. The example below illustrates balance sheet translation and the resulting gains or losses as they might be calculated on the day following a devaluation. A more complex example is presented in the appendix to this chapter. It applies translation rules to an income statement for Instruments Napoleon for an entire year during which business was conducted and the exchange rate gradually deteriorated.

Both examples are based on the following exchange rate assumptions, where the functional currency is the French franc and the reporting currency is the U.S. dollar:

1. *Historic exchange rate:* Plant and equipment, long-term debt, and common stock were entered on the corporate books at a time in the past when the exchange rate was FF6.00/$.
2. *Year-beginning exchange rate:* On December 31, 1985, the current exchange rate was FF8.00/$.
3. *Year-end exchange rate:* By December 31, 1986, the franc is presumed to have dropped 20% in value from its year-beginning value to a new value of FF10.00/$.

The following three examples illustrate how each of the three translation methods would treat a translation loss immediately after a drop in exchange rates from FF8.00/$ to FF10.00/$. No operations of the French affiliate are involved, and thus no corporate income statements need be translated.

Current Rate Method

Exhibit 6.4 illustrates translation loss using the current rate method. Under this method, assets and liabilities on the predevaluation balance sheet are translated at the current rate of FF8.00/$. Capital stock is translated at the historic rate of FF6.00/$, and retained earnings are translated at a composite rate that would be equivalent to having the additions to retained earnings of each past year translated at the exchange rate in effect in that year.

As shown in Exhibit 6.4, the "before-devaluation" dollar translation shows an accumulated translation loss from prior periods of $300,000. This balance is the cumulative gain or loss from translating franc statements into dollars in prior years, and is carried separately in a cumulative translation adjustment (CTA) account.

After devaluation, assets and liabilities are all translated at the new exchange rate of FF10.00/$. The equity accounts, including retained earnings, are translated just as they were before devaluation; the resulting translation adjustment increases to minus $500,000. The increase of $200,000 in the cumulative translation adjustment account (from minus $300,000 to minus $500,000) is the amount of translation loss measured by the current rate method on the day of devaluation.

EXHIBIT 6.4
Current Rate Translation Loss on Day of Devaluation, Instruments Napoleon, S.A. (no operations involved)

		BEFORE DEVALUATION		*AFTER DEVALUATION*	
	Francs	*Rate*	*Dollars*	*Rate*	*Dollars*
Cash	1,600,000	8.00	200,000	10.00	160,000
Accounts receivable	3,200,000	8.00	400,000	10.00	320,000
Inventory	2,400,000	8.00	300,000	10.00	240,000
Net plant and equipment	4,800,000	8.00	600,000	10.00	480,000
Total	12,000,000		1,500,000		1,200,000
Accounts payable	800,000	8.00	100,000	10.00	80,000
Short-term bank loan	1,600,000	8.00	200,000	10.00	160,000
Long-term debt	1,600,000	8.00	200,000	10.00	160,000
Capital stock	1,800,000	6.00	300,000	6.00	300,000
Retained earnings	6,200,000	(a)	1,000,000	(b)	1,000,000
Translation adjustment	n.a.		(300,000)		(500,000)
Total	12,000,000		1,500,000		1,200,000

(a) Dollar retained earnings before devaluation are the cumulative sum of additions to retained earnings of all prior years, translated at exchange rates in effect in those years.

(b) Translated into the same dollar amount as before devaluation.

n.a. Not applicable. A translation adjustment account would not appear in the franc statement of the affiliate.

Translation loss under any method can be viewed as a decrease in the value, stated in the reporting currency, of "net exposed assets," where "exposed" means that the reporting currency measurement of that asset drops with a devaluation or deterioration of the functional currency and rises with a revaluation or appreciation of the functional currency. "*Net* exposed assets" in this context means exposed assets minus exposed liabilities. Thus net assets are positive (long position) if exposed assets are greater than exposed liabilities, but are negative (short position) if exposed assets are smaller than exposed liabilities.

The translation loss of $200,000 under the current rate method came about as follows:

Loss due to decrease in dollar value of assets		
Cash (from $200,000 to $160,000)	$ 40,000	
Accounts receivable (from $400,000 to $320,000)	80,000	
Inventory (from $300,000 to $240,000)	60,000	
Net plant (from $600,000 to $480,000)	120,000	
Decrease in value of exposed assets		$300,000
Gain due to decrease in dollar value of liabilities		
Accounts payable (from $100,000 to $80,000)	$ 20,000	
Short-term bank loan (from $200,000 to $160,000)	40,000	
Long term debt (from $200,000 to $160,000)	40,000	
Less decrease in value of exposed liabilities		– 100,000
Net translation loss		$200,000

A simplified approach to determining translation loss is to multiply net exposed assets by the amount of the devaluation expressed as a decimal. Under the current rate method all assets and liabilities are deemed exposed, so the loss is as follows:

Exposed assets		
Cash	$200,000	
Accounts receivable	400,000	
Inventory	300,000	
Net plant	600,000	
Total exposed assets		$1,500,000
Exposed liabilities		
Accounts payable	$100,000	
Short-term bank debt	200,000	
Long-term debt	200,000	
Less total exposed liabilities		– 500,000
Net exposed assets		$1,000,000
Multiplied by amount of devaluation (as decimal)		× .20
Translation loss (current rate method)		$200,000

Monetary/Nonmonetary (Temporal) Method

Translation under the monetary/nonmonetary (temporal) method is illustrated in Exhibit 6.5. Under this method monetary assets and monetary liabilities in the predevaluation functional currency balance sheet are translated at the current rate of exchange, while other assets and equity accounts are translated at their historic rate. For Instruments Napoleon, the historic

EXHIBIT 6.5
Monetary/Nonmonetary (Temporal) Translation Loss on Day of Devaluation, Instruments Napoleon, S.A. (no operations involved)

		BEFORE DEVALUATION		*AFTER DEVALUATION*	
	Francs	*Rate*	*Dollars*	*Rate*	*Dollars*
Cash	1,600,000	8.00	200,000	10.00	160,000
Accounts receivable	3,200,000	8.00	400,000	10.00	320,000
Inventory	2,400,000	8.00	300,000	8.00	300,000
Net plant and equipment	4,800,000	6.00	800,000	6.00	800,000
Total	12,000,000		1,700,000		1,580,000
Accounts payable	800,000	8.00	100,000	10.00	80,000
Short-term bank loan	1,600,000	8.00	200,000	10.00	160,000
Long-term debt	1,600,000	8.00	200,000	10.00	160,000
Capital stock	1,800,000	6.00	300,000	6.00	300,000
Retained earnings	6,200,000	(a)	900,000	(b)	900,000
Translation loss					(20,000)
Total	12,000,000		1,700,000		1,580,000

(a) Dollar retained earnings before devaluation are the cumulative sum of additions to retained earnings of all prior years, translated at exchange rates in effect in those years.

(b) Translated into the same dollar amount as before devaluation. In the actual statement, the translation loss of $20,000 would be closed into retained earnings, leaving a net retained earnings balance of $880,000.

rate for inventory differs from that for net plant and equipment because inventory was acquired at a different date.

Under the monetary/nonmonetary method, past translation losses are not accumulated in a separate equity account, but are closed out to retained earnings. Thus in the predevaluation dollar balance sheet, retained earnings are the cumulative result of earnings from all prior years translated at the historic rates in effect each year, plus translation gains or losses from all prior years. In Exhibit 6.5, no translation loss appears in the predevaluation dollar balance sheet because any losses would have been closed to retained earnings.

The effect of a devaluation is to create an immediate translation loss of $20,000. This amount is shown as a separate line item in Exhibit 6.5 in order to focus attention on it for this textbook example. Under FAS #8, the translation loss of $20,000 would be passed through the income statement, reducing net income and reducing retained earnings. In our example, then, ending retained earnings would in fact be $880,000 (i.e., $900,000 minus $20,000). Other countries using the monetary/nonmonetary method do not necessarily require all gains and losses to pass through the income statement.

When translation loss is viewed in terms of changes in the value of exposed accounts, the loss of $20,000 under the monetary/nonmonetary (temporal) method comes about as follows:

Exposed assets; i.e., monetary assets		
Cash	$200,000	
Accounts receivable	400,000	
Total exposed assets		$600,000
Exposed liabilities; i.e., monetary liabilities		
Accounts payable	$100,000	
Short-term bank debt	200,000	
Long-term debt	200,000	
Less total exposed liabilities		− 500,000
Net exposed assets		$100,000
Multiplied by amount of devaluation (as decimal)		× .20
Translation loss (monetary/nonmonetary method)		$ 20,000

The reason that translation loss is less under the monetary/nonmonetary method than under the current rate method in this example is that different assets are considered exposed—or not exposed. The managerial implications of this factor are very important, because management can reduce translation loss by reducing exposed assets or by increasing exposed liabilities. Depending on the accounting method of the moment, management might select different asset categories for reduction or different liability categories for an increase. Thus "real" decisions about investments and financing might be dictated by selection of the methods for reporting results, when in fact the reporting method should be neutral in its influence on operating and financing decisions.

Current/Noncurrent Method

Translation under the current/noncurrent method is illustrated in Exhibit 6.6. Under the current/noncurrent method, current assets and current liabilities in the predevaluation functional currency balance sheet are translated at the current rate of exchange, while other assets and equity accounts are translated at historic rates.

In Exhibit 6.6, the translation loss is $120,000. As we described earlier, when the current/noncurrent method was used in the United States net translation gains were normally carried in a "reserve for future translation losses." Net losses were first written off against any balance in this reserve, and only when the reserve was depleted were any residual net losses charged to retained earnings. Not all countries using the current/noncurrent method follow this U.S. practice.

The translation loss of $120,000 under the current/noncurrent method comes about as follows:

Exposed assets; i.e., current assets		
Cash	$200,000	
Accounts receivable	400,000	
Inventory	300,000	
Total exposed assets		$900,000
Exposed liabilities; i.e., current liabilities		
Accounts payable	$100,000	
Short-term bank debt	200,000	
Less total exposed liabilities		−300,000
Net exposed assets		$600,000
Multiplied by amount of devaluation (as decimal)		× .20
Translation loss (current/noncurrent method)		$120,000

COMPARISON OF TRANSLATION LOSS WITH ECONOMIC LOSS

Translation loss can now be compared with economic loss. Translation loss for Instruments Napoleon, as calculated in Exhibits 6.4 through 6.6, is as follows:

	Change in cumulative translation adjustment account	*Derived from*
Current rate method	$200,000 loss	page 177
Monetary/nonmonetary method	20,000 loss	page 179
Current/noncurrent method	120,000 loss	page 180

Economic gain or loss, by comparison, was as follows (from Exhibit 6.2):

	Change in net present value
Case 1	$ 83,700 loss
Case 2	153,300 gain
Case 3	360,200 gain
Case 4	138,300 gain
Case 5	69,200 loss

EXHIBIT 6.6
Current/Noncurrent Translation Loss on Day of Devaluation, Instruments Napoleon, S.A. (no operations involved)

		BEFORE DEVALUATION		*AFTER DEVALUATION*	
	Francs	*Rate*	*Dollars*	*Rate*	*Dollars*
Cash	1,600,000	8.00	200,000	10.00	160,000
Accounts receivable	3,200,000	8.00	400,000	10.00	320,000
Inventory	2,400,000	8.00	300,000	10.00	240,000
Net plant and equipment	4,800,000	6.00	800,000	6.00	800,000
Total	12,000,000		1,700,000		1,520,000
Accounts payable	800,000	8.00	100,000	10.00	80,000
Short-term bank loan	1,600,000	8.00	200,000	10.00	160,000
Long-term debt	1,600,000	6.00	266,667	6.00	266,667
Capital stock	1,800,000	6.00	300,000	6.00	300,000
Retained earnings	6,200,000	(a)	833,333	(b)	833,333
Translation loss					(120,000)
Total	12,000,000		1,700,000		1,520,000

(a) Dollar retained earnings before devaluation are the cumulative sum of additions to retained earnings of all prior years, translated at exchange rates in effect in those years.

(b) Translated into the same dollar amount as before devaluation. In the actual statement, the translation loss of $120,000 would be closed into retained earnings, leaving a net retained earnings balance of $713,333.

The gain or loss amounts above illustrate that economic exposure may be extremely different—not only in amount but also in sign—from translation exposure measured by any of the prevailing accounting methods.

A manager guided by accounting measures of loss or gain might, in this situation, avoid France because of the possibility of a translation loss. Such a manager might fear loss of a bonus tied to reported profits, or possibly loss of a job if the investment in France were made and a translation loss were subsequently reported.

Under three of the five assumptions about volume, cost, and price, France became a very desirable location for investment precisely because of the economic consequences that followed devaluation. This example illustrates the importance of focusing decisions primarily on the economic consequences of changes in exchange rates, and only secondarily on any short-run accounting reports.

CONSOLIDATION OF ACCOUNTS

Financial statements of Instruments Napoleon, S.A., must be combined with those of its parent and sister affiliates to prepare a consolidated balance sheet and income statement. Translation of its statements is necessary not only as an accounting procedure but also as the first step in preparing corporatewide exposure reports for management use.

Balance sheets for Washington Controls, Inc., the U.S. parent, and its two wholly owned affiliates, Instruments Napoleon, S.A., and Canadian Instruments, Ltd., are shown in Exhibit 6.7. The nonconsolidated balance sheet of the parent is shown in column 1; column 2 shows the balance sheet of Instruments Napoleon; and column 3 shows the balance sheet of Canadian Instruments. All balance sheets are for December 31, 1985, before any changes in exchange rates. The symbol *C$* is used to designate Canadian dollars, while *$* by itself means U.S. dollars.

The footnotes to Exhibit 6.7 give details of the financial situation. The U.S. parent has £100,000 on deposit in a London bank; Canadian Instruments owes its U.S. parent C$600,000; the parent carries its investments in Instruments Napoleon and Canadian Instruments at $1,000,000 and $3,340,000, respectively; the U.S. parent has borrowed £200,000 from a London bank; and Canadian Instruments has long-term debt denominated in French francs of FF6,400,000. On December 31, 1985, the various spot exchange rates are as follows:

$1.00 = FF8.0000	or	FF1.00 = $0.1250
$1.00 = C$1.2500	or	C$1.00 = $0.8000
$1.00 = £0.6667	or	£1.00 = $1.5000
C$1.00 = £0.5333	or	£1.00 = C$1.8750
FF1.00 = C$0.1562	or	C$1.00 = FF6.4000

The process of creating a consolidated balance sheet is shown in Exhibit 6.8. Intracompany accounts are canceled; the remaining foreign currency accounts are translated into U.S. dollars; and the dollar amounts are added horizontally to create, in the right-hand column, the consolidated balance sheet. Translation has been accomplished by the current rate method. Details of the translation for intracompany accounts are given in the notes to Exhibit 6.8.

The net effect of consolidation is to create a worldwide consolidated balance sheet that reports, in U.S. dollar terms, assets of $18,140,000, liabilities of $9,600,000, and shareholders' equity of $8,540,000. The main purpose of translation is to create such a consolidated balance sheet.

INTERNAL MANAGEMENT REPORTS

Financial managers have devised internal reports to present one or another facet of foreign exchange exposure in a format that will facilitate deciding how to manage such exposure. These internal reports are derived from the

EXHIBIT 6.7
Washington Controls, Inc., and Affiliates, Nonconsolidated Balance Sheets, December 31, 1985 (in thousands of currency units)

	Washington Controls (parent only)	*Instruments Napoleon*	*Canadian Instruments*
Assets			
Cash	$ 800[a]	FF 1,600	C$ 600
Accounts receivable	2,400[b]	3,200	2,000
Inventory	3,000	2,400	1,800
Net plant and equipment	5,000	4,800	3,000
Investment in Instruments Napoleon, S.A.	1,000[c]		
Investment in Canadian Instruments, Ltd.	3,340[d]		
	$15,540	FF12,000	C$7,400
Liabilities and Net Worth			
Accounts payable	$ 2,000	FF 800	C$1,400[b]
Short-term bank loan	2,000	1,600	825[f]
Long-term debt	3,000	1,600	1,000[g]
Capital stock	4,000	1,800	1,200
Retained earnings	4,540	6,200	2,975
	$15,540	FF12,000	C$7,400

[a]U.S. parent has £100,000 in a London bank, carried on its books as $150,000. This amount is part of the total cash balance of $800,000 shown on the parent's books.

[b]Canadian Instruments owes the U.S. parent C$600,000, included in accounts payable and carried on the U.S. books at $480,000. Remaining accounts receivable (parent books) and accounts payable (Canadian Instrument's books) are in U.S. and Canadian dollars, respectively.

[c]The U.S. parent carries its 100% ownership of Instruments Napoleon at $1,000,000, this being the sum of capital stock ($300,000) and retained earnings ($1,000,000), minus translation adjustment ($300,000), before devaluation, as shown in Exhibit 6.4 under the current rate method of translation.

[d]The U.S. parent carries its 100% ownership of Canadian Instruments at $3,340,000, this being the sum of capital stock (C$1,200,000) and retained earnings (C$2,975,000), the sum times $0.80/C$. (C$175,000 × 0.80 = $3,340,000).

[e]The U.S. parent has borrowed, on a short-term basis, £200,000 from a London bank, carried on its books as $300,000. Remaining parent short-term bank debt is denominated in U.S. dollars.

[f]Canadian Instruments' short-term bank loan consists of £440,000, carried on Canadian books as C$825,000. (C$825,000 = $660,000.)

[g]Canadian Instruments' long-term debt consists of FF6,400,000 in Eurofrancs, carried on Canadian books as C$1,000,000.

data used to prepare companywide consolidated financial statements. Three typical internal management reports are:

1. a translation exposure report,
2. a transaction exposure report, and
3. a schedule of cash flows by currency; i.e., a currency cash budget.

EXHIBIT 6.8
Washington Controls, Inc., Consolidated Balance Sheet, December 31, 1985 (accounts translated into thousands of U.S. dollars with intracompany accounts removed)

	Washington Controls (parent)	*Instruments Napoleon*	*Canadian Instruments*	*Consolidated balance sheet*
Assets				
Cash	$ 800[a]	$200	$ 480	$ 1,480
Accounts receivable	1,920[b]	400	1,600	3,920
Inventory	3,000	300	1,440	4,740
Net plant and equipment	5,000	600	2,400	8,000
Investment in Instruments Napoleon, S.A.	0[c]			
Investment in Canadian Instruments, Ltd.	0[c]			
				$18,140
Liabilities and Net Worth				
Accounts payable	$2,000	$100	$ 640[e]	$ 2,740
Short-term bank loan	2,000	200	660[f]	2,860
Long-term debt	3,000	200	800[g]	4,000
Capital stock	4,000	0[c]	0[c]	4,000
Retained earnings	4,540	0[c]	0[c]	4,540
				$18,140

[a]The U.S. parent has £100,000 on deposit in a London bank, carried on its books as $150,000. This amount is part of the total cash balance of $800,000 shown on the parent's books.

[b]$2,400,000 − $480,000 intracompany debt = $1,920,000.

[c]Investments in affiliates cancel with the equity of the affiliates in consolidation. If the carrying value on the books of the parent is not equal to the translated equity value of the affiliate, the difference is closed to retained earnings.

[d]Includes £200,000 carried at $300,000.

[e]

Original company balance sheet amount	C$1,400,000
less intracompany debt	− 600,000
	C$ 800,000
times exchange rate ($0.80/C$)	× .80
U.S. dollar amount	$ 640,000

[f]Consists of £440,000 carried as C$825,000. C$825,000 × 0.80 = $660,000. (Alternatively, £440,000 × 1.50 = $660,000.)

[g]Consists of FF6,400,000 carried as C$1,000,000. C$1,000,000 × 0.80 = $800,000. (Alternatively, FF6,400,000/8 = $800,000.)

In general, internal management reports are oriented toward measuring the near-term earnings and cash flow impact of a change in exchange rates. "Near-term" looks beyond the immediate, next-day translation impact, but does not go so far as to forecast potential long-run changes in cash flows caused by devaluation-induced changes in prices, unit volume, or costs. In other words, "near-term" stops short of attempting to measure full economic exposure.

Translation Exposure Report

A translation exposure report measures the exposed position of a firm at one point in time in each of the currencies used. *Currencies,* rather than countries, are the focus. As in the example for Washington Controls, which has both debt and assets in pounds but has no operations in the United Kingdom, the currencies used by a multinational firm need not be those of the countries of operations.

Depending on the translation method used, the format will vary. Exhibit 6.9 shows a translation exposure report for Washington Controls using the current rate method. The account headings are all accounts deemed "exposed" under this method, while the columns show the total amount by currency. In this example, all foreign currency amounts are shown as dollar equivalents so that the relative size of various exposures can be judged. Some firms prepare exposure reports in their functional currencies instead of their reporting currency. Computerized systems can easily prepare the reports in either currency.

Details of the various calculations are given in the notes to Exhibit 6.9. Observe that a column exists for pounds, even though Washington Controls has no affiliate in the United Kingdom. This column is used to emphasize the fact that the columns represent *currencies,* not countries or affiliates.

On page 177 in this chapter, Instruments Napoleon was shown to have net exposure of $1,000,000 under the current rate method. However, because Canadian Instruments has a French franc debt of FF6,400,000, translated as $800,000, the total worldwide exposure for Washington Controls in French francs is reduced to only $200,000. A system of delegating exposure management to each affiliate that allowed—or even worse, encouraged—the financial manager of Instruments Napoleon to eliminate a million dollars of net franc exposure would be counterproductive for the worldwide enterprise because a large amount of the French affiliate's exposure has already been offset by the Canadian affiliate's franc-denominated debt. The financial manager of the French affiliate, acting alone, would probably overcompensate.

Worldwide exposure in Canadian dollars, measured in U.S. dollars, is $5,280,000. This value results when foreign currency amounts are removed from the various Canadian accounts. Worldwide exposure in pounds is

EXHIBIT 6.9
Washington Controls, Inc., and Affiliates, Translation Exposure Report, December 31, 1985 (report based on current rate method; foreign currency amounts expressed in thousands of U.S. dollars)

	French francs	*Canadian dollars*	*British pounds*
Exposed Assets			
Cash	$ 200	$ 480	$150[a]
Accounts receivable	400	1,600	—
Inventory	300	1,440	—
Net plant and equipment	600	2,400	—
Exposed assets	$1,500	$5,920	$150
Exposed Liabilities			
Accounts payable	$ 100	$ 640	$ —
Short-term bank loan	200	—	960[b]
Long-term debt	1,000[c]	—	—
Exposed liabilities	$1,300	$ 640	$960
Net exposure	$ 200	$5,280	−$810

[a]£100,000 cash balance held by U.S. parent and carried on U.S. books as $150,000. This amount is part of the total cash balance of $800,000 shown on the parent's books.

[b]Consists of £200,000 owed by the U.S. parent and £440,000 owed by Canadian Instruments, Ltd. The Canadian affiliate has no short-term bank debt denominated in Canadian dollars. Translation of the two sterling debts into U.S. dollars is as follows:

Parent debt: £200,000 × $1.50 =		$300,000
Canadian debt:	£440,000 × C$1.875/£ = C$825,000	
	C$825,000 × $0.80/C$ =	$660,000
(Alternatively, £440,000 × $1.50/£ = $660,000)		
		$960,000

[c]Consists of FF1,600,000 on books of Instruments Napoleon, translated as $200,000, plus FF6,400,000 on books of Canadian Instruments, translated as $800,000. ($200,000 + $800,000 = $1,000,000.) The Canadian affiliate has no long-term debt denominated in Canadian dollars.

negative $810,000, the result of the fact that the U.S. parent holds a relatively small pound cash balance while both the parent and the Canadian affiliate have large pound debts. No column exists for U.S. dollars, because U.S. dollars cannot create translation exposure when the reporting currency is the U.S. dollar.

Transaction Exposure Report

Transaction exposure is measured by affiliate as well as by currency, and intracompany accounts do *not* cancel out. Thus transaction exposure differs from translation exposure, which is properly measured only by currency and only from the perspective of the parent.

A transaction exposure report for Washington Controls is shown in Exhibit 6.10. The report is a matrix showing on one dimension the unconsolidated parent and each affiliate. The other dimension shows transaction exposure in each currency. Note that the cells that might show each affiliate's transaction exposure in its home currency are empty; each affiliate can have transaction exposure only in other currencies.

Transaction exposure arises partly from accounts receivable, any other monetary receivables, and all monetary debts. Cash balances do not contribute to transaction exposure. In addition to exposed balance sheet accounts, four off-balance sheet items create transaction exposure and so are included in the report:

1. *Contracts to buy foreign exchange forward.* Such contracts obligate the affiliate to deliver at some future date its home currency and receive a predetermined amount of a foreign currency at an already established exchange rate. Since the amount of foreign currency to be received is fixed, the contract creates an exposed position very similar to that of a foreign currency denominated account receivable.
2. *Contracts to sell foreign exchange forward.* These contracts are the reverse of the contracts above, and they create an exposed position similar to an account payable. In the example in Exhibit 6.10, the U.S. parent entered into a contract to receive $100,000 worth of pounds at a future date. Presumably this contract was made for the purpose of reducing a portion of the exposed obligation to repay a short-term pound loan equivalent to $300,000.
3. *Unfilled customer orders at fixed foreign prices.* Such contracts are essentially accounts receivable not yet recorded on the affiliate's books. When denominated in a foreign currency, they constitute a fixed amount of such currency to be received at a future date, regardless of the exchange rate at that time.
4. *Purchase commitments at fixed foreign prices.* These are obligations denominated in a foreign currency to purchase such items as raw materials, components, energy, or physical facilities. In Exhibit 6.10 Instruments Napoleon has a purchase commitment denominated in U.S. dollars of $100,000.

Note that intracompany accounts do *not* cancel in transaction exposure. Canadian Instruments owes its U.S. parent C$600,000, carried as $480,000. This debt creates transaction exposure for the U.S. parent, which will receive Canadian dollars of uncertain U.S. dollar value, but it creates no transaction exposure for the Canadian affiliate. Had the loan been denominated instead as US$480,000, the transaction exposure would have been

EXHIBIT 6.10
Washington Controls, Inc., and Affiliates, Transaction Exposure Report, December 31, 1985 (in thousands of U.S. dollar amounts of functional currencies)

	U.S. dollars	*French francs*	*Canadian dollars*	*British pounds*
U.S. Parent				
Accounts receivable	no report		+480[a]	
Accounts payable				
Short-term bank loans				−300[b]
Long-term debt				
Forward exchange contracts				+100
Fixed price customer orders, net of purchase commitments				
Net exposure			+480	−200
Instruments Napoleon				
Accounts receivable		no report		
Accounts payable				
Short-term bank loans				
Long-term debt				
Forward exchange contracts				
Fixed price customer orders, net of purchase commitments	+100			
Net exposure	+100			
Canadian Instruments				
Accounts receivable			no report	
Accounts payable				
Short-term bank loans				−660[c]
Long-term debt		−800[d]		
Forward exchange contracts				
Fixed price customer orders, net of purchase commitments				
Net exposure		−800		−660

[a]C$600,000 (= $480,000) owed by Canadian Instruments to U.S. parent.

[b] £200,000 (= $300,000) owed by U.S. parent to London bank.

[c]£440,000 (= $660,000) owed by Canadian Instruments to London bank.

[d]FF6,400,000 (= $800,000) owed by Canadian Instruments in Eurofrancs.

shifted to the Canadian affiliate. Since intracompany debt creates transaction exposure for one or the other of the parties, management should denominate intracompany obligations to position a potential loss or gain where desired for tax or other purposes.

Overall, Exhibit 6.10 shows that the U.S. parent by itself (i.e., unconsolidated) has a positive ("long") transaction exposure in Canadian dollars, and a negative ("short") exposure in pounds. Instruments Napoleon has a positive exposure in U.S. dollars, and Canadian Instruments has a negative exposure in both francs and pounds. As we stated earlier, "positive" exposure means a net foreign currency claim that will drop in home currency value if the foreign currency depreciates and will rise if it appreciates. "Negative" exposure means a net foreign currency debt that will drop in home currency value if the foreign currency depreciates and will rise if it appreciates.

Schedule of Cash Flow by Currency

To overcome the static nature of the foreign exchange exposure report, a multinational firm should prepare a schedule of cash flows for each of the various currencies in which it does business. Such a schedule is really a cash budget subdivided by type of currency. Exhibit 6.11 is an example for Washington Controls, Inc., simplified to show only gross receipts and disbursements by currency without the underlying detail.

Exhibit 6.11 is based on quarters, but monthly or other periodic schedules might be more appropriate for any given company.

Budgeted receipts in each currency reflect cash collections from anticipated credit sales and from collecting outstanding accounts receivable. The transaction exposure report in Exhibit 6.10 considered only *already existing* accounts receivable. A schedule of cash flows by currency also accommodates all other expected receipts by currency type, such as proceeds from disposal of assets or from the issuance of new securities. Disbursements reflect not only already existing payables, but also other disbursements anticipated in future quarters. Such disbursements might include payments reducing outstanding debt, an item of detail not reflected in the transaction exposure report, and any intended acquisitions of assets. For these reasons, the amounts in Exhibit 6.11 are not derived directly from previous exhibits.

In Exhibit 6.11 we see that Washington Controls, Inc., generates future inflows in U.S. dollars, French francs, and British pounds that are more than adequate to cover anticipated disbursements. The fact that pound balances will be generated by operations indicates that Washington Controls and its Canadian affiliate are not as vulnerable to actual loss due to an appreciation of the pound as might appear from the translation and transaction exposure reports. In fact, part of the negative pound exposure of the parent of $300,000 is hedged by the forward exchange contract reported in the transaction exposure report, and the remainder by the net inflow over one year of $200,000 worth of pounds shown in the schedule of cash flow by currency. The schedule of cash flow indicates a continual shortage of Canadian dollars.

EXHIBIT 6.11
Washington Controls, Inc., and Affiliates, Schedule of Cash Flow by Currency (foreign currency amounts expressed in thousands of U.S. dollars)

	First quarter	*Second quarter*	*Third quarter*	*Fourth quarter*	*Year total*
U.S. Dollars					
Budgeted receipts	5,000	5,000	5,000	5,000	20,000
Budgeted disbursements	−4,600	−4,500	−4,400	−4,300	−17,800
Net dollar receipts	400	500	600	700	2,200
French Francs					
Budgeted receipts	450	500	450	400	1,800
Budgeted disbursements	−400	−400	−400	−400	−1,600
Net franc receipts	50	100	50	0	200
Canadian Dollars					
Budgeted receipts	1,000	1,200	1,800	2,000	6,000
Budgeted disbursements	−1,150	−1,350	−1,900	−1,900	−6,300
Net Canadian dollar receipts	(150)	(150)	(100)	100	(300)
British Pounds					
Budgeted receipts	55	55	55	55	220
Budgeted disbursements	−5	−5	−5	−5	−20
Net pound receipts	50	50	50	50	200
Net receipts, all currencies	350	500	600	850	2,300

The key point illustrated in the schedule of cash flows by currency is that exposure is not a matter of financial statement data alone, but must also consider probable future cash flows from operations. Because future cash flows are conjectural, true exposure is also a matter of estimate and managerial judgment.

One caveat is important. Any schedule of cash flow by currency is presumably based on the anticipated volume of business without an unexpected change in exchange rates. Should any of the currencies unexpectedly change in foreign exchange value, subsequent sales or sourcing practices might have to be revised, creating related changes in the currency cash budget. These changes in turn might lead to altered cash flows and working capital requirements. Therefore the best way to measure exposure is to estimate cash flows based on a range of possible future exchange rates over a long period, such as five years. These results can then be compared with the static exposed positions reflected in the translation and transaction exposure reports. A complete set of schedules of anticipated cash flow by currency for all possible devaluation/revaluation assumptions approaches a schedule that measures economic exposure as it was defined at the beginning of this chapter.

SUMMARY

A change in exchange rates can cause a loss or gain on operations. A key responsibility of financial management is to anticipate the type of gain or loss, when it might occur, how much it might be, and what to do about it.

This chapter explains the differences between translation, transaction, and economic exposure. Particular attention is devoted to the difference between translation (accounting) measures and economic measures.

Procedures, including FAS #52, by which financial statements of foreign affiliates are translated into consolidated reports are described and compared. Finally, management's use of three internal reports is explained. The three reports are a translation exposure report, a transaction exposure report, and a schedule of cash flow by currency.

NOTES

1. This four-level approach is developed more fully in theory and with an extended case (Novo Industri A/S) in Arthur I. Stonehill, Niels Ravn, and Kåre Dullum, "Management of Foreign Exchange Economic Exposure," in *International Financial Management,* Stockholm: Norstedt & Soners, 1982, pp. 128–148.

2. Price Waterhouse International, *International Survey of Accounting Principles,* New York: Butterworth, 1979.

3. *Ibid.*

4. *Ibid.*

5. Russell A. Taussig, "Impact of SFAS No. 52 on the Translation of Foreign Financial Statements of Companies in Highly Inflationary Economies," *Journal of Accounting, Auditing, and Finance,* Winter 1983, pp. 145–146.

Chapter 6: Appendix Translation Loss Measured during a Year of Operations

The Instruments Napoleon example given in this chapter was necessarily simple in order to avoid the complications of translating an income statement. In this Appendix, the translation loss created by Instruments Napoleon will be measured at the end of 1986, a year during which it is assumed that the franc depreciates steadily from FF8.00/$ (on December 31, 1985) to FF10.00/$ (on December 31, 1986). The historic exchange rate remains at FF6.00/$.

Translation of an income statement requires calculation of average exchange rates for the year. Instruments Napoleon has an inventory turnover of three months—i.e., inventory sold in any quarter was manufactured in the previous quarter. Instruments Napoleon uses first-in, first-out (FIFO) accounting for cost of goods sold. Using average exchange rates for each quarter, we can calculate 1986 average exchange rates for current operating expenses and for cost of goods sold as follows:

Period of time	*Operating expense calculation*	*Cost of goods sold calculation*
4th quarter 1985 average exchange rate	—	FF 7.50/$
1st quarter 1986 average exchange rate	FF 8.00/$	8.00
2nd quarter 1986 average exchange rate	8.50	8.50
3rd quarter 1986 average exchange rate	9.00	9.00
4th quarter 1986 average exchange rate	9.50	—
Total	35.00	33.00
Average	FF 8.75/$	FF 8.25/$

During 1986 the following business activities occur:

- Instruments Napoleon sells 1,000,000 units at the rate of 250,000 units per quarter. Unit sales price is FF12.80, and annual sales revenue is thus FF12,800,000.
- During the year collections from accounts receivable consist of year-beginning receivables (FF3,200,000) and proceeds from sales of

the first three quarters (FF9,600,000). Year-end accounts receivable consist of sales of the fourth quarter: 250,000 units at FF12.80 = FF3,200,000.

- Cost of goods sold is FF9.60 per unit. During 1986 year-beginning inventory (250,000 units) is sold. New manufacturing consists of 250,000 units per quarter, and inventory on hand at the end of the year is that manufactured during the fourth quarter: 250,000 units at FF9.60 = FF2,400,000.
- General and administrative expenses of FF1,200,000 are incurred and paid in cash during 1986. Annual depreciation is FF240,000.
- The French corporate income tax rate is 50%, and income taxes are paid on a cash basis throughout every year.
- No cash dividends are paid.
- Accounts payable and short-term bank debt are rolled over and renewed, respectively, for the same amount as that at the end of 1985. (For this example, interest on bank debt is ignored.)

As a consequence of the above events, changes in Instruments Napoleon's cash balance during 1986 are as follows:

Year-beginning cash balance (Dec. 31, 1985)	FF 1,600,000
Plus:	
Collection of year-beginning accounts receivable	3,200,000
Collection of receivables from sales of first three quarters	9,600,000
Available	14,400,000
Less:	
General and administrative expenses paid	1,200,000
Income taxes paid	880,000
Manufacturing costs for new inventory	9,600,000
Year-end cash balance (Dec. 31, 1986)	FF 2,720,000

The income statement for the year ended December 31, 1986, is shown in Exhibit 6A.1, and balance sheets for both December 31, 1985, and December 31, 1986, are shown in Exhibit 6A.2.

In 1986, Instruments Napoleon earned net income of FF880,000. Because no dividends were paid, retained earnings rose from FF6,200,000 to FF7,080,000. This increase is shown both at the bottom of the franc income statement in the surplus reconciliation (Exhibit 6A.1), and also as the increase between the year-beginning and year-ending retained earnings accounts in the franc balance sheet (Exhibit 6A.2).

CURRENT RATE METHOD

Under the current rate method of translation, all revenue and expense accounts are translated at the *average* exchange rate in effect during the year. This process leads to net income translated into dollars of $100,600 and to year-end retained earnings of $1,100,600. These numbers appear in the current rate translation column of Exhibits 6A.1 and 6A.2.

Under the current rate method, translation gains and losses are not shown in the income statement, nor are they reflected in the retained earnings account. Rather, any imbalance in the dollar balance sheet from the prior year shows as a change in the cumulative translation adjustment account. Exhibit 6A.2 shows that the cumulative translation adjustment account changes from a credit balance of $300,000 to a credit balance of $512,600. The difference of $212,600 is a translation loss for the year. It is carried forward to future years in the cumulative translation adjustment account in the equity section of the balance sheet.

MONETARY/NONMONETARY METHOD

Under the monetary/nonmonetary (temporal) method of translation, sales and cash operating expenses are translated at the average exchange rate of FF8.75/$. However, cost of goods sold and depreciation are translated at the historic rate of exchange appropriate for each asset category within those groups. A rate of FF8.25/$ was used for cost of goods sold and a rate of FF6.00/$ for depreciation.

Under the monetary/nonmonetary method, pretax operating profit is calculated to be $122,100 (the difference between sales revenue and the various expenses, each translated individually). Income tax expense is translated directly from the franc accounts at the average rate of exchange as $100,600. Aftertax profit is calculated to be $21,500. Translation of the balance sheet (Exhibit 6A.2) shows that year-end retained earnings must be $904,600, up $4,600 from year-beginning retained earnings of $900,000. Since translated earnings were $21,500, a translation loss of $16,900 was experienced under the monetary/nonmonetary method.

The translation loss of $16,900 is the amount necessary to reconcile the net income figure with the change in retained earnings shown in Exhibit 6A.2. Because the temporal method requires that this translation loss pass through the net income calculation, the loss shows up in Exhibit 6A.1 as a subtraction before the calculation of net income. Note that under the monetary/nonmonetary method year-end inventory has been translated at FF9.50/$, the "historic" rate derived from the last quarter of 1985 when that inventory was manufactured.

EXHIBIT 6A.1

Translation Loss during a Year of Operations

Instruments Napoleon, S.A., income statements, year ended December 31, 1986 (dollars and francs in thousands)

Item	Income statement in francs	CURRENT RATE TRANSLATION		MONETARY/ NONMONETARY (TEMPORAL) TRANSLATION		CURRENT/ NONCURRENT TRANSLATION	
		Rate	Dollars	Rate	Dollars	Rate	Dollars
Sales (1,000,000 units @ FF12.8/unit)	12,800	8.75[a]	1,462.9	8.75[a]	1,462.8	8.75[a]	1,462.8
Direct costs (1,000,000 units @ FF9.6/unit)	9,600	8.75[a]	1,097.2	8.25[b]	1,163.6	8.25[b]	1,163.6
Cash operating expenses	1,200	8.75[a]	137.1	8.75[a]	137.1	8.75[a]	137.1
Depreciation	240	8.75[a]	27.4	6.00[c]	40.0	6.00[c]	40.0
Total operating expenses	11,040		1,261.7		1,340.7		1,340.7
Pretax profit	1,760		201.2		122.1		122.1
Income tax expense	880	8.75[a]	100.6	8.75[a]	100.6	8.75[a]	100.6
Profit after tax	880		100.6		21.5		21.5
Foreign exchange gain (loss)	n.a.		n.a.		(16.9)		(69.5)
Net income	880		100.6		4.6		(48.0)
Retained earnings, Dec. 31, 1985	6,200		1,000.0		900.0		833.3
less dividends paid	0	8.75[a]	0.00	8.75[a]	0.00	8.75[a]	0.00
Retained earnings, Dec. 31, 1986	7,080		1,100.6		904.6		785.3

n.a. Not applicable. This line would not appear in this statement.

[a] Average exchange rate for current year.

[b] Historic exchange rate for inventory.

[c] Historic exchange rate for plant and equipment.

EXHIBIT 6A.2

Translation Loss during a Year of Operations

Instruments Napoleon, S.A., balance sheets, December 31, 1985 and 1986 (dollars and francs in thousands)

	Balance sheet in francs	CURRENT RATE TRANSLATION		MONETARY/ NONMONETARY (TEMPORAL) TRANSLATION		CURRENT/ NONCURRENT TRANSLATION	
		Rate	Dollars	Rate	Dollars	Rate	Dollars
Balance Sheet, December 31, 1985							
Cash	1,600	8.00	200.0	8.00	200.0	8.00	200.0
Accounts receivable	3,200	8.00	400.0	8.00	400.0	8.00	400.0
Inventory	2,400	8.00	300.0	8.00	300.0	8.00	300.0
Net plant and equipment	4,800	8.00	600.0	6.00	800.0	6.00	800.0
	12,000		1,500.0		1,700.0		1,700.0
Accounts payable	800	8.00	100.0	8.00	100.0	8.00	100.0
Short-term bank loan	1,600	8.00	200.0	8.00	200.0	8.00	200.0
Long-term debt	1,600	8.00	200.0	8.00	200.0	6.00	266.7
Capital stock	1,800	6.00	300.0	6.00	300.0	6.00	300.0
Retained earnings	6,200		1,000.0		900.0		833.3
Cumulative translation adjustment	n.a.		(300.0)		n.a.		n.a.
	12,000		1,500.0		1,700.0		1,700.0

Balance Sheet, December 31, 1986

Cash	2,720	10.00	272.0	10.00	272.0	10.00	272.0
Accounts receivable	3,200	10.00	320.0	10.00	320.0	10.00	320.0
Inventory	2,400	10.00	240.0	9.50	252.6	10.00	240.0
Net plant and equipment	4,560	10.00	456.0	6.00	760.0	6.00	760.0
	12,880		1,288.0		1,604.6		1,592.0
Accounts payable	800	10.00	80.0	10.00	80.0	10.00	80.0
Short-term bank loan	1,600	10.00	160.0	10.00	160.0	10.00	160.0
Long-term debt	1,600	10.00	160.0	10.00	160.0	6.00	266.7
Capital stock	1,800	6.00	300.0	6.00	300.0	6.00	300.0
Retained earnings	7,080		1,100.6		904.6		785.3
Cumulative translation adjustment	n.a.		(516.6)		n.a.		n.a.
	12,800		1,288.0		1,604.6		1,592.0

n.a. Not applicable. This line would not appear in this statement.

CURRENT/NONCURRENT METHOD

Under the current/noncurrent method of translation, income statement accounts are translated in the same manner as they are under the temporal method, resulting in the same reported aftertax income of $21,500. However, translation of the balance sheet by the current/noncurrent method leads to year-end retained earnings of only $785,300, a decrease of $48,000 from the year-beginning balance of $833,300. The foreign exchange translation loss is thus $69,500, the amount necessary to reduce aftertax income of $21,500 to the requisite overall loss of $48,000.

BIBLIOGRAPHY

Adler, Michael, "Translation Methods and Operational Foreign Exchange Risk Management," in Goran Bergendahl, ed., *International Financial Management,* Stockholm: Norstedt & Soners, 1982, pp 87–103.

Adler, Michael, and Bernard Dumas, "Should Exposure Management Depend on Translation Accounting Methods?" *Euromoney,* June 1981, pp. 132–138.

———, "Exposure to Currency Risk: Definition and Measurement," *Financial Management,* Spring 1984, pp. 41–50.

Aggarwal, Raj, "FASB No. 8 and Reported Results of Multinational Operations: Hazard for Managers and Investors," *Journal of Accounting, Auditing and Finance,* Spring 1978, pp. 197–216.

Aliber, R. Z., and C. P. Stickney, "Accounting Measures of Foreign Exchange Exposure: The Long and Short of It," *Accounting Review,* January 1975, pp. 44–57.

Bindon, Kathleen R., *Inventories and Foreign Currency Translation Requirements,* Ann Arbor: UMI Research Press, 1983.

Choi, Frederick D. S., Howard D. Lowe, and Reginald G. Worthley, "Accountors, Accountants, and Standard No. 8," *Journal of International Business Studies,* Fall 1978, pp. 81–87.

Donaldson, Howard, and Alan Reinstein, "Implementing FAS No. 52: The Critical Issues," *Financial Executive,* June 1983, pp. 40–50.

Donaldson, J. A., *Corporate Currency Risk,* London: Financial Times Business Information, Ltd., 1980.

Dukes, Ronald, *An Empirical Investigation of the Effects of Statement of Financial Accounting Standards No. 8 on Security Return Behavior,* Stamford, Conn.: Financial Accounting Standards Board, 1978.

Eaker, M. R., "The Numeraire Problem and Foreign Exchange Risk," *Journal of Finance,* May 1981, pp. 419–426.

Financial Accounting Standards Board, *Accounting for the Translation of Foreign Currency Transactions and Foreign Currency Financial Statements,* Statement of Financial Accounting Standards No. 8, October 1975, Stamford, Conn.: Financial Accounting Standards Board, 1975. Reprinted, except for Appendix D, in *Journal of Accountancy,* December 1975, pp. 78–89.

———, *Foreign Currency Translation,* Statement of Financial Accounting Standards No. 52, December 1981, Stamford, Conn.: Financial Accounting Standards Board, 1981.

Foreign Currency Translation: Understanding and Applying FAS 52, New York: Price Waterhouse and Company, 1981.

George, Abraham M., "Cash Flow versus Accounting Exposures to Currency Risk," *California Management Review*, Summer 1978, pp. 50–55.

Giddy, Ian H., "Exchange Risk: Whose View?" *Financial Management*, Summer 1977, pp. 23–33.

Goodman, Hortense, and Leonard Lorensen, *Illustrations of Foreign Currency Translation*, New York: American Institute of Certified Public Accountants, 1982.

Hekman, Christine R., "A Financial Model of Foreign Exchange Exposure," *Journal of International Business Studies*, Summer 1985, pp. 83–99.

———, "Foreign Exchange Exposure: Accounting Measures and Economic Exposure," *Journal of Cash Management*, February/March 1983, pp. 34–45.

———, "Measuring Foreign Exchange Exposure: A Practical Theory and Its Application," *Financial Analysts Journal*, September/October 1983, pp. 59–65.

Ijiri, Yuji, "Foreign Currency Accounting and Its Transition," in R. J. Herring, ed., *Management of Foreign Exchange Risk*, Cambridge, England: Cambridge University Press, 1983.

Levi, Maurice D., "Underutilization of Forward Markets or Rational Behavior," *Journal of Finance*, September 1979, pp. 1013–1017.

Militello, Frederick C., Jr., "Statement No. 52: Changes in Financial Management Practices," *Financial Executive*, August 1983, pp. 48–51.

Rayburn, Frank R., and G. Michael Crooch, "Currency Translation and the Funds Statement: A New Approach," *Journal of Accountancy*, October 1983, pp. 51–62.

Sapy-Mazello, Jean-Pierre, Robert M. Woo, and James Czechowicz, *New Directions in Managing Currency Risk: Changing Corporate Strategies and Systems under FAS No. 52*, New York: Business International, 1982.

Srinivasulu, S. L., "Classifying Foreign Exchange Exposure," *Financial Executive*, February 1983, pp. 36–44.

Stanley, Marjorie T., and Stanley B. Block, "Response by United States Financial Managers to Financial Accounting Standard No. 8," *Journal of International Business Studies*, Fall 1978, pp. 89–99.

Stonehill, Arthur, Niels Ravn, and Kåre Dullum, "Management of Foreign Exchange Economic Exposure," in *International Financial Management*, Stockholm: Norstedt & Soners, 1982, pp. 128–148.

Taussig, Russell A., "Impact of SFAS No. 52 on the Translation of Foreign Financial Statements of Companies in Highly Inflationary Economies," *Journal of Accounting, Auditing and Finance*, Winter 1983, pp. 142–156.

Veazey, Richard F., and Suk H. Kim, "Translation of Foreign Currency Operations: SFAS No. 52," *Columbia Journal of World Business*, Winter 1982, pp. 17–22.

Wurst, Charles M., and Raymond H. Alleman, "Translation Adjustments for a Strong Dollar," *Financial Executive*, June 1984, pp. 38–41.

Wyman, Harold E., "Analysis of Gains and Losses from Foreign Monetary Items: An Application of Purchasing Power Parity Concepts," *Accounting Review*, July 1976, pp. 545–558.

7

Managing Foreign Exchange Exposure

When and how should a multinational firm react to economic, transaction, and translation exposure? Techniques are available to offset each of these exposures, but whether an offset is desirable depends on management's financial objectives. If the firm's goal is to maximize long-run stockholder wealth, reacting to economic exposure is most important because it alone is concerned with the effect foreign exchange rate changes have on future cash flows. If maximizing reported near-term aftertax earnings per share is the goal, reacting to transaction and translation exposure becomes of prime importance.

In deciding when and how to react, management must recognize whether the international equilibrium model introduced in Chapter 5 is functioning according to its underlying theories. In the international equilibrium model, purchasing power parity, the International Fisher Effect, and interest rate parity may all approximate reality in the long run but deviate considerably from equilibrium in the short run because of lags in the adjustment process. If management believes that these markets are usually in equilibrium, it may concentrate on eliminating unexpected deviations through active transaction and translation exposure policies. If disequilibrium is the normal state of affairs, management should concentrate on economic exposure management.

Management must also understand how the firm's own cash flows adjust to inflation, interest, and exchange rate changes. Cash flows may not move as predicted by the macroeconomic indices because of the industry's competitive characteristics, location of the firm's production facilities, or price and income elasticities of demand in its markets. The various possible reactions to an exchange rate change were illustrated by the Instruments Napoleon example in Chapter 6.

The purpose of this chapter is to describe and evaluate those techniques which are commonly used to manage each of the three main types of exposure. The main technique to manage economic exposure is to diversify internationally with respect to sales, production, and financing. Transaction exposure can be offset by hedges in the forward market, money market, and options market. A balance sheet hedge is most appropriate for managing translation exposure. Some firms also use forward and money market hedges for translation exposure, but incur some speculative risk in so doing. A technique called "leads and lags" is useful in managing all three types of exposure. "Swaps" are used to avoid incurring foreign exchange exposure in the first place rather than as a means to offset existing exposure. A final important consideration is whether the benefits derived from managing foreign exchange exposure are worth the costs of such a program.

MANAGING ECONOMIC EXPOSURE

The objective of economic exposure management is to anticipate and influence the effect of unexpected changes in exchange rates on a firm's future cash flows.[1] This objective requires that management recognize a disequilibrium condition when it occurs and that it prepare the firm to react. In keeping with the theme of this book, we feel this task can best be accomplished if a firm diversifies internationally both its operations and its financing base. Diversifying operations means that a firm should diversify internationally its sales, location of production facilities, and raw material sources. Diversifying the financing base means that a firm should source its funds in more than one capital market and in more than one currency.

Depending on management's risk preference, a diversification strategy permits the firm to react either actively or passively to opportunities presented by disequilibrium conditions in the foreign exchange, capital, and product markets. Furthermore, such a strategy does not require management to predict disequilibrium but only to recognize it when it occurs.

Diversifying Operations

If a firm's operations are diversified internationally, management is prepositioned both to recognize disequilibrium when it occurs and to react competitively. Consider the case where purchasing power parity is temporarily in disequilibrium. Although the disequilibrium may have been unpredictable, management can often recognize its symptoms as soon as they occur. For example, management might notice a change in comparative costs in the firm's own plants located in different countries. It might also observe changed profit margins or sales volume in one area compared to another, depending on price and income elasticities of demand and competitors' reactions.

Recognizing this temporary change in worldwide competitive conditions permits management to make changes in operating strategies. Management might make marginal shifts in sourcing raw materials, components, or finished products. If spare capacity exists, production runs can be lengthened in one plant and reduced in another. The marketing effort can be strengthened in export markets where the firm's products have become more price competitive because of the disequilibrium condition.

Even if management does not actively distort normal operations when exchange rates change, the firm should experience some beneficial portfolio effects. The variability of its cash flows is probably reduced by international diversification of its production, sourcing, and sales because exchange rate changes under disequilibrium conditions are likely to increase the firm's competitiveness in some markets while reducing it in others. In that case economic exposure would be neutralized.

In contrast to the internationally diversified multinational firm, a purely domestic firm might be subject to the full impact of foreign exchange economic exposure even though it does not have foreign currency cash flows. For example, it could experience intense import competition in its domestic market from competing firms producing in countries with undervalued currencies. Domestic U.S. television producers were certainly made aware of this problem when Japanese producers captured the U.S. market at a time when the yen was probably undervalued.

A purely domestic firm does not have the option to react to an international disequilibrium condition in the same manner as a multinational firm. In fact, a purely domestic firm will be mispositioned to recognize that a disequilibrium exists because it lacks comparative data from its own internal sources. By the time external data are available from published sources, it is often too late to react. Even if a domestic firm recognizes the disequilibrium condition, it cannot quickly shift production and sales into foreign markets in which it has had no previous presence.

Diversifying Financing

If a firm diversifies its financing sources, it will be pre-positioned to take advantage of temporary deviations from the International Fisher Effect. If interest rate differentials do not equal expected changes in exchange rates, opportunities to lower a firm's cost of capital will exist. However, to be able to switch financing sources, a firm must already be well known in the international investment community, with banking contacts firmly established. Once again, this is not an option for a domestic firm that has limited its financing to one capital market.

In addition to diversifying capital market sources to take advantage of unexpected interest differentials, a multinational firm can reduce its default risk by matching the mix of currencies it borrows to the mix of currencies it expects to receive from operations. A number of firms already use this strategy to neutralize transaction and translation exposure. Nevertheless, this strategy is difficult to implement in practice because a firm cannot predict cash flows very far into the future. In fact, unexpected changes in exchange rates may alter the very flows management is trying to predict, thus changing the currency mix to be matched.

Although we recommend diversification as a strategy of foreign exchange risk management, such a strategy has a potentially favorable impact on other risks as well. In particular, it could reduce the variability of future cash flows due to domestic business cycles, provided these are not perfectly correlated with international flows. It could increase the availability of capital, also reducing its cost, by diversifying such risks as restrictive capital market policies or government borrowing competition in the capital market. It could diversify political risks such as expropriation, war, blocked funds, or just unfavorable changes in laws that reduce or eliminate profitability. The list of advantages from international diversification can even be extended to such areas as spreading the risk of technological obsolescence and reducing portfolio risk in the context of the capital asset pricing model—but now we are preempting the diversification strategy recommendation that will appear throughout the rest of this book.

Constraints exist that may limit the feasibility of a diversification strategy for foreign exchange risk management or one of the other risks just mentioned. For example, the technology of a particular industry may require such large economies of scale that it is not economically feasible to diversify production locations. Firms in this industry could still diversify sales and financing sources, however. On the other hand, the firm may be too small or too unknown to attract international equity investors or lenders. Yet it could at least diversify its sales internationally. Thus a diversification strategy can only be implemented as far as is feasible.

International Automobile Industry: A Case Example of Economic Exposure

The case of the international automobile industry illustrates diversification strategy as a reaction to economic exposure. Prior to World War II several of the largest U.S. automobile manufacturers elected to produce and sell automobiles worldwide. General Motors established manufacturing facilities through acquisitions in Germany (Adam Opel), the United Kingdom (Vauxhall), and Australia (Holden's Pty., Ltd.). These acquisitions created permanent economic exposure in Deutschemarks, British pounds, and Australian pounds (later Australian dollars). In the postwar era, manufacturing plants were also built in such countries as Mexico, Brazil, and Argentina, adding economic exposure in those currencies. Likewise, Ford established an even larger overseas manufacturing base, particularly in Germany and the United Kingdom, thus creating a corresponding degree of economic exposure.

Consequently General Motors and Ford have operated throughout the past four decades with internationally diversified sales and production, as well as a portion of their financing raised in foreign currencies. They were pre-positioned to take advantage of deviations from purchasing power parity. They could, when they wished, shift component sourcing and labor-intensive operations to take advantage of periodic changes in comparative costs. However, the cost advantage of longer production runs and rationalization of component production in countries with a comparative advantage could offset the advantage of temporary foreign exchange rate disequilibria. Political and labor relations also limited the degree of flexibility to shift production.

In contrast, most European and Japanese automobile manufacturers entered the post–World War II period with devastated plants and lost prewar export markets. Their strategy was to rebuild their plants in the home country and attempt to export to obtain badly needed hard currencies for reconstruction. Economies of scale certainly played a role in this decision to centralize production at home. Access to subsidized financing and societal pressures to maximize employment also were motivations.

During the period of fixed exchange rates (1945–1971), both the diversification and nondiversification strategies were viable. U.S. automobile manufacturers benefited from reconstruction and rapid growth of the European market. The real effective dollar exchange rate was relatively high so they produced an increasing share of their European, Australian, and Latin American sales in local plants. On the other hand, European and Japanese manufacturers recaptured significant shares of their home markets and established strong export markets. Their exports were aided by the strong U.S. dollar, which made their export prices relatively attractive, and by the weakness of their home currencies, which made home country production costs relatively low.

The foreign exchange crisis of 1971–1973 and subsequent weakening of the dollar, which changed the competitive equilibrium, illustrates the advantages of international diversification. European manufacturers lost their export advantage, particularly in the U.S. market, because of high European real effective exchange rates compared with a relatively low real effective exchange rate for the dollar. Japanese manufacturers were not as severely affected because the real effective rate for the yen stayed about the same and the Japanese were making rapid improvements in productivity and quality. U.S. manufacturers benefited from a weak dollar. They increased exports to Europe and third markets while remaining competitive in the U.S. market. Their European manufacturing subsidiaries maintained market share in Europe, but faced the same export problems as their European competitors.

The prolonged weakness of the dollar until late 1979 forced European and Japanese manufacturers to change tactics. At first they were able to offset some of the economic exposure damage by improving productivity and taking advantage of economies of scale. Marketing strategies were altered. Instead of featuring low cost, advertising programs emphasized quality control and advanced engineering design. Swedish Volvo, for example, showed its cars negotiating dangerous snow and ice conditions on difficult, winding roads. Volkswagen resale values were cited as proof of quality and endurance. Product policies were altered to feature new luxury models in order to compete in the less price-sensitive segment of the market. Finally, financing was partially shifted from home currency sourcing to dollar sourcing to match more closely dollar inflows from sales. Volkswagen alone raised $150 million in the Eurobond market in 1977.[2]

Despite these tactical attempts to offset economic exposure, European manufacturers in particular gradually lost their export market share outside Europe and began to run operating losses on a consolidated basis. At this point they reevaluated their postwar strategy of centralizing production in the home country with heavy emphasis on exports. Volkswagen decided to produce in Pennsylvania and began operations there in 1978. Renault expanded its equity interest in American Motors and eventually began producing their models in Wisconsin. Volvo and Fiat elected to stay out of U.S. production and lost nearly all their U.S. market share.

Japanese manufacturers were aided by the yen, which was undervalued in real terms, economies of scale, quality improvements, and productivity gains. They also increased their dollar borrowing in the Eurobond market for the same reasons as Volkswagen. Nevertheless they initially chose not to attempt to reduce economic exposure by producing in the United States. A few years later, however, they were forced to reconsider this decision because of political pressure from U.S. labor unions. Voluntary quotas on Japanese automotive exports to the United States and the threat of mandatory U.S. content regulations eventually pressured the Japanese to start U.S. production. Nissan established a manufacturing plant in Tennessee in 1980, and in 1984 Toyota negotiated a joint venture with General Motors for production in California.

Ironically, Japanese entry into U.S. manufacturing came at a time of unprecedented strength for the dollar in real terms. It would have been an ideal time to export everything from Japan. Nevertheless, the day may arrive when the dollar declines in real terms, in which case Japanese and European firms will then benefit from diversification of their economic exposure in the United States.

MANAGING TRANSACTION EXPOSURE

Transaction exposure typically arises when payments must be made or received in a foreign currency. The two most common methods to offset transaction exposure are a forward market hedge and a money market hedge. In recent years an options market hedge has become a third alternative for some types of exposure.

To illustrate how these techniques may be used to protect against transaction exposure, consider an example in which Alvarez, a U.S. manufacturing firm, sells a gas turbine generator to Mercator, a British firm, in March for £1,000,000. Payment is due three months later in June. Alvarez's cost of capital is 15%. The following quotes are available:

Spot exchange rate: $1.4000/£

Three-month forward rate: $1.4175/£ (a 5% per annum premium)

U.K. three-month interest rate: 8.0% per annum (or 2.0%/quarter)

U.S. three-month interest rate: 13.1% per annum (or 3.275%/quarter)

June put option on the Philadelphia Stock Exchange at strike price of 140: 2.50 cents per pound premium

June put option in the over-the-counter (bank) market at strike price of 140: 2.00% premium

Alvarez's foreign exchange advisory service forecasts that the spot rate in three months will be $1.4350, a premium of 10%. That is, they forecast that the pound will strengthen more rapidly in the next three months than the implicit "unbiased forecast" of $1.4175 that exists in the forward quotation.

Four alternatives are available to Alvarez:

- remain unhedged,
- hedge in the forward market,
- hedge in the money market, or
- hedge in the options market.

Unhedged Position

Alvarez may decide to accept the transaction risk. If the firm believes its foreign exchange advisor, it expects to receive £1,000,000 × $1.4350 = $1,435,000 in three months. However, that amount is at risk. If the pound should fall to, say, $1.3800, Alvarez would receive only $1,380,000. This amount is $55,000 less than expected and might be insufficient to cover the manufacturing cost of the gas turbine. Exchange risk is not one-sided, however; if the transaction were left uncovered and the pound strengthened even more than forecast by the advisor, Alvarez could receive considerably more than $1,435,000.

Forward Exchange Market Hedge

A forward exchange market hedge, or "forward hedge," involves a forward contract and a source of funds to fulfill that contract. The forward contract is entered into at the time the transaction exposure is created. In Alvarez's case, that would be in March, when the sale to Mercator was booked as an account receivable. Funds to fulfill the contract will be available in June when Mercator pays £1,000,000 to Alvarez. If funds to fulfill the forward contract are on hand or are due because of a business operation, the hedge is considered "covered," "perfect," or "square" because no residual foreign exchange risk exists. Funds on hand or to be received are matched by funds to be paid.

In some situations funds to fulfill the forward exchange contract are not already available or due later, but must be purchased in the spot market at some future date. Such a hedge is "open" or "uncovered." It involves considerable risk because the hedger must take a chance on purchasing foreign exchange at an uncertain future spot rate in order to fulfill the forward contract. Purchase of such funds at a later date is referred to as "covering." There is an old financial saying that is appropriate for an uncovered forward obligation:

> He who sells what isn't his'n
> Must cover up or go to prison!

Should Alvarez wish to hedge its transaction exposure in the forward market, it will sell the £1,000,000 today at the three-month forward quotation of $1.4175 per pound. This is a "covered transaction" in which the firm no longer has any foreign exchange risk. In three months the firm will receive £1,000,000 from the British buyer, deliver that sum to the bank against its forward sale, and receive $1,417,500. This certain sum is less than the uncertain $1,435,000 expected from the unhedged position because the forward market quotation differs from the firm's three-month forecast.

If Alvarez's forecast of future rates were identical to that implicit in the forward quotation, i.e., $1.4175, expected receipts would be the same whether or not the firm hedges. However, realized receipts under the unhedged alternative could vary considerably from the certain receipts when the transaction is hedged. Belief that the forward rate is an unbiased estimate of the future spot rate does not preclude use of the forward hedge to eliminate the risk of an unexpected change in the future spot rate.

Money Market Hedge

Like a forward market hedge, a money market hedge also involves a contract and a source of funds to fulfill that contract. In this instance the contract is a loan agreement. The firm seeking the money market hedge borrows in one currency and exchanges the proceeds for another currency. Funds to fulfill the contract—i.e., to repay the loan—may be generated from business operations, in which case the money market hedge is "covered." Alternatively, funds to repay the loan may be purchased in the foreign exchange spot market when the loan matures. In this instance the money market hedge is "uncovered" or "open."

The structure of a money market hedge resembles that of a forward exchange hedge. The difference is that the cost of the money market hedge is determined by differential interest rates, while the cost of the forward exchange market hedge is a function of the forward rate quotation. In efficient markets interest rate parity should ensure that these costs are nearly the same, but not all markets are efficient at all times. Furthermore, the difference in interest rates facing a private firm borrowing in two separate national markets may be different than the difference in risk-free government bill rates in these same markets. It is the latter differential that is relevant for interest rate parity.

To hedge in the money market, Alvarez will borrow pounds in London at once, immediately convert the borrowed pounds into dollars, and repay the pound loan in three months with the proceeds from the sale of the generator. How much should Alvarez borrow? It will need to borrow just enough to repay both the principal and interest with the sale proceeds. The interest will be 8% per annum, or 2% for three months. Therefore, assuming that x is the amount of pounds to borrow, we obtain:

$$\begin{aligned} 1.02x &= £1{,}000{,}000 \\ x &= £\ \ 980{,}392 \end{aligned}$$

Alvarez will borrow £980,392 and in three months repay that amount plus £19,608 of interest with the sale proceeds.

Alvarez will exchange the £980,392 for dollars at the current spot rate of $1.4000, receiving $1,372,549 at once. If this sum were invested in the U.S. money market at the three-month rate of 3.275% (13.1% per annum), proceeds of $1,372,549 × 1.03275 = $1,417,500 would be received at the end of three months. This sum is identical to the sum received in the forward exchange hedge explained earlier. The forward exchange hedge and the money market hedge yield identical solutions because quarterly exchange rate differentials are assumed to be identical to quarterly interest differentials. If the forward market and the money market are *not* in equilibrium, one alternative will be superior to the other.

In an example such as this, one should question why Alvarez would invest the dollar proceeds of the pound loan in the U.S. money market instead of using those dollars within the firm, especially since the firm's 15% cost of capital is greater than the U.S. money market rate. Alvarez should prefer the money market hedge to the forward hedge because it can earn internally more than the money market rate of 13.1% per annum. Indeed, if Alvarez's marginal opportunity cost is greater than 18.2% per annum, or 4.55% for three months, it should prefer the certain $1,372,549 at the present time, received via the money market hedge, over the even larger $1,435,000 expected (but not assured) by the unhedged alternative.

The break-even investment rate can be calculated as follows: Assume that r is the unknown internal opportunity cost for three months, expressed as a decimal. We have:

$$\$1{,}372{,}549\ (1 + r) = \$1{,}435{,}000$$
$$r = .0455$$

If the certain $1,372,549 were invested internally for three months at 4.55%, its value would grow to the $1,435,000 expected three months hence from the unhedged alternative.

Options Market Hedge

Alvarez could cover its £1,000,000 exposure by purchasing a *put* option. This technique allows Alvarez to speculate on the upside potential for appreciation of the pound while limiting downside risk to a known amount.

Based on the quotes shown earlier, Alvarez could purchase a put option on the Philadelphia Stock Exchange having a June expiration date, a strike price of 140, a premium cost of 2.50 cents per pound, and a contract size of £12,500. The cost of this option is as follows:

Premium cost per option ($0.025 × £12,500)	$312.50
Brokerage cost per option	25.00
Total cost per option	$337.50
Option cost per pound ($337.50 /£12,500)	$0.0270
Number of options needed (£1,000,000/£12,500)	80
Total cost for 80 options (80 × $337.50)	$27,000

Alvarez could also purchase a similar put option from its bank for a 2.00% premium. Its cost would be $1,400,000 × .02 = $28,000. Therefore Alvarez would choose the Philadelphia put option, which costs $1,000 less. When the £1,000,000 is received in June, the value in dollars depends on the spot rate at that time. The upside potential is unlimited, the same as in the unhedged alternative. At any exchange rate above $1.4000 Alvarez would allow its option to expire unexercised and would exchange the pounds for dollars at the spot rate. That rate might be $1.4175 (the forward rate), $1.4350 (the expected rate), or even a higher rate.

If the expected rate of $1.4350/£ materializes, for example, Alvarez would exchange the £1,000,000 in the spot market for $1,435,000. Net proceeds would be $1,435,000 minus the $27,000 cost of the options, or $1,408,000.

In contrast to the unhedged alternative, however, downside risk is limited with an option. If the pound depreciates below $1.4000, Alvarez would exercise its option to sell (put) £1,000,000 at $1.4000/£, receiving

$1,400,000 gross, but $1,373,000 net of the $27,000 cost of the option. Although this downside result is worse than the downside of the forward or money market hedges, the upside potential is not limited the way it is with those hedges. Thus, whether the option strategy is superior to a forward or money market hedge depends on the degree to which management is risk averse.

We can calculate a trading range for the pound that defines the break-even points for the option compared with the other strategies. The upper bound of the range is determined by comparison with the forward rate. The pound must appreciate enough above the $1.4175 forward rate to cover the $0.0270/£ cost of the unexercised option. Therefore the break-even upside spot price of the pound must be $1.4175 + $0.0270 = $1.4445. If the spot pound appreciates above $1.4445, proceeds under the option strategy will be greater than under the forward hedge. If the spot pound ends up below $1.4445 the forward hedge would be superior in retrospect.

The lower bound of the range is determined by a comparison with the unhedged strategy. If the spot price falls below $1.4000, Alvarez will exercise its put option and sell the proceeds at $1.4000. The net proceeds per pound will be $1.4000 less the $0.0270 cost of the option, or $1.3730. If the spot rate falls below $1.3730, the net proceeds from exercising the option will be greater than the net proceeds from selling the unhedged pounds in the spot market. At any spot rate above $1.3730 the spot proceeds from the unhedged alternative will be greater.

Strategy Comparison

The four alternatives available to Alvarez are shown in Exhibit 7.1. If forward rates and money market rates are in equilibrium and Alvarez invests temporary cash balances in the money market, both hedged positions produce a certain $1,417,500 in three months. The forward market hedge does not allow variation on this result, but the money market hedge permits the firm to change the risk situation and invest temporary cash balances at some other rate. To the extent that different end results are achieved by changing the risk situation, the two hedges are not directly comparable.

If Alvarez does not hedge, it can "expect" $1,435,000 in three months. However, this sum is at risk and might be greater or smaller. If, for example, the spot rate in three months were $1.4175, the rate implied in the forward quotation, the unhedged alternative would also provide $1,417,500. Under conditions when the forward rate is accepted as the most likely future spot rate, the expected results from an unhedged position are identical to the certain results from either of the two hedged positions. Under such circumstances the advantage of hedging over remaining unhedged is the reduction of uncertainty.

EXHIBIT 7.1
Comparison of Alternative Hedging Strategies

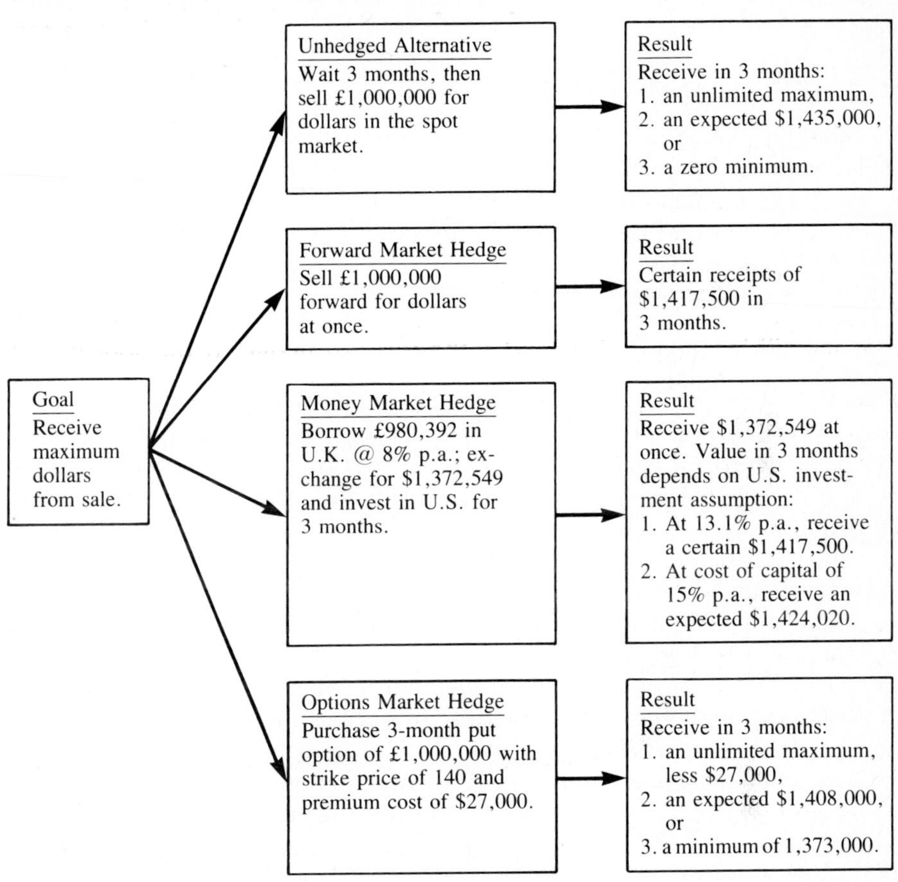

The options market hedge has nearly the same upside potential as the unhedged alternative, except for the cost of the option, but limits the downside risk to receiving $1,373,000.

Foreign currency options have a variety of hedging uses beyond the one illustrated by Alvarez. A put option can be useful to construction firms or other exporters when they must submit a fixed price bid in a foreign currency without knowing until some later date whether their bid is successful. A put option can be used to hedge the foreign exchange risk either for the bidding period alone or for the entire period of potential exposure if the bid is won. If the bid is rejected, the loss is limited to the cost of the option. In contrast, if the risk is hedged by a forward contract and the bid is rejected, the forward contract must be reversed or eventually fulfilled at an unknown potential loss or gain. The bidder has an uncovered forward contract.

MANAGING TRANSLATION EXPOSURE

Translation exposure arises from consolidating assets and liabilities measured in foreign currencies with those in the reporting currency. The main technique to manage translation exposure is called a "balance sheet hedge." Forward hedges and money market hedges can also be used, but only with speculative overtones.

Balance Sheet Hedge

A balance sheet hedge calls for having an equal amount of exposed foreign currency assets and liabilities on a firm's consolidated balance sheet. If this can be achieved for each foreign currency, net translation exposure will be zero. A change in exchange rates will change the value of exposed assets in an equal but opposite direction to the change in value of exposed liabilities. If a firm translates by the monetary/nonmonetary method, a zero net exposed position is called "monetary balance."

Since translation exposure is measured by currency, not by country, equality of exposed assets and liabilities need be achieved only on a worldwide basis and not on the individual balance sheets of each foreign affiliate. Although FAS #52 generally prescribes the current rate method of translation, it should be remembered that the balance sheet of a foreign affiliate whose functional currency is the dollar creates translation exposure by the monetary/nonmonetary method rather than the current rate method.

The cost of a balance sheet hedge depends on relative borrowing costs. If foreign currency borrowing costs, after adjusting for foreign exchange risk, are higher than parent currency borrowing costs, the balance sheet hedge has a positive cost, and vice versa. It should be noted, however, that normal operations already involve decisions about the magnitude and currency denomination of specific balance sheet accounts. Thus, balance sheet hedges are a compromise in which the denomination of balance sheet accounts is altered, perhaps at a cost in terms of borrowing costs and operating efficiency, to achieve some degree of foreign exchange protection.

To illustrate a balance sheet hedge, assume that Pindus is the Greek affiliate of Henley, a U.S. firm. Pindus has the balance sheet shown in Exhibit 7.2. All local accounts are in drachmas (symbol *Dr*), and translation exposure by the current rate method and the monetary/nonmonetary method is Dr7,500,000 and Dr1,200,000, respectively, as shown.

At the current spot rate of $0.0200/Dr (Dr50/$), the parent's exposure in dollars is as follows:

EXHIBIT 7.2
Pindus Company Balance Sheet and Exposure (in thousands of drachmas)

	Balance sheet accounts	*Current rate exposure*	*Monetary/ nonmonetary exposure*
Assets			
Cash	1,800	1,800	1,800
Accounts receivable	3,600	3,600	3,600
Inventory	2,700	2,700	
Net fixed plant and equipment	3,600	3,600	
Total assets	11,700		
Total exposed assets		11,700	5,400
Liabilities and Capital			
Accounts payable	900	900	900
Notes payable	900	900	900
Long-term debt	2,400	2,400	2,400
Shareholder's equity	7,500		
Total liabilities and capital	11,700		
Total exposed liabilities		4,200	4,200
Net exposed assets		7,500	1,200

Current rate method: Dr7,500,000 × $0.0200/Dr = $150,000

Monetary/nonmonetary method: Dr1,200,000 × $0.0200/Dr = $ 24,000

Management believes that within one year the drachma will drop in value relative to the dollar by 20% to $0.0160/Dr. Should such a devaluation occur, Henley will have a translation loss equal to 20% of the net exposed assets:

Translation loss, current rate method: $150,000 × .20 = $30,000

Translation loss, monetary/nonmonetary method: $24,000 × .20 = $ 4,800

Under the current rate method the translation loss will be reflected directly in the cumulative translation adjustment account, while under the monetary/nonmonetary method the substantially smaller loss will flow through the income statement and reduce current earnings.

If Henley wishes to avoid translation exposure in drachmas, two types of balance sheet hedges are available. On the asset side, it can reduce exposed drachma assets without a corresponding reduction in drachma liabilities. For example, it can exchange drachma cash or receivables for dollars, if this is allowed by the monetary authorities. On the liability side, two steps are necessary: (1) drachmas must be borrowed by Pindus, by Henley, or by a third affiliate, and (2) those drachmas must be exchanged for nonexposed assets.

Current rate method Under the current rate method, Dr7,500,000 should be borrowed. If Pindus borrows drachmas, the effect of the first step is to increase both an exposed asset (cash) and an exposed liability (notes payable) on the balance sheet of Pindus, with no effect on net exposed assets. The required second step has two possibilities: (1) Pindus could exchange the acquired drachmas for dollars, which Pindus could continue to hold if allowed by Greek foreign exchange regulations; (2) Pindus could transfer the borrowed drachmas to Henley, perhaps as a drachma dividend or repayment of intracompany debt. Then Henley would exchange the drachmas for dollars.

Drachmas may also be borrowed by Henley (or a third affiliate), thus keeping the drachma debt off of Pindus's books. However, again the second step is essential if worldwide exposure in drachmas is to be eliminated. Henley must exchange the borrowed drachmas for dollars or other nonexposed assets.

Any such borrowing should be coordinated by Henley to avoid the possibility that one affiliate is borrowing drachmas while another is repaying a drachma loan. This may not seem likely with drachmas, since that currency is used only in Greece, but it could easily happen with the widely traded currencies.

Monetary/nonmonetary method If translation is by the monetary/nonmonetary method, Dr1,200,000 should be borrowed. As before, Pindus could borrow these drachmas and use them to acquire dollars. However, it could also use the loan proceeds to acquire inventory or fixed assets. Under the monetary/nonmonetary method these assets are not exposed.

Forward Exchange Market Hedge

To hedge translation exposure in the forward market, a firm must sell the exposed currency in the forward market now, purchase that currency in the spot market later, and deliver the purchased currency against the forward contract. The size of the necessary forward contract is determined by the following formula:

$$\text{Forward contract size} = \frac{\text{potential translation loss in dollars}}{\begin{array}{c}\text{forward rate in}\\ \text{dollars per local}\\ \text{currency unit}\end{array} - \begin{array}{c}\text{expected future spot}\\ \text{rate in dollars per}\\ \text{local currency unit}\end{array}}$$

The denominator, the difference between the forward rate and the expected future spot rate, with rates expressed on a direct basis, gives expected profit per unit of the parent's reporting currency. Dividing this profit per unit into the potential translation loss gives the amount of exposed currency that must be sold forward.

In the case of Pindus, the financial manager forecasts a spot rate one year hence of \$0.0160/Dr at a time when the one-year forward quote is \$0.0180/Dr. Application of the formula to protect against the expected translation loss under each of the translation methods gives the following contract sizes:

$$\text{Current rate method} = \frac{\$30{,}000}{\$0.0180/\text{Dr} - \$0.0160/\text{Dr}} = \begin{array}{l}\text{Dr15,000,000}\\ \text{contract size}\end{array}$$

$$\begin{array}{l}\text{Monetary/}\\ \text{nonmonetary method}\end{array} = \frac{\$4{,}800}{\$0.0180/\text{Dr} - \$0.0160/\text{Dr}} = \begin{array}{l}\text{Dr2,400,000}\\ \text{contract size}\end{array}$$

If Pindus sells drachmas at \$0.0180, the current quote on the forward market, and buys them later in the spot market at their expected price of \$0.0160, it will make a profit of \$0.0020 on each drachma. Total profit on the hedge, using the contract size of Dr15,000,000 specified by the current rate method, would be calculated as follows:

Sell drachmas forward at present forward quotation (Dr15,000,000 × \$0.0180/Dr):	\$270,000
Less cost of drachmas purchased next year for delivery against contract (Dr15,000,000 × \$0.0160/Dr):	240,000
Net profit on forward hedge:	\$ 30,000

By a similar calculation, profit on a contract size of Dr2,400,000 would be \$4,800.

If the drachma devalues as anticipated, the forward hedge provides profit equal to the expected translation loss. One must note, however, that the size of the contract is determined by the accounting rules in force. If the company is to avoid translation losses and if it reports by the current rate method, a contract substantially larger than that required with use of the monetary/nonmonetary method is needed. The fact that a "real" event, the purchase of a forward contract of a different size, is caused by selection of an accounting rule emphasizes that steps taken to remove translation loss may not be accomplishing a basic economic purpose.

In the above example two important complications exist: taxes and speculation. For simplicity the following example will be based on the Dr15 million contract needed under the current rate method. The reader may wish to work out similar calculations for the monetary/nonmonetary method.

Taxes Translation losses are not deductible from taxable income, but profits on forward contracts create taxable income. In this respect hedging to protect against a translation loss differs from hedging to protect against a transaction loss. In the transaction hedge, profit in the forward market exactly offsets an operating loss and vice versa. Thus the hedge preserves an existing profit situation and does not change overall taxable income. In the translation hedge, if the firm's marginal income tax rate is 50%, the contract size must be doubled—to Dr30,000,000 in the above example. This action would produce a pretax profit on the contract of $60,000, which, after payment of half as income tax, would leave $30,000 to offset the translation loss.

The income tax effect can be minimized by having the forward contract carried out by any affiliate of the multinational parent that is located in a low-tax jurisdiction. If, for example, both Greece and the United States had a 50% income tax, but an affiliate in Switzerland, whose statements would also be consolidated into those of the parent, had only a 20% tax liability, the Swiss affiliate could carry out the forward exchange market hedge with a much smaller contract. The aftertax effect on the parent's consolidated financial statement would be the same.

From a practical point of view a very large forward contract is often necessary to cover a potential translation loss after taxes. Sometimes such a contract will be too big for the financial resources of the hedging firm. Even though no cash transaction takes place when the forward contract is negotiated, the negotiating bank is extending credit on the basis of the firm's ability to pay at maturity. If the contract is too large relative to the firm, the bank may decline to enter into the contract.

Speculation The second complication arises because use of a forward market hedge to reduce translation loss creates an "uncovered" position. In the previous tax-free example the $30,000 profit on the forward contract offsets the $30,000 translation loss *only* when the ending spot exchange rate is $.0160 per drachma. At any other ending spot exchange rate gains and losses on translation and on the forward hedge will be different. This outcome is illustrated in Exhibit 7.3. If the amount of drachma devaluation is less than forecast, or if the drachma appreciates rather than devalues, Henley will experience a net loss that could be very large. If the drachma should devalue more than forecast, Henley will profit more on the forward contract than it will lose in translation.

A forward contract is a matched hedge against a translation loss *only* if the firm correctly forecasts the future spot exchange rate. Any error in this forecast will lead to a mismatch in the hedge, with the firm either losing or gaining depending on the direction of the error. *Thus an uncovered forward market hedge is pure speculation, which could just as easily be negotiated without regard to the amount of translation exposure.*

EXHIBIT 7.3
Pindus Company: Forward-Hedging Results in Relation to Exchange Rate Changes

Amount of change in spot rate	*Spot rate after change*	*Profit (loss) on forward transaction*	*Translation gain (loss)*	*Net gain (loss)*
40% devaluation	$.0120	$90,000	$(60,000)	$30,000
30% devaluation	.0140	60,000	(45,000)	15,000
20% devaluation	.0160	30,000	(30,000)	0
10% devaluation	.0180	0	(15,000)	(15,000)
No change	.0200	(30,000)	0	(30,000)
10% appreciation	.0220	(60,000)	15,000	(45,000)
20% appreciation	.0240	(90,000)	30,000	(60,000)
30% appreciation	.0260	(120,000)	45,000	(75,000)
40% appreciation	.0280	(150,000)	60,000	(90,000)

Assumptions: Initial exchange rate = $.0200/Dr; Dr15,000,000 sold forward at $.0180/Dr; no income taxes. The alternative in the box is the expected result.

Money Market Hedge

A particular variation of a balance sheet hedge for reducing translation exposure is a money market hedge. To hedge its drachma translation exposure, either Pindus or Henley could borrow drachmas, exchange the drachmas for dollars, and invest the dollars.

At maturity the dollar proceeds of the investment would be exchanged into drachmas to repay the drachma loan. The maturity of the dollar investment must match the maturity of the drachma loan, and the amount borrowed should be the exact amount of translation exposure.

To illustrate the technique, assume that the interest rate paid to borrow drachmas is 16% and the interest rate earned on dollars is 12%. Also assume, as we did earlier, that the drachma is expected to devalue by 20% within one year, and income taxes are not a concern. Either Pindus or Henley should do the following:

Step 1. Borrow Dr7,500,000 for one year at 16%, promising to repay principal and interest one year hence of (Dr7,500,000)(1.16) = Dr8,700,000.

Step 2. Exchange the drachmas for dollars at the current spot rate: (Dr7,500,000)($.0200) = $150,000.

Step 3. Invest the dollars for one year at 12%, receiving at maturity ($150,000)(1.12) = $168,000.

Step 4. One year hence exchange sufficient dollars for drachmas to repay the drachma loan plus interest. If the ending exchange rate is \$.0160/Dr as anticipated, the dollars needed will be (Dr8,700,000)(\$.0160) = \$139,200.

The net profit on the money market operation would be as follows:

Amount received at maturity of dollar investment	\$168,000
Less amount needed to repay drachma loan and interest	139,200
Profit on money market operation	\$ 28,800
Less translation loss	0
Net profit on money market hedge	\$ 28,800

Several comments on the use of the money market hedge to protect against translation losses are in order. The total operation consists of two parts: a covered hedge against translation exposure and a speculative position taken in relationship to interest rate differentials and probable devaluation. The translation exposure is hedged completely because the amount of exposed currency borrowed is exactly equal to net exposed assets. During the entire period exposed drachma assets will be equal to exposed drachma liabilities.

The money market portion of the operation is speculative because a profit or loss will be made, depending on the ending spot exchange. This relationship is summarized in Exhibit 7.4 using the interest rates assumed earlier. Devaluations of 10% or greater cause Pindus to gain on the money market operation. The break-even exchange rate is \$.0193/Dr, a devaluation of 3.5%. The larger the devaluation the larger the gain, because fewer dollars are needed to repay the drachma loan. If there is no change in the value of the drachma, or if the drachma appreciates in value, Pindus will lose on the money market operation, because more dollars will be needed to repay the drachma loan than were generated by the dollar investment. Since translation exposure is zero, the net gain or loss on the hedge operation is equal to the gain or loss on the money market portion alone.

LEADS AND LAGS—THE TIMING OF FUND TRANSFERS

Firms can reduce foreign exchange exposure by accelerating or decelerating the timing of payments that must be made in a different currency, i.e., by "leading" or "lagging" the movement of funds. Leading and lagging may be done between affiliates or with independent firms. Assuming that payment would be made eventually, leading or lagging always results in changing the assets or liabilities in one firm, with the reverse effect on the other firm. It thus results in a change of balance sheet positions and so can be considered as a technique for achieving a hedged balance sheet position.

EXHIBIT 7.4
Pindus Company: Money Market Hedge in Relation to Exchange Rate Changes

Amount of change in spot rate	*Spot rate after change*	*Profit (loss) on money market operation*	*Translation gain (loss)*	*Net gain (loss)*
40% devaluation	$.0120	$63,600	0	$63,600
30% devaluation	.0140	46,200	0	46,200
20% devaluation	.0160	28,800	0	28,800
10% devaluation	.0180	11,400	0	11,400
No change	.0200	(6,000)	0	(6,000)
10% appreciation	.0220	(23,400)	0	(23,400)
20% appreciation	.0240	(40,800)	0	(40,800)
30% appreciation	.0260	(58,200)	0	(58,200)
40% appreciation	.0280	(75,600)	0	(75,600)

Assumptions: Initial exchange rate = $.0200/Dr; Dr7,500,000 borrowed at 16% for one year, exchanged for dollars, and invested at 12% for one year; no income taxes. The alternative in the box is the expected result.

Leading or lagging between independent firms requires that the time preference of one firm be imposed to the detriment of the other firm. For example, a German firm may wish to lead in collecting its Italian accounts receivable that are denominated in lira because it expects the lira to drop in value compared with the Deutschemark. But why should the Italian customers prepay their accounts payable? Credit was part of the inducement for them to purchase from the German firm. The only way the Italians would willingly lead their accounts payable would be for the German creditor to offer them a discount about equal to the forward discount on the lira or, in equilibrium, the difference between Italian and German interest rates for the period of prepayment.

Leading and lagging between related firms is more feasible because they presumably embrace a common set of goals for the consolidated group. Furthermore, periodic payments are often made between units of a multinational firm, providing the opportunity for many types of leads or lags. Reasons for such flows are shown in Exhibit 7.5. Some are for basic operational purposes, such as the shipment from one affiliate to another of raw material, goods, or partially assembled components. Payments may be made for the use of corporate facilities, such as ships, aircraft, and communication services, or for the use of technology or management services. Because opportunities for leading or lagging payments depend on the requirement for payments of this nature, the device is more readily adaptable to a company that operates on an integrated worldwide basis. If each unit functions

EXHIBIT 7.5
Natural Fund Flows within a Multinational Corporate Network

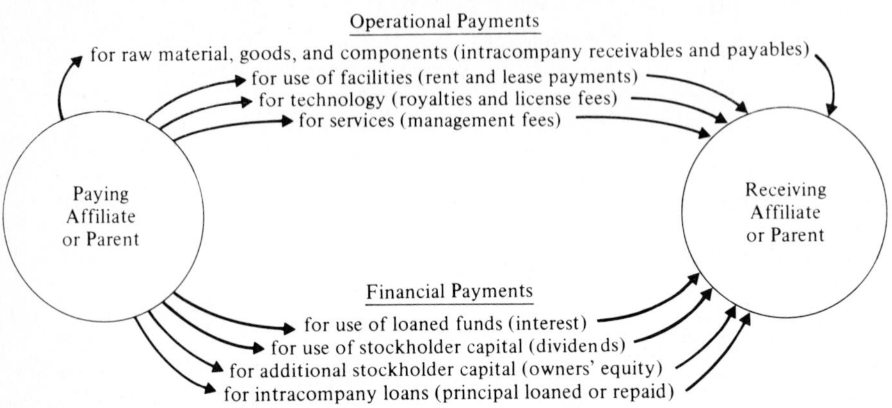

as a separate and self-sufficient entity, opportunities for leading or lagging disappear.

Another set of payment opportunities arises from the financing of foreign affiliates. As shown at the bottom of Exhibit 7.5, these may include interest payments, repaying principal on intracorporate loans, supplying owners' equity, and paying dividends to the owners. In addition to foreign exchange rate considerations, however, the motivation for early or late financial payments could be to position funds for liquidity reasons. Indeed, liquidity considerations may predominate, because under equilibrium conditions nothing can be gained from leading or lagging.

A necessary condition for efficient use of leads and lags is the ability of the parent to adjust its techniques for measuring profit or controlling investment in assets by its various affiliates so that the performance rating of units or of managers is not changed when one unit "helps" another for the good of the overall enterprise.This strategy is discussed in Chapter 16.

Because the use of leads and lags is an obvious technique for minimizing foreign exchange exposure and for shifting the burden of financing, most governments impose some limits on the allowed range. Exhibit 7.6 shows the limits on leads and lags as well as on intracompany netting allowed by a set of selected countries.

USING FOREIGN EXCHANGE SWAPS TO REDUCE EXPOSURE

A foreign exchange swap is an agreement between two parties to exchange a given amount of one currency for another and, after a period of time, to give back the original amounts swapped. A transaction in the spot market

EXHIBIT 7.6

Limits on Leads and Lags and Netting in Selected Countries*

(Periods given below are maximum possible terms)

Country	Export lag	Export lead	Import lag	Import lead	Netting
Argentina	180 days	Allowed–no limit	Allowed–no limit	Not allowed	Not permitted
Australia	180 days[1]	30 days	180 days[2]	30 days[2]	Permission required
Belgium	180 days[3]	90 days[3]	180 days[3]	90 days[3]	Permission required
Brazil	Not allowed	Allowed–no limit	180 days	Not allowed[4]	Not permitted
Canada	Allowed–no limit	Allowed–no limit	Allowed–no limit	Allowed–no limit	Permitted
Denmark	30 days[5]	Allowed–no limit[6]	Allowed–no limit[6]	30 days[5]	Permitted
France	180 days[7]	Allowed–no limit	Allowed–no limit	Permission required[8]	Permission required but difficult
Germany	Allowed–no limit	Allowed–no limit	Allowed–no limit	Allowed–no limit	Permitted
Ireland	180 days	Allowed–no limit	Allowed–no limit[9]	Not allowed[10]	Permission required but readily available
Italy	120 days[11]	360 days	360 days	60 days	Not permitted[12]
Japan	180 days	180 days[13]	120 days[14]	120 days[14]	Not permitted[15]
Korea	Permitted but not encouraged	Permission required	Permitted but not encouraged	Permission required but rare	Permitted
Malaysia	180 days[16]	Allowed–no limit[16]	Allowed–no limit	Allowed–no limit	Permitted[17]
Mexico	Allowed–no limit	Allowed–no limit	Allowed–no limit	Allowed–no limit	Permitted
Netherlands	Allowed–no limit	Allowed–no limit	Allowed–no limit	Allowed–no limit	Permitted
New Zealand	180 days	Allowed–no limit[18]	Allowed–no limit[19]	Not allowed[20]	Permission required[21]
Pakistan	120 days	Allowed–no limit	Not allowed	Not allowed	Not permitted
Philippines	60 days[32]	Allowed–no limit	90 days	Not allowed	Permission required
Singapore	180 days[22]	Allowed–no limit	Allowed–no limit	Allowed–no limit	Permitted[23]
South Africa	180 days[24]	Allowed–no limit	Allowed–no limit	Not allowed[25]	Not permitted except with special permission
Spain	90 days	180 days	180 days[26]	Not allowed[27]	Permission required but difficult
Sweden	Commercial practice[28]	Allowed–no limit	180 days[28]	Permission required[29]	Permission required[30]
Switzerland	Allowed–no limit	Allowed–no limit	Allowed–no limit	Allowed–no limit	Permitted
Taiwan	Generally not permitted[31]	Tolerated[31]	Tolerated[31]	Permitted in some cases[31]	Not possible
UK	180 days	Allowed–no limit	Allowed–no limit	Not allowed	Permitted
US	Allowed–no limit	Allowed–no limit	Allowed–no limit	Allowed–no limit	Permitted

* Based on information primarily obtained locally from finance ministries, central and commercial banks.

FOOTNOTES (1) Deferred terms are approved for export of capital equipment and in some instances where goods are sent abroad on consignment; foreign currency proceeds are permitted to be held overseas for a maximum of one month to meet firm commitments falling due abroad; (2) Longer periods may be granted by Reserve Bank if normal commercial practice with goods is involved; (3) Belgium/Luxembourg Exchange Institute requires permission for all commercial payments above Bfr10 million; (4) Except with special permission from exchange department of central bank for a maximum of 25% of value of imports; (5) Maximum allowed deviation from original date of payment stipulated by trading partners in the contracts, which must be in conformity with normal commercial practices for the particular line of business involved; (6) When customary within the trade; (7) Receipts must now be converted into francs within 8 days, although in practice an extension of a few days is tolerated; (8) Allowances are made for 30% down payment on imported capital goods and 10% down payment for noncapital goods; (9) Officially there is a 9-month limitation, but this is never followed in practice; (10) Sometimes allowed for capital goods; (11) Once payment is received, Italian exporters must convert proceeds into lire within 15 days; (12) Italian exchange office of Foreign Trade Ministry can authorize exceptions; for firms that are both importers and exporters, "compensations" can be effected between their exchange receipts and payments, allowing more flexibility in leads and lags; (13) But exporters are allowed to receive advances for up to 12 months on export contracts of less than $500,000; (14) But importers are usually bound by the contracted time of payment; (15) Except for "invisible" trade-related items, such as harbor charges, warehouse fees, etc.; (16) Payments must be in certain specified currencies; (17) Except for payment of exports as noted and for receipt of loan funds by Malaysian companies; (18) But not customary, except in the wool trade; (19) If more than 12 months, consent of the Overseas Investment Commission must be obtained; (20) In special cases, the Reserve Bank will allow early deposits—down payments—on capital equipment where called for by usual trade practice; (21) But is not usual—in general, exceptions or qualifications to the above rules are unusual and authorities are reluctant to make concessions; (22) Permission of the Monetary Authority of Singapore necessary if proceeds are expected to be received more than 6 months after shipment date; (23) For transactions relating to payments for goods and services; offsetting in relation to loans requires specific MAS approval; (24) Once payment is received, exporter can hold foreign exchange for 7 days; (25) Except with special exchange control approval, and after specially designed equipment is ordered; (26) Includes a 90-day grace period; permission may be obtained for lags up to a year rather easily, but is more difficult for longer periods; (27) Special permit may allow down payment of up to 25% when the order is placed; higher down payments may at times be negotiated; (28) Normally follows customary conditions of payment; otherwise 180 days maximum; (29) Allowed only for normal one-third down payment on machinery and related goods, and consignments of under Skr50,000; (30) Must be based on current payments, and is authorized only if it involves balancing out of accounts between Swedish parents and their foreign subsidiaries; (31) Technically these practices are allowed, since there are no specific regulations concerning leads and lags; however, the country's all-embracing exchange control system ordinarily makes leads and lags impractical; (32) The full value of exports is normally required to be remitted within 60 days, but lags of up to 180 days are allowed for new exports or sales to new markets.

Source: Reprinted from the April 1, 1977, issue of *Business International* with permission of the publisher, Business International Corporation (New York).

matched by an offsetting transaction in the forward market—e.g., covered interest arbitrage—is one type of swap arrangement. Other types of foreign exchange swap arrangements are the "back-to-back" or "parallel loan," the "currency swap," and the "credit swap." These are used to reduce foreign exchange translation and transaction exposure prior to entering into a potentially risky venture. Hence they are usually negotiated before an exposed situation is created.[3]

An interest rate swap is a similar technique used to reduce financial costs. Interest rate swaps are explained in Chapter 11.

Back-to-Back, or Parallel, Loans

A back-to-back, or parallel, loan involves two business firms in separate countries arranging to borrow each other's currency for a specific period of time. At an agreed terminal date they return the borrowed currencies. The operation is conducted outside the foreign exchange markets, although spot quotations may be used as the reference point for determining the amount of funds to be swapped. Such a swap creates a covered hedge against exchange loss, since each company, on its own books, borrows the same currency it repays. Back-to-back loans are also used at a time of actual or anticipated legal limitations on the transfer of investment funds to or from either country.

The structure of a typical back-to-back loan is illustrated in Exhibit 7.7. In the basic swap, shown at the top of the exhibit, a British parent firm wanting to invest funds in its Dutch affiliate locates a Dutch parent firm that wants to invest funds in Britain. Avoiding the exchange markets entirely, the British parent lends pounds to the Dutch affiliate in the United Kingdom, while the Dutch parent lends guilders to the British affiliate in the Netherlands. The two loans would be for equal values at the current spot rate and for a specified maturity. At maturity the two separate loans would each be repaid to the original lender, again without any need to use the foreign exchange markets. Neither loan carries any foreign exchange risk, and neither loan normally needs the approval of any governmental body regulating the availability of foreign exchange for investment purposes.

Parent company guarantees are not needed on the back-to-back loans because each loan carries the right of offset in the event of default of the other loan. A further agreement can provide for maintenance of principal parity in case of changes in the spot rate between the two countries. For example, if the pound dropped by more than, say, 6% for as long as 30 days, the British parent might have to advance additional pounds to the Dutch affiliate so as to bring the principal value of the two loans back to parity. A similar provision would protect the British if the guilder should weaken. Although this parity provision might lead to changes in the amount

EXHIBIT 7.7
Structure of a Back-to-Back, or Parallel, Loan

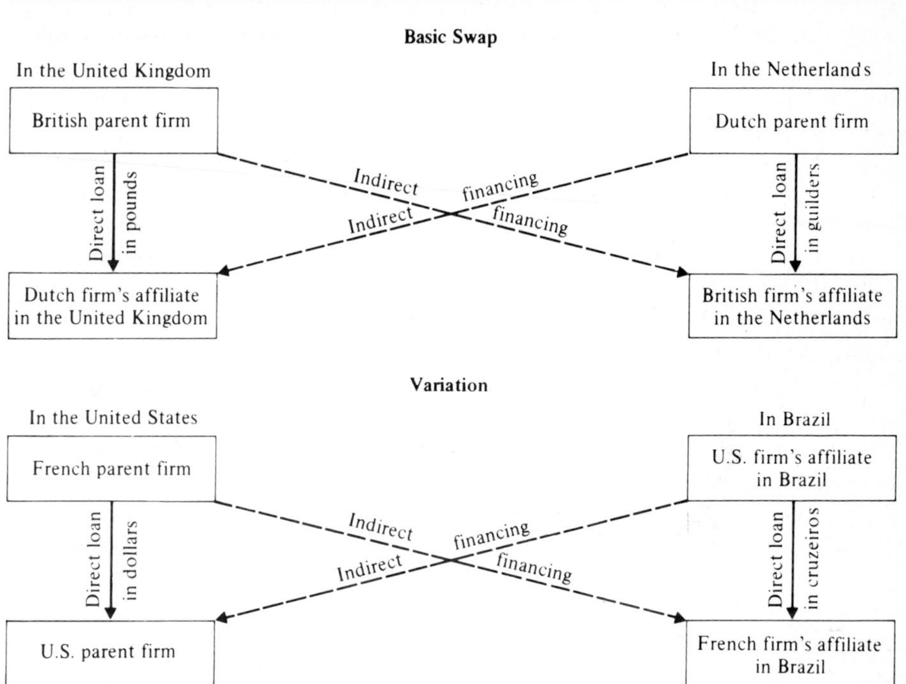

of home currency each party must lend during the period of the agreement, it does not increase foreign exchange risk, because at maturity all loans are repaid in the same currency loaned.

A number of variations may be developed on the basic swap theme, including use of foreign finance subsidiaries and triangular relationships. A variation involving blocked funds is shown in the bottom half of Exhibit 7.7. Assume that the Brazilian affiliate of a U.S. firm has cruzeiros in Brazil that it cannot remit to the United States because of Brazilian restrictions on the repatriation of funds. The Brazilian affiliate of the U.S. firm locates another foreign firm in Brazil that needs cruzeiros for expansion. In the example this is a French affiliate. In the example the U.S. affiliate in Brazil lends cruzeiros to the French affiliate, while in the United States the French parent lends dollars to the U.S. parent. Of course, it would be equally possible for the French parent to loan francs to the U.S. parent's affiliate in France. One can even imagine the French parent arranging for its affiliate in Egypt to loan Egyptian pounds to a U.S. affiliate in that country.

Interest may or may not be involved in a back-to-back loan, depending on whether internal interest rates in the two countries are similar or widely divergent. In one instance, for example, an interest rate differential of .75% was reported for such a loan between the United States and the United Kingdom, in comparison to a rate for hedging in the forward market of 2.75%.[4] In this particular instance a U.S.-based leasing firm loaned $10 million to a major U.S. machine tool manufacturer on behalf of a British firm that owed that sum to the U.S. equipment firm. The parallel part of the swap involved the British firm lending the pound equivalent of $10 million to the British affiliate of the U.S. leasing company. The British firm agreed to pay the U.S. leasing company 10% interest per annum in the United States, while the U.S. leasing affiliate in the United Kingdom paid interest at the rate of 10.75%. Some back-to-back loans are arranged with floating interest rates.

Although the concept of back-to-back loans is simple, difficulties do arise in locating the other side of a transaction. Commercial banks, for whom such loans are a form of competition, seldom attempt to broker arrangements, although on occasion they do facilitate negotiations between firms that are clients of the bank. Usually parties must locate each other directly or through some other type of financial institution such as investment banks.

Currency Swap

A currency swap resembles a back-to-back loan except that it does not appear on a firm's balance sheet. Typically, two firms agree to exchange an equivalent amount of two different currencies for a specified period of time. Currency swaps can be negotiated for a wide range of maturities up to at least ten years. If funds are more expensive in one country than another, a fee may be required to compensate for the interest differential.

Accountants in the United States treat the currency swap as a foreign exchange transaction rather than as debt and treat the obligation to reverse the swap at some later date as a forward exchange contract. Forward exchange contracts can be matched against assets under FAS #52, but they are entered in a firm's footnotes rather than as balance sheet items. The result is that translation and transaction exposures are avoided, but neither a long-term receivable nor a long-term debt is created on the balance sheet. The risk of changes in currency rates to the implied collateral in a long-term currency swap can be treated with a clause similar to the maintenance of principal clause in a back-to-back loan. If exchange rates change by more than some specified amount, say 10%, an additional amount of the weaker currency might have to be advanced.

Currency swaps are sometimes used with interest rate swaps, as explained in Chapter 11, to reduce the cost of borrowing.

Credit Swaps

A credit swap is an exchange of currencies between a business firm and a bank (often the central bank) of a foreign country, which is to be reversed at some future date.

The basic concept of a credit swap has been used for more than half a century between commercial banks, and between commercial banks and central banks, to satisfy temporary bank needs for foreign exchange. However, use of credit swaps between business firms and banks is a post–World War II development that arose when U.S. firms were financing affiliates in weak currency countries. The allure of a credit swap is its ability to reduce the need to finance a weak currency operation from a hard currency source.

An example would be a U.S. multinational firm wishing to finance its affiliate in Colombia. The U.S. parent deposits dollars to the account of a Colombian bank's New York correspondent, and in return, the Colombian bank in Bogota makes an equivalent loan in pesos to the U.S. firm's affiliate in Colombia. At a specified future date the transaction will be reversed; the U.S. firm's Colombian affiliate will repay the Colombian bank in Bogota the original quantity of pesos, and the Colombian bank will return the original dollar deposit in New York to the U.S. parent. Thus, the U.S. parent recovers the original dollar principal advanced, regardless of what happens during the interim to the exchange rate between pesos and dollars. The Colombian bank receives an interest-free dollar deposit in its New York correspondent bank.

The swap rate at which dollars are deposited to obtain the foreign currency, and later the foreign currency exchanged to repay dollars, may or may not equal the market spot rate at the time the swap contract is negotiated. Usually the swap rate is disadvantageous to the business firm relative to the market spot rate. Thus if $1 could be exchanged for 20 pesos in the spot market, $1 might obtain only 12 pesos via the swap agreement. Consequently, the dollar amount required to finance a foreign affiliate through a credit swap may substantially exceed the dollars needed to make the same investment through the foreign exchange market.

In a typical credit swap the foreign bank will charge local currency interest on the local currency loan extended to the U.S. affiliate. However, interest may or may not be paid by the foreign bank on the dollar credit made available to it.

A credit swap only protects the principal amount involved. It does not protect earnings on that principal that might be remitted to the parent, either as a return on the parent's investment or as a payment of any dollar interest charges incurred.

ACTIVE VS. PASSIVE MANAGEMENT OF FOREIGN EXCHANGE EXPOSURE

Should management follow an *active* policy of foreign exchange risk management or *passively* accept the outcome of the marketplace? This chapter has shown that the tools exist to protect against most kinds of foreign exchange risk, but they almost always exact a countervailing cost.

A number of theoretical arguments have been made both for and against active management of foreign exchange risk.[5] In general, those in favor of an active strategy believe that international markets for products, factors of production, financial capital, and foreign exchange are characterized by significant imperfections and inefficiencies. Those who favor a passive strategy believe that these markets are reasonably efficient. Surveys of managerial attitudes reveal that managers usually side with the market imperfections theorists.

Economic Exposure

The case for active management of economic exposure hinges on the degree to which purchasing power parity holds. As was shown earlier, purchasing power parity may hold in the long run, but significant deviations occur in the short run. Furthermore, even if purchasing power parity holds when measured by a particular macroeconomic price index, the market prices faced by an individual firm, which probably represent a different mix of goods and services, can create a competitive disequilibrium from that firm's perspective. Since disequilibria situations cannot be predicted accurately, management should pre-position the firm through diversification so it can recognize and take advantage of a disequilibrium situation when it occurs.

Transaction and Translation Exposure

The case for managing transaction and translation exposure depends on two factors: (1) the degree to which foreign exchange and money markets are efficient, and (2) management's risk aversion to higher variability in cash flow and reported earnings per share due to foreign exchange gains and losses.

Although some well-designed theoretical studies have shown that the foreign exchange and money markets for some major trading currencies have been efficient for particular time periods, this conclusion cannot be automatically extended to all currencies at all times. Indeed, many theorists and most managers believe that markets for a particular currency at a particular point in time may be inefficient and that the multinational firm is equipped to take advantage of these inefficiencies. They believe this situation exists not only for the very large number of currencies that are pegged but even for some of the widely traded major currencies. Inefficiencies can occur because of speculation, government intervention in the foreign exchange or money markets, political instability, tax law changes, or other government restrictions. If the market is inefficient, mispriced local borrowing, forward contracts, or option contracts may yield a positive return to those firms equipped to find the loopholes, avoid the restrictions, or just plain speculate.

Even if foreign exchange and money markets are always efficient, however, management is often strongly motivated to protect the firm against *unexpected* changes in future spot rates. The fact that in an efficient market the forward rate may be an *unbiased* predictor of future spot rates does not mean that the forward rate is also an *accurate* predictor of future spot rates. "Unbiased" only means that on average over the long run actual future spot rates will be above forward quotations about as often as they will be below. Management wants to ensure that whatever exchange rate may exist in the future, be it the expected rate or an unexpected rate, the variability of reported earnings per share and cash flow will be minimized. Protective techniques may thus be used to guard against the unknown—in effect, to minimize the variance—rather than to respond to a particular belief about the probable future value of a particular currency.

A further benefit of reduced variability in cash flow is the possibility that this will increase the firm's debt capacity because of lower financial risk.

Management's motivation to reduce variability is sometimes reinforced for cosmetic reasons if management believes it will be criticized more severely for incurring foreign exchange losses on the income statement than for incurring similar or even higher costs in avoiding the foreign exchange loss. The belief is reinforced by the firm's income statement, where foreign exchange losses may appear as a highly visible separate line item or footnote, while the costs of protection are buried in operating or interest expense.

This accounting-based motivation to reduce variability has been strongly attacked by efficient market theorists. They believe that investors can see through the "accounting veil" and therefore have already factored the foreign exchange effect into a firm's market valuation. Furthermore, they believe investors do not value the firm's costly efforts to reduce the foreign exchange effect because investors can do this themselves through diversifying their portfolios internationally. The efficient market arguments are treated more fully in Chapters 8 and 12.

Choice between Minimizing Transaction or Translation Exposure

If management does decide to offset both transaction and translation exposure, it will find it virtually impossible to offset both exposures at the same time. For example, the easiest way to offset translation exposure is to require the parent firm and all affiliates to denominate all exposed assets and liabilities in the parent's reporting currency. For U.S. firms and affiliates all assets and liabilities would be held in dollars. Such a firm would have no translation exposure, but it would have transaction exposure. Each foreign affiliate, which normally prepares its own financial statements in local currency terms before translating into dollars, would experience transaction gains or losses on its local currency financial statements as it settled various dollar-denominated obligations. These "realized" transaction gains or losses would affect taxable income in the country of domicile, and the transaction gains or losses net of tax effect would be translated into dollars as "foreign exchange gain or loss" when the affiliate's income statement was consolidated into that of the parent. The consolidated multinational corporation would thus show some net gain or loss on foreign exchange accounts even though these were transaction gains or losses incurred by affiliates operating in dollars.

To illustrate, assume that a U.S. parent instructs its Japanese affiliate to bill an export to the parent in dollars. The account receivable on the Japanese affiliate's books would be shown in the yen equivalent of the dollar amount and yen profit on the sale would be recorded. If prior to payment for the import by the parent the yen appreciates 5%, the parent will pay only the contracted dollar amount. The Japanese affiliate will receive 5% fewer yen than were expected and booked earlier as profit, and so will have to show a 5% foreign exchange loss on dollar-denominated transactions. This foreign exchange loss will eventually be translated into dollars when the affiliate's income statement is consolidated with that of the parent. The consolidated U.S.-based multinational firm will show a foreign exchange loss—on dollars!

Similar reasoning will show that if a firm chooses to eliminate transaction exposure, translation exposure is likely. The easiest way to be rid of transaction exposure is to require the parent and all affiliates to denominate all accounts subject to transaction exposure in local currency. Thus each affiliate would avoid any transaction gains or losses when those accounts are settled. However, each affiliate would be creating net translation exposure by being either long or short in terms of local currency exposed assets or liabilities. The consolidated financial statement of the parent firm would show translation exposure in each local currency.

Taxes complicate the decision to seek protection against transaction or translation exposure. Transaction losses are normally considered "realized" losses and are therefore deductible from taxable income. However, translation losses are only "paper" losses, which, under the current rate method, flow directly to the equity section of the balance sheet. Because they result only from accounting definitions of exposure, and thus involve no cash flows, translation losses are not deductible from taxable income. It is highly debatable whether protective techniques that necessitate cash payments, and so reduce net cash flow, should be incurred to avoid noncash losses.

SUMMARY

This chapter has analyzed when and how a multinational firm should react to economic, transaction, and translation exposures. International diversification of sales, production, and financing is the best way to manage economic exposure. Hedges in the forward market, money market, or options market are alternative techniques to manage transaction exposure. A balance sheet hedge is the best technique to offset translation exposure. Leads and lags can be used to react to all three types of exposure. Swaps are used to avoid incurring foreign exchange exposure in the first place.

The chapter also discussed whether or not managers should actively manage foreign exchange exposure. Although techniques are available to implement such a strategy, each has a cost. Those favoring an active strategy believe that international markets for products, factors of production, financial capital, and foreign exchange are sometimes imperfect or inefficient, and the multinational firm is equipped to gain from such a situation. However, even if markets are efficient, and no gains can be made, they prefer to pay a known cost for protection rather than be exposed to a probabilistic outcome.

Those who favor a passive strategy believe that markets are reasonably efficient. They also believe that investors do not value a firm's costly efforts to minimize the foreign exchange effect because investors can do this themselves through international portfolio diversification.

NOTES

1. For a good description of reacting to economic exposure, see Gunter Dufey, "Corporate Finance and Exchange Rate Variations," *Financial Management,* Summer 1972, pp. 51–57; Alan Shapiro and David Rutenberg, "Managing Exchange Risks in a Floating World," *Financial Management,* Summer 1976, pp. 48–58; and Arthur I. Stonehill, Niels Ravn, and Kåre Dullum, "Management of Foreign Exchange Economic Exposure," in Goran Bergendahl, ed., *International Financial Management,* Stockholm: Norstedts, 1982, pp. 128–148.

2. For an interesting case study of Volkswagen's foreign exchange exposure problems, see S. L. Srinivasulu, "Strategic Response to Foreign Exchange Risk," *Columbia Journal of World Business,* Spring 1981, pp. 13–23.

3. For a definitive study of swaps, see Carl R. Beidleman, *Financial Swaps: New Strategies in Currency and Coupon Risk Management,* Homewood, Ill.: Dow Jones–Irwin, 1985.

4. Mark E. Battersby, "Avoiding Risks by 'Parallel Lending,'" *Finance Magazine,* September–October 1975, pp. 56–57.

5. A good summary of these arguments can be found in Gunter Dufey and S. L. Srinivasulu, "Corporate Management of Foreign Exchange Risk," *Financial Management,* Winter 1983, pp. 54–62.

BIBLIOGRAPHY

Aggarwal, Raj, *Financial Policies for the Multinational Company: The Management of Foreign Exchange,* New York: Praeger, 1976.

Aliber, Robert Z., *Exchange Risk and Corporate International Finance,* New York: Wiley, 1979.

Ankrom, Robert K., "Top Level Approach to the Foreign Exchange Problem," *Harvard Business Review,* July/August 1974, pp. 79–90.

Antl, Boris, and Richard Ensor, eds., *Currency Risk and the Corporation,* London: Euromoney Publications, 1982.

———, *The Management of Foreign Exchange Risk,* London: Euromoney Publications, 1982.

Antl, Boris, ed., *Swap Financing Techniques,* London: Euromoney Publications, 1983.

Aubey, R. T., and R. H. Cramer, "Use of International Currency Cocktails in the Reduction of Exchange Rate Risk," *Journal of Economics and Business,* Winter 1977, pp. 128–134.

Arnold, Tanya S., "How to Do Interest Rate Swaps," *Harvard Business Review,* September/October 1984, pp. 96–101.

Babbel, David F., "Determining the Optimum Strategy for Hedging Currency Exposure," *Journal of International Business Studies,* Spring/Summer 1983, pp. 133–139.

Batra, Raveendra N., Shabtai Donnenfeld, and Josef Hadar, "Hedging Behavior by Multinational Firms," *Journal of International Business Studies,* Winter 1982, pp. 59–70.

Beidleman, Carl R., *Financial Swaps: New Strategies in Currency and Coupon Risk Management,* Homewood, Ill.: Dow Jones–Irwin, 1985.

Beidleman, Carl R., John L. Hillary, and James A. Greenleaf, "Alternatives in Hedging Long-Date Contractual Foreign Exchange Exposure," *Sloan Management Review,* Summer 1983, pp. 45–54.

Biger, Nahum, "Exchange Risk Implications of International Portfolio Diversification," *Journal of International Business Studies,* Fall 1979, pp. 64–74.

Booth, Laurence D., "Hedging and Foreign Exchange Exposure," *Management International Review,* Vol. 22, No. 1, 1982, pp. 26–42.

Chalupa, Karel V., "Foreign Currency Futures: Reducing Foreign Exchange Risk," *Economic Perspectives* (Federal Reserve Bank of Chicago), Winter 1982, pp. 3–11.

Christofides, N., R. D. Hewins, and G. R. Salkin, "Graph Theoretic Approaches to Foreign Exchange Operations," *Journal of Financial and Quantitative Analysis,* September 1979, pp. 481–500.

Controlling Risk with Foreign Currency Options: Supplement to Euromoney, February 1985.

Donaldson, J. A., *Corporate Currency Risk,* London: Financial Times Business Information, Ltd., 1980.

Dufey, Gunter, "Corporate Finance and Exchange Rate Variations," *Financial Management,* Summer 1972, pp. 51–57.

———, "Funding Decisions in International Companies," in Goran Bergendahl, ed., *International Financial Management,* Stockholm: Norstedts, 1982, pp. 29–53.

Dufey, Gunter, and Ian Giddy, "International Financial Planning: The Use of Market Based Forecasts," *California Management Review,* Fall 1978, pp. 54–62.

Dufey, Gunter, and S. L. Srinivasulu, "The Case for Corporate Management of Foreign Exchange Risk," *Financial Management,* Winter 1983, pp. 54–62.

Eaker, Mark R., "Denomination Decision for Multinational Transactions," *Financial Management,* Autumn 1980, pp. 23–29.

———, "The Numeraire Problem and Foreign Exchange Risk," *Journal of Finance,* May 1981, pp. 419–427.

Eaker, Mark R., and Dwight Grant, "Optimal Hedging of Uncertain and Long-Term Foreign Exchange Exposure," *Journal of Banking and Finance,* June 1985, pp. 222–231.

Fitzsimons, Robert B., "Exposure Management Is Too Important to Be Left to the Treasurer," *Euromoney,* March 1979, pp. 103–112.

Folks, William R., Jr., "Decision Analysis for Exchange Risk Management," *Financial Management,* Winter 1972, pp. 101–112.

———, "The Optimal Level of Forward Exchange Transactions," *Journal of Financial and Quantitative Analysis,* January 1973, pp. 105–110.

———, "Optimal Foreign Borrowing Strategies with Operations in the Forward Exchange Markets," *Journal of Financial and Quantitative Analysis,* June 1978, pp. 245–254.

Frankel, J. A., "The Diversifiability of Exchange Risk," *Journal of International Economics,* No. 9, 1979, pp. 379–393.

Giddy, Ian H., "Why It Doesn't Pay to Make a Habit of Forward Hedging," *Euromoney,* December 1976, pp. 96–100.

———, "The Foreign Exchange Option as a Hedging Tool," *Midland Corporate Finance Journal,* Fall 1983, pp. 32–42.

Hagemann, Helmut, "Anticipate Your Long-Term Foreign Exchange Risks," *Harvard Business Review,* March/April 1977, pp. 81–88.

Herring, R. J., ed., *Managing Foreign Exchange Risk,* Cambridge, England: Cambridge University Press, 1983.

Hill, Joanne, and Thomas Schneeweis, "Forecasting Hedging Effectiveness of Pound and Mark Forward and Futures Markets," *Management International Review,* Vol. 22, No. 1, 1982, pp. 43–52.

Jacque, Laurent L., *Management of Foreign Exchange Risk: Theory and Practice,* Lexington, Mass.: Heath, 1978.

———, "Management of Foreign Exchange Risk: A Review Article," *Journal of International Business Studies,* Spring/Summer 1981, pp. 81–101.

Jilling, Michael, *Foreign Exchange Management in U.S. Multinational Corporations,* Ann Arbor, Mich.: UMI Press, 1980.

Kemp, Donald S., "Hedging a Long-Term Financing," *Euromoney,* February 1981, pp. 102–105.

Kohlhagen, Steven W., "A Model of Optimal Foreign Exchange Hedging without Exchange Rate Projections," *Journal of International Business Studies,* Fall 1978, pp. 9–19.

Korsvold, Paul, "The Futility of Currency Hedging Models," in Goran Bergendahl, ed., *International Financial Management,* Stockholm: Norstedts, 1982, pp. 104–127.

Lassen, Richard, *Currency Management,* Cambridge, Mass.: Woodhead-Faulkner, 1982.

Levich, Richard M., and Clas G. Wihlborg, eds., *Exchange Risk and Exposure,* Lexington, Mass.: Lexington Books, 1980.

Logue, Dennis E., and George S. Oldfield, "Managing Foreign Assets When Foreign Exchange Markets Are Efficient," *Financial Management,* Summer 1977, pp. 16–22.

McRae, T. W., and D. P. Walker, *Foreign Exchange Management,* Englewood Cliffs, N.J.: Prentice-Hall, 1980.

Makin, John H., "The Portfolio Method of Managing Foreign Exchange Risk," *Euromoney,* August 1976, pp. 58–64.

———, "Portfolio Theory and the Problem of Foreign Exchange Risk," *Journal of Finance,* May 1978, pp. 517–534.

Mathur, Ike, "Managing Foreign Exchange Risks Profitably," *Columbia Journal of World Business,* Winter 1982, pp. 23–30.

Naidu, G. W., and Tai Shim, "Effectiveness of Currency Futures Market in Hedging Foreign Exchange Risk," *Management International Review,* Vol. 21, No. 4, 1981, pp. 5–16.

Park, Yoon S., "Currency Swaps as a Long-Term International Financing Technique," *Journal of International Business Studies,* Winter 1984, pp. 47–54.

Reier, S., "The Boom in Long-Dated Forwards," *Institutional Investor,* October 1983, pp. 353–354.

Riehl, Heinz, and Rita M. Rodriguez, *Foreign Exchange and Money Markets,* New York: McGraw-Hill, 1983.

Rodriguez, Rita M., *Foreign Exchange Management in U.S. Multinationals,* Lexington, Mass.: Lexington Books, 1980.

———, "Corporate Exchange Risk Management: Theme and Aberrations," *Journal of Finance,* May 1981, pp. 427–439.

Sapy-Mazello, Jean-Pierre, Robert M. Woo, and James Czechowicz, *New Directions to Managing Currency Risk: Changing Corporate Strategies and Systems under FAS No. 52,* New York: Business International, 1982.

Schwab, Bernhard, and Peter Lusztig, "Apportioning Foreign Exchange Risk through the Use of Third Currencies: Some Questions on Efficiency," *Financial Management,* Autumn 1978, pp. 25–30.

Serfass, William D., Jr., "You Can't Outguess the Foreign Exchange Market," *Harvard Business Review,* March/April 1976, pp. 134–137.

Shapiro, Alan C., and David P. Rutenberg, "When to Hedge against Devaluation," *Management Science,* August 1974, pp. 1514–1530.

———, "Managing Exchange Risks in a Floating World," *Financial Management,* Summer 1976, pp. 48–58.

Soenen, Luc A., "Foreign Exchange Exposure Management," *Management International Review,* Vol. 19, No. 2, 1979, pp. 31–38.

———, *Foreign Exchange Exposure Management: A Portfolio Approach,* Alpen aan den Rijn, the Netherlands: Sijthoff & Noordhoff, 1979.

Soenen, Luc A., and E. G. F. van Winkel, "The Real Costs of Hedging in the Forward Exchange Market," *Management International Review,* Vol. 22, No. 1, 1982, pp. 53–59.

Srinivasulu, S. L., "Strategic Response to Foreign Exchange Risks," *Columbia Journal of World Business,* Spring 1981, pp. 13–23.

Stanley, Marjorie T., and Stanley B. Block, "Portfolio Diversification of Foreign Exchange Risk: An Empirical Study," *Management International Review,* Vol. 20, No. 1, 1980, pp. 83–92.

Stonehill, Arthur I., Niels Ravn, and Kare Dullum, "Management of Foreign Exchange Economic Exposure," in Goran Bergendahl, ed., *International Financial Management,* Stockholm: Norstedts, 1982, pp. 128–148.

Tait, Simon, "It Takes Two to Tango," *Euromoney,* February 1983, pp. 75–81.

Tran, Vinh Quang, *Foreign Exchange Management in Multinational Firms,* Ann Arbor, Mich.: UMI Press, 1980.

Waters, Somerset R., "Exposure Management Is a Job for All Departments," *Euromoney,* December 1979, pp. 79–82.

Wheelwright, Steven, "Applying Decision Theory to Improve Corporate Management of Currency-Exchange Risks," *California Management Review,* Summer 1975, pp. 41–49.

Wihlborg, Clas, "Economics of Exposure Management of Foreign Subsidiaries of Multinational Corporations," *Journal of International Business Studies,* Winter 1980, pp. 9–18.

Yang, Ho C., "The Value of a Forward Contract in Foreign Currencies," *Journal of Business, Finance, and Accounting,* Winter 1984, pp. 575–578.

Problems for Part II

1. *The Daimyo's Palace*

   You have just rented an ancient palace in Japan for a vacation 12 months hence. Your landlord wants to preserve his real income in Japanese yen, and so the present monthly rent of ¥2,500,000 will be adjusted upward or downward for any change in the Japanese cost of living between now and then.

   You expect U.S. inflation to be 12% and Japanese inflation to be 3% over the coming year. You believe implicitly in the theory of purchasing power parity, and you note from the *Wall Street Journal* that the current spot rate is ¥250/$. How many U.S. dollars will you need one year hence to pay your first month's rent?

2. *The Nations of Alpine and Bayshore*

   Alpine and Bayshore are both large countries with efficient capital and money markets. The currency of Alpine is the alp (A^) and that of Bayshore is the bay (B¯). For both countries the Fisher Effect, purchasing power parity, and interest rate parity are in equilibrium and are expected to remain in equilibrium.

   Recently the *Financial Times* published the following data:

	In Alpine	*In Bayshore*
Spot foreign exchange quotation	A^8.0000/B¯	B¯0.1250/A^
12-month Treasury bill rate	10%	not given

   The general consensus of informed economists is that inflation in Alpine during the coming year will be 5% and that in Bayshore inflation will be 11%. As chief international financial officer for your company you are asked to determine and/or forecast the following:

   a. The 12-month Treasury bill rate in Bayshore.

   b. The 12-month forward exchange quote, direct basis, for both Alpine and Bayshore.

c. The 12-month forward exchange quote on a percent-per-annum basis for both Alpine and Bayshore.

d. Reconciliation of the differential inflation rates between the two countries with forward foreign exchange quotations expressed as annual percent premium or discount.

3. *Kelton Industries*

Kelton Industries is scheduled to receive a CR$8,640 million dividend from its affiliate in Campinas, Brazil, in three months. (*CR$* is the symbol for Brazilian cruzeiros.) The current spot rate is CR$8,640/US$, and the three-month forward rate is CR$9,600/US$. Inflation in Brazil is about 4.5% per month, and the cruzeiro is devalued about once a month. The U.S. inflation rate is 1% per month. Kelton's affiliate in Campinas can borrow at 48% per annum interest. What should Kelton Industries do about its forthcoming dividend?

4. *Hithergreen Products*

Hithergreen Products is completing a new factory building in Canada and must make a final construction payment of C$28,000,000 in six months. Foreign exchange and interest rate quotations are as follows:

Present spot rate:	C$1.4000/US$
Six-month forward rate:	C$1.4200/US$
Canadian six-month interest rate:	13% per annum
U.S. six-month interest rate:	10% per annum

The financial manager's own analysis suggests that in six months the following spot rates can be expected:

Highest expected rate:	C$1.4000/US$
Most likely rate:	C$1.4300/US$
Lowest expected rate:	C$1.4500/US$

Hithergreen Products does not presently have any excess dollar cash balances. However, it expects to obtain adequate cash from an income tax refund due in six months. Hithergreen's weighted average cost of capital is 20% per annum. What alternatives are available for making payment, and what are the advantages or disadvantages of each?

5. *New Haven Tools, Inc.*

New Haven Tools, Inc., is filling an order from a Korean industrial company for machinery worth 160,000,000 won. The export sale is denominated in Korean won and is on a one-year open account basis. The opportunity cost of funds for New Haven Tools is 8%.

The current spot rate between won and dollars is 800 won/$. The forward won sells at a discount of 12% per annum, but the finance staff of New Haven Tools believes that the won will drop only 9% in value over the next year. New Haven Tools faces the following choices:

a. Wait one year to receive the won amount and exchange won for dollars at that time.

b. Sell the won proceeds of the sale forward today.

c. Borrow won from a Seoul bank at 20% per annum against the expected future receipts of the Korean importer's payment.

What do you recommend and why?

6. *Bakersfield Bland*

Your brewery produces Bakersfield Bland, a low-calorie, low-taste beer that has not yet developed a national or international following. (As a matter of fact, no one in Bakersfield drinks it either!) In mid-March you receive an order for 10,000 cartons from Munich, Germany, for next fall's Oktoberfest, with payment of DM672,000 due in mid-September, before the beer is consumed. In your opinion the Deutschemark will rise from its present rate of DM2.8000/$ to DM2.6500/$ by September, and you learn you can borrow marks for six months at 6% per annum.

What should you do? Discuss issues as necessary.

7. *Intelledex, Inc.*

Intelledex, Inc., a robotics manufacturer based in Corvallis, Oregon, has won a bid to deliver robotics equipment to the French automobile company Renault. The bid is FF8 million. Intelledex will receive the entire FF8 million upon delivery of the equipment six months from now. The present spot rate for the French franc is FF8.000/$, and the six-month forward rate is FF8.2000/$. Intelledex can borrow U.S. dollars at 12% per annum or French francs at 17% per annum. Its opportunity cost of capital is 14% per annum.

a. Explain the various ways in which Intelledex could cover its foreign exchange exposure.

b. What would the break-even opportunity cost of capital have to be for them to be indifferent between the various alternatives?

c. Explain how economic exposure might change the expected profitability of this order.

8. *Pacific Power and Light Company*

Pacific Power and Light Company (PP&L) has purchased an electric power generator from Mitsui Trading Company of Japan. PP&L owes Mitsui ¥250 million in six months. The present spot rate is ¥250/$. The six-month forward rate is ¥248/$. PP&L can borrow or invest yen at 8% and U.S. dollars at 10% (annual rates). PP&L can also purchase a six-month call option on the Philadelphia Stock Exchange at a strike price of ¥250 for a premium of 0.004 cents per yen. Compare the alternative ways PP&L can make its payment. Which way do you recommend?

9. *Hyster Corporation*

Hyster Corporation of Portland, Oregon, received an order from Volkswagen in Germany for an automated materials handling system. Receipt of DM5 million is due upon the expected completion date six months from today. Foreign exchange, interest rate, and foreign currency option quotations from Hyster's bank are as follows:

Present spot rate:	DM2.8585/$
Six-month forward rate:	DM2.7990/$
German six-month interest rate:	6.25% per annum
U.S. six-month interest rate:	10.50% per annum
Premium on six-month put option on DM at 2.8585:	3.000%

The financial manager's own analysis suggests that in six months the following spot rates can be expected:

Highest expected rate:	DM2.6000/$
Most likely rate:	DM2.8000/$
Lowest expected rate:	DM2.9100/$

Hyster's cost of capital is 12%.

Compare the different alternatives for Hyster to manage his foreign exchange risk. What are the advantages and disadvantages of each?

10. *Khao-I-Dang Corporation*

Khao-I-Dang Corporation is the Thai affiliate of a U.S. machine tool manufacturer. Khao-I-Dang assembles some machine tools from parent-supplied components and manufactures other models entirely within Thailand. Sales are throughout Southeast Asia. Khao-I-Dang's balance sheet in thousands of Thai bahts (symbol ฿) as of December 31, year 1, is as follows:

Assets	
Cash	฿ 3,600
Accounts receivable	4,800
Inventory	4,800
Net plant and equipment	6,000
	฿19,200
Liabilities and Net Worth	
Accounts payable	฿1,200
One-year bank loan	1,200
Ten-year development loan	3,600
Common stock	6,000
Retained earnings	7,200
	฿19,200

Relevant exchange rates for the translation of Khao-I-Dang's balance sheet into U.S. dollars are:

Historic exchange rate (for plant and equipment, long-term debt, and common stock): ฿16/$

December 31, year 1, exchange rate (inventory was acquired at this rate): ฿20/$

December 31, year 2, exchange rate (following devaluation of 16⅔%): ฿24/$

Assuming no change in baht balance sheet amounts during the year, calculate translation gain or loss on December 31, year 2, by the current rate method (or by the monetary/nonmonetary method, if more appropriate). Explain translation loss in terms of changes in the value of individual exposed accounts.

11. *Syarikat Payung*

Syarikat Payung, the 100% owned Malaysian subsidiary of Drizzle, Inc., of Seattle, manufactures umbrellas for its U.S. parent. The functional currency of Syarikat Payung is the Malaysian ringgit (symbol R), and the reporting currency of Drizzle is the U.S. dollar. The current spot rate, which has not changed since Drizzle invested in Malaysia, is R2.5/$.

Nonconsolidated financial statements of Drizzle, Inc., and Syarikat Payung, in thousands of currency units, are as shown on the following page.

a. Prepare a consolidated balance sheet for Drizzle and its Malaysian affiliate.

b. Assume the Malaysian ringgit changes in value from R2.5/$ to R3.0/$. What is the percentage change in the dollar value of the ringgit?

	Drizzle, Inc.	Syarikat Payung
Assets		
Cash	$ 1,000	R 750
Accounts receivable	2,000	1,500[a]
Inventory	3,000	2,250
Net plant and equipment	5,000	3,000
Investment in shares of Syarikat Payung	1,700[b]	
	$12,700	R7,500
Liabilities and Net Worth		
Accounts payable	$ 4,000[c]	R1,500
Long-term debt	—	1,750[d]
Common stock	5,000	2,000
Retained earnings	3,700	2,250
	$12,700	R7,500

[a]Includes R975,000 due from parent. The intracompany loan is denominated in ringgits.

[b]The parent's investment in the common stock of Syarikat Payung is carried at the dollar translated value of the subsidiary's equity: R4,250/2.5 = $1,700.

[c]Includes R975,000 payable to Syarikat Payung and translated as $390,000. This is the intracompany loan referred to in note *a*.

[d]The entire long-term debt is denominated in U.S. dollars.

c. Calculate any translation gain or loss to Drizzle, Inc., using the current rate method. Does this gain or loss appear only in the income statement, only in the balance sheet, or in both statements?

d. What transaction gain or loss did Drizzle, Inc., or Syarikat Payung experience as a result of the devaluation?

12. *Durable Corporation*

Durable Corporation believes that the outlook for the Portuguese escudo is not good, and that the escudo will drop from its present value of Es150/$ to Es180/$ by year end. Durable's finance staff is thus more pessimistic than the market as a whole, since the current one-year forward quote for the escudo is Es165/$.

Durable's translation exposure in Portugal on January 1 is a positive Es4,455,000, and the finance staff decides to hedge this exposure by selling escudos forward. Reasoning that the profit on the transaction will be taxed at the U.S. rate of 46%, they sell forward Es4,455,000 divided by 0.54 (i.e., 1 − 0.46), or Es8,250,000. They expect the aftertax gain to exactly offset their non–tax-deductible loss from translation.

When Durable closes its books on December 31, one year later, the spot rate is Es148/$. Assess the reasonableness of Durable's actions.

13. *Colombian Coffee Company*

The balance sheet of Colombian Coffee Company, the wholly owned Colombian subsidiary of the Catalina Coffee Company, is shown below. The Colombian currency is the peso, which has an exchange rate as follows:

Current spot rate:	Ps105.00/$
Current one-year forward rate:	Ps122.50/$
Catalina's forecast for spot rate one year hence:	Ps140.00/$

Colombian Coffee Company Balance Sheet (in thousands of Colombian pesos)

Assets	
Cash, denominated in pesos	Ps 420,000
Cash, denominated in dollars	210,000
Receivables, denominated in pesos	630,000
Receivables, denominated in dollars	105,000
Inventory	1,470,000
Net plant and equipment	1,260,000
	Ps4,095,000
Liabilities and Net Worth	
Accounts payable, denominated in pesos	Ps 210,000
Notes payable, denominated in pesos	315,000
Notes payable, denominated in dollars	630,000
Long-term debt, denominated in pesos	105,000
Shareholders' equity	2,835,000
	Ps4,095,000

a. The Colombian subsidiary is the only foreign operation of Catalina Coffee Company, whose reporting currency is the U.S. dollar. What is the subsidiary's contribution to the parent's translation exposure by the current rate method (or by the monetary/nonmonetary method, if more appropriate)?

b. What would be Catalina Coffee Company's translation loss should the Colombian peso devalue as expected?

c. Assuming an income tax–free environment, what size forward contract should Catalina Coffee Company enter into if it decides to hedge its translation exposure, based on its own forecast of next year's spot rate?

d. Would the above hedge give complete protection? Discuss.

14. *H. C. Andersen Enterprises*

The parent and Danish affiliate balance sheets of H. C. Andersen Enterprises are as follows (in thousands of monetary units):

	H. C. Andersen Enterprises (parent only)	Danish affiliate
Assets		
Cash	$ 600	DKr 3,600
Accounts receivable	1,200[a]	1,800
Inventory	1,200	3,240
Net plant and equipment	1,800	3,600
Investment in affiliate	684	
	$5,484	DKr12,240
Liabilities and Net Worth		
Accounts payable	$ 300	DKr 5,400[a]
Shareholders' equity	5,184	6,840
	$5,484	DKr12,240

[a]Includes DKr1,800,000 owed to H. C. Andersen parent by Danish affiliate.

The current (and historic) exchange rate is DKr10.00/$. H. C. Andersen Enterprises translates by the current rate method and uses the U.S. dollar as its reporting currency.

a. Is there any translation exposure within H. C. Andersen Enterprises worldwide? If so, how much and where?

b. Is there any transaction exposure within H. C. Andersen Enterprises worldwide? If so, how much and where?

c. What should be the effect on H. C. Andersen Enterprises if the Danish krone strengthened to DKr8.00/$? Show monetary amounts, and assume the intracompany payables/receivables are not paid off until after revaluation.

15. *Cleveland Lock Company*

Cleveland Lock Company has supplied ignition locks for American automobile manufacturers since the late 1930s. In the early 1970s, Cleveland Lock opened wholly owned affiliates in Germany and Italy, and at the end of last year balance sheets of the U.S. parent (unconsolidated) and the two subsidiaries were as follows (in thousands):

	Cleveland Lock, U.S.	*German affiliate*	*Italian affiliate*
Assets			
Cash	$ 2,000	DM 4,000	Lit 1,800,000
Accounts receivable	6,000[a]	8,000[b]	3,600,000
Inventory	4,000	4,000	3,600,000
Net plant and equipment	7,800	4,000	5,400,000
Investments	7,200		
	$27,000	DM20,000	Lit14,400,000
Liabilities and Net Worth			
Accounts payable	$ 4,000	DM 8,000[a]	Lit 1,800,000
Notes payable	6,000	2,000	5,400,000[c]
Term loans	4,000	2,000	
Common stock	6,000	4,000	3,600,000
Retained earnings	7,000	4,000	3,600,000
	$27,000	DM20,000	Lit14,400,000

[a]Of the $6,000,000 accounts receivable on the books of Cleveland Lock, U.S., $4,800,000 is denominated in dollars and due from independent customers. The remainder consists of DM3,000,000 owed by the German affiliate to its U.S. parent and carried on the U.S. books at $1,200,000.

[b]The German affiliate has accounts receivable in French francs of FF9,000,000 from nonrelated customers. These are carried on the German books as DM2,500,000 and are included within the total balance of DM8,000,000.

[c]The Italian affiliate owes a London bank $1,000,000 (in dollars), and it owes a French bank FF4,500,000 (in francs). The lire equivalent of these debts, Lit2,700,000, is included in the Lit5,400,000 of notes payable.

Exchange rates are presently as follows:

Spot:	$1.00 =	DM2.50 =	FF9.00 =	Lit1800.
One year forward:	$1.00 =	DM2.40 =	FF8.20 =	Lit2000.

a. Prepare a consolidated balance sheet in U.S. dollars for Cleveland Lock at current exchange rates.

b. What is Cleveland Lock's translation exposure by the current rate method?

c. What is Cleveland Lock's worldwide transaction exposure?

d. What might Cleveland Lock do about its translation and transaction exposure?

PART III

Long-Run Investment Decisions

8

The Foreign Investment Decision

The foreign investment decision results from a complex process that differs in many respects from that governing the domestic investment decision. Foreign investments are usually motivated by a wider and more complicated set of strategic, behavioral, and economic considerations. The investigation process is often longer, more costly, and yields less information on which to evaluate opportunities. Financial evaluations of initial foreign investments using traditional discounted cash flow techniques are not relied on as heavily as they are in domestic investments because of greater perceived business, political, and foreign exchange risks. In this chapter we examine the strategic, behavioral, and economic motives for direct foreign investments. In Chapter 9 we examine the political risk implications of direct foreign investment. In Chapter 10 we show how traditional capital budgeting analysis must be modified for foreign project analysis.

An immense body of literature has emerged in the last 25 years to explain the rapid growth of direct foreign investment. Many theories have been proposed and tested. Each theory typically explains why direct foreign investment occurs in certain industries or in particular types of firms. No one theory has been able to explain direct foreign investment for all types of industries, firms, and countries. Nevertheless, in the last 10 years significant attempts have been made to synthesize the various theories into one grand theory. Our approach in this chapter is to summarize these various theories and attempts at synthesis, because in combination they constitute a good explanation of most direct foreign investment.

To place the theories in perspective, we note that they have one theme in common. They all attempt to explain why a firm resorts to direct foreign investment rather than relying on exporting, licensing, or management contracts. The original classical theory of international trade was based only on exporting and importing as determined by comparative advantage and the law of factor proportions. Since direct foreign investment, licensing, and management contracts were not part of the classical theory, why have they become so important in recent years? More specifically, why does a firm establish direct foreign investments rather than license foreign firms or operate abroad under a management contract? To answer these questions, we will now examine the various strategic, behavioral, and economic theories that have been proposed and tested during the last 25 years. In the case of economic theories we will contrast them with the classical theory of international trade.

STRATEGIC MOTIVES FOR DIRECT FOREIGN INVESTMENT

Surveys and case studies of multinational firms indicate that their motivations for making direct foreign investments are based on strategic considerations of five main types:

1. market seekers,
2. raw material seekers,
3. production efficiency seekers,
4. knowledge seekers, and
5. political safety seekers.[1]

Market seekers produce in foreign markets either to satisfy local demand or to export to markets other than their home market. U.S. automobile firms manufacturing in Europe for local consumption are an example of market-seeking motivation.

Raw material seekers extract raw materials wherever they can be found, either for export or for further processing and sale in the host country. Firms in the oil, mining, plantation, and forest industries fall into this category.

Production efficiency seekers produce in countries where one or more of the factors of production are underpriced relative to their productivity. Labor-intensive production of electronic components in Taiwan, Malaysia, and Mexico are examples where these conditions apparently occur.

Knowledge seekers operate in foreign countries to gain access to technology or managerial expertise. For example, German and Dutch firms have purchased U.S.-located electronics firms for their technology.

Political safety seekers acquire or establish new operations in countries such as the United States that are considered unlikely to expropriate or interfere with private sector firms. For example, Canadian firms in the energy sector have shown interest in U.S. acquisitions as a partial response to Canadian government policies in the energy field.

The five types of strategic considerations just described are not mutually exclusive. For example, forest products firms seeking wood fiber in Brazil would also find a large Brazilian market for a portion of their output.

Why do strategic rather than financial considerations seem to be very important motivations for direct foreign investment? Perceived political and foreign exchange risks often cloud the determination of an appropriate risk-adjusted required rate of return for a foreign project. As a result, the range of expected outcomes may be so large as to reduce the credibility of any financial discounted cash flow analysis that attempts to find a single-valued expected rate of return. Therefore, although discounted cash flow analysis is still used appropriately to analyze specific projects, it is not usually the deciding factor in choosing the original countries in which a multinational firm will invest. Empirical studies of large samples of multinational firms lend support to this conclusion.

Based on a sample of 100 detailed questionnaires and 50 in-depth interviews, a study of multinational firms undertaken by the Conference Board concluded the following:

> Even in discussions of the technical application of various financial criteria the ever-present main point proved to be that considerations of market position *dominate* the decision-making process. They determine the need, the urgency, and the desirability of an investment, while financial evaluations are used mainly to test the validity of marketing assumptions and to determine both the financial requirements and the financial means for attaining marketing goals. Thus, for the most part, financial considerations are pertinent to the *how to* rather than to the *whether to* finance a foreign investment.[2]

A second, independent study surveyed 92 U.S. and 18 non-U.S. multinational corporations. The results showed the following:

> Financial investment criteria were used most often in evaluating relatively small cost-saving projects, replacement projects, and other projects which would fall under the purview of local managers. For relatively large or strategic investments, however, financial investment criteria were used only as a rough screening device to prevent obviously unprofitable projects from wasting the time of the board of directors.
>
> Foreign investment proposals were almost always relatively large and strategic. The decision at the board level was usually determined by the competitive situation, case by case, on the assumption that the financial homework had been done down the line.
>
> Interviews with officers at different levels in the same corporation indicated that the financial homework was done, but with varying degrees of sophistication.
>
> At the industrial engineering level the calculations were quite consistent with capital budgeting theory. The same generalization could be made about projects which were screened at lower levels of the financial organization.

As projects moved up the line for approval, however, theoretical financial investment criteria seemed to be less well understood and often subordinated to other considerations. In fact, officers at various levels of the same organization offered conflicting opinions as to the extent of use of financial investment criteria and rarely agreed on the exact way the actual calculations were made.[3]

BEHAVIORAL MOTIVES FOR DIRECT FOREIGN INVESTMENT

Yair Aharoni's study of the behavioral aspects of the foreign investment decision process found two sets of motives. One set arose from a stimulus from the external environment and the other from within an organization on the basis of personal biases, needs, and commitments of individuals and groups.[4] His study of 38 primarily market-seeking U.S. firms that had considered investing in Israel found the following important external stimuli:

1. An outside proposal, provided it comes from a source that cannot be easily ignored. The most frequent sources of such proposals are foreign governments, the distributors of the company's products, and its clients.
2. Fear of losing a market.
3. The "bandwagon" effect: very successful activities abroad of a competing firm in the same line of business, or a general belief that investment in some area is "a must."
4. Strong competition from abroad in the home market.[5]

In addition to the above four motives, Aharoni found some auxiliary motives:

> When some unutilized resources exist in the company, or when fixed costs can be spread over additional areas, these facts can be used as a "point of sale" by a proposer or by an executive interested in foreign investments. The existence of such factors will not by itself cause a decision to look abroad, but it may work as a catalyst toward such a decision. These factors augment the impact of the initiating force and may therefore be regarded as auxiliary forces.
>
> The auxiliary forces uncovered in the field research were:
>
> 1. Creation of a market for components and other products.
> 2. Utilization of old machinery.
> 3. Capitalization of know-how; spreading of research and development and other fixed costs.
> 4. Indirect return to a lost market through investment in a country that has commercial agreements with these lost territories.[6]

Aharoni's study is a good example of the behavioral theory of a firm, first articulated by Herbert Simon (1947) and improved by Richard Cyert and James March (1963).[7] As was true for the domestic case, the behavioral approach to the foreign investment decision is usually a specific decision on a specific opportunity evaluated sequentially in response to a specific motivating force. It is not, typically, a program to search for all possible foreign investment opportunities, gather all the relevant data for each, compare and rank them, and choose those which rank highest. Of course, there can be numerous alternatives involved in one opportunity, or perhaps several foreign and domestic opportunities are evaluated at the same time. Thus there is a need for ranking, but the constraint is more likely to be lack of management time and ability than lack of funds. In this case the ranking process may really be decided by the choice of which alternatives to investigate. *The sequence and intensity of investigation, including the strength of the motivating force, thus becomes the major determinant of the foreign investment decision.*

The following excerpts from Aharoni's study describe the investigation process and its influence on the final foreign investment decision:

> An investigation is carried out in successive phases, with built-in check points. Therefore, the sequence of investigation is of crucial importance. Indeed, the field research clearly shows that a very distinct pattern exists in the way information is collected, scrutinized, communicated, and evaluated. The first phase is carried out at the company's office. Various readily available crude general indicators are consulted to form some opinion on the risk and uncertainty involved, to estimate the size of the market, and to test whether the proposed project accords with existing company practices and resources.
>
> The preliminary screening at this juncture may result in a decision to abandon the project. If it does not, one or more executives are directed to go to the foreign country for a more thorough and costly on-the-spot investigation. More detailed surveys of market size and analyses of costs of production and technical feasibility of the proposed venture are undertaken. During these and later stages projects are reviewed by various echelons in the corporation hierarchy. The presentation of the project for assessment by higher echelons may necessitate the gathering of more information and additional, more elaborate calculations. Negotiations are undertaken both inside and outside the company to resolve conflicts, and both goals and estimates are continually revised.
>
> Thus, the amount and complexity of information gathered grow as the investigation advances. In the first phases, assessment is based on "hunches," "rules of thumb," and "general corporate policies" and the information is very crude, meager, and of a very general character. In the more advanced phases, information pertaining directly to the investment becomes more abundant.
>
> Because of the cost, some variables are fixed in advance and a certain value, based on previous experience in another environment, is assigned to them. Even in the last phases of investigation, not all the information that may be available is gathered, digested, and analyzed.
>
> Other things being equal, the greater the amount of information that is easily and readily available, the higher the probability that a corporation will

be willing to investigate. The high cost of obtaining information is a barrier to investment in less developed countries. In general, it is much harder to gather information on these countries from generally available sources. Furthermore, the available crude indicators hardly make those countries "look right." It is therefore most unlikely that United States manufacturing concerns will invest in these countries unless a special effort is made to induce these concerns to do so. . . .

The inevitable uncertainty about detailed circumstances in which the investment is to be implemented compels decision makers to assign a high priority to flexibility. They look askance at an investment opportunity that is lacking in this dimension. Thus, investors shy away from situations involving rigid government controls or small markets and will inject many elements of pessimistic prejudice into the evaluation.

. . . In an organizational setting, three additional points, not necessarily connected with cost, should be stressed.

First, investigators tend to avoid areas of possible friction with other executives and with prior organizational policies and commitments. This fact adds to the tendency already mentioned above to assume many variables fixed at a given value. For instance, an investigator working for a company whose policy is to have 100% control of its subsidiaries generally will not consider the possibility of joint ventures. Also, the investigator generally will assume that the production processes and the size of the plant will be the same as in the United States. By so doing, the investigator not only makes the investigation more manageable in scope, but also makes sure it fits into the general frame of his organization. Changing too many things at once may create a clash with too many vested interests inside the organization. By keeping some things constant, the investigator can narrow the area of disagreement while reducing the cost of investigation.

The only exception to this is encountered when the initiating force creates a strong impact, and the investigator cannot reconcile this impact with the facts found in the field without having to change some of these "constants." A strong initiating force may compel a company to consider a joint venture despite its general aversion to such situations, or may compel it to consider and accept construction of a much smaller plant than the one it is used to operating.

Second, the investigation is carried out by many people, at different points of time. Those making the investigation are not necessarily those carrying the final responsibility for the decision. The relationships among various individuals and groups taking part in the decision process become important variables that should be carefully analyzed and evaluated.

Third, because of the diffusion of decision making in organizations, results of an investigation are presented in written form. There is, however, a significant difference between the evaluation procedures used throughout the investigation and the manner in which the results are presented. For purpose of presentation, a complex document is written. Both its structure and contents are dictated by the company's standard operating procedures, as well as by the writer's desire that his conclusions be accepted by the receiver of the report. Often, the report includes considerably more information than was available when the investigator made up his own mind. It also includes quantitative data prepared for no other reason than to comply with the standard operating procedure.

Thus, the written report does not reflect directly the manner in which the writer has reached his decision. It is a full-dress re-analysis of the situation in terms that are considered to be both completely rational and persuasive in presenting its writer's point of view. Therefore, it is very difficult to identify the beginning and end points of the investigation. The division of the decision process into well-defined stages is quite ambiguous. These stages are used only for purposes of exposition because in real situations they overlap. An investigation may be finished and a certain echelon of executives may come to a decision, but the question has to be referred to a higher echelon that may require more information, and thus a new investigation must be undertaken. A decision may be reached on the basis of available information, and this decision may open a new path of investigation.[8]

ECONOMIC MOTIVES FOR DIRECT FOREIGN INVESTMENT

Although survey and case studies of the foreign investment decision emphasize strategic and behavioral motives, these may very well be consistent with rational, profit-seeking, economic motives. According to modern extensions of international economic theory, executives of multinational firms may be operating in a manner that is consistent with maximizing long-run profit (net earnings or cash flow) and market value of common stock, often under conditions of worldwide oligopolistic competition. However, to understand the recent theories, we find it useful to review briefly classical trade theory. This theory explained very well why firms should export and import. More recent theories explain why firms should undertake direct foreign investment, licensing, and management contracts instead of continuing to rely only on exporting and importing.

Comparative Advantage

The theory of comparative advantage and its corollary, the theory of factor proportions, provide a basis for explaining and justifying international trade in a model world assumed to enjoy free trade, perfect competition, no uncertainty, costless information, and no government interference. The theory contains the following features:

- Exporters in country A sell goods or services to *unrelated* importers in country B (any other country).
- Firms in country A specialize in making products that can be *relatively* efficiently produced given country A's endowment of factors of production, i.e., land, labor, capital, and technology. Firms in country

B do likewise given the factors of production found in country B. In this way the total combined output of A and B is maximized.

- Since the factors of production cannot be freely moved from country A to country B, the benefits of specialization are realized through international trade.
- How the benefits of the extra production are shared depends on the terms of trade. Each share is determined by supply and demand in perfectly competitive markets in the two countries. Neither country A nor B is worse off than before trade, and typically both are better off, albeit perhaps unequally.

For an example of the benefits of free trade based on comparative advantage, assume that country A is relatively efficient at producing food and country B is relatively efficient at producing cloth. Assume that each unit of production (land, labor, capital, and technology) in country A can produce either 6 tons of food or 12 yards of cloth, whereas each unit of production in country B can produce either 2 tons of food or 10 yards of cloth. In other words, a production unit in A has an *absolute advantage* over a production unit in B in both food and cloth. Nevertheless, country A has a larger *relative advantage* over country B in producing food (6 to 2) than cloth (12 to 10). As long as these ratios are unequal, *comparative advantage* exists.

Assume that both countries have one million units of production and the production and consumption situations before trade are as follows:

	Units of production	*Total production (millions of tons or yards)*	*Total consumption (millions of tons or yards)*
Country A			
Food	700,000 × 6 =	4.2	4.2
Cloth	300,000 × 12 =	3.6	3.6
Country B			
Food	700,000 × 2 =	1.4	1.4
Cloth	300,000 × 10 =	3.0	3.0

Now assume that trade is allowed, with the barter ratio between food and cloth being 4 yards of cloth equal 1 ton of food. The barter ratio must end up between the ratios in each of the countries since without trade nobody in country A would pay more than 2 yards of cloth for 1 ton of food, while in country B nobody would pay more than 5 yards of cloth for 1 ton of food. Assume that country A transfers all units of production from producing cloth to producing food and country B transfers all units of production from producing food to producing cloth. The resulting output is then bartered so that both countries consume more food or cloth than they consumed before trade was allowed. The new production and consumption situations after trade could be as follows:

	Units of production	*Total production (millions of tons or yards)*	*Trade (millions of tons or yards)*	*Total consumption (millions of tons or yards)*
Country A				
Food	1,000,000 × 6 =	6.0	−1.6	4.4
Cloth	—	—	+6.4	6.4
Country B				
Food	—	—	+1.6	1.6
Cloth	1,000,000 × 10 =	10.0	−6.4	3.6

Both countries have benefited from specializing and trading. Country A consumes 200,000 tons more of food and 2.8 million yards more of cloth. Country B consumes 200,000 tons more of food and 600,000 yards more of cloth. Total combined production of both food and cloth has increased through the specialization process, and it only remains for the exchange ratio to determine how the larger output is distributed between the countries.

Although international trade might have approached the comparative advantage model during the nineteenth century, it certainly does not today, for the following reasons:

- Countries do not appear to specialize only in those products that could be most efficiently produced by that country's particular factors of production. Instead governments interfere with comparative advantage for a variety of economic and political reasons, such as full employment, economic development, national self-sufficiency in defense-related industries, and protection of an agricultural sector's way of life. Government interference takes the form of tariffs, quotas, and other nontariff restrictions.
- At least two of the factors of production, capital and technology, flow directly between countries rather than only indirectly through traded goods and services. This direct flow occurs between related affiliates of multinational firms, as well as between unrelated firms via loans, licenses, and management contracts.
- Although the terms of trade are ultimately determined by supply and demand, the process by which this trade occurs is different from that visualized in traditional trade theory. The terms of trade are determined partly by administered pricing in oligopolistic markets.

- Comparative advantage shifts over time as less developed countries become more developed and realize their latent opportunities. For example, comparative advantage in producing cotton textiles shifted from the United Kingdom to the United States, to Japan, to Hong Kong, and now to Taiwan.
- The classical model of comparative advantage did not really address certain other issues such as the effect of uncertainty and information costs, the role of differentiated products in imperfectly competitive markets, and economies of scale.

Nevertheless, although the world is a long way from the classical trade model, the principle of comparative advantage is still valid. The closer the world gets to true international specialization, the more world production and consumption can be increased, provided the problem of equitable distribution of the benefits can be solved to the satisfaction of consumers, producers, and political leaders. Complete specialization, however, remains an unrealistic limiting case, just as perfect competition is a limiting case in microeconomic theory.

International Capital Movements

Classical theory postulated that international capital movements were motivated either by interest differentials for securities of equal risk or by trade imbalances. It should be remembered that both foreign exchange rates and domestic money supplies were tied to gold. In the classical model interest differentials signaled the existence of different balances between investment opportunities and resources available for investment. As a result, the theory held, capital would flow from those countries with few investment opportunities relative to investable resources to countries with many opportunities relative to funds.

Trade imbalances were self-correcting if each country abided by the so-called rules of the game, which in a nutshell meant noninterference. For example, if country A developed an export surplus with country B, country A's money supply would automatically increase as a result of the inflow of gold to settle the accounts. Under the quantity theory of money the increase in money supply would lead to an increase in domestic prices in country A and a decrease in interest rates. Just the opposite would occur in country B.

Higher domestic prices in country A would lead to fewer exports and more imports of goods and services from country B. Lower interest rates in country A would lead to a flow of capital to country B, where interest rates had become higher. Thus the trade imbalance would eventually be reversed as country A continued to inflate and country B to deflate. The same process in reverse would automatically correct an import surplus in country A.

During the twentieth century, if not earlier, countries have refused to play by the rules of the game. Domestic money supplies have not been allowed to vary in response to trade imbalances. On the contrary, each country has attempted to pursue an independent monetary policy designed to achieve domestic economic goals rather than balance in the external accounts. Furthermore, prices are determined by a much more complex process than that assumed in the quantity theory of money.

Under today's floating exchange rates countries are even more able to pursue independent economic policies. For example, if domestic economic policy leads to rapid inflation in country A, the foreign exchange rate should eventually deteriorate in rough proportion, thereby maintaining country A's external price competitive position.

International economic theorists are now extending the classical theory of international trade and capital movements under free-trade conditions in perfectly competitive markets with a theory of worldwide oligopolistic competition in imperfect markets. This shift is parallel to the shift in attention in domestic microeconomic theory from the limiting cases of perfect competition and monopoly to imperfect competition and oligopoly. The actors in the revised theory are the multinational firms rather than the independent national manufacturers, exporters, and importers. The activity that must be explained by the updated theory is the economic rationale for direct foreign investment.

Product and Factor Market Imperfections

The modern theory of direct foreign investment can be traced to Stephen Hymer's doctoral dissertation at the Massachusetts Institute of Technology in 1960.[9] Hymer was the first person to identify imperfections in national and international markets for products and factors of production as preconditions for most direct foreign investment. His work was later extended by Charles Kindleberger (1969) and became the basis for numerous other theories based on product and factor market imperfections.[10] The more notable of these theories are associated with Harvard economists Richard Caves (1971) and Raymond Vernon (1966).[11]

The most recent extensions of the market imperfections theory have been developed by economists at the University of Reading in the United Kingdom, namely, Peter Buckley and Mark Casson (1976) and John Dunning (1977).[12] In addition to theories based on imperfections in product and factor markets, complementary theories based on financial market imperfections have been developed by a number of scholars, no one of whom has emerged as the dominant spokesperson.

According to the Hymer-Kindleberger theory, product and factor market imperfections open the door to direct foreign investment. Market imperfections may occur naturally, but they are usually attributed to policies of firms and governments. For example, firms in oligopolistic industries seek to create unique competitive advantages through product differentiation and/or preemptive investments to capture foreign raw material sources. Governments create market imperfections through tariff and nontariff barriers to trade, preferential purchasing policies, tax incentives, capital market controls, and similar policies.

One of the most important market imperfections created by governments was the formation of the European Economic Community (EEC) in 1957. The six original members agreed to remove internal tariffs, erect a common external tariff, and coordinate their monetary and fiscal policies. Although these goals were to be accomplished over a ten-year transition period, it was obvious to many U.S.- and European-based multinational firms that an opportunity existed to participate through direct foreign investment in the growth and profit that would surely come from such a large, protected market. A similar opportunity developed when the European Free Trade Association (EFTA) was established in 1958. Opportunities have also been created by governments in less developed countries that have potentially large, protected markets, such as Brazil, Indonesia, Nigeria, and India. It should be noted, however, that government policies to create protected markets can attract direct foreign investment only if the market is sufficiently large, or protected, to overcome diseconomies of scale from production units of less than optimal size.

Although government policies, oligopolistic competition, or natural barriers may create potentially large, protected markets, foreign firms operating manufacturing plants in these markets must enjoy some competitive advantages not possessed by local firms in order to be compensated for such inherent disadvantages as lack of knowledge about local customs, differing local tastes, and unfamiliar legal systems, as well as greater communication and control costs. Furthermore, the competitive advantages must allow the firm to earn a higher rate of return from direct foreign investment or licensing than would be earned by similar projects of comparable risk in the home market, assuming there is competition for capital funds within the firm. If these conditions are not met, the firm will prefer to cover foreign markets through exporting and importing, as justified by classical trade theory.

The most important competitive advantages enjoyed by multinational firms are (1) economies of scale arising from their large size; (2) managerial and marketing expertise; (3) superior technology owing to their heavy emphasis on research; (4) financial strength; and (5) differentiated products. We will discuss each of these in turn.

Economies of scale Economies of scale can be developed in production, marketing, finance, research and development, transportation, and purchasing. In each of these areas there are significant competitive advantages to being *large,* whether because of international or just domestic operations. Production economies can come from the use of large-scale, automated plant and equipment or from an ability to rationalize production through worldwide specialization. For example, some automobile manufacturers, such as Ford, produce engines in one country, transmissions in another, bodies in another, and assemble still elsewhere, with the location often being dictated by *comparative advantage.* Marketing economies occur when firms are large enough to use the most efficient advertising media to create worldwide brand identification, as well as to establish worldwide distribution, warehousing, and servicing systems. Financial economies derive from access to the full range of financial instruments and sources of funds, such as the Eurocurrency and Eurobond markets. In-house research and development programs are typically restricted to large firms because of the minimum-size threshold for establishing a laboratory and scientific staff. Transportation economies accrue to firms that can ship in carload or shipload lots. Purchasing economies come from quantity discounts and market power.

Empirical studies lend some support to the hypothesis that multinationals must be large to succeed. In comparing U.S. manufacturing multinationals with U.S. domestic firms in the same industry, Horst found that the only statistically significant variable was firm size.[13] Wolf found size linked with profitability for a large sample of U.S. multinationals when using 1962 data but not 1966 data.[14] The problem with such studies is the difficulty of determining causality. Are multinationals larger and more profitable than domestic firms because they are multinational, or are they multinational because they are larger and more profitable?

Managerial and marketing expertise Managerial expertise includes skill in managing large industrial organizations from both a human and technical viewpoint. It also encompasses knowledge of modern analytical techniques and their application in functional areas of business. Virtually no empirical studies exist to test whether managerial expertise leads to success in large, protected, worldwide oligopolistic markets. Servan-Schreiber popularized the managerial expertise (and technology) thesis in *The American Challenge,* but this book was based on case studies and intuitive reasoning.[15] For example, he cited the great depth of management in U.S. firms due to the U.S. educational opportunities to study business administration (management) at both the undergraduate and graduate levels. This situation contrasted with the elitist approach to management education in Europe. Nevertheless, a scientifically based study of the effect of managerial expertise is still lacking, a task that will be extremely difficult because of its nonquantifiable aspects.

Subsets of managerial expertise include well-developed marketing and production skills such as prior experience in similar foreign markets. In almost all surveys and case studies multinational firms have been observed to export to a market before establishing a production facility there. Likewise, they have prior experience sourcing raw materials and human capital in other foreign countries either through imports, licensing, or direct foreign investments. In this manner the multinational firms can partially overcome the supposed superior local knowledge of host country firms.

Technology Technology includes both scientific and engineering skills. It is not limited to multinationals, but U.S. firms in general have had an advantage in terms of access to continuing new technology spin-offs from the military and space programs. Empirical studies have supported the importance of technology as a characteristic of multinational firms. Raymond Vernon's product cycle theory, which is discussed later, is based on the fact that multinational firms are the originators of much of the new technology because of research and development activities on new products initially launched in their home markets.[16] Empirical tests of this theory by Gruber, Mehta, and Vernon, and Hirsch seem to confirm the relationship between research and development and direct foreign investment.[17] Still another empirical study by Severn and Laurence links direct foreign investment with research and development intensity but concludes that the higher rate of profitability of the multinationals is due to research and development rather than to their multinationality.[18] Expansion abroad merely increases the return on the fixed research and development expenditures.

Financial strength Financial strength includes not only economies of scale but the ability to reduce risk through diversification of operations and borrowing sources. Typically multinationals have had both lower cost and better availability of capital than foreign and domestic competitors. This topic will be covered later in this chapter and in the appendix to this chapter.

Differentiated products An important extension of the market imperfections theory was made by Richard Caves (1971), who studied direct foreign investment from the perspective of the economics of industrial organizations.[19] Caves noted that multinational firms are typically in industries characterized by research or marketing intensity or both. These firms create their own firm-specific advantages by producing and marketing *differentiated products*. Such products originate from research-based innovations or heavy marketing expenditures to gain brand identification. Furthermore, the research and marketing process continues to produce a steady stream of new differentiated products. It is difficult and costly for competitors to copy such products, and they must always face a time lag if they try. Having developed differentiated products for the domestic home market, the firm may decide to market them worldwide, a decision consistent with the desire to maximize return on heavy research and marketing expenditures.

Product differentiation does not necessarily mean that worldwide markets must always be serviced by direct foreign investment. Caves classifies differentiated products into three groups. If the costs of a product benefit from economies of scale in production and the product can be marketed without significant adaptation to local market conditions, Caves predicts that exports will be the preferred method of selling. If the product does not enjoy economies of scale, or if the product involves a proprietary process, licensing of foreign firms may occur. However, if the firm's main competitive advantage is embodied in research, marketing, and managerial expertise, rather than in any specific existing differentiated products, then expansion may take the form of direct foreign investment.

Product cycle theory At the same time as Caves was working on his theory of product differentiation in the economics department at Harvard University, across the river at the Harvard Business School Raymond Vernon and his colleagues were proposing another version of direct foreign investment theory based on product differentiation with a time lag.[20] Vernon's *product cycle theory* requires imperfections in both the market for products and for factors of production. It suggests that direct foreign investment is a natural stage in the life cycle of a new product from its inception to its maturity and eventual decline. The socioeconomic development, economies of scale, and oligopolistic competition, which are found in the most advanced industrial countries, lead firms in these countries to undertake intensive research and development efforts. New technologically advanced, or differentiable, products are discovered.

The new products are first introduced in the home market. Close coordination of production and sales is required while the product is improved and the production process standardized. After a short time lag the product is exported. As the new product reaches maturity, competition from nearly similar products narrows profit margins and threatens both export and the home markets.

At this stage foreign manufacturing locations are sought where market imperfections in the cost of factors of production create a chance for lower unit production costs. Thus the foreign investment is essentially a *defensive* investment designed to preserve profit margins in both export and home markets.

Examples of defensive investments can be found in many labor-intensive less developed countries. For example, the price of labor in Mexico, Puerto Rico, Hong Kong, Korea, Malaysia, and Taiwan is low compared to productivity. This feature has attracted direct foreign investment in labor-intensive industries. If laborers in these countries earn the local currency equivalent of $2 per hour compared to their U.S. counterparts, who earn $4 per hour, but their productivity is equal, a firm could cut its per-unit labor cost in half. Of course, other factors of production, such as shipping, tariffs, equipment, plant, and land, may cost much more in these countries, thereby offsetting the labor differential. Furthermore, over time labor costs may increase more rapidly in these countries than in the United States because of foreign demand for their services. In the meantime, however, a temporary market imperfection for labor exists and attracts direct foreign investment.

Richard Moxon has studied the motivation for U.S. investment in offshore electronics plants, which is an example of investment based on a combination of product cycle theory and the behavioral theory of direct foreign investment.[21] The bulk of the offshore electronics plants in the study were owned by 20 U.S. parent firms and located primarily in Mexico and Taiwan, with a smaller number in Hong Kong, Korea, and Singapore. They were exporting their output to their U.S. parents under Items 806.30 and 807.00 of the U.S. Tariff Schedules, under which U.S. duties are assessed only on their foreign value added. In most cases the parent exported materials to the subsidiary, which then conducted the labor-intensive operations and shipped the assemblies back to the parent.

On the basis of interviews with executives of the parent firms, confirmed by regression studies of the characteristics of the imports and the electronics industry, Moxon found the following motivations and behavior:

- The offshore investments were defensive in nature, being a response to strong price competition in the U.S. market from low-priced imports from foreign producers, especially from Japan. Without the offshore investment the U.S. market might have been entirely lost to imports.
- Labor-intensive products not requiring too much skill were selected for offshore production. Not only were the foreign wages lower than U.S. wages, but the workers had a more acceptable attitude toward tedious assembly work. Their productivity was higher, turnover lower, and quality standards better on standardized tasks than for their U.S. counterparts.
- Shipping costs were an important determinant of which products and operations were conducted offshore. Small, lightweight assemblies were feasible. Products that were heavy, bulky, easily damaged in shipping, or required rapid delivery were not manufactured offshore.
- Tarriffs were not an important consideration because of the low overall U.S. tariffs on electronics and the favorable provisions on imports under Items 806.30 and 807.00.
- Sales growth in the United States encouraged offshore production since it permitted U.S. facilities to remain in production and not put U.S. workers out of work.

- Products that were simple, standardized, and in high-volume production were produced offshore. These were products where automation had gone as far as it could in the United States. Custom-made and highly engineered products were produced in the United States.
- Political and economic risks were offset by use of multiple sourcing both offshore and in the United States, despite loss of economies of scale.
- Subcontracting to foreign producers occurred only when the product's volume was too low for the parent to gain the inherent economies of scale, or when fluctuations in the parent's production required peak load backup. Only the simplest products, with minimum technology transfer, were subcontracted. The foreign subcontractors could realize economies of scale and reduce fluctuation by producing for several firms as well as themselves.
- As U.S. firms gained favorable experience in offshore production, more complex offshore production operations were undertaken, such as full assembly and testing.

Follow the leader Although the product cycle theory initiated the idea of defensive investments, many other theories of defensive investments followed. Frederick Knickerbocker (1973) developed a *follow the leader theory* of defensive direct foreign investment.[22] He noted that in oligopolistic industries when one competitor undertakes a direct foreign investment, other competitors follow very quickly with defensive direct investments into that market. He hypothesized that the followers were motivated by a desire to deny any competitive advantages, such as the benefits of economies of scale, to the others.

Knickerbocker's theory does not explain why the leader initiates the original direct foreign investment, but presumably the reason springs from the opposite side of the same coin. For example, firms are observed entering potentially large markets prematurely with direct foreign investments in an attempt to gain economies of scale and preempt economies of scale from the other competitors. Some of the manufacturing investments in large, growing, less developed countries fall into this category. Even in countries where the size and growth potential of the market are permanently limited, multinationals will make direct investments or acquisitions of firms that are less profitable and riskier than themselves because of the favorable impact on economies of scale and diversification of risk for the firms as a whole, and denial of these advantages to other oligopolistic competitors. Multinationals sometimes make direct investments of a defensive nature in the home markets of competitors even though such investments appear in accounting statements to be unprofitable. The purpose is to disrupt the easy market share of competitors in their home market in order to reduce their economies of scale and thereby their competitiveness in other markets. U.S., European, and Japanese automobile manufacturing firms have sometimes considered defensive investments in each other's markets in this light.

Defensive investments are even more apparent in the raw material–producing industries, such as in oil, tin, copper, bauxite, rubber, and forest products. Control over sources of raw material, and conversely denial of these sources to competitors, causes a number of preemptive, defensive-type investments, similar to those of market-seeking oligopolists.

Another characteristic that is an important motivation for direct investments in raw materials is the need to develop economies of scale through both horizontal and vertical integration. The raw materials are typically just one stage in a multistage production process reaching all the way from raw materials to final consumers. The independents who perform only one stage in the process are often in a poor bargaining position. The fully integrated producers have alternative sources of supply and control the final markets. Thus, although an investment in raw materials may not be profitable in itself, it creates the opportunity for downstream profits that are not available to the independents.

Credibility Defensive investments also occur when *credibility* with an existing customer base becomes important. For example, this factor motivated NOVO Industri, A/S, a Danish manufacturer of industrial enzymes and pharmaceuticals (particularly insulin), to establish a plant to manufacture industrial enzymes in the United States (in North Carolina).[23] NOVO enjoyed a large export market for industrial enzymes in the United States. However, enzymes are intermediate products that are used in the production of such end products as detergents and fructose. Enzymes are living organisms that are typically custom-tailored to each manufacturer's process. Quality control and guaranteed availability are critical in the continuous processes employed in such industries. Therefore despite the loss of economies of scale in Denmark, and suboptimal economies of scale in the United States, NOVO felt obligated to establish a manufacturing presence in the United States to maintain its credibility in the marketplace.

Growth to survive Another version of defensive investments suggests that firms invest abroad because they have saturated the domestic market and any further expansion domestically would lead to destructive retaliation by the other oligopolists or antitrust action (in the United States).[24] Growth abroad, either through new investments or acquisitions, is the natural reaction of firms that have a "grow to survive" attitude. In these firms, however, there could also be an intuitive understanding that growth leads to improving economies of scale relative to competitors and therefore ultimately to superior financial performance.

Knowledge seekers Multinational firms that have been identified as *knowledge seekers* are still another example of defensive investments. These are firms trying to maintain or acquire a better position in one or more of the key competitive variables. In particular, they are trying to improve managerial expertise, technology, or knowledge of product and factor markets. This goal is accomplished most efficiently by acquisition of foreign firms that already possess some of these attributes. There may also be an element of improving economies of scale and financial strength in these types of acquisitions. Phillips (the Netherlands), Siemens (Germany), and Nippon Electric (Japan) have all made important acquisitions of U.S. firms in the integrated circuit and semiconductor business. Most acquisitions were located near San Francisco in the area known popularly as "Silicon Valley." This area is one of several centers of excellence in the electronics field.

Follow the customer The growing presence abroad of service firms is a final example of defensive investments. Banking, advertising, legal, and accounting firms have typically followed their clients abroad. Their motivation is to counter efforts by other international and local service firms to steal their clients. They are forced to invest in facilities and staff in key foreign locations both for credibility and for convenience.

Internalization During the past ten years economists at the University of Reading (United Kingdom), followed by others, have attempted to synthesize and extend those theories of direct foreign investment that are based on market imperfections. Peter Buckley and Mark Casson (1976) and John Dunning (1977) hypothesize that the mere existence of imperfect markets and competitive advantages for oligopolistic firms is not sufficient to guarantee direct foreign investment.[25] As was pointed out by Caves earlier, they claim that the advantaged firms could cover foreign markets through exports, licensed production, or management contracts. Thus for direct foreign investment to occur, competitive advantages must be firm-specific, not easily copied, and in a form that allows them to be transferred to foreign affiliates. For example, economies of scale and financial strength are not necessarily firm-specific because they can and are achieved by many firms throughout the world. Certain kinds of technology can be purchased, licensed, or copied. Even differentiated products can lose their advantage to slightly altered versions given enough marketing effort and the right price.

According to the theory of internalization, the key ingredient for maintaining a firm-specific competitive advantage is possession of proprietary information and control of the human capital that can generate new information through expertise in research, management, marketing, and technology. Needless to say, once again large research-intensive firms are most likely to fit this description.

Why does possession of information lead to direct foreign investment? In the words of Alan Rugman, one of the theory's strong proponents:

> Information is an intermediate product *par excellence.* It is the oil which lubricates the engine of the MNE [multinational enterprise]. There is no proper market for the sale of information created by MNE and therefore no price for it. There are surrogate prices; for example, those found by evaluating the opportunity cost of factor inputs expended in the production and processing of a new research discovery or by an *ex post* evaluation of the extra profits generated by that discovery, assuming all other costs to remain the same. Yet there is no simple interaction of supply and demand to set a market price. Instead the MNE is driven to create an internal market of its own in order to overcome the failure of an external market to emerge for the sale of information. This internal market of the MNE is an efficient response to the given exogenous market imperfection in the determination of the price of information. Internalization allows the MNE to solve the appropriability problem by assigning property rights in knowledge to the MNE organization.
>
> The creation of an internal market by the MNE permits it to transform an intangible piece of research into a valuable property specific to the firm. The MNE will exploit its advantage in all available markets and will keep the use of information internal to the firm in order to recoup its initial expenditures on research and knowledge generation. Production by subsidiaries is preferable to licensing or joint ventures since the latter two arrangements cannot benefit from the internal market of an MNE. They would therefore dissipate the information monopoly of the MNE, unless foreign markets were segmented by effective international patent laws or other protective devices.[26]

Although the theory of internalization is appealing as a high-level synthesis of market imperfections theories, it lacks empirical verification. Testing such a theory is difficult where no observable market exists external to the firm. Furthermore, we do observe cases where multinational firms have been willing to license information in one market at the same time as they are exploiting it through export or direct foreign investment in other markets. John Dunning has proposed an *eclectic theory* of international production in which location-specific factors explain why a firm might serve a particular market by direct foreign investment or export or management contract or licensing.[27]

Management contracts and licensing as alternatives to direct foreign investment In recent years a number of host countries have demanded that multinational firms sell their services in "unbundled form" rather than only through direct investment. For instance, they would like to purchase managerial expertise and knowledge of product and factor markets through management contracts, technology through licensing agreements, and financial strength through loans.

The answer to these demands depends on the price host countries are willing to pay for the unbundled services. If the price were high enough, many firms would prefer to take advantage of market imperfections in an unbundled way, particularly in view of the *lower political, foreign exchange, and business risks*. Since we observe multinationals continuing to prefer direct investments, we must assume that the price for selling unbundled services is still too low.

Why is the price of unbundled services too low? The answer may lie in the synergy created when services are bundled as direct investments in the first place. Managerial expertise is often dependent on a delicate mix of organizational support factors that cannot be transferred externally efficiently. Technology is a continuous process, but licensing usually captures only the technology of a particular point in time. Most important of all, however, economies of scale cannot be sold or transferred in small bundles. By definition they require large-scale operations. How can even a relatively large operation in a small market achieve the same economies of scale as a large operation in a large market?

Despite the handicaps some multinationals have successfully sold unbundled services. An example would be the current sales of managerial expertise and technology to the OPEC countries. In this case, however, the OPEC countries are both willing and able to pay a price high enough to approach the returns on direct foreign investment (bundled services), while only receiving the lesser benefits of the unbundled services.

Imperfections in the Market for Financial Assets

Modern portfolio theory suggests that an investor can improve risk versus return performance by holding an internationally diversified portfolio of securities as compared with a domestically diversified portfolio.[28] An explanation of thinking on internationally diversified portfolios by Donald Lessard is contained in the appendix to this chapter.

Unfortunately, barriers to international capital flows and imperfections in national securities markets reduce the ability of investors to hold optimally diversified international portfolios. A comprehensive study by Gunter Dufey for the U.S. Treasury Department summarizes these imperfections under three categories: incentives, constraints, and investor perceptions.[29]

Incentives for portfolio investment Incentives in favor of portfolio investment include intelligent regulation of securities markets and new issues; good experience, depth, breadth, and resilience of certain capital markets; and market efficiency as measured by a low level of transaction costs. With respect to regulation of the market the United States is far more advanced than the others, followed by the United Kingdom. The same is true of depth and breadth of the markets and low transactions costs. These encourage foreign portfolio investment in the United States and the United Kingdom.

Constraints on portfolio investment Constraints on portfolio investment include taxes, foreign exchange, and capital market controls. The most important tax barrier is the withholding tax on dividends and interest. Foreign investors used to pay a withholding tax to the United States of up to 30% (until 1984) on income received on U.S. securities. Similar withholding taxes are imposed by many other countries. Other potential tax barriers are caused by the differential incidence of foreign domestic taxes and bureaucratic difficulty in claiming foreign tax credits, both of which can lead to unintended double taxation.

Foreign exchange controls that are barriers to portfolio investment include an outright ban on the purchase of foreign securities, such as Japan has imposed periodically, or a ban on foreign purchase of domestic securities, like that imposed by Germany and Switzerland in 1973. Special taxes on the purchase of foreign securities, such as the interest-equalization tax imposed by the United States in the period 1963–1974, also are significant constraints. Another barrier is a split foreign exchange market, such as that in the United Kingdom (until 1978), where U.K. investors were required to purchase "investment sterling" at a premium over "resident sterling" if they wished to buy foreign securities.

Capital market control systems can also be barriers. They include restricting access to the capital market by operating a "queue" (wait in line), as in the United Kingdom, France, Germany, and Switzerland; requiring complete and complex disclosure (United States); requiring ceilings on the amount of domestic securities that can be owned by foreigners in total and for individual firms (Japan); and restricting the composition of institutional portfolios, such as those of insurance companies in the United States.

Investor perceptions can be an effective barrier to international portfolio investment. Investors typically have only limited knowledge about foreign securities because of inadequate disclosure and unfamiliarity with foreign investment institutional practices and securities markets. Investors also lack confidence in their ability to forecast sales and profit potentials in foreign markets, as well as foreign exchange and political risks. On the other hand, these perceived risks may be compensated for by opportunities for a higher rate of return relative to risk than that in domestic securities, particularly if systematic risk is recognized.

The multinational firm as a surrogate for an internationally diversified portfolio If securities market imperfections make it difficult for the investor to hold an optimally diversified international portfolio, can the shares of a multinational corporation, whose activities are already internationally diversified, serve as a surrogate investment vehicle? The answer probably is yes. There is almost bound to be some reduction in a portfolio's overall and systematic risk because project returns in different countries are not likely to be perfectly correlated with each other even if the projects are in the same industry. Furthermore, many multinationals are diversified both by industry and by country. A further benefit they provide is diversification of foreign exchange risk and political risk.

Not only can investors overcome imperfections in the worldwide market for financial assets by holding shares in multinational firms, they can simultaneously benefit from the multinational firms' aforementioned ability to exploit imperfections in the markets for real assets and factors of production. Although it is difficult empirically to separate and test the effect of each of these benefits, they in combination contribute to a better risk versus return performance for multinational firms compared to domestic firms.

It has been suggested that large individual or institutional investors might capture the benefits of imperfections in the market for real assets, and avoid securities market imperfections, by buying an internationally diversified share of specific projects. This strategy would probably not be successful, however, because the investors offer only financial capital. To really capitalize on the opportunities, they would need to provide at least some of the other key competitive variables in oligopolistic markets that were described earlier. Kobrin and Lessard used this very reasoning to forecast that investors from the OPEC countries would not benefit from making direct foreign investments in the industrialized countries, particularly the United States, because they offer only financial capital.[30] They could expect only the normal market rate of return for a given level of risk and therefore might as well buy an efficiently diversified portfolio.

In fact, the bulk of foreign investment in the United States is in the form of portfolio investment rather than direct foreign investments. This situation is partly due to the competitive difficulty of capturing returns from market imperfections on real assets but also to the fact that there are fewer imperfections in the U.S. market for financial assets. In other words, there are few impediments to capital inflow and the securities markets are relatively efficient and well regulated in the United States.

If the shares of multinational firms indeed provide an investor with the benefits of market imperfections, and the investor recognizes this advantage, one would expect the shares of multinational firms to sell at a premium compared to shares of domestic firms. The premium should be roughly equal to the cost to investors of capturing the benefits of market imperfections themselves. Whether the cost of equity of multinational firms is actually lower than that of a collection of uninational firms with comparable investments is an empirical question that is drawing considerable attention. Studies by Agmon and Lessard, Rugman, Aggarwal, and Kohers support the lower cost of equity hypothesis.[31] However, their conclusions are challenged by Jacquillat and Solnik, as well as Adler.[32] We will return to this question in the appendix to this chapter and again in Chapter 12.

Imperfections in the foreign exchange market Robert Aliber (1970) suggested that some foreign direct investment is motivated by imperfections in the foreign exchange markets.[33] He noted that foreign direct investment is attracted to countries that have undervalued currencies and from countries that have overvalued currencies. This statement assumes, of course, that purchasing power parity is perceived to be in disequilibrium. Despite the foreign exchange benefits, however, foreign investment seems unlikely to occur unless imperfections also exist in product or factor markets and unless the investing firms have competitive advantages, as previously described. Nevertheless, Aliber's theory may have some relevance for the timing of direct foreign investment. Firms that are already considering an investment might actually start the process at a time when they believe their currency is overvalued or a potential host country's currency is undervalued.

Several empirical tests of the foreign exchange rate hypothesis have been undertaken, with inconclusive results.[34] However, overvaluation of the U.S. dollar relative to European currencies during the late 1950s and the 1960s may have contributed, perhaps modestly, to decisions by U.S. firms to invest in the EEC and EFTA countries. Indeed, purchasing power parity was quite likely not functioning properly during this period because of fixed exchange rates.

With the advent of floating rates, opportunities to recognize and take advantage of deviations from purchasing power parity appear less likely than they were during the period of fixed exchange rates that Aliber studied. Nevertheless, as pointed out in Chapter 5, temporary disequilibria do occur. For example, note the unpredicted weakness of the U.S. dollar in 1978 followed by its exceptional strength 1980–1985. We have already suggested in Chapter 7 that one way for firms to manage their foreign exchange economic exposure is to diversify internationally their sales, sourcing, and financing. Direct foreign investment is one method to accomplish this diversification.

Synthesis

Synthesizing all the theories of direct foreign investment based on market imperfections is difficult. In our opinion the theory of internalization, as extended by the eclectic theory of production, is the most advanced attempt so far, but it suffers from the same empirical testing problems as the other theories. Nearly all the empirical tests show that direct foreign investment originates in firms that are large, research-intensive, and subject to oligopolistic competition from both domestic and foreign firms. However, these characteristics are consistent with nearly all the theories proposed.

Even if the market imperfections theory could be conclusively tested, some types of direct foreign investment would probably fall outside its purview.[35] For example, none of the theories have attempted to explain the increasingly important direct foreign investment by service firms. It is believed that they follow their customers abroad, but we are unaware of empirical tests of this hypothesis.

Another type of direct foreign investment that seems to fall outside the market imperfections classification relates to political safety. Firms we have previously defined as *political safety seekers* invest in politically safe countries, but their main motivation is to *disinvest* from politically unsafe countries. Although individual and institutional investors, and some industrial firms, would typically place these kinds of flight funds in portfolio investments in foreign countries, at least some of the investment ends up in direct foreign investment. Testing the political safety motivation is almost impossible, because firms will not reveal political motives while some of their assets or interests remain behind. Nevertheless it is common knowledge in the business and banking communities that such flights occur. Although we often picture politically motivated foreign investments as emanating from unstable Latin American, African, and Asian countries, apprehension about socialism in Europe at the beginning of the 1980s led to significant movements of funds from Europe to the United States.

Diversification of political risk is a motive for multiple sourcing of raw material. A raw material shortage might develop because of expropriations, strikes, war, boycotts, and other interruptions. These have periodically created worldwide shortages in copper and oil. Changes in foreign exchange rates or exchange controls could also make one source of raw material more costly or less available than another in the short run.

SUMMARY

The direct foreign investment decision results from a complex process motivated by strategic, behavioral, and economic considerations. Surveys and case studies of multinational firms indicate that their strategic motivations can be classified into five main types: market seekers; raw material seekers; production efficiency seekers; knowledge seekers; and political safety seekers.

Behavioral studies show that the foreign investment decision is often motivated by a strong stimulus from the external environment, or from within an organization on the basis of personal biases, needs, and commitments of individuals and groups. The investigation process itself, particularly the choice of projects to be investigated, is a major determinant of the foreign investment decision.

The economic rationale for direct foreign investment is based on a theory of imperfections in individual national markets for products, factors of production, and financial assets. Product and factor market imperfections provide an opportunity for multinational firms to outcompete local firms, particularly in industries characterized by worldwide oligopolistic competition, because the multinational firms have superiority in economies of scale, managerial expertise, technology, differentiated products, and financial strength. Oligopolistic competition also motivates firms to make defensive investment abroad to save both export and home markets from foreign competition. The product cycle theory suggests that new products are first developed in the most advanced countries by large firms that have the ability to undertake research and development. The new products are introduced into the home market and later exported. As the product matures and the production process becomes standardized, foreign competition reduces profit margins and threatens the home market. Part of the production process is then defensively relocated abroad to take advantage of lower unit costs of labor or other factors of production.

Defensive direct foreign investments may also be motivated by "follow the leader" behavior; a desire to establish credibility with local customers; a "grow to survive" philosophy; a desire to gain knowledge by acquiring firms with valuable expertise; and a need to follow the customer in the case of service firms.

The theory of internalization holds that firms having a competitive advantage because of their ability to generate valuable proprietary information can only capture the full benefits of innovation through direct foreign investment. A desire to control the use of proprietary information explains the reluctance of multinational firms to unbundle their services to host countries in the form of management contracts and licensing agreements. However, economies of scale, location-specific factors, and the price of such unbundled services also play a role in this decision.

Imperfections in the market for financial assets make it difficult for an investor to hold an optimally diversified international portfolio of securities. Holding shares in a multinational firm may be the second-best alternative open to investors. The multinational firm is already diversified internationally, although not necessarily in an optimal way. The investor also has the opportunity to capture the benefits of imperfections in the markets for products and factors of production through the multinational firm.

Imperfection in the foreign exchange market may influence the timing of direct foreign investment. In addition, some motivations for direct foreign investment cannot easily be classified under market imperfections theory. One example is disinvestment emanating from countries where political risk is a factor.

NOTES

1. The first four classifications were suggested in W. Dickerson Hogue, "The Foreign Investment Decision Making Process," *Association for Education in International Business Proceedings,* December 29, 1967, pp. 1–2. They were also contained in Lee Nehrt and W. Dickerson Hogue, "The Foreign Investment Decision Process," *Quarterly Journal of AISEC International,* February–April 1968, pp. 43–48.

2. *U.S. Production Abroad and the Balance of Payments,* New York: The Conference Board, 1966, p. 63.

3. Arthur Stonehill and Leonard Nathanson, "Capital Budgeting and the Multinational Corporation," *California Management Review,* Summer 1968, p. 40.

4. Yair Aharoni, *The Foreign Investment Decision Process,* Boston: Harvard Graduate School of Business Administration, Division of Research, 1966.

5. *Ibid.,* pp. 54–55.

6. *Ibid.,* pp. 70–71.

7. Herbert Simon, *Administrative Behavior,* New York: Macmillan, 1947; and Richard Cyert and James March, *A Behavioral Theory of the Firm,* Englewood Cliffs, N.J.: Prentice-Hall, 1963.

8. Aharoni, *The Foreign Investment Decision Process,* pp. 79–82.

9. Stephen Hymer, Ph.D. dissertation, Massachusetts Institute of Technology, 1960. This study was later published as *The International Operations of National Firms: A Study of Direct Foreign Investment,* Cambridge, Mass.: MIT Press, 1976.

10. Charles P. Kindleberger, *American Business Abroad: Six Lectures on Direct Investment,* New Haven: Yale University Press, 1969.

11. Richard E. Caves, "International Corporations: The Industrial Economics of Foreign Investment," *Economica,* February 1971, pp. 1–27; and Raymond Vernon, "International Investment and International Trade in the Product Cycle," *Quarterly Journal of Economics,* May 1966, pp. 190–207.

12. Peter J. Buckley and Mark Casson, *The Future of the Multinational Enterprise,* London: Macmillan, 1976; and John H. Dunning, "Trade Location of Economic Activity and the MNE: A Search for an Eclectic Approach" in Bertil Ohlin, Per-Ove Hesselborn, and Per Magnus Wijkman, eds., *The International Allocation of Economic Activity,* New York: Holmes and Meier, 1977, pp. 395–418.

13. Thomas Horst, "Firm and Industry Determinants of the Decision to Invest Abroad: An Empirical Study," *Review of Economics and Statistics,* August 1972, pp. 258–266.

14. Bernard N. Wolf, "Size and Profitability among U.S. Manufacturing Firms: Multinational versus Primarily Domestic Firms," *Journal of Economics and Business,* Fall 1975, pp. 15–22.

15. J. J. Servan-Schreiber, *The American Challenge,* London: Hamish Hamilton, 1968.

16. Raymond Vernon, "International Investment and International Trade in the Product Cycle," *Quarterly Journal of Economics,* May 1966, pp. 190–207.

17. W. Gruber, D. Mehta, and R. Vernon, "The R & D Factor in International Trade and International Investment of United States Industries," *Journal of Political Economy,* February 1967, pp. 20–37. Also see Se'ev Hirsch, *Location of Industry and International Competitiveness,* Oxford: Oxford University Press, 1967; S. Hirsch, "Multinationals:

How Different Are They?" in G. Y. Bertin, ed., *The Growth of the Large Multinational Corporation,* Paris: Centre Nationale de la Recherche Scientifique, 1973.

18. A. Severn and M. M. Laurence, "Direct Investment, Research Intensity, and Profitability," *Journal of Financial and Quantitative Analysis,* March 1974, pp. 181–190.

19. Caves, "International Corporations."

20. Vernon, "International Investment"; Gruber, Mehta, and Vernon, "R & D Factor in International Trade."

21. Richard W. Moxon, "The Motivation for Investment in Offshore Plants: The Case of the U.S. Electronics Industry," *Journal of International Business Studies,* Spring 1975, pp. 51–66. Also see Richard W. Moxon, "Offshore Production in the Less-Developed Countries: A Case Study of Multinationality in the Electronics Industry," *The Bulletin,* Nos. 98–99, New York University, July 1974, pp. 1–90.

22. A good synthesis of oligopoly theory and its relation to multinational firms can be found in Fred T. Knickerbocker, *Oligopolistic Reaction and the Multinational Enterprise,* Boston: Harvard Graduate School of Business Administration, 1973.

23. This information came from a close working relationship between one of the authors and officials of the firm.

24. For studies of the "growth" version of international oligopoly theory, see Bela Belassa, "American Direct Investment in the Common Market," Banca Nazionale del Lavoro, *Quarterly Review,* June 1966, pp. 121–146. Also see Stephen Hymer and Robert Rowthorn, "Multinational Corporations and International Oligopoly: The Non-American Challenge," in Charles P. Kindleberger, ed., *The International Corporation: A Symposium,* Cambridge, Mass.: MIT Press, 1970, pp. 57–91.

25. Buckley and Casson, *Future of the Multinational Enterprise;* and Dunning, "Trade Location."

26. Alan Rugman, "Internalization as a General Theory of Foreign Direct Investment: A Re-Appraisal of the Literature," *Weltwirtschaftliches Archiv,* Vol. 116, No. 2, June 1980, pp. 368–369.

27. See all of the John Dunning bibliographical citations.

28. See H. G. Grubel, "Internationally Diversified Portfolios," *American Economic Review,* December 1968, pp. 1229–1314. Also see Haim Levy and Marshall Sarnat, "International Diversification of Investment Portfolios," *American Economic Review,* September 1970, pp. 668–675; Donald R. Lessard, "World, Country and Industry Relationships in Equity Returns: Implications for Risk Reduction through International Diversification," *Financial Analysts Journal,* January–February 1976, pp. 32–38.

29. Gunter Dufey, "Institutional Constraints and Incentives on International Portfolio Investment," *International Portfolio Investment,* U.S. Department of the Treasury OASIA, 1975.

30. Stephen J. Kobrin and Donald R. Lessard, "Large Scale Direct OPEC Investment in U.S. Enterprise and the Theory of Foreign Direct Investment—A Contradiction," *Weltwirtschaftliches Archiv,* December 1976, pp. 660–673.

31. See Tamir Agmon and Donald Lessard, "Investor Recognition of Corporate International Diversification," *Journal of Finance,* September 1977, pp. 1049–1055. Also see Alan R. Rugman, "Motives for Foreign Investment: The Market Imperfections and Risk Diversification Hypothesis," *Journal of World Trade Law,* September–October 1975, pp. 567–573; Raj Aggarwal, "Multinationality and Stock Market Valuation," *Management International Review,* Vol. 19, February 1979, pp. 5–21;

Theodor Kohers, "The Effect of Multinational Operations on the Cost of Equity Capital of U.S. Corporations: An Empirical Study," *Management International Review,* Vol. 15, Nos. 2–3, 1975, pp. 121–124.

32. Bertrand Jacquillat and Bruno Solnik, "Multinationals Are Poor Tools for Diversification," *Journal of Portfolio Management,* Winter 1978, pp. 8–12; and Michael Adler, "Investor Recognition of Corporation International Diversification: Comment," *Journal of Finance,* March 1981, pp. 187–190.

33. Robert Aliber, "A Theory of Foreign Direct Investment," in Charles P. Kindleberger, ed., *The International Corporation,* Cambridge, Mass.: MIT Press, 1970, pp. 17–34.

34. A fairly recent test was made by Dennis E. Logue and Thomas D. Willett, "The Effects of Exchange Rate Adjustment on International Investment," in Peter B. Clark, Dennis E. Logue, and Richard J. Sweeney, eds., *The Effects of Exchange Rate Adjustments,* Washington, D.C.: Department of the Treasury, 1977, pp. 137–150.

35. Several good articles on the state of the art in direct foreign investment theory provide descriptions of additional theories that we have not discussed and sometimes are not dependent on a market imperfections assumption. See, for example, Jamuna P. Agarwal, "Determinants of Foreign Direct Investment: A Survey," *Weltwirtschaftliches Archiv,* No. 4, 1980, pp. 739–773; Giorgio Ragazzi, "Theories of the Determinants of Direct Foreign Investment," International Monetary Fund, *Staff Papers,* July 1973, pp. 471–498; and A. L. Calvet, "A Synthesis of Foreign Direct Investment Theories and Theories of the Multinational Firm," *Journal of International Business Studies,* Spring–Summer 1981, pp. 43–59.

Chapter 8: Appendix International Diversification and Direct Foreign Investment

Donald R. Lessard
Associate Professor
Sloan School of Management, MIT

Although there is general agreement that the principal motivations for direct foreign investment (DFI) lie in the realm of the theory of industrial organization, many hold that there also are financial motivations for DFI.[1] Among these financial motivations, international diversification of risks has received the greatest attention. This appendix develops the rationale for international diversification.

THE DIVERSIFICATION MOTIVE

It is generally accepted that investors should and can expect higher rates of return on risky investments than they can earn on less risky investments. Thus the required rate of return applicable to a particular investment will consist of the interest rate, reflecting society's time preference as well as a premium for inflation, and a risk premium.

$$R_j = r + \text{risk premium},$$

where R_j is the required rate of return on asset j, a project, firm, or security issued by a firm, and r is the nominal interest rate on a riskless security.

As long as returns from different assets are not subject to exactly the same risks, the risk of a portfolio of these assets will be less than the risk of the typical security in the portfolio. This implies that the risk of an asset in the context of a well-diversified portfolio, termed its *systematic risk,* will be less than its *total risk*. Recognizing this, risk-averse investors will hold diversified portfolios of assets. As a result, in equilibrium the premiums which individuals demand for bearing risks will reflect only systematic risk, that portion of a risk which cannot be diversified away within an economy. The relationship between these three components of risk and the extent of risk reduction possible through diversification is illustrated in Exhibit 8A.1.

EXHIBIT 8A.1
Risk Reduction through Diversification: The Domestic Case

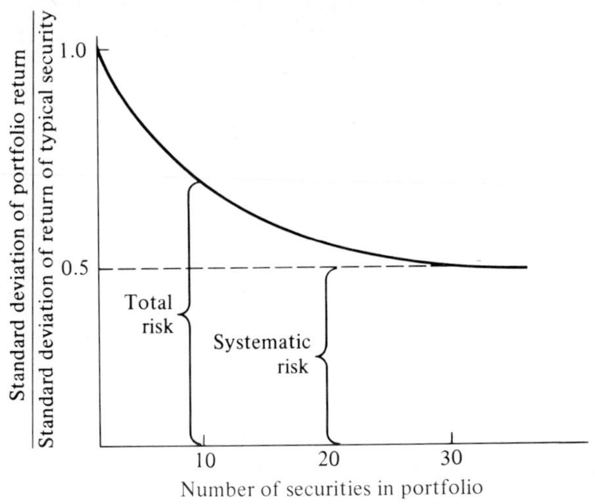

THE MAGNITUDE OF RISK REDUCTION THROUGH DIVERSIFICATION

The proportion of total risk which is systematic depends on the degree of correlation among the outcomes of the various projects, firms, or securities which represent claims on firms. For the U.S., the degree of correlation between returns on shares of individual firms and the completely diversified portfolio, the market aggregate of all risky securities, typically is around .5.[2] This means that on average, the systematic risk of a security is 50% of its total risk. Figures for a variety of other countries are presented in Exhibit 8A.2.

In general, the proportion of risk of securities which is systematic in other countries is higher than in the U.S. This reflects the fact that these countries typically have a less diverse industrial base than the U.S. and, in some cases, a more volatile political environment. This is particularly true for less-developed countries where there is little room for risk reduction through domestic diversification.

When diversification is extended across national boundaries, a substantial proportion of the risk which is systematic within each country can be averaged out. Exhibit 8A.3 shows this, comparing the risk reduction through diversification within the U.S. to that obtainable through international diversification. In the international case, portfolio risk drops to 33% of that of the typical stock, one-third less than the U.S. figure.

EXHIBIT 8A.2
Risk Reduction through Domestic Diversification

	STANDARD DEVIATION OF MARKET PORTFOLIO DIVIDED BY STANDARD DEVIATION OF TYPICAL STOCK		
Country	*Solnik 1966–1971 (a)*	*Lessard 1969–1973 (b)*	*Lessard 1958–1968 (c)*
Argentina	—	—	.81
Brazil	—	—	.69
Chile	—	—	.71
Colombia	—	—	.84
France	.57	.68	—
Germany	.66	.66	—
Japan	—	.52	—
The Netherlands	.49	.63	—
Switzerland	.66	.71	—
U.K.	.59	.61	—
U.S.	.52	—	—

Sources: (a) B. H. Solnik, "Why Not Diversify Internationally?" *Financial Analysts Journal* (July–August 1974); (b) D. R. Lessard, "World, National, and Industry Factors in Equity Returns: Implications for Risk Reduction through International Diversification," *Financial Analysts Journal* (January–February 1976); and (c) D. R. Lessard, "International Portfolio Diversification: A Multivariate Analysis for a Group of Latin American Countries," *Journal of Finance* (June 1973).

EXHIBIT 8A.3
Risk Reduction through National and International Diversification

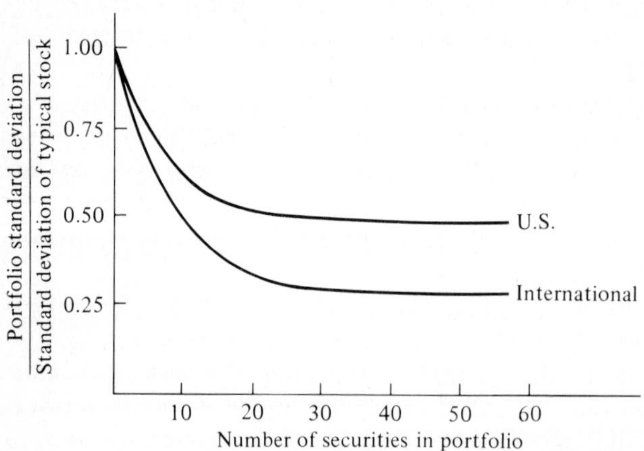

The reason for this additional diversification is that returns on diversified single-country portfolios display considerable independence. This can be seen by examining the correlations between returns on the stock markets of seven major countries and the U.S. for different periods of time through 1977, reported in Exhibit 8A.4.

In interpreting these correlations, it should be kept in mind that each of these single-market portfolios is completely diversified within the country, reflecting only 50 to 70% of the risk of the individual securities which it includes. As a result, a useful benchmark for comparison is the typical correlations between well-diversified portfolios such as mutual funds in the U.S. and the overall U.S. market portfolio. These correlations average around .90.[3]

Canada, as would be expected, moves most closely with the U.S. This reflects the close physical and financial integration of the two economies and the fact that both have similar, broadly diversified industrial structures. The correlations have decreased in recent years, perhaps reflecting the greater importance of political factors within Canada that distinguish it from its North American neighbor.

The Netherlands and Switzerland also display relatively high correlations with the U.S. over most time periods. This reflects their openness and integration with the world economy, but also the fact that both are headquarters for major multinational firms. As a result, the domestic stock market includes claims on a significant proportion of foreign activities. The only exception is the 1971–1973 period where the major currency realign-

EXHIBIT 8A.4
Correlation of Major Foreign Markets with U.S.—Selected Periods

Country	*61–65*	*64–68*	*67–71*	*70–74*	*73–77*	*7/71–6/73*	*7/73–6/75*	*7/75–6/77*
Canada	.828	.830	.813	.836	.727	—	—	—
France	.364	.016	.081	.349	.499	−.240	.683	.392
Germany	.563	.120	.343	.349	.431	.161	.487	.500
Japan	.181	.070	.224	.301	.396	.364	.293	.727
The Netherlands	.695	.602	.570	.463	.609	.154	.671	.618
Switzerland	.559	.346	.532	.501	.629	.148	.689	.718
U.K.	.428	.187	.278	.483	.507	.312	.596	.256

Source: Based on monthly changes in market indexes in *Capital International Perspective,* Geneva, Switzerland, Capital International, S.A., various issues.

Note: All periods are 60 months long, except 7/71–6/73, with 54 observations, and the last three subperiods, each of 24 months.

ments and associated adjustments caused the value of the U.S. portfolio to diverge from that of most other countries.

Correlations of the U.S. market returns with those of France, Germany, and the U.K. display considerable variability over time. This reflects changes in the degree of uncertainty regarding domestic, political, and economic developments as well as changes in the volatility of economic factors affecting the entire world economy. Only Japan shows a continuing upward trend, reflecting its greater industrial and financial integration into the world economy.

An important question is whether the correlations among markets are increasing over time and thus whether the advantages of international diversification have decreased in recent years. There is little question that worldwide political and economic influences have become more volatile. The oil crisis affected all industrial economies, and the repercussions continue. The degree of independence among returns in various stock markets has decreased as a result. As shown in Exhibit 8A.4, the correlations among markets have been rising in recent years. However, they also have varied considerably from period to period. In the early 1960s they were nearly as high as they are now. They fell in the mid-1960s as the world economy experienced relative stability, and continued at relatively high levels into the late 1960s as the performance of the U.S. and European economies diverged.

When the most recent period is broken into shorter periods, an interesting pattern emerges. Correlations of major foreign markets with the U.S. were low from July 1971 to June 1973, reflecting major currency adjustments and divergent economic performance by the U.S. From July 1973 to June 1975 they rose dramatically, reflecting the common impact of the energy crisis and subsequent developments, and they remained relatively high in the most recent 24-month period. The correlations among the various foreign countries, which are not reported in the table, also tell an interesting story. The continental EEC countries have tended to move more closely together, with the exception of France, which has had a series of internal upheavals. The U.K. has moved in and out of synchronization as international and domestic influences have varied in importance.

Empirical evidence suggests that the potential for risk reduction through international diversification is even greater for less-developed countries. Variations in the returns from projects in these countries are even less related to international factors than is the case for developed countries. Domestic uncertainties and, in particular, political factors appear to dominate. Further, there is little interconnection of capital markets since local private investors are often restricted to the domestic capital market and foreign investors do not have ready access to local security markets because of official restrictions and the undeveloped state of the markets themselves.

RELEVANCE OF FINANCIAL MOTIVES TO DFI

There is no question that the diversification motive is an important determinant of desired capital flows. However, there is considerable controversy regarding the role it plays in DFI. The arguments against its relevance are essentially of two types: (1) Relatively few barriers exist to capital flows, and therefore investors can obtain the same benefits by holding internationally diversified portfolios of shares; or (2) managers of MNCs (multinational corporations) do not act according to the assumptions of the economic model on which diversification gains are premised. Each of these arguments is discussed below.

Investors Can Do It Themselves

When an MNC invests internationally, it typically transfers capital as well as management and technology. Even when it borrows locally to finance the expansion, DFI almost always involves a transfer of risk capital. Thus, in investing internationally the MNC serves as a financial intermediary. In a world with no barriers to capital flows, this intermediation could take place through a variety of channels, including bank loans and portfolio investment, and the MNC's ability to diversify internationally would not result in a competitive advantage. Thus only when there are impediments or costs to market-minded international financial transactions are financial considerations a motive for DFI. This argument parallels the generally accepted view that imperfections in markets for technology or other real factors of production are what make these factors relevant to multinationalism. In each case there are underlying economic forces that motivate an international transfer of some factor, and barriers or impediments to market-mediated transfers that make DFI the most attractive channel.

Financial markets by and large are among the most efficient of all markets since there are many possible transactors, information is widely disseminated, and transactions costs tend to be quite low. Nevertheless, there are a number of sovereign and institutional impediments to international capital flows, as explained earlier in this chapter.

A further impediment to international diversification at an investor level is the fact that due to industrial organization or other considerations, many ventures are directly owned by MNCs and as a result are not open to investors. In a strict sense, this cannot be termed a financial motivation for DFI. However, it does serve to illustrate the interaction between real and financial motivations. Determining the extent to which these impediments encourage capital flows via DFI is a difficult empirical question. However, given the powerful motives for financial transfers, it would appear that financial market imperfections should be included in the list of factors favoring DFI.

Managers Don't Act That Way

Much of the literature on DFI stresses behavioral rather than economic motives for multinationalism. The tastes and desires of managers, it is argued, far outweigh considerations of shareholder wealth maximization. Ironically, if this is the case, diversification is even a stronger motive for DFI than with shareholder wealth maximization. In this case, diversification will be a motivation whether or not there are barriers to portfolio capital flows. Managers typically are risk averse and, as a result, will prefer a more stable stream of earnings to a more volatile one. International diversification provides a natural way to accomplish this since it does not require that the firm diversify into businesses in which it has little expertise.

EMPIRICAL EVIDENCE ON THE RELEVANCE OF THE DIVERSIFICATION MOTIVE

Even a casual examination of DFI patterns shows that diversification is not the sole motivation for MNC expansion. If it were, the world would be dominated by global holding companies and DFI would not be concentrated in research and advertising-intensive industries. However, this does not rule out diversification as a joint determinant of DFI. If it is a joint determinant, then a valid test of its relevance must be capable of separating its effects from those of real market imperfections. To date, there are no direct tests of the diversification motive which do this.

An example of a false test of the diversification motive is an examination of the "portfolios" of foreign projects held by MNCs to see if they are efficient in terms of expected return and (total) variance.[4] Such a test would reject the diversification motive since MNC portfolios tend to be concentrated in countries where returns are highly correlated with the U.S., especially Canada. However, it fails to take into account the real considerations that motivate DFI. Further, it misinterprets the diversification argument. Barring behavioral considerations, MNCs should not be expected to form portfolios which are efficient in terms of expected returns and total risk. Rather, they should invest more heavily, relative to the level justified by real advantages, in those countries or industries where investors cannot readily diversify for themselves, thus enabling investors to improve the risk-return composition of their portfolios.[5]

Indirect evidence of the relevance of the diversification motive is provided by Hughes, Logue, and Sweeney (1975), and Agmon and Lessard (1977), who show that MNC security price behavior does reflect the extent of corporate international diversification.[6] In other words, investors at a minimum recognize the diversification provided by MNCs. Whether they place a value on this MNC diversification is yet to be determined. In either case, the fact that many risks can be diversified away internationally, whether at the firm or investor level, should be taken into account in evaluating specific foreign projects.

NOTES

1. Grubel first introduced the diversification motive into the theory of international capital flows: see Herbert G. Grubel, "Internationally Diversified Portfolios, Welfare Gains and Capital Flow," *American Economic Review,* December 1968, pp. 1299–1314. Further empirical evidence was provided by Levy and Sarnat; see Haim Levy and Marshall Sarnat, "International Diversification of Investment Portfolios," *American Economic Review,* September 1970, pp. 668–675.

2. See, for example, William F. Sharpe, *Investments,* Englewood Cliffs, N.J.: Prentice-Hall, 1985.

3. See, for example, Michael C. Jensen, "Risk, the Pricing of Capital Assets, and the Evaluation of Investment Portfolios," *Journal of Business,* April 1969.

4. Prachowny and Stevens attempt to confirm the diversification motive, but focus on the optimality of the total MNC portfolio rather than on the ability of the MNC to widen the opportunity set available to investors. See M. F. Prachowny, "Direct Investment and the Balance of Payments of the U.S.: A Portfolio Approach," and G. V. G. Stevens, "Capital Mobility and the International Firm," both in F. Machlup, W. S. Salant, and L. Tarshis, eds., *International Mobility and Movement of Capital,* New York: Columbia University Press, 1972.

5. Alan R. Rugman (1977) seeks to show that greater risk reduction is available via real diversification rather than through portfolio investment. He does this by comparing correlations among stock market returns and correlations of "real" factors including indexes of industrial production and interest rates.

6. John S. Hughes, Dennis E. Logue, and Richard J. Sweeney, "Corporate International Diversification and Market Assigned Measures of Risk and Diversification," *Journal of Finance and Quantitative Analysis,* November 1975, pp. 627–637. Also see T. Agmon and Donald R. Lessard, "Investor Recognition of Corporate International Diversification," *Journal of Finance,* September 1977, pp. 1049–1055.

BIBLIOGRAPHY

Adler, Michael, "Investor Recognition of Corporation International Diversification: Comment," *Journal of Finance,* March 1981, pp. 187–190.

Adler, Michael, and Bernard Dumas, "Optimal International Acquisitions," *Journal of Finance,* March 1975, pp. 1–19.

Agarwal, Jamuna P., "Determinants of Foreign Direct Investment: A Survey," *Weltwirtschaftliches Archiv,* 116(4), 1980, pp. 739–773.

Agmon, Tamir, and Se'ev Hirsch, "Multinational Corporations and the Developing Economies: Potential Gains in a World of Imperfect Markets and Uncertainty," *Oxford Bulletin of Economics and Statistics,* Vol. 41, 1979, pp. 333–344.

Agmon, Tamir, and Donald Lessard, "Investor Recognition of Corporate International Diversification," *Journal of Finance,* September 1977, pp. 1049–1055.

———, "Investor Recognition of Corporate International Diversification: Reply," *Journal of Finance,* March 1981, pp. 191–192.

Aharoni, Yair, *The Foreign Investment Decision Process,* Boston: Harvard Graduate School of Business Administration, Division of Research, 1966.

Aliber, Robert Z., "A Theory of Foreign Direct Investment," in Charles P. Kindleberger, ed., *The International Corporation,* Cambridge, Mass.: MIT Press, 1970, pp. 17–34.

Arpan, Jeffrey S., Edward B. Flowers, and David A. Ricks, "Foreign Direct Investment in the United States: The State of Knowledge in Research," *Journal of International Business Studies,* Spring–Summer 1981, pp. 137–154.

Batra, R. N., and R. Ramachandran, "Multinational Firms and the Theory of International Trade and Investment," *American Economic Review,* June 1980, pp. 178–190.

Boddewyn, Jean J., "Foreign and Domestic Divestment and Investment Decisions: Like or Unlike?" *Journal of International Business Studies,* Winter 1983, pp. 23–35.

———, "Foreign Divestment: Magnitude and Factors," *Journal of International Business Studies,* Spring–Summer 1979, pp. 21–27.

Buckley, Peter J., "A Critical Review of Theories of the Multinational Enterprise," *Aussenwirtschaft,* March 1981, pp. 70–87.

———, "New Theories of International Business: Some Unresolved Issues," in Mark C. Casson, ed., *The Growth of International Business,* London: Allen and Unwin: 1983, pp. 34–50.

Buckley, Peter J., and Mark Casson, *The Future of the Multinational Enterprise,* London: Macmillan, 1976.

———, *The Economic Theory of the Multinational Enterprise,* London and Basingstoke: Macmillan, 1985.

Calvet, A. Louis, "A Synthesis of Foreign Direct Investment Theories and Theories of the Multinational Firm," *Journal of International Business Studies,* Spring–Summer 1981, pp. 43–59.

Casson, Mark, *Alternatives to the Multinational Enterprise,* London: Macmillan, 1979.

Casson, Mark, ed., *The Growth of Internatioanl Business,* London: George Allen and Unwin, 1983.

Casson, Mark C., "Transaction Costs and the Theory of the Multinational Enterprise," in Alan M. Rugman, ed., *New Theories of the Multinational Enterprise,* London: Croom Helm and New York: St. Martin's Press, 1982.

Caves, Richard E., "International Corporations: The Industrial Economics of Foreign Investment," *Economica,* February 1971, pp. 1–27.

———, "The Causes of Direct Investment: Foreign Firms' Shares in Canadian and United Kingdom Manufacturing Industries," *Review of Economics and Statistics,* August 1974, pp. 270–293.

Coase, Ronald H., "The Nature of the Firm," *Economica,* N.S., Vol. 4, 1937, pp. 386–405.

Contractor, Farok J., "In Defence of Licensing: Its Increased Role in International Operations," *Columbia Journal of World Business,* 1981, pp. 73–83.

Davidson, William H., "The Location of Foreign Direct Investment Activity: Country Characteristics and Experience Effects," *Journal of International Business Studies,* Fall 1980, pp. 9–22.

———, *Experience Effects in International Investment and Technology Transfer,* Ann Arbor, Mich.: UMI Research Press, 1981.

Dufey, Gunter, "Institutional Constraints and Incentives on International Portfolio Investment," *International Portfolio Investment,* U.S. Department of the Treasury, OASIA, 1975.

Dunning, John H., "The Determinants of International Production," *Oxford Economic Papers,* November 1973, pp. 289–336.

———, "Explaining Changing Patterns of International Production: In Defense of the Eclectic Theory," *Oxford Bulletin of Economics and Statistics,* November 1979, pp. 269–296.

———, *International Production and the Multinational Enterprise,* London: Allen and Unwin, 1981.

———, *The Multinational Enterprise,* London: Allen and Unwin, 1971.

———, "Trade, Location of Economic Activity and the MNE: A Search for an Eclectic Approach," in Bertil Ohlin, Per-Ove Hesselborn, and Per Magnus Wijkman, eds., *The International Allocation of Economic Activity,* New York: Holmes and Meier, 1977, pp. 395–418.

———, "Towards an Eclectic Theory of International Production: Some Empirical Tests," *Journal of International Business Studies,* Spring–Summer 1980, pp. 9–31.

Dunning, John H., and Alan M. Rugman, "The Influence of Hymer's Dissertation on the Theory of Foreign Direct Investment," *American Economic Review,* May 1985, pp. 228–232.

Errunza, Vihang R., "Gains from Portfolio Diversification into Less Developed Countries' Securities," *Journal of International Business Studies,* Fall–Winter 1977, pp. 83–99.

———, "Gains from Portfolio Diversification into Less Developed Countries' Securities: A Reply," *Journal of International Business Studies,* Spring–Summer 1978, pp. 117–123.

Flowers, Edward B., "Oligopolistic Reactions in European and Canadian Direct Investment in the United States," *Journal of International Business Studies,* Fall–Winter 1976, pp. 43–55.

Franko, Lawrence G., "Foreign Direct Investment in Less Developed Countries: Impact on Home Countries," *Journal of International Business Studies,* Winter 1978, pp. 55–65.

Giddy, Ian H., "The Demise of the Product Cycle Model in International Business Theory," *Columbus Journal of World Business,* Spring 1978, pp. 90–97.

Gordon, Sara L., and Francis A. Lees, "Multinational Capital Budgeting: Foreign Investment under Subsidy," *California Management Review,* Fall 1982, pp. 22–32.

Grosse, Robert, "The Theory of Foreign Direct Investment," *Essays in International Business,* Columbia: University of South Carolina, Center for International Business Studies, December 1981.

Grubel, Herbert G., "Internationally Diversified Portfolios: Welfare Gains and Capital Flows," *American Economic Review,* December 1968, pp. 1299–1314.

Grubel, Herbert G., and Kenneth Fadner, "The Interdependence of International Equity Markets," *Journal of Finance,* March 1971, pp. 89–94.

Gruber, W., D. Mehta, and R. Vernon, "The Research and Development Factor in International Trade and International Investment of U.S. Industry," *Journal of Political Economy,* February 1967, pp. 20–37.

Hanink, Dean M., "A Mean-Variance Model of MNF Location Strategy," *Journal of International Business Studies,* Spring 1985, pp. 165–170.

Helpman, Elhanan, "A Simple Theory of International Trade with Multinational Corporations," *Journal of Political Economy,* 1984, pp. 451–471.

Hennart, Jean-Francois, *A Theory of Multinational Enterprise,* Ann Arbor: University of Michigan Press, 1982.

Hood, Neil, and Stephen Young, *The Economics of Multinational Enterprise,* London and New York: Longmans, 1979.

Horst, Thomas, "Firm and Industry Determinants of the Decision to Invest Abroad: An Empirical Study," *Review of Economics and Statistics,* August 1972, pp. 258–266.

Hughes, John S., Dennis E. Logue, and Richard J. Sweeney, "Corporate International Diversification and Market Assigned Measures of Risk and Diversification," *Journal of Financial and Quantitative Analysis,* November 1975, pp. 627–637.

Hymer, Stephen H., *The International Operations of National Firms: A Study of Direct Foreign Investment,* Cambridge, Mass.: MIT Press, 1976.

Ibbotson, Roger C., Richard Carr, and Anthony Robinson, "International Equity and Bond Returns," *Financial Analysts Journal,* July–August 1982, pp. 61–83.

Jacquillat, Bertrand, and Bruno Solnik, "Multinationals Are Poor Tools for Diversification," *Journal of Portfolio Management,* Winter 1978, pp. 8–12.

Kelly, Marie Wicks, *Foreign Investment Practices of U.S. Multinational Corporations,* Ann Arbor, Mich.: UMI Research Press, 1981.

Kim, Seung H., "Financial Motives of U.S. Corporate Investment in Korea," *California Management Review,* Summer 1976, pp. 60–68.

Kindleberger, Charles P., *American Business Abroad: Six Lectures on Direct Investment,* New Haven, Conn.: Yale University Press, 1969.

Kindleberger, Charles P., ed., *The International Corporation: A Symposium,* Cambridge, Mass.: MIT Press, 1970.

Knickerbocker, Fred T., *Oligopolistic Reaction and the Multinational Enterprise,* Boston: Harvard Graduate School of Business Administration, 1973.

Kobrin, Stephen J., "The Environmental Determinants of Foreign Direct Manufacturing Investment: An Ex Post Empirical Analysis," *Journal of International Business Studies,* Fall–Winter 1976, pp. 27–42.

Kobrin, Stephen J., and Donald R. Lessard, "Large Scale Direct OPEC Investment in Industrialized Countries and the Theory of Foreign Direct Investment—A Contradiction," *Weltwirtschaftliches Archiv,* December 1976, pp. 660–673.

Kojima, K., *Direct Foreign Investment: A Japanese Model of Multinational Business Operations,* London: Groom Helm, 1978.

Krugman, Paul R., "The New Theories of International Trade and the Multinational Enterprise," in Charles P. Kindleberger and David B. Audretch, eds., *The Multinational Corporation in the 1980s,* Cambridge, Mass.: MIT Press, 1983.

Lall, Sanjaya, "Monopolistic Advantages and Foreign Involvement by U.S. Manufacturing Industry," *Oxford Economic Papers,* N.S., Vol. 32, 1980, pp. 102–122.

Lessard, Donald R., "World, National, and Industry Factors in Equity Returns," *Journal of Finance,* May 1974, pp. 379–391.

———, "World, Country, and Industry Relationships in Equity Returns: Implications for Risk Reduction through International Diversification," *Financial Analysts Journal,* January–February 1976, pp. 32–38.

———, "The Structure of Returns and Gains from International Diversification," in N. Elton and M. Gruber, eds., *International Capital Markets,* Amsterdam: North-Holland, 1976.

———, "Transfer Prices, Taxes and Financial Markets: Implications of Internal Financial Transfers within the Multinational Firm," in Robert G. Hawkins, ed., *Economic Issues of Multinational Firms,* Greenwich, Conn.: JAI Press, 1979.

Levy, Haim, and Marshall Sarnat, "International Diversification of Investment Portfolios," *American Economic Review,* September 1970, pp. 668–675.

Litvak, I. A., and C. J. Maule, eds., *Foreign Investment: The Experience of Host Countries,* New York: Praeger, 1970.

Logue, Dennis E., and Thomas D. Willet, "The Effects of Exchange Rate Adjustment on International Investment," in Peter B. Clark, Dennis E. Logue, and Richard J. Sweeney, eds., *The Effects of Exchange Rate Adjustments,* Washington, D.C.: Department of the Treasury, 1977, pp. 137–150.

Magee, Stephen P., "Information and the Multinational Corporation: An Appropriability Theory of Direct Foreign Investment," in Jagdish N. Bhagwati, ed., *The New International Economic Order: The North–South Debate,* Cambridge, Mass.: MIT Press, 1977, pp. 317–340.

Maldonado, Rita, and Anthony Saunders, "International Portfolio Diversification and the Inter-Temporal Stability of International Stock Market Relationships 1957–1978," *Financial Management,* Autumn 1981, pp. 54–63.

Markusen, J. P., "Multinationals, Multi-Plant Economies, and the Gains from Trade," *Journal of International Economics,* 1984, pp. 205–226.

Mathur, Ike, and Kyran Hanagan, "Are Multinational Corporations Superior Investment Vehicles for Achieving International Diversification?" *Journal of International Business Studies,* Winter 1983, pp. 135–146.

McClain, David, "Foreign Direct Investment in the United States: Old Currents, New Waves and the Theory of Direct Investment," in Charles P. Kindleberger and David Audretch, eds., *The Multinational Corporation in the 1980s,* Cambridge, Mass.: MIT Press, 1983.

Miller, N. C., and Marina Von Neumann Whitman, "A Mean-Variance Analysis of United States Long-Term Portfolio Foreign Investment," *Quarterly Journal of Economics,* May 1970, pp. 175–196.

Miller, Robert R., and Dale R. Weigel, "The Motivation for Foreign Direct Investment," *Journal of International Business Studies,* Fall 1972, pp. 67–79.

Mirus, Rolf, "A Note on the Choice between Licensing and Direct Foreign Investment," *Journal of International Business Studies,* Spring–Summer 1980, pp. 86–91.

Moxon, Richard W., "The Motivation for Investment in Offshore Plants: The Case of the U.S. Electronics Industry," *Journal of International Business Studies,* Spring 1975, pp. 51–66.

Nigh, Douglas, "The Effect of Political Events on United States Direct Foreign Investment: A Pooled Time-Series Cross-Sectional Analysis," *Journal of International Business Studies,* Spring 1985, pp. 1–17.

Ozawa, T., "International Investment and Industrial Structure, New Theoretical Implications from the Japanese Experience," *Oxford Economic Papers,* March 1979, pp. 72–92.

Parry, Thomas G., "Internalization as a General Theory of Foreign Direct Investment: A Critique," *Weltwirtschaftliches Archiv,* September 1985.

Ragazzi, Giorgio, "Theories of Determinants of Direct Foreign Investment," *IMF Staff Papers,* July 1973, pp. 471–498.

Root, Franklin R., and Ahmed A. Ahmed, "The Influence of Policy Instruments on Manufacturing Direct Foreign Investment in Developing Countries," *Journal of International Business Studies,* Winter 1978, pp. 81–93.

Rugman, Alan M., "Risk Reduction by International Diversification," *Journal of International Business Studies,* Vol. 7, No. 2, 1976, pp. 75–80.

———, *International Diversification and the Multinational Enterprise,* Lexington: Heath, 1979.

———, "Internalization as a General Theory of Foreign Direct Investment: A Re-Appraisal of the Literature," *Weltwirtschaftliches Archiv,* Vol. 116, No. 2, 1980, pp. 365–379.

———, "Internalizational Theory and Corporate International Finance," *California Management Review,* Winter 1980, pp. 73–79.

———, *Inside the Multinationals: The Economics of Internal Markets,* London: Croom Helm, and New York: Columbia University Press, 1981.

———, "Multinational Enterprises and World Product Mandates," in Alan M. Rugman, ed., *Multinationals and Technology Transfer: The Canadian Experience,* New York: Praeger, 1983.

———, "The Determinants of Intra-Industry Direct Foreign Investment," in Asim Erdilek, ed., *Multinationals as Mutual Invaders: Intra-Industry Direct Foreign Investment,* London: Croom Helm, 1985, pp. 38–59.

———, "Internalization Is Still a General Theory of Foreign Direct Investment," *Weltwirtschaftliches Archiv,* September 1985.

Rugman, Alan M., ed., *New Theories of the Multinational Enterprise,* London: Croom Helm, and New York: St. Martin's Press, 1982.

Salehizadeh, Mehdi, "Regulations of Foreign Direct Investment by Host Countries," *Essays in International Business,* Columbia: University of South Carolina, Center for International Business Studies, May 1983.

Saunders, Anthony, and Richard S. Woodworth, "Gains from International Portfolio Diversification: U.K. Evidence 1971–75," *Journal of Business Finance and Accounting,* Autumn 1977, pp. 299–309.

Scaperlanda, A. E., and L. J. Manner, "Determinants of U.S. Direct Investment in the E.E.C.," *American Economic Review,* September 1969, pp. 558–568.

Senchak, Andrew J., Jr., and W. L. Beedles, "Is Indirect International Diversification Desirable?" *Journal of Portfolio Management,* Winter 1980, pp. 49–57.

Servan-Schreiber, J. J., *The American Challenge,* London: Hamish Hamilton, 1968.

Severn, A. K., and M. M. Laurence, "Direct Investment, Research Intensity, and Profitability," *Journal of Financial and Quantitative Analysis,* March 1974, pp. 181–190.

Stehle, Richard, "An Empirical Test of the Alternative Hypotheses of National and International Pricing of Risky Assets," *Journal of Finance,* May 1977, pp. 493–502.

Stobaugh, Robert, Jr., "Where in the World Should We Put That Plant?" *Harvard Business Review,* January/February 1969, pp. 129–136.

Vernon, Raymond, "International Investment and International Trade in the Product Cycle," *Quarterly Journal of Economics,* May 1966, pp. 190–207.

———, "The Location of Economic Activity," in John H. Dunning, ed., *Economic Analysis and the Multinational Enterprise,* London: Allen and Unwin, 1974, pp. 89–114.

———, "The Product Cycle Hypothesis in a New International Environment," *Oxford Bulletin of Economics and Statistics,* Vol. 41, 1979, pp. 255–267.

Wilkins, Mira, ed., *Foreign Investment in the United States,* New York: Arno Press, 1977.

Wilson, Brent D., *Disinvestment of Foreign Subsidiaries,* Ann Arbor, Mich.: UMI Research Press, 1980.

———, "The Propensity of Multinational Companies to Expand through Acquisitions," *Journal of International Business Studies,* Spring–Summer 1980, pp. 59–65.

Wolf, Bernard M., "Industrial Diversification and Internationalization: Some Empirical Evidence," *Journal of Industrial Economics,* Vol. 26, 1977, pp. 177–191.

Zagaris, Bruce, *Foreign Investment in the U.S.,* New York: Praeger, 1980.

9

Political Risk Management

A multinational firm may be influenced by political events within a host country or by a change of political relationship between the host country and some other country. The possibility of such events occurring and having an influence on the economic well-being of the firm is called *political risk*. Conceptually the effect on the firm could be either positive or negative; however, most managerial attention focuses on possible negative effects.

Management of political risk refers to steps taken by firms to anticipate political events, to protect against loss (or to attempt to gain) from such events, or lastly to attempt to recover as much compensation after an adverse political event as possible.

Political risk is often viewed in terms of potential conflict between corporate goals and the national aspirations of a host country. Historically conflicts have arisen over such issues as the firm's impact on economic development, perceived infringements on national sovereignty, foreign control of key industries, sharing or nonsharing of ownership and control with local interests, impact on a host country's balance of payments or the foreign exchange value of its currency, access to and control over export markets, and "exploitation" of natural resources. Attitudes about conflicts are often colored by views toward free enterprise versus socialism, the degree of nationalism or internationalism present, or the place of religious views in determining appropriate economic behavior.

TYPES OF POLITICAL RISK AND THE FOREIGN INVESTMENT DECISION

Stephen Kobrin points out that multinational firms face a broad range of political-economic risks that can best be viewed along two dimensions. The first dimension, derived from the work of Stefan Robock, distinguishes between macro or environmental risks, which affect all foreign firms in a country without regard to how they are organized, and micro risks, which are specific to an industry, a firm, or a project. The second differentiation is between those political events that affect ownership of assets, such as full or partial divestment, and those that affect the operations of a firm and thus its cash flows and returns.[1] Kobrin argues that most of the political risk problems of multinational firms involve micro risk, and most current political problems involve operations rather than ownership.

Kobrin also notes that various risks have different degrees of importance depending on whether the firm is operating in a developing or an industrialized country. In a survey of senior international managers of U.S.-based multinational firms respondents were asked to rank the relative importance of various kinds of political risk. Civil disorder and expropriation were seen as most important in less developed countries, whereas in industrial countries price controls and labor disruptions were seen as most important. Results of the survey are shown in Exhibit 9.1.

In an investigation of the effect of political events on the direct foreign investment decisions of U.S. manufacturing firms, Douglas Nigh studied 24 firms for 21 years.[2] He tested four hypotheses based on the idea that both *intra*-nation events in the host country, such as a coup d'état, and *inter*-nation events, such as breaking diplomatic relations with the United States, would influence the amount of direct foreign investment by U.S. multinational firms in that host country. The two variables were determined after Nigh observed the following contradiction: Interviews and surveys of corporate executives showed that they regarded political events as a most

EXHIBIT 9.1
Relative Importance of Risks, Ranked by Median Rankings

LESS DEVELOPED COUNTRIES		*INDUSTRIALIZED COUNTRIES*	
Mean ranking	*Risk*	*Mean ranking*	*Risk*
1.8	Civil disorder	3.2	Price controls
2.4	Expropriation	3.7	Labor disruptions
3.6	War	4.4	Remittance restrictions
5.3	Remittance restrictions	5.5	Civil disorder
5.5	Labor disruptions	5.5	Fiscal changes
5.7	Partial expropriation	6.0	Expropriation
6.0	Price controls	6.9	Partial expropriation
7.3	Fiscal changes	7.2	Contract cancellation
7.6	Contract cancellation	8.4	War

Source: Stephen J. Kobrin, *Managing Political Risk Assessment: Strategic Response to Environmental Change,* Berkeley: University of California Press, 1982. Adapted from p. 118. The survey was based on 80 replies.

important factor in the direct foreign investment decision, but econometric studies of environmental discriminants of direct foreign investment generally show little relationship between political events and the amount of direct foreign investment.

Nigh found that conflict in the host country has a direct influence on manufacturing direct foreign investment when that country is a less developed country, but no effect when that country is developed. Intra-nation conflict in a less developed country appears to investors to be associated with instability of that country.

Nigh also found that inter-nation conflict from both less developed and developed countries is of concern to those making direct investment decisions. Apparently hostility toward the U.S. government carries over into hostility toward U.S. multinational firms. This results in part from the U.S. government's regulation of the foreign affiliates of U.S. firms in such matters as antitrust policy, East-West trade, and capital flows. U.S. firms in foreign countries are also the most visible targets for anti-U.S. feeling motivated by other causes.

FORMS OF HOST GOVERNMENT INTERFERENCE

At issue in all political conflicts is the question of which side's views will dominate. From a legalistic point of view the host country's views always dominate, because it is a sovereign nation that may set whatever rules it wishes for the behavior of foreign firms operating on its soil. From an economic point of view the issue is less clear, since some types of political interference may draw reprisals from the parent firm or even from that firm's home government. For this reason host governments have developed an array of techniques to influence the behavior of foreign firms operating within their country. Whether such techniques constitute true "interference" or are simply the just and fair activities of a governing body is an emotionally charged issue not easily susceptible to neutral resolution. For convenience of exposition we will group government activities that constrain the free actions of a multinational firm under the heading "interference."

Much of the literature on foreign environmental risks has concentrated on the extreme cases of expropriation or nationalization. In fact, a whole spectrum exists of types of interference that host governments have adopted to control real or imagined dangers of foreign investments.

Nondiscriminatory Interference

Nondiscriminatory interference is often relatively mild and not particularly directed against foreign-controlled operations. It may impact equally on joint ventures or even local firms having management or licensing agreements with foreign businesses. Some forms of nondiscriminatory interference are the following:

- Requiring the use of local nationals in management positions.
- Negotiating transfer prices designed to favor the host country's tax base.
- Requiring export industries to sell in the home market at a break-even price in order to subsidize local consumption of the particular product.
- Requiring social and economic overhead facilities to be constructed by the investing firm.
- Requiring the use of a given percentage of local content in assembly of knocked-down imported components.
- Temporarily making the host country currency inconvertible.

Although these forms do not inherently discriminate against foreign investment, they are often more rigidly enforced against highly visible, large multinational firms.

Discriminatory Interference

Discriminatory interference is intended to give local firms or national groups specific advantages over foreign firms. Its forms include the following:

- Allowing only joint ventures, with the foreign firm being limited to a minority position. As an example, the laws of Malaysia provide that by the year 1990 the national wealth should be owned 30% by Malays, who are the ethnic majority but who have been rural workers rather than business entrepreneurs; 40% by other Malaysians who are of Chinese or Indian extraction; and 30% by foreigners. Present proportions in the commercial and manufacturing sectors are approximately 10% Malays, about 44% Malaysian, and the remaining 46% foreign.
- Requiring special taxes, excessive fees, high utility charges, or other hidden forms of extra compensation from foreign-owned firms but not from domestic-owned firms.
- Legal harassment such as requiring special permits, excessive pollution control requirements, bias in labor arbitration or mediation, over-documentation of all transactions, etc.
- Encouraging a national boycott of a firm's goods, or encouraging a strike of its workers. The Falklands/Malvinas war between the United Kingdom and Argentina in 1982 led not only to such pressure against British firms in Argentina, but also to pressure against U.S. firms. This is an example of how firms from an originally uninvolved third country

(the United States) may experience politically inspired loss because of their country's inability to stay totally neutral.

Discriminatory Sanctions

Discriminatory sanctions involve very strong pressures undertaken so that the foreign enterprise will no longer be able to operate profitably and will thus gradually go out of business. Motivation may be purely political and nationalistic or it may be to provide more business opportunities and to capture more business profits for national entrepreneurs. Practices include the following:

- "Creeping expropriation," such as has occurred under various regimes in Latin America. Laws may prevent profits belonging to foreigners from being remitted and foreign-owned capital (including funds generated via depreciation) from being repatriated. Laws may also force foreign firms to invest these blocked funds in specific local governmental obligations, which quickly lose their value because of rampant inflation.
- Levying taxes, royalties, or other charges against foreign firms to the point at which profits are no longer possible.
- Claiming huge compensation for past inequities arising out of a concession agreement granted by a previous government but now ruled invalid.

Wealth Deprivation

A fourth level of interference would be the outright takeover of individual foreign firms. The practice is sometimes referred to as foreign wealth deprivation, and it can take the form of selective expropriation of individual foreign firms, nationalization of an entire industry, or socialization of the whole country.

Expropriation is the term used to describe the official seizure of foreign property by a host country whose intention is to use the seized property in the public interest. Expropriation is recognized by international law as the right of sovereign states, provided the expropriated firms are given *prompt* compensation at *fair market value* in *convertible currencies*. Therein lies the rub. Promptness is often delayed by extensive negotiations and appeals. Fair market value is in the eyes of the beholder, with the firms arguing for "going-concern" value and the countries arguing for depreciated book value as the measure of market value. Sufficient convertible currency reserves are often not available to the expropriating country for full and prompt payment of a negotiated settlement. Some examples of selective expropriation are the following:

- Chile's 1971 takeover of the U.S.-owned copper mining affiliates of Kennecott, Anaconda, and Cerro, as well as affiliates of Ford, ITT, Boise Cascade, Dupont, and Ralston-Purina. Compensation for the copper mining expropriations was eventually negotiated with Chile after the overthrow of the Allende government in 1973. The remaining firms are mostly back under U.S. management.
- Peru's 1968 takeover of International Petroleum Company (Exxon) followed by expropriations of affiliates of Cerro, W. R. Grace, and Utah International. Peru agreed to partial compensation payments in 1974.
- Bolivia's 1969 takeover of affiliates of Gulf Oil and U.S. Steel.
- Libya's 1969 takeover of Occidental Petroleum's oil fields.

Nationalization is the term used to describe the transfer of a whole industry from private to public ownership. In this case there is ostensibly no discrimination against foreign-owned firms, although often the whole industry that is nationalized is foreign-owned. Recent events involving nationalization include the following:

- Nationalization of firms and industries in Iran following the ouster of the shah in 1979.
- The nationalization of some French industries and the remaining private banks in France after the 1981 election of Socialist President Francois Mitterand.
- In 1974 Venezuela announced its intention to nationalize both its iron mining and oil industries. The affected firms included U.S. Steel, Bethlehem Steel, Exxon, Texaco, and several other oil companies. This action was a relatively "friendly" expropriation, because Venezuela had the financial ability to provide adequate compensation in convertible currencies and was not motivated by any ideological extremism.
- Saudi Arabia and Aramco concluded another "friendly" expropriation. Aramco is a consortium of foreign oil firms, which produces almost all Saudi Arabia's oil.

Socialization (or communization) is the term used to describe the nationalization of all industries in a country. Cuba's 1960 takeover of all private firms, whether foreign or domestic, is the best known and most costly case for foreign firms since World War II.

HISTORICAL RECORD

No comprehensive listing of government interference exists. Cases of "voluntary" forced sales of foreign firms to either host country governments or private firms are usually reported in the press but not compiled by an official source at the time of the event. Nevertheless, several surveys of expropriations, conducted with hindsight, shed some light on the number of expropriations since World War II and estimates of value of properties expropriated.

A comprehensive survey of takeovers of foreign firms during the period 1960–1974, conducted by an agency of the United Nations, reported 875 cases, with just 10 countries accounting for two-thirds of the takeovers.[3]

A second study completed in 1970 by Frederick Truitt concentrated on expropriation of U.S. and British firms since World War II.[4] Exhibit 9.2 summarizes these results by industry sector and number of firms taken over. Note that the extractive and service sectors have been the most vulnerable to takeover, with relatively few cases having occurred in the manufacturing sector.

A more recent study of foreign government takeovers of 170 U.S. foreign affiliates during the period 1946–1975 by Robert Hawkins, Norman Mintz, and Michael Provissiero makes a rough estimate that the value of U.S. affiliates taken over since 1961 approaches the $2 to $3 billion range.[5] Although this amount is relatively small compared to total U.S. direct foreign investment, it is concentrated by industry and geographic area. For example, Latin American countries, particularly Argentina, Chile, and Peru, took over U.S. affiliates during 1967–1973 equal in number to 2.2% of the U.S. affiliates in Latin America in 1966. The corresponding number for Africa is 6.4% and for the Middle East, 3.0%. Their conclusions are as follows:

- Takeovers of U.S. firms since World War II have been increasing in annual number.
- Only a few developing countries account for a large share of the takeovers.
- Latin American countries are the most prone to take over foreign firms.
- Expropriation with some compensation is the most typical form of takeover, but negotiation of contract and direct intervention (without following local laws) have been increasing in importance.
- Takeovers occur most frequently to firms in the extractive industries of oil, mining, and plantations.
- The motivation for the takeovers was typically a recent change to a leftist government, but a significant number were economically motivated either to gain control over the country's natural resources or to eliminate the drain of foreign ownership in mature industries.

A study by David Bradley, using the Harvard Business School's "Multinational Enterprise Project" data base, sheds some more light on the common characteristics of his sample of 114 affiliates of U.S. firms expropriated during the period 1960–1974.[6] The most important characteristics are the composition of ownership, technology barriers, degree of vertical integration, and size of assets.

EXHIBIT 9.2
Expropriation and Nationalization by Sector

Sector	*Expropriation and/or nationalization programs*			*Number of American and British firms taken*		
Extractive						
Petroleum:						
Integrated operations[a]	5			7		
Refining or distribution only	7			22		
Total petroleum		12			29	
Plantation agriculture	3			3		
Mining	1			1		
Total extractive			16			33
Manufacturing			7			8
Public Utilities			5			3
Service						
Trade[b]	5			12		
Commercial banking	7			22		
Insurance	6			131		
Miscellaneous and unknown[c]				160		
Total service			18			325

Source: J. Frederick Truitt, "Expropriation of Foreign Investment: Summary of the Post World War II Experience of American and British Investors in Less Developed Countries, " *Journal of International Business Studies,* Fall 1970, p. 30.

[a]Any petroleum investment except refining or distribution.

[b]Retail and export-import.

[c]Indicates that author is not sure how companies affected should be allocated between categories.

Although many academic and business leaders believe that a joint venture with the host government reduces political risk, Bradley's study concludes quite the opposite. He concludes, "Historically, the rate of expropriation has been ten times greater for a joint venture with the host government than for a 100% U.S.-owned subsidiary. Similarly, the probabilities are increased eightfold for joint ventures with foreign multinational corporations. The joint venture may, however, increase the likelihood of receiving compensation."[7] Joint ventures with local private parties, as distinct from governments, apparently reduce the risk of expropriation.

Bradley also concludes that firms with dynamic high technology of a proprietary nature, such as IBM, have little chance of being expropriated because the host country cannot duplicate the product or service. On the other hand, he also finds that firms with a very low level of technology, such as textiles or food processing, are not likely to be expropriated because they lack the glamour or aura of technological development sought by host governments for political reasons. Firms with a middle level of technology are most exposed to political risk.

Foreign affiliates that are part of a vertically integrated firm, with the parent controlling the affiliates' supply or market, are unlikely to be expropriated. The Chrysler plant in Peru is given as an example. Only 50% of its car and truck components are made in Peru. Thus it would be valueless for the Peruvian government to own the plant if it could not make the rest of the components itself.

Finally, Bradley's study shows that large visible firms are much more likely to be expropriated than are small firms. The benefits deriving from expropriation of a small firm would hardly be worth the trouble it would cause with foreign investors and the international banking community.

In a 1980 study of expropriations in 76 less developed countries over the period 1960–1976, Kobrin found that ideologically motivated mass expropriation actually took place in less than ten of the countries studied.[8] Elsewhere expropriation was primarily used as a selective instrument of economic policy. Kobrin notes that forced divestment has fallen off in the years since 1976.[9]

FORECASTING POLITICAL INTERFERENCE

Forecasting political interference requires a twofold approach. One approach is to forecast a particular country's propensity to interfere or expropriate. The second approach is to forecast a particular firm's propensity to be interfered with or expropriated.

The just-described history of expropriations shows that countries with a high propensity to expropriate have certain characteristics in common. These include being less developed, having recently shifted to leftist governments, and being located in Latin America, Africa, or the Middle East. Yet there are many countries with these surface characteristics that have not expropriated foreign firms. A deeper insight into the political, social, and historical makeup of countries is necessary for predictions of political risk.

History also shows that firms most likely to be expropriated are in the extractive or service (banking and insurance) industries, are highly visible, and do not possess exceptionally advanced technology that is difficult for host governments to replace. Nevertheless, many firms with these characteristics located in countries with a high propensity to expropriate have not in fact been expropriated. Part of the reason for this situation might be attributed to differences in firms' operating policies, which impact on the degree of political risk they will face.

Four approaches are used to forecast political interference:[10]

1. "grand tours" and "old hands,"
2. opinion surveys,
3. quantitative approaches, and
4. market-derived forecasts.

"Grand Tours" and "Old Hands"

The "grand tour" involves an inspection visit to the potential host country by an executive or team of people from the investing firm. Meetings are held with local officials and businessmen. The visitors then brief headquarters management on their "firsthand" impressions. Needless to say, firsthand impressions can be superficial. Also the visit may be carefully orchestrated by host country officials who are eager for the investment.

The "old hands" approach is to rely on the advice of outside consultants who are seasoned experts on the country in question—for example, other businessmen, diplomats, educators, journalists, or local politicians. The investing firm is at the mercy of the consultant's supposed expertise, which sometimes is fortunate and sometimes unfortunate. But at least these experts are usually an improvement over the "instant experts" of the "grand tour."

Opinion Surveys

Opinion surveys, combining the opinions of "experts" in a formally weighted system, are conducted as follows. First, a checklist of variables that are thought to influence political risk is identified. Next, a group of experts rank these variables and form a composite index of political risk based on the weighted variables. Finally, countries are ranked with respect to political risk on the basis of the composite index. Sometimes the index and ranking are sponsored by independent organizations. Examples of these are the Business Environmental Risk Index published by BERI, Business International's Country Risk Assessment Service, and Frost and Sullivan's World Political Risk Forecasts. Sometimes a multinational firm prepares its own index and ranking. Whether the index is a good predictor of political risk depends on whether the variables that influence political risk in a particular host country are correctly identified, whether the experts have formed valid opinions of the values of these variables in that environment, and finally whether they have correctly weighted these variables.

Opinion surveys of business executives sometimes reveal that the executives have a polarized attitude toward the political risks of investing in foreign countries. If the perceived level of political risk is low, they will invest and probably give only minor consideration to future political risk unless some single event subsequently pushes political risk to the forefront of their consciousness. One often-cited item of evidence in support of this view is the fact that before the 1959–1960 expropriations in Cuba, most U.S. businesses did not bother to take out the investment insurance available at that time through the Agency for International Development.

If the perceived level of political risk is above some ill-defined threshold level, the business executive is likely to eliminate investment in that particular country from further consideration without giving serious attention to ways that the perceived level of risk might be lessened.

In 1969 Robert Stobaugh, Jr., reported the results of a survey about the ways 40 international companies analyze foreign investment climates.[11] He found that the survey sample could be classified by four approaches: (1) go/no go; (2) premium for risk; (3) range of estimates; (4) risk analysis.

In the go/no go approach the firm refuses to consider investments in countries deemed to have too unfavorable an investment climate.

In the premium-for-risk approach the firm requires a higher return on investment from projects in countries with unfavorable investment climates. The higher return is often established with the use of risk indices. Stobaugh reported that 80% of the U.S.-based managers interviewed used the premium-for-risk approach.

In the range-of-estimates approach management provides its best estimate of values for the various factors that will affect the project's profitability. This estimate is calculated by identifying crucial variables, estimating the value of the variables at different times in the future, and projecting an estimate of the resulting cash flow. Other target variables, such as accounting net profit, may also be used. Estimates of the crucial variables are then varied to determine the sensitivity of the projected cash flow to changes in each factor. By focusing on those factors having the greatest impact on cash flow, and by measuring the sensitivity of projected cash flow to various combinations, management is able to reduce its forecast of cash flow to a likely range.

In the risk analysis approach an estimate is made of the probability of various events occurring. Exhibit 9.3 is Stobaugh's diagram showing the use of the risk analysis approach to appraise the chances of expropriation with or without compensation, under varying assumptions as to political control. By following the various branches of the diagram, one can see that there is a .500 probability that the government will be overthrown. If the new government is left wing, there is an additional .500 probability that the plant will not be nationalized; while if the new government is right wing, there is a .800 probability of the plant not being nationalized.

If the probabilities are multiplied along the various branch lines, the summary of outcomes is as shown in the right column. If these outcomes are regrouped by event, it can be shown, for example, that the overall probability of the plant not being nationalized is .810. The regrouped probabilities of other outcomes are shown at the bottom of the diagram. Such

EXHIBIT 9.3
Probability Analysis—Year 1: Government Overthrow

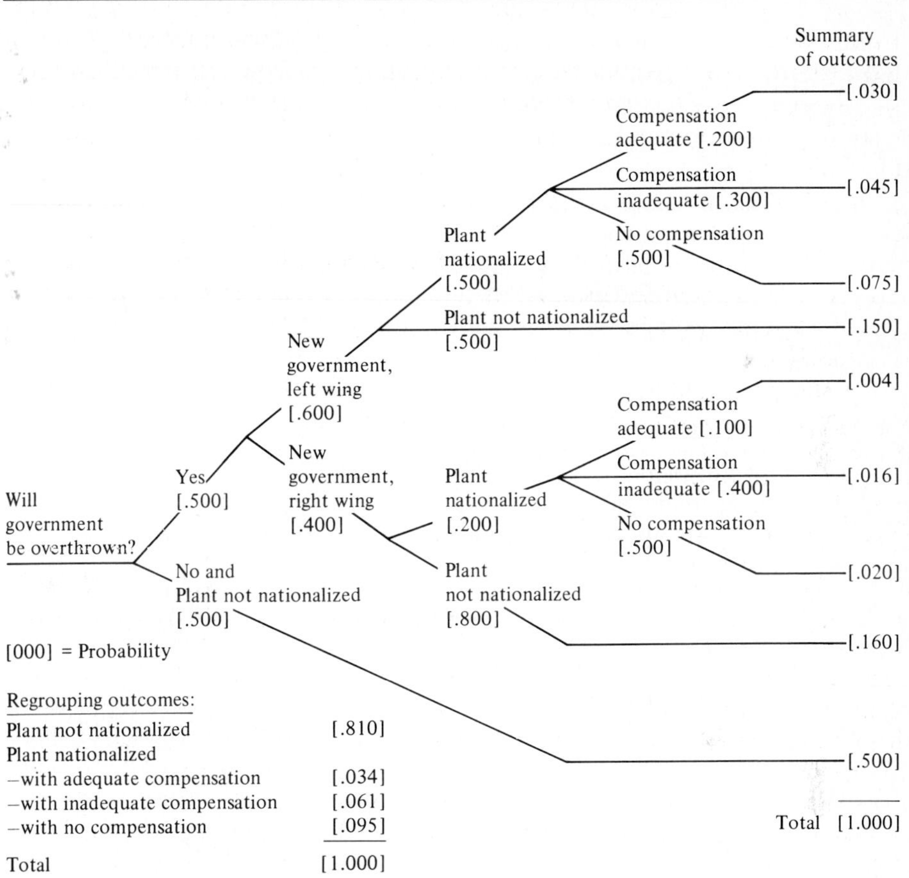

Regrouping outcomes:	
Plant not nationalized	[.810]
Plant nationalized	
–with adequate compensation	[.034]
–with inadequate compensation	[.061]
–with no compensation	[.095]
Total	[1.000]

Source: Robert Stobaugh, Jr., "How to Analyze Foreign Investment Climates," *Harvard Business Review,* September/October 1969, p. 108.

probabilistic estimates may lead to managerial decisions different from the unweighted guesses by the manager. The technique itself is capable of including changed estimates for future years.

Quantitative Methods

In recent years political scientists have attempted to apply their understanding of such topics as politics, nationalism, conflict resolution, and the law to forecasting political risk for multinational firms. With the aid of advanced statistical techniques they have constructed some fairly elaborate models to explain political risk. One such model will be explained after a few notes of caution.

Limits to accuracy of quantitative models None of the existing models have been able to descend from the macro level of forecasting a country's propensity to expropriate, which they do well, to the micro level of forecasting a particular firm's propensity to be expropriated, which they do badly. One of the reasons is that some of the best models were designed for other purposes, such as State Department use, rather than use by multinational firms. However, even those that profess to help multinational firms often suffer from another basic flaw. The flaw is that such models often assume that a country's *political stability*, as measured by various indicators of violence and unrest, is the key to forecasting its propensity to expropriate foreign firms.

Political instability does not necessarily lead to a greater danger of expropriation. In fact, an empirical study by Kobrin concludes:

> First, it is clear that not all forms of political violence equally threaten foreign investors. Neither unorganized turmoil nor all but the most wide-spread internal warfare appear to be a major source of constraints on foreign enterprise. On the other hand, what we called subversion, direct, highly organized and covert actions against the regime can, under appropriate conditions, result in increased political risk.[12]

Kobrin notes that Gulf Oil Company was able to operate successfully in Angola during a period of violent conflict and under the control of a Marxist government. At one time Gulf's rigs were being protected by Cuban troops![13] He also points out that a political or military coup in Latin America, for example, would not necessarily be a destabilizing event that threatens foreign investments since it is one of the historical ways governments are changed. On the other hand, a similar coup in the United Kingdom or the United States would be a revolutionary act fraught with danger and destabilizing tendencies.

The Haendel-West-Meadow Political System Stability Index Dan Haendel, Gerald West, and Robert Meadow have developed a specific quantitative approach to measuring political risk, which they believe is free of attitude inputs.[14] In this respect their approach differs markedly from the technique of surveying attitudes of respondents. Citing the sharp drop in U.S. investment flows to all of Latin America after the 1959–1960 Cuban confiscation of U.S. investment in that country, Haendel, West, and Meadow (H-W-M) suggest that a more sophisticated method of evaluating political risk might have prevented such a panicky aftermath. H-W-M define political risk as "the risk or *probability* of occurrence of some political event(s) that will change the prospects for the profitability of a given investment." Ability to measure risk more precisely, they note, would benefit multinational firms and host countries alike by permitting investors to reduce the discount rate they apply to various foreign ventures. Additionally, firms considering an investment would be better able to compare risk among various countries on a systematic basis, and managers of already operating foreign affiliates would be better able to respond to risk-increasing events.

The H-W-M approach is to identify and measure the discrete components of political risk and then reaggregate these measures into an overall index suitable for a particular enterprise. H-W-M apply equal weight to each of three subindexes in their own compilation of an index, but they suggest that any particular management might combine the various components into other mixes more suitable for its own venture. For example, one blend might be more appropriate for investors concerned with continued repatriation of profits, another blend might be more relevant for continued successful operations within the host country, while a third might be desirable for a firm heavily dependent on import of raw material or components, or export of final products.

The basic H-W-M political system stability index is shown schematically in Exhibit 9.4. The index is composed of an equal weighting of three basic subindexes on (1) socioeconomic characteristics, (2) societal conflicts, and (3) governmental processes. The societal conflict index is, in turn, derived from three sub-subindexes on public unrest, internal violence, and coercion potential. All these indexes are derived from 15 underlying indicators, which can be measured on a quantitative basis without reliance on "soft" data such as attitudes or opinions of individuals.

To illustrate, the H-W-M sub-subindex on political unrest is derived from numerical counts of demonstrations, riots, and government crises. A demonstration is defined as a "peaceful public gathering of at least 100 people for the primary purpose of displaying opposition to government policies or authority." A riot is defined as "a demonstration involving the use of force and resulting in material damage or bloodshed." A government crisis is defined as a "rapidly developing situation that threatens to bring about the immediate downfall of the government."

Each of three major subindexes is also given a confidence estimate, on a scale from 1 to 5, as follows:

1. Very high confidence in the accuracy, reliability, and comparability of the score to those of other nations.

2. High confidence in the accuracy and reliability of the score. A few doubts as to the comparability of the statistic to other nations because of missing data, underreporting, or overreporting of events.

3. Moderate confidence in the accuracy and reliability of the score. Some doubts about the comparability of the statistic because of missing data, underreporting, or overreporting of events.

EXHIBIT 9.4
Formation of Political System Stability Index (PSSI)

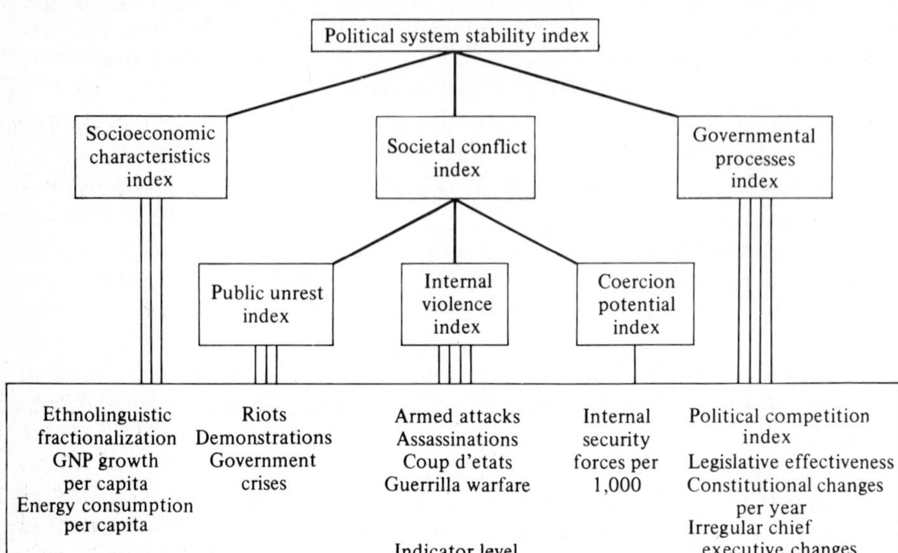

Source: Reproduced from *Overseas Investment and Political Risk,* by Dan Haendel and Gerald T. West, with Robert G. Meadow, FPRI Monograph Series, Number 21, 1975, p. 64, with permission of the Foreign Policy Research Institute, Philadelphia.

4. Low confidence in the accuracy and reliability of the score. Serious doubts as to the comparability of the statistic to those of other nations because of missing data, underreporting, or overreporting of events.
5. Minimal confidence in the accuracy and reliability of the score. Very severe doubts about the comparability of the statistic to those of other nations because of missing data, underreporting, or overreporting of events.

Whereas the statistical indexes themselves are based on quantitative data, the confidence estimate allows compensation for missing data, evaluation of the reliability of data sources, and general knowledge of the country.

Forecasts Derived from Financial Market Data

Market-derived forecasts assume efficient markets exist, in which all available information is utilized by competitive security buyers and sellers to establish a security's price. A country risk forecast based on bond market assessments is published annually by *Euromoney*. The results of the October 1985 analysis are shown in Exhibit 9.5.

EXHIBIT 9.5
Euromoney Country Risk Ratings

Rank in 1985	*Rank in 1984*	*Country*	*Index*	*Rank in 1985*	*Rank in 1984*	*Country*	*Index*
1=	1=	Australia	100.00	42	39=	Algeria	60.05
1=	1=	Canada	100.00	43	42	Qatar	59.85
1=	1=	Germany, West	100.00	44	38	Portugal	58.70
1=	1=	Japan	100.00	45	49	Jordan	58.05
1=	1=	Netherlands	100.00	46	46	India	58.00
1=	1=	Sweden	100.00	47	45	Colombia	55.70
1=	1=	Switzerland	100.00	48	43	UAE	53.75
1=	1=	United Kingdom	100.00	49	35	Hungary	53.55
1=	1=	United States	100.00	50	58	Bulgaria	51.75
10	1=	Finland	99.75	51	64=	Barbados	50.00
11=	12	Austria	91.60	52	53	Solomon Islands	46.80
11=	11	Belgium	91.60	53=	51	Egypt	46.55
11=	—	Luxembourg	91.60	53=	44	Trinidad & Tobago	46.55
14	13	Norway	91.50				
15	15	New Zealand	91.05	55	54	Mexico	45.55
16	16	Denmark	90.95	56	50	Turkey	43.20
17	14	France	88.75	57	48	Papua New Guinea	40.65
18	18	Saudi Arabia	85.95				
19	27	China	85.45	58	55	Burma	39.15
20	17	Singapore	84.25	59	62	Fiji	37.65
21	22	Hong Kong	83.75	60	64=	Paraguay	37.45
22	19	Ireland	82.35	61	63	Israel	37.40
23	26	Italy	81.90	62	64=	Nauru	36.85
24	29	Spain	81.75	63	61	Yugoslavia	35.10
25	24	Kuwait	81.05	64	68	Gabon	34.55
26	20	Iceland	78.90	65	56	Sri Lanka	33.00
27=	23	Bahrain	78.35	66	67	Congo	31.75
27=	28	Malaysia	78.35	67	60	Syria	30.95
29	21	USSR	76.50	68	69	Cameroon	30.85
30	32	Taiwan	72.00	69	59	Botswana	30.50
31	25	South Africa	70.95	70	57	Panama	27.90
32	33	Korea	70.65	71	75	Mozambique	27.70
33	31	Thailand	70.60	72	70=	Malta	27.20
34	41	Germany, East	70.50	73	52	Pakistan	26.55
35	30	Greece	68.55	74	70=	Romania	25.95
36	36	Tunisia	65.95	75	80=	Angola	25.55
37	34	Indonesia	63.95	76	80=	Cuba	25.20
38	37	Cyprus	63.75	77	73	Zimbabwe	25.15
39	39=	Bermuda	63.55	78	89=	Senegal	23.75
40	—	Oman	63.15	79	86=	Argentina	23.35
41	47	Czechoslovakia	61.95	80	76=	Philippines	22.30

EXHIBIT 9.5 (Cont.)

Rank in 1985	*Rank in 1984*	*Country*	*Index*	*Rank in 1985*	*Rank in 1984*	*Country*	*Index*
81	74	Mauritius	21.00	100=	89=	Malawi	15.45
82	76=	Venezuela	20.65	100=	99=	Niger	15.45
83	84	Jamaica	20.30	102	96	Liberia	15.05
84	85	Ghana	20.25	103	101=	Iran	14.45
85	70=	Morocco	20.20	104	101=	Haiti	14.30
86	82=	Poland	20.15	105	98	Uruguay	13.55
87	—	Zaire	20.10	106	97	Zambia	11.80
88	89=	Brazil	20.00	107	114	Chile	11.60
89	86=	Costa Rica	19.95	108	95	Lebanon	11.50
90	78=	Swaziland	19.65	109	106=	Ecuador	11.25
91	78=	Bangladesh	19.40	110	115	Tanzania	11.20
92	94	Ivory Coast	19.20	111	109=	Nigeria	10.45
93	82=	Kenya	18.75	112	99=	Lesotho	10.35
94	88	Dominican Republic	16.55	113=	109=	Peru	10.35
				113=	104=	Bolivia	10.00
95=	93	Honduras	16.35	115=	104=	Sudan	10.00
95=	112	Mauritania	16.35	115=	113	Uganda	10.00
97	89=	Guatemala	16.15	117	101=	Guyana	9.00
98=	109=	Iraq	15.75	118	106=	Ethiopia	6.80
98=	106=	Libya	15.75	119	116	El Salvador	4.00

Source: Euromoney, October 1985, pp. 327–329.

Euromoney bases its ratings on comparative terms for international bond and money market instruments. Yields and conditions in these markets are weighted 50% for access to the market by the country, 25% for the spread and maturity terms obtained, and 25% for the sales success of the offering.

The *Euromoney* rankings, as well as a similar effort by *Institutional Investor,* are published on a regular basis but most other rankings are sold to clients by private advisory services.

Country vs. Firm-Specific Political Risk Analysis

A trend in political risk analysis that has evolved since the 1979 overthrow of the shah of Iran and the political turmoil of the early 1980s in Central America stems from a realization that different firms operating within the same country may have quite different exposure to political risks. Hence a desire to evaluate political risk on a firm-specific basis has begun to supplement pure country risk analysis. The desire for such "tailor-made" analyses by political risk analysts working in-house also springs in part from the observation that country risk analysts do not necessarily agree.

For example, *Business Week* compared Business International's Country Assessment Service, which surveys 71 countries twice a year, with Frost and Sullivan's World Political Risk Forecasts, which surveys 60 countries every month. These two services were selected because they are among the better-known political risk services in the United States. Their listings of the ten best political risks and the ten worst political risks are shown in Exhibit 9.6. Five countries (West Germany, Japan, Malaysia, Singapore, and the Netherlands) appear in both lists of the best ten, and only three countries (Iran, Nicaragua, and the Philippines) appear in both lists of the ten worst.

In-house political risk analysts relate the general risk attributes of specific countries to the particular characteristics and vulnerabilities of their client firms. Dan Haendel notes that the framework for such analysis depends on such attributes as the ratio of a firm's foreign to domestic investments, the political sensitivity of the particular industry, and the degree of diversification.[15] Mineral extractive firms, manufacturing firms, multinational banks, private insurance carriers, and worldwide hotel chains are all exposed in fundamentally different ways to politically caused losses. Stephen Blank, a political risk analyst for the Conference Board, is quoted as saying, "The idea of rating (an entire) country's risk is silly. An extractive firm, such as oil or mining, is almost always going to run a higher risk than some one selling ice cream."[16]

Foreign-owned firms cannot eliminate completely the risk of host country political interference within its borders. Whenever foreign-owned firms are perceived, rightly or wrongly, to operate in such a way as to inhibit host

EXHIBIT 9.6
Ten Best and Ten Worst Political Risk Countries, 1980, as Ranked by Frost and Sullivan and Business International

TEN BEST POLITICAL RISKS		*TEN WORST POLITICAL RISKS*	
Frost and Sullivan	*Business International*	*Frost and Sullivan*	*Business International*
United States	Singapore	El Salvador	Iran
Denmark	Netherlands	Iran	Yugoslavia
Singapore	Norway	Nicaragua	South Korea
Finland	Kuwait	Zaire	Algeria
West Germany	Saudi Arabia	Zambia	Brazil
Austria	Switzerland	Libya	Nicaragua
Canada	West Germany	Bolivia	India
Japan	Britain	Turkey	China
Malaysia	Malaysia	Pakistan	Thailand
Netherlands	Japan	Philippines	Philippines

Source: Business Week, December 1, 1980, p. 69.

country national economic, political, or social goals, there is likely to be conflict and political interference. It is just a question of where on the spectrum of possibilities mentioned earlier particular government interference will fall at a particular point in time. It is therefore necessary to plan protective steps in advance, to minimize the likelihood of political interference and the damage that might thus be incurred.

The protective steps can be divided into three categories:

1. negotiating the environment prior to foreign investment,
2. operating strategies after the investment is made, and
3. compensation strategies after expropriation or nationalization has occurred.

NEGOTIATING THE ENVIRONMENT PRIOR TO INVESTMENT

Preinvestment negotiation takes such forms as concession agreements, planned divestment, and investment insurance and guarantees.

Concession Agreements

In the early stages of the colonial era, foreign-owned firms were frequently assured of a friendly political environment because the host country was often controlled, directly or indirectly, by the investors' governments. Many firms operated under a royal charter granted by the home country government. The British East India Company and the Hudson's Bay Company are cases in point. Their charters stipulated their rights and responsibilities in terms of the home country legal, political, and social values. In return, the investing firms received political and military protection from their home countries.

Toward the end of the colonial era, approximately 1913 to 1945, foreign investors responded to the increasing pressures of nationalism abroad and the rejection of colonialism by socialist governments at home by negotiating concession agreements with host country governments. The concession agreements spelled out specific rights and responsibilities of both the foreign firms and the host country government. Both home country and host country legal, political, and social values were presumably considered in arriving at an agreement. For instance, the United Fruit Company operated under a number of individual concession agreements with each Latin American host country.

Many of the early concession agreements were negotiated with fairly weak or autocratic governments. Frequently the agreements were refuted by later "popular" governments on the basis that the former concession was signed under duress by nonrepresentative political leaders. Unfortunately for the multinational firms many host countries either do not accept the Western legal traditions honoring concession agreements as international contracts, or do not believe the concession agreements were made between representative parties acting without duress.

Although concession agreements have proved to be weak arrangements in many of the former colonial possessions, they continue to be negotiated for new foreign investments in both industrialized and developing countries. For instance, there can be no foreign-owned investments in Norway, Japan, India, and Mexico, among others, without a formal concession agreement with the host government. A typical concession agreement would spell out policies on potential sources of conflict such as those listed below.

- The basis on which funds may be remitted (dividends, management contracts, royalties, patent fees, loan repayments, etc.).
- The basis for setting transfer prices, if applicable.
- The right to export to third-country markets.
- Social and economic overhead required to be built.
- Method of taxation, including both the rate base and method of assessing taxable income and property.
- Access to the host country capital market, particularly for long-term borrowing.
- Provision for local equity participation, if any.
- Price controls, if any, applicable to sales in the host country market.
- Limitations on securing of raw materials and components.
- Limitations on nationality of personnel.
- A clause prohibiting the foreign-owned firm from calling on its home country government to intervene in disputes with the host country government ("Calvo clause").
- Provision for arbitration of disputes.

Planned Divestment

Another suggested preinvestment strategy is planned divestment. Raul Prebisch, former director-general of the U.N. Commission for Trade and Development, and A. O. Hirschman, of Princeton University, have proposed that foreign firms in Latin America plan to sell majority ownership in their affiliates to local nationals during a previously agreed period of time.[17]

In some instances planned divestment is a necessary condition of entry or has been imposed on already existing firms. The Cartagena Agreement of May 1969, which established the Andean Common Market, classified enterprises as *domestic* (80% or more of the ownership capital owned within the host country), *mixed* (between 51% and 80% of the capital locally owned), and *foreign* (less than 51% of the capital owned locally). Foreign companies in the Andean nations are expected to transform themselves into mixed companies having effective managerial control in the hands of Andean nationals within 15 years, for Chile, Colombia, and Peru, and within 20 years, for Bolivia and Ecuador.[18]

The main argument for planned divestment is that the benefits to the host country of foreign direct investment come in the early years. These benefits include an infusion into the local economy of capital, entrepreneurship, management, and new technology. In the later years, however, there is a possibility that successful firms replace potential local firms, which have been made possible because of the benefits stemming from the original foreign investment. Thus, although local capital, entrepreneurship, management, and technology have started to develop, thanks in part to foreign investment, all the profitable growth areas have been preempted by successful foreign firms. Increasingly host countries are asking foreign firms the question, "What have you done for us lately?"

In a critique of planned divestment Jack Behrman points out the following fallacies inherent in this strategy.[19]

- Divestment does not seek to change the behavior of foreign-owned firms. The only economic objective is to prevent capital outflow in the form of dividends and other returns. Local owners may be able to transfer more funds abroad than the foreign-owned firms previously repatriated as profits.
- If public national ownership is merely substituted for private foreign ownership, what evidence is there that the affiliates would be able to attract better management, technology, etc.?
- One result of divestment would be to disintegrate the affiliate from the world economy. This is particularly true in Latin American extractive industries, since the raw material extraction is but one stage in a vertically integrated international production function.
- The question of valuation of the foreign investment for purposes of buy out is almost unsolvable. If the price is agreed on beforehand and the investment turns out to be unprofitable, the government would not want to go through with the deal. If the price is negotiated at the time of divestment, the threat of expropriation makes objective bargaining over price difficult to carry out.
- The existing foreign investor faced by impending divestment is not likely to build up a potential competitor. It would probably not establish research and development facilities, undertake elaborate management training programs voluntarily, invest in physical facilities with a long-run payout, or develop an export market.
- Foreign firms considering investment would likely be scared off under the go/no go philosophy, particularly since the profit potential of the

investment would have to be available in the first few years to justify investment in facilities with a long life.

Investment Insurance and Guarantees

As well as instituting concession agreements, adaptation to host country goals, and possibly planned divestment, multinational firms can sometimes transfer political risk to a public agency through an investment insurance and guarantee program. As of 1985, programs to protect investments by their nationals in less developed countries have been created by Australia, Austria, Belgium, Denmark, Finland, France, Germany, India, Israel, Italy, Japan, the Netherlands, New Zealand, Norway, Spain, Sweden, Switzerland, the United Kingdom, and the United States.

The U.S. investment insurance and guarantee program was originally authorized by the Economic Cooperation Act of 1948. Coverage at first was limited to inconvertibility of foreign currencies into dollars. Protection against expropriation was added in 1952; protection against war, revolution, and insurrection between 1960 and 1962; and protection against civil strife in 1981. Before 1955 most of the insurance applied to investments in Europe, but gradually the emphasis changed toward investments in the less developed countries. The Agency for International Development (AID) took over the program in 1961, and thereafter coverage was limited to the less developed countries. Public Law 91-175 of December 30, 1969, provided for the establishment of the government-owned Overseas Private Investment Corporation (OPIC) to take over AID's responsibility for the investment insurance and guarantee program.

OPIC's stated purpose at the time it was created was to mobilize and facilitate the participation of United States private capital and skills in the economic and social progress of less developed friendly countries and areas, thereby complementing the developmental assistance of the United States. However, OPIC was also charged with conducting its operations on a self-sustaining basis, as well as with protecting the interests of U.S. firms abroad. These goals are sometimes in conflict, making assessment of OPIC difficult.

The Overseas Private Investment Corporation Act of 1978 and the OPIC Amendments Act of 1981 together specified that preferential treatment be given to projects in countries with per capita incomes of $680 or less (measured in 1979 U.S. dollars), and that OPIC activities in countries with per capita incomes of $2,950 or more should be restricted. Previous legislative language preventing OPIC support for copper exploration and mining projects was removed in the 1981 amendment. In addition, no claim under contracts will be honored if the investor or its agents have been convicted under the 1977 Foreign Corrupt Practices Act. OPIC obviously is charged with serving an array of political interests.

OPIC operates two main programs: insurance of U.S. private investments in less developed countries, and project financing. Project financing consists of assisting U.S. lenders and business firms in searching out and financing worthwhile projects, and is carried out through an investment guaranty program. This program provides (1) protection against loss from political and commercial risks by arranging for repayment of principal and interest on loans made to eligible borrowers, (2) a direct investment fund that offers dollar financing from OPIC's own resources, and (3) a feasibility study program that assists in the financing of studies to determine the viability of new projects in developing nations.

OPIC provides insurance coverage for three separate types of political risk: inconvertibility; expropriation; and war, revolution, insurrection, and civil strife.

Inconvertibility Inconvertibility is the risk that the investor will not be able to convert profits, royalties, fees, or other income, as well as the original capital invested, into dollars. If inconvertibility should occur, OPIC will convert at the current exchange rate. Claims can be filed because of active blockage if the host government passes a regulation preventing a transfer; because of passive blockage if a host government simply fails to act or approve a transfer; or because of a discriminatory exchange rate imposed on the investor. Inconvertibility insurance does not provide protection against depreciation or appreciation of the currency of investment.

Expropriation Expropriation is the risk that the host government takes a specific step that for one year prevents the investor or the foreign affiliate from exercising effective control over use of the property. Also covered is so-called "creeping" expropriation, wherein host government action less severe or overt than outright expropriation nevertheless forces the foreign-owned enterprise to withdraw, close, or be taken over by the state. Such expropriation may be effected by such actions as restrictive regulations, suspension of licenses, a burdensome tax, or discriminatory government action.

War, revolution, insurrection, and civil strife This coverage applies primarily to the damage of physical property of the insured, although in some cases inability of a foreign affiliate to repay a loan because of a war may be covered. War may exist without a formal declaration. Coverage does not extend to executives who may be kidnapped. Since 1983, physical damage resulting from civil strife has been covered.

Costs OPIC's base rates for manufacturing and service projects are shown below. Fees for expropriation insurance on large or sensitive projects may be slightly higher. Fees may also be increased or decreased by up to one-third depending on the risk profile of the specific project. For all coverages a standby fee of 0.25% will be charged on equity amounts prior to investment or on undisbursed portions of loan agreements. OPIC's base rates are as follows:

Coverage	*Annual base rate per $100 of coverage*
Inconvertibility	30 cents
Expropriation	60 cents
War, revolution, and insurrection (WRI)	60 cents
Civil strife rider	15 cents

Other features of the U.S. investment insurance and guarantee program are as follows:

- Eligible countries must have signed a bilateral agreement with the United States recognizing that the insured investor's rights will be transferred to the U.S. government if payment is made under the insurance contract, and agreeing to arbitrate conflicts arising from the insurance program.
- Each specific insured project must be approved for insurance purposes by the host country.
- Only new projects, including modernization or expansion of an existing investment, can be insured.
- Only U.S. citizens, U.S. firms owned at least 50% by U.S. citizens, or 95% U.S.-owned foreign firms can be covered by the insurance program.
- Insurance of equity investments is for a maximum of 20 years, but shorter maturities are applied in certain sensitive cases. Insurance of loans is for the length of the loan period, which must run three years or longer.
- Partial coverage can be bought on a project-by-project basis; i.e., inconvertibility only, war risk only, etc.
- The maximum insured amount is normally limited to 270% of the insured equity investment and 90% of principal and interest on any long-term loans.

OPERATING STRATEGIES AFTER THE INVESTMENT DECISION

Although an investment agreement may create an obligation on the part of both foreign investor and host country, conditions change and the agreements are often revised "voluntarily," but under pressure. As pointed out in Chapter 1, this is part of the continuing process by which foreign-owned firms are expected to adapt to changing host country priorities. The firm that sticks to the legal interpretation of its agreement usually finds that the host country government first applies pressure in areas not covered by the agreement and then possibly reinterprets the agreement as necessary to force desired changes on the foreign-owned firm. Thus most multinational firms out of self-interest follow a policy of adaptation to changing host country priorities whenever this is possible.

Anticipation of host country priorities is the key to a successful operating strategy. Future political risk can be reduced by careful consideration of policies in the following five areas:

1. production and logistics,
2. marketing,
3. financial,
4. organizational, and
5. personnel.

Production and Logistics

Production and logistics techniques to reduce political risk include local sourcing, location of facilities, control of transportation, and control of patents and processes.

Local sourcing The degree of local sourcing is the key decision variable as far as political risk is concerned. Economic development goals encourage host countries to insist on maximum value added by local production. From the viewpoint of the foreign-owned firm trying to adapt to host country goals, local sourcing would reduce the likelihood of political interference but would increase the loss if interference did occur. If the foreign firm produced the local components itself, the size of its local investment, and correspondingly financial exposure, would have to be larger than if these components were imported. If local producers supplied the components, there might be poorer quality control, higher price from lack of economies of scale, unreliable delivery schedules, etc. Thus the foreign-owned firm might be trading a lower political risk for an increase in financial and commercial risk.

Unrealistic local sourcing requirements also interfere with the recent trend for some multinational firms to rationalize production on a worldwide basis. Costs can be reduced by gaining economies of scale through larger production runs and by utilizing comparative advantage in whatever countries it occurs. For example, in late 1965 Argentina and Chile negotiated a two-way trade in automobile components.[20] However, Argentina agreed to allow only an interchange of components not exceeding 6% of the value of an Argentine vehicle and constituting less that 30% of any one local item.

Chile, for its part, insisted on the development of parts manufacturing that would contribute to the country's technological improvement. Hence Argentina was able to export only a few high-value items, such as engines, transmissions, and rear-axle assemblies, while Chile was able to export only low-value items, such as hub caps and air cleaners. Neither country could export cars to the other, yet in 1967 Argentina had 11 automobile-manufacturing firms producing 177,500 vehicles, and Chile had 19 firms producing 16,400 vehicles. By comparison, a Ford Motor Company assembly plant in Los Angeles, California, produced 106,548 automobiles in 1968.

Even if rationalization of production is encouraged, political risk is involved. On the one hand, expropriation of a plant producing a component that needs to be combined with many others to produce a finished product would have little value by itself. On the other hand, if one plant were the only source for a particular component, there could be a strike, civil disturbance, or government interference; the whole rationalized production system would grind to a halt without the missing component. Needless to say, most firms are careful to have alternative sources of supply in different countries to avoid just such a pitfall.

Location of facilities A variation of the purposeful rationalization of production is found in those extractive industries in which the natural location of different stages of production is either source-oriented, footloose, or market-oriented. For instance, oil is drilled in the Middle East, Latin America, Indonesia, etc. There is no choice as to the location of this stage of production. The refining stage is footloose. Whenever possible, the oil companies have built their refineries in politically safe countries, such as Western Europe, even though costs might be reduced by refining near the oil fields. In other words, there is a trade-off of reduced political risk and financial exposure for possibly higher refining costs. The transportation and main market distribution stages of production are also located outside the area of high political risk.

The oil-exporting countries were kept in a weak bargaining position for many years as a result of the geographical separation of production stages. Since the oil-exporting countries were not united, if one oil-producing country threatened expropriation, it was faced with the difficult task of arranging for refining, transportation, and marketing of its own crude oil. In addition, the international oil companies had alternative sources of crude oil if one source were expropriated. Soviet bloc countries were oil exporters and so did not present an alternative market.

Formation of the Organization of Petroleum Exporting Countries (OPEC) in the 1960s and its cohesiveness in organizing a successful cartel in 1974 changed the balance of power between the oil-exporting countries, the international petroleum companies, and the many oil-importing nations of the world. Acting as a unified whole, OPEC members were able to more than quadruple world oil prices. The OPEC nations and the international oil companies are now mutually dependent on each other.

Control of transportation In a few cases control of transportation has been an important means of reducing the likelihood of expropriation. For many years the United Fruit Company and the Standard Steamship Company had a powerful lever on those Latin American countries which were dependent on banana production. The companies owned the refrigerator ships and controlled the market outlets. Control of oil pipelines that cross national frontiers, oil tankers, ore carriers, and railroads have all been used at some time to influence the political behavior of a host country.

Control of patents and processes Control of key patents and processes has been a viable way to reduce the likelihood of political interference. If a host country is unable to operate an expropriated plant because it does not have technicians capable of running the process, or of keeping up with the changing technology of the industry, expropriation might not occur. If the plant were expropriated, there would be a good chance that adequate compensation and a continuing management contract might be negotiated to keep the plant operating.

The international oil companies were thought to have control of key patents and processes in their relationships with oil producers in the Middle East. However, Iraq's takeover and subsequent operation of the foreign oil companies in the 1950s cast doubt on the effectiveness of this strategy. Nasser's takeover and subsequent operation of the Suez Canal was another case in which foreign investors miscalculated the ability of local nationals to run a technologically complex operation. After all, any host country can hire outside technicians on a management contract to teach local nationals how to run a specific operation.

In individual cases the key patent or process strategy has worked. Coca-Cola still controls its secret ingredient, even though all bottling is local. In general, the companies that have been most successful in employing this strategy are in industries in which the technology changes rapidly. Companies in data processing, electronics, aircraft manufacturing, atomic energy, and pollution control have had a continuing comparative advantage because of their research and development work. Expropriation of plants in these industries would soon be valueless because the product would become obsolete.

Marketing

Marketing techniques to reduce political risk include control of markets, brand names, and trademarks.

Control of markets Control of markets is a common strategy to reduce the likelihood of expropriation in many industries. As effective as the OPEC cartel has been in raising the price received for crude oil by its member countries, marketing is still controlled by the international oil companies. The fact that the OPEC nations still need the oil companies limits the degree to which they can go in taking over all the functions previously performed by the companies. Similar market constraints have limited the degree to which copper, tin, and other metal ore–producing countries have gone in taking over foreign assets. Although legal title by foreign firms to mineral resources and the plant and equipment needed locally to extract those resources is undoubtedly a thing of the past, the need of national governments and market-controlling firms to work together should ensure the continued survival of most extraction-oriented firms. In many instances the market control lever will provide the incentive for technical assistance contracts for the "expropriated" firm.

Control of export markets for manufactured goods is also a source of either conflict or cooperation between host countries and foreign-owned firms. From the viewpoint of the multinational firm, world markets should be served from sources of its own choosing, depending on considerations of production cost, transportation, tariff barriers, political risk exposure, competition, etc. The sourcing pattern that maximizes long-run profit from the total systems viewpoint of the multinational firm rarely maximizes exports (or value added) from the viewpoint of any of the host countries in which the plants are located. The argument has often been stated that if the same plants were owned by local nationals who were not part of a worldwide integrated system, there would be more exports from the host country. For example, the electrotechnical industry has often been accused of limiting foreign production to the home market of its foreign subsidiaries. It has been able to do this indirectly by granting the rights to use patents and licenses to produce goods for the host country market only.

Brand name and trademark control Control of a brand name or trademark can have an effect almost identical to that of controlling patents or processes. It gives the multinational firm a monopoly on something that may or may not have much value. If a plant were expropriated, the value of the brand name or trademark would most likely be lost to the host country.

Financial

A great many financial strategies can be adopted to reduce the risk of loss in case of political interference. These are covered elsewhere, so for the moment it is enough to list some of the more popular methods.

- Foreign affiliates can be capitalized with a thin equity base and a large local debt proportion. If the debt is borrowed from locally owned banks, any expropriation of local assets, or inconvertibility of local currency, would be partially offset by a corresponding reduction in local debt liability (which would also be expropriated as far as most foreign firms are concerned). Raising a large proportion of debt from host country banks, however, is very difficult to accomplish in practice.
- Localizing a subsidiary's capital structure will be discussed in Chapter 12 as a means of meeting local competitive and economic norms.
- There are a number of contractual protection devices, discussed in Chapters 7 and 14. These include hedging, swaps, linked financing, and export credit insurance.
- Major noncontractual protection devices, discussed in Chapter 15, focus on efficient management of working capital. Exposure to loss can be reduced by attention to the timing of intracompany fund transfers and to the level and location of investments in cash balances, receivables, and inventories.

Organizational

The key organizational strategy to have a bearing on political risk is the form and proportion of ownership sought by the investing firm. Some countries, such as Mexico, Japan, and India, do not normally permit a foreign investor to maintain majority ownership of affiliates within their borders.

There are several ways for a multinational firm to organize so as to minimize the possibility of loss from political reasons. It might lower its ownership profile through the use of joint ventures, through judicious location of regional headquarters, through licensing a local firm to produce its products, or by managing a local business on a management contract basis.

Joint ventures Joint ventures between multinationals and host country firms are one answer to a nation's demands for an ownership share in its own industries. The right local partner can contribute equity capital, access to local borrowing, technology, competent management, and a positive local image. On the other hand, the 1984 experience of Union Carbide in Bhopal, India, shows that in the event of a disaster, the multinational firm whose name is associated with the joint venture absorbs virtually all of the political fallout. Union Carbide owned only 50.9% of Union Carbide India, Ltd., but generally was given 100% of the blame for the Bhopal chemical spill. Companies whose operations involve even the smallest risk of an operating disaster may decide against joint ventures on the basis that only with 100% control can they be positive they are in control of the operations.

One of the underlying principles of political risk minimization is to deter nationalization by increasing the potential cost of such action to the host country. One strategy is to establish joint ventures with investors from other nations. A Latin American joint venture owned by parent firms in Japan, France, and the United States would be an example. Nationalization would distress private investors in all three countries, thus impairing good economic relations with three national groups of businesspeople, and creating at least the possibility of three separate diplomatic protests. Additionally, the venture is not clearly marked as to parent nationality and so is less vulnerable to fallout from international political events, such as unpopular United Nations votes, unrelated to the business.

Joint ventures with an agency of the host government are becoming more common. The theory is that at least if the "out" political party becomes the "in" party, it would be less likely to expropriate a company in which it owns a share. If public approval is the motive for the joint venture, what better way than to join with the approver? Naturally the choice of a public partner has many other advantages and disadvantages to be considered, but it would be foolish to rule out such a partnership on ideological grounds alone. There are in existence public-private foreign joint ventures, for example, in Norway, Ghana, India, Colombia, Mexico, Yugoslavia, and a number of other countries. On the other hand, according to the Bradley survey mentioned earlier, joint ventures with host governments are much more likely to be expropriated than other forms of joint ventures or 100% ownership.

Regardless of whether the host country partner is public or private, there are negative aspects of joint ventures from the viewpoint of the investing firm. If the wrong partner is chosen, the political risk could be increased rather than reduced. Imagine the embarrassment of a foreign investor who picked a prominent Chilean capitalist as a joint-venture partner just prior to the nationalization program of the Allende government. How about a joint venture with dictator Trujillo in the Dominican Republic just before his assassination or with the shah of Iran before his overthrow? A local partner who cannot contribute good government relations, capital, technology, or management is probably worse than no partner at all.

Conflict over dividend policy is likely, since there is no assurance that both parties will have the same need for funds, or the same outlook on growth prospects in the case of reinvestment. Transfer pricing on products or components bought from or sold to related companies presents a particularly knotty problem. This topic is covered in Chapter 15. Control of financing is another problem area. The foreign-owned firm would have a hard time justifying the use of cheap or available funds in one country to finance its operations in other countries. Ability of a firm to rationalize its production on a worldwide basis would be jeopardized. This was the reason that the Ford Motor Company bought out the 45% minority interest in British

Ford in 1960 despite very unfavorable reaction in both the U.S. and U.K. press.

In some cases financial disclosure of local results would be increased by having local partners. This disclosure would give competitors knowledge about the business that they would not ordinarily possess, since operations in a given country are usually not disclosed in required financial reports but are consolidated with other foreign or regional results.

Finally, the problem of valuation of equity shares is difficult, as is discussed in Chapter 12. How much should the local partner pay for its share? It is not likely that the opportunity cost of capital, expectations about required rate of return, or other valuation variables would be the same for the local partner as for the investing firm.

In summary, if the right local partner is chosen, the political risk might be reduced, but there is a trade-off. The investing firm's freedom to operate the joint venture as part of a multinational system is likely to be restricted. What is optimal from the viewpoint of the joint-venture operation might be suboptimal for the multinational operation as a whole.

Location of regional headquarters In recent years many U.S. and European firms have found it advantageous to locate their Latin American regional headquarters in Coral Gables, Florida, rather than in Latin America itself. Nearness to the Miami International Airport, cost savings such as avoiding cost-of-living payments and school tuition for executives and families, lack of vulnerability to pressure for bribes and payoffs, and an efficient telephone system are some of the advantages cited. However, equally important is to avoid offending countries that would not have the regional headquarters. Because of jealousies between the various Latin American countries, individual political leaders have less objection to a regional headquarters in Florida than in a neighboring nation. In addition, the regional headquarters is no longer a hostage to local politics and never has to be moved. If the political climate in any individual country deteriorates, the firm can simply hold back on local operations or pull out with a minimum of publicity until conditions improve.

Licensing Licensing has been a popular method for nonmultinational firms to profit from foreign markets without the need to commit sizable funds. Since the foreign producer is typically 100% locally owned, political risk is minimized.

The main disadvantage of licensing is that licensing fees are likely to be lower than direct investment profits (although return on the minimal investment might be higher). Other disadvantages include possible loss of quality control, establishment of a potential competitor in third-country markets, and possible loss of opportunity to enter the market with a direct investment later on.

Multinational firms have not typically used licensing to minimize political risk. On the contrary, most licensing arrangements have been with their own foreign affiliates or joint ventures. License fees have been a way to spread the corporate research and development cost among all operating units, and a means of repatriating profits in a form typically more acceptable than dividends to host countries.

Management contracts Management contracts are similar to licensing insofar as they provide for some foreign profits without significant foreign investment or exposure. Political risks would be minimal, but the same might be true of profits, particularly if the use of scarce managerial talent were valued at its full worth. Some international consulting and engineering firms, however, have traditionally conducted their foreign business on the basis of a management contract.

If planned divestment ever becomes a reality, multinational firms may be forced to convert direct investments into management contracts. For example, Cerro Corporation signed a contract in August 1971 to act as purchasing agent in the United States for equipment needed at three large mines that Chile had just seized from Anaconda Copper. Cerro was supposed to train technical workers at the mines. This action seemed to presage a new wave of flexibility on the part of multinational firms and host governments, since the Cerro Corporation had just had its own copper mines expropriated by Chile. Unfortunately, less than six months later the contract was canceled by Chile.

Personnel

Use of local nationals to staff foreign affiliates is an almost universal policy of all multinational firms. The main controversy comes when choosing top executives. Use of local nationals as top executives can reduce political risk, but might increase business risk if they are less competent or loyal than parent company nationals. There is a trend toward increasing use of local nationals in key positions. This trend is helped by the greatly increased number of non-U.S. nationals who have received MBA or other equivalent management training.

COMPENSATION STRATEGIES AFTER EXPROPRIATION OR NATIONALIZATION

Recovery of value for assets lost through expropriation or nationalization is, in almost every instance, a far less attractive alternative than resolving the controversy beforehand. Nevertheless, certain remedies or counteractions can be taken after a confiscation has occurred. William R. Hoskins has outlined four action phases that typically follow a confiscation under conditions indisputably creating a right to compensation under international law.[21] These are as follows:

Phase I: rational negotiation.

Phase II: negotiation flavored with power tactics.

Phase III: exploration of legal remedies.

Phase IV: surrender by management and decision to seek only salvage value.

Rational Negotiation

Confiscation seldom occurs without some warning for the involved enterprise, which therefore has some opportunity to dissuade the host government from its intended action. Once expropriation occurs, however, the initial steps of the affected company are likely to be directed toward persuading the host government that the expropriation was in error and should be reversed. During this initial period of rational negotiation the firm frequently concentrates on keeping the channels of communication open and on reiterating any points put forward prior to the negotiations.

On the positive side, such points are usually a catalog of the advantages and benefits that have flowed and can be expected to flow in the future from continued operations of the firm. The firm can also approach this initial postconfiscation bargaining from a negative point of view, stressing the economic damage that will inevitably follow cessation of the company's activities. During this period the firm may well offer concessions as an inducement to the country to permit continued operations. The range of concessions is presented in Exhibit 9.7.

Some concessions, such as in Group A of Exhibit 9.7, might be willingly offered, while others, such as in Group C, might be sought by the country but regarded as too damaging by the company. Negotiation of concessions is therefore most likely to center around the alternatives in Group B.

Application of Power Tactics to the Bargaining

If rational negotiations fail to produce a satisfactory solution, the controversy is likely to escalate into Phase II, the exercise of power. Power tactics on a political level may take the form of soliciting political support from opposing political parties or from friendly neighboring countries, or seeking the intercession of the parent country's government officials on an informal basis. Because the era of foreign investor–dominated countries has faded into history, power responses at the political level may well bring about stronger negative reaction from the host country rather than the desired agreement.

EXHIBIT 9.7
Types of Concessions That a Firm Can Offer in Phase I

Group A: Steps willing to take	*Group B: Steps will take under duress*	*Group C: Steps will not take*
1. Hire national managers	*1.* Invest more capital for expansion	*1.* Suspend payment of dividends
2. Raise transfer prices charged to U.S. parent	*2.* Contribute to political campaigns	*2.* Surrender majority control
3. Accept local company as minority partner	*3.* Release government from concession agreements	*3.* Remove all U.S. personnel
4. Change expatriate management	*4.* Support government programs	*4.* Distort global organization

Source: William R. Hoskins, "How to Counter Expropriation," *Harvard Business Review,* September/October 1970, p. 104.

An example of power negotiations is the "Chileanization" of Anaconda's copper operations in Chile during the last years of the administration of Eduardo Frei. Even though Anaconda's properties were subsequently expropriated by the Marxist regime of Salvatore Allende at the time of the "Chileanization" agreement it seemed that Anaconda had deflected demands for immediate expropriation in return for a policy of gradual transfer of its operations to Chilean ownership.

As mentioned earlier in this chapter, economic rather than political power may be exerted, especially to the extent that the investing firm controls technological skills, export markets, component parts, or raw materials, or has tied the local affiliate into a worldwide network so that the local affiliate is not self-sustaining. Application of economic power threats may lead to settlement when the host government's bargaining position is weak. However, such threats may also produce a political backlash, further damaging relationships between the multinational firm and the host country and destroying any possibility of eventual salvage value. In most respects the timing and subtlety with which power bargaining is exercised will be critical to the success or failure of this approach.

Legal Remedies

At some point either concurrent with or following Phases I and II, a firm whose properties have been confiscated will begin to explore legal redress of its grievances. Normally action will first be sought in the court of the host country, especially if there is a reasonable possibility of success in this channel. Proceeding in local courts is likely to be faster, less expensive, and more efficient than other legal courses. Success in a local court action is not likely to damage the local reputation of the firm.

A second alternative is to seek legal redress in the parent country's court system, possibly filing claims against property owned by the seizing nation. A general principle of international law holds that the acts of sovereign nations within their own borders may not be questioned in the courts of other nations. In the case of the United States this doctrine was strictly upheld by the U.S. Supreme Court in *Banco Nacional de Cuba* v. *Sabbatino,* 376 U.S. 398 (1961). Subsequently the U.S. Foreign Assistance Act was amended (the Sabbatino Amendment) to deny the application of this principle in any action based on confiscation in violation of international law, unless the president of the United States determines that application of the amendment would be against the interests of U.S. foreign policy. At present, the possibility of successful action within the U.S. court system is uncertain because the constitutionality of the Sabbatino Amendment has not been clearly established.

Within the framework of legal action, investors can also seek to have the parent country's government forbid imports from countries that have expropriated their property. Expropriation can also result in compensation under provisions of investment insurance and guarantee programs. The existence of investment insurance permits executives to negotiate with greater strength, because they know they can fall back on the insurance protection.

Other possibilities for legal redress consist of seeking diplomatic intervention by the government of the parent country, or of having it present a claim through the International Court of Justice.

International Centre for Settlement of Investment Disputes (ICSID)

In addition to these legal avenues, multinational firms now have recourse to binding arbitration by the International Centre for Settlement of Investment Disputes, located at the World Bank offices in Washington, D.C. This institution was established in October 1966, as a result of discussions (1961 to 1965) sponsored by the World Bank and leading to the Convention of Settlement of Investment Disputes. Some 84 countries have signed the convention. These include most African nations, many Asian nations, and most of the industrial countries. Unfortunately, except for Guyana, Jamaica, Trinidad, and Tobago, no Latin American country has signed the convention. Since the Latin American countries tend to be among the most volatile politically, their absence measurably reduces the potential of the ICSID.

The International Centre was created to provide a conciliation and arbitration mechanism to settle legal disputes between member states and foreign investors. The underlying purpose of the organization is to encourage the growth of private foreign investment for economic development, by creating an impartial international forum to which disputing parties may turn for conciliation or arbitration. The International Centre obtains jurisdiction *only* when both parties to an investment dispute consent. Such consent may be reached when a new investment agreement is entered into, and in fact may be part of the formal investment agreement, or arguments over existing investment agreements may be referred to the International Centre. Once given, such consent cannot be withdrawn by either party, even if one of the member states withdraws from the International Centre. After consent is given, however, either party to an investment dispute may file a request for conciliation or arbitration. Within a rather flexible framework a conciliation commission or an arbitral tribunal will be constituted to judge the issues.

An example of ICSID arbitration is the tribunal's 1984 decision requiring Indonesia to pay $4 million to a group of foreign investors who had undertaken to build a hotel in Jakarta in partnership with an Indonesian army cooperative. After a quarrel over division of profits, armed military personnel occupied the hotel, and it was subsequently taken over by Indonesia. Many foreign investment agreements with Indonesia provide for ICSID arbitration of disputes, but this was the first example of its use. Honoring the ICSID decision will probably enhance Indonesia in the eyes of foreign investors.[22]

Management Surrender and the Seeking of Salvage

Greater recovery is likely if management of the expropriated firm concedes defeat and seeks to salvage what it can from the situation. Hoskins suggests that the investor may best settle for a continued economic relationship without undue concern for legal ownership. He suggests three possibilities:

1. the investor handles exports as in the past, but under a commission arrangement;
2. technical and managerial skills are furnished under a management contract;
3. raw materials and components are sold to the foreign state by the investor.

Loss of the foreign investor's ownership of the property in the host country need not mean the loss of profitable business. In fact, if it is technology and skills rather than monetary capital that is the unique contribution of the foreign investor, contracts providing for compensation for the supplying of such technology and skills, rather than reliance on a return on invested capital, may prove more profitable in the long run.

SUMMARY

Multinational firms must face the risk that host governments may interfere in their operations. Politically motivated interference may take several forms:

- It may simply be a nondiscriminatory type having an equal effect on both domestic and foreign firms.
- It may discriminate against foreign firms by giving specific advantage to national enterprises.
- It may be intended to drive the foreign enterprise out gradually by impairing its ability to earn a reasonable profit.
- It may involve the outright takeover of foreign firms.

A look at the historical record of expropriations since World War II reveals that firms that have been expropriated possess one or more of the following characteristics:

- large size;
- medium level of technology;
- not vertically integrated;
- extractive industries, banking, or insurance;
- located in Latin America, Africa, or the Middle East;
- joint ventures with host government or another multinational firm.

Techniques for forecasting political risk include on-site visits, opinion surveys, quantitative models, and financial market signals. Most techniques do a better job of forecasting a country's political instability than its propensity to expropriate. No technique handles the problem of identifying a firm's propensity to be expropriated, particularly if the firm's own operating policies are considered as variables that affect political risk.

Techniques for dealing with political risk were described and classified into three categories:

- Negotiating the environment prior to investment. This category includes concession agreements, adaptation to host country goals, planned divestment, and investment guarantees.
- Operating strategies after the investment is made. These strategies dictate operating policies in production, logistics, marketing, finance, organization, and personnel.

- Compensation strategies after expropriation. This category includes rational negotiation, application of power tactics to bargaining, legal remedies, use of the International Centre for Settlement of Investment Disputes, and management surrender in the interest of seeking salvage.

NOTES

1. Stephen J. Kobrin, *Managing Political Risk Assessment: Strategic Response to Environmental Change,* Berkeley: University of California Press, 1982, p. 35. Stefan Robock's original dichotomy appeared in Stefan Robock, "Political Risk: Identification and Assessment," *Columbia Journal of World Business,* July/August 1971, pp. 6–20.

2. Douglas Nigh, "The Effect of Political Events on United States Direct Foreign Investment: A Pooled Time Series Cross-Sectional Analysis," *Journal of International Business Studies,* Spring 1985, pp. 1–17.

3. Economic and Social Council to the Secretary-General, *Permanent Sovereignty over Natural Resources,* New York: United Nations, September 1974, pp. 1–3.

4. J. Frederick Truitt, "Expropriation of Foreign Investment: Summary of the Post World War II Experience of American and British Investors in Less Developed Countries," *Journal of International Business Studies,* Fall 1970. The basic source for this article—and an excellent study of expropriation—is Truitt's doctoral dissertation on the same subject completed at Indiana University in 1970, revised and published under the name "Expropriation of Private Foreign Investment," *International Business Series No. 3,* Bloomington: Indiana University, 1974.

5. Robert G. Hawkins, Norman Mintz, and Michael Provissiero, "Government Takeovers of U.S. Foreign Affiliates," *Journal of International Business Studies,* Spring 1976, pp. 3–15.

6. David G. Bradley, "Managing against Expropriation," *Harvard Business Review,* July/August 1977, pp. 75–83.

7. *Ibid.,* p. 80.

8. Stephen J. Kobrin, "Political Assessment by International Firms: Models or Methodologies?" *Journal of Policy Modeling,* May 1981, p. 253.

9. *Ibid.*

10. R. J. Rummel and David A. Heenan suggested the first three of these approaches in "How Multinationals Analyze Political Risk," *Harvard Business Review,* January/February 1978, pp. 67–76.

11. Robert B. Stobaugh, Jr., "How to Analyze Foreign Investment Climates," *Harvard Business Review,* September/October 1969, pp. 100–108.

12. Stephen J. Kobrin, "The Conditions under Which Political Disruption Results in Increased Political Risk," Cambridge, Mass.: MIT, Sloan School of Management, working paper 900–1977, January 1977, p. 33. This paper was later published in Stephen J. Kobrin, "When Does Political Instability Result in Increased Investment Risk?" *Columbia Journal of World Business,* Fall 1978, pp. 113–122.

13. Kobrin, "Political Assessment," p. 253.

14. Dan Haendel and Gerald T. West, with Robert G. Meadow, *Overseas Investment and Political Risk,* Philadelphia: Foreign Policy Research Institute, 1975. (Published in association with Lexington Books, Heath.) This book has been revised and expanded as Dan Haendel, *Foreign Investment and the Management of Risk,* Boulder, Colo.: Westview Press, 1979.

15. Haendel, *Foreign Investment,* p. 5.

16. *Los Angeles Times,* Business Section, February 17, 1980, p. 9.

17. Raul Prebisch, "The Role of Foreign Private Investment in the Development of Latin America," *Sixth Annual Meeting of the IA-ECOSOC (June 1969),* OEA/Ser. H/X14; and in "La Marca de la Integracion," *Boletin de la Integracion,* INTAL, March 1970, No. 51. Also Albert O. Hirschman, "How to Divest in Latin America, and Why," *Essays in International Finance,* No. 76, Princeton University, International Finance Section, November 1969.

18. Two articles discussing the Andean Common Market's rules are Joseph Pincus and Donald E. Edwards, "The Outlook for United States Foreign Direct Investment in the Andean Pact Countries in the Seventies," *Journal of International Business Studies,* Spring 1972, pp. 69–94; and James K. Weekly, "The Andean Common Market Foreign Investment Code," *MSU Business Topics,* Autumn 1971, pp. 19–24.

19. Jack N. Behrman, "International Divestment: Panacea or Pitfall," *Looking Ahead,* National Planning Association, November–December 1970.

20. Jack Baranson, "Integrated Automobiles for Latin America?" *Finance and Development,* fourth quarter 1968, pp. 25–29.

21. William R. Hoskins, "How to Counter Expropriation," *Harvard Business Review,* September/October 1970, pp. 102–112.

22. Karene Witcher, "Tribunal Rules against Indonesia in Hotel Dispute," *Asian Wall Street Journal,* January 25–26, 1985, p. 3.

BIBLIOGRAPHY

Blitzer, Charles R., Panos E. Cavoulacos, and Donald R. Lessard, "Contract Efficiency and Natural Resource Investment in Developing Countries," *Columbia Journal of World Business,* Spring 1984, pp. 10–18.

Boddewyn, J. J., "Divestment: Local vs. Foreign and U.S. vs. European Approaches," *Management International Review,* 1979/1, pp. 21–28.

———, "Foreign Divestment: Magnitude and Factors," *Journal of International Business Studies,* Spring–Summer 1979, pp. 21–27.

Bradley, David G., "Managing against Expropriation," *Harvard Business Review,* July–August 1977, pp. 75–83.

Brewer, Thomas L., "The Instability of Governments and the Instability of Controls on Funds Transfers by Multinational Enterprises: Implications for Political Risk Analysis," *Journal of International Business Studies,* Winter 1983, pp. 147–157.

Bulcke, D. Vanden, and J. J. Boddewyn, *Investment and Divestment Policies in Multinational Corporations in Europe,* London: Saxon/Teakfield; New York: Praeger, 1979.

Bunn, D. W., and X. Mustafaoglu, "Forecasting Political Risk," *Management Science,* November 1978, pp. 1557–1567.

Doz, Yves L., Christopher A. Bartlett, and C. K. Prahalad, "Global Competitive Pressures and Host Country Demands," *California Management Review,* Spring 1981, pp. 63–74.

Doz, Yves L., and C. K. Prahalad, "How MNCs Cope with Host Government Demands," *Harvard Business Review,* March/April 1980, pp. 149–160.

Eiteman, David K., "A Model for Expropriation Settlement: The Peruvian-IPC Controversy," *Business Horizons,* April 1970, pp. 85–91.

Frank, Isaiah, *Foreign Enterprise in Developing Countries,* Baltimore: Johns Hopkins University Press, 1980.

Ghadar, Fariborz, Stephen J. Kobrin, and Theodore H. Moran, eds., *Managing International Political Risk: Strategies and Techniques,* Washington, D.C.: Ghadar and Associates, 1983.

Gladwin, Thomas N., and Ingo Walter, *Multinationals under Fire,* New York: Wiley, 1980.

Goldstein, Elizabeth, and Jan Vanous, "Country Risk Analysis: Pitfalls of Comparing the Eastern Bloc Countries with the Rest of the World," *Columbia Journal of World Business,* Winter 1983, pp. 10–16.

Green, Robert T., "Political Structures as a Predictor of Radical Political Change," *Columbia Journal of World Business,* Spring 1974, pp. 28–36.

Green, Robert T., and Christopher M. Korth, "Political Instability and the Foreign Investor," *California Management Review,* Fall 1974, pp. 23–31.

Haendel, Dan, *Foreign Investment and the Management of Political Risk,* Boulder, Colo.: Westview Press, 1979.

Haendel, Dan, and Gerald T. West, with Robert G. Meadow, *Overseas Investment and Political Risk,* Philadelphia: Foreign Policy Research Institute, 1975.

Haner, F. T., "Rating Investment Risks Abroad," *Business Horizons,* April 1979, pp. 18–23.

Hawkins, Robert G., Norman Mintz, and Michael Provissiero, "Government Takeovers of U.S. Foreign Affiliates," *Journal of International Business Studies,* Spring 1976, pp. 3–15.

Holton, Richard H., "Making International Joint Ventures Work," in Lars Otterbeck, ed., *The Management of Headquarters-Subsidiary Relationships in Multinational Corporations,* New York: St. Martin's Press, 1981, pp. 255–267.

Hu, Henry T. C., "Compensation in Expropriations: A Preliminary Economic Analysis," *Virginia Journal of International Law,* Fall 1979, pp. 61–95.

Ingram, George M., *Expropriation of U.S. Property in South America,* New York: Praeger, 1974.

Johnson, Howard C., *Risk in Foreign Business Environments: A Framework for Thought and Management,* Cambridge, Mass.: Arthur D. Little, 1980.

Kennedy, J. Whitcomb, "Risk Assessment for Affiliates Based in Less Developed Countries," *Columbia Journal of World Business,* Summer 1984, pp. 76–79.

Killing, Peter J., "How to Make a Global Joint Venture Work," *Harvard Business Review,* May/June 1982, pp. 120–127.

Kobrin, Stephen J., "The Environmental Determinants of Foreign Direct Manufacturing Investment: An Ex-Post Empirical Analysis," *Journal of International Business Studies,* Fall–Winter 1976, pp. 29–42.

———, "When Does Political Instability Result in Increased Investment Risk?" *Columbia Journal of World Business,* Fall 1978, pp. 113–122.

———, "Political Risk: A Review and Reconsideration," *Journal of International Business Studies,* Spring–Summer 1979, pp. 67–80.

———, "Foreign Enterprise and Forced Divestment in LDC's," *International Organization,* Winter 1980, pp. 65–88.

———, "Political Assessment by International Firms: Models or Methodologies?" *Journal of Policy Modeling,* May 1981, pp. 251–270.

———, *Managing Political Risk Assessment: Strategic Response to Environmental Change,* Berkeley: University of California Press, 1982.

Kobrin, Stephen J., John Basek, Stephan Blank, and Joseph La Palombara, "The Assessment and Evaluation of Noneconomic Environments by American Firms: A Preliminary Report," *Journal of International Business Studies,* Spring–Summer 1980, pp. 32–47.

Knudsen, Harald, "Explaining the National Propensity to Expropriate: An Ecological Approach," *Journal of International Business Studies,* Spring 1974, pp. 51–71.

Mandel, Robert, "The Overseas Private Investment Corporation and International Investment," *Columbia Journal of World Business,* Spring 1984, pp. 89–95.

Mascarenhas, Briance, and Ole Christian Sand, "Country Risk Assessment Systems in Banks: Patterns and Performance," *Journal of International Business Studies,* Spring 1985, pp. 19–35.

Merrill, James, "Country Risk Analysis," *Columbia Journal of World Business,* Spring 1982, pp. 88–91.

Muller, Maarten H., "Compensation for Nationalization: A North–South Dialogue," *Columbia Journal of Transnational Law,* No. 1, 1981, pp. 35–78.

Nagy, Pancras J., "Quantifying Country Risk: A System Developed by Economists at the Bank of Montreal," *Columbia Journal of World Business,* Fall 1978, pp. 135–147.

———, *Country Risk,* London: Euromoney, 1984.

Neville, M. K., Jr., "Present Status of Compensation by Foreign States for the Taking of Alien-Owned Property," *Vanderbilt Journal of Transnational Law,* Winter 1980, pp. 51–74.

Nigh, Douglas, "The Effect of Political Events on United States Direct Foreign Investment: A Pooled Time Series Cross-Sectional Analysis," *Journal of International Business Studies,* Spring 1985, pp. 1–17.

Otterbeck, Lars, "The Management of Joint Ventures," in Lars Otterbeck, ed., *The Management of Headquarters-Subsidiary Relationships in Multinational Corporations,* New York: St. Martin's Press, 1981, pp. 269–296.

Overholt, William H., *Political Risk,* London: Euromoney Publications, 1982.

Perlitz, Manfred, "Compensatory Arrangements in International Licensing Agreements: Effects on Market Penetration Abroad, Foreign Pricing Policy, and Conflict Areas between Licensee and Licensor," *Management International Review,* 1980/1, pp. 75–82.

Poynter, Thomas A., "Government Intervention in Less Developed Countries: The Experience of Multinational Companies," *Journal of International Business Studies,* Spring/Summer 1982, pp. 9–25.

Robinson, Richard D., *National Control of Foreign Business Entry,* New York: Praeger, 1976.

Robock, Stefan, "Political Risk: Identification and Assessment," *Columbia Journal of World Business,* July/August 1971, pp. 6–20.

Rogers, Jerry, ed., *Global Risk Assessments: Issues, Concepts and Applications,* Riverside, Calif.: Global Risk Assessments, 1983.

Root, Franklin R., "U.S. Business Abroad and Political Risks," *MSU Business Topics,* Winter 1968, pp. 73–80.

Rummel, R. J., and David A. Heenan, "How Multinationals Analyze Political Risk," *Harvard Business Review,* January/February 1978, pp. 67–76.

Ryans, J. K., and J. C. Baker, "The International Centre for Settlement of Investment Disputes," *Journal of World Trade Law,* January–February 1976, pp. 65–79.

Saini, Krishan, "A Survey of the Quantitative Approaches to Country Risk Analysis," *Journal of Banking and Finance,* June 1984, pp. 341–356.

Salehizadeh, Mehdi, *Regulation of Foreign Direct Investment by Host Country,* Essays in International Business No. 4, Columbia: University of South Carolina, 1983.

Simon, Jeffrey D., "Political Risk Assessment: Past Trends and Future Prospects," *Columbia Journal of World Business,* Fall 1982, pp. 62–71.

Stein, Philip J., "Should Your Firm Invest in Political Risk Insurance?" *Financial Executive,* March 1983, pp. 18–22.

Stobaugh, Robert B., "How to Analyze Foreign Investment Climates," *Harvard Business Review,* September–October 1969, pp. 100–108.

Stoever, William A., "LDC Governments: Takeovers and Renegotiations of Foreign Investments," *California Management Review,* Winter 1979, pp. 5–14.

Thunell, Lars H., *Political Risks in International Business: Investment Behavior of Multinational Corporations,* New York: Praeger, 1977.

Tipgus, Manuel A., "Compliance with the Foreign Corrupt Practices Act," *Financial Executive,* August 1981, pp. 38–48.

Torneden, Roger L., *Foreign Disinvestment by U.S. Multinational Corporations,* New York: Praeger, 1975.

Wells, Louis T., Jr., "Negotiating with Third World Governments," *Harvard Business Review,* January/February 1977, pp. 72–80.

Wilson, Brent D., *Disinvestment of Foreign Subsidiaries,* Ann Arbor, Mich.: UMI Research Press, 1980.

Yonah, Alexander, and Robert A. Kilmarx, *Political Terrorism and Business: The Threat and Response,* New York: Praeger, 1979.

10

Multinational Capital Budgeting

Although the original decision to undertake an investment in a particular foreign country may be determined by a mix of strategic, behavioral, and economic decisions, the specific project, as well as all reinvestment decisions, should be justified by traditional financial analysis. For example, a production efficiency opportunity may exist for a U.S. firm to invest abroad, but the type of plant, mix of labor and capital, kinds of equipment, method of financing, and other project variables must be analyzed within the traditional financial framework of discounted cash flows.

On the basis of the compromise viewpoint of financial goals developed in Chapter 1, consideration must also be given to the impact of the proposed foreign project on consolidated net earnings and on the market value of the parent firm.

FOREIGN COMPLEXITIES

Capital budgeting for a foreign project uses the same theoretical framework as domestic capital budgeting: Project cash flows are discounted at the firm's weighted average cost of capital, or the project's required rate of return, to determine net present value; or, alternatively, the internal rate of return that equates project cash flows to the cost of the project is sought. However, capital budgeting analysis for a foreign project is considerably more complex than the domestic case for a number of reasons:

- Parent cash flows must be distinguished from project cash flows. Each of these two types of flows contributes to a different view of value.

- Parent cash flows often depend upon the form of financing. Thus cash flows cannot be clearly separated from financing decisions, as is done in domestic capital budgeting.
- Remittance of funds to the parent must be explicitly recognized because of differing tax systems, legal and political constraints on the movement of funds, local business norms, and differences in how financial markets and institutions function.
- Cash flows from affiliates to parent can be generated by an array of nonfinancial payments, including payment of license fees and payments for imports from the parent.
- Differing rates of national inflation must be anticipated because of their importance in causing changes in competitive position, and thus in cash flows over a period of time.
- The possibility of unanticipated foreign exchange rate changes must be remembered because of possible direct effects on the value to the parent of local cash flows, as well as an indirect effect on the competitive position of the foreign affiliate.
- Use of segmented national capital markets may create an opportunity for financial gains or may lead to additional financial costs.
- Use of host government subsidized loans complicates both capital structure and the ability to determine an appropriate weighted average cost of capital for discounting purposes.
- Political risk must be evaluated because political events can drastically reduce the value or availability of expected cash flows.
- Terminal value is more difficult to estimate because potential purchasers from the host, parent, or third countries, or from the private or public sector, may have widely divergent perspectives on the value to them of acquiring the project.

Since the same theoretical capital budgeting framework is used to choose among competing foreign and domestic projects, a common standard is critical. Thus all foreign complexities must be quantified as modifications to either expected cash flow or the rate of discount. Although in practice many firms make such modifications arbitrarily, readily available information, theoretical deduction, or just plain common sense can be used to make less arbitrary and more reasonable choices.

PROJECT VS. PARENT VALUATION

A strong theoretical argument exists in favor of analyzing any foreign project from the viewpoint of the parent. Cash flows to the parent are ultimately the basis for dividends to stockholders, reinvestment elsewhere in the world, repayment of corporatewide debt, and other purposes that affect the firm's many interest groups. However, since most of a project's cash flows to its parent, or to sister affiliates, are financial cash flows rather than operating cash flows, the parent viewpoint usually violates a cardinal concept of capital budgeting, namely, that financial cash flows should not be mixed with operating cash flows. Sometimes the difference is not important because the two are almost identical, but in some instances a sharp divergence in these cash flows will exist. For example, funds that are permanently blocked from repatriation, or "forcibly reinvested," are not available for dividends to the stockholders or for repayment of corporate debt. Therefore shareholders will not perceive the blocked earnings as contributing to the value of the firm, and creditors will not count on them in calculating interest coverage ratios and other evidence of ability to service debt.

Evaluation of a project from the local viewpoint serves some useful purposes, but should be subordinated to evaluation from the parent's viewpoint. In evaluating a foreign project's performance relative to the potential of a competing project in the same host country, one must pay attention to the project's local return. Almost any project should at least be able to earn a cash return equal to the yield available on host government bonds with a maturity the same as the project's economic life, if a free market exists for such bonds. Host government bonds ordinarily reflect the local risk-free rate of return, including a premium equal to the expected rate of inflation. If a project cannot earn more than such a bond yield, the parent firm should buy host government bonds rather than invest in a riskier project—or, better yet, invest somewhere else!

If the theory of direct foreign investment is correct, multinational firms should invest only if they can earn on a project a risk-adjusted return greater than local-based competitors can earn on the same project. If they are unable to earn superior returns on foreign projects, their stockholders would be better off buying shares in local firms, where possible, and letting those companies carry out the local projects.

Apart from these theoretical arguments, surveys over the last eighteen years show that in practice multinational firms continue to evaluate foreign investments from both the parent and project viewpoint. Responses of multinational firms to surveys by Stonehill and Nathanson (1968), Baker and Beardsley (1973), Oblak and Helm (1980), Bavishi (1981), Kelly and Philippatos (1982), and Stanley and Block (1983) reveal that firms calculate and evaluate rates of return by using cash flows to and from the parent alone, as well as to and from the foreign project alone.[1] In a 1978–1979 study of 156 U.S. multinationals, Bavishi reported that in appraising foreign projects, 42% of the firms use cash flow from the foreign project's viewpoint, 21% use cash flow from the parent's viewpoint, and 37% use both.[2] In their study of 121 U.S. multinational firms, conducted in the early 1980s, Stanley and Block found that 48% of their 121 respondents evaluate foreign projects on the basis of the project's cash flows, 36% on the basis of parent cash flows, and 16% on both.[3]

The attention paid to project returns in the various survey results probably reflects emphasis on maximizing reported consolidated net earnings per share as a corporate financial goal. As long as foreign earnings are not blocked, they can be consolidated with the earnings of the remaining affiliates and of the parent.[4] Even in the case of temporarily blocked funds, some of the most mature multinational firms do not necessarily eliminate a project. They take a very long-run view of world markets.

If reinvestment opportunities in the country where the funds are blocked are at least equal to the parent firm's required rate of return (after adjusting for anticipated exchange rate changes), temporary blockage of transfer may have little practical effect on the capital budgeting outcome because future project cash flows will be increased by the returns on forced reinvestment. Since the large multinationals hold a portfolio of domestic and foreign projects, corporate liquidity is not impaired if a few projects have blocked funds; alternate sources of funds are available to meet all planned uses of funds. Furthermore, a long-run historical perspective on blocked funds does indeed lend support to the belief that funds are almost never permanently blocked. However, waiting for the release of such funds can be frustrating, and sometimes the blocked funds lose value because of inflation or unexpected exchange rate deterioration while blocked, even though they have been reinvested in the host country to protect at least part of their value in real terms.

In conclusion, most firms appear to evaluate foreign projects from both parent and project viewpoints. The parent's viewpoint gives results closer to the traditional meaning of net present value in capital budgeting. Project valuation provides a closer approximation of the effect on consolidated earnings per share, which all surveys indicate is of major concern to practicing managers.

ADJUSTING FOR RISK—PARENT VIEWPOINT

In analyzing a foreign project from the parent point of view, the additional risk that stems from its "foreign" location can be handled in at least two ways. The first method is to treat all foreign risk as a single problem by increasing the discount rate applicable to foreign projects relative to the rate used for domestic projects to reflect the greater foreign exchange risk, political risk, and other uncertainties perceived in foreign operations.

In the second method, which we prefer, all foreign risks are incorporated in adjustments to forecasted cash flows of the project. The discount rate for the foreign project is risk-adjusted only for overall business and financial risk, in the same manner as that for domestic projects.

Adjusting the Discount Rate

Adjusting the discount rate applied to a foreign project's cash flow to reflect political and foreign exchange uncertainties does not penalize net present value in proportion to either the actual amount at risk or to possible variations in the nature of that risk over time. Combining all risks into a single discount rate discards much information about the uncertainties of the future.

For example, political uncertainties are a threat to the entire investment, not just to annual cash flows. Potential loss depends partly on the terminal value of the unrecovered parent investment, which will vary depending upon how the project was financed and whether political risk insurance has been obtained. Furthermore, if the political climate were expected to be unfavorable in the near future, any investment would probably be unacceptable. Political uncertainty usually relates to possible adverse events that might occur in the more distant future, but that cannot be foreseen at the present. Adjusting the discount rate for political risk thus penalizes early cash flows too heavily while not penalizing distant cash flows enough.

In the case of foreign exchange risk, changes in exchange rates have a potential effect on future cash flows because of economic exposure. The direction of the effect, however, can either decrease or increase net cash inflows, depending on where the products are sold and where inputs are sourced. The variety of outcomes under economic exposure was explained in the Instruments Napoleon example in Chapter 6. To increase the discount rate applicable to a foreign project, on the assumption that the foreign currency might depreciate more than expected, ignores the possible favorable effect of a foreign currency depreciation on the project's competitive position. Increased sales volume might more than offset a lower value of the local currency.

Apart from anticipated political and foreign exchange risks, multinational firms sometimes worry that taking on foreign projects might increase the firm's overall cost of capital because of investors' perceptions of foreign risk. This worry seems reasonable if the firm is investing in Libya, Iran, Lebanon, or Angola in the 1980s, especially if the firm's operations are heavily centered in one such unreliable country, and if that country is in the news frequently in a context of rampant xenophobia. However, the argument loses persuasiveness when applied to diversified foreign investments with a heavy balance in the industrial countries of Canada, Western Europe, Australia, and Asia, where in fact the bulk of direct foreign investment is located. These countries have a reputation for treating foreign investments by consistent standards, and empirical evidence confirms that a foreign presence in these countries may not increase the cost of capital. In fact, some studies indicate that required returns on foreign projects may even be lower than those for domestic projects, as is shown in the appendices to Chapters 8 and 12.

Adjusting Cash Flows

In the rest of this chapter we will use the method that adjusts cash flows rather than the discount rate in treating risk. Cash flows to the parent will be discounted by the rate of return appropriate for the business and financial risks of comparable domestic projects. Any risk unique to the foreign location of the project will be incorporated into project cash flows.

It should be noted that many multinational firms do adjust the discount rate for foreign projects despite the theoretical limits of this method. The aforementioned Baker and Beardsley survey found that 49% of the responding multinationals add a premium percentage for risk to their required rate of return on foreign investments.[5] The authors remark that these tended to be firms with a relatively small percentage of foreign sales. Firms with a larger foreign commitment did not typically change the discount rate, but instead presumably adjusted cash flows. The Oblak and Helm survey also reported that slightly more than half of the responding firms varied the discount rate for foreign projects, but the other half did not.[6] Of those that varied the discount rate, 40% subjectively varied their weighted average cost of capital, while 44% used the local (that is, foreign) weighted average cost of capital.

In their 1983 study, Stanley and Block found that 62% of their respondents used some risk-adjustment technique, but that risk-adjusted discount rates and risk-adjusted cash flows were used with similar frequency. They also found that the use of risk adjustment techniques is independent of the percentage of foreign sales to total sales.[7]

ADJUSTING FOR RISK—PROJECT VIEWPOINT

From the project point of view, "foreign" risks also exist. A foreign affiliate has foreign exchange exposure on both its imports and exports. Since the prime purpose of finding a project rate of return is to compare it with alternative opportunities to invest funds locally, the appropriate discount rate should be the one required by *local* investors for projects of the same business and financial risk class. This approach forces the parent to remember that local inflation and risk must be reflected in the required rate of return for local projects.

For comparisons within the host country, a project's actual financing or parent-influenced debt capacity should be overlooked, since these would probably be different for local investors than they are for a multinational owner. In addition, the risks of the project to local investors might differ from those perceived by a foreign multinational owner because of the opportunities a multinational firm has to take advantage of market imperfections. Moreover, the local project may be only one out of an internationally diversified portfolio of projects for the multinational owner, whereas it might have to stand alone, without international diversification, if undertaken by local investors. Since diversification reduces risk, the multinational firm can require a lower rate of return than is required by local investors.

Thus the discount rate used locally must be a hypothetical rate based on a judgment as to what independent local investors would probably demand were they to own the business. Consequently, application of the local discount rate to local cash flows provides only a rough measure of the value of the project as a stand-alone local venture, rather than an absolute valuation.

ILLUSTRATIVE EXAMPLE: MULTINATIONAL ELECTRICAL CORPORATION

To illustrate the foreign complexities of multinational capital budgeting, we will analyze a "market seeking" investment by a U.S. firm investing in France. To keep the example simple, we will introduce details of the investment opportunity as needed in the analysis rather than all at once. In this way, "foreign" complications can be discussed and analyzed one at a time. Eventually the uniqueness of multinational capital budgeting should become clear. Note, however, that a definitive normative model for capital budgeting analysis of foreign projects has not yet been fully agreed upon by either theoreticians or practitioners. Therefore, wherever possible, alternative approaches will be introduced even though the authors prefer one over the other.

Multinational Electrical Corporation (MEC-USA), a hypothetical, U.S.-based, multinational firm with sales and assets in the billion dollar class, is considering establishment of a freezer manufacturing plant in France (MEC-France). It has previously exported freezers to France from the United States, but these exports have become less competitive in price because of the increased strength of the U.S. dollar compared to the EMS currencies.

The French facility will supply the French market as well as the rest of the EEC. MEC-France will remit 5% of sales in French francs as a license fee to MEC-USA. About 20% of raw materials and components used in the manufacturing process will be imported from MEC-USA's plants in the United States and be billed in dollars at market price. All other inputs will be sourced in France.

As an inducement to locate in an existing but vacant plant in an area of high unemployment within France, a French Development Bank (FDB) is willing to provide a five-year loan for 50% of the acquisition cost of the plant at 6% interest, with the principal to be repaid in five equal installments at the end of each year. Because of the subsidy, the interest is not deductible for tax purposes in France but is deductible for U.S. tax purposes.

MEC-France's income will be taxed at a 50% rate in France. Contingent U.S. tax on this same income will be explained later. MEC-USA is taxed at a 46% rate.

MEC-USA uses a 14% risk-adjusted required rate of return for evaluating freezer plants domestically. This rate reflects their perception of the business and financial risks of this kind of investment but does not reflect any risks of foreign operations.

About one month will be needed to attain full-scale operation, since the existing plant and work force had been producing refrigerators, and conversion to freezers should be relatively simple.

To make comparisons between alternative capital investment opportunities on the same time scale, MEC-USA uses a five-year time horizon for capital budgeting analysis, even for projects with very uneven lives. This approach tends to emphasize the importance of calculating the project's terminal value. Nevertheless, many firms prefer the short time horizon, especially for analyzing foreign projects, because of the perceived increase in political and foreign exchange risks as time passes.

The MEC-USA project investigation team believes that similar projects in France at this time have a required rate of return of about 15% after French taxes for an all-equity investment. French government long-term bonds have a 5% aftertax yield to maturity. The 10% difference reflects the project's business risk as seen by French investors.

PROJECT INVESTMENT OUTLAYS AND FINANCING

MEC-USA's project investigation team must estimate project cash flows from both local and parent perspective. Conceptually, these flows can be illustrated as shown in Exhibit 10.1.

From the parent's perspective, outflows consist of the original dollar investment to purchase a French plant, send used equipment, and transfer working capital. In addition, the parent has a French franc outflow for local purchase of equipment and working capital with funds borrowed from a French bank.

Inflows back to the parent include a contribution to profit and overhead from exports to the EEC through MEC-France, license fees paid by MEC-France, an interest subsidy from the French Development Bank, net operating income in MEC-France if it is fully transferable, eventual recapture of working capital tied up in MEC-France, and the terminal market value of MEC-France after capital gains taxes. Inflows to the parent are reduced by tax payments to the United States for capital gains on the sale of equipment to MEC-France, and income tax on foreign source income remitted as dividends and license fees from MEC-France. In addition, withholding taxes are paid to the French government on dividends remitted by MEC-France to MEC-USA.

From the viewpoint of MEC-France, cash outflows are for the original investment in plant, equipment, and working capital. This is the French franc equivalent of the original investment by MEC-USA. In addition,

EXHIBIT 10.1
Cash Flows: A Conceptual View

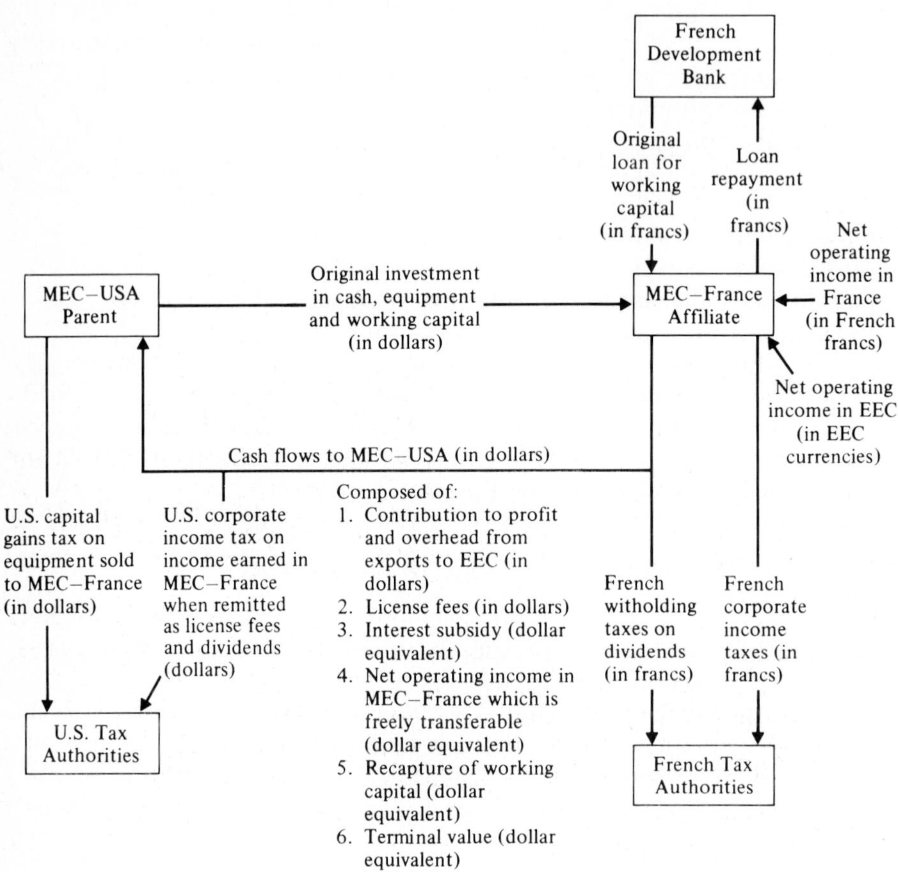

MEC-France pays French corporate income taxes on its net operating income and requires periodic additions to required working capital.

MEC-France's cash inflows come from net operating income earned on exports to the EEC and on sales in France. In addition, it has cash inflows from the tax shield on depreciation, eventual recapture of required net working capital, and its terminal value after capital gains taxes.

Initial Investment

MEC-USA's project investigation team must first estimate what outlays will be required to get MEC-France underway. The main investment will be in plant, equipment, and working capital. A summary of the investment is shown in Exhibit 10.2.

EXHIBIT 10.2
Original Investment in MEC-France (in Year 0)
Original exchange rate is FF8 = $1.00

	Thousands of francs	*Thousands of dollars*
1. Purchase and conversion of plant	FF30,000	$3,750
2. Used equipment from the United States	5,000	625
3. New equipment from France	5,000	625
4. Components and raw material provided by MEC-USA	5,000	625
5. Cash provided by French banks	5,000	625
6. Total original investment	FF50,000	$6,250

An existing French refrigerator manufacturing plant will be purchased and converted to freezers for FF30 million. At the present exchange rate of FF8 = $1.00 this amount is equivalent to $3,750,000. Half of the amount is being provided as a five-year loan by the French Development Bank (FDB) at a low 6% interest. The other half will be paid for in cash by MEC-USA. Plant capacity will be large enough to handle foreseeable output for the next ten years. The plant can be depreciated on a straight-line basis over a five-year life to a zero salvage value.

Equipment worth FF10 million ($1,250,000) is needed to start operations. Half of this will be imported as used equipment from another MEC-USA plant and the rest will be purchased locally in France. The used equipment is carried on MEC-USA's books at zero book value but will be transferred at its market value of $625,000 (FF5 million). A 30% capital gains tax will be levied by the United States on the book gain.[8] The transfer value represents the true market value of the used equipment if sold in the United States or purchased in France. If this were not the case, the accounting value on the MEC-France books would differ from the value used for capital budgeting purposes, which should be the opportunity cost (market value) of the equipment. All equipment can be depreciated on a straight-line basis over a five-year life to a zero salvage value in MEC-France.

Working capital investments in cash, accounts receivable, and inventory are expected to average 20% of net sales once MEC-France is operating normally. Accounts payable to local suppliers are expected to average 10% of net sales. Therefore net working capital investment will equal 10% of net sales. As part of its equity contribution, MEC-USA will provide initial net working capital in the form of components and raw materials. The components and raw materials will be transferred to MEC-France at $625,000, which includes a 30% contribution to profit and overhead of the parent. Future transfers of components and raw materials will be based on the same contribution margin. MEC-USA expects to have considerable spare capacity in the United States and therefore uses contribution margin (sales minus variable costs) as its measure of gain rather than net income on a full-cost basis. All additions to net working capital beyond the original inventory will be financed through local borrowing from French banks. An initial working capital loan for cash of FF5 million ($625,000) will be provided by the local banks.

Financial Structure of MEC-France

Exhibit 10.3 shows financing of the initial investment in MEC-France. As is normal in capital budgeting, all assets, including net working capital, are considered part of the initial investment *regardless of how they are financed.* In this case the French Development Bank and local banks have provided 40% of the initial capital. This 40% debt ratio (total debt ÷ total assets) is approximately the same as the consolidated worldwide debt ratio of MEC-USA. The fact that MEC-France borrows the funds does not change the fact that these debts will be consolidated with the debt of the parent and other affiliates for reporting purposes. Therefore the same argument that justifies use of a weighted average cost of capital rather than the marginal cost of

EXHIBIT 10.3
Initial Balance Sheet of MEC-France (in thousands of French francs)

Assets	
1. Cash	FF 5,000
2. Accounts receivable	—
3. Inventory	5,000
4. Total current assets	FF10,000
5. Net plant	30,000
6. Equipment	10,000
7. Total	FF50,000
Liabilities and Net Worth	
8. Accounts payable	FF —
9. Notes payable to local banks	5,000
10. Total current liabilities	FF 5,000
11. Loan payable to French Development Bank	15,000
12. Common stock	30,000
13. Total	FF50,000

project-specific funds in the domestic case holds here. There is no point in giving MEC-France the benefit of the already existing corporate debt capacity unless this project actually changes the worldwide MEC-USA debt capacity. French debt is merely a substitute for other debt that MEC-USA could have raised.

If for some reason MEC-France did indeed increase MEC-USA's debt capacity, it would then be proper to recognize this advantage by one of two popular methods. One method would be to lower the risk-adjusted discount rate for MEC-France by including a higher proportion of debt. The other method would be to discount MEC-France's cash flows by an all-equity cost of capital appropriate for a firm of the same business risk, and then add to its discounted cash flows the discounted tax shield provided by debt. The risk-free rate should be used to discount the tax shield, since this benefit is a certainty.[9]

The fact that MEC-France's debt does not reduce its initial investment does not mean the debt is immaterial. The debt structure and source of debt have a bearing on how funds may be repatriated to the parent. This factor could be important in the event of blocked funds or other future political risks.

Project-Specific Financing

Although the project-specific loan by FDB does not change the debt capacity of MEC-USA, the favorable interest rate represents a subsidy. In effect, the French government is allowing its capital market to be segmented for certain purposes. From MEC-USA's viewpoint similar long-term debt borrowed in the United States would carry a 10% interest rate. The project investigation team believes that the long-run outlook is for the French franc to depreciate 3% annually with respect to the dollar. Therefore a French franc loan at 6% would represent a 3% beforetax effective cost to MEC-USA compared to borrowing dollars at 10%. The subsidy before tax is therefore worth the difference between the U.S. borrowing rate at 10% and the effective 3% French borrowing rate, or a subsidy of 7%. Since interest on this loan is deductible for U.S. tax purposes, the net after-tax subsidy to MEC-USA is 7% × (1 − U.S. tax rate of 46%) = 3.78% per year for five years.

There are three ways to handle project-specific subsidies in capital budgeting. One method is to add the subsidy to project cash inflows and discount at the weighted average cost of capital to the parent. A second way is to discount the subsidy at some other rate, e.g., the risk-free rate. A third method is to lower the risk-adjusted discount rate for the project to reflect the lower cost of debt. The main difference conceptually depends on the assumption about the rate of return on reinvestment of the funds from the project.

We prefer the method that adjusts the cash flows and discounts by the parent's weighted average cost of capital. This method makes the normal assumption that funds from the French project will be reinvested at the corporatewide cost of capital for MEC-USA. If the cost of capital of the French project were lowered, it would assume that funds from the project would be reinvested at the lower cost of capital rate. This event is unlikely, since higher returns would exist elsewhere, as implied by the higher cost of capital (hurdle rate) for MEC-USA.

Cash flows from MEC-France should be credited with the interest subsidy as follows:

	YEAR				
	1	*2*	*3*	*4*	*5*
1. Loan balance, in thousands of francs	FF15,000	FF12,000	FF9,000	FF6,000	FF3,000
2. Annual interest charge at 6%	FF 900	FF 720	FF 540	FF 360	FF 180
3. Loan balance, expressed in thousands of dollars	$1,875	$1,500	$1,125	$750	$375
4. Interest subsidy after tax (line 3 × .0378)	$71	$57	$43	$28	$14

CASH FLOWS FROM PROJECT

The first step in estimating operating cash flows from the proposed MEC-France project is to forecast a five-year operating plan on the basis of the most likely assumptions of marketing and production policies, remittance of funds, inflation, foreign exchange rate changes, and the political outlook. Later, these "most likely" assumptions should be altered in order to test the sensitivity of expected cash flows to changes in the key assumptions.

Basic Demand

The project investigation team estimates that MEC-France will be able to sell 20,000 freezer units in France and another 20,000 units in the rest of the EEC during the first year at a price of FF2,000 each. They estimate that the basic demand for freezers in France is growing at 5% per year and in the rest of the EEC at 8% per year. This is also the most likely forecast for growth in unit sales for MEC-France based on their proposed marketing strategy and the outlook for inflation and exchange rates in the EEC. It could differ from the industry average growth rate but only if MEC-France purposely changes their pricing strategy in response to inflation or devaluation.

Inflation, Exchange Rates, and Pricing Strategy

The project investigation team believes that annual inflation in France will average 10% over the next five years. The comparable figure for a trade-weighted average of the rest of the EEC is 5%. Freezer prices in each national market seem to increase at a pace equal to national inflation. MEC-France's pricing strategy is to follow local prices. This strategy is based on the observation that the freezer industry in France and the rest of the EEC is characterized by well-behaved oligopolists. Few price-cutting wars occur because the industry seems to have found a competitive equilibrium where the price elasticity of demand is about 1.0 in each direction in each country.

With the pricing strategy based on local prices in each national market, changes in exchange rates would change the effective price of MEC-France's exports in terms of French franc receipts. If MEC-France's freezers sell for DM1,000 each today when FF2 = DM1, their receipts when converted to French francs would be FF2,000 each. If the exchange rate should change to FF3 = DM1, receipts would increase to FF3,000 upon conversion. This is a good example of economic exposure benefits. Although the French franc devalues, French franc revenues increase.

There is a mistaken tendency on the part of some observers and even government officials to overestimate the effect of devaluation of the national currency on the balance of payments and employment. A favorable effect can only happen if firms have been following a suboptimal pricing strategy prior to devaluation. The devaluation is an *excuse* to change prices, but if firms have been paying attention to price elasticity of demand in each national market, they should already be at the optimal local price. For example, there is no reason for MEC-France to change its freezer prices in Germany as a result of devaluation of the French franc. If they did actually cut prices in proportion to the devaluation, they would surely start a price war and all competitors would make less total revenue and profits. While it is true that MEC-France would probably be in a better position to weather the price war than their other EEC competitors, depending on what happens to comparative costs, they would still make less profit than when the industry was at the previous equilibrium price and all the benefit of devaluation was registered as windfall profits to MEC-France.

It would also be suboptimal for German firms to react to the French franc devaluation by raising their freezer prices in France if they are not the price leaders there. Depending on price elasticity of demand, and the pricing reaction of competitors in France, they could simply lose relatively more in volume than they gained in price (elastic demand). There is the other possibility, of course, that French competitors would raise their prices under the German "umbrella," but this action assumes that the whole industry should have been charging the higher price all along. The industry must not have been at the best equilibrium position to maximize total revenue prior to the change in prices by German firms.

Since market structures and competitive reactions to price changes differ by industry, it is very difficult for most observers to predict the actual effect of an exchange rate change on international trade, employment, and profits. On the other hand, the competitors in each industry have been observing each others' reactions for years and are probably in a better position to guess at the likely results of exchange rate changes on their own competitive position. Spending some effort at the firm level to anticipate economic exposure to exchange rate changes is a desirable activity.

The investigation team forecasts that over the next five years the French franc will depreciate by 5% annually relative to the trade-weighted EEC currencies (ECUs). This forecast is based on the purchasing-power-parity theory, which would predict that the change in exchange rates would equal the 5% differential in inflation rates.

The team's forecast for the dollar is that the French franc will depreciate annually by only 3% relative to the dollar even though the inflation differential they predict is also 5% (U.S. inflation = 5% per year). The reason for this apparent contradiction of purchasing power parity is that the dollar's value is based on many factors other than trade with France or even with the EEC. It is based on U.S. trade with the rest of the world, as well as the use of the dollar by many other countries as a trading, financing, and reserve currency. The MEC-France project investigation team feels that the dollar will gradually become more competitive in the EEC because of a 2% annual depreciation of the dollar relative to the ECU, despite the fact that the two rates of inflation are equal.

The team's calculation of exchange rates for the franc vis-à-vis both the ECU and the U.S. dollar are as follows:

Year	*French francs per ECU*	*French francs per U.S. dollar*
1	2.0000, as given	8.0000, as given
2	2.0000/.95 = 2.1053	8.0000/.97 = 8.2474
3	2.1053/.95 = 2.2161	8.2474/.97 = 8.5025
4	2.2161/.95 = 2.3327	8.5025/.97 = 8.7655
5	2.3327/.95 = 2.4555	8.7655/.97 = 9.0366

Sales Forecast

As a result of their analysis of basic demand, inflation, exchange rates, and pricing strategy, the investigation team has prepared Exhibit 10.4 as a summary of sales projections for MEC-France.

EXHIBIT 10.4
Sales Projections for MEC-France

	YEAR				
	1	*2*	*3*	*4*	*5*
Sales in France					
1. Unit sales of freezers	20,000	21,000	22,050	23,153	24,310
2. Franc price per unit	2,000	2,200	2,420	2,662	2,928
3. Total revenue (lines 1 × 2), in thousands of francs	40,000	46,200	53,361	61,633	71,180
Sales in EEC					
4. Unit sales of freezers	20,000	21,600	23,328	25,194	27,210
5. ECU unit price	1,000	1,050	1,103	1,158	1,216
6. Number of French francs per ECU	2.0000	2.1053	2.2161	2.3327	2.4555
7. Unit price in francs (lines 5 × 6)	2,000	2,211	2,444	2,701	2,986
8. Total revenue (lines 4 × 7), in thousands of francs	40,000	47,758	57,014	68,049	81,250
Combined Sales					
9. Number of freezer units (lines 1 + 4)	40,000	42,600	45,378	48,347	51,520
10. Total revenue (lines 3 + 8), in thousands of francs	80,000	93,958	110,375	129,682	152,430

Unit sales in France are expected to grow at a 5% rate from 20,000 units in year 1 to 24,310 units in year 5. French franc prices will increase at a 10% rate from FF2,000 in year 1 to FF2,928 in year 5. As a result, total revenues will rise from FF40 million in year 1 to FF71,180,000 in year 5.

Unit sales in the EEC are expected to grow at 8% per year from 20,000 units in year 1 to 27,210 units in year 5. The price, expressed in ECUs, will increase at a 5% rate. As a result of the 5% annual devaluation of the French franc relative to EEC currencies, the French franc price for sales in the EEC rises at approximately a 10% rate, i.e., 5% from EEC inflation and 5% from French franc devaluation. Note that the French franc domestic price is approximately equal to the French franc export price. This is reasonable considering both prices are increasing by the differential national inflations, and the devaluation of the French franc in this case is based on purchasing power parity between France and the EEC.

Production Costs in MEC-France

Production costs in MEC-France will be influenced by local inflation and the depreciation of the French franc relative to the dollar. Twenty percent of components and raw materials are imported from MEC-USA.

The investigation team expects locally sourced variable costs per unit, such as raw materials, components, and labor, to increase at the 10% French annual inflation rate. Local variable costs are expected to start at FF1,000 per unit during year 1.

Imported raw materials and components from the United States will increase in price in proportion to expected U.S. inflation of 5% annually plus a 3% annual increase due to depreciation of the French franc relative to the dollar. MEC-France could protect itself against its transaction exposure in dollars—e.g., by buying dollars in the forward market—but the expected cost of buying such protection should just about equal the expected transaction loss if the forward markets are functioning as predicted in efficient market theory. Therefore the cost of foreign exchange protection operations is not added to MEC-France's production costs.

The license fee payable to MEC-USA is based on 5% of total revenue payable in French francs. Thus any increase in sales, either domestic or export, will automatically increase the license fee cost in the same proportion. The license fee cost is assumed to be really a contribution for existing technology, and no additional cash expenses are involved in transferring this technology. In other words, the 5% fee is the net cash benefit to MEC-USA.

Selling and administrative costs are mostly a function of French expenses but are partly fixed and partly variable. They are expected to average about FF5 million in year 1 and increase at 5% annually.

Depreciation on plant and equipment is totally fixed in French francs. The plant and equipment costing FF40 million at the start of year 1 will be written off over 5 years to a zero salvage value. This amounts to depreciation of FF8 million per year.

Exhibit 10.5 is a summary of production cost projections for MEC-France.

Income Taxes

MEC-France will pay French income taxes at 50% on net income earned in France. Taxable income includes all sales, domestic and export, since they have no separate marketing subsidiaries in the rest of the EEC. If they did, the tax calculation would be much more complicated, since income tax in those subsidiaries would be deferred until profits were remitted back to France. Tax-deductible expenses include all costs of production including the license fee to MEC-USA. If the license fee were much higher than the 5% of sales level, it is doubtful that the entire fee could be deducted. The

EXHIBIT 10.5
Production Cost Projections for MEC-France

	YEAR				
	1	*2*	*3*	*4*	*5*
1. ***Units Produced*** (line 9 from Exhibit 10.4)	40,000	42,600	45,378	48,347	51,520
Variable Costs					
Raw materials, components, and labor sourced in France:					
2. Unit cost in francs	1,000	1,100	1,210	1,331	1,464
3. Total cost (lines 1 × 2), in thousands of francs	40,000	46,860	54,907	64,350	75,425
Raw materials and components imported from MEC-USA:					
4. Unit cost in dollars	50.00	52.50	55.12	57.88	60.78
5. Total cost (lines 1 × 4), in thousands of dollars	2,000	2,237	2,501	2,798	3,131
6. Exchange rate, francs per dollar	8.0000	8.2474	8.5025	8.7655	9.0366
7. Total cost (lines 5 × 6), in thousands of francs	16,000	18,449	21,265	24,526	28,294
8. Total variable costs (lines 3 + 7), in thousands of francs	56,000	65,309	76,172	88,876	103,719
License Fees, in Thousands of Francs					
9. Total revenue (line 10 from Exhibit 10.4)	80,000	93,958	110,375	129,682	152,430
10. Fees at 5% of revenue (line 9 × .05)	4,000	4,698	5,519	6,484	7,621
11. ***Selling and Administrative, in Thousands of Francs***	5,000	5,250	5,512	5,788	6,078
12. ***Depreciation, in Thousands of Francs***	8,000	8,000	8,000	8,000	8,000
13. ***Total Production Costs, in Thousands of Francs*** (lines 8 + 10 + 11 + 12)	73,000	83,257	95,203	109,148	125,418

excess would be considered a constructive dividend and therefore not deductible. Although interest paid to the banks would be deductible, the cost of financing and tax shield from interest are normally included in the weighted average aftertax cost of capital used to discount cash flows rather than included in cash flows. Moreover, in this case cash flows are being discounted by an all-equity required rate of return, with the tax advantage of debt purposely ignored for ease of comparison to other similar French projects.

Exhibit 10.6 presents a summary of expected taxable income, expenses, and corporate income taxes for capital budgeting purposes from the view-

EXHIBIT 10.6
Pro Forma Income Statement for MEC-France (in thousands of French francs)

	YEAR				
	1	*2*	*3*	*4*	*5*
All-Equity Basis Calculations					
1. Total revenue (line 10 from Exhibit 10.4)	80,000	93,958	110,375	129,682	152,430
2. Total production costs (line 13 from Exhibit 10.5)	73,000	83,257	95,203	109,148	125,418
3. Operating income, all-equity basis (lines 1 − 2)	7,000	10,701	15,172	20,534	27,012
4. French corporate income tax @ 50% (line 3 × .5)	3,500	5,350	7,586	10,267	13,506
5. Net income on all-equity basis (lines 3 − 4)	3,500	5,350	7,586	10,267	13,506
Income Tax Calculations—Accounting Basis					
6. Operating income (line 3)	7,000	10,701	15,172	20,534	27,012
7. Interest expense on bank loan (line 9 from Exhibit 10.3 × .10)	500	500	500	500	500
8. Interest expense on French Development Bank loan	900	720	540	360	180
9. Taxable income	5,600	9,481	14,132	19,674	26,332
10. Income tax @ 50%	2,800	4,740	7,066	9,837	13,166
11. Net accounting income	2,800	4,740	7,066	9,837	13,166

point of MEC-France. Withholding taxes on both dividends and license fees to MEC-USA are not included as charges to MEC-France since they arise from the manner in which MEC-USA chooses to remit funds from MEC-France. The evaluation of MEC-France's performance relative to its potential in France should not be reduced by taxes that relate to the "foreign" residence of its stockholders. Its French competitors would presumably have French stockholders who would not be subject to those withholding taxes.

The bottom half of Exhibit 10.6 shows net income on an accounting basis, calculated after payment of the 50% French corporate income tax on income after interest expense. Although this is not the format commonly used in domestic capital budgeting, the information is essential because only *actual* French income taxes, rather than the hypothetical all-equity taxes shown in line 4 in the top half of the exhibit, may be used by the parent as a credit against U.S. taxes levied on dividends from the affiliate.

Working Capital in MEC-France

Working capital needs in MEC-France (cash, accounts receivable, and inventory) are projected to average 20% of total revenue, but accounts payable to suppliers will reduce the net working capital need to 10% of sales. Since accounts payable is "free" debt, it is not normally included in the cost of capital or debt capacity calculation. Therefore we are not relaxing the concept of giving this project extra debt capacity. Depreciation and retained earnings will provide the additional funds needed for additions to working capital. Seasonal needs will be supplied under the line of credit with local French banks. Exhibit 10.7 shows the anticipated additions to net working capital investment of MEC-France.

Terminal Value

Estimation of terminal value is a subjective task at best. The usual procedure requires an estimate of MEC-France's market value at the end of year 5 from three different perspectives:

1. What will be its value if retained as a going concern by MEC-USA?
2. What will be its value if purchased by outside investors?
3. What will be its value if liquidated?

Whichever approach yields the highest value will normally be used as terminal value on the assumption that a profit-maximizing firm will opt for that choice when the time arrives. For simplicity, we assume that MEC-France will be sold to French investors at the end of five years (approach 2).

To estimate market value at the end of year 5, the investigation team needs to assume a future time horizon beyond year 5. Then, in accordance

EXHIBIT 10.7
Net Working Capital Investment in MEC-France (in thousands of French francs)

	YEAR					
	0	*1*	*2*	*3*	*4*	*5*
1. Total revenue (line 10 from Exhibit 10.4)	—	80,000	93,958	110,375	129,682	152,430
2. Net working capital investment (line 1 × .10)	—	8,000	9,396	11,037	12,968	15,243
3. Annual addition to net working capital (given in year 0; subsequent year's change from prior year)	10,000	(2,000)	1,396	1,641	1,931	2,275
4. Addition financed by MEC-USA (inventory)	5,000	—	—	—	—	—
5. Addition financed by MEC-France	5,000	(2,000)	1,396	1,641	1,931	2,275

with traditional valuation theory, they can calculate the present value of all future expected net cash inflows, including a liquidating cash inflow, using a risk-adjusted discount rate. Normally they would discount future dividends to stockholders, but in the case of a 100%-owned foreign affiliate "dividends" are only one of several alternative ways to transfer funds internally within the multinational firm. Therefore in this case terminal value should be based on expected cash inflows to MEC-France.

Terminal value policy of MEC-France If MEC-France is expected to continue indefinitely, its future cash inflows would be an annuity growing at some annual percentage. Most capital budgeting analysts are uncomfortable with indefinite time horizons and the related need to estimate cash flows and inflation far into the future. Therefore for pragmatic reasons MEC-USA uses a consistent policy for all projects of assuming that terminal value is equal to the present value at the end of year 5 of a 10-year annuity discounted at the local required rate of return. The annuity amount is equal to the net cash inflow in year 5. In other words, they assume that the net cash inflows in year 5 will continue at the same level for 10 more years and will be reinvested at the local rate of return. The rationale for using the local required rate of return is that if the project is sold to French investors, the price will probably be based on their opportunity costs.

In the case of MEC-France, net cash inflows in year 5 are estimated to be FF19,231,000 (see note b to Exhibit 10.8). The cost of capital for MEC-France is 15% after tax. Therefore the terminal value expressed in French francs is equal to FF19,231,000 × 5.019 (10-year annuity at 15%) or FF96,520,000. Partially offsetting the terminal value are some contingent tax liabilities equal to about 30% or FF28,956,000 (FF96,520,000 × .3) payable to France and the United States. If MEC-France were sold or liquidated, these taxes would be levied on capital gains, recaptured depreciation, and capital transfer to the United States. The calculation is complex and beyond the scope of this book. Since most of these taxes would also be paid by French investors in a similar project, the taxes should be included as a charge against MEC-France when evaluating performance against potential.

Break-even terminal value Since calculation of terminal value is arbitrary, an alternative is to utilize a technique called "break-even terminal value." This technique involves answering the question "What must the terminal value be in order to break even on the investment?" For example, if the cumulative net present value of MEC-France's cash flows discounted at 15% turns positive before the end of year 5, the answer to the question is zero terminal value. The project is already justified prior to year 5. However, if the cumulative net present value is still negative at the end of year 5, a break-even terminal value can be calculated that would increase cumulative net present value to zero at the end of year 5. With a zero net present value the project would be just barely acceptable. The following formula can be used to calculate the break-even terminal value:

$$\text{Break-even terminal value, year}_n = \frac{\text{cumulative net present value, year}_n \text{ (ignore the sign)}}{\text{present value factor, year}_n}$$

At the end of year 5 the cumulative net present value of MEC-France, excluding terminal value and working capital recapture, is a negative FF1,140,193. This is calculated as follows:

1. Cumulative net present value year 4 (line 13 of Exhibit 10.8)	(FF10,698,000)
2. Operating cash flows in year 5	FF19,231,000
3. Present value factor for year 5	.497
4. Present value of cash flows in year 5 (lines 2 × 3)	FF9,557,807
5. Cumulative net present value year 5 (lines 1 + 4)	(FF1,140,193)

In order to find the break-even terminal value, substitute into the formula:

$$\begin{array}{l}\text{Break-even terminal value} \\ \text{at the end of year 5}\end{array} = \frac{\text{FF1,140,193}}{.497} = \text{FF2,294,151}$$

In other words, if MEC-France's market value is FF2,294,151 at the end of year 5, its net present value discounted at 15% would equal zero. The project would be just barely acceptable from the MEC-France viewpoint.

The main advantage of using break-even terminal value is that management may feel more comfortable about predicting whether market value will exceed a certain figure than predicting an exact figure for market value. On the other hand, projects compete with one another, especially under conditions of capital rationing. In such circumstances it is important to predict the full net present value and internal rate of return for each project rather than the conditions under which they would all have zero net present value.

RATE OF RETURN—MEC-FRANCE VIEWPOINT

The project investigation team now has enough information to calculate the rate of return from MEC-France's viewpoint, as shown in Exhibit 10.8. Line 13 shows the project to have a very favorable net present value of FF40,015,000 using the 15% discount rate, which represents the all-equity required rate of return for French investors for projects of similar business risk. Remember that this version of the discount rate is used to facilitate an evaluation of the expected performance of MEC-France compared to the project's potential if undertaken by local French investors. It also automatically takes French inflation into account, since the local required rate of return on all-equity investments should be higher than the rate of inflation by a premium for the perceived business risk in the project. The internal rate of return to MEC-France is 34.9% (Exhibit 10.8, line 14), considerably above the 15% required rate of return.

RATE OF RETURN—MEC-USA VIEWPOINT

The parent rate of return from the viewpoint of MEC-USA depends on four additional factors: (1) the availability for transfer of net cash flows from MEC-France; (2) U.S. and French taxes on remitted funds; (3) contribution to MEC-USA's profit and overhead from exports to the EEC; (4) the change in value of the French franc relative to the dollar.

Availability for Transfer of Net Cash Inflows from MEC-France

The most important test of the desirability of MEC-France is its rate of return from the viewpoint of MEC-USA. Assume for the moment that there is no perceived danger of funds being blocked in MEC-France, and

EXHIBIT 10.8
Rate of Return from Viewpoint of MEC-France (in thousands of French francs)

	YEAR					
	0	*1*	*2*	*3*	*4*	*5*
Cash Inflows						
1. Net income (line 5 from Exhibit 10.6)	—	3,500	5,350	7,586	10,267	13,506
2. Depreciation (line 12 from Exhibit 10.5)	—	8,000	8,000	8,000	8,000	8,000
3. Recapture of net working capital in terminal year (line 2 from Exhibit 10.7)	—	—	—	—	—	15,243T[a]
4. Terminal value[b]	—	—	—	—	—	96,520T[a]
5. Total inflows	—	11,500	13,350	15,586	18,267	133,269
Cash Outflows						
6. Original investment in plant and equipment (lines 5 + 6 from Exhibit 10.3)	40,000	—	—	—	—	—
7. Additions to net working capital (line 3 from Exhibit 10.7)	10,000	(2,000)	1,396	1,641	1,931	2,275
8. Capital gains tax on terminal value (line 4 × .3)	—	—	—	—	—	28,956T[a]
9. Total outflows	50,000	(2,000)	1,396	1,641	1,931	31,231
10. ***Net Inflows***	(50,000)	13,500	11,954	13,945	16,336	102,038
11. PV factor @ 15%	1.000	.870	.756	.658	.572	.497
12. Net present value (lines 10 × 11)	(50,000)	11,745	9,037	9,176	9,344	50,713
13. Cumulative net present value	(50,000)	(38,255)	(29,218)	(20,042)	(10,698)	40,015
14. Internal rate of return: 34.9%						

[a]Cash flow in terminal year only.

[b]Operating cash flow in the fifth year is calculated as follows:

Net income (line 1)	FF13,506,000
Depreciation (line 2)	8,000,000
Total inflows	FF21,506,000
Less additions to working capital (line 7)	−2,275,000
Operating cash flow	FF19,231,000

Terminal value in the fifth year is operating cash flow of FF19,231,000 times 5.019 for the present value of a ten-year annuity at 15%: FF19,231,000 × 5.019 = FF96,520,000.

that net cash inflows in MEC-France (Exhibit 10.8, line 10) can be positioned freely by MEC-USA. For example, they can be remitted to the parent as dividends, loaned to another affiliate, reinvested in France, or invested from France in projects in other countries.

The key concept in capital budgeting for measuring rate of return from the parent's viewpoint is that if the funds *are available* for transfer out of the host country, they should count in full as cash inflows to the parent. The choice of how to position the funds, however, may cause a leak into tax payments to the host country and parent country.

U.S. and French Taxes on the Transfer of Income from MEC-France

To estimate the timing of cash leaks into the payment of contingent national taxes, the project investigation team must assume a particular fund-positioning policy by MEC-USA. For purposes of analysis they assume that 80% of annual net accounting income in MEC-France will be paid as dividends to MEC-USA. The rest of net cash inflows will be reinvested at a 15% internal rate of return in France in other manufacturing plants with similar business risk characteristics.

Exhibit 10.9 shows how to estimate U.S. and French taxes on the transfer of income from MEC-France. Dividends are subject to two taxes. The French will collect a 5% withholding tax on dividends paid to nonresidents of France; i.e., MEC-USA. This is shown in Exhibit 10.9, line 3. The United States will collect a tax if the French net income behind the dividend has been subject to lower French income and withholding taxes than it would be if subject to U.S. income taxes. Chapter 18 (Tax Planning) explains in detail how the United States taxes foreign-source income, but for the moment the calculation shown in Exhibit 10.9 should suffice.

The calculation of the U.S. tax on dividends from MEC-France involves two steps:

1. MEC-USA will receive a "foreign tax credit" for any income tax or withholding tax already paid to France. The withholding tax is not really "withheld" since it is never returned to the payer. Since only 80% of the accounting net income is paid as dividends, MEC-USA would receive a tax credit for only 80% of the income taxes "deemed paid" on that income to France. The mechanical procedure for calculating this deemed-paid tax is shown in Exhibit 10.9, line 6. The total foreign tax credit is shown in Exhibit 10.9, line 7. It is the sum of the deemed-paid tax for French income taxes plus the 5% French withholding tax on dividends.
2. MEC-USA will be subject to 46% U.S. income taxes on the income before tax in MEC-France, which made possible the dividends. Exhibit

EXHIBIT 10.9
U.S. and French Taxes on the Transfer of Income from MEC-France

	YEAR				
	1	*2*	*3*	*4*	*5*
Dividends at 80% of Net Accounting Income, in Thousands of French Francs					
1. Net accounting income of MEC-France (line 11 from Exhibit 10.6)	2,800	4,740	7,066	9,837	13,166
2. Dividend paid to MEC-USA (line 1 × .80)	2,240	3,792	5,653	7,870	10,533
3. Less French withholding tax (line 2 × .05)	−112	−190	−283	−393	−527
4. Net dividend to MEC-USA (lines 2 − 3)	2,128	3,602	5,370	7,477	10,006
Foreign Tax Credit, in Thousands of French Francs					
5. French withholding tax (line 3)	112	190	283	393	527
6. Deemed-paid credit in United States for income taxes paid by MEC-France [dividend as percentage of net accounting income, times amount of French income taxes (lines 2 ÷ 1 × line 10 from Exhibit 10.6)]	2,240	3,792	5,653	7,870	10,533
7. Total foreign tax credit (lines 5 + 6)	2,352	3,982	5,936	8,263	11,060
Included in U.S. Income Tax for Tax Purposes, in Thousands of French Francs					
8. Dividend to MEC-USA (line 2)	2,240	3,792	5,653	7,870	10,533
9. Plus foreign deemed-paid tax (line 6)	2,240	3,792	5,653	7,870	10,533
10. Gross dividend included (lines 8 + 9)	4,480	7,584	11,306	15,740	21,066
11. U.S. income tax due (line 10 × .46)	2,061	3,489	5,201	7,240	9,690
12. Less foreign tax credit (line 7)	−2,352	−3,982	−5,936	−8,263	−11,060

EXHIBIT 10.9 (Cont.)

	YEAR				
	1	*2*	*3*	*4*	*5*
13. U.S. income tax due (lines 11 − 12), in thousands of French francs	(291)	(493)	(735)	(1,023)	(1,370)
License Fees, in Thousands of French Francs					
14. License fees paid to MEC-USA (line 10 from Exhibit 10.5)	4,000	4,698	5,519	6,484	7,621
15. U.S. income tax due (line 14 × .46)	1,840	2,161	2,539	2,983	3,506
16. Less French withholding taxes paid on license fees (line 14 × .05)	−200	−235	−276	−324	−381
17. Net U.S. income tax due on license fees (lines 15 − 16)	1,640	1,926	2,263	2,659	3,125
Total U.S. Income Tax on Income from MEC-France, in Thousands of French Francs					
18. Excess tax credit on dividends (line 13)	(291)	(493)	(735)	(1,023)	(1,370)
19. Tax on license fees (line 17)	1,640	1,926	2,263	2,659	3,125
20. Total tax due (lines 18 + 19)	1,349	1,433	1,528	1,636	1,755
Conversion of French Franc Amounts to U.S. Dollars					
21. Exchange rate, francs per U.S. dollar (line 6 from Exhibit 10.5)	8.0000	8.2474	8.5025	8.7655	9.0366
22. Total U.S. tax due, in thousands of dollars (lines 20 ÷ 21)	$169	$174	$180	$187	$194

10.9, lines 8, 9, and 10, show how to find the income in MEC-France that is subject to U.S. tax at the time of dividends. The procedure used is called "grossing up." The dividend received in the United States is added to the French deemed-paid tax to determine the income subject to U.S. income tax. Then the U.S. tax is levied on that income (Exhibit 10.9, line 11) but is reduced by the amount of the foreign tax credit

(Exhibit 10.9, line 12). In this case the foreign tax credit on taxes paid to France is higher than the U.S. income tax liability. This results in a tax credit surplus (Exhibit 10.9, line 13), which can be used to offset U.S. taxes due on other foreign source income.

In addition to taxes on dividends, MEC-USA would need to pay taxes on the license fees paid to them by MEC-France. These have already been deducted as an expense in MEC-France (Exhibit 10.5, line 10) but would be subject to a 5% French withholding tax when transferred to MEC-USA, as shown in Exhibit 10.9, line 16. In general, whether or not withholding taxes are levied on transfers, such as license fees, royalties, and contribution to corporate overhead, varies from country to country as modified by bilateral tax treaties. License fees would also be subject to the full 46% corporate income tax in MEC-USA minus a tax credit for the withholding taxes paid to France. The net U.S. tax on license fees is shown in Exhibit 10.9, line 17.

The total tax bill to the U.S. on dividends and license fees is calculated in Exhibit 10.9, lines 18, 19, and 20. To make the calculations easier to follow, all U.S. tax calculations have been denominated in French francs up to this point, but naturally U.S. taxes will be paid in U.S. dollars. The relevant exchange rate for conversion is the current rate at the time of transfer. The dollar tax liabilities are shown in Exhibit 10.9, line 22.

Contribution to MEC-USA's Profit and Overhead from Exports to the EEC

In addition to net inflows available from MEC-France after deducting contingent taxes, MEC-USA is receiving an inflow of cash from export sales of raw materials and components to MEC-France. On the other hand, the project investigation team estimates that the MEC-France project will actually replace some exports of freezers from MEC-USA, which would have been realized without this project.

Exhibit 10.10 presents the net contribution after U.S. taxes to MEC-USA's profit and overhead from export sales to the EEC. Thirty percent of the value of raw material and component sales to MEC-France is a beforetax contribution to profit and overhead (sales less variable costs) in MEC-USA, as shown in Exhibit 10.10, lines 1 and 2. Since spare manufacturing capacity will exist for the foreseeable future in MEC-USA, this contribution should count as a marginal cash benefit of the French project. By the same reasoning, lost freezer export sales, which are estimated to be $2 million annually with a 30% contribution margin, should count as a marginal cash cost of the French project. This is shown in Exhibit 10.10, line 3. This approach assumes that these export sales really would have been made if the MEC-France project were not undertaken. If they would have been lost anyway—for example, due to the increased EEC competition that instigated the MEC-France investigation—then they are not relevant to the MEC-France decision.

EXHIBIT 10.10
Contribution to MEC-USA's Profit and Overhead from Exports to the EEC, after U.S. Tax (in thousands of dollars)

	YEAR					
	0	*1*	*2*	*3*	*4*	*5*
1. Sale of initial inventory to MEC-France (line 4 in dollars from Exhibit 10.2 × .3)	187	—	—	—	—	—
2. Exports of raw materials and components to MEC-France (line 5 from Exhibit 10.5 × .3)	—	600	671	750	839	939
3. Less contribution no longer earned on displaced export sales to EEC ($2 million × .3)	—	−600	−600	−600	−600	−600
4. Gross contribution (lines 1 + 2 + 3)	187	0	71	150	239	339
5. Less U.S. corporate income tax (line 4 × .46)	−86	0	−33	−69	−110	−156
6. Net contribution (lines 4 − 5)	101	0	38	81	129	183

The whole value of contribution would be subject to the U.S. corporate income tax at 46% in order to determine the net value of export sales to MEC-USA (Exhibit 10.10, lines 5 and 6). Since fixed costs will not change because of these exports, their marginal contribution will increase taxable income by an equal amount.

Net Present Value and Internal Rate of Return under "Most Likely" Assumptions

Given the most likely assumptions made by the project investigation team, Exhibit 10.11 presents the expected rate of return from the viewpoint of MEC-USA. Once again, MEC-France will have a very favorable $6,101,000 net present value, using the 14% weighted average cost of capital that MEC-USA uses for projects of similar business and financial risk. The expected internal rate of return is 38.4%, or slightly higher than the 34% internal rate of return from the viewpoint of MEC-France.

A closer inspection of the results shows that the value of operating net inflows into MEC-France (Exhibit 10.11, line 1) and license fee payments (Exhibit 10.11, line 2) is reduced somewhat from the parent's viewpoint because of the depreciation of the French franc relative to the dollar, as

EXHIBIT 10.11
Rate of Return from Viewpoint of MEC-USA

	YEAR					
	0	*1*	*2*	*3*	*4*	*5*
Cash Inflows, in Thousands of French Francs						
1. Net inflows to MEC-France (line 10 from Exhibit 10.8)	(50,000)	13,500	11,954	13,945	16,336	102,038
2. License fees before U.S. taxes (line 10 from Exhibit 10.5)	—	4,000	4,698	5,519	6,484	7,621
3. Total inflows (lines 1 + 2)	(50,000)	17,500	16,652	19,464	22,820	109,659
Cash Outflows, in Thousands of French Francs						
4. French withholding taxes (lines 3 + 16 from Exhibit 10.9)	—	312	425	559	717	908
5. Total outflows	—	312	425	559	717	908
6. ***Net Inflows, in Thousands of French Francs*** (lines 3 − 5)	(50,000)	17,188	16,227	18,905	22,103	108,751
7. ***Number of French Francs per Dollar*** (line 6 from Exhibit 10.5)	8.0000	8.0000	8.2474	8.5025	8.7655	9.0366
Cash Inflows, in Thousands of Dollars						
8. Net inflows in MEC-France (lines 6 ÷ 7)	(6,250)	2,148	1,968	2,223	2,522	12,035
9. Net contribution from exports to the EEC (line 6 from Exhibit 10.10)	101	0	38	81	129	183
10. Subsidized interest on FDB loan	0	71	57	43	28	14
11. Total inflows	(6,149)	2,219	2,063	2,347	2,679	12,232

EXHIBIT 10.11 (Cont.)

	YEAR					
	0	*1*	*2*	*3*	*4*	*5*
Cash Outflows, in Thousands of Dollars						
12. U.S. capital gains tax on used equipment sale (line 3 in dollars from Exhibit 10.2 × .3)	187	—	—	—	—	—
13. U.S. corporate income tax on income remitted from MEC-France (line 22 from Exhibit 10.9)	—	169	174	180	187	194
14. Total outflows	187	169	174	180	187	194
15. ***Net Inflows, in Thousands of Dollars*** (lines 11 − 14)	(6,336)	2,050	1,889	2,167	2,492	12,038
Net Present Value, in Thousands of Dollars						
16. Present value factor at 14%	1.000	.877	.769	.675	.592	.519
17. Present value (lines 15 × 16)	(6,366)	1,798	1,453	1,463	1,475	6,248
18. Cumulative net present value	(6,336)	(4,538)	(3,085)	(1,622)	(147)	6,101
19. Internal rate of return ≈ 38.4%						

well as French and U.S. withholding and income taxes on the remittances. This is partially offset by the net dollar contribution from exports of raw materials and components from MEC-USA and the modest interest subsidy.

SENSITIVITY ANALYSIS

So far the project investigation team is using a set of "most likely" assumptions to forecast rates of return. It is now time to subject the most likely outcome to sensitivity analyses. The same probabilistic techniques are available to test the sensitivity of results to political and foreign exchange risks as are used to test sensitivity to business and financial risks. Popular techniques include the use of decision tree analysis, reducing cash flows to certainty equivalents, adjusting the discount rate to reflect the degree of riskiness of the project, and measuring the statistical dispersion of expected returns. Many decision makers feel more uncomfortable about the necessity to guess probabilities for unfamiliar political and foreign exchange events than they do about guessing their own more familiar business or financial risks. Therefore it is more common to test sensitivity to political and foreign exchange risk by simulating what would happen to net present value and earnings under a variety of "what if" scenarios.

To illustrate how simulation is used, we will show what might happen to the rate of return if certain political risks materialize. The project investigation team is assuming that all net cash inflows to MEC-France are immediately available for transfer out of France if desired by MEC-USA. What if some or all of the net cash inflows are blocked from transfer? The impact on project rate of return from the viewpoint of MEC-USA will depend on when the blockage occurs, the reinvestment opportunities for the blocked funds in France, and when the blocked funds can eventually be transferred out of France.

Dividends Partially Blocked

A typical case of partially blocked funds would be a French policy that limits the amount of dividends that can be paid. For example, the French might limit dividends to 80% of net income. Assume that license fees can be paid but funds from depreciation and 20% of net income must be reinvested in France. Opportunities for reinvestment of excess cash yield 5% after French income taxes. Assume that the blocked funds can be repatriated at the end of year 5 when the project is sold to French investors.

In the case of blocked funds it is critical to analyze MEC-France's cash budget to identify the amount of funds blocked, their reinvestment return, and ways other than dividends in which funds can be transferred under French law. Exhibit 10.12 presents a cash budget under these assumptions of partially blocked funds.

An examination of cash outflows in Exhibit 10.12 shows that funds are actually being transferred out of MEC-France to service the bank debt and to pay the allowable dividend (80% of net income) and associated French withholding taxes. In addition, the license fees are being paid to MEC-USA. Furthermore, some funds would be reinvested regardless of controls to permit additions to required working capital including the cash balance needed for operating purposes. The latter is assumed to be growing at 10% annually. Thus the practical effect of this partial blockage of funds transfer causes only a modest excess cash balance (Exhibit 10.12, line 16), which is reinvested at a 5% aftertax yield.

EXHIBIT 10.12
Cash Budget in MEC-France (FF thousands)—Dividends Partially Blocked

	YEAR				
	0–1	*2*	*3*	*4*	*5*
Cash Inflows					
1. Net income (Exhibit 10.8, line 1)	3,500	5,350	7,586	10,267	13,506
2. Depreciation (Exhibit 10.8, line 2)	8,000	8,000	8,000	8,000	8,000
3. Total inflows	11,500	13,350	15,586	18,267	21,506
Cash Outflows					
4. Loan principal repayment to French Development Bank	3,000	3,000	3,000	3,000	3,000
5. Loan principal repayment to local French banks	2,000	3,000			
6. Interest to French banks after tax	900	720	540	360	180
7. Dividends to MEC-USA at 80% of net income (Exhibit 10.9, line 2)	2,240	3,792	5,653	7,870	10,533
8. Withholding tax on dividends at 5% (Exhibit 10.9, line 5)	112	190	283	393	527
9. Withholding tax on license fees at 5% (Exhibit 10.9, line 16)	200	235	276	324	381
10. Additions to working capital (Exhibit 10.7, line 5)	3,000	1,396	1,641	1,931	2,275
11. Total outflows	11,452	12,333	11,393	13,878	16,896
12. ***Net Change in Cash from Operations*** (lines 3 − 11)	48	1,017	4,193	4,389	4,610
13. Starting cash balance (lines 14 + 17 for previous year)	5,000	5,050	6,095	10,500	15,301
14. Ending cash balance (lines 12 + 13)	5,048	6,067	10,288	14,889	19,911
15. Desired cash balance (5.0×1.1^n) ($n = 1 - 4$)	5,000	5,500	6,050	6,655	7,320
16. Excess cash balance (lines 14 − 15)	48	567	4,238	8,234	12,591
17. Return after tax on excess cash balance at 5% (line 16 × .05)	2	28	212	412	630

The main reason that the partial blockage of funds has little impact on project rate of return from MEC-USA's viewpoint is that most of the blocked funds are used to repay bank debt. In fact, if the bank debt had been somewhat larger, repayment would have used all excess cash. This result illustrates the importance of finance structure when funds may be blocked. Repayment of bank debt is equivalent to a return of funds to MEC-USA because the reduced debt in France theoretically creates an equivalent amount of debt capacity that MEC-USA can borrow elsewhere. This assumes that MEC-USA has a target debt ratio for its consolidated balance sheet, and it is only a matter of cost and availability of funds that determines where debt will be raised.

Exhibit 10.13 shows the net effect of the partially blocked funds on project rate of return from MEC-USA's viewpoint. The only difference is that the excess cash balances are reinvested at 5% after tax, whereas previously they were assumed to be reinvested at 15%, the project's French discount rate. Thus the lost opportunity cost is 10% after tax. The excess cash is returned as part of working capital at the end of year 5 and can be assumed for simplicity's sake to be already included in the previous figure. It is obvious from Exhibit 10.13, line 5, that the impact of partially blocked funds in this case is negligible.

EXHIBIT 10.13
Rate of Return from the Viewpoint of MEC-USA when Dividends Are Partially Blocked

	YEAR					
	0	*1*	*2*	*3*	*4*	*5*
1. Net inflows ($ thousands) (Exhibit 10.11, line 15)	(6,336)	2,050	1,889	2,167	2,492	12,036
2. Excess cash balance in France (FF thousands) (Exhibit 10.12, line 16)	—	48	567	4,238	8,234	12,591
3. Net opportunity cost of holding excess cash (FF thousands) (line 2 × .10)[a]	—	5	57	424	823	1,259
4. Number of FF/$	8.0000	8.0000	8.2474	8.5025	8.7655	9.0366
5. Net opportunity cost of holding excess cash ($ thousands)	—	1	7	50	94	139

[a]The opportunity cost is the aftertax rate at which the funds were assumed to be reinvested (the 15% discount rate), minus the actual aftertax reinvestment rate (5%).

Dividends and License Fees Fully Blocked

Assume that France experiences a foreign exchange crisis and blocks all remittances of dividends and license fees for five years. They are recaptured on sale of MEC-France to French investors at the end of year 5 when controls are lifted. In this case excess cash accumulates rapidly and the opportunity cost is significant. Exhibit 10.14 shows the revised cash budget for MEC-France. Exhibit 10.15 shows the impact on project rate of return from the viewpoint of MEC-USA.

Although the French project still shows a positive net present value of $4,434,000 (Exhibit 10.15, line 17), almost all the return comes on sale at the end of five years. The net present value depends heavily on the assumption that the accumulated $7,004,000 of blocked funds (Exhibit 10.15, line 7) will be released at the end of year 5. The relatively low reinvestment rate on blocked funds causes the internal rate of return to MEC-USA to fall to 28.8%, compared to 38.4% when no funds are blocked.

If there is a clear threat that funds may be blocked, MEC-USA must use other options for moving funds out of MEC-France. The problem is that each of these options has costs in terms of built-in inefficiencies, lost managerial motivation, and the risk of antagonizing the French government. These less tangible costs need to be quantified for purposes of capital budgeting analysis, a task that is very difficult to accomplish. The easiest policy variables to measure are changes in the proportion of debt financing and the unbundling of fund remittances. Changes in the transfer price, for example, on sales of components from MEC-USA to MEC-France, are hard to quantify because of the managerial motivation and government interface problems.

Expropriation

The ultimate in political risk is expropriation of MEC-France by the French government. The effect of expropriation on project rate of return from the viewpoint of MEC-USA will depend on the following four factors:

1. How much compensation will the French government pay and how long after expropriation will this occur?
2. How much debt is still outstanding to French lenders?
3. What are the tax consequences of the expropriation?
4. What are the future cash flows foregone?

As we explained in Chapter 9, many expropriations eventually result in some form of compensation to the former owners. This compensation can come from a negotiated settlement with the host government or from

EXHIBIT 10.14
Cash Budget in MEC-France (FF thousands)—Dividends and License Fees Blocked

	YEAR				
	0–1	*2*	*3*	*4*	*5*
Cash Inflows					
1. Net income (Exhibit 10.12, line 1)	3,500	5,350	7,586	10,267	13,506
2. License fees after tax (Exhibit 10.5, line 10 × .5)	2,000	2,348	2,760	3,242	3,810
3. Depreciation	8,000	8,000	8,000	8,000	8,000
4. Total inflows	13,500	15,698	18,346	21,509	25,316
Cash Outflows					
5. Principal and interest (Exhibit 10.12, lines 4 + 5 + 6)	5,900	6,720	3,540	3,360	3,180
6. Additions to working capital (Exhibit 10.12, line 10)	3,000	1,396	1,641	1,931	2,275
7. Total outflows	8,900	8,116	5,181	5,291	5,455
8. ***Net Change in Cash from Operations*** (lines 4 − 7)	4,600	7,582	13,165	16,218	19,861
9. Starting cash balance (lines 10 + 13 for previous year)	5,000	9,830	18,008	32,429	50,747
10. Ending cash balance (lines 8 + 9)	9,600	17,412	31,173	48,647	70,608
11. Desired cash balance (Exhibit 10.12, line 15)	5,000	5,500	6,050	6,655	7,320
12. Excess cash balance (lines 10 − 11)	4,600	11,912	25,123	41,992	63,288
13. Return after tax on excess cash balance at 5% (line 12 × .05)	230	596	1,256	2,100	3,164

payment of political risk insurance by the parent government. In this particular case political risk insurance is not available from the U.S. government for investments in developed countries such as France. Negotiating a settlement takes time, and the eventual compensation is sometimes paid in installments over a further period of time. Thus the present value of the compensation is often much lower than its nominal value. Furthermore, most settlements are based on book value of the firm at the time of expropriation rather than the firm's market value.

Repayment of local debt would usually receive first claim on any compensation funds paid. Thus the debt remaining to the French Development

EXHIBIT 10.15
Rate of Return from the Viewpoint of MEC-USA when Dividends and License Fees Are Blocked

	YEAR					
	0	*1*	*2*	*3*	*4*	*5*
Cash Inflows						
1. Principal and interest payments to French banks (FF thousands) (Exhibit 10.12, lines 4 + 5 + 6)		5,900	6,720	3,540	3,360	3,180
2. Number of FF/$		8.0000	8.2474	8.5025	8.7655	9.0366
3. Principal and interest payments ($ thousands) (lines 1 ÷ 2)		737	815	416	383	352
4. Net contribution from exports to the EEC ($ thousands) (Exhibit 10.11, line 9)	101	0	38	81	129	183
5. Interest subsidy (Exhibit 10.11, line 10)		71	57	43	28	14
6. Recapture of required working capital Exhibit 10.8, line 3 ÷ 9.0366)						1,687
7. Recapture of excess cash (Exhibit 10.14, line 12 ÷ 9.0366)						7,004
8. Terminal value (Exhibit 10.8, line 4 ÷ 9.0366)						10,681
9. Total inflows (lines 3 + 4 + 5 + 6 + 7 + 8	101	808	910	540	540	19,921
Cash Outflows ($ thousands)						
10. Original investment in plant, equipment, and working capital Exhibit 10.2, line 6)	6,250					

EXHIBIT 10.15 (Cont.)

	YEAR					
	0	*1*	*2*	*3*	*4*	*5*
11. U.S. capital gains tax on used equipment (Exhibit 10.11, line 12)	187					
12. Capital gains tax on terminal value (Exhibit 10.8, line 8 ÷ 9.0366)						3,204
13. Total outflows (lines 10 + 11 + 12)	6,437					3,204
14. ***Net Inflows*** (lines 9 − 13)	(6,336)	808	910	540	540	16,717
Net Present Value						
15. Present value factor at 14%	1.0	.877	.769	.675	.592	.519
16. Present value (lines 14 × 15)	(6,336)	709	700	365	320	8,676
17. Cumulative net present value	(6,336)	(5,627)	(4,927)	(4,562)	(4,242)	4,434
18. Internal rate of return ≈ 28.8%						

Bank would be paid before MEC-USA could receive the balance of settlement funds. If no compensation agreement can be negotiated, it might be possible for MEC-USA to default on French debt. In the more general case, however, local debt might be supplied by a subsidiary of a U.S. bank in the host country. The parent bank would probably expect to be repaid by the parent firm from funds outside the expropriating country if necessary.

The tax consequences of expropriation would depend on the timing and amount of capital loss recognized by the U.S. government. This loss would usually be based on the uncompensated book value of the French investment. The problem is that there is often some doubt as to when a write-off is appropriate for tax purposes, particularly if negotiations for a settlement drag on. In some ways a nice clear expropriation without hope of compensation, such as occurred in Cuba in the early 1960s, is preferred to a slow "bleeding to death" in protracted negotiations. The former leads to an earlier use of the tax shield and a one-shot write-off against earnings, whereas the latter tends to depress earnings for years, as legal and other costs continue and no tax shelter is achieved.

The value of future cash inflows foregone is really the key to the effect of expropriation on project rate of return in capital budgeting. Refer back to the discussion of break-even terminal value earlier in this chapter; the same technique can be applied to political risk analysis. According to Exhibit 10.11, MEC-France's cumulative net present value turns positive during the fifth year. If expropriation comes after the fourth year, the project would have only a slightly negative cumulative net present value. If it comes during the third year or earlier, the project would have a break-even net present value of zero only if its terminal value is high enough to compensate for cash inflows foregone. In this case terminal value is composed of net compensation plus any tax shield. For example, if expropriation occurs at the beginning of the third year, net compensation plus tax shield would need to have a net present value of $3,085,000 for MEC-USA to realize the required 14% rate of return on MEC-France. This result occurs because the cumulative net present value (Exhibit 10.11, line 18) is a negative $3,085,000 after two years of operation. The same type of analysis can be used to find a break-even year or terminal value if funds are permanently blocked. Blocked funds reduce net present value in the same manner as expropriation, but without the benefit of a tax shield or compensation.

IMPACT ON OTHER FINANCIAL GOALS

Although capital budgeting analysis of a project's discounted cash flow to the parent is the theoretically correct method for calculating the economic value of a project, including allowances for the time value of money and project risks, many financial executives are still concerned about the *timing* of a project's impact on their firm's consolidated net earnings and common stock price. In keeping with the compromise viewpoint adopted earlier, foreign projects should be analyzed from three different perspectives: impact on a firm's cash flow, net earnings (per share), and market value. Analysis of a project's net present value or internal rate of return is, of course, from the cash flow perspective.

Impact on Consolidated Net Earnings

Exhibit 10.16 summarizes the impact of MEC-France on consolidated net earnings of MEC-USA. Since MEC-France is a 100%-owned affiliate, any net earnings on its books are consolidated after translation to dollars with MEC-USA's worldwide income. In addition, MEC-USA's own earnings will be larger than otherwise because of the contribution to overhead and profit made by license fees, exports of components, and the interest subsidy from the French Development Bank. The net earnings of MEC-USA are in-

EXHIBIT 10.16
Impact of MEC-France on Consolidated Net Earnings of MEC-USA, Excluding Terminal Value

	YEAR				
	0–1	*2*	*3*	*4*	*5*
Income from MEC-France (FF thousands)					
1. Net income in MEC-France (Exhibit 10.8, line 1)	3,500	5,350	7,586	10,267	13,506
2. License fees before U.S. taxes (Exhibit 10.5, line 10)	4,000	4,698	5,519	6,484	7,621
3. Less French withholding taxes on dividends and license fees (Exhibit 10.11, line 4)	−312	−425	−559	−717	−908
4. Total income (FF thousands) (lines 1 + 2 − 3)	7,188	9,623	12,546	16,034	20,219
5. Number of FF/$ (Exhibit 10.5, line 6)	8.0000	8.2474	8.5025	8.7655	9.0366
6. ***Income from MEC-France ($ thousands)*** (lines 4 ÷ 5)	898	1,167	1,476	1,829	2,237
7. Net contribution from exports to the EEC (Exhibit 10.11, line 9)	101	38	81	129	183
8. Subsidized interest on French Development Bank loan (Exhibit 10.11, line 10)	71	57	43	28	14
9. Less U.S. corporate income tax on foreign source income (Exhibit 10.11, line 13)	−169	−174	−180	−187	−194
10. Net impact on consolidated net income of MEC-USA ($ thousands) (lines 6 + 7 + 8 − 9)	901	1,088	1,420	1,799	2,240
11. Return on original investment (line 10 ÷ Exhibit 10.2, line 6, in $)	14.4%	17.4%	22.7%	28.8%	35.8%

creased each year, beginning with $901,000 in year 1 and rising to $2,240,000 in year 5. The accounting return on original investment is another measure of the net earnings effect of MEC-France. It shows a favorable return of 14.4% in year 1 and increases each year to 35.8% in year 5.

Impact on Market Value

Analysis of the impact of MEC-France on market value is more controversial. The traditional theoretical viewpoint has been that the market value of a firm's common stock is equal to the present value of all expected future dividends, including a liquidating dividend, discounted at a rate reflecting the required rate of return for firms of similar risk. This rate is mainly a function of the net present value of all the firm's projects, present and future, using the appropriate risk-adjusted discount rate for each project. On the other hand, because investors are not privy to details of a firm's capital budgeting analysis, nor projected cash flows for each project, they have tended to rely on extrapolations of historical net earnings (per share) and dividends as a proxy for potential future dividends. The appropriate capitalization rate for these earnings is usually based on the price/earnings ratios of other firms of similar risk, rather than the discount rate used in internal capital budgeting. Thus many executives, who hope to maximize the market value of their firm's common stock, analyze projects both from the viewpoint of impact on cash flow and net earnings.

Proponents of the capital asset pricing model suggest that project cash flows should be discounted by a rate that reflects only the project's systematic risk in a portfolio context (Chapter 8 Appendix). This is the only risk for which investors will be compensated. Therefore it is important to determine the degree of covariance between project cash flows and cash flows (or other measures of return) of an efficient portfolio. Thus it may be impossible to tell what kind of impact MEC-France will have on market price of MEC-USA by using only the net present value and net earnings data presented up to now. On the other hand, we have left open the question of how the 14% risk-adjusted discount rate used by MEC-USA is determined in the first place. It might be based on total risk or just systematic risk. Chapter 12 presents an analysis of how the cost of capital and risk-adjusted discount rates can be determined. We will delay until then further discussion of the impact of specific project rates of return on market value of common stock.

SUMMARY

Capital budgeting for foreign projects involves many complexities that do not exist in domestic projects. A foreign project should be judged on its net present value from the viewpoint of funds which can be freely remitted to the parent. Comparison of a project's net present value to similar projects in the host country is useful for evaluating expected performance relative to potential.

Debt raised in the host country does not reduce the investment outlay from the parent's viewpoint. It is merely a substitute for debt raised elsewhere. If local debt carries a subsidized interest rate, the subsidy element should be included as a cash inflow.

Risks that are peculiar to foreign operations, such as political risk and foreign exchange risk, can be best accommodated by adjusting project cash flows rather than adjusting the project's risk-adjusted discount rate.

The effect of foreign projects on consolidated net earnings and the market value of common stock is also important. The impact on market value is dependent on how investors perceive the risk of foreign operations and how they value the diversification advantages.

NOTES

1. Arthur Stonehill and Leonard Nathanson, "Capital Budgeting and the Multinational Corporation," *California Management Review,* Summer 1968, pp. 39–54. James C. Baker and Laurence J. Beardsley, "Multinational Companies' Use of Risk Evaluation and Profit Measurement for Capital Budgeting Decisions," *Journal of Business Finance,* Spring 1973, pp. 38–43. David J. Oblak and Roy J. Helm, Jr., "Survey and Analysis of Capital Budgeting Methods Used by Multinationals," *Financial Management,* Winter 1980, pp. 37–41. Vinod B. Bavishi, "Capital Budgeting Practices at Multinationals," *Management Accounting,* August 1981, pp. 32–35. Marie E. Wicks Kelly and George C. Philippatos, "Comparative Analysis of the Foreign Investment Evaluation Practices by U.S.-Based Manufacturing Multinational Corporations," *Journal of International Business Studies,* Winter 1982, pp. 19–42. Marjorie Stanley and Stanley Block, "An Empirical Study of Management and Financial Variables Influencing Capital Budgeting Decisions for Multinational Corporations in the 1980s," *Management International Review,* Vol. 23, No. 3, 1983, pp. 61–71.

2. Bavishi, "Capital Budgeting Practices," p. 34.

3. Stanley and Block, "Management and Financial Variables."

4. U.S. firms must consolidate foreign affiliates that are over 50% owned. If an affiliate is between 20% and 50% owned, it is usually consolidated on a pro-rata basis. Affiliates less than 20% owned are normally carried as unconsolidated investments.

5. Baker and Beardsley, "Risk Evaluation and Profit Measurement," p. 39.

6. Oblak and Helm, "Capital Budgeting Methods," p. 39.

7. Stanley and Block, "Management and Financial Variables," pp. 66–67.

8. The 30% capital gains tax is an oversimplification since part of the tax would be at the full 46% rate applicable to recaptured depreciation.

9. For an excellent analysis of the use of this method, called the "adjusted present value approach," see Donald R. Lessard, "Evaluating Foreign Projects: An Adjusted Present Value Approach," in Donald R. Lessard, ed., *International Financial Management: Theory and Application,* New York: Wiley, 1985, pp. 570–584.

BIBLIOGRAPHY

Aharoni, Yair, *The Foreign Investment Decision Process,* Boston: Harvard Graduate School of Business Administration, Division of Research, 1966.

Baker, James C., "Capital Budgeting in West European Companies," *Issues in Financial Management,* Vol. 19, No. 1, 1981, pp. 3–10.

Baker, James C., and Laurence J. Beardsley, "Multinational Companies' Use of Risk Evaluation and Profit Measurement for Capital Budgeting Decisions," *Journal of Business Finance,* Spring 1973, pp. 38–43.

Bavishi, Vinod B., "Capital Budgeting Practices at Multinationals," *Management Accounting,* August 1981, pp. 32–35.

Booth, Laurence D., "Capital Budgeting Frameworks for the Multinational Corporation," *Journal of International Business Studies,* Fall 1982, pp. 113–123.

Freitas, Lewis P., "Investment Decision Making in Japan," *Journal of Accounting, Auditing & Finance,* Summer 1981, pp. 378–382.

Gordon, Sara L., and Francis A. Lees, "Multinational Capital Budgeting: Foreign Investment under Subsidy," *California Management Review,* Fall 1982, pp. 22–32.

Kelly, Marie E. Wicks, *Foreign Investment Evaluation Practices of U.S. Multinational Corporations,* Ann Arbor: UMI Research Press, 1983.

Kelly, Marie E. Wicks, and George C. Philippatos, "Comparative Analysis of the Foreign Investment Evaluation Practices by U.S.-based Manufacturing Multinational Corporations," *Journal of International Business Studies,* Winter 1982, pp. 19–42.

Kim, Suk H., and Edward J. Farragher, "Current Capital Budgeting Practices," *Management Accounting,* June 1981, pp. 26–30.

Lessard, Donald R., "Evaluating International Projects: An Adjusted Present Value Approach," in Donald R. Lessard, ed., *International Financial Management: Theory and Application,* New York: Wiley, 1985, pp. 570–584.

Mehta, Dileep R., "Capital Budgeting Procedures for a Multinational," in P. Sethi and R. Holton, eds., *Management of Multinationals,* New York: Free Press, 1974, pp. 271–291.

Oblak, David J., and Roy J. Helm, Jr., "Survey and Analysis of Capital Budgeting Methods Used by Multinationals," *Financial Management,* Winter 1980, pp. 37–41.

Shapiro, Alan C., "Capital Budgeting for the Multinational Corporation," *Financial Management,* Spring 1978, pp. 7–16.

———, "International Capital Budgeting," *Midland Corporate Finance Journal,* Spring 1983, pp. 26–45.

Stanley, Marjorie, and Stanley Block, "An Empirical Study of Management and Financial Variables Influencing Capital Budgeting Decisions for Multinational Corporations in the 1980s," *Management International Review,* No. 3, 1983.

Stonehill, Arthur, and Leonard Nathanson, "Capital Budgeting and the Multinational Corporation," *California Management Review,* Summer 1968, pp. 39–54.

Zenoff, David, and Jack Zwick, *International Financial Management,* Englewood Cliffs, N.J.: Prentice-Hall, 1969, Chap. 5.

Problems for Part III

1. *Sarasota Corporation*

   After all foreign and U.S. taxes, Sarasota Corporation of the United States expects to receive cash dividends of 180 French francs per share from its wholly owned French affiliate during the coming year. The current exchange rate is nine French francs to the U.S. dollar, and the franc is expected to depreciate at an average annual rate relative to the dollar of 6%.

   The franc dividend is also expected to grow at an annual rate of 10% forever. Sarasota Corporation owns 20 million shares of its French affiliate, and Sarasota's weighted average cost of capital is 18%. What is the present value of Sarasota's equity in its French affiliate?

2. *Hideyoshi, K.K.*

   Hideyoshi, K.K., of Shizuoka, Japan, manufactures office duplicating equipment. Early in 1986 the company received a proposal that it establish a wholly owned manufacturing affiliate in Sindolaysia, a country of 50 million people located near several ASEAN countries. The proposal was advanced by P. K. Fong, manager of Hideyoshi's distribution subsidiary in Sindolaysia, who argued that Sindolaysia would be ideal for manufacturing because of its comparatively low costs, the high level of education of its work force, and the fact that it aspires to become a major light manufacturing center.

   Fong recognized that political sentiment in Sindolaysia toward foreign investment was lukewarm, in part because the country had once been a European colony and in part because it was occupied by Japan during World War II. The Sindolaysian government was trying to emphasize industrialization from within, with only temporary assistance from foreign investors, and it had recently passed a law that all foreign investments become the property of the government of Sindolaysia after seven years. Nevertheless, Fong argued, the project would pay for itself in five years and so was worthwhile.

The Sindolaysian currency is the durian (symbol D`), which is currently worth about 50 yen. Future exchange rates between the yen and durian are forecast as follows:

Year	*Yen per durian*
1987	45
1988	40
1989	35
1990	30
1991	25
1992	20
1993	15

To justify the proposal, Fong submitted the capital budgeting analysis shown on the following page. All financial amounts are in thousands of durians.

Revenue and expense forecasts. Unit demand and local sales price forecasts are incorporated in the schedule on the following page. Variable costs are 40% of sales, fixed cash costs are D`40 million per year, and depreciation and other noncash expenses are D`20 million per year.

Capital outlay and recovery. Hideyoshi, K.K., would invest 4.5 billion yen in inventory, plant, and equipment at the end of 1986. The project would begin generating earnings in 1987, and at the end of 1993 all plant, equipment, and working capital would be given to Sindolaysia.

Cash dividends equal to annual profits may be repatriated to Japan each year. Cash flow from depreciation may not be repatriated annually, but may be invested in Sindolaysian money market instruments to yield 15% tax free. In 1993 the value of this fund (principal and interest) may be repatriated to Japan free of both Sindolaysian and Japanese taxes.

Taxes. The Sindolaysian corporate income tax rate is 30%. The Japanese corporate tax rate is 50% on the grossed-up pretax profit of foreign affiliates. However, a Japanese company may take a tax credit for income taxes already paid to a foreign government. Neither Sindolaysia nor Japan has any provision for carrying losses forward or backward for tax purposes.

Weighted average cost of capital. Hideyoshi, K.K., has always used a discount rate of 20% per annum to evaluate cash flows from proposed investment projects.

What is your recommendation for the proposal, and why?

	1986	*1987*	*1988*	*1989*	*1990*	*1991*	*1992*	*1993*
Unit sales volume (000)		80	100	120	130	135	140	145
Unit sales price (D`)		1,000	1,100	1,200	1,250	1,300	1,320	1,340
Sales revenue (D`000)		80,000	110,000	144,000	162,250	175,500	184,800	187,600
Variable costs (40%)		32,000	44,000	57,000	65,000	70,200	73,920	75,040
Cash fixed costs		40,000	40,000	40,000	40,000	40,000	40,000	40,000
Depreciation		20,000	20,000	20,000	20,000	20,000	20,000	20,000
Pretax profit		−12,000	6,000	26,400	37,500	45,300	50,880	52,560
Income tax @ 30%		0	1,800	7,920	11,250	13,590	15,264	15,768
Net income		−12,000	4,200	18,480	26,250	31,710	35,616	36,792
Add back depreciation		20,000	20,000	20,000	20,000	20,000	20,000	20,000
Cost of project	−90,000							
Project cash flows	−90,000	8,000	24,200	38,480	46,500	51,710	55,616	56,792
20% present value factor	1.000	.833	.694	.579	.482	.402	.335	.291
Present value of flows	−90,000	6,664	16,795	22,280	22,296	20,787	18,631	16,544
Cumulative present value	−90,000	−83,336	−66,541	−44,261	−21,965	−1,178	17,453	33,997

3. *Cordillera de los Andes*

Development officers from Cordillera, a modern South American republic in the Andes, recently approached Olympia Manufacturing Company about expanding their affiliate in Cordillera. They asked Olympia to manufacture products that had heretofore been imported.

Cordillera has been a functioning democracy since the late nineteenth century, and has had no revolutions or *golpes*. Politicians of both parties support the policy of encouraging progressive foreign firms to invest in Cordillera for a limited time, after which the affiliate must be sold to local investors at net book value. Inflation in Cordillera is 12% per annum, and the present exchange rate is eight cords (symbol ₡) per dollar. The following information about the project is known.

Investment. Plant and equipment to be provided by Olympia will cost $62,500,000 (₡500,000,000). Working capital will be financed 100% by Cordillera banks. Earnings will be generated at the end of years 1 through 5, and after five years all remaining assets will be turned over to local investors at net book value. However, Olympia will be allowed to depreciate the investment over five years on a straight line basis, so ending book value is expected to be zero.

Demand, price, and exchange rate forecasts. Forecasts for unit demand, sales prices, and foreign exchange rates are as follows:

Year	*Anticipated unit demand*	*Expected unit sales price*	*Forecast exchange rate, ₡/$*
0			₡ 8/$
1	800,000	₡1,000	10
2	900,000	1,120	12
3	1,000,000	1,254	14
4	1,200,000	1,405	16
5	1,400,000	1,574	18

The table above reflects an expected price increase of 12% per annum. Variable costs will be 50% of sales revenue, and cash fixed costs will be ₡100 million in year 1 and will probably rise at 12% per year in keeping with general inflation. Depreciation will be ₡100 million per year.

Repatriation. An annual cash dividend equal to 100% of accounting profits may be repatriated to the United States at the end of each year. Depreciation funds may not be repatriated, but they may be invested in Cordillera treasury deposits established especially for foreign firms. These deposits yield 6% per annum free of taxes. When the operating assets are turned over to the Cordillera government, the balance of these deposits may be repatriated at the then-existing exchange rate. Any portion of such funds received in the United States in excess of the original investment will be subject to a capital gains tax of 25%.

Taxation. Corporate income in Cordillera is taxed at 35%, while dividends received in the United States are subject to a 50% tax with credit allowed for taxes already paid in Cordillera.

Cost of capital. Olympia uses an 18% weighted average cost of capital for all projects, domestic and foreign. Within Cordillera, projects of this risk class are normally expected to earn 30% per annum in local currency terms.

a. What is your recommendation for this proposal? Assume that all cash flows occur at the end of each year, and consider both parent and project viewpoints.

b. Suppose that Olympia finds it can use its depreciation funds in Cordillera to purchase local handicrafts, which in turn can be sold in the United States at cost, including freight and selling expenses. That is, Olympia has an opportunity to enter into a profitless venture selling handicrafts from Cordillera at cost in the United States. Is this opportunity of any use to Olympia?

4. *Madras Processing Company*

Jason Smith, director of marketing for Adelaide Food Corporation of Australia, was convinced it would be profitable for Adelaide to open a wholly owned fish processing plant in Madras. If the investment were made, the subsidiary, to be known as Madras Processing Company, would buy fish caught in the Indian Ocean, freeze the fish, and distribute to food vendors in Australia and New Zealand. Smith forecast the following in Australian dollars:

Annual sales		$72,000,000
Cost of fish sold	$58,000,000	
Administrative expenses	6,000,000	64,000,000
Profit		$ 8,000,000

Smith, a former salesman, remembered from a training session on finance he had attended that only cash flow mattered when investment decisions were being made, so he ignored depreciation.

Further investigation showed that purchase and installation of a complete canning factory manufactured in Singapore would cost $20 million, and that land and docking facilities would cost an additional $4 million. Indian income taxes are 36%, a rate that seemed favorable in comparison with the 50% corporate income tax rate in Australia.

Smith showed his calculations to Tracey Jones, a recent college graduate in finance, who revised Smith's profit calculations to include both depreciation and income taxes. Jones assumed a 16-year life for the canning plant and equipment, and projected annual net income after tax as follows:

Annual sales		$72,000,000
Cost of fish sold	$58,000,000	
Administrative expenses	6,000,000	
Depreciation	1,250,000	65,250,000
Profit before taxes		$6,750,000
Indian income taxes @ 36%		2,430,000
Net profit after tax		$ 4,320,000

Knowing that Adelaide Foods's board of directors regarded 20% as the weighted average cost of capital, Jones prepared the following table (in thousands of Australian dollars):

Year	*Aftertax profit*	*Depreciation*	*Cash flow*	*20% PV factor*	*Cash flow*	*Cumulative present value*
1	4,320	1,250	5,770	0.883	4,806	4,806
2	4,320	1,250	5,770	0.694	4,004	8,810
3	4,320	1,250	5,770	0.579	3,341	12,151
4	4,320	1,250	5,770	0.482	2,781	14,932
5	4,320	1,250	5,770	0.402	2,320	17,252
6	4,320	1,250	5,770	0.335	1,933	19,185
7	4,320	1,250	5,770	0.279	1,610	20,795
8	4,320	1,250	5,770	0.233	1,344	22,139
9	4,320	1,250	5,770	0.194	1,119	23,258
10	4,320	1,250	5,770	0.162	935	24,193
11	4,320	1,250	5,770	0.135	779	24,972
12	4,320	1,250	5,770	0.112	646	25,618
13	4,320	1,250	5,770	0.093	537	26,155
14	4,320	1,250	5,770	0.078	450	26,605
15	4,320	1,250	5,770	0.065	375	26,980
16	4,320	1,250	5,770	0.054	312	27,292

Jones took her calculations to Richard Dobbins, vice-president of finance. Dobbins made the following observations and asked Jones to rework her calculations:

a. Working capital needs in a fish freezing plant are typically 10% of annual sales.

b. Adelaide Foods's weighted average cost of capital for domestic operations had been calculated as follows:

	Cost	*Proportion*	*Weighted cost*
Long-term debt @ 16%, before tax @ 50%	0.08	0.40	0.032
Equity @ 28%	0.28	0.60	0.168
			0.200

c. Adelaide Foods could finance the subsidiary directly from Australia, using its own 20% weighted average cost of capital as a cutoff point. However, Adelaide Foods could also have the subsidiary borrow $15 million from an Indian development bank at a subsidized rate of 10%. The loan would be for ten years with interest payable annually and the entire principal due at the end of the tenth year. Adelaide Foods would not have to cosign the development loan.

d. Because all of Madras's sales would be in hard currencies, India would allow annual dividends equal to 100% of accounting income. Invested capital could not be repatriated, but after 16 years Adelaide Foods could sell the operation to Indian investors. Dobbins estimated that such a sale would include working capital on a dollar-for-dollar basis, land for twice the amount originally paid, and about $5 million for the 16-year-old canning plant.

What type of recommendation should Jones make to the board of directors? What conditions and assumptions should she make?

PART IV

Financing Decisions

11

International Financial Markets

To show how the cost and availability of short- and long-term capital is determined for a multinational firm, we must review the most important features of international financial markets. A number of sources of capital exist in international markets, the most important of which are the Eurocurrency and Eurobond markets. In addition, multinational firms often have access to domestic long-term debt and equity markets, both in countries where they operate and in countries whose capital markets are open to world competition. Easy access to foreign sources of funds is one of the many comparative advantages, or if you prefer, market imperfections, enjoyed by multinational firms.

The basic conditions necessary for any successful external money or capital market are that nonresidents of the country whose currency is used be free to transfer their holdings of that currency at will and that the market have some significant cost advantage over the purely domestic market. The cost advantage is typically derived from an absence of government interference, such as taxes, reserve requirements, deposit insurance premiums, interest rate regulations, and government policies to influence credit allocation, and the fact that the market is basically a "wholesale" market. In addition, a demand must exist on the part of nonbank entities for the currencies obtained in the external financial market.

EXTERNAL MARKETS

International financial market activity is concentrated in certain cities that have come to be identified as international financial centers. London and New York City are the most important, but since the mid-1960s other locations have become prominent. Four major types of transactions occur in an international financial center that is also an important domestic financial center. These are depicted in Exhibit 11.1.

Any important national financial center will depend on the presence of a large body of domestic investors or depositors supplying funds to domestic users (Relationship A). Investors supply funds directly to users by purchasing securities such as bonds, commercial paper, or shares of stock, while depositors supply their funds to financial intermediaries (banks, insurance companies, mutual funds, etc.) who pool these receipts and make loans or equity investments from the pool. Most financial intermediaries guarantee the deposit, so the depositor looks to the intermediary rather than to the ultimate borrower for security.

An international financial center exists when domestic funds are supplied to foreign users or when foreign funds are supplied to domestic users. These are the diagonal Relationships B and C. A healthy international financial center will almost always develop business along line D, in which foreign funds are supplied to foreign users.

London and New York, as the world's most important international financial markets, perform all four of the possible functions, and as of the mid-1980s Tokyo appears to be joining this group. Other cities perform two or three of the four functions quite well and are important regional financial centers. These include Paris, Zurich, Geneva, Amsterdam, Singapore, and Hong Kong.[1]

EXHIBIT 11.1
Schematic View of Transactions in an International Financial Center

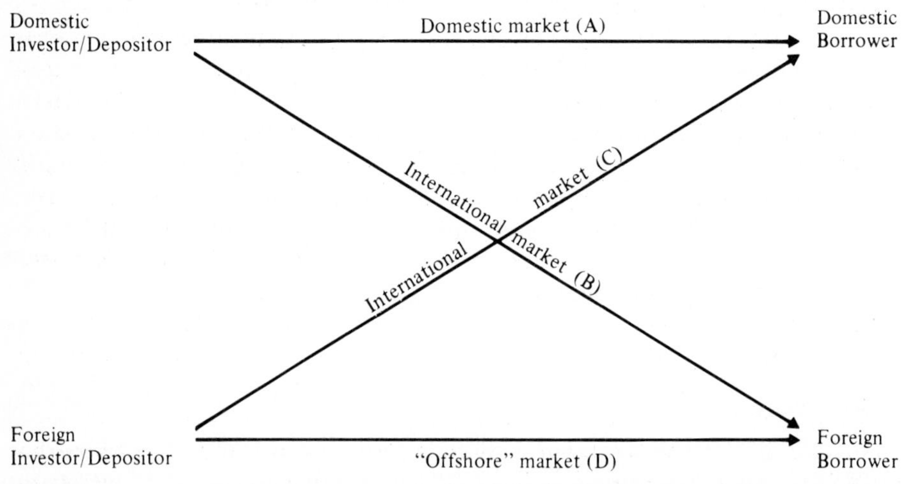

Note: The terms "offshore" and "overseas" are often used in the English language as synonyms for "foreign," presumably because England, the home country of the language, is an island. Describing Luxembourg as an "offshore" financial center seems contrary to a literal meaning of the word, since it is England that is "offshore."

Still other centers perform only Relationship D. They are usually referred to as "offshore" financial centers. They exist by providing a service for nonresidents while (usually) keeping their international business separate from their domestic business. The best-known offshore financial centers are Luxembourg, Cayman Islands, the Bahamas, the Netherlands Antilles, Bahrain, Kuwait, and Panama. Jersey, Guernsey, and the Isle of Man function as offshore financial centers for London-based financing.[2]

The major requirements for success as an offshore financial center are the following:[3]

- Economic and political stability, which gives confidence to nonresidents that fund movements will not be restricted.
- An efficient and experienced financial community, able to carry out necessary technical operations with skill.
- Good communication and support services, so that market information can be quickly and efficiently transmitted to participants.
- A regulatory climate that protects investors and depositors but is not unduly restrictive to financial institutions.

EURODOLLARS AND OTHER EUROCURRENCIES

A Eurodollar is a U.S. dollar time deposit in a bank outside the United States. The bank may be a foreign bank or the overseas branch of a U.S. bank. Eurodollar time deposit maturities range from call money and overnight funds to longer periods; certificates of deposit are usually for three months or more and in million-dollar increments. Note that a Eurodollar deposit is *not* a demand deposit; it is not created on the bank's books by writing loans against required fractional reserves, and it cannot be transferred by a check drawn on the bank having the deposit. Eurodollar deposits are transferred by wire or cable transfer of an underlying balance held in a correspondent bank located within the United States. A domestic analogy would be the transfer of deposits held in savings and loan associations, which is done by having the association write a check on a commercial bank.

Any convertible currency can exist in "Euro-" form. Thus there are Euromarks (Deutschemarks deposited in banks outside Germany), Eurosterling (British pounds deposited in banks outside the United Kingdom), and Euroyen (Japanese yen deposited outside Japan), as well as Eurodollars.

The banks in which Eurocurrencies are deposited are often referred to as "Eurobanks." Dufey and Giddy define a Eurobank as "a financial intermediary that simultaneously bids for time deposits and makes loans in a currency other than that of the country in which it is located."[4] Eurobanks are major world banks that, in addition to their Eurobusiness, generally conduct a domestic banking business. Thus the Eurocurrency operation that qualifies a bank for the name "Eurobank" is in fact a department of a large commercial bank, and the name "Eurobank" springs from the function performed.

The Eurocurrency market serves three valuable purposes. Eurocurrency deposits are an efficient and convenient money market device for holding excess corporate liquidity; the Eurocurrency market is a major source of short-term bank loans to finance corporate working capital needs, including the financing of imports and exports; and the market is useful for arbitrage purposes.

Size and Location

The prefix "Euro" does not mean that the bank must be in Europe. The location of a Eurocurrency deposit might be London, which is the center of the Eurocurrency market (except for Eurosterling), or Paris, Frankfurt, Zurich, Amsterdam, and other European financial centers. However, Euromarkets also exist in Nassau (the Bahamas), Hong Kong, Singapore ("Asiandollars"), and even in the United States through a special entity called an "International Banking Facility (IBF)." These will be described in more detail in Chapter 13, but for the moment it is sufficient to note that they are physically located in the United States in parent bank facilities but are treated by both federal and state governments as if they were located abroad. They were authorized in 1981 by the Federal Reserve Board to enable U.S. banks to compete more effectively in the Eurodollar market.

The exact size of the Eurocurrency market is difficult to measure because it depends on daily decisions by depositors on where to hold readily transferable liquid funds, and particularly whether to deposit dollars within or outside the United States. Eurocurrency statistics are provided both in the *Annual Report* of the Bank for International Settlements (BIS), in Basle, Switzerland, and by Morgan Guaranty Trust Company in its monthly *World Financial Markets*. Exhibit 11.2 from Morgan Guaranty shows that as of June 1983 the size of the Eurocurrency market was $2,056 billion, a fourfold increase since 1976. Breaking the total down geographically, 60% was deposited in Europe, 8% in the United States, 6% in Japan, 3% in Canada, and 22% in seven offshore banking centers.

Exhibit 11.2 also shows the currency of denomination of Eurocurrencies. The U.S. dollar at $1,641 billion is almost 80% of the total market. It is for this reason that the Eurocurrency market is often referred to as the Eurodollar market. The Deutschemark is second in importance, at $175 billion or 8.5% of the market. Of the total $2,056 billion of gross deposits, some $1,483 billion or 72% is deposited in a Eurobank by another bank. Only $489 billion or 24% of deposits are from nonbank firms. When interbank liabilities are canceled, the gross market size drops from $2,056 billion to $945 billion.

Creation of Eurodollars

A Eurodollar is not a currency separate from a dollar in the United States. Similarly, every Eurocurrency has an exchange value identical with its domestic or home currency counterpart. If the domestic counterpart devalues or revalues, the rate of exchange between its corresponding Eurocurrency and other foreign currencies changes by the same amount.

Eurocurrency deposits differ from their domestic money market counterparts only in terms of their geographic location and in terms of the interest rates that might be paid on deposits or loans relative to home currency interest rates.

The process by which Eurocurrencies come into existence can be illustrated with dollars. Eurodollars are created when a dollar deposit is transferred from a bank within the United States to a bank outside the country, or when someone outside the United States acquires dollars, perhaps because of a commercial transaction or a purchase in the foreign exchange market, and deposits those dollars in a bank outside the United States. Eurodollar creation can be illustrated by following the "T-account" entries that arise when U.S. dollars are deposited in foreign banks.

Step 1 Assume that before the creation of any Eurodollars a Dutch multinational corporation acquires $100 on demand deposit in a New York bank. Eurodollar transactions are usually $500,000 or more, but we are using $100 to simplify the presentation. The demand deposit of the Dutch corporation would be reflected on the books of the New York bank, the Dutch corporation, and the Federal Reserve Bank of New York as follows:

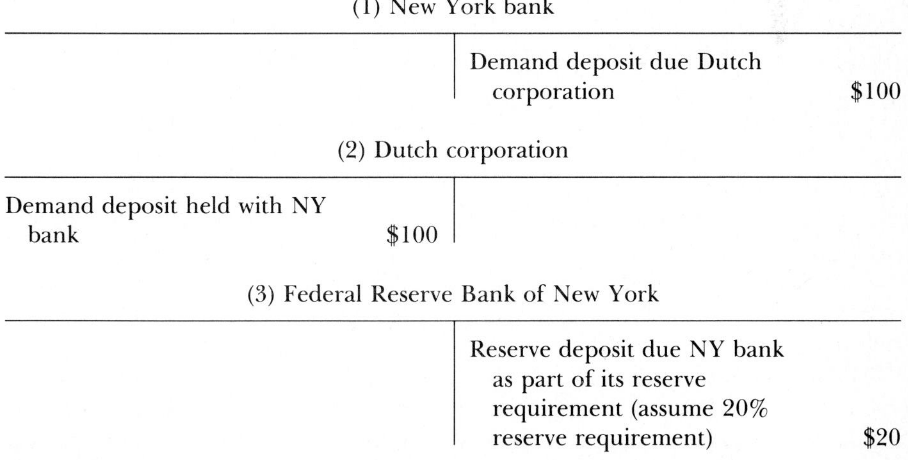

(1) New York bank

		Demand deposit due Dutch corporation	$100

(2) Dutch corporation

Demand deposit held with NY bank	$100		

(3) Federal Reserve Bank of New York

		Reserve deposit due NY bank as part of its reserve requirement (assume 20% reserve requirement)	$20

Step 2 Assume that the Dutch corporation decides to convert its dollar demand deposit into an interest-earning form. The corporation might in-

EXHIBIT 11.2
Eurocurrency Market Size
Measured by foreign-currency liabilities at end of period, billions of dollars

	1976	*1977*	*1978*	*1979*	*1980*	*1981*	*1982*	*June 1983*
By Market Center:								
European centers	**406**	**511**	**656**	**867**	**1,045**	**1,202**	**1,273**	**1,239**
United Kingdom	201	232	290	385	485	590	636	635
France	50	64	80	101	124	134	140	127
Luxembourg	34	46	55	76	84	82	83	79
Belgium	20	22	37	48	62	73	72	74
Netherlands	21	27	38	47	55	57	55	52
Italy	17	23	30	37	46	49	43	37
Switzerland	17	20	30	34	35	35	34	34
Austria	—	10	13	18	23	23	25	25
Germany	14	16	21	25	25	26	24	23
Spain	7	9	12	17	21	24	19	17
Sweden	3	4	5	8	11	13	13	14
Denmark	—	2	2	3	3	4	4	4
Ireland	—	2	2	2	4	4	4	4
Unallocated	22	34	41	66	67	88	121	114
United States[a]	—	—	—	—	—	46	147	171
Japan	35	36	48	61	100	123	124	126
Canada	21	25	33	40	54	66	65	67
Offshore banking centers	**133**	**168**	**212**	**265**	**325**	**424**	**448**	**453**
Bahamas	79	90	105	112	126	150	132	137
Singapore	17	21	27	38	54	86	103	105
Bahrain	6	16	23	29	38	51	59	57
Hong Kong	6	8	16	21	32	43	53	54

Cayman Islands[b]	12	16	18	27	33	42	47	46
Panama	11	15	20	33	35	42	43	43
Netherlands Antilles	2	2	3	5	7	10	11	11
By Currency of Denomination:								
U.S. dollar	476	562	703	887	1,138	1,446	1,633	1,641
Deutschemark	70	104	141	193	190	184	189	175
Swiss franc	24	35	43	62	83	110	100	98
Japanese yen	2	4	9	15	17	24	27	29
British pound	6	10	15	23	36	30	26	25
French franc	5	7	11	17	22	17	18	20
Dutch guilder	5	8	11	13	12	14	17	20
Other currencies[c]	7	10	16	23	26	36	47	48
By Type of Entity:								
Nonbanks	109	135	174	245	327	428	474	489
Official monetary institutions	80	100	115	145	150	132	90	84
Other banks[c]	406	505	660	843	1,047	1,301	1,493	1,483
Gross Market Size	**595**	**740**	**949**	**1,233**	**1,524**	**1,861**	**2,057**	**2,056**
Interbank liabilities within market area	**281**	**361**	**471**	**655**	**819**	**1,002**	**1,125**	**1,111**
Net market size	**314**	**379**	**478**	**578**	**705**	**859**	**932**	**945**

Source: Morgan Guaranty Trust Company, *World Financial Markets,* January 1984, p. 9.

[a]International banking facilities only.

[b]U.S. bank branches only.

[c]Includes unallocated.

struct the New York bank to invest the sum in money market instruments such as U.S. Treasury bills or time certificates of deposit with the New York bank. Possibly for reasons of higher yield, however, the Dutch corporation decides to deposit its dollars in a dollar-denominated time deposit at a London bank. The result is as follows:

(4) New York bank

		Demand deposit due Dutch corporation	−$100
		Demand deposit due London bank	+$100

(5) London bank

Demand deposit in NY bank	+$100	Time deposit due Dutch corporation	+$100

(6) Dutch corporation

Demand deposit in NY bank	−$100		
Time deposit in London bank	+$100		

By this step a Eurodollar, that is, a U.S. dollar deposit liability of a foreign bank, has been created. Note, however, that the $100 liability of the London bank is matched by the bank's $100 claim on a demand deposit in New York. Total deposit levels in the United States have not changed, but ownership of the U.S. deposit has shifted from a foreign corporation to a foreign bank. The reserve requirement at the Federal Reserve Bank and the U.S. money supply is unchanged.

Step 3 Because the London bank is paying interest on its dollar time-deposit liability to the Dutch corporation, it wishes to invest the underlying dollars to earn a return on them. Assume that the London bank decides, as a matter of prudence, to retain $10 of its deposit in the New York bank as a liquid reserve and to loan $90 to a Paris bank. This is an interbank loan and will usually take the physical form of the London bank instructing the New York bank by wire to transfer funds out of its own account and into the account of the Paris bank. It will be noted that because Eurodollars are not demand deposits they are transferred by orders given to the New York bank and not by writing checks or other transfer of the Eurodollar deposit balances on the books of the European bank.

The London bank's loan to the Paris bank is reflected in the T-accounts that follow:

(7) London bank

Demand deposit in NY bank	−$90		
Loan to Paris bank	+$90		

(8) Paris bank

Demand deposit in NY bank	+$90	Dollar loan repayable to London bank	+$90

(9) New York bank

		Demand deposit due London bank	−$90
		Demand deposit due Paris bank	+$90

No change has occurred in the amount of demand deposit liabilities of the New York bank. However, title to $90 of such deposits has been shifted from the London bank to the Paris bank. Contrary to some views of the Eurodollar market, there has not been a pyramiding or expansion of Eurodollar deposits *within* Europe. Total Eurodollar deposits remain at $100, the time deposit of the Dutch corporation. Additionally, ownership of a New York–based deposit has been transferred to a new owner, and a repayment obligation (the Eurodollar loan) created in Europe.

Step 4 Assume that the Paris bank reloans its $90 to a French importer, who is seeking a dollar loan to pay for imports from the United States. The transactions to record the loan would be as follows:

(10) Paris bank

Demand deposit in NY bank	−$90		
Dollar loan to French importer	+$90		

(11) French importer

Dollar check drawn on NY bank	+$90	Loan payable in dollars to Paris bank	+$90

If the French importer owned a New York bank account, the importer might deposit the loan proceeds in New York rather than hold the physical check as has been assumed in this example. The French importer might also instruct the Paris bank to wire dollar funds directly to the New York exporter, thus combining T-account transaction (11) with transaction (12) below. For simplicity we will assume separate transactions and the holding of the physical check by the French importer as an asset.

Assume that the New York exporter has a bank account in the same New York bank and deposits all receipts in that bank. When the French importer pays the New York exporter, the transaction would be recorded thus:

(12) French importer

Dollar check drawn on NY bank	−$90		
Inventory	+$90		

(13) New York exporter

Demand deposit in NY bank from deposit of check received	+$90		
Inventory	−$90		

As soon as the check clears the New York bank, that bank would adjust its books as follows:

(14) New York bank

		Demand deposit due Paris bank	−$90
		Demand deposit due NY exporter	+$90

Use of the proceeds of the Paris bank's Eurodollar loan to the French importer to pay the U.S. exporter does not cause any change in the volume of demand deposits of U.S. banks. The only change is that an obligation to a foreigner (the Paris bank) is changed to an obligation to a domestic business (the New York exporter).

Step 5 Eventually the French importer must accumulate or acquire dollars to repay its Eurodollar loan from the Paris bank, possibly by selling the imported goods for dollars or by selling them for francs and using the francs to buy dollars on the foreign exchange market. Assume, for our example, that the goods have been sold for French francs and the French importer now buys $90 of U.S. currency with accumulated French francs and uses the $90 to repay the loan. The resulting transactions would be as follows (accounting for the sale within France is ignored, as is interest on the loan):

(15) French importer

(a) French francs (dollar equivalent	−$90	(b) Loan payable in dollars to Paris bank	−$90
(a) U.S. currency	+$90		
(b) U.S. currency	−$90		

(16) Paris bank

Dollar loan to French importer	−$90		
Dollar deposit in NY bank (to reflect deposit of dollar currency received)	+$90		

(17) New York bank

Currency	+$90	Demand deposit due Paris bank	+$90

Step 6 Finally the Paris bank repays its loan from the London bank by wiring a transfer of New York funds held by the Paris bank (the example ignores interest):

(18) Paris bank

Dollar deposit in NY bank	−$90	Loan from London bank	−$90

(19) London bank

Dollar deposit in NY bank	+$90		
Loan to Paris bank	−$90		

(20) New York bank

		Demand deposit due London bank	+$90
		Demand deposit due Paris bank	−$90

Summary Most of these transactions cancel out, as shown in Exhibit 11.3, in which each of them is summarized in T-account form and the ending balance indicated.

At the end of the series of transactions, the New York bank owes the London bank $100, this demand deposit having originally been acquired from the Dutch corporation and then transferred first to the London bank, then to the Paris bank, and then back to the London bank. Additionally,

EXHIBIT 11.3
T-Accounts Summarizing Eurodollar Transactions

New York Bank

		(1) DD Dutch corp.	100
(4) DD Dutch corp.	100	(4) DD London bank	100
(9) DD London bank	90	(9) DD Paris bank	90
(14) DD Paris bank	90	(14) DD NY exporter	90
(17) Dollar currency	90	(17) DD Paris bank	90
(20) DD Paris bank	90	(20) DD London bank	90
Dollar currency	90	DD London bank	100
		DD NY exporter	90

London Bank

(5) DD NY bank	100	(5) TD Dutch corp.	100
(7) Loan Paris bank	90	(7) DD NY bank	90
(19) DD NY bank	90	(19) Loan Paris bank	90
DD NY bank	100	TD Dutch corp.	100

Paris Bank

(8) DD NY bank	90	(8) Loan London bank	90
(10) Loan Paris importer	90	(10) DD NY bank	90
(16) DD NY bank	90	(16) Loan Paris importer	90
(18) Loan London bank	90	(18) DD NY bank	90

Dutch Corporation

(2) DD NY bank	100		
(6) TD London bank	100	(6) DD NY bank	100
TD London bank	100		

French Importer

(11) Dollar check	90	(11) Loan Paris bank	90
(12) Inventory	90	(12) Dollar check	90
(15a) US$ currency	90	(15a) French francs	90
(15b) Loan Paris bank	90	(15b) US$ currency	90
Inventory	90	French francs	90

EXHIBIT 11.3 (Cont.)

New York Exporter

(13) DD NY bank	90	(13) Inventory	90
DD NY bank	90	Inventory	90

Federal Reserve Bank of New York

		(3) Reserves, NY bank	20
		Reserves, NY bank	20

Note: DD means demand deposit balance; TD means Eurodollar time-deposit balance.

the New York bank received $90 in currency to match the eventual increase in demand deposits due the exporter. This transaction is no different from one resulting if the exporter sells its merchandise for cash on Manhattan Island and deposits the sales proceeds.

The London bank ended where it started, owning a $100 demand deposit in New York and owing a $100 time deposit to the Dutch corporation. Similarly, the Paris bank, which started with no dollar balances or loans, ended up with all its accounts closed out.

The Dutch corporation ended with a $100 time deposit in London rather than a $100 demand deposit in New York. The French importer ended up with an additional $90 of inventory purchased and with its French franc cash balances reduced by the equivalent of US$90. Had the French importer sold the acquired inventory for US$90 or more of French francs, the ending balance would have been cash sales proceeds less whatever French francs were needed to acquire the dollars to repay the Eurodollar loan from the Paris bank.

The New York exporter ended with $90 of additional cash in the New York bank from the proceeds of the sale. In the example inventory was reduced by $90, implying a sale at cost with no profit. In fact, inventory might have been reduced by some (lesser) cost and the balance shown as an increase in retained earnings.

Throughout the entire example reserve balances at the New York Federal Reserve Bank remained at $20, the backing required for the single $100 of demand deposit balances which circulated among various European holders. No additional reserve balance is shown for the additional deposit of the New York exporter because that balance is matched 100% by currency deposited.

Development of the Eurodollar Market

Historically, the Eurodollar market was born shortly after World War II, when Eastern European holders of dollars, including the various state trading banks of the Soviet Union, were afraid to deposit their dollar holdings in the United States because these deposits might be attached by U.S. residents with claims against Communist governments. Therefore Eastern European holders deposited their dollars in Western Europe, particularly with two Soviet banks: the Moscow Narodny Bank, in London, and the Banque Commerciale pour L'Europe du Nord, in Paris. These two banks redeposited the funds in other Western banks, especially in London.

Additional dollar deposits came from various central banks in Western Europe, which elected to hold part of their dollar reserves in this form to obtain a higher yield. Commercial banks also placed their dollar balances in the market for the same reason as well as because specific maturities could be negotiated in the Eurodollar market. Additional dollars came to the market from European insurance companies with a large volume of U.S. business (who found it financially advantageous to keep their dollar reserves in the higher-yielding Eurodollar market) and from the various holders of international refugee funds.

These historical precedents sometimes distract observers from the forces that have led to the strong and large market of the present time. The modern Eurodollar market "represents the highly efficient response of international banks to the desires of investors for high-yielding, safe and liquid investments, and the needs of businesses and governments for low-cost funds with assured availability."[5]

Although the basic causes of the growth of the Eurodollar market are economic efficiency, a number of unique institutional events during the 1950s and 1960s helped its growth. In 1957 British monetary authorities responded to a weakening of the pound by imposing tight controls on U.K. bank lending in sterling to nonresidents of the United Kingdom. Encouraged by the Bank of England, U.K. banks turned to dollar lending as the only alternative that would allow them to maintain their leading position in world finance. Although New York had the advantage of being "home base" for the dollar, as well as having a large domestic money and capital market, international trading in the dollar centered in London because of that city's expertise in international monetary matters as well as time and distance proximity to major customers.

Additional support for a European-based dollar market came from the balance of payments difficulties of the United States during the 1960s, which temporarily segmented the U.S. domestic capital market from that of the rest of the world. Passage of the U.S. interest equalization tax in 1963 effectively closed the U.S. capital markets to foreign issues. This action encouraged the creation of alternative sources of medium- and long-term funds in the Eurocurrency and newly created Eurobond markets. The Federal Reserve System's foreign credit restraint program prevented foreign borrowers, including U.S.-owned foreign affiliates, from medium-term borrowing in the United States, thus reinforcing the need for banking alternatives in Europe. Finally, restrictions on U.S. foreign direct investment, which began on a voluntary basis in 1965 but became mandatory in 1968, forced U.S. multinational firms to source funds needed for overseas operations outside the United States, i.e., in the Eurocurrency and Eurobonds markets. Although these restrictions were removed in 1974, their effect at the time was to direct attention to the efficiency of the Eurodollar market.

The key factor attracting both depositors and borrowers to the Eurodollar market is the narrower interest rate spread within that market. The difference between deposit and loan rates is often less than 1%. As shown conceptually in Exhibit 11.4, depositors can earn more in the Eurodollar market than in the United States, while, at the same time, borrowers can borrow for less.

Interest spreads in the Eurodollar market are small for a number of reasons. Low lending rates exist because the Eurodollar market is a

EXHIBIT 11.4
Concept of Narrower Spread between Lending and Deposit Rates in the Eurodollar Market

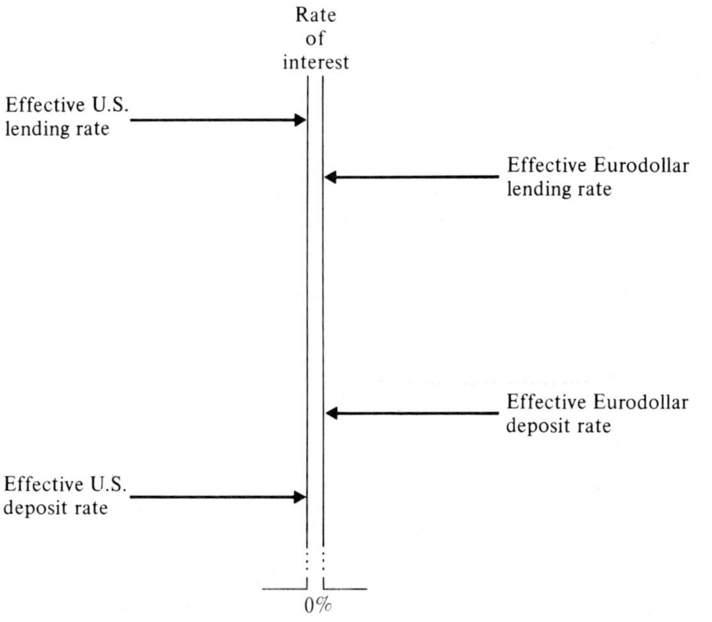

"wholesale" market, where deposits are made in amounts of $500,000 or more on an unsecured basis. Borrowers are usually large corporations or government entities that qualify for low rates because of their credit standing and because the transaction size is large. In addition, overhead assigned to the Eurodollar operation by participating banks is small.

Deposit rates are higher in the Eurodollar market than in the U.S. domestic market because banks need not comply with U.S. reserve requirements, nor are they subject to "jawboning" guidance in the interest of domestic monetary policy. Prior to July 1, 1973, all time and savings deposits in U.S. banks were subject to interest rate ceilings under Regulation Q. Since that date single-maturity time deposits in denominations of $100,000 or more have been free of interest rate ceilings, but all other deposits remain regulated. Eurodollar deposits are not subject to such regulation. In addition, Eurodollar deposits are not subject to the Federal Deposit Insurance Corporation assessments paid on domestic dollar deposits.

Eurodollar Bank Loans

Eurodollar bank loans are also called "Eurodollar credits" or simply "Eurocredits." The latter title is broader because it encompasses nondollar loans in the Eurocurrency market. Eurocredits are bank loans to business firms, sovereign governments, and to other banks, denominated in Eurocurrencies and extended by banks in countries other than the country in whose currency the loan is denominated.

The basic borrowing rate for Eurodollar loans has long been tied to the London Interbank Offered Rate (LIBOR), which is the deposit rate applicable to interbank loans within London. In the early 1980s, however, use of this LIBOR base was supplemented by use of a U.S. money market rate base. Consequently, as of the mid-1980s both rates serve as the base for different credits. Borrowers pay a premium over the base rate determined by their creditworthiness and the terms of the credit.

Eurodollars are lent for both short- and medium-term maturities, with transactions for six months or less regarded as routine. Most Eurodollar loans are for a fixed term with no provision for early repayment. Eurobanks may do three things with their deposits. First, they may redeposit them in another Eurobank. This process, which can be repeated a number of times, creates a chain of interbank deposits that gives the appearance of more Eurodollars than can be borrowed. No fundamental extension of bank credit to final commercial users has taken place.

The second possibility is to make a loan to a nonbank user, who may use the dollars to pay obligations, or may exchange them for local currency. The cost of such a loan, including the cost of forward cover, may be less than the cost of a direct local currency loan. Imperfect markets create such apparent arbitrage opportunities. Only large firms have access to Eurodollar loans, but interest rates in domestic markets are determined with reference to all borrowers, including those with no access to the Eurodollar market. Domestic interest rates are also influenced by domestic monetary policies, and, in addition, taxes may differ in the two jurisdictions. Lastly, local banks may be required to hold reserves or pay for deposit insurance, costs which do not exist in the Eurodollar market.

The third possible use of a Eurodollar bank deposit is for the receiving bank, if not a U.S. branch, to redeposit the Eurodollars in a U.S. branch bank. U.S. branches also receive Eurodollar deposits directly from nonbank sources. In either instance, the U.S. branch may relend the dollars to its U.S. parent for ultimate relending to U.S. clients of the home office, especially during periods of tight money in the United States.

Standby Eurodollar credits are of two types: "a Eurodollar line of credit" and a "Eurodollar revolving commitment." Under a Eurodollar line of credit, a bank promises to lend Eurodollars up to the credit limit, with the interest rate determined by market conditions when the loan is made. Because the line of credit can be canceled by the bank at any time, the arrangement is essentially one of preparing for borrowing in advance.

Under a Eurodollar revolving commitment, a bank agrees to lend for a period of perhaps three to five years by accepting a series of sequential notes of short maturity. For example, the borrower may renew a series of 180-day notes at each maturity at the interest rate then in effect. Banks charge a fee of about 0.5% per annum on the unused portion of such a revolving, nonrevokable commitment.

Floating Interest Rates and Loan Syndication

Development of the concept of floating interest rates during the 1970s was a major force in the development of the Eurodollar market, as well as the Eurobond market. The combination of floating rates, premiums over LIBOR, and the creation of large syndicated loans kept the Eurocredit market viable during a period of variable interest rates and inflation in most major countries.[6]

The floating rate formula provides for a periodic change in the rate of interest charged on loans as well as in the rate paid on time deposits. Interest rates are negotiated on the basis that the rate will be changed every three or six months in response to any change in a defined base rate. The most common base rate is LIBOR; however, as mentioned earlier, U.S. money market rates, such as the U.S. Treasury bill or prime rates, are sometimes used as a base. Contractual floating rates for loans or for deposits are expressed as a spread, or premium, above the base rate.

The major result of the shift to floating rates is that creditors and depositors alike have been willing to commit funds for longer maturities. Under the older fixed rate system, a bank that loaned funds long term, but sourced the funds for that loan from short-term deposits, ran a risk that its funding sources would dry up, or that costs would escalate while the funds were committed at a fixed rate for a longer maturity. Depositors hesitated to place funds for longer maturities because of the risk that they would not be able to benefit from any rise in interest rates.

The syndication of most loans in recent years has enabled banks to spread the risk of very large loans among a number of banks. Syndication has been particularly important because many large multinational firms needed credit in excess of a single bank's loan limit. A syndicated bank loan is arranged by a lead bank on behalf of its client. Before finalizing the loan agreement, the lead bank seeks the participation of a group (syndicate) of banks, with each participant providing a portion of the total funds needed.

Eurodollar Deposits

Eurodollar deposits are either for a specific term, or are negotiable certificates of deposit (CDs). At one time the rates paid on straight term deposits were fixed for the maturity of the deposit. More recently, however, time deposits are accepted as "roll-over credits" on which interest is paid at a floating rate that is adjusted every three or six months to match changes in money market rates.

Under straight term deposits, if the depositor wants to withdraw funds before maturity, permission of the bank must be obtained. However, such permission is rarely sought because of embarrassment on the depositor's part for having to admit to poor liquidity planning. Most corporate depositors would prefer to borrow Eurodollars if caught short of funds.

A negotiable certificate of deposit, or "CD," is an instrument issued by a bank as a receipt for the deposit of a stated amount of money for a stated maturity at a fixed or floating rate of interest. Because the CD is negotiable, it may be traded in the money market. Consequently the original depositor need not wait until maturity to recover funds represented by the principal amount of the deposit; the depositor simply sells the CD in the money market.

Eurodollar CDs, also called "London dollar CDs," were first offered in 1966 by the London Branch of Citibank. Currently, well over 100 banks issue negotiable CDs. An active secondary market is maintained by about 20 broker/dealer firms who are members of the International CD Market Association, established in London in 1968 to standardize dealing practices.

Two types of CDs are issued. A "tap" CD is the more normal version. The issuing bank "taps" the market by offering for sale CDs of a particular maturity or yield. Tap CDs are available for maturities of less than one year in multiples of $1,000, with a usual minimum purchase amount of $25,000. However, such small issues do not command rates as high as those available on larger purchases. Maturities are normally for exact terms of from 1 to 12 months, with 3- and 6-month maturities most popular. Maturities of 48 hours and of 7 days are possible, as are maturities up to 5 years, the maximum allowed by British monetary authorities. For maturities over a year, tap CDs are usually issued in total amounts above $250,000.

The second type of CD is a "tranche" CD. The tranche CD is not a single certificate but is rather a series of identical "tranches," each with a smaller denomination, such as $10,000 or $25,000, but with identical yields, interest payments dates, and maturities. Tranche issues are usually offered in amounts of from $15 million to $25 million in a public offering intended to be widely distributed in the financial world. Because individual parts of the tranche can be liquidated, the tranche CD resembles an intermediate-term bond issued by a commercial bank more than a pure money market instrument.

With the advent of the five-currency-based SDR in 1980, seven London banks began to issue CDs denominated in SDRs. The critical factor was the ease of calculating a market rate of interest on the SDR that was, in turn, the weighted average of prevailing interbank rates on dollars, Deutschemarks, yen, French francs, and the U.K. pound. SDR CDs are sold to institutional investors in minimum denominations of one million SDRs, and a secondary market is maintained by Credit Suisse–First Boston.

ASIAN CURRENCY MARKET

An Asian version of the Eurocurrency market was created in October 1968, when the government of Singapore granted permission to the Singapore branch of Bank of America to accept foreign currency deposits in the same manner as was being done in Europe. The logic for a separate Asian dollar market (ADM), as it is also called, came from the observation that many Asians, including large numbers of overseas Chinese, had dollars or other foreign currencies whose existence they did not wish to reveal to their local governments. Other holders of convertible currencies in Asia were U.S., Japanese, and other multinational firms operating in the area, and central banks and treasuries of Asian governments. Because Asian money markets were not developed, these funds were either held at no interest or deposited far away in the Eurodollar market. In either event, the excess funds were eventually loaned to businesses operating in Europe or the United States, rather than to the many capital-short industries of Asia.

In its early years the Asian currency market provided an intermediation function between the Asian dollar and the Eurocurrency markets, as Asian dollar deposits in Singapore were re-lent to banks in Europe. However, the Asian currency market soon developed its own network of regional lending opportunities that provided a way for surplus Asian funds as well as additional European funds to be channeled into Asian projects. The market also provides a mechanism for arbitrage between foreign exchange and money markets in Asia, the Middle East, and Europe.

Creation of the Market

Singapore created the Asian currency market by removing a then-existing withholding tax on interest paid on nonresident deposits, by reducing from 40% to 10% the income tax levied on interest earned from offshore loans, and granting Asian Currency Unit (ACU) licenses to qualifying banks located in Singapore. Singapore was willing to do this for three reasons: (1) income earned on the enlarged financial services would improve the city-state's balance of payments, (2) dependence on international trade as a source of economic growth would be reduced, and (3) Singapore would be one step ahead of potential competition for becoming a major Asian international financial center. Although at that time Hong Kong and Tokyo seemed more logical locations for a regional financial center, Hong Kong was not willing to remove its 15% withholding tax on interest earned from offshore currency transactions, and Japanese financial markets and institutions were rigidly protected from the influence of free markets. (Hong Kong has since removed its 15% tax, and Japan is in the process of liberalizing its capital market.)

Market Size

The Asian currency market is primarily an interbank market, as can be seen from the balance sheet in Exhibit 11.5. Almost 25% of total assets are in the form of loans to nonbank customers, primarily to manufacturing firms and to nonbank financial institutions outside Singapore. The majority of loans, some 47% of total assets, are to banks located outside Singapore but in the Asia-Pacific region.

The basic rate in the Asian dollar market is the Singapore Interbank Offered Rate, or SIBOR. Floating rate certificates of deposit are issued by Singapore banks and carry a small premium over SIBOR.

On the deposit side, some 16% of liabilities are derived from nonbank customers, with most of the remainder from banks, primarily from outside Singapore. The largest net supplier of funds to ACUs is the London Eurocurrency market, with Middle Eastern countries also an important source.

Most ACU deposits are in U.S. dollars, but Japanese yen, Dutch guilders, Swiss francs, Deutschemarks, and British pounds are accepted. Regular deposits are accepted in amounts as low as US$25,000. No withholding or other tax is deducted from interest paid on deposits, and no restrictions are applied to the inward or outward remittance of funds. The minimum deposit maturity is one month.

EXHIBIT 11.5
Asian Currency Units: Assets and Liabilities, March 31, 1985
(in millions of U.S. dollars)

Assets		
Loans to nonbank customers	$ 33,855.4	24.9%
Interbank funds		
In Singapore	3,591.4	2.6
Inter-ACU	24,364.6	18.0
Outside Singapore	64,156.0	47.3
	92,112.0	67.9
Other assets	9,729.2	7.2
Total	$135,696.6	100.0%
Liabilities		
Deposits of nonbank customers	$ 21,990.9	16.2%
Interbank funds		
In Singapore	2,218.4	1.6
Inter-ACU	24,375.2	18.0
Outside Singapore	80,534.8	59.3
	107,128.4	78.9
Other liabilities	6,577.3	4.9
Total	$135,696.6	100.0%

Source: Monetary Authority of Singapore, *Annual Report 1984/1985*, p. 37.

The Asian dollar market has one unique advantage—it exists as an offshore dollar market in an Asian time zone. By filling in the time gap between the U.S. Pacific Coast and Europe, the market contributes to the existence of 24-hour trading in dollar deposits. During the morning in Singapore, business is conducted with Sydney (two hours ahead), Tokyo (one hour ahead), and Hong Kong (same time zone). By afternoon business can be conducted with London (seven hours behind) and the rest of Europe.

INTERNATIONAL BOND MARKET

An *international bond* is initially offered to investors outside the country of the borrower. International bonds are either "Eurobonds" or "foreign bonds." A Eurobond is underwritten by an international syndicate of banks and other securities firms, and is sold exclusively in countries other than the country in whose currency the issue is denominated. For example, a bond issued by a U.S. corporation, denominated in U.S. dollars but sold to investors in Europe and Japan (not to investors in the United States) would be a Eurobond.

A foreign bond, in contrast, is underwritten by a syndicate composed of members from a single country, sold principally within that country, and denominated in the currency of that country. The issuer, however, is from another country. A bond issued by a Swedish corporation, denominated in dollars, and sold in the United States to U.S. investors by U.S. investment bankers, would be a foreign bond. Foreign bonds have nicknames: Foreign bonds sold in the United States are "Yankee bonds"; foreign bonds sold in Japan are "Samurai bonds"; and foreign bonds sold in the United Kingdom are "Bulldogs."

Size of the Market

Exhibit 11.6 shows both Eurobond and foreign bond issues from 1981 through 1984. In 1984, Eurobond issues totaled $80,240 million and foreign bond issues were $27,430 million, for a total $107,670 million of international bond issues. U.S. dollar denominated Eurobonds at $64,290 million were 80% of all Eurobond issues. Deutschemark Eurobonds were next in importance. In foreign bonds, Swiss franc issues equal to $13,120 million amounted to 48% of all issues. Other important currencies for foreign bonds are the U.S. dollar, Japanese yen, and Deutschemark.

The location of borrower for both Eurobonds and foreign bonds is shown in Exhibit 11.7, derived from data in Exhibit 11.6.

Some 41.5% of all Eurobonds were issued by European borrowers, with an additional 28.8% raised by U.S. borrowers. The rest of the world, which includes all developing countries, borrowed only 2.5% of total Eurobond issues. Australia, Japan, New Zealand, and South Africa borrowed 30.8% of all foreign bond issues, with Japan being most important. International institutions, such as the World Bank, are major borrowers in the foreign bond market since their issues are sometimes given priority access to domestic capital markets by government regulators.

Eurobond Market

Eurobonds are issued by multinational corporations, large domestic corporations, sovereign governments, governmental enterprises, and international institutions. They are offered simultaneously in a number of different national capital markets, but not in the capital market of the country, nor to residents of the country, in whose currency the bond is denominated. Almost all Eurobonds are in bearer form with call provisions and sinking funds.

The syndicate that offers a new issue of Eurobonds might be composed of underwriters from a number of countries, including European banks, foreign branches of U.S. banks, banks from offshore financial centers, in-

EXHIBIT 11.6
International Bond Issues[a] (in millions of U.S. dollars)

		EUROBOND ISSUES			*FOREIGN ISSUES*		
			of which			*of which*	
Borrowing countries or areas	*Years*	*Total*	*U.S. dollars*	*Deutsche-marks*	*Total*	*in United States*	*in Switzer-land*
Western Europe	1981	7,650	5,230	880	5,390	640	3,070
	1982	16,550	12,690	1,930	5,250	780	2,350
	1983	22,770	16,630	2,410	6,700	1,360	2,490
	1984	33,310	26,370	2,160	7,190	2,180	2,130
Canada	1981	5,500	4,550	130	5,450	4,310	870
	1982	6,920	5,600	100	4,440	2,700	1,330
	1983	3,840	2,660	360	2,910	1,630	1,220
	1984	4,490	2,650	180	1,760	450	1,040
United States	1981	6,050	5,890	30	700		700
	1982	13,020	12,340	530	1,790		1,470
	1983	6,070	5,680	220	1,240		1,180
	1984	23,100	21,210	540	1,460		1,220
Other developed countries[b]	1981	3,460	2,730	230	2,820	100	2,360
	1982	3,860	3,050	480	5,740	400	4,440
	1983	6,060	4,760	830	8,300	530	7,140
	1984	13,080	10,450	1,270	8,450	150	7,180
Rest of the world	1981	2,330	2,080	90	1,120	440	90
	1982	2,820	2,510	210	520	—	200
	1983	1,680	1,510	160	630	—	100
	1984	2,040	1,810	30	990	—	170
International institutions	1981	2,490	1,700	40	6,030	2,070	1,200
	1982	3,280	2,490	—	7,460	2,150	1,530
	1983	6,070	4,500	60	7,270	1,220	1,370
	1984	4,220	1,800	140	7,580	1,000	1,380
Total issues placed	1981	27,480	22,180	1,400	21,510	7,560	8,290
	1982	46,450	38,680	3,250	25,200	6,030	11,320
	1983	46,490	35,740	4,040	27,050	4,740	13,500
	1984	80,240	64,290	4,320	27,430	3,780	13,120

Source: Bank for International Settlements, *Annual Report,* Basle, Switzerland, June 10, 1985, p. 120.

[a]Data based on OECD sources, but excluding certificates of deposit.

[b]Australia, Japan, New Zealand, and South Africa.

EXHIBIT 11.7
Location of Borrower for International Bond Issues, 1984
(in millions of U.S. dollars and by percentages)

	EUROBONDS		*FOREIGN BONDS*	
	Amount	*Percentage*	*Amount*	*Percentage*
Western Europe	$33,310	41.5%	$ 7,190	26.2%
Canada	4,490	5.6	1,760	6.4
United States	23,100	28.8	1,460	5.3
Other developed countries[a]	13,080	16.3	8,450	30.8
Rest of the world	2,040	2.5	990	3.6
International institutions	4,220	5.3	7,580	27.6
Total	$80,240	100.0%	$27,430	100.0%

[a]Other developed countries are Australia, Japan, New Zealand, and South Africa.

vestment and merchant banks, and nonbank securities firms. In the United States, commercial banks may not underwrite corporate securities, but foreign branches may do so. This distinction does not exist in most of the world, where commercial banks also act as major underwriters and distributors of new issues of securities.

Although the Eurobond market evolved at about the same time as the Eurodollar market, the two markets exist for different reasons, and each could exist independently of the other. The Eurobond market owes its existence to several unique factors, some of which have changed recently. Three of the original factors still of importance are: absence of regulatory interference, less stringent disclosure practices, and favorable tax treatment.

Absence of regulatory interference National governments often impose tight controls on foreign issuers of securities denominated in the local currency and sold within their national boundaries. However, governments in general have less stringent limitations for securities denominated in foreign currencies and sold within their markets to holders of those foreign currencies. In effect, Eurobond sales fall outside the regulatory domain of any single nation.

Less stringent disclosure Disclosure requirements in the Eurobond market are much less stringent than those of the Securities and Exchange Commission for sales within the United States. U.S. firms often find that the registration costs of a Eurobond offering are less than those of a domestic issue and that less time is needed to bring a new issue to market. Non-U.S. firms often prefer Eurodollar bonds over bonds sold within the United

States because they do not wish to undergo the costs, and disclosure, needed to register with the Securities and Exchange Commission. For example, top foreign executives resist strongly the idea that their salaries should be public information, or that trading in the shares of their own company should be reported. Preparing foreign financial statements according to U.S. accounting principles is costly and requires more detailed disclosure of operations, such as industry segment breakdown, than is typically required in other countries.

Favorable tax status Eurobonds offer tax anonymity and flexibility. Interest paid on Eurobonds is generally not subject to an income withholding tax. As one might suspect, Eurobond interest is not always reported to tax authorities.

Prior to June 1984, U.S. corporations issuing Eurobonds were required to withhold up to 30% of each interest payment to foreigners for U.S. income taxes. The rate depended on the foreigner's country of residence and the bilateral tax treaty between that country and the United States. U.S. corporations wishing to issue Eurobonds had to do so through offshore finance affiliates, typically in the Netherlands Antilles, in order to avoid this tax. In 1984, however, the U.S. tax laws were revised to exempt foreign holders of bonds issued by U.S. corporations from any withholding tax. U.S. corporations found it feasible for the first time to sell Eurobonds directly to foreigners. Repeal of the U.S. withholding tax caused other governments, including those of France, West Germany, and Japan, to liberalize their tax rules as a defensive measure to avoid an outflow of capital from their markets.

Eurobonds are usually issued in bearer form, meaning that the name and country of residence of the owner is not on the certificate. To receive interest, the bearer cuts an interest coupon from the bond and turns it in at a bank. European investors are accustomed to the privacy provided by bearer bonds and are very reluctant to purchase registered bonds, which require holders to reveal their names before they receive interest. Bearer bond status, of course, is also tied to tax avoidance.

Euroyen Bonds

In 1984, the Japanese government relaxed its regulations to allow non-Japanese corporations to issue yen-denominated bonds outside of Japan, and in 1985 Japan removed a 20% withholding tax previously levied on interest paid to foreign bondholders by Japanese corporations. The withholding tax had prevented Japanese corporations from raising funds in the Euroyen market. Both of these steps have been interpreted as efforts by the Japanese government to open its capital market and make the yen a major international currency. Within months of the initial liberalization of the

Euroyen bond market, several large U.S. corporations, including Sears Roebuck & Company and Dow Chemical, issued Euroyen bonds.

Japanese companies find the Euroyen bond market attractive as a source of funds. Interest rates are slightly lower than rates on domestically issued yen bonds because they are in bearer form and international investors will accept a lower yield in return for anonymity. Additionally, collateral is usually required behind domestic Japanese bonds, but is not needed in the Euroyen bond market.[7]

Under the newly liberalized rules, syndicates offering Euroyen bonds may be headed by non-Japanese investment banking firms. The Euroyen market now enables non-Japanese corporations to raise funds in yen, whereas previously they could only issue Samurai bonds within Japan. The process of complying with Japanese requirements to issue Samurai bonds was very complicated and time-consuming.[8]

In the mid-1980s, Japanese and foreign banks were also permitted to issue Euroyen certificates of deposit in bearer form. Euroyen CDs are exempt from Japanese withholding tax and are traded in the secondary market.

Rating of Eurobonds and Other International Issues

Purchasers of Eurobonds do not typically rely on bond-rating services or on detailed analyses of financial statements. General reputation of the issuing corporation and its underwriters has been the major factor in obtaining favorable terms. For this reason, larger and better-known multinational firms, state enterprises, and sovereign governments are able to obtain the lowest interest rates. Firms whose names are better known to the general public, possibly because they manufacture consumer goods, are often believed to have an advantage over equally qualified firms whose products are less widely known.

Moody's and Standard & Poor's (S&P's) both provide ratings for selected international bonds for a fee.[9] S&P's ratings for international bonds imply the same creditworthiness as for domestic bonds of U.S. issuers. S&P's limits its evaluation to the issuer's ability to obtain the necessary currency to repay the issue according to the original terms of the bond, and excludes any assessment of risk to the investor caused by changing exchange rates.

S&P's rates international bonds on request of the issuer. Based on supporting financial statements and other material obtained from the issuer, a preliminary rating is made. The issuer is then informed and given an opportunity to comment. After S&P's determines its final rating, the issuer may decide not to have the rating published. Consequently a disproportionately large number of published international ratings fall into the highest categories, since issuers about to receive a lower rating often decide not to have the rating published.

S&P's review of political risk includes study of the government system, the social environment, and the nation's external relations. Its review of economic risk looks at debt burden, international liquidity, balance of payments flexibility, economic structure, growth performance, economic management, and economic outlook. S&P's also evaluates the bonds of sovereign-supported entities by looking first at their creditworthiness on a stand-alone basis, and then looking at the extent to which sovereign support either enhances or diminishes the borrower's financial strength.

Innovations in the Eurobond Market

The Eurobond market is the most competitive capital market in the world. Each year new innovations in the types of securities are devised to appeal to issuers and investors with particular needs. Some recent innovations are stripped bonds, floating rate notes, currency and interest rate swaps, partly paid bonds, dual currency bonds, and currency cocktail bonds.

Stripped bonds In 1985 the U.S. Treasury gave serious consideration to issuing U.S. government bonds in bearer form in order to sell them to foreigners. Congressional critics, however, argued that such bonds might be purchased by (or for) U.S. citizens to evade taxes. Eventually the Treasury decided against issuing bearer bonds. Nevertheless, new Treasury regulations permit U.S. corporations to sell bearer bonds to foreign residents. In addition, securities firms may buy U.S. Treasury securities, repackage them in trusts, and resell claims on the trust to foreigners in bearer form. These are called "stripped" bonds.

One form of stripped Treasury bonds sold by a syndicate headed by Salomon Brothers, Inc., goes by the acronym of "CATS," which stands for "Certificates of Accrual on Treasury Securities." CATS were first offered in August 1984 as deep discount bonds in bearer form to foreign investors and in registered form to U.S. investors. The two forms are interchangeable, so that bearer bonds resold by foreigners to U.S. residents will be exchanged for registered certificates, and vice versa. Deep discount bonds are sold at a fraction of their maturity value, with the investor's profit derived entirely from recovering the higher maturity value. Such bonds are particularly popular with investors from countries that consider all appreciation as capital gains subject to preferential tax treatment or no tax at all.

In a CATS offering, interest coupons are stripped from the maturity or "corpus" portion of the Treasury bonds. Certificates are then sold against each set of coupons for each interest date as well as against the corpus portion. Hence each CATS is a zero-coupon bond that pays no interest and is sold at a deep discount from maturity value. In its first CATS issue, Salomon Brothers offered $5.3 billion of coupon CATS due semiannually from February 15, 1985, to August 15, 2009; and a corpus CATS consisting of a claim on the $1.7 billion principal callable August 15, 2009, and maturing August 15, 2014. The corpus portion of the Salomon Brothers issue was offered at $595 for a $1,000 bond, to yield an effective 11⅝%.[10]

Floating rate notes Floating rate notes (FRNs) are marketable securities, issued by sovereign nations, state enterprises, and other top-quality borrowers, to raise funds directly from investors. FRNs are underwritten by investment bankers as an alternative to medium and long term syndicated bank loans in the Eurocurrency market. FRNs sell at lower interest rate margins over LIBOR, have slightly longer maturities than syndicated bank loans, and provide a higher yield to investors. Therefore, competition from FRNs is causing commercial bank syndicates to lose some of their highest quality borrowers and depositors. However, banks themselves have at times issued FRNs to raise additional capital.

Currency swaps and interest rate swaps A swap in the Eurobond market is an exchange of financial obligations between two parties, each of whom has incurred a financial obligation in a currency or in a type of interest payment that was not really desired, but was perhaps cheaper. A Eurobond swap agreement can be a currency swap, an interest rate swap, or both.

Currency swaps enable borrowers to exchange the debt service obligations on bonds denominated in one currency for the service on similar debt denominated in another currency. By swapping their future cash flow obligations, two parties are able to alter their currency exposure.

Currency swaps have been in existence for many years, and some of the early types were explained in Chapter 7. The usual motivation for a currency swap in the Eurobond market is to replace cash outflows scheduled in an "undesired" currency with outflows in a "desired" currency. The "undesired" currency was probably borrowed on better terms, but the "desired" currency is probably that in which the firm's future operating revenue will be generated. Preferential financial terms in a particular currency arise because of market imperfections caused by such factors as a firm's greater access to borrowing in its home currency, the novelty of a particular debt issue, governmental regulations, and investor preference for buying bonds of domestic firms.[11]

Interest rate swaps involve exchanging cash flows of a floating rate obligation for the cash flows of a fixed rate obligation. Interest rate swaps are sought when a firm has revenue that varies with the level of interest rates but costs of debt that are fixed. The counterpart for a trade might be another firm whose revenue does not change with interest rates, but which can borrow advantageously on a floating rate basis. Each firm can finance on its own best terms, and then exchange its financial obligations for an alternate set of financial obligations better suited to its expected revenue stream.[12]

Partly paid bonds Partly paid bonds have been issued in U.S. dollars and sold to foreign investors who want U.S.-denominated assets now but believe that both dollar interest rates and the foreign exchange value of the dollar will drop within a few months. The bonds are purchased in, say, January, by a down payment of 30% of the purchase price to the issuer. The remaining 70% is due six months later, in July. If the buyer's forecast is correct, the July payment will cost less in its home currency in July than it would have cost in January, while the higher interest rate of January is locked in. If, by July, interest rates have declined, the value of the bond will rise above par. Having paid in only 30%, the buyer has leveraged the return on the down payment upwards. In other words, if the bond rose in price from $1,000 to $1,050, an increase of 5%, the investor's equity has risen from $300 to $350, an increase of 16.7%. This could be partially offset by the lower value of the bond in terms of other currencies than the dollar.

Partly paid bonds have been issued by such firms as Coca-Cola Company, Sears Roebuck, Security Pacific National Bank, Deutsche Bank, and Volvo. The bonds have had particular appeal to Japanese investors.[13]

Dual currency bonds Dual currency bonds require the issuer to pay interest in one currency, but repay principal in another. The issuer achieves some of the advantages of an interest rate swap. In a 1985 offering, a subsidiary of Colgate-Palmolive sold ten-year Swiss-franc denominated bonds paying 7% interest in Swiss francs. However, the face amount, nominally SF5,000, will be redeemed only for US$2,600. Other dual currency bonds have been issued, for example, paying yen interest but redeemable in U.S. dollars.[14]

The dual currency bond allows the issuer to avoid part of the cost of swapping its liabilities into another currency. After exchanging the Swiss francs received on the sale of the bonds into U.S. dollars, the Colgate-Palmolive subsidiary need only swap its interest liability into dollars to have a complete dollar liability. By using dual currency bonds, Colgate-Palmolive calculated that it saved 17 basis points (0.17%) in interest charges. The issue was sold at a time when the dollar was declining in value relative to the Swiss franc, thus making investors more willing to acquire a dual currency bond. Investors in such issues are reported to be small investors based in Switzerland who like the Swiss franc yield, which is higher than the yield available on domestic Swiss issues. They are willing to risk a change in the Swiss franc value of the dollar at redemption.

Currency cocktail bonds Currency cocktail bonds are denominated in one of several currency baskets, such as SDRs or ECUs. Currency cocktail bonds have been issued from time to time since the mid-1970s. They appeal to investors because interest and principal payments should be more stable than the value of any one of the component currencies because of currency diversification. Such bonds are particularly useful for corporations whose cash receipts from sales are in a variety of currencies. Conceptually some of those currencies will be rising in value while others will be dropping. The net result could parallel the value of the currency cocktail bond.

THE INTERNATIONAL MARKET FOR EQUITIES

More and more, firms of one country are listing their shares on the stock exchanges of other countries. The London Stock Exchange now has over 500 foreign listings, of which about 200 are U.S. firms. Shares of 10 U.S. firms are listed on the Tokyo Stock Exchange, and about 50 non-U.S. firms are listed on the New York Stock Exchange. Some 250 foreign stocks are registered with the U.S. Securities and Exchange Commission. Those not listed on any of the organized U.S. exchanges are traded in the U.S. over-the-counter market.

American Depositary Receipts

In the United States, foreign shares are usually traded through American Depositary Receipts, or ADRs. These are negotiable certificates issued by a U.S. bank in the United States to represent the underlying shares of stock, which are held in trust at a custodian bank in the foreign country. ADRs are sold, registered, and transferred in the United States in the same manner as any share of stock, with each ADR share representing some multiple of a share of the underlying foreign stock. This permits ADRs to trade in an appropriate price range for the U.S. market even if the price of the foreign share is inappropriate when converted to U.S. dollars.

ADRs can be exchanged for the underlying foreign shares, or vice versa, so arbitrage activities keep foreign and U.S. prices of any given share the same. For example, investor demand in one market will cause a price rise there, which will cause an equivalent price in the other market even when investors there are not as bullish on the stock.

ADRs convey certain technical advantages to U.S. shareholders. Dividends paid by a foreign firm are passed to its foreign custodial bank and then to the U.S. bank that issued the ADR. The U.S. bank exchanges the foreign currency dividends for U.S. dollars and sends the dollar dividend to the ADR holders. ADRs are in registered form, rather than in bearer form. Transfer of ownership is facilitated because it is done in the United States in accordance with U.S. laws and procedures, and in the event of the death of a shareholder the estate need not go through probate in a foreign court system.

ADRs are either "sponsored" or "unsponsored." Sponsored ADRs are created at the request of a foreign firm wanting its shares traded in the United States. The firm applies to the Securities and Exchange Commission and a U.S. bank for registration and issuance of ADRs. The foreign firm pays all costs of creating such sponsored ADRs. If a foreign firm does not seek to have its shares traded in the United States but U.S. investors are interested, a U.S. securities firm may initiate creation of the ADRs. Such an ADR would be unsponsored.

Size of International Equity Markets

Statistics on U.S., Japanese, and European stock exchanges at the end of 1983 are given in Exhibit 11.8, which shows that almost all of the major stock exchanges of the world have sizable listings of foreign stocks. The number of foreign firms listed on the Amsterdam exchange even exceeds the number of domestic firms. The New York Stock Exchange is the largest exchange in terms of market value and trading volume value of domestic firms, but the London Stock Exchange has the greatest number of firms listed. Trading volume in shares (not shown in the exhibit) is largest on the Tokyo Stock Exchange, which is also the second largest in the world in terms of market capitalization of shares listed.

Unique Attributes of World Stock Exchanges

U.S. investors might assume that other stock exchanges operate in a style similar to that of the New York Stock Exchange. Nothing could be further from the truth, as can be seen from the following list of unique attributes of some of the world's major exchanges. Many of these attributes influence how prices in that market respond to buying and selling pressure.

In Frankfurt, a 5% limit on price movement in any day is imposed by the exchange. In both Frankfurt and Zurich only banks may provide brokerage services. Independent stock brokers and dealers do not exist, and the banks consequently monopolize access to the exchanges. German banks also have a monopoly on investment banking, so that sale of both new and already-issued shares is handled by the same institution.

Japanese investors are accustomed to paying much higher price-earnings ratios than U.S. investors. However, the yen price of a Japanese stock is very low, and certificates are issued only in multiples of one thousand shares. One thousand shares is also the unit of trading on the Tokyo Stock Exchange, and odd lots are recorded only on the company's books without issuance of a certificate. Odd lots are sold back to the company at the then-current stock price.

The Paris Stock Exchange has a "spot" and a "forward" section. Prices on the Paris spot market are set at a daily fixing, at which an exchange employee, or a member who does no trading, collects all unfilled bids and offers, including orders with price limits attached, and then selects the price that will accommodate the most orders. After the fixing, shares may be

EXHIBIT 11.8

Market Statistics on U.S., Japanese, and European Stock Exchanges in 1983

All values translated to U.S. dollar at year-end rates

Country	*Stock exchange*	*Market value of domestic firms*[a] *(US$ millions)*	*NO. LISTED FIRMS*		*Trading volume of domestic firms (US$ millions)*	*VOLUME*	*VALUE*[d]	*Concentration of ten largest domestic firms*[e]
			Domestic	*Foreign*		*Value*	*No. firms*	
United States	New York	1,522,160 (48%)	1,500	50	765,275[b]	50.28%	1,015	15% of total value
	American	57,574	774	48	31,848[b]	55.32%	74	Not available
Japan	Tokyo	545,848 (17%)	1,441	11	230,906	42.30%	379	18% of total value
U.K.	London	225,837 (7%)	2,217	515	42,576[b]	18.87%	102	28% of total value
Germany	Association of German Exchanges	82,870 (2.6%)	442	173	32,949	39.76%	187	45% of total value
Switzerland	Zurich	44,081 (1.4%)	120	164	Not available	—	367	59% of total value
France	Paris	38,139 (1.2%)	518	179	8,345	21.88%	74	24% of total value
Netherlands	Amsterdam	33,742 (1.1%)	215	256	10,182	30.18%	157	81% of total value
Sweden	Stockholm	30,245 (<1%)	145	5	9,847	32.56%	209	47% of total value
Italy	Milan	20,909 (<1%)	138	0	3,872	18.52%	152	54% of total value
Belgium	Brussels	10,879 (<1%)	204	138	1,432	13.29%	53	52% of total value
Spain	Madrid	10,861 (<1%)	394	0	956	8.80%	28	52% of total value
Denmark	Copenhagen	10,557 (<1%)	211	4	182	1.72%	50	Not available
Norway	Oslo	4,585 (<1%)	113	6	445	9.71%	41	Not available
Finland	Helsinki	4,134 (<1%)	48	0	250	6.05%	86	Not available
Austria	Vienna	1,528 (<1%)	62	36	133[b]	8.70%	25	36% of total value

Source: Gabriel Hawawini, *European Equity Markets: Price Behavior and Efficiency*, New York: Salomon Brothers Center for the Study of Financial Institutions and the Graduate School of Business Administration of New York University, Monograph 1984-4/5.

[a]Percentage based on a total world market value of equity of 3,153,800 millions of U.S. dollars. The source of the original statistics used to draw the table is: *The International Federation of Stock Exchanges* (22, Boulevard de Courcelles, 75017 Paris, France)

[b]All firms. No data available for domestic firms.

[c]Trading volume is from the preceding column. Market value is for domestic firms (third column).

[d]This average market value is calculated for domestic firms.

[e]As a percentage of the total market value of equity on April 26, 1985, according to *Capital International Perspective*, Geneva, Switzerland (1985).

traded at other prices as brokers attempt to complete unfilled orders. However, the daily fixing price is the official price reported in the newspapers. Consequently investors may find their orders executed at prices that cannot be verified from the daily newspaper as having occurred.

In Zurich, and in the Paris forward market, stocks are "called" for trading. This is referred to as "open outcry" trading, or *à la criée*. All trading in a given stock must take place when its name is called, and stocks may not be traded afterwards. The list of stocks to be traded is called twice a day.

Stock trading in Singapore is by means of an electric trading board. Orders are put into the computer, and the highest bid and lowest offer are displayed on a quote board. When a bid and offer that match are entered into the computer system by an exchange member, the computer effects the trade.

DEVELOPMENT BANKS

A development bank is a financial institution whose lending policy is guided by the perceived economic, social, or political needs of a country or region rather than by commercial goals alone. International and regional development banks loan mainly to governmental borrowers, although some programs by these organizations provide funds for private business. National and private development banks lend almost exclusively to private businesses. Even when development banks are financing governmental projects, such as dams or highways, private businesses may benefit through opportunities to bid on parts of the construction activity.

In general, development banks make intermediate- to long-term loans. If development banks take equity participation in private ventures, their intent is usually to sell that participation to private investors as soon as the venture proves itself viable.

Development banks can be divided into two categories: those associated with the World Bank Group, and regional and national development banks.

World Bank Group

The World Bank Group is a term used to describe three related international financial institutions whose purpose is to help member countries develop their economies. The three institutions are the International Bank for Reconstruction and Development, more frequently called the World Bank, the International Development Association (IDA), and the International Finance Corporation (IFC). Each of the three functions as a specialized agency of the United Nations, having certain international privileges and immunities.

The group is headquartered in Washington, D.C., with other major offices in Paris, London, New York, and Tokyo. The World Bank and IDA are of interest to private multinational businesses primarily because they provide much of the planning and financial impetus for international development projects for which private businesses may be contractors, suppliers, or engineers. By creating improved economic infrastructures, World Bank and IDA projects help create environments in which a wide variety of private businesses may find it advantageous to make follow-up investments in various projects. The IFC is an international organization engaged in a broad range of projects in conjunction with private businesses.

Regional Development Banks

Throughout the world there are many regional development banks, established somewhat in the image of the World Bank and the International Development Association. The six major such banks, in order of date of establishment, are:

1. The European Investment Bank (EIB), established in 1958 by the Treaty of Rome as part of a series of efforts by European countries toward achieving political, economic, and technical integration and cooperation. The EIB's offices are at 2, Place de Metz, Luxembourg, Grand Duchy of Luxembourg.
2. The Inter-American Development Bank (IDB), also known by its Spanish name, Banco Interamericano Desarrollo (BID), established in 1959 by 19 Latin American countries and the United States. The bank's headquarters is at 808 17th Street, N.W., Washington, D.C. 20577.
3. The African Development Bank (AfDB), established in 1964 under the aegis of the United Nations Economic Commission for Africa. Its headquarters is at B.P. 1387, Abidjan, Ivory Coast.
4. The Asian Development Bank (ADB), formed in 1966 by 31 countries. The bank's headquarters is P.O. Box 789, Manila, Philippines 2800.
5. The East African Development Bank (EADB), established in 1967 at the same time as the East African Community. It has three members, Kenya, Uganda, and Tanzania, and is headquartered at Box 1001, Arusha 3181, Tanzania.
6. The Arab Bank for Economic Development in Africa (BADEA), created by the Arab League in 1975. The bank's headquarters is Sharaa el Baladia, P.O.B. 2640, Khartoum, Sudan.

SUMMARY

Multinational corporations and sovereign governments raise significant amounts of capital in international money and capital markets. International financial centers have developed to service these capital needs. They are located in such important centers as New York, London, Tokyo, Zurich, Paris, Frankfurt, Singapore, and Hong Kong and in numerous offshore tax shelters.

The most important international capital market is that based on Eurocurrencies. Not only is the Eurocurrency market a source of short-term credit and a place for short-term deposits, it has evolved into a medium-term market for syndicated loans to finance larger sums.

The Eurobond market has developed in tandem with the Eurocurrency market, although for different reasons. An absence of regulatory interference, less stringent disclosure requirements, and favorable tax treatment have helped the Eurobond market. Recent innovations in the Eurobond market include stripped bonds, floating rate notes, currency swaps, interest rate swaps, partly paid bonds, dual currency bonds, and currency cocktail bonds.

International trading in equities is also growing. In the United States the ADR system is particularly useful for trading in foreign stocks. The most important stock exchanges are located in New York, Tokyo, and London, but numerous smaller exchanges exist. Trading procedures differ widely.

The World Bank Group and various regional and national development banks provide needed infrastructure loans to member countries. This facilitates world trade and direct foreign investment as well as providing a market for private firms to act as contractors and suppliers.

NOTES

1. Excellent overall descriptions of international financial centers can be found in Howard C. Reed, *The Preeminence of International Financial Centers,* New York: Praeger, 1981; and Gunter Dufey and Ian H. Giddy, *The International Money Market,* Englewood Cliffs, N.J.: Prentice-Hall, 1978. For a more concise discussion of the development of Asian financial centers, see Howard C. Reed, "The Ascent of Tokyo as an International Financial Center," *Journal of International Business Studies,* Winter 1980, pp. 19–35.

2. R. A. Jones, "The British Isle Offshore Financial Centres," *National Westminster Bank Quarterly Review,* November 1982, pp. 53–65.

3. Dufey and Giddy, *The International Money Market,* p. 39.

4. *Ibid.,* p. 10.

5. Gunter Dufey and Ian H. Giddy, *Credit Creation and the Growth of the Eurodollar Market,* Research Paper No. 127, New York: Columbia University Graduate School of Business, 1976.

6. Yoon S. Park and Jack Zwick, *International Banking in Theory and Practice,* Reading, Mass.: Addison-Wesley, 1985, pp. 17–18.

7. *Wall Street Journal,* January 1, 1985, p. 33.

8. *Ibid.,* November 30, 1984.

9. A detailed description of Standard & Poor's procedure for determining credit ratings for all securities, including international securities, is given in their booklet,

Credit Overview. Corporate and International Ratings, published by Standard & Poor's Corporation, 25 Broadway, New York, N.Y. 10004.

10. Wall Street Journal, August 10, 1984.

11. Catherine L. Mann, "U.S. International Transactions in 1984," *Federal Reserve Bulletin,* May 1985, p. 280.

12. For an explanation of the various types of swaps, see Tanya S. Arnold, "How to Do Interest Rate Swaps," *Harvard Business Review,* September–October 1984, pp. 96–101; and Frederick C. Militello, Jr., "Swap Financing, A New Approach to International Transactions," *Financial Executive,* October 1984, pp. 34–39.

13. Business Week, January 31, 1983, p. 83.

14. Wall Street Journal, August 12, 1985, p. 23.

BIBLIOGRAPHY

Allan, Iain, "Return and Risk in International Capital Markets," *Columbia Journal of World Business,* Summer 1982, pp. 3–23.

Arnold, Tanya S., "How to Do Interest Rate Swaps," *Harvard Business Review,* September–October 1984, pp. 96–101.

Bhattacharya, Anindya, *The Asian Dollar Market,* New York: Praeger, 1977.

Brock, David, and Christine I. Wallich, *Currency Swaps: A Borrowing Technique in a Public Policy Context,* Washington, D.C.: World Bank, 1984.

Choi, Frederick D. S., and Arthur I. Stonehill, "Foreign Access to U.S. Securities Markets: The Theory, Myth and Reality of Regulatory Barriers," *The Investment Analyst* (London), July 1982, pp. 17–26.

Coats, Warren L., Jr., "The Weekend Eurodollar Game," *Journal of Finance,* June 1981, pp. 649–659.

Courtadon, Carol L., *The Competitive Structure of the Eurobond Underwriting Industry,* New York: Salomon Brothers Center for the Study of Financial Institutions and the Graduate School of Business Administration of New York University, Monograph 1985-1.

Dufey, Gunter, and Ian H. Giddy, *The International Money Market,* Englewood Cliffs, N.J.: Prentice-Hall, 1978.

———, "Innovation in the International Financial Markets," *Journal of International Business Studies,* Fall 1981, pp. 33–51.

Eiteman, David K., "International Capital Markets," in N. Roussakis, *International Banking: Principles and Practices,* New York: Praeger, 1983, pp. 57–80.

Elton, Edwin J., and Martin J. Gruber, eds., *International Capital Markets,* Amsterdam: North-Holland, 1976.

Emery, Robert F., *The Japanese Money Market,* Lexington, Mass.: Lexington Books, 1984.

Errunza, Vihang R., "Efficiency and the Programs to Develop Capital Markets: The Brazilian Experience," *Journal of Banking and Finance,* December 1979, pp. 355–382.

Euromoney, monthly issues, current data, surveys and articles on the Euromarkets.

Finnerty, Joseph E., and Thomas Schneeweis, "Time Series Analysis of International Dollar Denominated Interest Rates," *Journal of International Business Studies,* Spring–Summer 1979, pp. 39–52.

———, "Determinations of Eurodollar Interest Rates under Fixed and Floating Exchange Rates," *Nebraska Journal of Economics and Business,* Autumn 1981, pp. 51–61.

Finnerty, Joseph E., Thomas Schneeweis, and Shantaram P. Hegde, "Interest Rates in the $Eurobond Market," *Journal of Financial and Quantitative Analysis,* September 1980, pp. 743–755.

Folks, William R., and Ramesh Avanti, "Raising Funds with Foreign Currency," *Financial Executive,* February 1980, pp. 44–49.

Frydl, Edward J., "The Eurodollar Conundrum," *Federal Reserve Bank of New York Quarterly Review,* Spring 1982, pp. 11–19.

Germany, J. David, and John E. Morton, "Financial Innovation and Deregulation in Foreign Industrial Countries," *Federal Reserve Bulletin,* October 1985, pp. 743–753.

Goodstadt, Leo, "How Hong Kong Came of Age as a Euromarket Centre," *Euromoney,* February 1982, pp. 54–63.

Hawawini, Gabriel, *European Equity Markets: Price Behavior and Efficiency,* New York: Salomon Brothers Center for the Study of Financial Institutions and the Graduate School of Business Administration of New York University, Monograph 1984-4/5.

Hawkins, Robert G., Richard M. Levich, and Clas G. Wihlborg, eds., *The Internationalization of Financial Markets and National Economic Policy,* Volume 3 of *Research in International Business and Finance,* Greenwich, Conn.: JAI Press, 1982.

Ibbotson, Roger C., Richard C. Carr, and Anthony W. Robinson, "International Equity and Bond Returns," *Financial Analysts Journal,* July–August 1982, pp. 61–83.

Johns, R. A., "The British Isle Offshore Finance Centres," *National Westminster Bank Quarterly Review,* November 1982, pp. 53–65.

Kemp, Lynette J., *A Guide to World Money and Capital Markets,* New York: McGraw-Hill, 1982.

Kerr, Ian, *A History of the Eurobond Market: The First 21 Years,* London: Euromoney Publications, 1984.

Kim, Seung H., and Stephen W. Miller, *Competitive Structure of the International Banking Industry,* Lexington, Mass.: Lexington Books, 1983.

Kirkland, Richard I., Jr., "The Stock Market," *Fortune,* October 14, 1985, pp. 159–164.

Lees, Francis A., "Developing Country Access to the International Capital Markets," *Columbia Journal of World Business,* Fall 1979, pp. 71–84.

Logue, Dennis E., and Lemma W. Senbet, "External Currency Market Equilibrium and Its Implications for Regulation of the Eurocurrency Market," *Journal of Finance,* May 1983, pp. 435–447.

Lomax, D. F., and P. T. Gutmann, *The Euromarkets and International Financial Policies,* New York: Halsted, 1980.

Militello, Frederick C., Jr., "Swap Financing, A New Approach to International Transactions," *Financial Executive,* October 1984, pp. 34–39.

Park, Yoon S., "The Economics of Offshore Financial Centers," *Columbia Journal of World Business,* Winter 1982, pp. 31–35.

Park, Yoon S., and Jack Zwick, *International Banking in Theory and Practice,* Reading, Mass.: Addison-Wesley, 1985.

Quinn, Brian S., "The International Bond Market for the U.S. Investor," *Columbia Journal of World Business,* Fall 1979, pp. 85–90.

Reed, Howard C., "The Ascent of Tokyo as an International Financial Center," *Journal of International Business Studies,* Winter 1980, pp. 19–35.

———, *The Preeminence of International Financial Centers,* New York: Praeger, 1981.

Robbins, Sidney, and Robert Stobaugh, *Money in the Multinational Enterprise,* New York: Basic Books, 1973, especially Chapter 4, "Financing Foreign Affiliates."

Skully, Michael T., ed., *Financial Institutions and Markets in the Far East,* New York: St. Martin's Press, 1982.

Starr, Danforth W., "Opportunities for U.S. Corporate Borrowers in the International Bond Markets," *Financial Executive,* June 1979, pp. 50–59.

Tan, Chwee Huat, *Financial Institutions in Singapore,* 3rd ed., Singapore: Singapore University Press Pte., 1984.

Thomas, B. S., "Internationalization of the Securities Markets," *George Washington Law Review,* January 1982, pp. 155–190.

van Agtmael, Antoine, *Emerging Securities Markets,* Washington, D.C.: World Bank, 1982, pp. 60–62.

Yassukovich, S. M., "Eurobonds and Debt Rescheduling," *Euromoney,* January 1982, pp. 60–62.

12

Cost of Capital and Financial Structure

In analyzing the foreign investment decision (Chapter 8), we suggested that one important economic rationale for the existence of a multinational firm is that it is able to take advantage of *international and national financial market imperfections* through a process called *internalization.* This comparative advantage should theoretically result in a lower cost of capital for a multinational firm compared to that of competing domestic firms. Whether or not multinational firms actually enjoy a lower cost of capital is an empirical question that is still under intense investigation. We will cite some of the evidence later.

Our approach in this chapter will be to analyze how market imperfections and other foreign influences are theoretically likely to affect a firm's cost of capital as well as project-specific discount rates. Although the main concepts used to analyze cost of capital in the domestic case provide the foundation for the multinational case, it is necessary to analyze the unique impact of foreign risks and foreign institutional variables.

WEIGHTED AVERAGE COST OF CAPITAL

A firm's weighted average cost of capital is normally found by combining the cost of equity with the cost of debt in proportion to the relative weight of each in the firm's optimal long-term financial structure. More specifically,

$$K = K_e\frac{E}{V} + K_i(1 - t)\frac{D}{V} ,$$

where

K = weighted average aftertax cost of capital,
K_e = risk-adjusted cost of equity,
K_i = beforetax cost of debt,
t = marginal tax rate,
E = market value of the firm's equity,
D = market value of the firm's debt,
V = total market value of the firm's securities ($E + D$).

Cost of Equity

The cost of equity for a firm can be measured in at least two different ways.[1] The traditional approach, called the dividend capitalization model, measures the cost of equity by the following formula:

$$K_e = \frac{D_1}{P_0} + g,$$

where

K_e = required return on equity,
D_1 = expected dividends per share during year one,
P_0 = market value per share at time zero (beginning of year one),
g = expected growth rate of dividends or market price of a share of stock.

The traditional approach assumes that the required return on equity is determined by the market's preferred trade-off between risk and return. Risk is typically defined as either the standard deviation, σ, of returns on a share of stock or the coefficient of variation, γ, of returns on a share of stock.

The capital asset pricing model approach is to define the cost of equity for a firm (security) by the following formula:

$$K_e = r + \beta(K_m - r),$$

where

K_e = expected (required) rate of return on equity,
r = rate of interest on risk-free bonds (Treasury bills, for example),
β = coefficient of systematic risk for the firm,
K_m = expected (required) rate of return on the market portfolio of stocks (Standard & Poor's 500 Index, for example).

The main difference between the two approaches to cost of equity is that the dividend capitalization model emphasizes the total risk of expected returns, whereas the capital asset pricing model emphasizes only the systematic risk of expected returns. Systematic risk is a function of the total variability of expected returns of the firm relative to the market index and the degree to which the variability of expected returns of the firm is correlated to the expected returns on the market index. Empirical studies show that both approaches to the cost of equity have some validity, depending on the sample and time period tested. In any case, the important point is that the cost of equity is some function of the market's preference for return and risk, however risk is defined.

Cost of Debt

The normal procedure for measuring the cost of debt for a domestic firm requires a forecast of domestic interest rates for the next few years, the proportions of various classes of debt the firm expects to use, and the domestic corporate income tax rate. The interest costs of the different debt components are then averaged according to their proportion in the debt structure. This beforetax average, K_i, is then adjusted for corporate income taxes by multiplying it by the expression [1 − the tax rate], i.e., $K_i(1 - t)$, to find the weighted average aftertax cost of debt.

MARKET IMPERFECTIONS AND FOREIGN INFLUENCES

The weighted average cost of capital is normally used as the risk-adjusted discount rate whenever a firm's new projects are in the same general risk class as its existing projects. On the other hand, a project-specific required rate of return should be used as the discount rate if a new project differs from existing projects in business or financial risk. In Chapter 10 we recommended that "foreign" risks of a project be treated as adjustments to expected cash flows rather than as adjustments to the discount rate. If this prescription is followed, the choice of whether to use a firm's overall cost of capital or a project-specific discount rate for evaluating foreign projects should be based on the same considerations of business and financial risk as those used in the domestic case. No special adjustments need be made for foreign risks.

If one prefers to treat foreign risks as adjustments to the project-specific required rate of return, it will be necessary to understand how foreign operations are valued by a firm's shareholders. This area is controversial but Donald Lessard offers a current perspective on it in the appendix to this chapter. Meanwhile we will concentrate on the way being multinational might affect a firm's overall cost of capital.

The overall cost of capital for a multinational firm can be influenced by at least seven important variables that arise from its international environment:

1. The *availability of capital* is an important variable in the multinational case, whereas it is typically a given parameter in the domestic case. Does access to international capital markets, as well as access to local capital markets through foreign affiliates, lower the cost of capital for multinational firms relative to domestic firms?
2. *Segmented national capital markets* can distort the cost of capital for firms domiciled in these markets. Can firms that happen to reside in such markets lower their cost of capital by sourcing capital in international markets?
3. Are investors willing to pay a premium for shares of multinational firms that serve as proxies to satisfy their *international portfolio diversification* motive?
4. Should firms adjust their overall cost of capital to reflect *foreign exchange and political risks*? This activity is not the same as adjusting for project-specific risks, since all foreign projects would be analyzed with the same (higher) discount rate.
5. *Taxation policies* of both home and host countries will influence a firm's aftertax cost of capital. How should a firm include tax considerations when sourcing funds and making financial structure decisions?
6. How does the amount of *disclosure* of a firm's financial position affect its access to international equity and debt markets and thus its cost of capital?
7. Multinational operations may change a firm's *optimal financial structure*. How does the added international availability of capital and ability to diversify cash flows internationally affect a firm's optimal debt ratio? What should be the finance structure of affiliates, considering that different lending norms exist in different countries and that a compromise must be struck to reflect affiliate liquidity needs, foreign exchange risk, political risk, legal requirements, and tax minimization?

Each of these issues will be analyzed in the rest of this chapter. It should be noted beforehand, however, that consensus has not yet been reached on many of the issues relating to cost of capital, either domestically or internationally. Therefore we perceive this chapter's role to be to highlight the main arguments for the various conflicting viewpoints rather than to impose a single normative solution on the reader.

AVAILABILITY OF CAPITAL

In the domestic case an underlying assumption is that total availability of capital to a firm is determined at any time by supply and demand in the domestic capital markets. A firm should always expand its capital budget by raising funds in the same proportion as its optimal financial structure, but as its budget expands in absolute terms, its marginal cost of capital will eventually increase. In other words, a firm can only tap the capital market for some limited amount in the short run before suppliers of capital balk at providing further funds, even if the same optimal financial structure is preserved. In the long run this may not be a limitation, depending on *market liquidity*.

Although no consensus exists about the definition of market liquidity, it can be observed by noting the degree to which a firm can issue a new security without depressing the existing market price, as well as the degree to which a change in price of its securities elicits a substantial order flow. Market liquidity varies greatly from one capital market to another, with the U.S., U.K., and Eurocurrency markets being considered the most liquid.

In the multinational case a firm is able to circumvent individual market liquidity by raising funds in the Euromarkets, local foreign capital markets, or its own domestic capital market. This activity should logically expand the capacity of a multinational firm to raise funds in the short run over what might have been raised if the firm were limited to its home capital market. This situation still assumes that the firm's optimal financial structure is preserved. Exhibit 12.1 shows how the availability of capital in international markets helps the multinational firm obtain a lower marginal cost of capital and a larger budget than might otherwise have been the case.

Exhibit 12.1 shows that the multinational firm has a given marginal return on capital at different budget levels represented in line DD'. This demand is determined by ranking potential projects according to net present value or internal rate of return. Percentage rate of return to both users and suppliers of capital is shown on the vertical scale. If the firm is limited to raising funds in its domestic market, the line SS_D shows the marginal domestic cost of capital (vertical axis) at various budget levels (horizontal axis). Remember that the firm continues to maintain the same debt ratio as it expands its budget so that financial risk does not change. The optimal budget in the domestic case is $40 million, where the marginal return on capital (MRR) just equals the marginal cost of capital (MCC_D). At this budget the marginal domestic cost of capital, K_D, would be equal to 20%.

If the multinational firm has access to additional sources of capital outside an illiquid domestic capital market, the marginal cost of capital should shift to the right, as shown by line SS_F in Exhibit 12.1. In other words, foreign markets can be tapped for long-term funds at times when the domestic market is saturated because of heavy use by other borrowers

EXHIBIT 12.1
Availability of Funds and the Cost of Capital

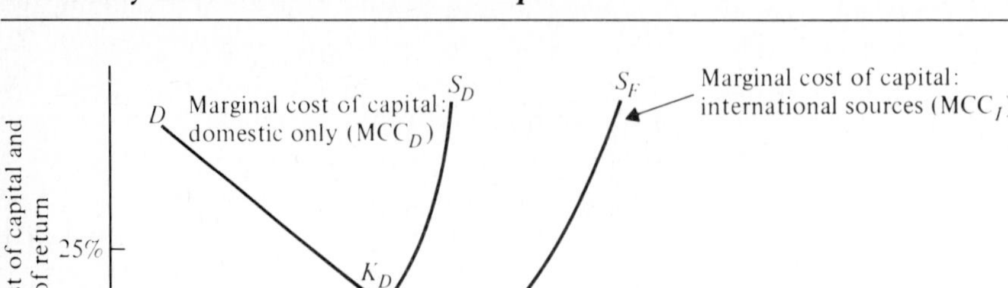

or equity issuers, or is unable to absorb another issue of the multinational firm in the short run. Exhibit 12.1 shows that by a tap of foreign capital markets the marginal international cost of capital, K_F, has been reduced to 15%, even while an additional $10 million is raised. This assumes that about $20 million is raised abroad, since only about $30 million could be raised domestically at a 15% cost of capital.

Availability of Equity Capital

Access to international equity markets can have a favorable impact on a firm's cost of equity. Equity is assumed to be raised in its normal proportion to debt as the budget expands. Although U.S.-based multinationals have raised only minute amounts of new equity capital abroad, non-U.S. multinationals have raised significant amounts in the United States. Both U.S. and non-U.S. multinationals have made active use of secondary equity markets by multiple listing on national stock exchanges. Note that the new issues and secondary markets for equity shares jointly determine the cost of equity.

Multinational firms list their shares on foreign stock exchanges to broaden their potential base for later new equity issues, to facilitate trading for existing foreign shareholders, to establish a market for potential stock swaps when acquiring a foreign firm, to increase the firm's visibility to its customers and employees, and to satisfy local ownership desires.

An active local market in a multinational firm's common stock facilitates later new issues and stock swaps when taking over foreign firms. In fact, more multinational firms would swap stock and list on foreign stock exchanges were it not for a general reluctance on the part of the public outside the United States to hold common stock of any kind. There is still a strong bias in favor of investing in land, gold, art treasures, and numbered Swiss bank accounts. Undoubtedly a history of political unrest and cultural distaste for money lending contribute to these preferences.

Another deterrent is that foreign exchange controls in some countries cause difficulties for citizens seeking to buy foreign securities. Controls have been relaxed somewhat in the last few years, but widespread individual ownership of any kind of common stock is untypical. Only the financial institutions are significant shareholders. The EEC has made it easier and less expensive for residents of European countries to buy foreign securities. In particular, in 1978 the United Kingdom dropped its controls on ownership of foreign securities by British residents. The growth of consumer-oriented financial institutions (such as mutual funds) and more adequate financial disclosure laws (especially in Germany) have also helped.

Multinational firms list on foreign stock exchanges to build their corporate image, advertise trademarks and products, and provide a convenient method for existing shareholders to trade their shares. Some firms publish foreign language versions of their annual reports.

As occurs in the domestic case, widespread foreign ownership of common stock encourages foreign shareholder, employee, and management loyalty. Companies producing consumer durables have always believed that stockholders are among their best potential customers, and foreign stockholders are likely to hold a similar view. Employee stock purchase plans and management stock options are effective motivators in the United States. Such compensation plans are now becoming popular abroad. In any case, to reap the loyalty benefits of foreign ownership of common stock, firms must make shares available for purchase by foreigners and establish a convenient method for trading the shares, i.e., local listing.

A desire to avoid nationalistic reactions to wholly owned foreign subsidiaries has led companies such as General Motors, Ford, and IBM to sell parent company shares worldwide as a substitute for local joint ventures.[2]

Availability of Debt Capital

Access to international capital markets should lower the cost of debt to a multinational firm relative to a firm limited to domestic sources of debt (see Exhibit 12.1). The multinational can borrow in the Eurocurrency market, the international bond market, or various national capital markets. Therefore to measure the beforetax cost of debt, K_i, one must forecast interest rates and the proportion of debt to be raised in each international and national capital market.

MARKET SEGMENTATION

Substantial research has been undertaken to address the following four questions:

1. To what extent are national capital markets segmented or integrated?
2. Can investors improve their portfolios' performance by diversifying internationally?
3. What is the effect of market segmentation or integration on the firm's cost of capital?
4. If markets are segmented, can investors satisfy their international diversification motive by holding the securities of multinational firms?

Definition of Market Segmentation

A national capital market is *segmented* if the required rate of return on securities in that market differs from the required rate of return on securities of comparable expected return and risk that are traded on other national securities markets (New York and London, for example). On the other hand, if all capital markets are fully *integrated,* securities of comparable expected return and risk should have the same required rate of return in each national market after adjusting for foreign exchange risk and political risk.

What causes a national capital market to be segmented? Market segmentation is a financial market imperfection caused by government constraints and/or investor perceptions. As we discussed in Chapter 8, government constraints include tax policies, controls on foreign exchange use, restrictions on the free transfer of capital, and interference in the functioning of domestic securities markets. Market segmentation due to investor perceptions is caused by information barriers, such as the quality of corporate disclosure and familiarity with securities markets and institutions. Investors are also influenced by transaction costs, alternative portfolio possibilities, financial risk, foreign exchange risk, and political risk.

Market Efficiency

A national securities market can be *efficient* in a domestic context and yet *segmented* in an international context. According to finance theory, a market is efficient if security prices in that market reflect all available relevant information and adjust quickly to any new relevant information. Therefore the price of an individual security reflects its "intrinsic value" and any price fluctuations will be "random walks" around this value. This statement assumes that transaction costs are low, that many participants are in the market, and that these participants have sufficient financial strength to move security prices. Empirical tests of market efficiency have been conducted on most of the major European securities markets, Japan, Canada, and, of course, the United States. The results show that many of these markets, and especially the U.S. and U.K. markets, are reasonably efficient.

An efficient national securities market might very well "correctly price" all securities traded in that market on the basis of information available to the investors who participate in that market. However, if that market is segmented, foreign investors would not be participants. Thus securities in the segmented market would be priced on the basis of domestic rather than international standards.

Effect of Market Segmentation on the Cost of Capital

The degree to which capital markets are segmented may have an important influence on a firm's cost of capital. At one extreme, if a firm is sourcing its capital in a fully segmented market, it is likely to have a higher cost of capital than if it had access to other capital markets. However, as will be shown later, a firm may be able to overcome this disadvantage by adopting financial policies that give it access to other capital markets.

At the other extreme, the cost of capital of a firm with access to fully integrated capital markets may be lower, because that cost may reflect a lower international price of risk. As we explained in Chapter 8 and its appendix, if economic activities are less than perfectly correlated among countries, investors can improve their portfolio performance by diversifying internationally. Adding foreign securities to a domestic portfolio should reduce that portfolio's systematic risk (beta). Therefore the required rate of return on internationally traded securities should reflect their higher value to internationally diversified portfolios rather than just their value to investors in the country in which the firm is located.

From a managerial perspective the difference between sourcing capital in a segmented versus integrated capital market can be shown diagrammatically by using the same example as was used in Exhibit 12.1. Exhibit 12.2 shows how escaping from dependence on a segmented capital market can lower a firm's cost of capital. The line $S'S_U$ represents the decreased marginal cost of capital for a firm that has gained access to other capital markets. As a result of the combined effects of greater availability of capital and international pricing of the firm's securities, the marginal cost of capital, K_U, declines to 13%, and the optimal capital budget climbs to $60 million.

International Diversification Premium

Segmented national capital markets create the imperfections that may allow multinational firms to enjoy a lower cost of capital. Investors may be willing to pay a premium for the ability to diversify their portfolios internationally.

EXHIBIT 12.2
Market Segmentation and the Cost of Capital

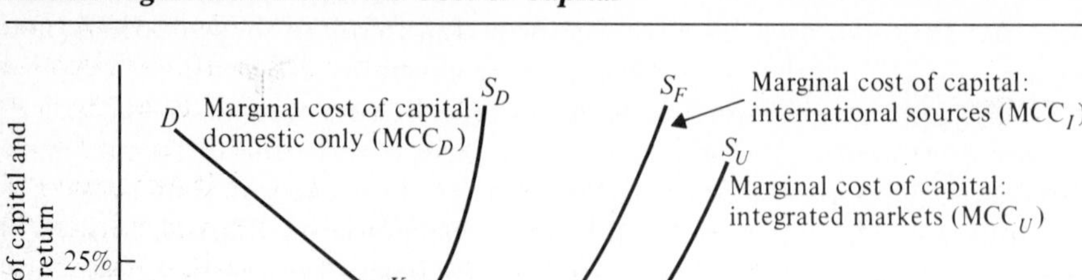

However, market segmentation may make it difficult for investors to find and purchase foreign securities to satisfy their diversification motive. Therefore they may be willing to pay a premium for the shares of multinational firms that thereby act as proxies for an internationally diversified portfolio.

In most cases foreign investors can purchase U.S. securities with relative ease. This extra supply of equity funds should have a favorable impact on U.S. stock prices in general rather than just on stock prices of U.S. multinational firms, although the latter might be favored because of their superior visibility abroad. In countries that restrict their citizens from purchasing foreign securities, however, resident investors might be tempted to purchase equity in their own multinational firms, thus lowering those firms' costs of capital.

Empirical Studies

Early research studies concentrated on establishing the fact that investors can benefit by diversifying their portfolios internationally because economic activities are imperfectly correlated between countries.[3] If investors can benefit by diversifying internationally, then it follows that securities that are traded internationally should be priced to reflect their contribution to lowering the systematic risk of an internationally diversified portfolio. This is the international version of the capital asset pricing model, which we will refer to as ICAPM.[4]

Tests of the ICAPM have been undertaken to determine the extent to which securities are priced according to national or international factors.[5]

The tests as a whole show some degree of both international and national factors in securities prices, leading to a conclusion that capital markets are partly integrated and partly segmented. This inconclusive result stems from the difficulty of correctly specifying a testable version of the ICAPM.[6] Indeed, some theoreticians have questioned whether it is theoretically possible to find a correct test for either the domestic or international versions of the model.[7]

The argument that multinational firms may serve as proxies for international diversification when capital markets are segmented is also controversial.[8] Although some tests show that multinational firms have historically had a lower cost of capital than have their domestic counterparts, this result could also be explained by investors perceiving that the multinational firm should benefit from imperfections in the product and factor markets. It seems to be impossible to segregate for testing purposes these real benefits from the purely financial benefits.

The corporate financial policy implications for firms residing in segmented capital markets were investigated by Stapleton and Subrahmanyan (1977). They concluded:

> In most cases, the effect of segmenting capital markets is to depress security prices and also to produce an incentive for corporations to increase the diversification opportunities available to investors. Three corporate financial policies that effectively reduce the effects of segmented markets are:
>
> a. Foreign portfolio/direct investment by firms.
>
> b. Mergers with foreign firms.
>
> c. Dual listing of the securities of the firm on foreign capital markets.[9]

Most of the tests of market segmentation and the proxy effect of multinational firms suffer from the usual problem of model builders, namely, the need to abstract from reality in order to have a testable model. In our opinion a realistic test would be to observe what happens to a single security's price when it has been traded only in a domestic market but then begins to be traded in a foreign market. Arbitrage should keep the market price equal in both markets. However, if during the transition one observes a significant change in the security's price uncorrelated with price movements in either of the underlying securities markets, one may infer that the domestic market was segmented.

In academic circles tests based on case studies are often considered to be "casual empiricism," since no theory or model exists to explain what is being observed. Nevertheless, something may be learned from such cases, just as scientists learn from observing nature in an uncontrolled environment. Furthermore, case studies that preserve real world complications may illustrate specific kinds of barriers to market integration and ways in which they might be overcome.

Unfortunately, few case studies have been documented where a firm has "escaped" from a segmented capital market. In practice, escape usually means listing on a foreign stock market such as New York or London, and/or selling securities in foreign capital markets. We will illustrate what can be learned from a case study by using the example of Novo Industri A/S, a Danish firm.

NOVO INDUSTRI A/S (NOVO)

Novo is a Danish multinational firm that produces industrial enzymes and pharmaceuticals (mostly insulin). It was previously introduced in some detail in Chapter 8 as a firm that made a direct foreign investment in the United States for "credibility" reasons.

In 1977 Novo's management decided to internationalize its capital structure and sources of funds. This decision was based on the observation that the Danish securities market was both illiquid and segmented from international markets.[10] In particular, the lack of availability and the high cost of equity capital in Denmark resulted in Novo having a higher cost of capital than its main multinational competitors, Eli Lilly (United States), Miles Laboratories (United States, owned by Bayer, Germany), and Gist Brocades (the Netherlands).

Apart from the cost of capital, Novo's projected growth opportunities signaled an eventual need to raise new long-term capital beyond what could be raised in the limited Danish market. Since Novo is a world technology leader in its specialties, planned capital investments in plant, equipment, and research could not be postponed until internal financing from cash flow became available. Novo's competitors would preempt any markets not served by Novo.

Even if an equity issue of the size required could have been raised in Denmark, the required rate of return would have been unacceptably high. For example, Novo's price/earnings ratio was typically around 5, while that of its foreign competitors was well over 10. Yet Novo's business and financial risk appeared to be about equal to that of its competitors. A price/earnings ratio of 5 appeared appropriate for Novo only within a domestic Danish context when Novo was compared with other domestic firms of comparable business and financial risk.

If Denmark's securities market were integrated with world markets, one would normally expect foreign investors to rush in and buy "undervalued" Danish securities. In that case firms like Novo would enjoy an international cost of capital comparable to their foreign competitors. Strangely enough, no Danish government restrictions existed that would have prevented foreign investors from holding Danish securities. Therefore one must look for investor perception as the main cause of market segmentation in Denmark at that time.

At least six characteristics of the Danish securities market were responsible for market segmentation:

1. disparity in the information base of Danish and foreign investors,
2. taxation,
3. alternative sets of feasible portfolios,
4. financial risk,
5. foreign exchange risk,
6. political risk.

Disparity in the Information Base

Certain Danish institutional characteristics caused Danish and foreign investors to be uninformed about each other's equity securities. The most important information barrier was the Danish regulation that prohibited Danish investors from holding foreign private sector securities.[11] Therefore Danish investors had no incentive to follow developments in foreign securities markets nor to factor such information into their evaluation of Danish securities. As a result, Danish securities might have been priced correctly in the efficient market sense relative to each other, considering the Danish information base, but priced incorrectly considering the combined foreign and Danish information base. Another detrimental effect of this regulation was that foreign securities firms did not locate offices or personnel in Denmark, since they had no product to sell. Lack of a physical presence in Denmark reduced the ability of foreign securities analysts to follow Danish securities.

A second information barrier was lack of enough Danish security analysts who followed Danish securities. Only one professional securities analysis service was published (Børsinformationen), and that was in the Danish language. A few Danish institutional investors employed in-house analysts, but their findings were not available to the public.

Other information barriers include language and accounting principles. Naturally financial information is normally published in Danish, using Danish accounting principles. A few firms, such as Novo, publish English versions, but almost none use U.S. or British accounting principles or attempt to show any reconciliation with such principles.

Taxation

Danish taxation policy had all but eliminated investment in common stock by individuals. Until a tax law change in July 1981, capital gains on shares held for over two years were taxed at a 50% rate. Shares held for less than two years, or for "speculative" purposes, were taxed at personal income tax rates, with the top marginal rate being 75%. In contrast, capital gains on bonds were tax-free. This situation resulted in bonds being issued at deep discounts, because the redemption at par at maturity was considered a capital gain. Thus most individual investors held bonds rather than stocks. This factor reduced the liquidity of the stock market and increased the required rate of return on stocks if they were to compete with bonds.

Feasible Set of Portfolios

Because of the prohibition on foreign security ownership at the time, Danish investors had a very limited set of securities from which to choose a portfolio. In practice, Danish institutional portfolios were composed of Danish stocks, government bonds, and mortgage bonds. Since Danish stock price movements are closely correlated with each other, Danish portfolios possessed a rather high level of systematic risk. In addition, government policy had been to provide a relatively high real rate of return on government bonds after adjusting for inflation. The net result of taxation policies on individuals and attractive real yields on government bonds was that required rates of returns on stocks were relatively high by international standards.

From a portfolio perspective Danish stocks provide an opportunity for foreign investors to diversify internationally. If Danish stock price movements are not closely correlated with world stock price movements, inclusion of Danish stocks in foreign portfolios should reduce their systematic risk. Furthermore, foreign investors are not subject to the high Danish income tax rates, since they are normally protected by tax treaties, which typically limit their taxes to 15% on dividends and capital gains. As a result of the international diversification potential, foreign investors might require a lower rate of return on Danish stocks than Danish investors, other things being equal. However, other things may not be equal, because foreign investors may perceive Danish stocks to carry more financial, foreign exchange, and political risk than their own domestic securities.

Financial, Foreign Exchange, and Political Risks

Financial leverage utilized by Danish firms is relatively high by U.S. and U.K. standards but not abnormal for Scandinavia, Germany, Italy, and Japan. In addition, most of the debt is short-term, with variable interest rates. Just how foreign investors would view financial risk in Danish firms depends on what norms they follow in their home countries. We know from Novo's experience in tapping the Eurobond market in 1978 that Morgan Grenfell, their British investment bankers, were eager for Novo to maintain a debt ratio (debt/total capitalization) closer to 50% rather than the traditional Danish 65–70%.

Foreign investors in Danish securities are subject to foreign exchange risk. Whether this is a plus or a minus factor depends on the investor's home currency, perception about the future strength of the krone, and its impact on a firm's economic exposure. Through personal contacts with foreign investors and bankers, Novo's management did not believe foreign exchange risk was a factor in Novo's stock price, because their operations were perceived as being well diversified internationally.

From the same interviews, with respect to political risk, Denmark is perceived as a stable Western democracy but with the potential to cause periodic problems for foreign investors. In particular, Denmark's national debt is regarded as too high for comfort, although this judgment has not yet shown up in the form of risk premiums on Denmark's Eurocurrency syndicated loans. The other threat perceived by foreign investors is that Denmark will move toward implementing "economic democracy" in a more substantial manner. Economic democracy would result in a mandatory profit-sharing plan whereby a central fund, governed by labor unions, would eventually become a major shareholder in private sector firms. Despite these general concerns about Denmark's political situation, investors in Novo in particular indicated that their evaluation of Novo's prospects was not influenced by political risk.

Barriers to Internationalization

Although Novo's management in 1977 wished to escape from the shackles of Denmark's segmented and illiquid capital market, many barriers had to be overcome. It is worthwhile to describe some of these, since they typify the barriers faced by other firms from segmented markets who wish to internationalize their capital structure.

Novo had been a family-owned firm, from its founding in the 1920s by the two Petersen brothers until 1974, when it went public and listed on the Copenhagen Stock Exchange. However, Novo was essentially unknown in investment circles outside Denmark. To overcome this *disparity in the information base,* Novo increased the level of its financial and technical disclosure in both Danish and English versions. This procedure was aided in late 1977 by Grieveson, Grant and Company, a British stock brokerage firm, which had started to follow Novo's stock and issued the first professional securities analysis report about Novo in English.

The information gap was further closed when Morgan Guaranty Trust Company of New York, Novo's main foreign commercial banker, was consulted about alternative strategies to tap international capital markets. Its advice was to try a Eurobond issue. It then introduced Novo to Morgan Grenfell, a leading U.K. investment bank, which confirmed the recommended strategy. In 1978 Morgan Grenfell successfully organized a syndicate to underwrite and sell a $20 million convertible Eurobond issue for

Novo. In connection with this offering Novo listed its shares on the London Stock Exchange to facilitate conversion and to gain visibility. These twin actions were the keys to dissolving the information barrier, and, of course, they also raised a large amount of long-term capital on favorable terms, which would have been unavailable in Denmark.

Despite the favorable impact of the Eurobond issue on availability of capital, Novo's cost of capital actually increased when Danish investors reacted negatively to the potential dilution effect of the conversion right. During 1979 Novo's stock price declined from around DKr300 per share to around DKr200–225 per share.

During 1979 a fortuitous event occurred. Biotechnology began to attract the interest of the U.S. investment community, with several sensationally oversubscribed stock issues by such start-up firms as Genentech and Cetus. Thanks to the aforementioned information gap, Danish investors were unaware of these events and continued to value Novo at a low price/earnings ratio of 5, compared to over 10 for its established competitors and 30 or more for these new potential competitors.

At this point Novo felt that it had to position itself with its customers in the U.S. market as a firm that had a proven track record in biotechnology, compared to the "blue sky" promises of the recent start-up firms. A failure to do so could lead to the faulty conclusion that Novo was not at the forefront in technology. Therefore, to protect its customer base, Novo organized a seminar in New York City on April 30, 1980. About 40 journalists and financial analysts attended the seminar. Soon after the seminar a few sophisticated individual U.S. investors began buying Novo's stock and convertibles through the London Stock Exchange. Danish investors were only too happy to supply this foreign demand. Therefore, despite relatively strong demand from U.S. and British investors, Novo's share price increased only gradually, reaching back to the DKr300 level by midsummer. However, during the following months foreign interest began to snowball, and by the end of 1980 Novo's stock price had reached the DKr600 level. Moreover, foreign investors had increased their proportion of share ownership from virtually nothing to around 30%. Novo's price/earnings ratio had risen to around 16, which was now in line with those of its international competitors but not with those of the Danish market. At this point one must conclude that Novo had succeeded in internationalizing its cost of capital. Other Danish securities remained locked in a segmented capital market. Indeed, movement in the Danish stock market in general did not parallel the rise in Novo's share price, nor could it be explained by movement in the U.S. or U.K. stock markets as a whole.

To improve the liquidity of its shares held by U.S. investors and to increase the availability of capital by tapping the U.S. new-issues market, Novo decided to sponsor an American depositary receipts (ADR) system in the United States, have its shares quoted on the over-the-counter market

(NASDAQ), and retain a U.S. investment banker to advise it about a U.S. stock issue. Goldman Sachs was selected for this purpose. Morgan Guaranty Trust Company of New York established the ADR system in April 1981. Novo's shares were split five for one in the U.S. market by issuing five times as many American depositary shares as there were underlying Danish krone shares held in the bank.

During the first half of 1981, under the guidance of Goldman Sachs and with the assistance of Morgan Grenfell and Copenhagen Handelsbank, Novo prepared a prospectus for SEC registration of a U.S. stock offering and eventual listing on the New York Stock Exchange. The main barriers encountered in this effort, which would have general applicability, were connected with preparing financial statements that could be reconciled with U.S. accounting principles and the higher level of disclosure required by the SEC. In particular, industry segment reporting was a problem both from a disclosure perspective and an accounting perspective because the accounting data were not available internally in that format. As it turned out, the investment barriers in the United States were relatively tractable, although expensive and time-consuming to overcome.

The more serious barriers were caused by a variety of institutional and government regulations in Denmark. The latter were never designed so that firms could issue stock at market value, since Danish firms typically issue stock at par value with preemptive rights. Even Novo's own stockholders had to be educated about the value of giving up their preemptive rights, but by this time Novo's stock price, driven by continued foreign buying, was so high that virtually nobody in Denmark thought it was worth the price foreigners were willing to pay. In fact, prior to the time of the share issue in July 1981, Novo's stock price had risen to over DKr1500, before settling down to a level around DKr1400. Foreign ownership had increased to over 50% of the shares outstanding.

Market segmentation was very apparent during the first half of 1981. Published and unpublished reports by Danish security analysts, bankers, and the popular press consistently claimed that Novo was seriously overvalued, while their foreign counterparts were consistently touting Novo as undervalued. The difference in views was based partly on investor perceptions of the importance of biotechnology and Novo's role in this field.

One final piece of evidence on market segmentation can be gleaned from the way Danish and foreign investors reacted to the announcement of the proposed new U.S. share issue on May 29, 1981. Novo's share price dropped 156 points in Copenhagen, equal to about 10% of its market value. As soon as trading started in New York six hours later, the share price immediately recovered all its loss. The Copenhagen reaction was typical for an illiquid market. Investors worried about the dilution effect of the new share issue since it would increase the number of shares outstanding by about 8%. They did not believe that Novo could invest the new funds at a rate of return that would not dilute future earnings per share. They also feared that the U.S. shares would eventually flow back to Copenhagen if biotechnology lost its glitter.

The U.S. reaction to the announcement of the new stock issue was consistent with what one would expect in a liquid and efficient market. U.S. investors viewed the new issue as creating additional demand for the stock as Novo became more visible because of the selling efforts of a large, aggressive syndicate. Furthermore, the marketing effort was directed at institutional investors who were previously underrepresented among Novo's U.S. investors. They had been underrepresented because U.S. institutional investors want to be ensured of a liquid market in a stock so that they may get out, if desired, without depressing the stock price. The wide distribution effected by the new issue, plus SEC registration and a New York Stock Exchange listing, all added up to more liquidity.

FOREIGN EXCHANGE RISK AND THE COST OF DEBT

When a multinational firm issues foreign currency–denominated debt, its effective cost equals the aftertax cost of repaying the principal and interest in terms of the parent's own currency. This amount includes the nominal cost of principal and interest in foreign currency terms, adjusted for any foreign exchange gains or losses. For example, if a U.S. multinational firm borrows Deutschemarks for one year at 6% interest, and during the year the mark appreciates by 8% relative to the dollar, the approximate beforetax cost of this debt is 14.48%. The calculation is as follows:

cost of debt	equals	interest in DM	times	additional interest due to exchange rate change	plus	additional principal due to exchange rate change.	
K_i	=	6%	×	1.08	+	8%	= 14.48%.

Another formula that is often used is

cost of debt	equals	principal and interest	times	exchange rate change	minus	principal	times 100.
K_i	=	[(1.06	×	1.08)	−	1.00]	× 100
	=	14.48%.					

The added 8.48% cost of this debt in terms of U.S. dollars would be reported as a foreign exchange transaction loss, and it would be deductible for tax purposes. Therefore the aftertax cost of this debt when the U.S. income tax rates are 46% would be

$$K_i(1 - t) = 14.48\% \times .54 = 7.82\%.$$

Multinational firms have discovered that borrowing foreign currency debt on a long-term basis creates considerable exposure to transactions gains or losses. For example, U.S. firms that borrowed long-term Deutschemarks or Swiss francs prior to December 1971 rue that day. In an article appropriately titled "Eurobond Currency Selection: Hindsight," Steven Dawson has shown what happened as of October 1973 to the nine Deutschemark-denominated bonds that were issued by U.S. firms during the period May 1967 to October 1969.[12] Exhibit 12.3, abstracted from his article, shows that in each case the borrower would have been much better off to have borrowed in dollars even though the initial nominal interest rate would have been higher for a dollar issue than for a Deutschemark issue.

Exhibit 12.4 shows a more recent study of a similar phenomenon by William Folks, Jr., and Josef Follpract, who picked up where Dawson left off.[13] Their study follows, until March 1976, the 35 nondollar-denominated long-term foreign currency debt issues that were floated by U.S. firms during the period July 1969 to December 1972. The study calculates both

EXHIBIT 12.3
New Issue Cost of Funds Compared with the Actual Cost

Issuer (parent)	*Date of issue*	*(A) Cost of funds at time of issue, mark-denominated*	*(B) Cost of funds at time of issue, dollar-denominated*	*(C) Effective cost of mark-denominated issue, adjustment for currency changes*
National Lead	5-26-67	6.58%	7.08%	12.38%
General Instrument	5-29-68	7.08	8.33	13.17
Gulf Oil	9-05-68	6.57	7.51	12.01
Occidental Petroleum	10-08-68	6.70	7.70	12.20
Tenneco	12-17-68	6.88	8.13	12.35
Chrysler	7-10-69	7.14	7.49	13.40
Studebaker-Worthington	7-31-69	7.65	8.81	14.00
Int. Standard Electric	9-01-69	7.14	8.40	13.38
TRW	10-15-69	7.82	8.70	13.17

Source: Steven M. Dawson, "Eurobond Currency Selection: Hindsight," *Financial Executive,* November 1973, p. 73.

Note: Column A presents the expected cost to maturity for the Deutschemark issues given the coupon, new issue price, maturity, and sinking fund repayment schedule. Column B makes a similar calculation, assuming that the issue was denominated in dollars instead. Here the actual coupon for the Deutschemark issue is increased by the difference between the Morgan Guaranty yield for dollar and Deutschemark bonds. In column C adjustment is made for the mark revaluations and dollar devaluations subsequent to the date of issue. Each payment of principal and interest is adjusted for the U.S. bank transfer rate in effect at the time of payment. All payments after October 1, 1973, are assumed to be made at the October 1 exchange rate.

EXHIBIT 12.4
Borrowing Costs of Foreign Currency Issues (Annual Coupon)

			COST OF BORROWING	
Currency	*Issue*	*Coupon*	*After tax*	*Before tax*
Deutsche-mark	Studebaker-Worthington	7¼	7.64	14.69
	International Standard Electric	7	6.40	12.31
	TRW	7½	6.44	12.38
	Tenneco (1)	7½	6.41	12.33
	Kraftco	7½	6.38	12.27
	Continental Oil	8	8.23	15.83
	Transocean Gulf[a]	7½	6.50	12.50
	Tenneco (2)	7¾	6.64	12.77
	Firestone	7¾	6.15	11.83
	Philip Morris	6¾	5.13	9.87
	Goodyear	6¾	5.13	9.87
	Teledyne	7¼	5.43	10.44
Swiss franc	Burroughs	6¼	6.40	12.31
	Standard Oil (California)	6¼	6.46	12.42
	Goodyear	7	7.12	13.69
	American Brands	6½	6.80	13.08
	Texaco	6¾	6.95	13.37
	Cities Service	7¼	10.02	19.27
Dutch guilder	General Electric	8¼	10.44	20.08
	GTE	8¼	10.11	19.44
	IBM	8	8.56	16.46
	Cities Service	8	9.18	17.65
	International Harvester	8	9.18	17.65
	Philip Morris	7½	6.59	12.67
	Sperry Rand	6½	5.43	10.44
	Holiday Inns	6½	5.52	10.62
	Teledyne	6¼	5.34	10.27
	Standard Brands	6½	5.64	10.85
	Textron Atlantic	6¾	5.83	11.21
Pound sterling	Amoco[a]	8	2.75	5.29
Luxembourg franc	International Standard Electric	6½	4.08	7.85

Source: William R. Folks, Jr., and Josef Follpract, "The Currency of Denomination Decision for Eurobonds: The American Experience," unpublished manuscript, Center for International Business Studies, University of South Carolina, 1976.

[a]Issued at 98.

before- and aftertax costs of these issues, assuming a 48% U.S. tax rate, and assuming that the remaining interest and principal payments to maturity would be paid at the exchange rate prevailing in March 1976. Once again the results with hindsight are startling. During this period all firms would clearly have been better off to issue dollar-denominated debt rather than Deutschemark, Swiss franc, Dutch guilder, or even Luxembourg franc bonds. Only Amoco's British pound issue proved less expensive than a U.S. dollar issue.

With the advantage of hindsight, why were the U.S. executives so misled? The economic theory presented in Chapter 5 would not have helped avoid this debacle, because the prefloat market conditions gave no indication of the violent structural changes that started in August 1971. Eventual abandonment of the fixed exchange rate system or the energy crisis of 1973–1974 could not reasonably have been anticipated. U.S. executives who decided to borrow in foreign currencies were apparently complying with the U.S. direct investment control program. They were also looking at the modest interest differentials in favor of foreign currency borrowing existing at the time, which they probably considered indicative of expected appreciation of the respective foreign currencies, just as the International Fisher Effect would predict. The problem is, of course, that the longer the period of future commitment, the more uncertain are any predictions about future exchange rates, inflation, and interest rates.

What can be done to prevent foreign exchange risk from increasing the effective cost of debt in the future? Some financial executives in the Folks and Follpract survey concluded from their experience that under no conditions should a firm borrow long-term in foreign currencies.[14] This policy would certainly eliminate the foreign exchange risk on the cost of debt, but in our opinion it would also throw away most of the advantage a multinational firm derives from its ability to increase the availability of capital to itself by borrowing in foreign capital markets.

Some of the financial executives in the survey took the position that borrowing long-term in foreign currencies is acceptable provided that the anticipated cash outflow on principal and interest is matched by anticipated operating receipts in that same currency.[15] In other words, General Motors could borrow Deutschemarks equal to its ability to repay them out of Deutschemark cash inflow, presumably from Opel in Germany. This approach has the advantage of minimizing the need to show transaction losses (or gains) on foreign exchange rate changes in the future. In our opinion, however, the approach has the disadvantage of not analyzing the financing decision separately from the investment decision. Because the *economic* exposure in Deutschemarks already exists for General Motors in Germany, a decision to borrow long-term in Deutschemarks does not change that exposure. Instead it creates a brand-new Deutschemark *transaction* and *translation* exposure that does not necessarily offset the economic exposure in Opel, as explained in Chapter 7. For example, if the Deutschemark appreciates, Opel could be in trouble in export markets and face more import competition, both of which would squeeze its Deutschemark profits and Deutschemark net cash inflows. At the same time General Motors would have committed these scarcer Deutschemarks to repaying its long-term Deutschemark debt. This is precisely the time when marks could have been converted to dollars at a more favorable rate, thus compensating General Motors in part for the lower overall Deutschemark cash inflow in Opel.

Some financial executives in the Folks and Follpract survey believed they were equipped to analyze interest rate differentials and compare these to expected exchange rate changes. They would borrow foreign currency if convinced that it would not appreciate vis-à-vis the dollar. This policy assumes once again that financial executives have superior insight into future foreign exchange rate prospects. A more tolerant interpretation of their response is that they believe inefficient markets exist and persist, and that they can circumvent the inefficiencies through the multinational firm's external financial network and ability to internalize some of the transfer costs.

Only two of the respondents in the survey indicated that their long-term foreign currency borrowing was designed to diversify their long-term currency commitments. This approach is perhaps the most defensible of all the approaches suggested. It has the advantage of not requiring superhuman ability to forecast and makes use of the traditional insurance principal. It is virtually identical conceptually with the approach that calls for internationally diversifying assets such as portfolio securities and direct foreign investments.[16]

Folks and Follpract recommended that a good theoretical approach would be to evaluate all foreign currency borrowing as if the annual principal and interest payments would be covered by hedging in the forward market at the beginning of the payment period.[17] The object is not actually to cover all transaction exposure on foreign debt in practice but merely to pretend that it is going to be hedged. Thus they use the cost of "insurance," which they could purchase if they wished, as a proxy for the foreign exchange risk involved. This approach has theoretical merit but is difficult to implement in practice because the financial executive must predict forward rates far into the future. The only rate that is known with certainty is the one-year forward rate. Predicting forward rates beyond one year is about as difficult as predicting future spot rates beyond one year.[18] On the other hand, this approach does have the advantage of forcing executives to make explicit assumptions about future exchange rates rather than minimize their importance, as they did in the past.

Folks and Follpract also suggest that management use the traditional break-even approach when comparing foreign currency to dollar borrowing over the same maturity. This approach requires "calculation of an annualized rate of foreign currency appreciation or depreciation vis-à-vis the dollar which would, if effected over the life of the bond, equalize the cost of borrowing." This approach has the advantage of only requiring management to specify whether they believe the future exchange rate change will be greater or less than the break-even rate calculated as suggested above, rather than requiring management to predict the specific percentage of annual exchange rate change.

In a later paper Folks extends the break-even approach to incorporate his earlier recommendation about always evaluating foreign borrowing on a hedged basis.[19] In this model the financial manager should calculate the break-even point as the discount rate that equates future payments of principal and interest on a foreign currency loan, on a *covered basis,* to the original proceeds from the loan, using a single currency such as the dollar as a "base" currency.

TAXATION

A multinational firm is subject to taxation in both the home market and in each host country in which it has affiliates or a commercial presence. Tax planning is the subject of Chapter 18, but for the moment we are interested in how it affects the calculation of cost of capital.

Taxation and the Cost of Retained Earnings and Depreciation

The way in which a parent firm's country of domicile taxes the firm's foreign source income may have an effect on the cost of equity. Normally the cost of funds from retained earnings and depreciation is considered to be about equal to the cost of equity from new issues of common stock, if we ignore the transactions costs involved in underwriting new issues. In the U.S. multinational case, however, earnings retained in foreign affiliates are not subject to U.S. corporate income tax, foreign withholding taxes, or transfer costs until those earnings are repatriated. Walter Ness has pointed out that this tax deferral privilege should therefore reduce the cost of equity for retained earnings of affiliates by the value of the tax deferral.[20] (This should also logically include funds retained due to the depreciation tax shield.) Thus Ness feels that the overall cost of equity for a U.S. multinational firm should be adjusted downward to reflect the advantage of tax deferral on retained earnings in affiliates.

One can contest this viewpoint on the grounds that U.S. multinational firms have many methods other than dividends of repatriating funds or repositioning them abroad. These methods, which will be discussed in Chapter 15, include transfer pricing, fees and royalties, intracompany loans, and leads and lags. In most cases they do not involve payment of either the

U.S. corporate income tax or foreign withholding tax on dividends. Therefore little difference exists between retained earnings and any other form of equity from the consolidated firm's viewpoint. Investors have already taken the tax deferral advantage into consideration when setting their required return on a multinational firm's equity. What is true, however, is that the U.S. multinational firm may in fact enjoy an effective overall tax rate that is lower than 46% as long as payment of the U.S. corporate income tax is deferred by efficient positioning of funds. Theoretically, of course, these funds might someday be returned to the parent and eventually the stockholders as a "final liquidating dividend," but in the meantime the U.S. Treasury is making an interest-free loan on the deferred taxes.

Taxation and the Cost of Debt

Determining the effective tax impact on the cost of debt for a multinational firm is complicated. First, the tax manager must forecast tax rates in each market in which the firm intends to borrow. Second, the deductibility of interest by each national tax authority must be determined. In some countries, such as the United Kingdom, interest paid to related foreign affiliates is not tax-deductible. Third, a determination must be made of which legal entities are most cost-effective as borrowers. For example, most U.S. firms would use a foreign finance affiliate to be the official borrower in the Eurobond market in order to minimize taxes on the investors. Fourth, any tax deferral privilege must be considered, although this has the same counterargument as was made for tax deferral on retained earnings.

DISCLOSURE

The worldwide trend toward requiring fuller and more standardized financial disclosure of operating results and balance sheet positions may have the desirable effect of lowering the cost of equity capital. Frederick D. S. Choi has presented a strong theoretical argument for this policy. He concludes:

> Increased firm disclosure tends to improve the subjective probability distributions of a security's expected return streams in the mind of an individual investor by reducing the uncertainty associated with the return stream. For firms which generally outperform the industry average, it is also argued that improved financial disclosure will tend to increase the relative weighting which an investor will place on favorable firm statistics relative to other information vectors which he utilizes in making judgments with respect to the firm. Both of the foregoing effects will entice an individual to pay a larger amount for a given security than otherwise, thus lowering a firm's cost of capital.[21]

The benefit of fuller disclosure was particularly important to firms desiring to raise debt in the Eurocurrency or Eurobond markets according to empirical findings by Choi reported in later studies.[22] A 1973 study of European firms, mostly multinationals, which were preparing to float bond issues on the Eurobond market, revealed that the majority preceded their flotation by increasing their volume and quality of financial disclosure. The inference is that this action was taken on the advice of their investment bankers in hopes of lowering the cost of debt and increasing the chance that the issue would be a successful sellout.

Another piece of evidence supporting the idea that executives believe fuller disclosure may reduce the cost of debt is a recent trend for European and Japanese firms to request bond ratings by Moody's and Standard & Poor's. Previously few non-U.S. firms asked for ratings because of the cost and degree of disclosure required. Now such firms feel they should follow the U.S. bond-rating practice if they expect to compete for funds successfully with U.S. firms in the Eurobond and U.S. bond markets. Bond-rating services have become quite cognizant of the variety of institutional, accounting, and legal differences that make fair comparisons of financial strength across national boundaries a very difficult task.[23] Nevertheless, Moody's and Standard & Poor's attempt to maintain the same quality of standards for non-U.S. bond issues as for U.S. issues.

OPTIMAL FINANCIAL STRUCTURE

The theory of optimal financial structure must be modified considerably to encompass the multinational firm. A number of new variables must be considered:

1. How does international availability of capital affect the optimal debt ratio of a multinational firm?
2. Can financial risk for a multinational firm be reduced through international diversification of cash flows?
3. What should be the finance structures of foreign affiliates, taking into consideration varying country norms, availability of funds, foreign exchange risk, political risk, and tax minimization?

After a brief review of the domestic theory of optimal financial structure, each of these questions will be treated in order.

Theory of Optimal Financial Structure

After many years of debate, finance theorists are still in disagreement on whether or not an optimal financial structure exists for a firm, and if so, how it can be determined. The great debate between the so-called traditionalists and the Modigliani and Miller school of thought has apparently ended in a compromise theory. When taxes and bankruptcy costs are considered, a firm has an optimal financial structure determined by that particular mix of debt and equity that minimizes the firm's cost of capital for a given level of business risk. If the business risk of new projects differs from the risk of existing projects, the optimal mix of debt and equity would change to recognize trade-offs between business and financial risks.

Exhibit 12.5 illustrates how the cost of capital varies with the amount of debt employed. As the debt ratio, defined as total debt divided by total assets, increases, the overall cost of capital (K) decreases because of the heavier weight of low-cost debt [$K_i(1 - t)$] compared to high-cost equity (K_e). The low cost of debt is, of course, due to the tax deductibility of interest shown by the term $(1 - t)$.

Partly offsetting the favorable effect of more debt is an increase in the cost of equity (K_e), because investors perceive greater financial risk. Nevertheless, the overall weighted average aftertax cost of capital (K) continues to decline as the debt ratio increases, until financial risk becomes so serious that investors and management alike perceive a real danger of *insolvency*. This result causes a sharp increase in the cost of new debt and equity, thus increasing the weighted average cost of capital. The low point on the resulting U-shaped cost of capital curve, which is at 14% in Exhibit 12.5, defines the debt ratio range in which the cost of capital is minimized.

Most theorists believe that the low point is actually a rather broad flat area encompassing a wide range of debt ratios, 30% to 60% in Exhibit 12.5,

EXHIBIT 12.5
Cost of Capital and Financial Structure

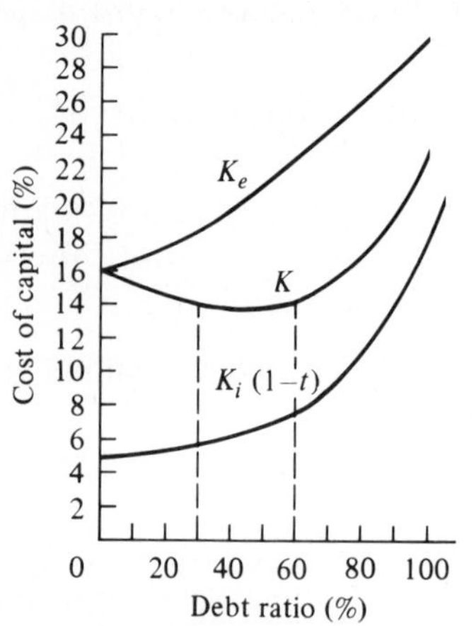

Key: debt ratio = $\frac{\text{total debt}}{\text{total assets}}$

K = weighted average aftertax cost of capital

K_e = cost of equity

$K_i(1 - t)$ = aftertax cost of debt

30%–60% = minimum cost of capital range

where little difference exists in the cost of capital. They also believe that, at least in the United States, the range of the flat area and the location of a particular firm's debt ratio within that range are determined by a variety of noncost variables. Two such variables have an important effect on the financial structure of multinational firms, namely, availability of capital and financial risk. These are discussed in the next two sections.

Availability of Capital

It was shown earlier in this chapter that international availability of capital to a multinational firm may allow it to lower its cost of equity and debt compared to most domestic firms. In addition, international availability permits a multinational firm to maintain its desired debt ratio, even when significant amounts of new funds must be raised. In other words, a *multinational firm's marginal cost of capital is constant for considerable ranges of its capital budget.* This statement is not true for most small domestic firms because they do not have access to the national equity or debt markets. They must either rely on internally generated funds or borrow short- and medium-term from commercial banks.

Multinational firms domiciled in countries that have illiquid equity markets are in almost the same situation as small domestic firms. They must rely on internally generated funds and bank borrowing, although the larger non-U.S. multinationals also have access to Eurobond and foreign bond markets. If they need to raise significant amounts of new funds to finance growth opportunities, they may need to borrow more than would be optimal from the viewpoint of minimizing their cost of capital. This is equivalent to saying that *their marginal cost of capital is increasing at higher budget levels.*

As an illustration of the effect of availability of capital on optimal financial structure and the marginal cost of capital, Exhibit 12.6 presents a graphical comparison between a U.S. multinational firm and either a non-U.S. multinational firm that faces an illiquid equity market at home or a small domestic U.S. firm.

In Exhibit 12.6a a U.S. multinational firm is depicted as enjoying a constant marginal cost of capital at all levels of its likely capital budget. Thus it is able to raise funds in the proportion desired for minimizing its cost of capital (K). In this example it can minimize its cost of capital by choosing any debt ratio between 30% and 60%, which is the lowest (flat) part of its cost of capital curve. If it chooses 45%, for example, it can raise all the funds it needs in the proportion of 45% debt and 55% equity without raising the cost of these funds. Even if internally generated funds are insufficient to maintain this proportion, it can sell new equity at about the same price as its existing equity. The optimal capital budget for the U.S. multinational firm in this example happens to be $90 million (Exhibit 12.6a). This is the point where its marginal return on capital just equals its marginal cost of capital. In other words, if it ranks all capital budgeting

EXHIBIT 12.6
Cost of Capital and Financial Structure: Constant versus Rising Marginal Cost of Capital

(a) U.S. Multinational Firm

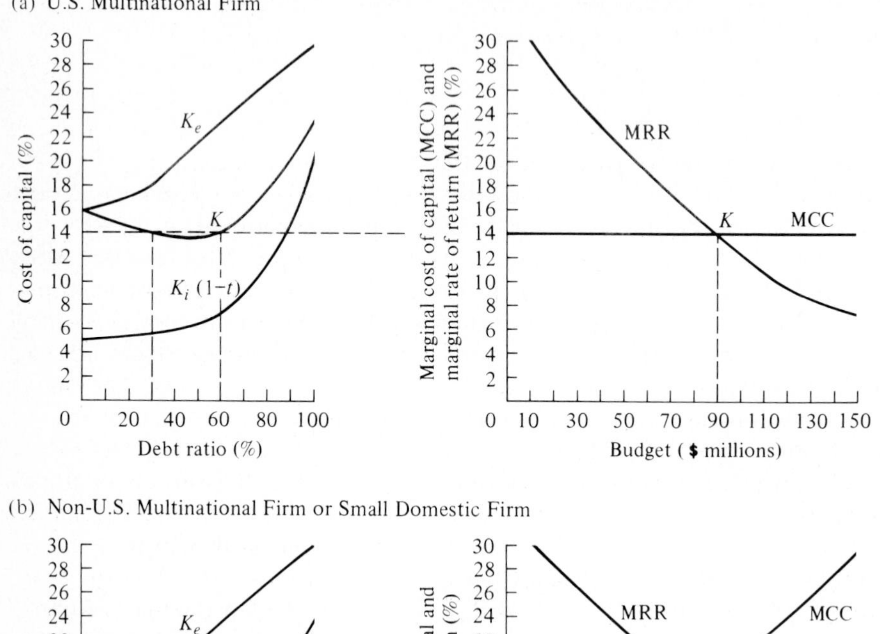

(b) Non-U.S. Multinational Firm or Small Domestic Firm

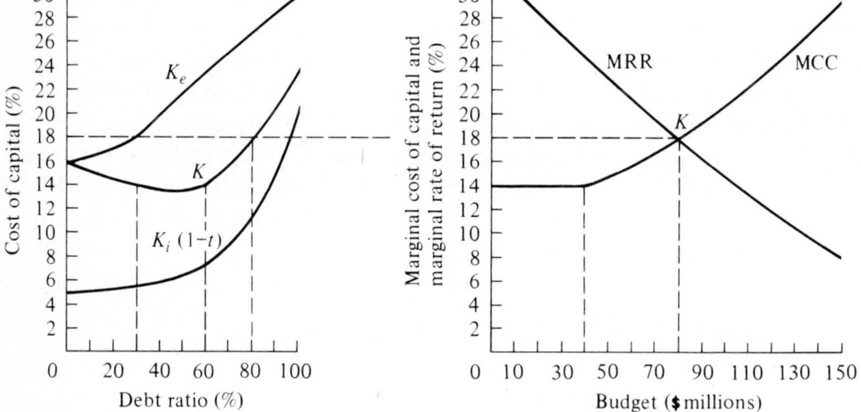

projects according to their internal rate of return (IRR), the last project to be accepted would be the one whose IRR just equals the firm's 14% marginal weighted average aftertax cost of capital (K).

Neither the non-U.S. multinational firm, which is assumed not to have access to a liquid national equity market, nor the small U.S. domestic firm can raise funds in the proportions desired to minimize their cost of capital

(K). Yet they are assumed to have the same relationship between their cost of capital (K) and their debt ratios as the U.S. multinational firm. In other words, the left-hand graphs are identical. Furthermore, all three firms are assumed to face the same opportunities, represented by the marginal return on capital curves (MRR). The difference is that the non-U.S. multinational firm and small U.S. domestic firm can maintain their optimal debt ratio range (30% to 60%) only for capital budgets up to $40 million. At that point they have committed all their internally generated funds plus the optimal proportion of additional debt. If they wish to reach their optimal budget, which is $80 million, they must borrow all the remaining $40 million. Neither firm can raise $40 million in their national equity markets, except perhaps at exorbitant rates or with unacceptable loss of control. Nevertheless, despite increasing their debt ratios to 80%, and thus their cost of capital (K) to 18%, both firms should borrow the additional $40 million in order to realize their profit potential. Their profit potential is maximized at the point in the capital budget where the marginal return on capital (MRR) equals the marginal cost of capital (MCC).

It should be noted that not only do the non-U.S. multinational firm and the small U.S. domestic firm have a higher cost of capital, which is 18% compared to 14% for the U.S. multinational firm, but their optimal capital budget is lower, $80 million compared to $90 million for the U.S. multinational firm. Thus it is not surprising that financial market imperfections have been cited frequently in this book as factors that give U.S. multinational corporations an advantage over U.S. domestic firms or non-U.S. multinationals that do not have access to liquid equity markets. It should also be noted, however, that a number of large non-U.S. multinational firms do indeed have access to U.S. equity markets for new issues and are also listed on U.S. stock markets. Furthermore, the equity markets in the United Kingdom are considered to be fairly liquid, and equity markets in the EEC are gradually improving.

Financial Risk Reduction through International Diversification of Cash Flows

The theoretical possibility exists that multinational firms are in a better position than domestic firms to support higher debt ratios because their cash flows are diversified internationally. The probability of a firm covering fixed charges under varying conditions in product, financial, and foreign exchange markets should improve if the variability of its cash flows is minimized.

By diversifying cash flows internationally, the multinational firm might be able to achieve the same kind of reduction in cash flow variability as portfolio investors receive from diversifying their security holdings internationally. The same argument applies, namely, that returns are not perfectly correlated between countries. For example, in 1980–1985 the economies of Germany and Japan were growing slowly, but the United States was experiencing comparatively healthy growth. Therefore one might have expected returns, either on a cash flow or earnings basis, to be depressed in Germany and Japan while being favorable in the United States. A multinational firm with operations located in all three of these countries could rely on its strong U.S. cash inflow to cover debt obligations, even if the German and Japanese affiliates produced weak net cash inflows.

In contrast, a domestic German or Japanese firm would not enjoy the benefit of cash flow international diversification but would have to rely entirely on its own depressed net cash inflow from domestic operations. Perceived financial risk for the German firm would have been greater than for a multinational firm because the variability of its German domestic cash flows could not be offset by positive cash flows elsewhere in the world.

FINANCIAL STRUCTURE OF FOREIGN AFFILIATES

If one accepts the theory that minimizing the cost of capital for a given level of business risk and capital budget is an objective that should be implemented from the perspective of the consolidated multinational firm, then the financial structure of each affiliate is relevant only to the extent that it affects this overall goal. In other words, an individual affiliate does not really have an independent cost of capital, and therefore its finance structure should not be based on an objective of minimizing its own independent cost of capital.

On the other hand, market imperfections and national institutional constraints dictate that *variables other than minimizing the cost of capital* are often major determinants of debt ratios for firms outside the United States. A question is thus raised about whether a multinational firm should consider these country norms that are not related to cost when it establishes finance structures for its foreign affiliates. In order to answer this question, we will present some empirical findings that describe financial structure norms in several representative countries. Then we will analyze whether a multinational firm should attempt to conform to these country norms within the broader constraint of minimizing their cost of capital on a consolidated worldwide basis.

Country Debt Ratio Norms

In the survey of financial executives in four industries and five countries, previously described in Chapter 1, the executives responded that in determining the optimal financial structure for their firms, the following factors were more important than minimizing the cost of capital:

1. risk: defined as the degree of cash flow coverage of fixed charges under varying market conditions,
2. availability of capital, and
3. international factors related to financing foreign operations, and reacting to foreign exchange and political risks.[24]

A number of institutional, cultural, and historical reasons explain why these noncost factors are important debt ratio determinants for both U.S. and non-U.S. firms.

French executives believed that *availability of capital* in both domestic and foreign markets was the key determinant of debt ratios. They were not as concerned with minimizing cost of capital as they were with guaranteeing availability of funds to meet all financial needs. They appear to perceive their firms as facing a rising marginal cost of capital curve, as depicted in Exhibit 12.6.

Japanese financial executives also responded that *availability of capital* was more important than cost of capital as a debt ratio determinant. This response was partly due to the lack of accumulated savings in Japan following World War II, combined with the rapid growth of Japanese firms in the postwar years. Rate of growth and variance of earnings were also cited as important determinants. These reflected management's concern for the inability of firms to generate enough funds through internal cash flow to match the existing potential for growth. The peculiar role of the Japanese stockholder, described earlier in Chapter 1, made issuing new equity far less desirable than borrowing from their banker-stockholders. As a result, debt ratios are extremely high in Japan. Nevertheless, in view of the high degree of mutual loyalty between Japanese bankers and their corporate clients, the perceived risk of default on loans would not conjure up visions of bankruptcy until conditions became really hopeless. Even then, if the firm is important to the economy, a reorganization is more likely to occur than complete liquidation. It appears that Japanese financial executives, like their French counterparts, believe that their firms face rising marginal-cost-of-capital curves.

Dutch financial executives were most concerned about *financial risk.* They worried that their cash flows might not cover their fixed charges such as principal, interest, and lease payments. They also placed emphasis on *minimizing the cost of capital* and ensuring the *availability of capital.* However, in the Netherlands, as was the case elsewhere outside the United States, financial executives felt that new equity issues were too difficult to sell at all—much less at a reasonable price. Their equity markets were simply too illiquid and segmented. Therefore their meaning of cost and availability of capital related primarily to the *cost and availability* of debt. This was a function of bargaining with their bankers, because the national bond market is

EXHIBIT 12.7
Debt Ratios in Selected Industries and Countries

Country	*No. of firms*	*Food and beverage*	*Metals*	*Mining and petroleum*	*Textiles and apparel*	*Paper*	*Chemicals*	*Electronics*	*Motor vehicles*	*Pharmaceuticals*	*Industrial farm equip.*
France	41	56.6	64.4	57.5	—	—	63.6	71.4	74.6	—	—
Germany	37	—	57.6	42.3	—	—	40.5	37.9	45.1	28.1	49.5
Japan	79	62.4	83.5	90.9	71.9	79.2	81.1	58.7	78.3	40.5	78.2
United Kingdom	90	49.3	51.5	42.7	51.7	60.3	48.2	53.2	54.0	42.1	54.8
United States	326	47.3	45.9	44.5	44.8	40.8	42.3	46.8	48.2	36.8	45.6
Total	573										

Source: Prepared by Vinod Bavishi, Frederick Choi, and Hany Shawky from the data bank at the Center for Transnational Accounting and Financial Research, University of Connecticut, Storrs, Connecticut, 1981.

Note: The number in the matrix represents average total debt as a percentage of total assets, based on book value for year end 1980. The numbers are computed by averaging the debt ratios for the individual firms in each category. The minimum number of firms in each industry is four.

also underdeveloped. Dutch bankers, needless to say, play a crucial role in determining the debt ratios of their clients regardless of the preference of their clients.

Norwegian financial executives also indicated that *financial risk* and *availability of capital* were the most important determinants of their debt ratios. Their situation was similar to that in Japan and the Netherlands insofar as the banks were the prime source of new capital. New equity issues were not a viable alternative in Norway, nor were stock market prices considered a reliable barometer of the market value of individual firms. The reliance on debt in Norway was so total that debt ratios approached 80% in the sample firms, with most debt being nominally short-term. In reality, however, short-term bank debt in countries such as Norway, Japan, and the Netherlands is commonly renewed almost indefinitely and therefore resembles long-term debt in the United States.

Even in the United States financial executives responded that the *financial risk* of not covering fixed charges under various cash flow forecasts was the primary determinant of their debt ratios. *International factors* were also quite important at the time of the survey because the U.S. foreign direct investment program was still in effect. U.S. multinational firms were forced into medium- and long-term borrowing in the Euromarkets to finance growth of their foreign affiliates. In some cases this feature increased the debt ratios of firms that normally financed all growth internally. Foreign borrowing was also undertaken by U.S. firms to reduce their exposure to foreign exchange risk. In contrast to financial executives in other countries, U.S. financial executives did not consider availability of capital to be an important determinant of their debt ratios. This is additional evidence of the comparative liquidity of U.S. capital markets. As occurred in other countries, U.S. financial executives did not place much emphasis on minimizing the cost of capital in deciding on their debt ratios. Perhaps they perceived their firms to be within the broad range of debt ratios where cost of capital would hardly change with a change in debt ratios. In other words, they are facing a constant marginal cost of capital for increasing budget levels as shown in Exhibit 12.6.

Because of national environmental characteristics, as illustrated in the above survey, average debt ratios for industrial firms vary considerably from country to country.[25] Exhibit 12.7 illustrates variations in debt ratios for selected industries and countries at the end of 1980.

Localized Financial Structures for Foreign Affiliates

Within the given constraint of minimizing its consolidated worldwide cost of capital, should a multinational firm take differing country debt ratio norms into consideration when determining its desired debt ratio for foreign affiliates? For example, should ITT have its Norwegian affiliate,

Standard Telefon og Kabelfabrikk, adopt a financial structure containing 80% debt, which is typical for its industry in Norway?

For definition purposes the debt considered here should be only that which is borrowed from sources outside the multinational firm. This debt would include local and foreign currency loans as well as Eurocurrency loans. The reason for this definition is that parent loans to foreign affiliates are often regarded as equivalent to equity investment both by host countries and by investing firms. A parent loan is usually subordinated to other debt and does not create the same threat of insolvency as an external loan. Furthermore, the choice of debt or equity investment is often arbitrary and subject to negotiation between host country and parent firm.

The main advantages of a finance structure for foreign affiliates that conforms to local debt norms are as follows:

1. A localized financial structure reduces criticism of foreign affiliates that have been operating with too high a proportion of debt (judged by local standards), often resulting in the accusation that they are not contributing a fair share of risk capital to the host country. At the other end of the spectrum, it would improve the image of foreign affiliates that have been operating with too little debt and thus appear to be insensitive to local monetary policy.
2. A localized financial structure helps management evaluate return on equity investment relative to local competitors in the same industry. In economies where interest rates are relatively high as an offset to inflation, the penalty paid reminds management of the need to consider price level changes when evaluating investment performances.
3. In economies where interest rates are relatively high because of a scarcity of capital, the penalty paid for borrowing local funds reminds management that unless return on assets is greater than the local price of capital—i.e., negative leverage—they are probably misallocating scarce domestic resources. This factor may not appear to be relevant to management decisions, but it will certainly be considered by the host country in making decisions with respect to the firm.

The main disadvantages of localized financial structures are as follows:

1. A multinational firm is expected to have a comparative advantage over local firms in overcoming imperfections in national capital markets through better availability of capital and the ability to diversify risk. Why should it throw away these important competitive advantages to conform to local norms that are established in response to imperfect local capital markets, historical precedent, and institutional constraints that do not apply to the multinational firm?
2. If each foreign affiliate of a multinational firm localizes its financial structure, the resulting consolidated balance sheet might show a

financial structure that does not conform to any particular country's norm. The debt ratio would be a simple weighted average of the corresponding ratio of each country in which the firm happened to operate. This feature could increase perceived financial risk and thus the cost of capital for the multinational firm, but only if two additional conditions are present:

a. The consolidated debt ratio must be pushed completely out of the discretionary range of acceptable debt ratios in the flat area of the cost of capital curve, shown previously in Exhibit 12.5.

b. The multinational firm must be unable to offset high debt in one foreign affiliate with low debt in other foreign or domestic affiliates *at the same cost.* If the International Fisher Effect is working, replacement of debt should be possible at an equal aftertax cost after adjusting for foreign exchange risk. On the other hand, if market imperfections preclude this type of replacement, the possibility exists that the overall cost of debt, and thus the cost of capital, could increase for the multinational firm if it attempts to conform to local norms.

3. The debt ratio of a foreign affiliate is in reality only cosmetic, since lenders ultimately look to the parent and its consolidated worldwide cash flow as the source of repayment. In many cases debt of affiliates must be guaranteed by the parent firm. Even if no formal guarantee exists, an implied guarantee usually exists since almost no parent firm would dare to allow an affiliate to default on a loan. If it did, repercussions would surely be felt with respect to the parent's own financial standing, with a resulting increase in its cost of capital.

In our opinion a compromise position is possible. Both multinational and domestic firms should try to minimize their overall weighted average cost of capital for a given level of business risk and capital budget, as finance theory suggests. However, if debt is available to a foreign affiliate at equal cost to that which could be raised elsewhere, after adjusting for foreign exchange risk, then localizing the foreign affiliate's financial structure should incur no cost penalty and yet would also enjoy the advantages listed above.

Naturally, if a particular foreign affiliate has access to local debt at a lower cost, after adjusting for foreign exchange risk, than other sources of debt available to the multinational firm, the multinational firm should borrow all it can through that foreign affiliate. The reverse would be true if the foreign affiliate only had access to higher-cost debt than available elsewhere. Nothing should be borrowed externally through that foreign affiliate.

These disequilibrium situations for a foreign affiliate can only occur in imperfect or segmented markets because otherwise the International Fisher

Effect should eliminate any such opportunities. The fact that opportunities to lower the cost of debt do exist is simply evidence of market imperfections or segmentation.

In summary, a multinational firm should probably follow a policy of borrowing at lowest cost, after adjusting for foreign exchange risk, anywhere in the world without regard to the cosmetic impact on any particular affiliate's financial structure. This policy assumes that local regulations permit this practice. The objective for a multinational firm is the same as that for a domestic firm, namely, to minimize its consolidated cost of capital for a given level of business risk and capital budget. On the other hand, if conforming to host country debt norms does not require a cost penalty, but merely replaces debt in one affiliate by debt in another, worthwhile advantages can be realized. These advantages include better public relations with host country monetary authorities and more realistic evaluation of performance of foreign affiliates relative to competition with host country firms.

CHOOSING AMONG SOURCES OF FUNDS TO FINANCE FOREIGN AFFILIATES

In addition to resolving the issue of choosing an appropriate financial structure for foreign affiliates, financial managers of multinational firms need to choose among alternative sources of funds to finance foreign affiliates.

Potential Sources of Funds

Sources of funds available to foreign affiliates can be classified as shown in Exhibit 12.8. In general terms they include the following:

- Funds generated internally by the foreign affiliates.
- Funds from within the corporate family.
- Funds from sources external to the corporate family.

The choice among the sources of funds ideally involves simultaneously *minimizing the cost* of external funds after adjusting for *foreign exchange risk,* choosing internal sources in order to *minimize worldwide taxes* and *political risk,* and ensuring that *managerial motivation* in the foreign affiliates is geared toward minimizing the firm's consolidated worldwide cost of capital, rather than the foreign affiliate's cost of capital. Needless to say, this task is almost impossible, and the tendency is to place more emphasis on one of the variables at the expense of others. Some notable theoretical attempts have been made to solve the problem, but all of these have had to ignore one or more of the variables in order to optimize a specific model.[26]

Minimizing the cost of new long-term external funds, after adjusting for foreign exchange risk, has already been analyzed earlier from the view-

EXHIBIT 12.8
Potential Sources of Capital for Financing a Foreign Affiliate

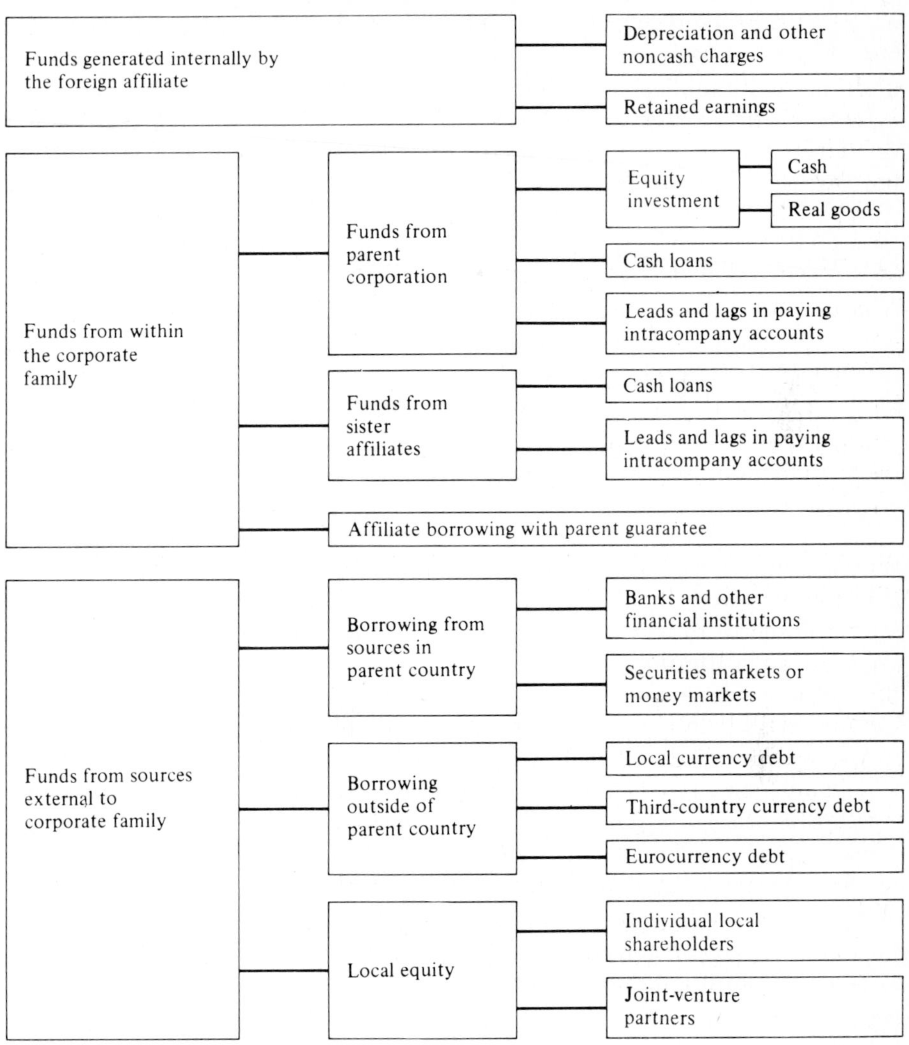

point of minimizing the cost of debt and equity to the consolidated worldwide firm. This is a more appropriate perspective than analyzing external funds from the viewpoint of a foreign affiliate.

The political risk implications of various strategies for financing foreign affiliates has been treated in Chapter 9. Political risk needs to be integrated with other considerations of cost, taxes, foreign exchange risk, and managerial motivation, but so far this integration has not been accomplished in theory or practice.

At least a portion of the financing problem is to provide short-term financing when and where it is needed by the affiliates. This problem can best be analyzed as an exercise in optimal positioning of funds within the multinational family group; that is the subject of Chapter 15. However, one issue that often arises in connection with short-term financing—and is not related to optimal positioning—is the question of parent guarantees of bank borrowing by foreign affiliates.

Parent Guarantees of Bank Loans to Foreign Affiliates

A large portion of bank lending to foreign affiliates is based on formal or informal guarantees by the parent firm. Parent guarantees can take a variety of forms. The strongest type is an "unlimited guarantee" in which the lender is protected on all loans to the affiliate without regard to amount or time limit. Other guarantees are limited to a single loan agreement between a lender and an affiliate and constitute only part of the specific loan agreement.

Yet another type of guarantee is a purchase agreement under which the parent commits itself to purchase the affiliate's promissory note from the lender in case the affiliate defaults. A weaker version of this is a "collection guarantee" in which the parent guarantees only that the lender will be able to collect the note. The lender must first try to collect the note from the affiliate before turning to the guarantor-parent. An even weaker arrangement, which is not a true guarantee, is for the parent to subordinate its own claims on the affiliate to those of the lender.

Many parents hesitate to guarantee the debts of their affiliates. According to the survey by Robbins and Stobaugh, parents whose international business is "small" (foreign sales of less than $100 million) prefer not to guarantee their affiliates' loan.[27] The financial statements of such affiliates are often not consolidated with the parent, and thus affiliate borrowing without a guarantee need not be reported to stockholders or lenders. In addition, such firms often want their affiliates to "stand on their own two feet."

Robbins and Stobaugh report that, in contrast, medium-sized firms (foreign sales between $100 million and $500 million) are often willing to give a guarantee, either for a small reduction in the cost of borrowing or to avoid the inclusion of complicating covenants in the loan agreement.

Large firms (foreign sales greater than $500 million) are similar to small firms; they prefer no guarantee. They often adopt a specific "no guarantee" rule, in part because they find it easier to be consistent than to try to differentiate among affiliates. Additionally they believe their affiliates can command the best interest rate without a guarantee, and they believe the affiliate is a better corporate citizen if it has the capital to stand on its own.

The substance of most parent guarantees is that the lender advances funds on the basis of the parent's credit standing. Although as a procedural matter the creditor will look first to the affiliate for repayment, in the eyes of the creditor repayment is ultimately the responsibility of the parent.

Robbins and Stobaugh note that some parents that will not provide a legal guarantee will nevertheless supply a "moral" guarantee, also referred to as a "monkey" or "Oklahoma" letter.[28] Such a letter indicates the willingness of the parent to stand behind its subsidiary to protect the reputation of the entire corporate system. Robbins and Stobaugh quote one such letter: "It is as inconceivable to us as it would be to you that we would change our ownership or draw out our investment without first notifying you and honoring our proportion of all debts."[29] Under a moral guarantee the parent might decide not to honor its obligation if the affiliate's difficulties were caused by political harassment rather than by adverse business fortunes.

A variation on borrowing with parent guarantee is the use of parent or network banking connections to obtain local loans. For example, New York banks may use their prestige and credit to help foreign affiliates of their U.S. customers find short-term or medium-term funds within a foreign country. Funds of the New York bank as such are not involved, except in the unusual circumstances that the foreign affiliate defaults to the local bank.

The technique works as follows: Assume that an Argentine affiliate of a U.S. firm wants short-term funds and that the U.S. parent would like to facilitate a loan to its affiliate by an Argentine bank. The U.S. parent arranges for its U.S. bank to open an irrevocable letter of credit in favor of the Argentine bank, authorizing the Argentine bank to draw sight drafts on the New York bank for sums not exceeding the total amount of the credit, to be drawn and honored only if the affiliate does not repay its loan.[30] This is called a "standby" letter of credit.

The result of this arrangement is that the Argentine bank makes a fully guaranteed loan to the affiliate. The affiliate receives the needed funds, but no exchange transaction is required and no exchange risk is incurred. The New York bank does not guarantee that the affiliate will repay the loan but agrees to make payment under its letter of credit if the affiliate defaults. Should the affiliate default, however, the New York bank will collect from the U.S. parent, which is presumed to be of outstanding reputation and credit standing.

When a parent is willing to guarantee a loan, that parent will often want the guarantee effective only under the home country legal jurisdiction. This policy ensures that any litigation will take place under a known set of laws and that the parent will not become a political whipping boy in a foreign court system. In the example above the parent had no obligation under the laws of Argentina.

If a direct parent guarantee to a bank is involved, that guarantee will often be to an entity in the home country. For example, the Italian affiliate of a U.S. manufacturing firm borrows in Italy with a parent guarantee. If the loan is from the Milan branch of a U.S. bank, the guarantee will be made to the U.S. parent bank. If the loan is from the parent office of an Italian bank, the guarantee will be made to the U.S. branch of that Italian bank.

It should be noted that parents are not the only source of guarantees. A given affiliate's loans may also be guaranteed by sister affiliates, perhaps for reasons of legal jurisdiction or perhaps to put a smaller limit on the effective amount of the guarantee.

SUMMARY

Measuring the cost of capital for a multinational firm is complicated by a number of environmental factors that distinguish multinational firms from domestic firms, as well as multinational firms headquartered in one country from those headquartered in another country. Access to international sources of both debt and equity increases the short-term availability of capital to multinational firms, thus allowing them to enjoy a constant marginal cost of capital over large variations in capital budgets.

Firms that must source their long-term funds in segmented national capital markets are likely to have a higher cost of capital than firms that can source funds in integrated capital markets.

Investors may be willing to pay a premium for the shares of multinational firms in order to satisfy their international diversification motives. This assumes that segmented capital markets prevent them from satisfying this motive through international portfolio diversification.

Long-term foreign currency debt is particularly exposed to foreign exchange risk, a fact that has had an adverse impact on the earnings of some firms in recent years.

Taxation policies of both home and host countries will influence a firm's aftertax cost of capital and the manner in which it finances its affiliates.

Full disclosure of operating results appears to have a favorable influence on the cost of capital of non-U.S. multinational firms that have raised capital in international markets. A difference in opinion exists about the effect on cost of capital of taxes on earnings retained abroad.

The optimal financial structure of multinational firms could differ from that of domestic firms because of the greater availability of capital to multinational firms as well as their ability to diversify internationally their cash flows. The optimal financial structure should be determined from the viewpoint of the consolidated worldwide multinational firm. Within this broad guideline the financial structure of a foreign affiliate might be determined in part by its host country norms. This assumes no increase in cost of capital to the multinational firm as a whole but rather substitution of debt in one country for debt in another.

To choose among the large variety of sources of funds available to finance foreign affiliates, the financial manager of a multinational firm must consider trade-offs among cost, foreign exchange risk, political risk, taxes, and managerial motivation.

NOTES

1. A third method to measure the cost of equity, the arbitrage pricing theory (APT), is presently being developed, as explained in Chapter 1. It is not yet operational but holds promise for future use.

2. Frederic G. Donner, "The World-Wide Corporation in a Modern Economy," Address to the 8th International Congress of Accountants, Waldorf-Astoria Hotel, New York, September 27, 1962.

3. Early studies were by Herbert G. Grubel, "Internationally Diversified Portfolios: Welfare Gains and Capital Flows," *American Economic Review,* December 1968, pp. 1299–1314; Hiam Levy and Marshall Sarnat, "International Diversification of Investment Portfolios," *American Economic Review,* September 1970, pp. 668–675; Herbert G. Grubel and Kenneth Fadner, "The Interdependence of International Equity Markets," *Journal of Finance,* March 1971, pp. 89–94; Tamir Agmon, "The Relations among Equity Markets: A Study of Share Price Co-Movements in the U.S., U.K., Germany, and Japan," *Journal of Finance,* September 1972, pp. 839–855.

4. See Fischer Black, "International Capital Market Equilibrium with Investment Barriers," *Journal of Financial Economics,* December 1974, pp. 337–352; Bruno H. Solnik, "An International Market Model of Security Price Behavior," *Journal of Financial and Quantitative Analysis,* September 1974, pp. 537–554; Michael Adler and Bernard Dumas, "Optimal International Acquisitions," *Journal of Finance,* March 1975, pp. 1–19; Frederick A. Grauer, Robert A. Litzenberger, and Richard F. Stehle, "Sharing Rules and Equilibrium in an International Capital Market under Uncertainty," *Journal of Financial Economics,* June 1976, pp. 233–256.

5. Early tests were by Donald R. Lessard, "World, National, and Industry Factors in Equity Returns," *Journal of Finance,* May 1974, pp. 379–391; Bruno H. Solnik, "The International Pricing of Risk: An Empirical Investigation of the World Capital Market Structure," *Journal of Finance,* May 1974, pp. 365–378; Richard F. Stehle, "An Empirical Test of the Alternative Hypothesis of National and International Pricing of Risk Assets," *Journal of Finance,* May 1977, pp. 493–502.

6. For a summary of testing problems, see Steven W. Kohlhagen, "Overlapping National Investment Portfolios: Evidence and Implications of International Integration of Secondary Markets for Financial Assets," in Donald R. Lessard, ed., *International Financial Management,* 2nd ed., New York: Wiley, 1985, pp. 97–117.

7. Richard Roll, "A Critique of the Asset Pricing Theory's Tests," *Journal of Financial Economics,* March 1977, pp. 129–176; Stephen A. Ross, "The Current Status of the Capital Asset Pricing Model (CAPM)," *Journal of Finance,* June 1978, pp. 885–901; Bruno H. Solnik, "Testing International Asset Pricing: Some Pessimistic Views," *Journal of Finance,* May 1977, pp. 503–512.

8. For a summary of empirical work on the multinational firm as a proxy for internationally diversified portfolios, see Marjorie T. Stanley, "Capital Structure and Cost of Capital for the Multinational Firm,"*Journal of International Business Studies,* Spring–Summer 1981, pp. 103–120. Important tests of this hypothesis have been undertaken by John S. Hughes, Dennis E. Logue, and Richard J. Sweeney, "Corporate International Diversification and Market Assigned Measures of Risk and Diversification," *Journal of Financial and Quantitative Analysis,* November 1975, pp. 627–637; Tamir Agmon and Donald R. Lessard, "Investor Recognition of Corporate International Diversification," *Journal of Finance,* September 1977, pp. 1049–1055; Wayne Y. Lee and Kanwal S. Sachdeva, "The Role of the Multinational Firm in the Integration of Segmented Markets," *Journal of Finance,* May 1977, pp. 479–492; Alan M. Rugman, "Risk Reduction by International Diversification," *Journal of International Business Studies,* Fall 1976, pp. 75–80; Bertrand Jacquillat and Bruno H. Solnik, "Multinationals Are Poor Tools for Diversification," *Journal of Portfolio Management,* Winter 1978, pp. 8–12; Vihang Errunza and Lemma W. Senbet, "The Effects of International Operations on the Market Value of the Firm: Theory and Evidence," *Journal of Finance,* May 1981, pp. 401–417.

9. Richard C. Stapleton and Marti G. Subrahmanyam, "Market Imperfections, Capital Market Equilibrium, and Corporation Finance," *Journal of Finance,* May 1977, p. 317.

10. The Novo case material is a condensed version of Arthur Stonehill and Kåre B. Dullum, *Internationalizing the Cost of Capital in Theory and Practice: The Novo Experience and National Policy Implications,* Copenhagen: Nyt Nordisk Forlag Arnold Busck, 1982; and New York: Wiley, 1983.

11. This prohibition has since been dropped with a corresponding reversal of its negative effects on Danish valuation of domestic securities.

12. Steven M. Dawson, "Eurobond Currency Selection: Hindsight," *Financial Executive,* November 1973, pp. 72–73.

13. William R. Folks, Jr., and Josef Follpract, "The Currency of Denomination Decision for Eurobonds: The American Experience," Unpublished manuscript, Center for International Business Studies, University of South Carolina, 1976.

14. *Ibid.,* pp. 20–21. The authors surveyed the executives responsible for the foreign currency debt issues shown in Exhibit 12.4.

15. This approach is defended on a theoretical level by Gunter Dufey and Ian H. Giddy, "International Financial Planning: The Use of Market-Based Forecasts," *California Management Review,* Fall 1978, pp. 69–81.

16. A formalized model for selecting optimal sources of foreign debt using the portfolio theory approach has been developed by James V. Jucker and Clovis de Faro, "The Selection of International Borrowing Sources," *Journal of Financial and Quantitative Analysis,* September 1975, pp. 381–407.

17. Folks and Follpract, "Currency of Denomination Decision," p. 22. Also see William R. Folks, Jr., "Optimal Foreign Borrowing Strategies with Operations in Forward Exchange Markets," *Journal of Financial and Quantitative Analysis,* June 1978, pp. 245–254.

18. Dufey and Giddy, in "International Financial Planning," demonstrate the use of differential interest rates on long-term bonds as one goes out on the yield curve to forecast future forward rates.

19. Folks, "Optimal Foreign Borrowing Strategies."

20. Walter L. Ness, Jr., "U.S. Corporate Income Taxation and the Dividend Remittance Policy of Multinational Corporations," *Journal of International Business Studies,* Spring 1975, pp. 67–77.

21. Frederick D. S. Choi, "Financial Disclosure in Relation to a Firm's Capital Costs," *Accounting and Business Research,* Autumn 1973, p. 279.

22. Frederick D. S. Choi, "European Disclosure: The Competitive Disclosure Hypothesis," *Journal of International Business Studies,* Fall 1974, pp. 15–23. Also see Frederick D. S. Choi, "Financial Disclosure and Entry to the European Capital Market," *Journal of Accounting Research,* Autumn 1973, pp. 159–175.

23. For a good description of how the ratings are done on non-U.S. firms, see Keith Wheelock, "An Aaa or a Baa—How Moody's Provides Its Ratings," *Euromoney,* June 1975, pp. 28–32.

24. Arthur Stonehill, Theo Beekhuisen, Richard Wright, Lee Remmers, Norman Toy, Antonio Parés, Alan Shapiro, Douglas Egan, and Thomas Bates, "Financial Goals and Debt Ratio Determinants: A Survey of Practice in Five Countries," *Financial Management,* Autumn 1975, pp. 27–41.

25. For details on typical debt ratios see Norman Toy, Arthur Stonehill, Lee Remmers, Richard Wright, and Theo Beekhuisen, "A Comparative International Study of Growth, Profitability, and Risk as Determinants of Corporate Debt Ratios in the Manufacturing Sector," *Journal of Financial and Quantitative Analysis,* November 1974, pp. 875–886.

26. See Alan C. Shapiro, "Evaluating Financing Costs for Multinational Subsidiaries," *Journal of International Business Studies,* Fall 1975, pp. 25–32; Clovis de Faro and James V. Jucker, "The Impact of Inflation and Devaluation on the Selection of an International Borrowing Source," *Journal of International Business Studies,* Fall 1973, pp. 97–104; William R. Folks, Jr., "The Analysis of Short-Term Cross-Border Financing Decisions," *Financial Management,* Autumn 1976, pp. 19–27.

27. Sidney M. Robbins and Robert B. Stobaugh, *Money in the Multinational Enterprise,* New York: Basic Books, 1973, pp. 67–69.

28. Ibid., p. 68.

29. Ibid.

30. Max Wasserman, Charles Hultman, and Lasz Zsoldes, *International Finance,* New York: Simmons-Boardman, 1963, pp. 172–173.

Chapter 12: Appendix Diversification and Required Rates of Return

Donald R. Lessard
Associate Professor
Sloan School of Management, MIT

A firm's cost of capital, or required return, for a specific project depends on the riskiness of the project's operating cash flows and on the contribution of the project to the firm's borrowing capacity. The weighted average formula presented in Chapter 12 provides a reasonable benchmark for projects that are similar to the majority of a firm's investments in both regards. For projects which differ in one or both regards, however, the weighted average formula presented gives little guidance since it provides no statement of how the cost of equity capital will vary with changes in business risk and financial structure. An alternative weighted average formula provides this link.[1]

$$K = k_u\left[1 - T\left(\frac{D}{V}\right)\right] \tag{1}$$

where

k_u = the cost of capital for the project if financed entirely with equity,
T = corporate tax rate,
D = project's contribution to borrowing capacity of the firm,
V = total market value of the project.

Foreign projects may differ from domestic projects either because of differences in business risk, reflected in k_u, or because of a different contribution to the corporation's debt capacity (not necessarily equal to the foreign borrowing undertaken to finance the project). Though k_u may be higher or lower than in the domestic case, the diversification arguments presented in the appendix to Chapter 8 suggest that even in cases where the total risk of a foreign project is higher than that of the typical domestic project, its systematic risk may be lower. Hence k_u may be lower. An illustration of this effect is provided below.

International Diversification and the Required Rate of Return: The simplest formal statement of the equilibrium trade-off between risk and expected return is the capital asset pricing model (CAPM).[2] It states that the required return on any project is composed of the interest rate on riskless debt plus a risk premium which is a linear function of the asset's systematic risk:

$$\underset{\substack{\text{required}\\ \text{return on}\\ \text{project}}}{R_j} = \underset{\substack{\text{risk-free}\\ \text{interest}\\ \text{rate}}}{r} + \underset{\substack{\text{risk}\\ \text{premium}}}{\beta_j(R_m - r)}, \tag{2}$$

where

R_j and R_m = expected (required) rates of return on security j and the market portfolio, respectively, both of which are random variables,

r = rate of interest on riskless bonds,

β_j = coefficient of systematic risk for security j = $\text{cov}(j,m)/\text{var}(m)$.

By restating the definition of the project's systematic risk as $\beta_j = \rho_{jm}(\sigma_j/\sigma_m)$, the correlation of j and m multiplied by the ratio of the standard deviations of j and m, it can be seen that there are two aspects which contribute to an asset's risk. One is the total variability of possible returns relative to those of the universe of risky assets. The other is the extent to which the variability is correlated with the returns on the universe of risky securities.

In order to see the impact of the differences in potential risk reduction through single-country and international diversification on risk premiums, we apply the CAPM to a single hypothetical situation. For each of eight countries we assume a standard project whose riskiness is characterized by a standard deviation of annual returns of 30 percent, roughly the average for the shares of large corporations in the U.S., and a correlation with the domestic market portfolio equal to an empirical estimate of the average correlation of individual stocks with the market portfolio for that country. The risk premium per unit of risk is assumed to be the same in all countries. Two risk premiums are calculated for each project, one from a domestic perspective and one from an international perspective. They are computed as follows:

$$\text{domestic risk premium} = .30 \times \rho_{dm} \times .5, \tag{3}$$

EXHIBIT 12A.1
Effect of International Diversification on Required Rate of Return

	Brazil	*France*	*Germany*	*Italy*	*Japan*	*Spain*	*Sweden*	*U.K.*	*U.S.*
Average correlation with domestic market portfolio[a]	.69	.68	.67	.66	.52	.63	.65	.61	.55
Risk premium from domestic perspective (%)	10.4	10.2	10.1	9.9	7.8	9.5	9.8	9.2	8.2
Average correlation with world market portfolio[b]	.14	.21	.31	.16	.15	.04	.19	.25	.44
Risk premium from world perspective (%)	2.1	3.2	3.7	2.5	2.2	0.6	2.8	3.8	6.6

[a]Figures for Brazil from Donald R. Lessard, "International Portfolio Diversification: A Multivariate Analysis for a Group of Latin American Countries," *Journal of Finance*, June 1973, pp. 619–633; others from Donald R. Lessard, "World, Country, and Industry Relationships in Equity Returns: Implications for Risk Reduction through International Diversification," *Financial Analysts Journal*, January–February 1976, pp. 32–38.

[b]Correlations with world obtained by multiplying the correlation with domestic market portfolio by the correlation of domestic market with the world market portfolio. This rests on the implicit assumption that the only relationship between individual securities and the world market is through their relationships with the domestic market portfolio. Figures for Brazil are based on subjective estimates of the correlation of the local market portfolio with the world market portfolio of .20.

where

$.30$ = project standard deviation,

ρ_{dm} = correlation of the project with the domestic market portfolio,

$.5$ = market price of one unit of nondiversifiable risk.[3]

$$\text{global risk premium} = .30 \times \rho_{wm} \times .5, \tag{4}$$

where

ρ_{wm} = correlation of the project with the world market portfolio.

The resulting estimates, reported in Exhibit 12A.1, are striking. The differences in risk premiums from domestic and international perspectives are very large. This is especially true for the smaller, more isolated markets included in the study—Brazil and Spain. Of course these are only rough estimates, but they suggest that a multinational firm could, in cases where there are barriers to portfolio capital flows to particular countries, accept a considerably lower rate of return on a project than could a purely local firm.

NOTES

1. This formula follows directly from the Modigliani-Miller proposition that the value of a levered firm financed with perpetual debt is as follows:

$$V_L = V_u + \text{TD},$$

where

V_u = market value of the firm if financed entirely with equity,

T = the corporate tax rate,

D = the face value of the perpetual debt.

See F. Modigliani and M. Miller, "The Cost of Capital, Corporation Finance and the Theory of Investment," *American Economic Review* 48, 1958, pp. 261–297; and "Corporate Income Taxes and the Cost of Capital: A Correction," *American Economic Review* 53, 1963, pp. 433–443. This formula is strictly true only with perpetual debt. S. Myers, in "Interactions of Corporate Financing and Investment Decisions—Implications for Capital Budgeting," *Journal of Finance,* March 1974, shows the extent of its bias when this assumption is relaxed.

2. In order to derive this model Sharpe assumed that financial markets are frictionless, claims against real investments are perfectly divisible and marketable, investors agree regarding possible future outcomes, and risky outcomes can be described appropriately only in terms of expected return and variance of return. For a more detailed development together with a thorough discussion of the empirical evidence regarding diversification and the market price of risk, see William F. Sharpe, *Investments,* Englewood Cliffs, N.J.: Prentice-Hall, 1985.

3. The market price of a unit of nondiversifiable risk is defined as $(R_m - r)/\sigma_m$. Over time the standard deviation of the U.S. market has been roughly 15% and the market risk premium has been around 7–8%. Thus, $(R_m - r)/\sigma_m = 7.5/15. = .5$.

BIBLIOGRAPHY

Adler, Michael, "The Cost of Capital and Valuation of a Two-Country Firm," *Journal of Finance,* March 1974, pp. 119–132.

———, "Investor Recognition of Corporation International Diversification: Comment," *Journal of Finance,* March 1981, pp. 187–190.

Adler, Michael, and Bernard Dumas, "Optimal International Acquisitions," *Journal of Finance,* March 1975, pp. 1–19.

———, "International Portfolio Choice and Corporation Finance: A Synthesis," *Journal of Finance,* June 1983, pp. 925–984.

Aggarwal, Raj, "Multinationality and Stock Market Valuation: An Empirical Study of U.S. Markets and Companies," *Management International Review,* No. 2, 1979, pp. 5–21.

———, "Investment Performance of U.S.-Based Multinational Companies: Comments and a Perspective of International Diversification of Real Assets," *Journal of International Business Studies,* Spring–Summer 1980, pp. 98–104.

———, "International Differences in Capital Structure Norms: An Empirical Study of Large European Companies," *Management International Review,* 1981/1, pp. 75–88.

Agmon, Tamir, "The Relations among Equity Markets: A Study of Share Price Co-Movements in the U.S., U.K., Germany and Japan," *Journal of Finance,* September 1972, pp. 839–855.

———, "Country Risk: The Significance of the Country Factor for Share-Price Movements in the United Kingdom, Germany and Japan," *Journal of Business,* January 1973, pp. 24–32.

Agmon, Tamir, and Donald Lessard, "Investor Recognition of Corporate International Diversification," *Journal of Finance,* September 1977, pp. 1049–1055.

———, "Investor Recognition of Corporate International Diversification: Reply," *Journal of Finance,* March 1981, pp. 191–192.

Areskoug, Kai, "Exchange Rates and the Currency of Denominations in International Bonds," *Economica,* May 1980, pp. 159–163.

Beidleman, Carl R., *Financial Swaps,* Homewood, Ill.: Dow Jones–Irwin, 1985.

Bertoneche, Marc L., "An Empirical Analysis of the Interrelationships among Equity Markets under Changing Exchange Rate Systems," *Journal of Banking and Finance,* December 1979, pp. 397–405.

Biger, Nahum, "Exchange Risk Implications of International Portfolio Diversification," *Journal of International Business Studies,* Fall 1979, pp. 64–74.

Black, Fischer, "International Capital Market Equilibrium with Investment Barriers," *Journal of Financial Economics,* December 1974, pp. 337–352.

Brewer, H. L., "Investor Benefits from Corporate International Diversification," *Journal of Financial and Quantitative Analysis,* March 1981, pp. 113–127.

Choi, Frederick D. S., "Financial Disclosure and Entry to the European Capital Market," *Journal of Accounting Research,* Autumn 1973, pp. 159–175.

———, "Financial Disclosure in Relation to a Firm's Capital Costs," *Accounting and Business Research,* Autumn 1973, pp. 272–282.

———, "European Disclosure: The Competitive Disclosure Hypothesis," *Journal of International Business Studies,* Fall 1974, pp. 15–23.

Choi, Frederick D. S., and Arthur Stonehill, "Foreign Access to U.S. Securities Markets: The Theory, Myth and Reality of Regulatory Barriers," *The Investment Analyst,* July 1982, pp. 17–26.

Cohen, Kalman, Walter Ness, Robert Schwartz, David Whitcomb, and Hitoshi Okuda, "The Determinants of Common Stock Returns Volatility: An International Comparison," *Journal of Finance,* May 1976, pp. 733–740.

Cohn, Richard A., and John J. Pringle, "Imperfections in International Financial Markets: Implications for Risk Premia and the Cost of Capital to Firms," *Journal of Finance,* March 1973, pp. 59–66.

Collins, J. Markham, and William S. Sekely, "The Relationship of Headquarters, Country, and Industry Classification to Financial Structure," *Financial Management,* Autumn 1983, pp. 45–51.

Dawson, Steven M., "Eurobond Currency Selection: Hindsight," *Financial Executive,* November 1973, pp. 72–73.

———, "How God's Gift Lost Its Gloss," *Euromoney,* May 1980, pp. 143–145.

de Faro, Clovis, and James V. Jucker, "The Impact of Inflation and Devaluation on the Selection of an International Borrowing Source," *Journal of International Business Studies,* Fall 1973, pp. 97–104.

Dufey, Gunter, "Institutional Constraints and Incentives on International Portfolio Investment," *International Portfolio Investment,* U.S. Department of the Treasury OASIA, 1975.

Dufey, Gunter, and Ian H. Giddy, "International Financial Planning: The Use of Market-Based Forecasts," *California Management Review,* Fall 1978, pp. 69–81.

Eaker, Mark R., "Denomination Decisions for Multinational Transactions," *Financial Management,* Autumn 1980, pp. 23–29.

Errunza, Vihang R., "Gains from Portfolio Diversification into Less Developed Countries," *Journal of International Business Studies,* Fall–Winter 1977, pp. 83–99.

———, "Determinants of Financial Structure in the Central American Common Market," *Financial Management,* Autumn 1979, pp. 72–77.

———, "Financing MNC Subsidiaries in Central America," *Journal of International Business Studies,* Fall 1979, pp. 88–93.

Errunza, Vihang, and Etienne Losq, "International Asset Pricing under Mild Segmentation: Theory and Test," *Journal of Finance,* March 1985, pp. 105–124.

Errunza, Vihang R., and Barr Rosenberg, "Investment in Developed and Less Developed Countries," *Journal of Financial and Quantitative Analysis,* December 1982, pp. 741–762.

Errunza, Vihang, and Lemma W. Senbet, "The Effects of International Operations on the Market Value of the Firm; Theory and Evidence," *Journal of Finance,* May 1981, pp. 401–417.

———, "International Corporate Diversification, Market Valuation, and Size-Adjusted Evidence," *Journal of Finance,* July 1984, pp. 727–743.

Eun, Cheol S., and Bruce G. Resnick, "Estimating the Correlation Structure of International Share Prices," *Journal of Finance,* December 1984, pp. 1311–1324.

Fatemi, Ali M., "Shareholder Benefits from Corporate International Diversification," *Journal of Finance,* December 1984, pp. 1325–1344.

Finnerty, Joseph E., and Thomas Schneeweis, "The Co-Movement of International Asset Returns," *Journal of International Business Studies,* Winter 1979, pp. 66–78.

Folks, W. R., Jr., "Analysis of Short-Term, Cross-Border Financing Decisions," *Financial Management,* Autumn 1976, pp. 19–27.

———, "Optimal Foreign Borrowing Strategies with Operations in Forward Exchange Markets," *Journal of Financial and Quantitative Analysis,* June 1978, pp. 245–254.

Grauer, Frederick A., Robert A. Litzenberger, and Richard E. Stehle, "Sharing Rules and Equilibrium in an International Capital Market under Uncertainty," *Journal of Financial Economics,* June 1976, pp. 233–256.

Grubel, Herbert G., "Internationally Diversified Portfolios: Welfare Gains and Capital Flows," *American Economic Review,* December 1968, pp. 1299–1314.

Grubel, Herbert G., and Kenneth Fadner, "The Interdependence of International Equity Markets," *Journal of Finance,* March 1971, pp. 89–94.

Guy, James R. F., "An Examination of the Effects of International Diversification from the British Viewpoint on Both Hypothetical and Real Portfolios," *Journal of Finance,* December 1978, pp. 1425–1438.

Hilliard, J., "The Relationship between Equity Indices on World Exchanges," *Journal of Finance,* March 1979, pp. 103–114.

Hong, H., "Predictability of Price Trends on Stock Exchanges: A Study of Some Far Eastern Countries," *Review of Economics and Statistics,* November 1978, pp. 619–621.

Hughes, John S., Dennis E. Logue, and Richard J. Sweeney, "Corporate International Diversification and Market Assigned Measures of Risk and Diversification," *Journal of Financial and Quantitative Analysis,* November 1975, pp. 627–637.

Ibbotson, Roger C., Richard C. Carr, and Anthony W. Robinson, "International Equity and Bond Returns," *Financial Analysts Journal,* July-August 1982, pp. 61–83.

Jacquillat, Bertrand, and Bruno H. Solnik, "Multinationals Are Poor Tools for Diversification," *Journal of Portfolio Management,* Winter 1978, pp. 8–12.

Jaffe, Jeffrey, and Randolph Westerfield, "The Week-End Effect in Common Stock Returns: The International Evidence," *Journal of Finance,* June 1985, pp. 433–454.

Jennergren, L. P., and P. E. Korsvold, "The Non-Random Character of Norwegian and Swedish Stock Market Prices," in E. J. Elton and M. J. Gruber, eds., *International Capital Markets,* Amsterdam: North-Holland, 1975, pp. 37–67.

Jucker, James V., and Clovis de Faro, "The Selection of International Borrowing Sources," *Journal of Financial and Quantitative Analysis,* September 1975, pp. 381–407.

Kenen, Peter B., "Capital Mobility and Financial Integration: A Survey," *Princeton Studies in International Finance,* No. 39, 1976.

Kohers, Theodor, "The Effect of Multinational Operations on the Cost of Equity Capital of U.S. Corporations: An Empirical Study," "Management International Review," February 1975, pp. 121–124.

Kohlhagen, Steven W., "Overlapping National Investment Portfolios: Evidence and Implications of International Integration of Secondary Markets for Financial Assets," in Donald R. Lessard, ed., *International Financial Management,* 2nd ed., New York: Wiley, 1985, pp. 97–117.

Lee, Wayne Y., and Kanwal S. Sachdeva, "The Role of the Multinational Firm in the Integration of Segmented Markets," *Journal of Finance,* May 1977, pp. 479–492.

Lessard, Donald R., "International Portfolio Diversification: A Multivariate Analysis for a Group of Latin American Countries," *Journal of Finance,* June 1973, pp. 619–633.

———, "World, National, and Industry Factors in Equity Returns," *Journal of Finance,* May 1974, pp. 379–391.

———, "World, Country, and Industry Relationships in Equity Returns: Implications for Risk Reduction through International Diversification," *Financial Analysts Journal,* January–February 1976, pp. 32–38.

Lessard, Donald R., and Alan C. Shapiro, "Guidelines for Global Financing Choices," *Midland Corporate Finance Journal,* Winter 1983, pp. 68–80.

———, "Principles of International Portfolio Selection," in Donald R. Lessard, ed., *International Financial Management,* New York: Wiley, 1985, pp. 16–30.

Levy, Hiam, and Marshall Sarnat, "International Diversification of Investment Portfolios," *American Economic Review,* September 1970, pp. 668–675.

Logue, Dennis E., Michael Salant, and Richard J. Sweeney, "International Integration of Financial Markets: Survey, Synthesis, and Results," in Carl H. Sten, John H. Makin, and Dennis E. Logue, eds., *Eurocurrencies and the International Monetary System,* Washington, D.C.: American Enterprise Institute, 1976, pp. 91–137.

McDonald, John, "French Mutual Fund Performance: Evaluation of Internationally Diversified Portfolios," *Journal of Finance,* December 1973, pp. 1161–1180.

Madura, Jeff, and E. Joe Nosari, "Utilizing Currency Portfolios to Mitigate Exchange Risk," *Columbia Journal of World Business,* Spring 1984, pp. 96–99.

Maldonado, Rita, and Anthony Saunders, "International Portfolio Diversification and the Inter-Temporal Stability of International Stock Market Relationships," *Financial Management,* Autumn 1981, pp. 54–63.

Minot, Winthrop G., "Tests for Integration between Major Western European Capital Markets," *Oxford Economic Papers,* November 1974, pp. 424–439.

Naumann-Etienne, Ruediger, "A Framework for Financial Decisions in MNC," *Journal of Financial and Quantitative Analysis,* November 1974, pp. 859–874.

Philippatos, G. C., A. Christofi, and P. Christofi, "The Inter-Temporal Stability of International Stock Market Relationships: Another View," *Financial Management,* Winter 1983, pp. 63–69.

Remmers, H. Lee, "A Note on Foreign Borrowing Costs," *Journal of International Business Studies,* Fall 1980, pp. 123–134.

Remmers, Lee, Arthur Stonehill, Richard Wright, and Theo Beekhuisen, "Industry and Size as Debt Ratio Determinants for Manufacturing Internationally," *Financial Management,* Summer 1974, pp. 24–32.

Ripley, Duncan M., "Systematic Elements in the Linkage of National Stock Market Indices," *Review of Economics and Statistics,* September 1973, pp. 356–361.

Robichek, Alexander A., and Mark R. Eaker, "Debt Denomination and Exchange Risk in International Capital Markets," *Financial Management,* Autumn 1976, pp. 11–18.

Roll, Richard, and Bruno H. Solnik, "A Pure Foreign Exchange Asset Pricing Model," *Journal of International Economics,* No. 7, 1977, pp. 161–179.

Rugman, Alan M., "Risk Reduction by International Diversification," *Journal of International Business Studies,* Fall 1976, pp. 75–80.

———, "International Diversification by Financial and Direct Investment," *Journal of Economics and Business,* Fall 1977, pp. 31–37.

———, *International Diversification and the Multinational Enterprise,* Lexington, Mass.: Lexington Books, 1979.

Sarathy, Ravi, and Sangit Chatterjee, "The Divergence of Japanese and U.S. Corporate Financial Structure," *Journal of International Business Studies,* Winter 1984, pp. 75–89.

Saunders, Anthony, and Richard S. Woodworth, "Gains from International Portfolio Diversification: U.K. Evidence 1971–1975," *Journal of Business Finance and Accounting,* Autumn 1977, pp. 299–309.

Senbet, Lemma W., "International Capital Market Equilibrium and the Multinational Firm Financing and Investment Policies," *Journal of Financial and Quantitative Analysis,* September 1979, pp. 455–480.

Severn, A. K., "Investor Evaluation of Foreign and Domestic Risk," *Journal of Finance,* May 1974, pp. 545–550.

Severn, Alan K., and David R. Meinster, "The Use of Multicurrency Financing by the Financial Manager," *Financial Management,* Winter 1978, pp. 45–53.

Shapiro, Alan C., "Exchange Rate Changes, Inflation, and the Value of the Multinational Corporation," *Journal of Finance,* May 1975, pp. 485–501.

———, "Evaluating Financing Costs for Multinational Subsidiaries," *Journal of International Business Studies,* Fall 1975, pp. 25–32.

———, "Financial Structure and Cost of Capital in the Multinational Corporation," *Journal of Financial and Quantitative Analysis,* June 1978, pp. 211–226.

———, "The Impact of Taxation on the Currency-of-Denomination Decision for Long-Term Borrowing and Lending," *Journal of International Business Studies,* Spring/Summer 1984, pp. 15–25.

Solnik, Bruno H., "Note on the Validity of the Random Walk for European Stock Prices," *Journal of Finance,* December 1973, pp. 1151–1159.

———, "The International Pricing of Risk: An Empirical Investigation of the World Capital Market Structure," *Journal of Finance,* May 1974, pp. 365–378.

———, "Why Not Diversify Internationally Rather Than Domestically?" *Financial Analysts Journal,* July/August 1974, pp. 48–54.

———, "An Equilibrium Model of the International Capital Market," *Journal of Economic Theory,* August 1974, pp. 500–524.

———, "An International Market Model of Security Price Behavior," *Journal of Financial and Quantitative Analysis,* September 1974, pp. 537–554.

———, "Testing International Asset Pricing: Some Pessimistic Views," *Journal of Finance,* May 1977, pp. 503–512.

Stanley, Marjorie T., "Capital Structure and Cost of Capital for the Multinational Firm," *Journal of International Business Studies,* Spring/Summer 1981, pp. 103–120.

Stapleton, Richard C., and Marti Subrahmanyam, "Market Imperfections, Capital and Market Equilibrium, and Corporation Finance," *Journal of Finance,* May 1977, pp. 307–319.

Stehle, Richard F., "An Empirical Test of the Alternative Hypothesis of National and International Pricing of Risk Assets," *Journal of Finance,* May 1977, pp. 493–502.

Stonehill, Arthur, Theo Beekhuisen, Richard Wright, Lee Remmers, Norman Toy, Antonio Parés, Alan Shapiro, Douglas Egan, and Thomas Bates, "Financial Goals and Debt Ratio Determinants: A Survey of Practice in Five Countries," *Financial Management,* Autumn 1975, pp. 27–41.

Stonehill, Arthur, and Thomas Stitzel, "Financial Structure and Multinational Corporations," *California Management Review,* Fall 1969, pp. 91–96.

Stulz, René M., "On the Effects of Barriers to International Investment," *Journal of Finance,* September 1981, pp. 923–933.

———, "Pricing Capital Assets in an International Setting: An Introduction," *Journal of International Business Studies,* Winter 1984, pp. 55–73.

Subrahmanyam, Marti G., "On the Optimality of International Capital Market Integration," *Journal of Financial Economics,* March 1975, pp. 3–28.

Suzuki, Sadahiko, and Richard W. Wright, "Financial Structure and Bankruptcy Risk in Japanese Companies," *Journal of International Business Studies,* Spring 1985, pp. 97–110.

Toy, Norman, Arthur Stonehill, Lee Remmers, Richard Wright, and Theo Beekhuisen, "A Comparative International Study of Growth, Profitability, and Risk as Determinants of Corporate Debt Ratios in the Manufacturing Sector," *Journal of Financial and Quantitative Analysis,* November 1974, pp. 875–886.

White, Betsy Buttrill, and John R. Woodbury III, "Exchange Rate Systems and International Capital Market Integration," *Journal of Money, Credit and Banking,* May 1980, pp. 175–183.

13

International Banking

The growth of multinational business since the end of World War II has been accompanied by a parallel expansion of the world banking system as banks from all major nations moved abroad aggressively to sustain their growth and to protect their domestic client bases from foreign competition. The terms *world bank* and *multinational bank* have come to mean a large bank with banking offices in many countries. Although the major focus of this book is on financial management of multinational firms, international banking is well worth discussing herein, as it facilitates and supports these firms. In addition, banking itself is a major multinational enterprise.

In this chapter we will look at how banks assess the unique risks of being international and how these risks can be incorporated into an appropriately diversified international lending portfolio. We will also look at how banks organize to conduct their international banking business, types of banking offices, and how charges and services differ among countries.

Multinational banks combine traditional banking structures and procedures with new instruments and techniques devised for more competitive worldwide service. Tasks undertaken by multinational banks include the following:

- Financing imports and exports (the traditional international banking task).
- Foreign exchange trading in a volume unprecedented a few decades ago.
- Underwriting both Eurobonds and foreign bonds.
- Borrowing and lending in the Eurocurrency market.
- Organizing or participating in international loan syndications.

- Project financing.
- International cash management, including new electronic ways of transferring funds from country to country.
- Soliciting local currency deposits and loans with an intent to operate as a full-service local bank.
- Supplying information and advice to clients, including multinational firms.

Some of the largest world banks attempt to do all of these things. Others have found it advantageous to specialize in a select few of the possible activities. Banks generalize or specialize according to their abilities and size, as well as their perception of what unique services their original home clients need.

International bank lending involves a more complex approach to assessing risk than that used in domestic banking, primarily because international banking is conducted in a different legal, social, political, and economic environment. The risks of international bank lending may be classified as *commercial risk* or *country risk.* Since banks often offer their advice to client firms on matters of country risk, their effectiveness in assessing that risk is important beyond the effect on the bank alone.

COMMERCIAL RISK IN INTERNATIONAL LENDING

Commercial risk involves assessing the likelihood that a foreign-based client will be unable to repay its debts because of business reasons. Although this risk has a direct domestic counterpart, differences exist. As in the domestic case, a multinational bank will attempt to judge the quality of a foreign client's products, management, and financial condition. Cultural differences and lack of information may inhibit an assessment of the firm's management, while differing accounting standards and disclosure practices may preclude the type of financial analysis common in the home country. The bank may find it difficult to evaluate foreign economic conditions that might affect the client firm, and may need legal advice to determine its position in any bankruptcy proceedings. In many countries, for example, firms cannot easily dismiss workers whose jobs have been rendered obsolete by a change in competition or the introduction of new technology. The magnitude of payments that must be made to redundant workers may have a significant negative impact upon a struggling firm's liquidity, and thus upon its ability to repay any bank loans.

COUNTRY RISK IN INTERNATIONAL LENDING

Country risk refers to the possibility that unexpected events within a host country will influence a client firm's or a government's ability to repay a loan. Country risk is usually divided into *sovereign risk* and *currency risk.* This division is useful when the borrower is a private firm, but when the borrower is the government itself, the distinction between sovereign risk and currency risk becomes blurred.

Sovereign risk, also called *political risk,* arises because a host government may exercise its sovereign power to unilaterally repudiate foreign obligations, or may prevent local firms from honoring their foreign obligations. The risk may derive from direct government action or from the indirect consequences of ineffective government, as when a government is unable to maintain law and order.

Currency risk, also called *foreign exchange risk,* arises from the possibility that an unexpected change in exchange rates will alter the home currency value of repayment of loans by foreign clients. If the loan is denominated in the home currency, say, U.S. dollars, the risk is shifted to the borrower. However, the bank still runs the currency risk that the borrower cannot obtain dollars to repay the loan. A bank may partially avoid this possibility by sourcing funds for foreign clients in local currencies. Repayment of principal will not then be subject to a currency risk. However, the profit margin between the lending rate and the local cost of sourcing the funds is of value to the parent bank only in terms of its home currency value. This component remains subject to currency risk.

Currency risk includes the possibility of foreign repayments being rescheduled because of a shortage of foreign exchange in the host country. It also includes the possibility of local currency devaluations of such magnitude that the financial condition of a private borrower is impaired. This latter circumstance may arise when the government has incurred such a large foreign currency debt that the limited foreign exchange must be rationed. Another possibility is that the government will arbitrarily influence the foreign exchange value of its currency.

Country Risk and the International Debt Problem

Since 1974 concern has grown that the large international banks are risking ruinous losses on syndicated loans to public and private entities in developing countries, particularly in Latin America. As was discussed in Chapter 3, the non-OPEC countries had a difficult time adjusting to energy price increases in 1974 and again in 1979. The problem was exacerbated by high interest rates on floating rate dollar loans during the early 1980s, and by the political difficulties of imposing the necessary monetary and fiscal discipline at home. As a result, many countries have defaulted or rescheduled their loans during the past six years. These include such large international borrowers as Brazil, Argentina, Mexico, and Poland, as well as a host of smaller borrowers.

EXHIBIT 13.1
U.S. Bank Exposure to Developing Country Debt

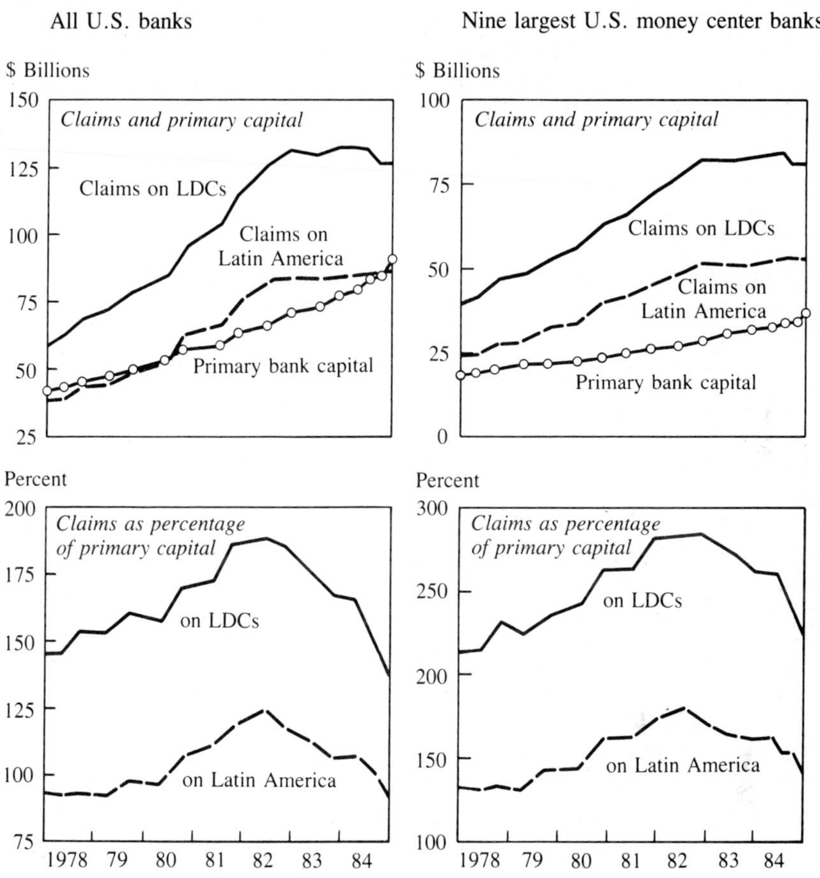

Source: Morgan Guaranty Trust Company of New York, *World Financial Markets,* July 1985, pp. 8–9.
Note: Non–local-currency claims of U.S. banks, adjusted for guarantees and other risk transfers.

Rescheduling is a polite, practical way for bankers to try to salvage their loans and avoid a write-off against their capital and surplus accounts. However, rescheduling has become an increasing embarrassment for banks, because many of them are overexposed to risk in one or more countries. Exhibit 13.1 shows the non–local-currency claims of U.S. banks on developing countries, adjusted for guarantees and other risk transfers. The peak of the exposure problem occurred in 1982, when developing country debt amounted to 186% of the primary capital of all U.S. banks, and about 275% of the primary capital of the nine largest U.S. money center banks. These ratios improved dramatically in 1983 and 1984 due to several factors. U.S. banks slowed down their lending to the developing countries and increased their primary capital (which includes loan loss reserves). The developing countries, with the help and insistence of the IMF, began to impose the necessary self-discipline to reduce their dependence on external borrowing.

Nevertheless, the continuing degree of bank exposure and well-publicized rescheduling by developing countries have stimulated increased regulation and disclosure upon the international banks. The pressure is on in the United States to increase bank primary capital, especially loan loss reserves, and to require banks to disclose their international loan portfolio composition by geographic area and type of loan. A lively academic debate also rages over the wisdom of the private sector financing developing countries rather than having public sector international institutions, such as the IMF and World Bank, do the financing.

Dangers of Lending to Sovereign Nations

Criticism of bank lending to developing countries runs along the following lines:[1]

1. Evaluation of country risk is extremely complex, because it depends on variables that are not normally analyzed by bankers when making domestic commercial loans. The new variables include unfamiliar political, sociological, macroeconomic, and financial variables.
2. Bankers have a poor track record in anticipating dramatic increases in sovereign risk until it is too late. Unexpected events such as wars (Nigeria, Ethiopia, and Lebanon) and social revolutions (Cuba and Iran) are also nearly impossible to forecast but are often a prime cause for national default on external debt.
3. Some critics believe that bankers have relaxed credit standards because of weak domestic and commercial demand for loans since 1974, compounded by an increasing supply of deposits.
4. In the event that a nation's foreign debt needs to be restructured, the fact that so many separate banks and international organizations are involved means that coordination is extremely difficult. *All* creditors must agree for any voluntary restructuring plan to be effective.
5. The concentration of syndicated loans in a relatively few "credit-worthy" developing countries, such as Brazil, Argentina, and Mexico, reduces the potential benefit of diversification.
6. The ability of debtor nations to service the growing burden of external debt is being questioned by both critics of the lenders and of the borrowers. Most bank debt is on a variable-interest-rate basis, thus causing the actual burden of interest payments to be uncertain but

potentially disastrous if interest rates should reach high levels. Most critics agree that no single or composite measure of debt-servicing ability can correctly forecast country risk, but the lack of such measures and even the lack of reliable data for the simplest indicators frustrates the ability of lenders to evaluate country risk. Moreover, borrowers are unable to judge their own ability to finance development plans.

7. If countries are unable to service their debt on time, the banks become effectively "locked in" and are forced to reschedule their loans indefinitely to prevent outright defaults. Such rollovers may disguise loans that should be written off and conceal severe depletions of banks' equity capital. Even if eventually repaid, rollovers impair the ability of banks to make new productive loans elsewhere.
8. Commercial banks usually fund medium-term loans by short-term borrowing (six months or less) in the Eurocurrency market. Although the profit margins on variable-interest-rate loans are semiprotected, the margin on fixed-interest-rate loans could be easily squeezed by a shift in the term structure of interest rates interacting with the mismatched maturities.
9. Since the collapse of the German Herstatt Bank in 1974 because of speculation in the foreign exchange market, some observers have been suspicious of the stability of the whole Eurocurrency interbank structure. If one major bank should fail, that event might have a domino effect on other banks because of the "tiering" of Eurocurrency deposits. The ability of syndicate banks of lesser stature to raise Eurocurrencies in the short run at reasonable rates to fund their share of "rollovers" to developing countries would be in jeopardy if confidence in the interbank market waned. At present, only the largest and most prestigious banks receive the bulk of new funds, especially petrodollars. The ability of secondary banks to maintain the spread between borrowing and lending rates is tenuous at best, because they often need to pay more than do prime banks for their funds in the interbank market.
10. The ultimate purpose of some loans is to provide financing for balance of payments deficits. This type of loan does not improve the exporting capability of the borrowing country and therefore does not generate the foreign exchange earnings needed to service the debt. Even some of the so-called project loans are substitutes for other foreign loans, which are then used to finance the deficit.

Benefits of Lending to Sovereign Nations

In spite of the negative criticism of commercial bank lending to developing nations, many positive features do exist for this type of lending, from the viewpoint of both the banks and the recipient countries. The benefits can be summarized as follows:

1. Actual loss ratios on international loans have been more favorable than those on domestic loans. A Federal Reserve Board study reported that during the decade ending in 1971, losses on international loans as a percentage of such loans outstanding averaged only .06%, compared with .18% on domestic loans.[2] The difference can be attributed in large measure to the low business and financial risk inherent in large state enterprises, banks, and governments, compared to the average private corporate borrower.
2. International lending has been a very profitable activity for many of the world's largest banks and has, for example, had a major impact on the earnings of such giants as Citicorp, Chase Manhattan, Bank of America, and Morgan Guaranty. Medium-term loans to private and sovereign foreign entities comprise only a modest part of their international portfolios.
3. Diversification of foreign lending by country and by type of customer reduces the risk of catastrophic losses to any one bank. In fact, this is the main reason advanced for syndicating large loans.
4. Precisely those banks with the most experience and capability in international lending are the ones that are most active in international lending. They are at least relatively better qualified to assess country risk than most banks.
5. The reason that loans to developing countries have been concentrated in a relatively few countries is that only those select countries have been able to pass the stringent credit test of international bank lenders. For example, India, Pakistan, and Bangladesh have large foreign debts to international public institutions, such as the World Bank and International Monetary Fund, but virtually no debt to private banks. They have not yet passed the credit test.
6. Developing countries badly need foreign banks to meet even relatively modest development plans. Most of the loans are indeed project loans, which are supposed to generate enough new foreign exchange to service the added foreign debt. If the private banking sector does not respond to the legitimate credit needs of responsible developing countries, an even greater burden will be placed on the international development institutions. Their limited funds will inevitably be diverted away from the poorest developing nations, which have no hope of qualifying for loans from private banks.
7. A number of safeguards exist that reduce the risk on a portion of international loans. These include guarantees by export credit insurance programs in the lenders' own countries, guarantees by a parent

on loans to its affiliates, and guarantees by host government agencies on loans to private firms within their country. The latter two do not apply to loans to sovereign states but do serve to reduce overall country risk.

8. Foreign governments and central banks have traditionally given highest priority to preserving their own credit standing, even if private firms within the country must default. Therefore lending to sovereign entities at least ensures first priority on whatever foreign exchange is available to repay external debts.

Analysis of Country Risk

Bank managers must develop a better approach to evaluation of both sovereign risk and currency risk. Approaches used vary somewhat depending on whether the borrower is the government itself, an industrial firm, or a private commercial bank within the foreign country.[3] The same variables are usually studied for all three client types, but the relative weight given one or another variable may differ substantially.

Sovereign risk analysis focuses on probable future willingness or ability of a government to honor past obligations or to allow firms and banks within the country to honor their obligations. Variables considered include political stability, since a new government may abrogate obligations incurred by its predecessor. Expected trends in the balance of payments are important because the ability to generate foreign exchange depends upon either a favorable current account or capital account. A third factor is the size of the foreign exchange obligations of the country relative to its GNP and international trade.

All of these seemed to play a part in Argentina's difficulties in honoring its foreign debt obligations in the mid-1980s. The military government, which led the country into the Falklands/Malvinas war with Great Britain, was replaced by a civilian government, which brought its disgraced military predecessors to trial for crimes against the Argentine people. The military government had incurred large foreign debts for projects of dubious economic benefit to the Argentine economy, and foreign exchange earnings were depressed in part due to the world economic situation of the mid-1980s. The debt and balance of payments situation of Argentina was not materially different from that of many other countries, as has been explained in Chapter 3. However, the replacement of a disgraced military government after an embarrassing attempt to invade the Falklands/Malvinas islands was uniquely Argentine.

Currency risk is judged primarily from projections of a country's balance of payments surplus or deficit on current account, its present and likely future holdings of foreign exchange reserves, which act as a buffer for a limited period of time in the country's ability to repay foreign debt, and the size and maturity structure of its foreign currency debt. These factors, in turn, are influenced by differential rates of domestic and foreign inflation and whether or not the country's exchange rates are allowed to adjust to the differential. In this context, foreign currency debt includes both governmental debt and the debt of private firms and banks within the country.

Bank Structure for Assessing Country Risk

Mascarenhas and Sand investigated the organizational structure used by the 50 largest U.S. banks to assess country risk. They studied the evaluation process within each bank, as distinct from assessments purchased from outside vendors on an ad hoc basis.[4] The following section is based on their study.

Banks set "country loan limits" to restrict exposure in any one country. Limits are established by a "country limit committee" composed of top bank executives. Country managers and staff analysts present recommendations to the country limit committee, of which they may or may not themselves be members.

A country limit decision is typically based on two separate pieces of information. One of these is the *country risk analysis study*, and the other is the *marketing plan* presented by the bank official in charge of operations in the country being reviewed.

Mascarenhas and Sand found that the organizational structure used by banks most often falls into one of four categories. In type 1, shown in Exhibit 13.2, the country manager includes a few paragraphs on country risk to accompany the loan limit proposal being recommended to the coun-

EXHIBIT 13.2
Type 1: Function and Role Differentiated; Position not Differentiated

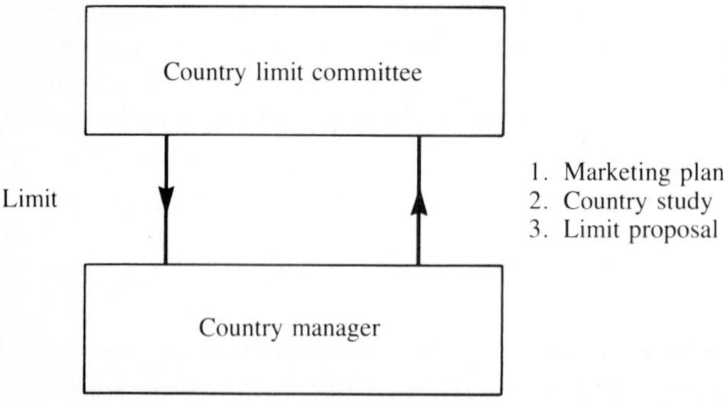

Source: Briance Mascarenhas and Ole Christian Sand, "Country Risk Assessment Systems in Banks: Patterns and Performance," *Journal of International Business Studies,* Spring 1985, p. 23.

try limit committee. In effect, the marketing plan, country study, and proposed loan limit all come from one person, the country manager.

This system is typically used by banks having little international exposure and/or experience. The country manager usually lacks an analytical framework or specialized training for evaluation of political and economic risks, and thus often depends "on an intuitive, subjective, gut-feeling approach."[5] Comparability in risk analyses between countries is difficult, and country managers are able to tailor their reports to include or exclude such information as they may wish in their desire to justify a particular limit proposal. In other words, the system does not have any checks or balances.

Type 2 organizations, shown in Exhibit 13.3, add a coordinator who provides standardization. The coordinator requests and collects information, standardizes content, and organizes and edits the final country risk report. Ultimate responsibility for the report, however, still lies with the country manager.

This system promotes comparability between countries and allows for frequent updates. Mascarenhas and Sand note that country managers have less opportunity to distort information. Information on related lines of exposure, such as a credit application to a U.S. bank from the African subsidiary of an Indian multinational, can be coordinated. However, the final loan limit proposal is still drafted by the country manager.

In type 3 organizations, shown in Exhibit 13.4, the coordinator is replaced by a formal assessment unit that reports directly to the country limit committee. This assessment unit makes its own independent study of the country and sends that report directly to the country limit committee, where the report is compared with the limit proposed by the country manager.

EXHIBIT 13.3
Type 2: Function, Role, and Position Differentiated; Use of a Coordinator

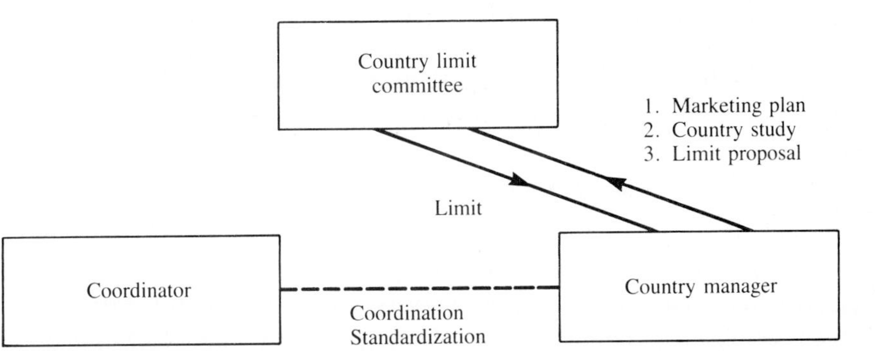

Source: Briance Mascarenhas and Ole Christian Sand, "Country Risk Assessment Systems in Banks: Patterns and Performance," *Journal of International Business Studies,* Spring 1985, p. 24.

EXHIBIT 13.4
Type 3: Function, Role, and Position Differentiated; Use of an Independent Assessment Unit

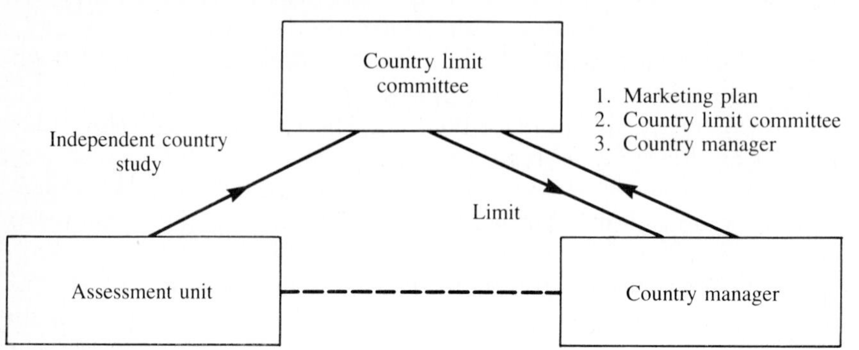

Source: Briance Mascarenhas and Ole Christian Sand, "Country Risk Assessment Systems in Banks: Patterns and Performance," *Journal of International Business Studies,* Spring 1985, p. 25.

This system includes the checks and balances inherent in an independent assessment unit. The country manager's report may now focus more directly on market opportunities, competition, and country-specific issues; the assessment unit is better able to evaluate sovereign and currency risks. The "gut-feeling" of the country manager can be offset by the "academic and technical" approach of the professional assessment staff.

In type 4 organizations, shown in Exhibit 13.5, staff specialists are added to the process. Separate assessment and coordination units exist, with staff specialists employed to report on political and economic matters to the coordinating unit, which in turn is separate from the assessment specialists. The staff specialists have professional expertise, while the coordination group acts as a bridge between the specialists and the rest of the organization. The coordination group tries to bring perspective to the process, and is often staffed by persons with strong interpersonal skills who, in addition, combine sufficient working knowledge of economics, politics, and banking so as to be effective mediators.

MANAGEMENT OF AN INTERNATIONAL LOAN PORTFOLIO

Modern portfolio theory can be applied to international bank portfolios, which are composed of a set of risky assets whose returns will vary due to both commercial and country risks. The unsystematic risk of the portfolio will be diminished if the bank successfully diversifies its assets among countries. Country limits are an attempt to guarantee diversification.

EXHIBIT 13.5
Type 4: Function, Role, and Position Differentiated; Use of Specialists

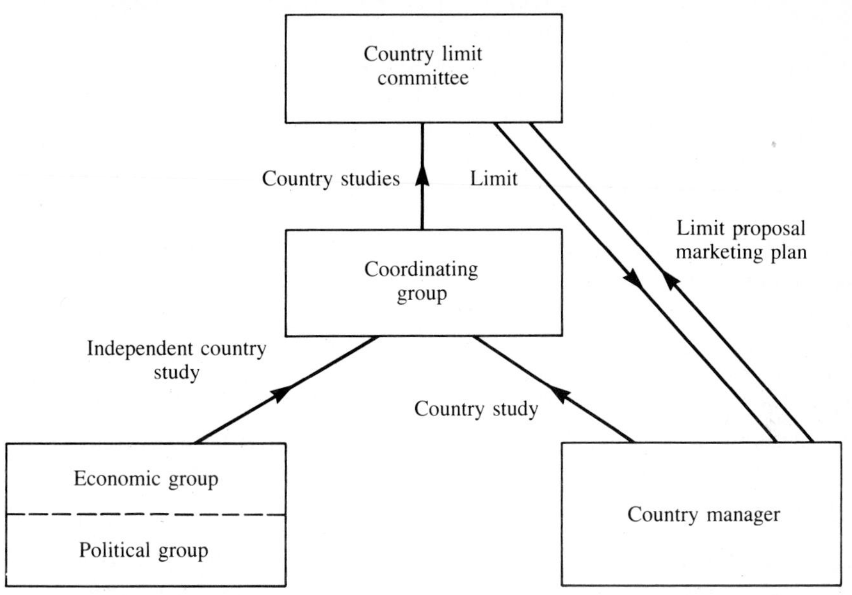

Source: Briance Mascarenhas and Ole Christian Sand, "Country Risk Assessment Systems in Banks: Patterns and Performance," *Journal of International Business Studies,* Spring 1985, p. 26.

From an international bank portfolio perspective, currency risk can cause a range of possible home currency returns that is likely to be normally distributed. The impact of sovereign risk, however, is more likely to have a binary distribution; either the bank is paid in full as agreed, or the loan experiences a major payment delay and possible default.

International loans are often just part of an ongoing relationship between a bank and its client. The bank may be receiving other compensation from the client, such as fees for foreign exchange transactions or international money management. Denying the loan may bring an end to such fees and may preclude the bank's participation in future loans when the client becomes worthy of credit again. These attributes do not fit neatly into portfolio theory, but they must be remembered in any intuitive application of the concepts of that theory.

Data for a meaningful *beta* for international loan portfolios is not available, which means that loan officers must use intuition in forecasting the future volatility and covariance of returns from each foreign country. Creation of an "efficient" loan portfolio is based as much on intuition as on the processing of hard statistical data.

Large money center banks cannot easily remove high-risk loans from their portfolios in order to reduce portfolio risk because no secondary market for such loans exists. It is possible to swap a risky loan to one country for a risky loan to another country, as mentioned in Chapter 11. However, when several Latin American governments found themselves unable to repay their debts as scheduled in the 1980s, large money center banks had to increase their risk. They had the choice of extending the maturity of defaulting loans or reporting a loss in earnings for that year. Smaller banks, on the other hand, were able to reduce their risk by refusing to extend the maturities of their Latin American loans. The larger banks were forced to assume the smaller banks' share of the credit to prevent the total loan from going into default.

Portfolio diversification works best if default risk in each country is independent of that in every other country, but often such defaults are closely correlated. For example, default risk for countries in geographical or ideological proximity might be correlated because of a common view of nationalism, as in the case of many Latin American countries; ideologically inspired invasion, as in the case of Kampuchea and Vietnam; drought and starvation, as in the case of East Africa; and civil strife with foreign intervention, as in the case of Nicaragua and El Salvador. Inter-nation dependency complicates the task of judging risk in an international loan portfolio, but it does not totally negate the advantages of international loan diversification.

In summary, Ingo Walter described the ideal person to analyze country risks: "a true 'renaissance person'—exceedingly intelligent, a holder of doctorates from respectable institutions in economics, political science, sociology, psychology and perhaps a few other fields as well, totally objective, with a great deal of common sense. In addition to being rather well-traveled, he or she is up-to-date on developments in all countries of interest to the bank (and in other countries that might affect them), and is personally acquainted with key policymakers."[6] Such a mix of skills is rare, so the managerial problem for a bank is to obtain all of these qualities from a mix of ordinary individuals and traditional organizational linkages.

TYPES OF BANKING OFFICES

Before deciding upon a form of organization through which to operate in foreign countries, a bank must define its objectives and develop a strategy. Giddy has identified three separate forms of international banking: arm's length international banking, offshore banking, and host-country banking. Most international bank operations fit into one or another of these categories.[7]

Arm's length international banking exists when the domestic bank carries on its international banking from within its home country, accepting foreign deposits and making foreign loans. International banking services involve developing relationships with correspondent banks in other countries. The home bank functions primarily as a center for clearing international payments and for financing imports and exports. The main customers are importers, exporters, tourists, and foreign banks.

In offshore banking, the bank accepts deposits and makes loans and investments in a Eurocurrency, and books these transactions in an offshore location. Examples are Eurodollars held in U.S. bank branches in Europe, the Bahamas, or the Cayman Islands. Offshore banks are active in the purchase and placement of short-term funds, in syndicated loans, and in foreign exchange trading. Their depositors and borrowers are usually located in countries other than the home country of the offshore bank. Some offshore banks specialize in taking deposits for relending in their home country. At times U.S. banks have used their branches in Europe to acquire Eurodollars, which could then be reloaned in the United States. Similarly, Midland Bank's acquisition of Crocker National Bank (California), Hong Kong and Shanghai Banking Corporation's acquisition of Marine Midland Bank (New York), and Mitsubishi Bank's acquisition of Bank of California were all partly motivated by a desire to gain access to dollar deposits in the United States to finance customers both in the United States and abroad.

Host-country banking typically involves full-service banking in a foreign country through a branch or subsidiary of the parent bank. Deposits and loans are made in the local currency to residents of the host country, in competition with local banks.

By combining correspondent banking, offshore banking, and host-country banking, a global network can be offered to meet the worldwide needs of client firms. Foreign banking offices of such a global network may be of five types: correspondent banks, representative offices, agencies, subsidiaries, and branch banks. In addition, U.S. banks now are able to operate international banking facilities and Edge Act corporations. Activities permitted under each form vary somewhat, according to the laws of the various host countries (or, in the case of foreign banks in the United States, according to state laws). The following discussion is necessarily general rather than specific to any single country.

Correspondent Banks

Most major banks of the world maintain correspondent banking relationships with local banks in each of the important foreign cities of the world. The two-way link between banks is essentially one of "correspondence," via cable and mail, and a mutual deposit relationship. For example, a U.S. bank may have a correspondent bank in Kuala Lumpur, Malaysia, and the U.S. bank will in turn be the correspondent bank for the Malaysian bank. Each will maintain a deposit in the other in local currency.

Correspondent services include accepting drafts, honoring letters of credit, and furnishing credit information. Services are centered around collecting or paying foreign funds, often because of import or export transactions. However, a visiting businessperson can use the home bank's introduction to meet local bankers.

Under a correspondent banking relationship neither of the correspondent banks maintains its own personnel in the other country. Direct contact between the banks is usually limited to periodic visits between members of the banks' management.

For the businessperson the main advantage of doing banking at home with a bank having a large number of foreign correspondent relationships is the ability to deal with financial matters in a large number of foreign countries with local bankers whose knowledge of local customs should be extensive. The disadvantage is the lack of ability to deposit in, borrow from, or disburse from a branch of one's own home bank, as well as the possibility that correspondents will put a lower priority on serving the foreign banks' customer than on serving their own permanent customers.

Representative Offices

A bank establishes a representative office in a foreign country primarily to help parent bank clients when they are doing business in that country or possibly in neighboring countries. It also functions as a geographically convenient location from which to visit correspondent banks in its region rather than sending bankers from the parent bank at greater financial and physical cost. A representative office is not a "banking office." It cannot accept deposits, make loans, commit the parent bank to a loan, or deal in drafts, letters of credit, or the Eurocurrency market. Indeed, a tourist cannot even cash a travelers check from the parent bank in the representative office.

The basic function of a representative office is to provide information, advice, and local contacts for the parent bank's business clients and to provide a location where businesspersons from either country can initiate inquiries about the parent bank's services. Representative offices introduce visiting executives to local banks, and they watch over correspondent banking relationships. They put parent bank customers in contact with local business firms interested in supplying, purchasing, or marketing products or services, and they arrange meetings with government officials if that is needed to obtain permissions, approvals, or government help. They provide credit analysis of local firms and economic and political intelligence about the country.

A representative office is usually small, often one executive, two or three assistants, and clerical help, all of whom work in an office that does not resemble a banking office in the physical sense. The representative and the assistants may have come to the office from the home country, but it is equally likely that they are citizens or permanent residents of the host country. The major advantage of a representative office is that the local representative will have a more precise understanding of the needs of home country clients than might local correspondents and can thus provide data and advice more suitable to their needs. The local representative will be bilingual, if that is needed, and can advise visitors about local customs and procedures.

If the parent bank eventually decides to open a local general banking office, the existence of a representative office for some prior period usually provides a valuable base of contacts and expertise to facilitate the change. However, representative offices are not necessarily a prelude to a general banking office, nor need an eventual general banking office be the major reason for opening a representative office. In some countries, such as Mexico, foreign banks are precluded from opening new general banking offices. Thus representative offices are the only possible presence in such countries.

The essential disadvantage of the representative office to the business firm is that it cannot conduct general banking activities. Although it can facilitate such transactions with local correspondents, the process may be slower or more cumbersome than a business firm might wish. Because a representative office is usually small, physical limitations do exist on the services that can be supplied to home office clients.

Agencies

In a few jurisdictions of the world, foreign banking may be conducted through an agency relationship. An agency resembles a branch bank except that it cannot accept deposits from the public. Some agencies may accept time deposits from other banks. Agencies perform a number of nondepository banking services, especially those related to international trade. They may arrange commercial and industrial loans, finance trade, issue letters of credit, accept, buy, and collect drafts or bills of exchange, conduct foreign exchange activities, and deal in the Eurocurrency market. Jurisdictional laws usually determine the choice between branch and agency.

Banking Subsidiaries and Affiliates

A subsidiary bank is a separately incorporated bank, owned entirely or in major part by a foreign parent, which conducts a general banking business. As a separate corporation, the banking subsidiary must comply with all the laws of the host country. Its lending limit is based on its own equity capital rather than that of the parent bank. This limits its ability to service large borrowers, but local incorporation also limits the liability of the parent bank to its equity investment in the subsidiary.

A foreign banking subsidiary often appears as a local bank in the eyes of potential customers in host countries and is thus often able to attract additional local deposits. This will especially be true if the bank was independent prior to being purchased by the foreign parent. Management may well be local, giving the bank greater access to the local business community. A foreign-owned bank subsidiary is more likely to be involved in both domestic and international business than is a foreign branch, which is more likely to appeal to the foreign business community but may well encounter difficulty in attracting banking business from local firms.

Related to a banking subsidiary is a banking affiliate. This operation is a locally incorporated bank owned in part, but not necessarily controlled, by a foreign parent. The remainder of the ownership may be local, or it may be other foreign banks. The affiliated bank itself may be newly formed, or it may be a local bank in which a foreign bank has purchased a part interest.

The major advantage of an affiliated banking relationship is that which springs from any joint venture between parties of different nationalities. The bank acquires the expertise of two or more sets of owners. It maintains its status as a local institution with local ownership and management, but it has continuing and permanent relations with its foreign part owner, including an ability to draw upon the international expertise of that part owner. The major disadvantage is also that common to joint ventures; the several owners may be unable to agree on particular policies important to the viability of the bank.

Branch Banks

A foreign branch bank is a legal and operational part of the parent bank, with the full resources of that parent behind the local office. A branch bank does *not* have its own corporate charter, its own board of directors, or any shares of stock outstanding. Although for managerial and regulatory purposes it will maintain its own set of books, its assets and liabilities are in fact those of the parent bank. Operating and credit policies of the branch are integrated into those of the parent.

Branch banks are subject to two sets of banking regulations. As part of the parent, they are subject to home country regulations. However, they are also subject to regulations of the host country, which may provide any of a variety of restrictions on their operations.

Branch banking is the form in which U.S. banks have opened offices in most foreign countries since the end of World War II. Four reasons are cited for this choice by U.S. banks:[8]

1. The entire asset structure and net worth of the U.S. bank is placed as a guarantee behind deposits in the branch.
2. Large corporate borrowers can be attracted by promotion of the idea that greater sums can be loaned to them than would be the case if the local office relied only on local deposits and money market funds.
3. The parent bank can maintain a maximum degree of control over operations of the branch.

4. The branch banking approach follows a traditional pattern of overseas expansion.

The major advantage to a business of using a branch bank is that the branch will conduct a full range of banking services under the name and legal obligation of the parent. A deposit in a branch is a legal obligation of the parent. Services to customers are based on the worldwide value of the client relationship rather than just on the relationship to the local office. Legal loan limits are a function of the size of the parent, not of the branch.

From the point of view of a banker the profits of a foreign branch are subject to immediate taxation at home, and losses of a foreign branch are deductible against taxable income at home. A new office expected to have losses in its early years creates a tax advantage if it is initially organized as a branch, even if eventually the intent is to change it to a separately incorporated subsidiary. From an organizational point of view a foreign branch is usually simpler to create and staff than is a separately incorporated subsidiary.

The major disadvantage of a branch bank is one that accrues to the bank rather than to its customers. The parent bank (not just the branch) may be sued at the local level for debts or other activities of the branch.

International Banking Facilities (IBFs)

As mentioned in Chapter 11, the Federal Reserve Board authorized (effective December 3, 1981) the establishment of U.S.-based international banking facilities (IBFs) in an effort to help U.S. banks capture a larger proportion of the Eurocurrency business. An IBF is not an institution separate from its parent, but is rather a separate set of asset and liability accounts maintained by the parent but segregated from regular bank books. An IBF is thus an accounting entity rather than a legal entity. The establishing entity may be a U.S.-chartered depository institution, a U.S. branch or agency of a foreign bank, or a U.S. office of an Edge Act corporation. Although physically located in the United States, IBFs are not subject to domestic reserve requirements, FDIC insurance premiums, or interest rate ceilings on deposits.

Federal Reserve concern about the possibility of reserve-free transaction accounts "leaking" into the domestic monetary system led to a number of limitations being imposed on IBFs. The limitations do not apply to foreign branches of U.S.-chartered banks. IBF loan and deposit customers are limited to foreign residents, including banks, other IBFs, and the parent bank. IBF time deposits may be offered to foreign banks and to other IBFs. However, nonbank foreign residents are subject to a minimum maturity or notice requirement of two business days.

Deposits and withdrawals of nonbank customers of IBFs must be at least $100,000 in size, except for transactions to withdraw accumulated interest or close the account. Bank customers, however, are not subject to any minimum transaction amount.

IBFs may not issue negotiable instruments, since such instruments could be transferred to U.S. residents who are not eligible to hold deposits in IBFs. Additionally, IBF loans to foreign nonbank customers are subject to a use-of-proceeds restriction, meaning that such funds may not be used to finance the borrower's operations within the United States. Time deposits of the customers may not be used to support the depositor's operations within the United States.

To attract IBFs, several states, including New York, have agreed to exempt them from state and local taxes. U.S.-owned IBFs are already exempt from federal taxes, but foreign-owned IBFs must pay federal taxes.

The number of IBFs has increased rapidly since 1981, and over 400 are now in existence, most of which are located in New York, California, and Florida. Some are owned indirectly by foreign banks through their U.S. agencies and branches. This is especially true for IBFs owned by Japanese and Italian banks, since those governments do not let their own banks own Caribbean "shell" corporations, which are otherwise attractive because of their favorable tax treatment of earned income. The IBF becomes a device to accomplish a similar end.[9]

IBFs have attracted a significant share of Eurodollar business away from other existing centers, especially those located in the Caribbean. By mid-1983 IBFs accounted for $171 billion of Eurocurrency deposits, or 8.3% of the total market. (See Exhibit 11.2.) From a political risk perspective, U.S. residents and firms would prefer to hold their deposits within the legal jurisdiction of the United States rather than offshore in the Caribbean. The same motive attracts some foreign funds seeking political safety. However, some foreign investors, particularly from the Middle East, were seriously disturbed by the U.S. freeze on Iranian funds when U.S. diplomats were being held hostage in Iran in 1979 and 1980. That action made these investors wary of moving funds into a U.S. legal jurisdiction. Some Eurodollar business has been attracted to the IBFs from London and other European centers because U.S. firms are able to transact business during the normal working day.

Edge Act and Agreement Corporations

Edge Act and Agreement corporations are subsidiaries of U.S. banks, incorporated in the United States under Section 25 of the Federal Reserve Act to engage in international banking and financing operations. Not only may such subsidiaries engage in general international banking, they may also finance commercial, industrial, or financial projects in foreign countries through long-term loans or equity participation. Such participation, however, is subject to the day-to-day practices and policies of the Federal Reserve System.

Edge Act and Agreement corporations are physically located in the United States. Because U.S. banks cannot have branches outside their own state, Edge Act and Agreement corporations are usually located in other states in order to conduct international banking activities. Growth in Edge Act banking was greatly facilitated in June 1979 when the Federal Reserve Board issued new guidelines that permitted interstate branching by Edge Act corporations. Previously an Edge Act corporation had to be separately incorporated in each state. By increasing their interstate penetration through Edge Act corporations, the large money center banks are establishing a physical presence in most of the important regional financial centers in order to prepare for the day when interstate branching will be permitted also for domestic business.

The International Banking Act of 1978 extended the Edge Act privilege to foreign banks operating in the United States. In return, the previous ability of foreign banks to conduct a retail banking business in more than one state was severely limited. They must pick a single state as home base. In that state they can conduct full-service banking. In all other states they must limit their activities to Edge Act banking in the same manner as U.S. banks. In many cases, however, foreign banks already had retail operations in more than one state. These were accorded "grandfather" protection but are not allowed to expand beyond what they had at the time the act was passed.

Origin Section 25 of the Federal Reserve Act was amended in 1916 to allow national banks and state banks belonging to the Federal Reserve System and having capital and surplus of $1 million (since increased to $2 million) or more to invest up to 10% of that capital and surplus in a subsidiary incorporated under state or federal law to conduct international or foreign banking. A bank forming such a subsidiary would enter into an "agreement" with the board of governors of the Federal Reserve System as to the type of activities in which they would engage—hence the name "Agreement corporation."

In 1919 Congress passed an amendment, proposed by Senator Walter E. Edge of New Jersey, that expanded the original provisions of the act to allow such subsidiaries to be chartered "for the purpose of engaging in international or foreign banking or other international or foreign financial operation . . . either directly or through the agency, ownership, or control of local institutions in foreign countries."[10] Subsidiaries chartered under this amendment, known as Edge Act corporations, can make equity investments abroad, an operation barred to domestic banks.

The major operational difference between the two types of organizations is that Agreement corporations must engage primarily in international or foreign banking, while Edge Act corporations may also engage in other foreign financial operations. Edge Act corporations are federally chartered and not subject to the banking laws of the various states. Agreement corporations are normally chartered under state law and operate under state jurisdiction.

Edge Act and Agreement corporations generally engage in two types of activities: direct international banking, including acting as a holding company for the stock of one or more foreign banking subsidiaries, and financing development activities not closely related to traditional banking operations. Before 1963 a single subsidiary could not engage in both "banking" and "financing" activities. Since that date a mixture has been possible.

International banking activities Edge Act and Agreement corporations may accept demand and time (but not savings) deposits from outside the United States (as well as from within, if such deposits are incidental to or for the purpose of transactions in foreign countries). Each corporation can also make loans, although commitments to any one borrower cannot exceed 10% of capital and surplus. They can issue or confirm letters of credit; make loans or advances to finance foreign trade, including production loans; create bankers' acceptances; receive items for collection; offer services such as remittance of funds abroad, or buying, selling, or holding securities for safekeeping; issue guarantees; act as paying agent for securities issued by foreign governments or foreign corporations; and engage in spot and forward foreign exchange transactions.

Edge Act subsidiaries whose primary activity is international banking may also function as holding companies by owning shares of foreign banking subsidiaries and affiliates. Domestic banks may have branches abroad, but they may not themselves own shares of foreign banking subsidiaries. Thus the Edge Act route permits U.S. banks to own foreign banking subsidiaries, either as wholly owned subsidiaries via an intermediary Edge Act corporation, or as part of a joint venture with foreign or domestic banks or with other nonbanking institutions.

International financing activities Edge Act and Agreement corporations differ from other U.S. banks in their ability to make portfolio-type investments in the equity of foreign commercial and industrial firms, either directly or through the intermediary of official or semiofficial development banks or corporations. Direct investment in a wide variety of local businesses can be made by intermediate-term loans, by purchase of shares of stock, or by a combination of these two methods.

Some longer-term development projects are typically initiated in the foreign country by local business and are referred to the Edge Act corporation by the parent bank. Analysis of the project follows standard approaches for longer-term investments, with commitments of from $100,000 to $1,000,000 or more resulting if investigation seems to warrant participation. Edge Act corporations engaged only in financing may invest up to 50% of their capital and surplus in a single venture. However, if the Edge Act corporation is also engaged in general banking, the limit is 10% of capital and surplus.

Profit on the project is from a combination of interest received on any debt portion of the investment, dividends received on the equity invested, and capital gains that might result if the venture is successful. It is usually contemplated that the equity investment will be sold after a time, to free capital for new ventures. If local markets do not exist in which the shares may be sold, the initial agreement can provide for the existing local owners to buy out the Edge Act corporation's interest at a price reached by some previously agreed formula.

Multinational Banking Consortia

A consortium bank is a joint venture, incorporated separately and owned by two or more banks, usually of different nationalities. The consortium bank takes customers referred to it by its parent banks and also develops its own business. Banking activities include arranging global syndicates for larger loans or longer-term loans than the parent banks might be willing to handle, underwriting corporate securities, operating in the Eurocurrency market, and arranging international mergers and acquisitions. Some consortium banks now operate as international merchant and investment banks, provide project financing, and give corporate financial advice.

Beginning in 1964, and with increased emphasis after about 1968, a number of multinational consortia of various national parentages were established in Europe. In the early 1980s some of these were restructured as single parent banks because the bank owners found the consortium bank competing with the shareholding parent bank for their most lucrative customers. Nevertheless, at the same time other consortium banks were being created, often in tax havens such as Luxembourg and the Bahamas.

Typical of such consortia banks is Société Financière Européenne (SFE), founded in April 1967 and owned in equal proportions by nine of the largest banks in the world, each from a separate country. The nine are:

- Algemene Bank Nederland N.V. (Netherlands),
- Banca Nazionale del Lavoro (Italy),
- Bank of America N.T. & S.A. (United States),
- Banque Bruxelles Lambert S.A. (Belgium),
- Banque Nationale de Paris (France),
- Barclays Bank International Limited (United Kingdom),
- Dresdner Bank A.G. (Germany),
- Sumitomo Bank Limited (Japan),
- Union Bank of Switzerland (Switzerland).

The SFE group itself consists of three principal companies. Société Financière Européenne Luxembourg is the holding company of the group and provides financial support for its principal subsidiaries. Banque de la Société Financière Européenne, Paris (BSFE), is the principal lending entity of the SFE group and functions as the group's central merchant banking unit. BSFE is owned 86.5% by the Luxembourg holding company and 13.5% by direct and equal investments of the nine SFE-Luxembourg shareholders. BSFE specializes in corporate finance services, loan management and syndication, bond underwriting and placements, mergers, and acquisitions. BSFE organizes, structures, and manages Eurocredits which are syndicated in the international market, has an active presence in the Eurobond market, and advises as well as participates in project financing. Project financing activities involve both consulting at the early stages and later implementation of a financial package, and BSFE has developed a special expertise in nuclear and other energy-related projects.

SFE Banking Corporation, Ltd., of Nassau, Bahamas, the third principal entity of the SFE group, was acquired in 1978 to broaden the group's geographical and service operating base. SFE Banking Corporation's Nassau presence allows it to function in the Eurocurrency market during business hours in both Europe and America. Other services of SFE Banking Corporation include incorporation and administration of companies, management of branch banks, invoicing services for international sales operations, international insurance company services, ship registration, pension fund and other corporate trustee services, and personal trustee services.

COMPARING BANK SERVICES

Banking structure and services vary by country. The following section looks at giro transfer systems, different ways by which banks calculate interest charges, and the range of services often available.

Giro Transfer Systems

In the major countries of western Europe, and in parts of Africa and Asia, individuals may make payments through a giro system. The word "giro" itself comes from the Greek *guros,* meaning circle or turn. A giro system is a money transfer network, usually operated by the post office, intended to facilitate the transfer of a high volume of transactions involving small sums.

Each individual or business has a giro account number. A person wishing to make a payment completes a giro transfer form with his or her own name and account number and the name and account number of the payee. The form is dropped into a postal collection box, and the giro transfer center in the post office reduces the balance in the payer's account, credits the account of the payee, and mails confirmations to both parties. Account holders may deposit directly into their own account at a post office, by mailing a check, or by having their employer deposit wages or salary directly into the account. Utilities, merchants, or others who normally receive payments from the public may maintain accounts into which their customers pay.

Interest is not paid on giro accounts, and overdrafts or other forms of credit are not a normal part of the system. Postage is free, and the cost of transactions is either free or very nominal.

Several advantages of giro systems over checks are suggested. It is not necessary to verify the presence of sufficient funds since the credit and debit are simultaneous. If the payer's account is short, no transfer can be made. Hence checks cannot bounce, and payers cannot kite against their future deposits. In addition, a giro is not a negotiable instrument and in fact never passes into the hands of the payee. Thus forgeries or altering the amount on the document are not possible. Lastly, giro transfer systems are easily computerized, providing for great efficiencies of time and cost. The first giro system, it should be noted, was introduced by the Austrian Post Office Savings Bank in 1883, so the concept predates computers by many decades.

Calculating Interest Charges

Local interest charges can be calculated in various ways. In Europe, banks tend to lend on an "overdraft" basis, with borrowers drawing against a previously established line of credit. Although some commissions or service charges may be imposed for establishment of the overdraft privilege, the basic cost is the interest rate levied on the daily overdraft balance. The borrower pays interest only on funds used, since there is no compensating balance requirement, and only for the period in days for which the funds are taken. For this reason, the effective interest cost of an overdraft "loan" is the nominal or stated interest rate paid on the overdraft balance.

By comparison, U.S. banks normally expect or require compensating balances and may at times loan only on the basis of notes with a specific maturity. Thus the effective cost of a U.S. bank loan is above its nominal cost. Of course, the "cost" of the compensating balance depends on whether such balances would in any event be maintained in the bank for operating purposes. Furthermore, it may be possible to arrange a loan from a branch of a U.S. bank in one country by arranging for compensating balances in another currency at a branch in another country. Thus comparison of effective interest cost is difficult.

Range of Services

Local banks generally have better access to informal contacts among local institutions and individuals, especially in countries in which business contacts are very much a matter of long-established social relationships. Local banks may also be better at dealing with local government red tape or at advising one how to handle situations involving bribery or other forms of corruption.

As a general matter, branches of multinational banks try to offer all services available from local banks, although the quality of such services may vary. Multinational banks are likely, however, to be more sophisticated at financing imports and exports and at handling foreign currency transactions, except when local banks are also involved to a considerable extent in the same activities. Banks with a global network of offices can frequently offer help on collection problems, worldwide credit checks, or advice facilities for worldwide clearing of funds with a minimum of float. Multinational banks are usually more interested, experienced, and aggressive in helping business firms with intermediate- and long-term industrial financing, whereas in many parts of the world local banks are more attuned to short-term financing of sales. Banks from various countries also have reputations for basing loans on different criteria. European bankers are often regarded as "asset lenders" who base their assessment of how much to loan on the existence of physical assets. By comparison, U.S. bankers tend to evaluate expected cash flow and to loan on the prospect that budgeted cash flow will be adequate to repay the loan. Japanese bankers have yet another approach. Although loans may be written for 90 days, Japanese banks see themselves as supplying more or less permanent capital, and what appear to be "short-term" loans are repeatedly rolled over.

SUMMARY

Management of multinational banks deals with problems more complex than those facing domestic banks because of differences in the legal, social, political, and economic environment. This chapter started with an analysis of how banks assess commercial and country risk in their lending activities. Country risk is composed of both sovereign (political) risk and currency (foreign exchange) risk. The chapter explained variables weighed in judging these risks. It also described internal bank organization structures used to set country loan limits.

Loan portfolios must be diversified among countries, a process accomplished by setting country loan limits in the context of portfolio theory. Difficulties in applying portfolio theory to international loan portfolios were discussed.

Types of bank offices used to provide services were explained, including those that are uniquely international such as IBFs, Edge Act and Agreement Subsidiaries, and multinational bank consortia. A description was also provided of giro transfer systems, different ways by which interest is calculated, and the range of services available.

NOTES

1. The following sources present summaries of the dangers and benefits: Irving S. Friedman, *The Emerging Role of Private Banks in the Developing World,* New York: Citicorp, 1977; Steven I. Davis, "How Risky Is International Lending?" *Harvard Business Review,* January/February 1977, pp. 135–143; Richard S. Dale and Richard P. Mattione, *Managing Global Debt,* Washington, D.C.: The Brookings Institution, 1983; and Sarkis J. Khoury, "Sovereign Debt: A Critical Look at the Causes and the Nature of the Problem," *Essays in International Business,* University of South Carolina, Center for International Business Studies, July 1985.

2. Steven I. Davis, "How Risky Is International Lending?" *Harvard Business Review,* January/February 1977, p. 140.

3. See Stephen V. O. Clarke, *American Banks in the International Interbank Market,* New York: Salomon Brothers Center for the Study of Financial Institutions, New York University Monograph Series in Finance and Economics, Monograph 1983-4, p. 28, for a listing of the criteria that bank managements should use in setting limits on lending to other banks in foreign countries.

4. Briance Mascarenhas and Ole Christian Sand, "Country-Risk Assessment Systems in Banks: Patterns and Performance," *Journal of International Business Studies,* Spring 1985, pp. 19–35.

5. *Ibid.,* p. 23.

6. Ingo Walter, "Country Risk, Portfolio Decisions and Regulation in International Bank Lending," *Journal of Banking and Finance,* March 1981, p. 85.

7. Ian Giddy, "The Theory and Industrial Organization of International Banking," New York: Columbia University Graduate School of Business Research Working Paper No. 343A, June 30, 1980.

8. Stuart W. Robinson, Jr., *Multinational Banking,* Leiden, The Netherlands: A. W. Sijthoff, 1972, p. 31.

9. Yoon S. Park and Jack Zwick, *International Banking in Theory and Practice,* Reading, Mass.: Addison-Wesley, 1985, p. 158.

10. Section 25(a) 1, Federal Reserve Act (12 U.S.C. 611–631).

BIBLIOGRAPHY

Abrams, Richard K., "The Role of Regional Banks in International Banking," *Columbia Journal of World Business,* Summer 1981, pp. 62–71.

Aggarwal, Raj, "Variations in Capital Ratios of the World's Largest Banks," *Management International Review,* No. 4, 1982, pp. 45–54.

Agmon, Tamir, and Yair E. Orgler, eds., "Proceedings of the International Conference on Multinational Banking in the World Economy," *Journal of Banking and Finance,* December 1983, pp. 445–648.

Aliber, Robert Z., "International Banking: Growth and Regulation," *Columbia Journal of World Business,* Winter 1975, pp. 9–15.

———, "Toward a Theory of International Banking," *Economic Review of the Federal Reserve Bank of San Francisco,* Spring 1976, pp. 5–8.

Baker, James C., "The IFC and European Banks: Key Factors in Development Aid," *Journal of World Trade Law,* May/June 1980, pp. 264–270.

Baker, James C., and M. Gerald Bradford, *American Banks Abroad, Edge Act Companies and Multinational Banking,* New York: Praeger, 1974.

Ball, Clifford A., and Adrian E. Tschoegl, "The Decision to Establish a Foreign Bank Branch or Subsidiary: An Application of Binary Classification Procedures," *Journal of Financial and Quantitative Analysis,* September 1982, pp. 411–424.

Bhattacharya, Anindya, "Offshore Banking in the Caribbean by U.S. Commercial Banks: Implications for Government-Business Interaction," *Journal of International Business Studies,* Winter 1980, pp. 37–46.

Blasi, Andrew B., "International Banking Facilities," *North Carolina Journal of International Law and Commercial Regulation,* Summer 1983, pp. 61–76.

Boatler, Robert W., "Bank Evaluation of LDC Country Risk," *Inter-American Economic Affairs,* Autumn 1984, pp. 71–76.

Brecher, Charles, and Vladimir Pucik, "Foreign Banks in the U.S. Economy: The Japanese Example," *Columbia Journal of World Business,* Spring 1980, pp. 5–13.

Clarke, Stephen V. O., *American Banks in the International Interbank Market,* New York: Salomon Brothers Center, New York University, 1984.

Crane, Dwight B., and Samuel L. Hayes III, "The New Competition in World Banking," *Harvard Business Review,* July–August 1982, pp. 88–94.

Dale, Richard S., and Richard P. Mattione, *Managing Global Debt,* Washington D.C.: The Brookings Institution, 1983.

Davis, Steven I., *The Management Function in International Banking,* New York: Wiley, 1979.

Dean, James W., and Ian H. Giddy, *Averting International Banking Crises,* New York: New York University Monograph Series in Finance and Economics, No. 1, 1981.

———, "Six Ways to World Banking Safety," *Euromoney,* May 1981, pp. 128–135.

Dod, David P., "Bank Lending to Developing Countries," *Federal Reserve Bulletin,* September 1981, pp. 647–656.

Edwards, Franklin R., "The New 'International Banking Facility': A Study in Regulatory Frustration," *Columbia Journal of World Business,* Winter 1981, pp. 6–18.

Eiteman, David K., "The Spread of Foreign Banks into the United States: Far Eastern Bank Operations in California," in R. Hal Mason, ed., *International Business in the Pacific Basin,* Lexington, Mass.: Heath, 1978.

Feiger, George, and Bertrand Jacquillat, *International Finance: Text and Cases,* Boston: Allyn and Bacon, 1981.

Fraser, Robert D., *International Banking and Finance,* 3rd ed., Washington, D.C.: R & H Publishers, 1977.

Goodman, Laurie S., "Bank Lending to Non-OPEC LDCs: Are Risks Diversifiable?" *Federal Reserve Bank of New York, Quarterly Review,* Summer 1981, pp. 10–20.

Griffith-Jones, Stephany, "The Growth of Multinational Banking, The Euro-Currency Market, and Their Effects on Developing Countries," *Journal of Development Studies,* January 1980, pp. 204–223.

Kammert, James L., *International Commercial Banking Management,* New York: AMACOM, 1981.

Kelly, Dennis E., "Edge Act Corporations after the International Banking Act and New Regulation K.: Implications for Foreign and Regional or Smaller Banks," *Virginia Journal of International Law,* Fall 1979, pp. 37–59.

Key, Sydney J., "Activities of International Banking Facilities: The Early Experience," *Economic Perspectives* (Federal Reserve Bank of Chicago), Fall 1982, pp. 37–45.

———, "International Banking Facilities," *Federal Reserve Bulletin,* October 1982, pp. 565–577.

Khoury, Sarkis J., "International Banking: A Special Look at Foreign Banks in the U.S.," *Journal of International Business Studies,* Winter 1979, pp. 36–52.

———, *Dynamics of International Banking,* New York: Praeger, 1980.

———, "Sovereign Debt: A Critical Look at the Causes and the Nature of the Problem," *Essays in International Business,* Columbia, S.C.: University of South Carolina, Center for International Business Studies, July 1985.

Kim, Seung H., and Stephen W. Miller, *Competitive Structure of the International Banking Industry,* Lexington, Mass.: Lexington Books, 1983.

Korth, Christopher M., "The Evolving Role of U.S. Banks in International Finance," *Bankers Magazine (U.S.),* July–August 1980, pp. 68–73.

———, "The Seat-of-the-Pants Analyst Needs Professional Help," *Euromoney,* May 1981, pp. 124–127.

———, "Risk Minimization for International Lending in Regional Banks," *Columbia Journal of World Business,* Winter 1981, pp. 21–28.

Krayenbuehl, Thomas E., *Country Risk: Assessment and Monitoring,* Lexington, Mass.: Lexington Books, 1985.

Lehr, Dennis J., and Benton R. Hammond, "Regulating Foreign Acquisition of U.S. Banks: The CBCA and the BHCA," *Banking Law Journal,* February 1980, pp. 100–152.

Lessard, Donald R., "North-South: The Implications for Multinational Banking," *Journal of Banking and Finance,* No. 7, 1983, pp. 521–536.

Madura, Jeff, "Credit Risk and the Multinational Corporation," *Bankers Magazine,* November–December 1983, pp. 69–72.

Mascarenhas, Briance, and Ole C. Sand, "Country-Risk Assessment Systems in Banks: Patterns and Performance," *Journal of International Business Studies,* Spring 1985, pp. 19–35.

Nagy, Pancras, *Country Risk,* London: Euromoney Publications, 1984.

Oppenheim, Peter J., *International Banking,* 3rd ed., Washington, D.C.: American Bankers Association, 1978.

Papadopoulos, P., "Measuring and Evaluation of Country Risk," *Canadian Banker,* December 1983, pp. 34–39, and February 1984, pp. 32–35.

Park, Yoon S., and Jack Zwick, *International Banking in Theory and Practice,* Reading, Mass.: Addison-Wesley, 1985.

Pringle, Andreas R., *Japanese Finance: A Guide to Banking in Japan,* New York: Wiley, 1981.

Rabino, Samuel, "The Growth Strategies of New York Based Foreign Banks," *Columbia Journal of World Business,* Winter 1981, pp. 29–35.

Retkwa, Rosalyn, "Bansais and Boos for the IBF's," *Euromoney,* February 1983, pp. 87–89.

Rhoades, Stephen A., "Concentration of World Banking and the Role of U.S. Banks among the 100 Largest, 1956–1980," *Journal of Banking and Finance,* September 1983, pp. 427–437.

Roussakis, Emmanuel N., "The Edges Come to Miami," *Bankers Magazine (U.S.),* May–June 1981, pp. 82–91.

Roussakis, Emmanuel N., ed., *International Banking, Principles and Practices,* New York: Praeger, 1983.

Shapiro, Alan C., "Risk in International Banking," *Journal of Financial and Quantitative Analysis,* December 1982, pp. 727–739.

———, "Currency Risk and Country Risk in International Banking," *Journal of Finance,* July 1985, pp. 881–891.

Skully, Michael T., *Merchant Banking in the Far East,* 2nd ed., London: Financial Times Business Publishing, 1980.

Stuhldreher, Thomas J., and James C. Baker, "Bankers' Attitudes toward U.S. Foreign Bank Regulation," *Banker,* January 1981, pp. 29–34.

Teeters, Nancy H., "The Role of Banks in the International Financial System," *Federal Reserve Bulletin,* September 1983, pp. 663–671.

Terrell, Henry S., "Bank Lending to Developing Countries: Recent Developments and Some Considerations for the Future," *Federal Reserve Bulletin,* October 1984, pp. 755–763.

Uggla, Christer, "International Means of Payments and Credits: What a Commercial Bank Can Offer," in Goran Bergendahl, ed., *International Financial Management,* Stockholm: P.A. Norstedt & Soners forlag, 1982, pp. 71–86.

Walter, Ingo, "Country Risk, Portfolio Decisions and Regulation in International Bank Lending," *Journal of Banking and Finance,* March 1981, pp. 77–92.

Weston, R., *Domestic and Multinational Banking,* New York: Columbia University Press, 1980.

World Banking 1985, New York: Business Press International, 1985.

Zenoff, David B., *International Banking Management and Strategies,* London: Euromoney Publications, 1985.

Zwick, Charles J., "Miami—The New International Banking Center," *Bankers Magazine (U.S.),* January–February 1982, pp. 19–22.

14

Import and Export Financing

Like those whose full effort is devoted to imports and exports, financial managers of multinational firms must be aware of the financial techniques involved in selling and shipping merchandise across national boundaries. Most multinational firms engage in importing and exporting, sometimes to affiliates and sometimes to independent customers.

THREE BASIC NEEDS OF IMPORT-EXPORT FINANCING

Importing and exporting involve certain ways of documenting transactions that have evolved over many centuries. The basic purpose of documentation is to assure the seller receives payment and the buyer receives the merchandise. More specifically, the system provides (1) assurance against the risk of noncompletion of a transaction, (2) protection against foreign exchange risk, and (3) a manner of financing the transaction.

Risk of Noncompletion

Once importer and exporter agree on terms, the seller usually wants to maintain legal title to the goods until paid, or at least until assured of payment. The buyer, however, is naturally reluctant to pay before receiving the goods, or at least before receiving title thereto.

Trust between buyer and seller complicates international trade more than domestic trade since in many cases parties to an international transaction will have limited knowledge about each other. Longer transportation and communication lines, and the possibility of misunderstanding because of a language or culture barrier, add uncertainty.

Much of the risk of noncompletion is reduced through the use of three key documents: (1) the *letter of credit,* which is a bank guarantee of payment if certain stipulated conditions are met; (2) the *draft,* which is the document by which payment is effected; and (3) the *bill of lading,* which is a shipping document issued by a common carrier. These documents are part of a carefully constructed system to determine who bears the risk of noncompletion in any transaction at any given time.

Protection against Foreign Exchange Risk

In international trade the basic foreign exchange risk is transaction risk, as that term was described in Chapter 6. If the transaction is invoiced in the exporter's currency, the importer carries the transaction risk. If the transaction is invoiced in the importer's currency, transaction risk resides with the exporter. Wherever different currencies and an interval of time between agreement on price and final payment exist, one or the other of the parties is exposed.

Transaction risk in international trade is usually covered by hedging, as described in Chapter 7. To acquire protection, however, the exposed party must know the amount and time of payment. The three key documents mentioned above specify both amount and time, and thus lay the groundwork for effective hedging.

Financing the Trade

Most international trade involves a time lag, which means that funds are tied up during the period the merchandise is in transit. Because the locus of risk of noncompletion is clear, and because foreign exchange risk can be hedged, commercial banks are often willing to finance goods in transit or even prior to shipment. A bank can deal with the financial aspects of a trade, as evidenced by documents, without exposing itself to questions about the quality of the merchandise or other physical aspects of the shipment.

In the next three sections we will examine each of the three key documents: the letter of credit, the draft, and the bill of lading. We will then discuss other documents and aspects of financing international trade.

LETTER OF CREDIT (L/C)

A letter of credit, often abbreviated L/C, is an instrument issued by a bank at the request of an importer, in which the bank promises to pay a beneficiary upon presentation of documents specified in the letter of credit. A letter of credit reduces the risk of noncompletion, since the bank agrees to pay against paper documents rather than actual merchandise. The relationship between the three parties can be seen in Exhibit 14.1.

EXHIBIT 14.1
Parties to a Letter of Credit

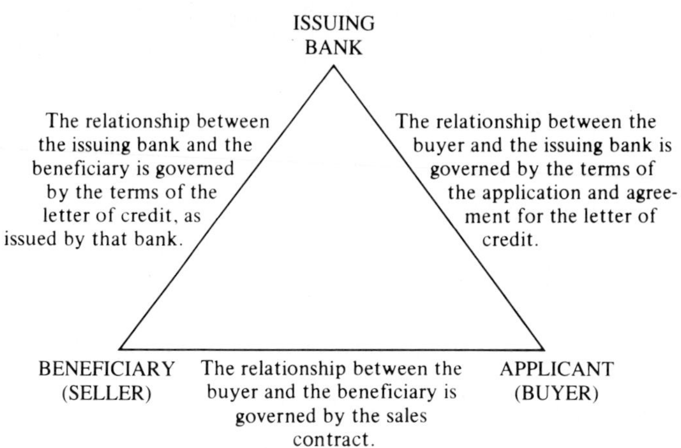

Source: First National Bank of Chicago, *Financing of U.S. Exports,* compiled by Patricia A. Ferris, January 1975, p. 21.

In international trade a letter of credit is sometimes referred to as a *commercial letter of credit,* a *documentary letter of credit,* or simply a *credit.* A commercial letter of credit is somewhat different from a *traveler's letter of credit,* since the latter is normally used for noncommercial transactions. Traveler's letters of credit usually call for clean (nondocumentary) drafts—a distinction that will be explained later in this chapter. Payment under a commercial letter of credit is usually by documentary drafts.

Normally a commercial letter of credit is used as part of the financing of a commercial transaction. Although details vary, depending on the type of letter of credit and its provisions, the following transaction is typical. An importer (buyer) and exporter (seller) agree on a transaction, and the importer applies to its local bank for the issuance of a letter of credit on a form such as shown in Exhibit 14.2. In Exhibit 14.2 a U.S. importer, XYZ, Inc., of Torrance, California, is applying to Security Pacific National Bank for a letter of credit good up to the amount of $7,690.20, to be issued to Japanese exporter, ABC Co., Ltd., of Tokyo.

The importer's bank, Security Pacific in Exhibit 14.2, will issue the letter of credit according to its assessment of the importer's credit-worthiness, or the bank might require a cash deposit or other collateral from the importer in advance. The importer's bank will want to know the type of transaction, the amount of money involved, and what documents must accompany the draft that will be drawn against the letter of credit. The application in Exhibit 14.2 is for the importation of PVC blue discharge hose, and the draft is to be payable 90 days after sight.

EXHIBIT 14.2
Application for Letter of Credit

TO: SECURITY PACIFIC NATIONAL BANK
INTERNATIONAL BANKING GROUP

LETTER OF CREDIT APPLICATION AND SECURITY AGREEMENT

DATE 9-22-xx

PLEASE ISSUE YOUR IRREVOCABLE LETTER OF CREDIT AND ADVISE THE BENEFICIARY BY [X] AIRMAIL [ ] CABLE SHORT DETAILS [ ] CABLE FULL DETAILS

IN FAVOR OF (NAME & ADDRESS) ABC Co., Ltd. No. 10 Mori Bldg 1-18-1, Toranomon, Minato-Ku, Tokyo, 105, Japan

FOR ACCOUNT OF (NAME & ADDRESS) XYZ, Inc. 55555 Hawthorne Blvd.,Suite 400-14 Torrance, California 90503

UP TO THE AGGREGATE SUM OF US$7,690.20 AVAILABLE BY DRAFTS ON YOU OR YOUR CORRESPONDENT AT 90 (USANCE) SIGHT FOR 100 % OF INVOICE VALUE ACCOMPANIED BY THE FOLLOWING DOCUMENTS (INDICATED BY "X")

[X] SIGNED COMMERCIAL INVOICE (S) 3 (INDICATE NUMBER OF COPIES) [X] SPECIAL CUSTOMS INVOICE (S) 3 [X] PACKING LIST 3

[X] NEGOTIABLE MARINE & WAR RISK INSURANCE POLICY/CERTIFICATE FOR 110 % OF CIF VALUE WITH CLAIMS PAYABLE IN THE UNITED STATES

[ ] OTHER DOCUMENTS

SPECIMEN

[X] FULL SET OF CLEAN ON BOARD OCEAN BILLS OF LADING [X] TO ORDER OF SHIPPER, BLANK ENDORSED. [ ] TO ORDER

[ ] AIRWAY BILL/AIR CONSIGNMENT NOTE CONSIGNED TO

[ ] RAILROAD/TRUCK BILL OF LADING CONSIGNED TO

SHOWING [X] FREIGHT PREPAID. [ ] FREIGHT COLLECT. MARKED "NOTIFY XYZ, Inc. 55555 Hawthorne Blvd., Suite 400-14 Torrance, California 90503

EVIDENCING SHIPMENT OF PVC Blue Discharge Hose (SPECIFY COMMODITY ONLY OMITTING DETAILS AS TO GRADE QUALITY PRICE ETC.)

FROM Nagoya, Japan (PORT OF SHIPMENT) TO CIF, Los Angeles, Calif. (DESTINATION) SHIPMENT TERMS (CHECK ONE √) [ ] FOB [X] CIF [ ] C&F [ ] (OTHER)

LATEST SHIPMENT DATE IS Oct. 30, 19xx PARTIAL SHIPMENTS PERMITTED [ ] YES [X] NO TRANSHIPMENT PERMITTED [ ] YES [X] NO

LATEST NEGOTIATION DATE IS Nov. 10, 19xx INSURANCE TO BE EFFECTED BY Seller (BUYER OR SELLER)

SPECIAL INSTRUCTIONS (INDICATE HERE ANY SPECIAL INSTRUCTIONS YOU WISH INCLUDED IN THE LETTER OF CREDIT.)

[X] COMMERCIAL INVOICES MUST CONTAIN SHIPPER'S SIGNED CERTIFICATION THAT GOODS ARE IN ACCORDANCE WITH BUYER'S PURCHASE ORDER NO. 2944 , PROFORMA INVOICE NO. DATED

[ ]

ADVISE CREDIT THROUGH BENEFICIARY'S BANK NAMED HERE • Security Pacific National Bank, Tokyo, Japan (IF BENEFICIARY'S BANK IS UNKNOWN WE WILL USE OUR CORRESPONDENT BANK.)

DEBIT TO: OFFICE NAME ACCOUNT NUMBER

MAIL SHIPPING DOCUMENTS TO DEF Co, Customs Broker, San Pedro

FOR BANK USE ONLY

EXTENSION OF THIS CREDIT UNDER CUSTOMER'S LIABILITY HAS BEEN APPROVED BY AN AUTHORIZED LOAN OFFICER OF SECURITY PACIFIC NATIONAL BANK.

OFFICE:

APPROVING OFFICER'S SIGNATURE & TITLE

L/C NO. 308,590 HEAD OFFICE I.B.G. APPROVAL

DIRECT INQUIRIES TO OUR MR. J. Smith PHONE NUMBER

WE, AND EACH OF US, AGREE THAT THE TERMS AND CONDITIONS SET FORTH ON THIS AND THE REVERSE HEREOF ARE HEREBY MADE A PART OF THIS APPLICATION AND ARE ACCEPTED AND AGREED TO BY US.

FIRM NAME XYZ, Inc. 55555 Hawthorne Blvd., Torrance

AUTHORIZED SIGNATURE (S)

TITLE

02331-7 2-76* 50 10Y

Source: Security Pacific National Bank.

If the importer's bank is satisfied with the credit standing of the applicant, it will issue a letter of credit guaranteeing to pay for the merchandise if shipped in accordance with the instructions and conditions contained in the credit. Exhibit 14.3 shows the letter of credit issued by Security Pacific National Bank for the import of PVC blue discharge hose. The credit specifies exactly what documents must accompany the draft drawn against the credit: commercial invoice, customs invoice, packing list, insurance policy or certificate, and a clean-on-board ocean bill of lading.

At this point the credit of the bank has been substituted for that of the importer, and the letter of credit becomes a financial contract between the issuing bank and the designated beneficiary, ABC Co., Ltd., of Tokyo. This financial contract is a separate transaction from the sale of the merchandise. If the terms of the letter of credit are met, any payment problems that develop at a later date are of concern only to the importer and the issuing bank. All other parties to the transaction may rely on the bank's credit without concern about the financial status of the importer.

The importer's bank issuing the letter of credit sends the document (or wires its terms) to a correspondent in the exporter's country, or to the exporter's bank, which advises the exporter (the beneficiary) of the establishment of a letter of credit in its name.

When the exporter ships the merchandise, the exporter draws a draft against the issuing bank in accordance with the terms of the letter of credit, attaches the required documents, and presents the draft to its own bank for payment. At this point different combinations of events are possible. Let us assume that the exporter's bank has not itself confirmed the credit. That is, the exporter's bank has not added its own promise to pay to the promise of the issuing bank. In this case the exporter's bank will accept the draft and accompanying documents and forward them to the bank of the importer, which issued the credit. If all the terms and conditions expressed on the letter of credit have been complied with and the required documents are attached, the importer's bank will honor the draft. In this instance it will pay the exporter's bank. When the exporter's bank receives the funds, it pays the exporter.

The importer's bank, in turn, collects from the importer in accordance with the terms agreed upon at the time the letter of credit was opened. The importer might have to pay at once in order to obtain the documents, including the order bill of lading that is needed to obtain physical possession of the merchandise. Alternatively, the bank may release the documents to the importer and the importer may promise to pay at some later date, usually under a trust receipt arrangement.

In the previous example the importer's bank decided to pay after inspecting the documents, and the exporter's bank functioned only as a collection organization. An alternative procedure would have been for the exporter's bank to *confirm* the letter of credit. The exporter's bank would

EXHIBIT 14.3
Letter of Credit

IRREVOCABLE
DOCUMENTARY
LETTER OF CREDIT

CABLE ADDRESS
SEPACBANK

SECURITY PACIFIC NATIONAL BANK
INTERNATIONAL BANKING GROUP

☐ Post Office Box 7637
San Francisco, California 94120

XX Head Office · Post Office Box 92890
Los Angeles, California 90009

☐ Post Office Box 1791
San Diego, California 92112

ABC Co., Ltd.
No. 10 Mori Bldg 1-18-1 Toranomon, Minato-Ku
Tokyo, 105, Japan

Advised by AIRMAIL/XXXXXX through:
Security Pacific National Bank
International Banking Office
Tokyo, Japan

WE ESTABLISH OUR IRREVOCABLE LETTER OF CREDIT NUMBER L C 308,590 DATED 9-22-xx IN YOUR FAVOR

FOR THE ACCOUNT OF XYZ, Inc., 55555 Hawthorne Blvd., Suite 400-14 Torrance, California 90503

UP TO THE AGGREGATE SUM OF SEVEN THOUSAND SIX HUNDRED NINETY AND 20/100 UNITED STATES DOLLARS*
* * * *($7,690.20)

AVAILABLE BY YOUR DRAFT (S) AT 90 days SIGHT FOR 100% INVOICE VALUE DRAWN ON US

AND ACCOMPANIED BY THE FOLLOWING DOCUMENTS:

1. Signed Commercial Invoices in triplicate, certifying that goods are in accordance with buyer's purchase order No. 2944.
2. Special Customs Invoices in triplicate.
3. Packing List in triplicate.
4. Negotiable Marine & War Risk Insurance Policy/Certificate for 110% of CIF value with claims payable in the United States.
5. Full set of clean on board Ocean Bills of Lading to the order of shipper, blank endorsed, showing "Freight Prepaid", marked Notify: XYZ, Inc., 55555 Hawthorne Blvd., Suite 400-14 Torrance, California 90503.

SPECIMEN

EVIDENCING SHIPMENT OF PVC Blue Discharge Hose

FROM Nagoya, Japan TO CIF, Los Angeles, California

PARTIAL SHIPMENTS ARE not PERMITTED

TRANSHIPMENT IS not PERMITTED. INSURANCE IS TO BE EFFECTED BY Seller

LATEST NEGOTIATION DATE OF THIS LETTER OF CREDIT IS November 10, 19xx

DRAFTS DRAWN AND NEGOTIATED UNDER THIS LETTER OF CREDIT MUST BE ENDORSED HEREON AND MUST BEAR THE CLAUSE: "DRAWN UNDER SECURITY PACIFIC NATIONAL BANK LETTER OF CREDIT NUMBER 308,590 DATED 9-22-xx
WE HEREBY ENGAGE WITH BONA FIDE HOLDERS THAT DRAFTS DRAWN STRICTLY IN COMPLIANCE WITH THE TERMS OF THIS CREDIT AND AMENDMENTS SHALL MEET WITH DUE HONOR UPON PRESENTATION *XXXXXXXXXXXXXXXXXXXXXXXXXXXXXXXXXX
THIS CREDIT IS SUBJECT TO THE UNIFORM CUSTOMS AND PRACTICE FOR DOCUMENTARY CREDITS (1974 REVISION), INTERNATIONAL CHAMBER OF COMMERCE PUBLICATION NUMBER 290.

*TO THE DRAWEE BANK

Authorized Signature

WHEN OPENED BY CABLE, THIS CREDIT IS ONLY AVAILABLE IF ATTACHED TO OUR CORRESPONDENT'S ADVICE OF CABLED CREDIT, THE TWO CONSTITUTING EVIDENCE OF THE OUTSTANDING AMOUNT OF THIS CREDIT.

051821 1-77 PS

Source: Security Pacific National Bank.

then itself honor drafts drawn against the credit when first presented and obtain reimbursement from the importer's bank. The distinction between confirmed and unconfirmed letters of credit will be explained more fully later in this section.

We emphasize here that a letter of credit is a promise to pay *against specified documents,* which must accompany any draft drawn against the credit. The letter of credit is not a guarantee of the underlying commercial transaction. To constitute a true letter of credit transaction, the following five elements must all be present with respect to the issuing bank:

1. The issuing bank must receive a fee or other valid business consideration for the letter of credit.
2. The bank's letter of credit must contain a specified expiration date or be for a definite term.
3. The bank's commitment must have a stated maximum.
4. The bank's obligation to pay must arise only on the presentation of specific documents, and the bank must not be called on to determine disputed questions of fact or law.
5. The bank's customer must have an unqualified obligation to reimburse the bank on the same condition as the bank has paid.

Types of Letters of Credit

Most commercial letters of credit are *documentary,* meaning that certain documents must be included with any drafts drawn under the terms of the credit. Documents required usually include an order bill of lading, a commercial invoice, and any of the following: consular invoice, insurance certificate or policy, certificate of origin, weight list, certificate of analysis, packing list. Commercial letters of credit are also classified as follows.

Irrevocable vs. revocable An irrevocable letter of credit obligates the issuing bank to honor drafts drawn in compliance with the credit and can be neither canceled nor modified without the consent of all parties, including in particular the beneficiary (exporter). A revocable letter of credit can be canceled or amended at any time before payment; it is intended to serve as a means of arranging payment but not as a guarantee of payment.

Confirmed vs. unconfirmed A letter of credit issued by one bank can be confirmed by another, in which case both banks are obligated to honor drafts drawn in compliance with the credit. An unconfirmed letter of credit is the obligation only of the issuing bank. An exporter is likely to want a foreign bank's letter of credit confirmed by a domestic bank when the exporter has doubts about the foreign bank's ability to pay. Such doubts may arise if the exporter is unsure of the financial standing of the foreign bank, or if political or economical conditions in the foreign country are unstable.

The desirability of confirmation was apparent from an event in 1975. The Bank of Nigeria, that country's central bank, refused to pay on irrevocable letters of credit that it had issued for the import of material ordered for Nigeria's development. Flush with income earned as a member of OPEC and desirous of furthering its economic development, Nigeria ordered more cement and other items than could be unloaded by available port facilities. By October 1975, some 400 ships were backed up in Lagos harbor, and the estimated delay for a newly arriving ship was 450 days. The governor of the Bank of Nigeria stated (*Business Week,* November 3, 1975): "It is the exporters and shipowners who are making things difficult," and the bank refused to honor its supposedly irrevocable letters of credit. Bankers termed the event virtually unprecedented in international trade, and exporters to Nigeria suffered major losses. Had the exporters insisted that their own banks confirm the Bank of Nigeria's "irrevocable" letters of credit, the losses would have been borne by the confirming bank rather than the exporters. An underlying assumption is that a confirming bank is better able to judge the credibility of a bank issuing a letter of credit than is a merchant.

Revolving vs. nonrevolving Most letters of credit are nonrevolving; they are valid for one transaction only. Under some circumstances, however, a revolving credit is issued. A $10,000 revolving weekly credit, for example, might mean that the beneficiary is authorized to draw drafts up to $10,000 each week until the credit expires. The period of a revolving credit might be daily, weekly, or monthly. Because the maximum exposure under an irrevocable revolving credit is very great (the buyer cannot stop its obligation to pay for future shipments even if it is dissatisfied with the merchandise), most revolving credits are issued in revocable form. A revolving credit may be *noncumulative,* in which case any amount not used by the beneficiary during the specified period may not be drawn against in a later period; or it may be *cumulative,* in which case undrawn amounts carry over to future periods. Under a cumulative revolving credit of, say, $10,000 per week, a beneficiary who drew only $7,000 in one week could draw up to $13,000 the following week.

Issuers of Letters of Credit

From an exporter's point of view a documentary letter of credit is one of the following:

1. An irrevocable letter of credit issued by a foreign bank and confirmed irrevocably by a domestic bank. (On occasion the credit may be confirmed by a third-country foreign bank. For example, a U.S.

exporter might receive a letter of credit from an African bank confirmed by a French or English bank.)

2. An irrevocable letter of credit issued by a domestic bank.
3. An irrevocable letter of credit issued by a foreign bank without the responsibility or endorsement of a domestic bank. In this situation the domestic bank transmits information (when the letter is opened) and forwards drafts for collection but does not lend its guarantee.
4. A revocable letter of credit established to arrange for payment.

Exporters generally prefer types 1 and 2 above, since they need look no further than a bank in their own country for compliance with the terms of the letter of credit. Although a letter of credit issued by a foreign bank alone (type 3) might well be of the highest esteem, most exporters are not in a position to evaluate or deal with foreign banks directly should difficulties arise.

Every irrevocable letter of credit must indicate an expiration date beyond which documents for payment or acceptance will not be accepted. Documents, such as drafts or bills of lading, must be presented within a reasonable time after issue, for if there is undue delay, the bank may refuse to accept them.

A bank issuing a letter of credit can designate the credit "transferable," in which case the beneficiary has the right to instruct the paying bank to make payment in whole or in part to one or more third parties (called "second beneficiaries"). However, a transferable credit can be transferred only once. Transfer of a fraction of a transferable credit can be made only if the letter of credit allows partial shipment of the merchandise.

Advantages and Disadvantages of Letters of Credit

The primary advantage of a letter of credit is that it facilitates international trade. The exporter gains because it can sell against the promise of a bank rather than a commercial firm. The exporter is also in a more secure position as to the availability of foreign exchange to pay for its sale. If the letter of credit is confirmed by a bank in the exporter's country, the problem of foreign exchange is eliminated. Even if the letter of credit is not confirmed, the issuing foreign bank is more likely to be aware of foreign exchange conditions and rules than is the importing firm itself. Lastly, should the importing country change its foreign exchange rules, it is likely to allow outstanding bank letters of credit to be honored for fear of throwing its own domestic banks into international disrepute.

The exporter may find that an order backed by an irrevocable letter of credit will facilitate obtaining domestic preexport financing. If the exporter's reputation for delivery is good, a local bank may lend funds to process and prepare the merchandise for shipment. Once the merchandise is shipped in compliance with the terms and conditions of the credit, payment for the business transaction is made and funds will be generated to repay the preexport loan.

The major advantage to the importing firm of a letter of credit is that the firm need not pay out funds until the documents have arrived and unless all conditions stated in the credit have been fulfilled. In addition, if acceptances are created under the letter of credit, an additional period of financing is provided. The main disadvantages are the fee charged by the importer's bank for issuing its letter of credit, and the likelihood that the letter of credit reduces the importer's borrowing line of credit from the importer's bank.

Liabilities of Banks under Letters of Credit

Since a letter of credit substitutes bank credit for merchant credit, banks incur obligations when they issue or confirm letters of credit. These are specified in detail in the "Uniform Customs and Practice for Documentary Credits," published by the United States Council of the International Chamber of Commerce.[1]

In documentary letters of credit various parties pay against documents, not against actual goods. Thus a bank is obligated to examine all documents with reasonable care to be sure that they appear on their face to be in accordance with the terms and conditions of the letter of credit. However, banks do not assume liability or responsibility for the form, sufficiency, accuracy, authenticity, falsification, or legal effect of any documents; nor for general and/or particular conditions stipulated in or superimposed on the documents; nor for the description, quantity, weight, quality, condition, packing, delivery, value, or existence of the goods; nor for the good faith or acts and/or omissions, solvency, performance, or standing of any of the parties to the transaction, including carriers and insurers.

Banks furthermore assume no liability or responsibility for the consequences of delays or losses in transit of messages, letters, or documents; or for errors arising in the transmission of cables, telegrams, or telex; or for errors in translating or interpreting technical terms. Furthermore, they are not liable or responsible for the consequences of strikes, lockouts, riots, civil commotions, insurrections, wars, acts of God, or other causes beyond their control.

DRAFT

A *draft,* sometimes called a *bill of exchange* (B/E), is the instrument normally used in international commerce to effect payment. A draft is simply an order written by an exporter (seller) requesting an importer (buyer) or its agent to pay a specified amount of money at a specified time.

The person or business initiating the draft is known as the *maker, drawer,* or *originator.* Normally this is the exporter who sells and ships the merchandise. The party to whom the draft is addressed is the *drawee.* The drawee is asked to *honor* the draft, i.e., to pay the amount requested according to the stated terms. In commercial transactions the drawee is either the buyer, in which case the draft is called a *trade draft,* or the buyer's bank, in which case the draft is called a *bank draft.* Bank drafts are usually drawn according to the terms of a letter of credit. A draft may be drawn as a bearer instrument, or it may designate a person to whom payment is to be made. This person, known as the *payee,* may be the drawer itself or it may be some other party such as the drawer's bank.

International practice, in which drafts are used to settle trade transactions, differs from domestic custom, in which sellers usually ship merchandise on open account, followed by a commercial invoice indicating the amount due and terms for payment. In domestic practice the buyer usually obtains possession of the merchandise without signing a formal document directly indicating its obligation to pay. International practice, in contrast, often requires payment or a formal promise to pay before the buyer can obtain the merchandise.

International practice differs in part because of traditions from an earlier day when buyers and sellers were less willing to trust each other—especially when they were in different countries with differing domestic commercial laws—and in part because drafts, which become *negotiable instruments,* provide a convenient instrument for financing the international movement of the merchandise.

Negotiable Instruments

To become a negotiable instrument, a draft or bill of exchange must conform to the following requirements:[2]

- It must be in writing and signed by the maker or drawer.
- It must contain an unconditional promise or order to pay a definite sum of money.
- It must be payable on demand or at a fixed or determinable future date.
- It must be payable to order or to bearer.

If the draft is drawn in conformity with the above requirements, a person receiving it is a *holder in due course* and is entitled to receive payment despite any personal disagreements between drawee and maker because of controversy over the underlying commercial transaction. If the drawee dishonors the draft, payment must be made to any holder in due course by any prior endorser or by the maker. This clear definition of the rights of parties who hold a negotiable instrument as a holder in due course has contributed significantly to the widespread acceptance of various forms of drafts, including personal checks.

Types of Drafts

Drafts are of two types: *sight drafts* and *time drafts.* Time drafts are also called *usance drafts.* A sight draft is payable on presentation to the drawee; the drawee must pay at once or dishonor the draft. A time draft allows a delay in payment. It is presented to the drawee who *accepts* it by writing or stamping a notice of acceptance on its face. Once accepted, the time draft becomes a promise to pay by the accepting party. When a time draft is drawn on and accepted by a bank, it becomes a *bankers' acceptance.* When a time draft is drawn on and accepted by a business firm, it becomes a *trade acceptance.*

A time draft drawn by ABC Co., Ltd., of Tokyo for its export of PVC blue discharge hose against the letter of credit shown earlier is illustrated in Exhibit 14.4. ABC Co., Ltd., is instructing Security Pacific National Bank to pay to the Commercial Bank, Ltd. (ABC's bank), the sum of $7,690.20 ninety days after the draft is first presented to Security Pacific. When the draft is presented to Security Pacific, that bank will check to see that all terms of the letter of credit have been complied with and will then stamp the face of the draft with the acceptance inscription shown with the draft in Exhibit 14.4. A bank officer will sign, and the draft becomes a bankers' acceptance maturing in 90 days. Because the draft in Exhibit 14.4 was accepted on October 11, it will mature on January 9.

Because payment on an acceptance is not made at the time of presentation, the acceptance serves as a device to finance merchandise in transit or held in inventory prior to sale. In practice, most time drafts are made payable 30, 60, 90, or some other specified number of days after (1) the date of the draft, in which case the date of payment is clearly established at the time the draft is drawn, or (2) the date of acceptance, in which case the drawee/acceptor is assured of a fixed time interval between the date when it accepts the draft and the time that payment must be made. Bankers' acceptances are usually sold in the short-term money market at a discount from face amount, thus providing a short-term liquid security for investors. The investor relies on the bank's promise to pay.

Trade acceptances are not normally marketable. However, they do constitute a written promise by the business firm that accepted the draft to pay on a specific date. On due date the holder (usually the exporter) can present the trade acceptance for collection through the accepting firm's bank. The bank itself is not obligated to pay, but when the importer is asked for payment by its own bank, the pressure to pay is great. A trade acceptance can be viewed as a documented, written account receivable, as compared with an open-book account receivable.

EXHIBIT 14.4
Time Draft and Stamp Including Acceptance by Bank

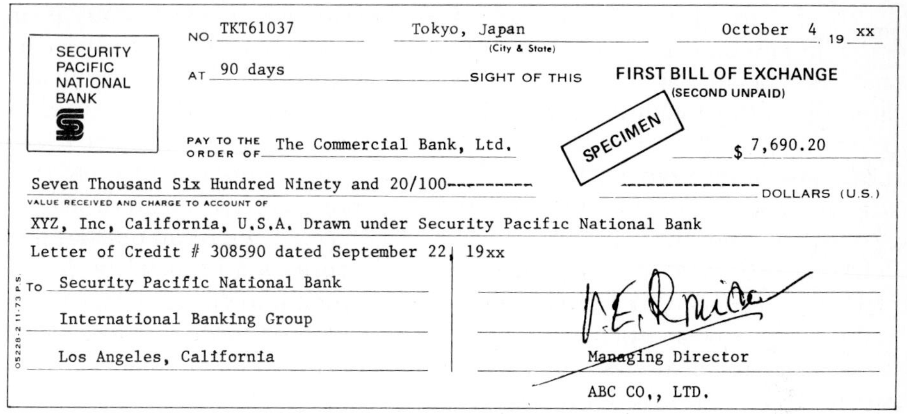

SECURITY PACIFIC NATIONAL BANK

NO. TKT61037 Tokyo, Japan (City & State) October 4 19 xx

AT 90 days SIGHT OF THIS FIRST BILL OF EXCHANGE (SECOND UNPAID)

SPECIMEN

PAY TO THE ORDER OF The Commercial Bank, Ltd. $ 7,690.20

Seven Thousand Six Hundred Ninety and 20/100---------- --------------- DOLLARS (U.S.)

VALUE RECEIVED AND CHARGE TO ACCOUNT OF

XYZ, Inc, California, U.S.A. Drawn under Security Pacific National Bank

Letter of Credit # 308590 dated September 22, 19xx

To Security Pacific National Bank

International Banking Group

Los Angeles, California

Managing Director

ABC CO., LTD.

05228-2 11-73 P.S.

The transaction which gives rise to this instrument is the

IMPORTATION

of PVC BLUE DISCHARGE HOSE

from NAGOYA, JAPAN

to LOS ANGELES, CALIFORNIA

No. $ 7,690.20

SPECIMEN

ACCEPTED

October 11, 19xx

PAYABLE AT

INTERNATIONAL BANKING GROUP

SECURITY PACIFIC NATIONAL BANK

LOS ANGELES, CALIFORNIA

By ....

Authorized Signature

Source: Security Pacific National Bank.

The time period of a draft is referred to as its *tenor* or *usance*. To qualify as a negotiable instrument, and so be attractive to a holder in due course, a draft must be payable on a fixed or determinable future date. For example, 60 days after sight is a determinable date, such a maturity being established precisely at the time the draft is accepted. However, payment "on arrival of goods" is not determinable since the date of arrival cannot be known in advance. Indeed, there is no assurance that the goods will arrive at all. Third parties would have no interest in investing in it because they could not be certain they would ever be paid. However, even a nonnegotiable acceptance can function as a device to obtain payment, since it is a legal obligation to pay unless there is some defect in the underlying commercial transaction.

Drafts are also classified as *clean* or *documentary*. A clean draft is an order to pay unaccompanied by any other documents. When it is used in trade, the seller has usually sent the shipping documents directly to the buyer, who thus obtains possession of the merchandise independent of its payment (on a clean sight draft) or acceptance (on a clean time draft). Clean drafts are often used by multinational companies shipping to their own affiliates, for matters of trust and credit are not involved. Clean drafts are also used for nontrade remittances, e.g., when collection of an outstanding debt is sought. Use of a clean draft puts pressure on a recalcitrant debtor by forcing it to convert an open-account obligation into documentary form. Failure to pay or accept such a draft when presented through a local bank can damage the drawee's reputation, and the existence of an accepted draft provides strong pressure for payment.

Where matters of international trade are concerned, most drafts are documentary, which means that various shipping documents are attached to the draft. Payment (for sight drafts) or acceptance (for time drafts) is required to obtain possession of the documents, which are in turn needed to obtain the goods involved in the transaction. If documents are to be delivered to the buyer on payment of the draft, it is known as a "D/P draft"; if the documents are delivered on acceptance, the draft is called a "D/A draft."

If no letter of credit exists but the exporter wants to control the merchandise until payment is made, the exporter will use a documentary sight draft drawn directly on the importer. However, this instrument does not eliminate all risk. An irresponsible buyer may refuse to accept the shipment for such reasons as a drop in prices or a loss of the market in which the buyer intended to resell. Then the exporter will have to find another buyer or pay to have the merchandise shipped back to the exporter's plant.

Bankers' Acceptances

When a draft is accepted by a bank, it becomes a *bankers' acceptance*. As such it is the unconditional promise of that bank to make payment on the draft when it matures. In quality the bankers' acceptance is practically identical to a marketable bank certificate of deposit (CD). The holder of a bankers' acceptance need not wait until maturity to liquidate the investment, but it may sell the acceptance in the money market, where constant trading in such instruments occurs.

The first owner of the bankers' acceptance created from an international trade transaction will be the exporter, who receives the accepted draft back after the bank has stamped it "accepted." The exporter may hold the acceptance until maturity and then collect. On an acceptance of, say, $100,000 for six months the exporter would receive the face amount less the bank's acceptance commission of 1.5% per annum:

Face amount of the acceptance	$100,000
Less 1.5% per annum commission for 6 months	– 750
Amount received by exporter in 6 months	$ 99,250

Alternatively, the exporter may "discount"—i.e., sell at a reduced price—the acceptance to its bank in order to receive funds at once. The exporter will then receive the face amount of the acceptance less both the acceptance fee and the going market rate of discount for bankers' acceptances. If the discount rate were 13.0% per annum, the exporter would receive the following:

Face amount of the acceptance		$100,000
Less 1.5% per annum commission for 6 months	$ 750	
Less 13.0% per annum discount rate for 6 months	6,500	7,250
Amount received by exporter at once		$ 92,750

The discounting bank may hold the acceptance in its own portfolio, thus earning for itself the 13% per annum discount rate, or the acceptance may be resold in the acceptance market. At present there are from 10 to 15 acceptance dealers in New York City who buy and sell acceptances at a spread (between buying and selling price) of ⅛% to ¼%. The dealers may hold the acceptances themselves, but more frequently they resell them to investors.

Within the United States, bankers' acceptances are either *eligible* or *ineligible*. An ineligible acceptance is a sound and marketable instrument, but it lacks certain characteristics that would make it eligible for purchase or discount by the Federal Reserve System. Requirements for eligibility are complex. The essence of the requirements is that eligible acceptances must have a maturity no longer than six months (for discount) or nine months (for purchase) and must arise out of specific commercial transactions, domestic trade, foreign trade, or the storage of commodities. Such acceptances must, in effect, finance self-liquidating transactions. Bankers' acceptances arising from international trade through letters of credit are almost always "eligible" within the U.S. classification.

BILL OF LADING

The third key document for financing international trade is the *bill of lading*, or B/L. The bill of lading is issued to the shipper by a common carrier transporting the merchandise. It serves three purposes: a receipt, a contract, and, if properly drawn, a document of title.

As a receipt, the bill of lading indicates that the carrier has received the merchandise described on the face of the document. Exhibit 14.5 shows a bill of lading issued by Mitsui O.S.K. Lines, Ltd., for shipment on the vessel America Maru of 90 rolls of PVC blue discharge hose from Nagoya, Japan, to Los Angeles, California. The carrier is not responsible for ascertaining that the containers hold what is alleged to be their contents, so descriptions of merchandise on bills of lading are usually short and simple. If shipping charges are paid in advance, the bill of lading will usually be stamped "freight paid" or "freight prepaid." If merchandise is shipped collect—a less common procedure internationally than domestically—the carrier maintains a lien on the goods until freight is paid.

As a contract, the bill of lading indicates the obligation of the carrier to provide certain transportation in return for certain charges. Common carriers cannot disclaim responsibility for their negligence through inserting special clauses in a bill of lading. The bill of lading, as a contract, may specify alternative ports in the event that delivery cannot be made to the designated port, or it may specify that the goods will be returned to the shipper at the shipper's expense.

As a document of title, the bill of lading can be used to obtain payment or a written promise of payment before the merchandise is released to the possession of the consignee. The bill of lading can also function as collateral against which funds may be advanced to the exporter by its local bank prior to or during shipment and before final payment by the importer.

Characteristics of the Bill of Lading

Bills of lading are either *straight* or *to order.* A straight bill of lading provides that the carrier deliver the merchandise to the designated consignee. A straight bill of lading is *not* title to the goods and is not required for the consignee to obtain possession. Because a straight bill of lading is not title, it is not good collateral for loans. In international transactions, therefore, a straight bill of lading is used when the merchandise has been paid for in advance, when the transaction is being financed by the exporter, or when the shipment is to an affiliate.

An order bill of lading directs the carrier to deliver the goods to the order of a designated party. An additional inscription may request the carrier to notify someone else of the arrival. The order bill of lading grants title to the merchandise only to the person to whom the document is addressed, and surrender of the order bill of lading is required to obtain the shipment.

As typically used, the order bill of lading is made to the order of the exporter, who thus retains title to the goods after they have been handed

EXHIBIT 14.5
Bill of Lading

(Forwarding Agent:)

B/L No. HO33-23758

Mitsui O.S.K. Lines. Ltd.

BILL OF LADING

Shipper
ABC Co., Ltd
No. 10 Mori Bldg
1-18-1 Toranomon, Minato-ku
Tokyo, 105, Japan

Consignee
TO ORDER OF SHIPPER

Notify Party
XYZ, Inc.
55555 Hawthorne Boulevard
Suite 400-14
Torrance, California 90503

Received by the Carrier from the shipper in apparent good order and condition unless otherwise indicated herein the Goods or the container (s) or package(s) said to contain the cargo herein mentioned, to be carried subject to all the terms and conditions appearing on the face and back of this Bill of Lading by the vessel named herein or any substitute at the Carrier's option and/or other means of transport, from the place of receipt or the port of loading to the port of discharge or the place of delivery shown herein and there to be delivered unto order or assigns. If required by the Carrier, this Bill of Lading duly endorsed must be surrendered in exchange for the Goods or delivery order.

In accepting this Bill of Lading, the Merchant agrees to be bound by all the stipulations, exceptions, terms and conditions on the face and back hereof, whether written, typed, stamped or printed, as fully as if signed by the Merchant, any local custom or privilege to the contrary notwithstanding, and agrees that all agreements or freight engagements for and in connection with the carriage of the Goods are superseded by this Bill of Lading.

In witness whereof, the undersigned, on behalf of Mitsui O.S.K. Lines, Ltd., the Master and the owner of the Vessel, has signed the number of Bill(s) of Lading stated below all of this tenor and date, one of which being accomplished, the others to stand void.

(Terms of Bill of Lading continued on the back hereof)

Pre-carriage by	Place of receipt	
I.C.T.	NAGOYA C.F.S.	
Ocean vessel / Voy. No.	**Port of loading**	
AMERICA MARU	NABOYA, JAPAN	
Port of discharge	**Place of delivery**	**Final destination for the Merchant's reference**
LOS ANGELES, CALIFORNIA, U.S.A.		LOS ANGELES C.F.S.

Particulars furnished by shipper

Container No.	Seal No. Marks and Numbers	No. of Containers or pkgs.	Kind of packages; description of goods	Gross weight	Measurement
MOLU2850842	41013509				
CTIU2565602	MOL35097				
			PVC BLUE DISCHARGE HOSE		
No. 1-90		90 ROLLS			
MADE IN JAPAN				4,980 KGS	6.836 CBM

SPECIMEN

Remark: L/C No. 308,590

• Total number of Containers or other packages or units received by the Carrier (in words): NINETY (90) ROLLS ONLY

Freight and charges	Revenue tons	Rate per	Prepaid	Collect
6.836 M3		$77.00/M3	US$525.60	
C.A.F.		6%	US$31.54	
			US$557.14	
C.F.S. CHARGE		¥12,650/M3	¥86,475	
	FREIGHT PREPAID			

Exchange rate	Prepaid at	Payable at	Place and date of issue
@ ¥ 267.75	TOYKO, JAPAN		TOKYO, JAPAN
	Total prepaid in Yen	**No. of original B(s)/L**	
	¥167,263	THREE (3)	MITSUI O.S.K. LINES, LTD.

LADEN ON BOARD THE VESSEL

Date Signature

by

Source: Security Pacific National Bank and Mitsui O.S.K. Lines, Ltd.

to the carrier. Title to the merchandise remains with the exporter until payment is received, at which time the exporter endorses the order bill of lading (which is negotiable) in blank, or to the party making the payment, usually a bank. The most common procedure would be for payment to be advanced against a documentary draft accompanied by the endorsed order bill of lading. After paying the draft, the exporter's bank forwards the documents through bank clearing channels to the bank of the importer. The importer's bank, in turn, releases the documents to the importer after payment (sight drafts), after acceptance (time drafts addressed to the importer and marked D/A), or after payment terms have been agreed (drafts drawn on the importer's bank under provisions of a letter of credit).

Variations in the Bill of Lading

A *clean* bill of lading indicates that the goods were received by the carrier in apparently good condition. The carrier is not obligated to check the condition of the merchandise beyond external visual appearance. A *foul* bill of lading indicates that the merchandise appeared to have suffered some damage before being received for shipment. A foul bill of lading lacks complete negotiability.

An *on-board* bill of lading indicates that the merchandise has been placed on board the vessel whose name is designated on the document. This form is preferred to a *received-for-shipment* bill of lading, which allows for the possibility that the goods are sitting on the dock and might remain there for some time. A received-for-shipment bill of lading is not an acceptable document unless it has been specifically authorized in the letter of credit. Similarly, unless authorized otherwise by the letter of credit, banks will refuse to accept *on-deck* bills of lading, indicating that the goods have been stowed on deck. Received-for-shipment bills of lading may be issued when goods are first received on the carrier's premises; they can be converted to an on-board form by an appropriate stamp showing the name of the vessel, the date, and the signature or initial of an official of the carrier.

ADDITIONAL DOCUMENTS

The draft, the bill of lading, and the letter of credit are the major documents required in most international transactions. However, additional documents may be needed as a condition of the letter of credit for honoring a draft. The more common additional documents include those described below.

A signed *commercial invoice* is issued by the seller and contains a precise description of the merchandise. Unit prices, financial terms of sale, and amount due from the buyer are indicated, as are shipping conditions related to charges, such as "FOB" (free on board), "FAS" (free alongside), "C & F" (cost and freight), or "CIF" (cost, insurance, freight). Commercial invoices are normally made out in the name of the applicant for the letter of credit, and the description of the merchandise must correspond with the description in the letter of credit.

Insurance documents must be as specified in the letter of credit and must be issued and/or signed by insurance companies or their agents or underwriters (an insurance broker's signature is unacceptable). The insurance may be issued to the exporter, who must then endorse the policy to the consignee, or it may be issued in the name of the consignee. The document must be expressed in the same currency as the credit and must not be dated later than the date of shipment carried on the face of the shipping documents. Insurance must be of types and for risks specified in the letter of credit.

Types of risk against which insurance can be placed include the following:[3]

1. Free-of-damage insurance, which covers only *total* loss of goods. Partial losses are not covered.
2. Fire and sea perils, free of particular average insurance. In marine insurance terms "average" means a loss less than a total loss, i.e., a partial loss. A "particular average" is a partial loss to the property of a particular owner and is borne entirely by that owner without contributions by other parties. "Free of particular average" thus means that a partial loss will not be paid. Free-of-particular-average clauses may be written with exceptions, such as in the provision "free of particular average unless caused by stranding, sinking, burning or collision with another vessel." Fire loss (other than that caused by lightning) is not considered a peril of the sea and so is mentioned specifically in order to be sure it is covered by an ocean marine policy. Perils of the sea include the action of wind and waves, lightning, collisions with other ships or objects, sinking, capsizing, and stranding.[4] "Fire and sea perils, free of particular average" thus means that total, but not partial, claims will be paid only if the damage is caused by fire or sea perils. Damage from other causes is not covered.
3. Fire and sea perils, with average. "Average" or "general average" is the practice of prorating a partial loss among all shippers on a vessel. It arose when some property was jettisoned to prevent the loss of the entire ship and all cargo. Shipowners and owners of the balance of the cargo would then contribute proportionally to the owners whose cargo was lost for the general good. Other voluntary sacrifices covered under general average would be damage to ship engines overworked in pulling the ship off a reef, or damage from water or chemicals used to extinguish a fire. "Fire and sea perils with average" means that the underwriter will pay charges assessed against undamaged property, under the general average principle, for damage caused by fire and sea perils.[5]

EXHIBIT 14.6
One Type of International Transaction

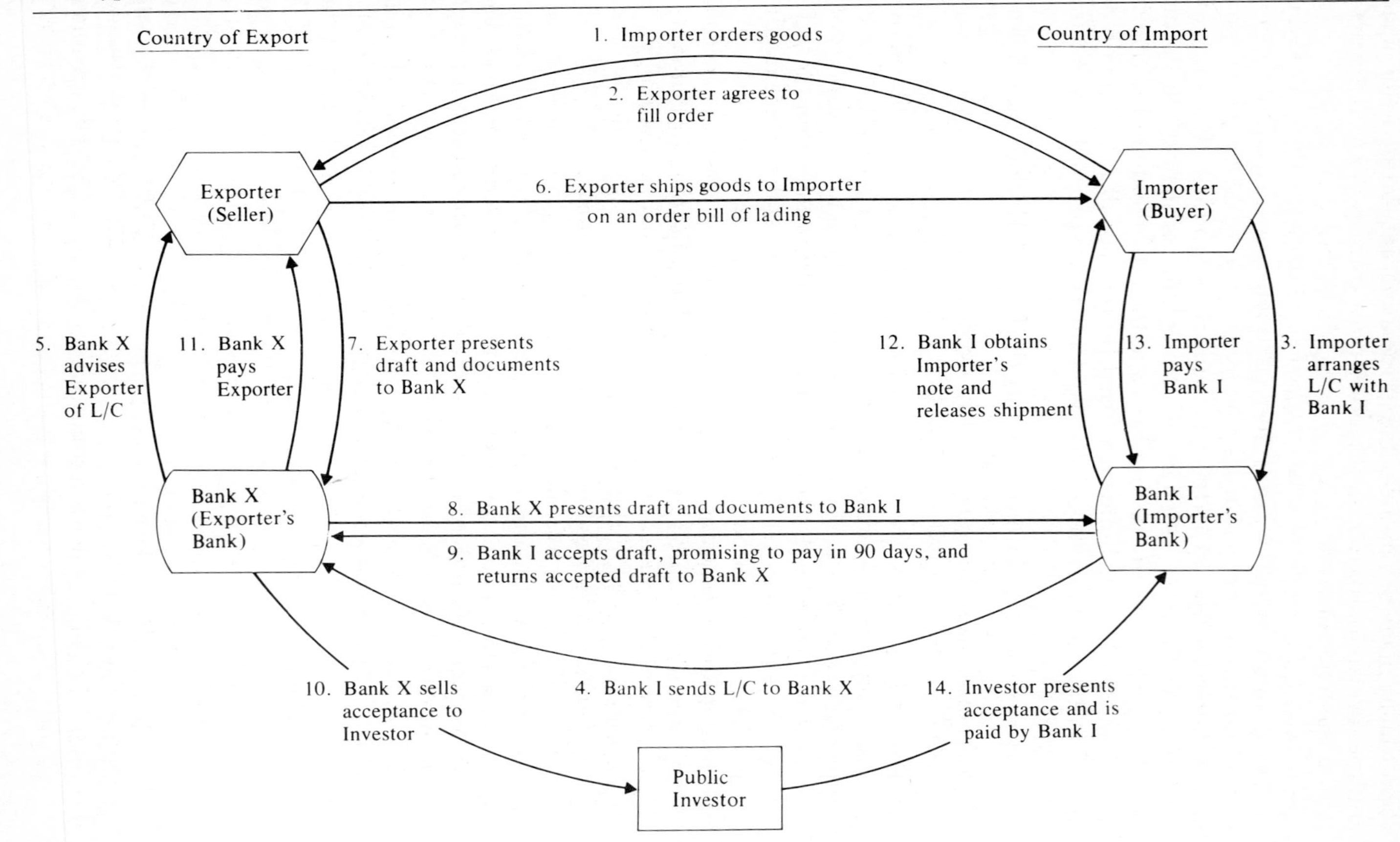

4. Named perils, which include fire and sea perils above, plus any number of specified additional perils such as freshwater damage, hook damage, fuel oil damage, theft, pilferage, nondelivery, or breakage.
5. All-risk insurance, which covers all losses from physical loss or damage from any external cause except war, strikes, riots, and civil commotion.

Coverage does not protect against losses due to the inherent nature of the goods or losses caused by delays in reaching a market.

Consular invoices are issued by the consulate of the importing country to provide customs information and statistics for that country, and again for customs purposes, to help prevent false declarations of value. The consular invoice may be combined with a *certificate of origin* of the goods.

Certificates of analysis may be required to ascertain that certain specifications of weight, purity, sanitation, etc., have been met. These conditions may be required by health or other officials of the importing country—especially in the case of foods and drugs—or they may be insisted on by the importer as assurance that it is receiving what it ordered. The certificates may be issued by government or private organizations, as specified in the letter of credit.

Packing lists may be required so that the contents of specific packages can be identified, either for customs purposes or for importer identification of the contents of separate containers.

Export declaration is a document prepared by the exporter to assist the government to prepare export statistics.

DOCUMENTATION IN A TYPICAL INTERNATIONAL TRANSACTION

In view of the variety of letters of credit, drafts, and bills of lading, an international transaction could conceivably be handled in several ways. The transaction that would best illustrate the interactions of the various documents would be an export financed under a documentary commercial letter of credit requiring an order bill of lading, with the exporter collecting immediately via a bank draft drawn on the importer's bank. Such a transaction is illustrated in Exhibit 14.6.

1. Importer places an order for the goods with Exporter, inquiring if Exporter would be willing to ship under a letter of credit.
2. Exporter indicates its willingness to ship under a letter of credit and indicates relevant information such as prices, terms, etc.
3. Importer applies to its bank, Bank I, for a letter of credit to be issued in favor of Exporter for the merchandise Importer wishes to buy.
4. Bank I issues the letter of credit in favor of Exporter and sends it to Bank X, Exporter's bank, or to a correspondent bank in the country of export.

5. Bank X advises Exporter of the opening of a letter of credit in the Exporter's favor. Bank X may or may not confirm the letter of credit to add its own guarantee to the document.
6. Exporter ships the goods to Importer on an order bill of lading made out to the order of Exporter so that title remains, at first, with Exporter.
7. Exporter presents a 90-day time draft to Bank X, drawn on Bank I in accordance with Bank I's letter of credit and accompanied by such other documents as required, including the order bill of lading. Exporter endorses the order bill of lading in blank so that title to the goods goes with the holder of the documents—Bank X at this point in the transaction.
8. Bank X presents the draft and documents to Bank I. Bank I accepts the draft, taking possession of the documents and promising to pay the now-accepted draft in 90 days.
9. Bank I returns the accepted draft to Bank X. Alternatively, Bank X could have asked Bank I to accept and discount the draft; then Bank I would have returned cash less a discount fee rather than the accepted draft to Bank X.
10. Bank X, having received back the accepted draft, now a bankers' acceptance, must choose between several alternatives. In the United States and the United Kingdom, where money markets are fully developed, Bank X may sell the acceptance in the open market at a discount to a public investor. The investor will typically be a corporation or financial institution with excess cash it wants to invest for a short period of time. Bank X may also hold the acceptance in its own portfolio.
11. If Bank X has discounted the acceptance with Bank I (mentioned in step 8 above) or has discounted it in the local money market, Bank X will transfer the proceeds less any fees and discount to Exporter. Another possibility would be for Exporter itself to take possession of the acceptance, hold it for 90 days, and present it for collection. Normally, however, exporters prefer to receive the discounted cash value of the acceptance at once rather than wait for the acceptance to mature and receive a slightly greater amount of cash.
12. Bank I notifies Importer of the arrival of the documents. Importer signs a note or makes some other agreed plan to pay the bank for the merchandise in 90 days, and Bank I releases the underlying documents so that Importer can obtain physical possession of the shipment.
13. In 90 days Bank I receives from Importer funds to pay the maturing draft.
14. On the same day—the 90th day after acceptance—the holder of the matured acceptance presents it for payment and receives its face value. The holder may present it directly to Bank I, as in the diagram, or

return it to Bank X and have Bank X collect it through normal banking channels.

EXPORT CREDIT INSURANCE

The exporter who insists on cash or letter of credit payment for foreign shipments is likely to lose orders to competitors from other countries that provide more favorable credit terms. Better credit terms are often made possible by means of export credit insurance, which provides assurance to the exporter or the exporter's bank that, should the foreign customer default on payment, the insurance company will pay for a major portion of the loss. Because of the availability of export credit insurance, commercial banks are willing to provide medium- to long-term financing (five to seven years) for exports.

Since credit has become an increasingly competitive component of the terms of export selling, governments of at least 35 countries have established entities that insure credit risks for exports. Details of these systems appear in the various editions of the *World's Principal Export Credit Insurance Systems* published by the International Export Credits Institute, New York.

Competition between nations to increase exports by lengthening the period for which credit transactions can be insured could lead to a credit war and to unsound credit decisions. To prevent such an unhealthy development, a number of leading trading nations joined together in 1934 to create the Berne Union (officially, the *Union d'Assureurs des Crédits Internationaux*) for the purpose of establishing a voluntary international understanding on export credit terms. The Berne Union recommends maximum credit terms for many items including, for example, heavy capital goods (five years), light capital goods (three years), and consumer durable goods (one year).

Export Credit Insurance in the United States

In the United States, export credit insurance is provided by the Foreign Credit Insurance Association (FCIA), an unincorporated association of private commercial insurance companies operating in association with the Export-Import Bank of the U.S. government.

The FCIA insures exporters for an agreed percentage of loss for commercial risks and indemnifies the exporter for 100% of a political loss. Losses due to commercial risk are those that result from the insolvency or protracted payment default of the buyer; political losses arise from political actions of governments beyond the control of buyer or seller. The FCIA will insure against the following political events:

- Cancellation or nonrenewal of a U.S. export license, or imposition of export restrictions prior to date of shipment under circumstances that are not the fault of the buyer.

- Cancellation of a previously issued and valid authority for the buyer to import the shipment involved, or by any action having the force of law that prevents importation, under circumstances that are not the fault of the buyer.
- War, hostilities, civil war, rebellion, revolution, insurrection, civil commotion, or similar disturbances, occurring on or before the due date.
- Requisition, expropriation, or confiscation of or intervention in the business of the buyer or guarantor by a government authority, occurring on or before the due date.
- Any action having the force of law that, under circumstances that are not the fault of the buyer, prevents the buyer from depositing the local currency or paying the bill.
- Transport or insurance charges occasioned after shipment by the interruption or diversion of voyage outside the United States from political causes and which charges are impracticable to recover from the buyer.
- Transfer risk, the inconvertibility of local currencies into U.S. dollars.

Note that devaluation losses are neither commercial nor political losses and *cannot* be insured against under FCIA policies.

Standard FCIA Policies

The FCIA issues short-term policies, involving payment terms up to 180 days, and medium-term policies with payment terms from 181 days to 5 years. Coverage up to 7 years may be arranged for aircraft, marine, and other sales, if necessary to meet government-supported foreign competition.

1. An overall *master policy* covers both commercial and political risks for a period of one year on all, or a reasonable spread, of an exporter's eligible sales, both short-term and medium-term. Coverage is essentially that described below under short-term and medium-term policies, except that medium-term coverage is comprehensive rather than on a case-by-case basis. A special master policy can also be issued that covers only political risk.
2. A *short-term comprehensive policy* covers commercial credit (normally up to 90%) and political risks (to 100%) on the sale of any type of product with at least 50% U.S. origin, on terms up to 180 days. U.S. agricultural commodities can be covered up to 98% for commercial risk and 100% for political risk under the same type of policy, on payment terms up to one year. Under certain conditions a short-term policy for political risk only can be issued, which covers up to 100% of the risk.

Short-term policies are normally written to cover *all* or *most* of the exporter's eligible shipments to all markets. Coverage of all shipments is required to avoid adverse selection; however, shipments to Canada and shipments paid in advance or financed under irrevocable letter of credit can be excluded by the exporter. In addition, shipments to the exporter's own affiliates can be excluded from short-term comprehensive policies but not from short-term political risk coverage. At the exporter's option such shipments can, under a comprehensive policy, be covered against political risks only.

3. A *medium-term comprehensive policy* covers 90% of commercial risk and 100% of political risk on sales of capital and quasi-capital goods solely of U.S. origin. Coverage may also include the U.S.-manufactured portion of goods partially manufactured abroad. Coverage is written on a case-by-case basis, and no requirement exists that the exporter insure all medium-term transactions. Buyers must make an initial cash payment, normally 15% of the purchase price, and the remainder must be covered by a specified form of promissory note. The FCIA also writes a medium-term political risk only policy.
4. A *combination policy* (different from a master policy) provides short- and medium-term coverage on the sale of capital and quasi-capital goods, related parts, and accessories to overseas franchised dealers and distributors. Coverage provides protection on parts and accessories up to 180 days, on inventory up to 270 days, and on accounts receivable up to three years.
5. A *new-to-export policy* is for companies new to exporting or those that have only occasionally exported in the past. FCIA indemnifies the insured for 95% of an insured obligation in the event of a commercial loss and for 100% on a political loss, for the first two years of the policy. If the new-to-export policy is renewed for a third year, coverage becomes 90%, which is the same as offered under all other policies. Also there is no deductible for one or two years and a lower minimum annual premium for new-to-export policies. Because this policy is a special program for new exporters, all companies applying for the policy must meet special requirements.
6. A *service policy* is available, on extended terms of repayment, to companies providing U.S. expertise and technology. FCIA indemnifies a company for 90% of an insured obligation in the event of a commercial loss and for 100% on a political loss.

Premium Costs

Premiums on short-term policies are based on each $100 of gross invoice value, including price, insurance, freight, and other charges. Premiums on medium-term policies are based on each $100 of the "financed portion," that is, on the principal amount covered by promissory notes. Medium-term policies cover the agreed percentage of the remaining outstanding balance on each note.

Composite premium rates are issued on all master and short-term policies. The rates are determined by the terms of sale being offered by the exporter, its previous experience with export sales, the risk associated with the countries to which it ships, and the spread of risk covered by the policy. On medium-term transactions the premium rates vary by length of repayment terms and buyer classification, private or sovereign. After a minimum cash down payment of 15%, the balance should be evidenced by a specified form of promissory note or notes, in the English language, and providing for approximately equal principal installments on a regular basis in dollars at a bank in the United States. Interest must be payable concurrently with principal.

Other Attributes of FCIA Export Credit Insurance

FCIA coverage differs from the export credit plans of many other countries in that FCIA assumes the burden of collecting from the buyer upon payment of a loss. The collection responsibility goes to FCIA's Corporate Recovery Department, which, after deducting expenses, returns to the insured a percentage of net recovery equal to the percentage loss sustained by the policyholder.

Coverage is limited to entities that are residents of or doing business in the United States. Short-term policies cover goods produced in the United States if at least one-half the value added by labor and materials but excluding markups is of U.S. origin. Medium-term policies cover export of heavy durables, machinery, plant equipment, etc., produced or manufactured in the United States.

GOVERNMENT PROGRAMS TO HELP FINANCE EXPORTS

Governments of most export-oriented industrialized countries have special financial institutions that provide some form of subsidized credit to their own national exporters. Traditionally these export finance institutions have offered terms that are better than those generally available from the competitive private sector. At times the subsidized rate has been as low as half the rates at which treasuries were borrowing—meaning, of course, that domestic taxpayers are subsidizing lower financial costs for foreign buyers. This subsidizing activity has been done in the name of creating employment and maintaining a technological edge. Particularly critical have been rates offered by French and U.S. credit programs to finance the exports of commercial aircraft, both countries believing that their position in worldwide aircraft manufacture would be lost were subsidized rates not available.

In the United States the chief government agency is the Export-Import Bank of the United States, headquartered in Washington, D.C. Other organizations include the Overseas Private Investment Corporation (OPIC) and the Private Export Funding Corporation (PEFCO), which will be discussed below.

Export-Import Bank

The Export-Import (Ex-Im) Bank is an independent agency of the U.S. government, established in 1934 to stimulate and facilitate the foreign trade of the United States. Interestingly, the Ex-Im Bank was originally created primarily to facilitate exports to the Soviet Union.

In 1945 the Ex-Im Bank was rechartered "to aid in financing and to facilitate exports and imports and the exchange of commodities between the United States . . . and any foreign country or the agencies or nationals thereof." The five full-time members of the board of directors of the Ex-Im Bank are appointed by the president of the United States with the advice and consent of the Senate. The bank has $1 billion of nonvoting stock paid in by the U.S. Treasury and has the option of borrowing an additional $6 billion from the Treasury if and when needed.

The Ex-Im Bank facilitates the financing of U.S. exports through various loan guarantee and insurance programs. The Ex-Im Bank guarantees repayment of medium-term (181 days to 5 years) export loans extended by U.S. banks to foreign borrowers.

The Ex-Im Bank will also agree ahead of time to purchase eligible medium-term obligations of foreign buyers of U.S. goods. By this process banks are able to fund at a fixed interest rate promissory notes, drafts, or contracts acquired from foreign customers of U.S. firms.

The Ex-Im Bank's long-term, direct-lending operation is based on participation with private sources of funds. Essentially the Ex-Im Bank lends dollars to borrowers outside the United States for the purchase of U.S. goods and services. Proceeds of such loans are paid to U.S. suppliers. The loans themselves are repaid with interest in dollars to the Ex-Im Bank. The Ex-Im Bank requires private participation in these direct loans, in part to ensure that it complements rather than competes with private sources of export financing, in part to spread its resources more broadly, and in part to ensure that private financial institutions will continue to provide export credit.

The Ex-Im Bank also guarantees lease transactions, finances the costs involved in the preparation by U.S. firms of engineering, planning, and feasibility studies for non-U.S. clients on large capital projects, and supplies counseling for exporters, banks, or others needing help in finding financing for U.S. goods.

Private Export Funding Corporation (PEFCO)

The Private Export Funding Corporation, or PEFCO, is a private corporation incorporated in 1970 for the purpose of making U.S. dollar loans to foreign importers to finance purchases of goods and services of U.S. manufacture or origin. PEFCO was established with the support of the U.S. Department of the Treasury and of Ex-Im Bank to assist in the financing of U.S. exports by mobilizing private capital as a supplement to the financing already available through Ex-Im Bank, commercial banks, and other lending institutions. PEFCO's loans are repayable in U.S. dollars and are unconditionally guaranteed by Ex-Im Bank. The attorney general of the United States, in turn, has ruled that all obligations of Ex-Im Bank are general obligations of the United States, backed by its full faith and credit. Because all PEFCO's loans are guaranteed, PEFCO itself does not evaluate credit risks, appraise economic conditions in foreign countries, or review other factors that might affect the collectibility of its loans.

Impetus for the formation of PEFCO came from the Bankers' Association for Foreign Trade, and PEFCO's stockholders consist of 54 commercial banks, including most of the major U.S. commercial banks involved in export financing, one investment banking firm, and seven manufacturing companies. The seven manufacturing firms are Boeing, Cessna, Combustion Engineering, General American Transportation, General Electric, McDonnell Douglas Finance, and United Technologies. All are major U.S. exporters, with aircraft and aircraft suppliers playing a prominent part.

Shareholders' equity provides approximately 2.4% of PEFCO's capital. Another 31.4% comes from current liabilities, primarily notes payable sold in the open market. The remainder of its capital comes from secured notes sold in the long-term securities market by investment banking firms.

FORFAITING

Forfaiting is a technique for arranging medium-term export financing. Forfaiting denotes the purchase of trade obligations falling due at some future date without recourse to any previous holder of the obligation. The word comes from the French *à forfait,* a term that implies "to forfeit or surrender a right." Under a typical arrangement an exporter receives immediate cash by discounting promissory notes or trade receivables on a "without recourse" basis to a specialized finance firm, called a "forfaiter." The forfaiter assesses and subsequently carries all political and commercial risk.

Forfaiting arose because the governments of Eastern Europe and certain other developing nations took an active role in seeking intermediate-term financing to pay for major items of imported capital equipment, including turnkey plants constructed by Western corporations. Such projects require up to a dozen years to complete, so financing was needed for a longer time than could be arranged by traditional bank export departments or even by the export credit guarantee programs of the various exporting countries. Forfaiting firms, most of which are in Switzerland, Austria, or Germany and are affiliated with commercial banks from other European countries, developed the technique of purchasing from the exporter all rights and claims to future cash receipts from the importer without any possibility of recourse to the exporting firm. Although the exporting firm remains responsible for the quality of delivered goods, it receives a clear and unconditional cash payment, while all political and commercial risk of nonpayment by the importer is carried by the forfaiter.

A typical forfaiting transaction involves five parties, as shown in Exhibit 14.7. The steps in the process are as follows:

EXHIBIT 14.7
Typical Forfaiting Transaction

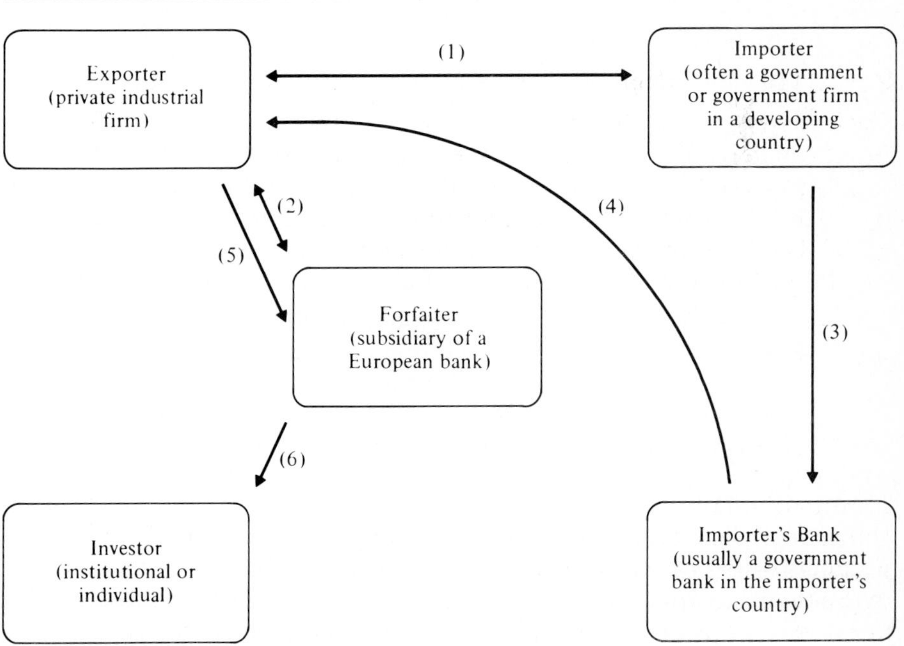

Step 1. Importer and exporter agree between themselves on a series of imports to be paid for over an intermediate (three- to seven-year) period. Periodic payments are to be made against progress in delivery or completion of the project.

Step 2. The exporter obtains the forfaiter's commitment to finance the transaction at a fixed discount rate, and payments are to be made when the exporter delivers to the forfaiter the appropriate promissory notes or other specified paper. The agreed-upon discount rate is one of the costs to the exporting firm. An additional standby fee of about .1% to .125% per month is charged by the forfaiter from the date of its commitment to finance until receipt of the actual discount paper issued in accordance with the finance contract. In anticipation of its standby obligation, the forfaiter might borrow the needed funds on a long maturity and reinvest them in short-term maturities, thus ensuring eventual availability of the funds to the exporter.

Step 3. The importer obligates itself to pay for the material by issuing a series of promissory notes, usually maturing every 6 or 12 months, against progress in delivery or completion of the project. These promissory notes are first delivered to the importer's bank, where they are endorsed (i.e., guaranteed) by that bank. In Europe the guarantee is sometimes referred to as an "aval." At this point the importer's bank becomes the primary obligor in the eyes of all subsequent holders of the notes.

Step 4. The now-endorsed promissory notes are delivered to the exporter.

Step 5. The exporter endorses the notes "without recourse" and discounts them with the forfaiter, receiving immediately the agreed-upon proceeds, less the amount of the discount taken out by the forfaiter. By endorsing them "without recourse," the exporter assumes no liability for future payment on the notes and thus in effect receives the discounted proceeds free of any further payment difficulties.

Step 6. The forfaiting firm endorses the notes and sells them in the European money market. The notes are now two-name paper (importer's bank and forfaiting firm); although investors can rely on either name, they are in fact attracted to the paper by the endorsement of the forfaiting firm.

In effect, the forfaiting firm functions as both a money market firm and a specialist in assessing country risk. As a money market firm, the forfaiter divides the discounted notes into appropriately sized packages and resells them to various investors having different maturity preferences. The forfaiter is supplying its own name as a guarantor of the notes. As a country risk specialist, the forfaiter assesses and bears the risk that the notes will eventually be paid by the importer or the importer's bank.

Success of the forfaiting technique resides in the belief that the external obligations of a government bank will have a higher priority for payment than will commercial debt, even when incurred by government entities. A government bank's default on an international agreement would destroy the country's credibility. In addition, the endorsing guarantee by the importer's bank is perceived to be "off the balance sheet" in that it is a contingent rather than a direct obligation. As an "off balance sheet" obligation, the debt is presumably not considered by other international organizations analyzing the credit risk of the importing country or its banking system.

COUNTERTRADE

The word *countertrade* refers to international trade arrangements that are variations on the ancient concept of barter. Countertrade became popular in the 1960s and 1970s as a way for the Soviet Union and Eastern European members of COMECON to finance their international trade without tapping their scarce hard currency reserves. The technique has recently been used by noncommunist less developed nations for the same reason.

Countertrade is a transaction "in which a seller provides a buyer with deliveries, and contractually agrees to purchase goods from the buyer equal to an agreed percentage of the original sales contract value."[6] In other words, an initial export sale is tied by contract to a flow of goods or services in the opposite direction. The countertrade component may take place at the same time as the original export, in which case credit is not an issue; or the countertrade may take place later, in which case financing becomes important. Countertrade takes several forms, depending on the type of goods and services involved and the financing arrangements.

Classical Barter

Classical barter is a direct exchange of physical goods between two parties. It is a one-time transaction carried out under a single contract that specifies both the goods to be delivered and the goods to be received. The two parts of the transaction occur at the same time, and no money is exchanged. Money may be used as the numeraire by which the two values are established and the quantities of each good are determined.

A recent example of classical barter is an arrangement whereby Pepsico exchanged Pepsi syrup for Stolichnaya vodka from the Soviet Union. Another example is a lambs-for-crude-oil deal negotiated between the New Zealand Meat Board and the government of Iran.

Counter-Purchase

A counter-purchase transaction involves an initial export, but with the exporter receiving back merchandise that is unrelated to items the exporter manufactures. One example is an agreement between McDonnell Douglas and Yugoslavia in 1966 under which McDonnell Douglas sold DC-9's to Yugoslovenski Aerotransport for $199 million cash and $26 million in Yugoslav goods. The Yugoslav products, imported into the United States over the subsequent decades, have included Zagreb hams, wines, dehydrated vegetables, and even some power transmission towers that were retransferred to the Los Angeles Department of Water and Power.[7] McDonnell Douglas reportedly houses a Yugoslav trading firm at one of its aircraft plants to deal with the goods acquired in countertrade.

Other counter-purchase examples are the purchase by West Germany's Volkswagenwerk of coal, oil, and machinery from East Germany in return for selling 10,000 automobiles to East Germany; and Rolls Royce's sales of jet parts to Finland in return for Rolls Royce's marketing Finnish TV sets and other consumer durables in the United Kingdom.

Compensation Arrangement, or Buy-Back

A third type of countertrade is called a compensation arrangement or buy-back transaction. In this instance the original seller is compensated by products that arise out of the original sale. A typical situation involves the initial export of an industrial plant, with the exporter accepting compensation in the form of future output from that plant. Such an arrangement has attributes that make it, in effect, an alternate form of direct investment. The value of the buy-back usually exceeds the value of the original sale, as would be appropriate to reflect interest.

A recent example of a buy-back is the agreement by several western European countries to provide materials and equipment for a gas pipeline from the Soviet Union to Europe, with compensation from gas from that pipeline. Another example is an agreement between Occidental Petroleum and the Soviet Union under which Occidental supplies the Soviet Union with one million tons of American super-phosphoric acid per year for 20 years and in turn receives 4 million tons of Soviet ammonia, urea, and potash. Occidental helped construct the extra ammonia production and pipeline capacity in the Soviet Union.

Switch Trade

Switch trade involves transferring use of bilateral clearing currencies from one country to another. For example, an original export from Canada to Romania is paid for with a cash balance deposited in a clearing account in

Romania. Although the clearing account may be *measured* in Canadian dollars (or in any other currency), the balance can be used only to purchase goods from Romania.

The original exporter from Canada might buy unrelated goods from Romania or it might sell the clearing balance at a substantial discount to a "switch trader," often located in Vienna, which in turn purchases goods from Romania for sale elsewhere. The Canadian exporter in effect exchanges the blocked clearing balance for hard currency at a substantial discount with a specialist firm equipped to export merchandise from Romania. The Romanian goods themselves are quite cheap, given the discount on the purchase of the blocked currency, and the switch trader resells the merchandise at a low price in world markets. Those who oppose this practice note that it is in effect dumping below true cost, which hurts competing manufacturers in other countries; however, because the "dumping" is not done by the original country of manufacture it escapes international agreements on dumping.

An example of a switch trade is a Polish/Greek clearing agreement that existed before Greece joined the EEC. Poland had sold Greece more goods than it had purchased, and so ended up with a dollar-denominated clearing balance in Greece. A switch trader bought the right to 250,000 clearing dollars from Poland for $225,000 and then resold them for $235,000 to a European sultana merchant, who in turn used them to purchase Greek sultanas through the Greek Foreign Trade Bank. (A sultana is a small white seedless grape used for both raisins and wine making.)[8]

Reasons for the Growth of Countertrade

In theory, countertrade is a movement away from free trade. It is a slow, expensive, and convoluted way of conducting trade that often forces firms (such as McDonnell Douglas) to set up operations to deal in products very remote from their expertise. The basic problem is that the agreement to take back goods in some form of barter suggests that those goods cannot be sold in the open market for as high a price as is being locked into the countertrade agreement.

Nevertheless, several reasons are advanced for the current growth of countertrade. First, from the perspective of either a Soviet bloc or developing country, countertrade often produces what are in effect hard currency sales that the country could not otherwise obtain. While it seems self-evident that McDonnell Douglas has little inherent expertise in selling hams, it is also probably true that the ham-producing entity within Yugoslavia has even less expertise in how to sell in the United States. McDonnell Douglas can probably acquire that marketing expertise more easily than can Yugoslavia.

Second, sales of hams or other imported goods by a U.S. corporation are probably less likely than direct import sales to run afoul of political tensions between the two countries or of domestic pressure against imports by affected domestic producers.

Third, countertrade enables a country to export merchandise of poor design or quality. The merchandise is often sold at a major discount in world markets. Whether or not this constitutes a discount on the original sale depends on how that original sale was priced.

Fourth, countertrade is compatible with the state planning systems of many socialist and communist countries. In these countries, production plans are made by a central authority, and the production system does not respond well to sudden changes in export demand. Countertrade provides an assured market for a period of time, and can be negotiated by governmental officials who set economic production quotas, rather than by the managers of individual plants who do not control the availability of resources.

SUMMARY

Over many years established procedures have arisen to finance foreign trade. The basic procedure rests on the interrelationship between three key documents, the letter of credit, the draft, and the bill of lading. Variations in each of these three key documents provide a variety of ways to accommodate any type of transaction.

In the simplest transaction in which all three documents are used and in which financing is desirable, an importer applies for and receives a letter of credit from its bank. In the letter of credit, the bank substitutes its pledge for that of the importer and promises to pay if certain documents are submitted to the bank. The exporter may now rely on the promise of the bank rather than on the promise of the importer.

The exporter typically ships on an order bill of lading, attaches the order bill of lading to a draft ordering payment from the importer's bank, and presents these documents, plus any of a number of additional documents, through its own bank to the importer's bank. If the documents are in order, the importer's bank either pays the draft (a sight draft) or accepts the draft (a time draft). In the latter case the bank promises to pay from 30 to 90 days or more in the future. At this step the importer's bank acquires title to the merchandise through the bill of lading, and it then releases the merchandise to the importer against payment or some agreed form of future payment.

If a sight draft is used, the exporter is paid at once. If a time draft is used, the exporter receives the accepted draft, now a bankers' acceptance, back from the bank. The exporter may hold the bankers' acceptance until maturity, or the exporter may sell the acceptance at a discount in the open market in order to receive immediate cash.

The entire process of international trade is facilitated by various national programs to provide export credit insurance and, under some circumstances, direct financial support. Intermediate import-export financing is also provided by private firms, called forfaiters, which purchase promissory notes arising from a trade transaction on a nonrecourse basis. Countertrade provides an alternative to hard currency financing.

NOTES

1. The address of the International Chamber of Commerce is 1212 Avenue of the Americas, New York, New York 10036.

2. *Uniform Commercial Code,* Section 3104(1).

3. For a more detailed discussion of marine insurance, see William H. Rodda, *Marine Insurance: Ocean and Inland,* 3rd ed., Englewood Cliffs, N.J.: Prentice-Hall, 1970.

4. *Ibid.,* pp. 20–21 and 34.

5. *Ibid.,* p. 22.

6. Pompiliu Verzariu, *Countertrade Practices in East Europe, the Soviet Union and China: An Introductory Guide to Business,* Washington, D.C.: U.S. Department of Commerce, International Trade Administration, Office of East-West Trade Development, April 1980, p. 7.

7. Chris MacKenzie, "How Many Canned Hams Buy a Jet?" *The Travel Agent,* January 28, 1982, pp. 90–92.

8. Rupert Birley, "Can't Pay? Will Pay, but in Sultanas," *Euromoney,* May 1983, p. 187.

Chapter 14: Appendix A
Commercial Abbreviations

AAR	Against all risks
A.B.	Aktiebolag. Swedish; stock company
A.G.	Aktiengesellschaft. German; incorporated (stock company)
A/P	Authority to purchase, or authority to pay
ASP	American selling price
B/E	Bill of exchange
B/L	Bill of lading
B.M.	Board measure
CAD	Cash against documents
C&D	Collection and delivery
C&F	Cost and freight to named port of import
CF&I	Cost, freight, and insurance
Cia.	Compania. Spanish; company
CIF	Cost, insurance, and freight to named port of import
CIF&C	Cost, insurance, freight, and commission (or charges)
CIF&E	Cost, insurance, freight, and exchange
CIF&I	Cost, insurance, freight, commission (or charges), and interest
C&I	Cost and insurance
cwt	Hundredweight
D/A	Documents against acceptance
D/D	Days after date
DF	Dead freight
DN	Debit note
D/P	Documents against payment
D/S	Days after sight
D/TR	Documents against trust receipt
E&OE	Errors and omissions excepted
EOM	End of month
EX DOCK	Named port of import

Adapted from *International Trade Information.* By permission of Bank of America, National Trust and Savings Association, San Francisco, California 94104, pp. 25–26.

FAF	Fly away free
FAQ	Free at quay
FAS	Free alongside a ship at named port of export
FC&S	Free from capture and seizure
FI	Free in (all expenses for loading into the hold of the vessel are for the account of the consignee)
FO	Free out (all expenses covering unloading from the hold of the vessel are for the account of the consignee)
FOB	Free on board
FOR	Free on rails
FPA	Free of particular average
FPAAC	Free of particular average American conditions
FPAEC	Free of particular average English conditions
GA	General average
GATT	General Agreement on Tariffs and Trade
Gebr.	German; Brothers
G.m.b.H	Gesellschaft mit beschraenkter Haftung. German for limited liability company
GT	Gross ton
Hijo(s)	Spanish; Son(s)
Hnos	Spanish; Brothers
Inc.	Incorporated
Kd	Knocked-down
KK	Kabushiki-Kaisha. Japanese; stock company
L/C	Letter of credit
Ltd.	Limited. British; limited liability company
MEC	Marine extension clause
MFN	Most favored nation
m.n.	moneda nacional. Spanish; any local currency
M/R	Mate's receipt
M/V	Motor vessel
NOE	Not otherwise enumerated
n.s.f.	not sufficient funds
N.V.	Naamloze vennootschap. Dutch; stock company (corporation)
O/A	Open account
OCP	Overland common points
ORL	Owner's risk of leakage
P/N	Promissory note
Pty. Ltd.	Proprietary Limited. Australian; privately owned corporation
RR	Railroad
SACI or SAIC	Sociedad de Capital e Industria. Spanish; company of capital and industry

SA	Sociedad Anonima or Société Anonyme. Spanish and French; corporation
SARL	Societa a Responsabilita Limitada or Société a Responsabilité Limitée. Italian or French; company with limited liability
S/D	Sight draft
S/D–B/L	Sight draft, bill of lading attached
S/D–D/P	Sight draft, documents against payment
S de RL	Sociedad de Responsabilidad Limitada. Spanish; limited partnership
S. en C.	Sociedad en Comandita. Spanish; silent partnership
SL&C	Shipper's load and count
SPA	Societa per Azioni. Italian; corporation
SPRL	Société de Personnes a Responsabilité Limitée. Belgian; company of persons with limited liability
SR&CC	Strikes, riots, and civil commotion
SS	Steamship
T/A	Trade acceptance
TT	Telegraphic transfer
VAT	Value added tax
Vda de	Spanish; widow of
WA	With average
WR	War risk
W/R	Warehouse receipt
Wwe.	German; Widow
Y.K.	Yugen-Kaisha. Japanese; limited liability company
Zoonen	Dutch; Sons

Chapter 14: Appendix B Glossary of Terms Related to International Trade

Ad valorem duty: A customs duty levied as a percentage of the assessed value of a product.

American selling price (ASP): Value applied to four groups of products (benzenoid chemicals, rubber-soled footwear with fabric uppers, canned clams, and certain wool knit gloves). The ASP consists of the adoption, for customs valuation purposes, of the domestic price of competing ("like or similar") merchandise in the United States, which is generally higher than that prevailing in other countries.

Binding: Refers to products on which the maximum level of duties has been fixed by negotiation and formally incorporated in a binding GATT legal instrument. These duties can be raised only through renegotiation or the granting of a temporary waiver.

Border tax adjustments: The fiscal practices under which imported goods are subject to some or all of the tax charged in the importing country and reexported goods are exempt from some or all of the tax charged in the exporting country. The issue of border taxes rests on a GATT provision that permits full compensation of indirect taxes at the border but does not permit compensation of direct taxes. The rationale underlying this provision is that the burden of indirect taxes is fully shifted forward to the final price of the taxed goods, whereas that of the direct taxes is not. Thus indirect taxes, unless fully compensated, would erode the taxing country's competitive position. In practice, the effect is not as clear as the proposition states.

"Buy American" policy: Domestic producers get government contracts if their prices are "reasonable," meaning that the U.S. price is not more than 6% higher than the foreign bid. Another 6% is allowed in certain cases. The Pentagon uses a 50% differential!

Cost and freight (C&F): Under this term the seller quotes a price including the cost of transportation to the named point of destination. An example would be "C&F (named point of destination)."

Cost, insurance, and freight (CIF): The FOB value (see below) plus the cost of packaging, freight or carriage, insurance premium, and other charges paid in respect of the goods from the time of loading in the country of export to their arrival at the named port of destination or place of transshipment.

Countervailing duty: An import charge designed to offset an export subsidy by another country, including rebates on exports connected with indirect taxes (the value-added tax [VAT], in particular) and all the forms of relief (tax on customs exemptions, special tariffs for public services, loans at low rates of interest, etc.) that reduce industrial costs, especially in depressed areas.

Découpage: The Kennedy Round formula for splitting tariff reductions on chemicals into two parts, one conditional on elimination of the American selling price (ASP), the other unconditional.

Disparity: A significant difference in tariff rates between countries on a particular product.

Double écart: The disparity formula proposed by the EEC in the Kennedy Round. A significant disparity would exist if one country's rate were at least twice that of another country and the difference in rates were at least 10 percentage points. The minimum 10-point spread was not applicable to semimanufactures.

Dumping: Goods offered for sale in a foreign market are said to be "dumped" if the price is lower than that of the same product in the home market or in a third country. As used in the GATT, it is simply a special case of "differential pricing."

Ex (point of origin): Under this term the price quoted applies only at the point of origin, and the seller agrees to place the goods at the disposal of the buyer at the agreed place on the date or within the period fixed. Examples are "Ex Factory" and "Ex Warehouse."

Exception: A nonagricultural product for which the Kennedy Round linear tariff cut was not offered.

Ex dock: Under this term seller quotes a price including the cost of the goods and all additional costs necessary to place the goods on the dock at the named port of importation, duty paid, if any. An example would be "Ex Dock (named port of importation)." Variations are "Ex Quay" and "Ex Pier."

Free alongside (FAS): Under this term the seller quotes a price including delivery of the goods alongside overseas vessel and within reach of its loading tackle. An example would be "FAS Vessel (named port of shipment)."

Free on board vessel (FOB): Cost of the goods to the purchaser abroad including packaging, inland and coastal transport in the exporting country, dock dues, loading charges, and all other costs, profits, charges, and expenses (such as insurance and commissions) accruing up to the point where the goods are deposited on board the exporting vessel or aircraft. Variations include the following:

a. "FOB (named inland carrier at named inland point of departure)." Under this term the price quoted applies only at the inland shipping point, and the seller arranges for loading of the goods on or in railway cars, trucks, lighters, barges, aircraft, or other conveyance furnished for transportation.

b. "FOB (named inland carrier at named inland point of departure) freight prepaid to (named point of exportation)." Under this term the seller quotes a price including transportation charges to the named point of exportation and prepays freight to named point of exportation, without assuming responsibility for the goods, after obtaining a clean bill of lading or other transportation receipt at named inland point of departure.

c. "FOB (named inland carrier at named inland point of departure) freight allowed to (named point)." Under this term the seller quotes a price including the transportation charges to the named point, shipping freight collect and deducting the cost of transportation, without assuming responsibility for the goods, after obtaining a clean bill of lading or other transportation receipt at named inland point of departure.

d. "FOB (named inland carrier at named point of exportation)." Under this term the seller quotes a price including the costs of transportation of the goods to named point of exportation, bearing any loss or damage, or both, incurred up to that point.

e. "FOB vessel (named port of shipment)." Under this term the seller quotes a price covering all expenses up to, and including, delivery of the goods on the overseas vessel provided by, or for, the buyer at the named port of shipment.

f. "FOB (named inland point in country of importation)." Under this term the seller quotes a price including the cost of the merchandise and all costs of transportation to the named inland point in the country of importation.

GATT: The General Agreement on Tariffs and Trade was established in 1947. It is a framework of rules for nations to manage their trade policies. It also provides a forum in which disputes can be negotiated.

Linear tariff cut: A reduction in all tariffs by the same percentage. In the Kennedy Round the general linear cut for nonagricultural tariffs was 50%.

Most-favored-nation treatment: Application of duties on the same, most-favored basis to all countries afforded such treatment; i.e., any tariff reduction granted in a bilateral negotiation when extended or "generalized" on a nondiscriminatory basis. It is customary to refer to a tariff being applied on an "MFN basis" as if it were applied without discrimination to all imports. But when a country maintains a two-column tariff (the lower tariff being charged on imports from countries receiving preferences), the higher, and less favorable, rate is known as the "MFN rate."

Nontariff barrier: Trade restrictive practices other than custom tariffs employed either by governments (in the form of import quotas, voluntary restrictions, variable levies, exceptional customs valuation procedures, or health regulations, for example), or by private firms (in the form of price control, division of markets, restriction of supplies, patent agreements, or control of technology, for example). The GATT distinguishes between nontariff barriers that hamper or produce distortions in world trade and those that have "incidental restricting effects" on trade.

Paratariff barrier: A distinctive form of nontariff barrier whose incidence is felt through the effect on the amount of duty collected. Paratariff barriers include arbitrary standards of valuation or of classification for customs purposes and can restrict trade only where there is a duty. Any reduction in duty also has the effect of reducing the additional protection afforded by the paratariff barrier.

Quota: A physical limit, mandatory or voluntary, set on the import of a product. It is a common form of nontariff barrier. GATT rules are more permissive on quotas than on tariffs.

Safeguard clause: A clause laying down conditions under which tariffs and nontariff barriers to trade, previously reduced and bound in negotiations, may be reintroduced.

Sales tax registration: A system under which entitled traders (but not consumers) may buy goods for subsequent resale (and sometimes for their own use) without paying tax.

Specific duty: A duty levied as a fixed money charge per physical unit, such as cents per kilogram.

Tariff: A duty or tax on imports that can be either a percentage of cost or a specific amount per unit of import.

Tariff harmonization: The process of making tariffs more homogeneous by eliminating or reducing pronounced disparities in tariff rates on the same item. There are four harmonization techniques: (1) reduction of rates by an agreed percentage that would depend on the initial height of the tariff in the country concerned; (2) reduction of rates by a percentage that would depend on the initial height of the tariff in the other participating countries; (3) reduction or elimination of differences between actual rates and lower "normative" or "target" rates; and (4) reduction of average duties in a given sector.

Tariff preferences: A scheme of tariff treatment favoring certain products of a country or group of countries. A generalized system of preferences, or GSP, involves preferential tariff treatment by developed countries for products originating in developing countries.

Variable levy: Tax used in the European Community on agricultural imports. As international commodity prices drop, the levy rises.

BIBLIOGRAPHY

Banks, Gary, "The Economics and Politics of Countertrade," *The World Economy,* June 1983, pp. 159–182.

Barovick, Richard, "National Foreign Trade Council Conference Spotlights Export Trading Companies," *Business America,* October 18, 1982, pp. 7–14.

Bayalic, Arthur E., "The Documentation Dilemma in International Trade," *Columbia Journal of World Business,* Spring 1976, pp. 15–22.

Bilkey, Warren J., "Variables Associated with Export Profitability," *Journal of International Business Studies,* Fall 1982, pp. 39–55.

Birley, Rupert, "Can't Pay? Will Pay, but in Sultanas," *Euromoney,* May 1983, pp. 187–189.

Bloch, Henry S., "Export Financing Emerging as a Major Policy Problem," *Columbia Journal of World Business,* Fall 1976, pp. 85–95.

Brady, Donald L., and William O. Bearden, "The Effect of Managerial Attitudes on Alternative Export Methods," *Journal of International Business Studies,* Winter 1979, pp. 79–84.

Celi, Louis J., and I. James Czechowicz, *Export Financing, A Handbook of Sources and Techniques,* Morristown, N.J.: Financial Executives Research Foundation, 1985.

Chew, Ralph H., "Export Trading Companies: Current Legislation, Regulation and Commercial Bank Involvement," *Columbia Journal of World Business,* Winter 1981, pp. 36–47.

Curtin, Donal, "The Uncharted $4 Billion World of Forfaiting," *Fortune,* August 1980, pp. 62–70.

Czinkota, Michael R., and George Tesar, *Export Management: An International Context,* New York: Praeger, 1982.

Dizard, John W., "The Explosion of International Barter," *Fortune,* February 7, 1983, pp. 88–95.

Dun, Angus, and Martin Knight, *Export Finance,* London: Euromoney Publications, 1982.

Dufey, Gunter, and Ian H. Giddy, "Innovation in the International Financial Markets," *Journal of International Business Studies,* Fall 1981, pp. 33–51.

Export-Import Bank: Financing for American Exports—Support for American Jobs, Washington, D.C.: Export-Import Bank of the United States, 1980.

Export-Import Bank of the United States, "EXIMBANK Program Summary," February 1984, pp. 1–12.

Forfaiting, Zurich, Switzerland: Credit Suisse, CS, 1980.

Hervey, Jack L., "Bankers' Acceptances Revisited," *Economic Perspectives,* Federal Reserve Bank of Chicago, May/June 1983, pp. 21–31.

Khoury, Sarkis J., "Countertrade: Forms, Motives, Pitfalls, and Negotiation Requirements," *Journal of Business Research,* June 1984, pp. 257–270.

Loeber, Dietrich Andre, and Ann Porter Friedland, "Soviet Imports of Industrial Installations under Compensation Agreements: West Europe's Siberian Pipeline Revisited," *Columbia Journal of World Business,* Winter 1983, pp. 51–62.

MacKenzie, Chris, "How Many Canned Hams Buy a Jet?" *The Travel Agent,* January 28, 1982, pp. 90–92.

Melton, William C., and Jean M. Mahr, "Bankers Acceptances," *Federal Reserve Bank of New York, Quarterly Review,* Summer 1981, pp. 39–52.

Plaut, Steven E., "Export-Import Follies," *Fortune,* August 25, 1980, pp. 74–77.

Posner, Alan R., "The States and Overseas Export Promotion," *MSU Business Topics,* Summer 1980, pp. 43–49.

Ryder, Frank R., "Challenges to the Use of the Documentary Credit in International Trade Transactions," *Columbia Journal of World Business,* Winter 1981, pp. 36–47.

Schuster, Falko, "Barter Arrangements with Money: The Modern Form of Compensation Trading," *Columbia Journal of World Business,* Fall 1980, pp. 61–66.

Scouton, William, "Export Trading Companies—A New Tool for American Business," *Business America,* October 18, 1982, pp. 3–6.

Stolz, Richard, "Eximbank: What It Does for American World Traders," *Cashflow,* November–December 1980, pp. 34–39.

Uniform Customs and Practices for Documentary Credits, New York: United States Council of the International Chamber of Commerce, 1974.

Verzariu, Pompiliu, *Countertrade Practices in East Europe, the Soviet Union and China,* Washington, D.C.: U.S. Department of Commerce, International Trade Administration, Office of East-West Trade Development, April 1980.

———, *Countertrade, Barter, and Offsets: New Strategies for Profit in International Trade,* New York: McGraw-Hill, 1984.

Weigand, Robert E., "International Trade without Money," *Harvard Business Review,* November/December 1977, pp. 28–30, 34, 38, 42, 166.

PART V

Working Capital Management and Control

15

Working Capital Management

Management of working capital requires both a *flow* and a *stock* perspective. From a flow perspective, managing the location of liquid funds is the most important task. *Location* means both the currency in which liquid funds are held and the country where such holdings are placed. From a stock perspective, managing the appropriate levels and composition of cash balances, accounts receivable, and inventories is the main task.

The first part of this chapter discusses techniques to move liquid funds from one location to another, including dividend remittances, royalties and other fees, and transfer pricing. The second part deals with the internationally unique aspects of managing cash, accounts receivable, and inventory.

CONSTRAINTS ON POSITIONING FUNDS

In domestic business, fund flows among units of a large company are generally unimpeded, and decisions about where to locate working cash balances or excess liquidity are usually based on marginal rates of return and gains from operating with minimal cash. With possibly minor exceptions all funds are denominated in the currency of the home country.

If a firm operates multinationally, political, tax, foreign exchange, and liquidity considerations impose significant restrictions on the idea that funds may easily and without cost be moved anywhere in the world. These constraints create the environment for special consideration of the problem of positioning funds multinationally.

Political constraints can block the transfer of funds either overtly or covertly. Overt blockage occurs when a currency becomes inconvertible or subject to other exchange controls that prevent its transfer at reasonable exchange rates. Covert blockage occurs when dividends or other forms of fund remittances are severely limited, heavily taxed, or prevented by other means.

Tax constraints arise because of the complex and interacting tax structures of various national governments through whose jurisdictions funds might pass.

Foreign exchange transaction costs are incurred when changing funds from one currency to another. These costs, in the form of fees and the difference between bid and offer prices, are profit for the commercial banks and dealers that maintain the foreign exchange market. Although usually a small percentage of the amount of money exchanged, such costs become quite significant for large sums or frequent transfers.

Liquidity constraints must be satisfied for each affiliate while maintaining good banking relationships locally and worldwide. This local interface is easily forgotten when trying to optimize worldwide corporate liquidity.

UNBUNDLING INTERNATIONAL FUND TRANSFERS

Multinational firms sometimes "unbundle" their transfer of funds into separate flows for each purpose. Host countries are more likely to perceive that part of what might otherwise be called "remittance of profits" constitutes an essential purchase of specific benefits that command worldwide values and benefit the host country. Unbundling allows a multinational corporation to recover funds from its affiliates without piquing host country sensitivities with large "dividend drains." An item-by-item matching of remittance to input, in the form of royalties for patents, fees for services, etc., is equitable to host country and foreign investor alike. If all investment inputs are unbundled, part of what might appear to be residual profits may turn out to be tax-deductible expenses related to a specific purchased benefit. Unbundling also facilitates allocation of overhead from a parent's international division to each operating affiliate in accordance with a predetermined formula. Unbundling also facilitates the entry of local capital into joint-venture projects because *total* remuneration to different owners can be in proportion to the value of their different types of contribution rather than only in proportion to monetary investment.

In the following sections we consider fund transfer techniques to pay for the bundle of contributions a parent might make to an affiliate and vice versa. Specifically we examine dividend policy, royalties, fees, contributions to overhead, transfer pricing, and reactions to blocked funds.

INTERNATIONAL DIVIDEND REMITTANCES

Payment of dividends is the most common method by which firms transfer funds from affiliate to parent. Determinants of dividend policy include tax considerations, political risk, foreign exchange risk, age and size of affiliate, availability of funds, and joint venture partners.

Taxes

Host country tax laws influence the dividend decision. Countries such as Germany tax retained earnings at one rate while taxing distributed earnings at a lower rate. Some countries levy withholding taxes on dividends paid to foreign parent firms. Parent country taxes also influence the decision, especially when they are higher than taxes in the foreign country and the eventual aim of the firm is to reinvest funds.

Political Risk

Political risk can motivate parent firms to require foreign affiliates to remit all locally generated funds in excess of stipulated working capital requirements and planned capital expansions. Such policies, however, are not universal. To enhance the financial self-reliance of affiliates, some parent firms abstain from demanding remittances. In most cases neither of these extremes is followed. Instead the normal corporate response to potential government restrictions is to maintain a constant dividend payout ratio so as to demonstrate that an established policy is in effect. Host governments are more likely to accept the idea of regular dividend payments because it provides a framework based on precedent against which to judge whether a particular dividend is "normal," or is an attempt to flee from the currency to the detriment of host country foreign exchange reserves.

Foreign Exchange Risk

If a foreign exchange loss is anticipated, affiliates might speed up the transfer of funds to their parent through dividends. This is part of a larger strategy of moving from weak currencies to strong currencies.

Age and Size of Affiliates

Sidney Robbins and Robert Stobaugh, in their survey of multinational firm financial practices, found that age and size of a business have a bearing on affiliate dividend practice.[1] Older affiliates provide a greater share of their earnings to the parent, presumably because as the affiliate matures, it has fewer reinvestment opportunities while, at the same time, marginal returns elsewhere are greater. Small firms were less likely to establish any underlying principles for determining dividend policy. They tended to "play it by ear."[2] Medium-sized firms were flexible, using dividend policy as one of several techniques for positioning funds throughout the system. Large firms used a rule-of-thumb guideline for all affiliates with exceptions when justified by circumstances.

Availability of Funds

Another factor cited by Robbins and Stobaugh is the availability of internally generated funds. Some affiliates must borrow to continue an established dividend policy.

Joint-Venture Partners

Existence of joint-venture partners or of local stockholders is also an important factor influencing dividend policy. Optimal positioning of funds internationally cannot dominate the valid claims of partners or local stockholders for dividends. They do not necessarily benefit from the world perspective of the multinational parent. Robbins and Stobaugh found evidence that local stock ownership leads to more stable dividend payments regardless of earnings. Firms hesitate to reduce dividends when earnings falter, but they also hesitate to increase dividends following a spurt in earnings. It might be difficult to reduce dividends later should earnings be lower.

ROYALTIES, FEES, AND HOME OFFICE OVERHEAD

Royalties represent remuneration paid to the owners of technology, patents, or trade names for the use of the technology or the right to manufacture or sell under the patents or trade names. A royalty rate may be expressed as a fixed monetary amount per unit or as a percentage of gross revenue.

A fee is compensation for professional services and expertise supplied to an affiliate by a parent or another affiliate. Fees are sometimes differentiated into management fees, for general managerial expertise and advice, and technical assistance fees, for guidance in technical matters. Fees are usually paid for identifiable benefits received by the affiliate, in contrast to overhead charges, to be discussed below, which are for more general benefits. Fees are usually a fixed charge, either in total for supplying the services for a stated period of time, or on a time-rate basis varying with the number of man-hours devoted to the affiliate. Fee provisions usually require an affiliate to pay travel and per diem expenses of the individuals involved.

A home office overhead allocation is a charge to compensate the parent for costs incurred in the general management of international operations and for other corporate overhead that must be recovered by the operating units. Overhead may be charged for regional cash management, research and development, corporate public relations, legal and accounting costs for the entire enterprise, or a share of the salaries and other costs of top management. Home office overhead is often levied throughout an entire company as a predetermined percentage of sales. In other instances the charge may be based on a pro rata sharing of specific costs, which can be matched to the various units.

Licensing Contract

If a parent is to preserve its rights to receive funds from affiliates as royalties, fees, or overhead allocations, the licensing contract that establishes the terms should consider the following points:[3]

1. If the payments are calculated as a percentage of the affiliate's sales price, "net sales price" must be carefully defined. Ideally net sales price means invoice price net of any trade discounts and excluding packing charges, sales, excise, and use taxes. Also excluded should be any allowances for freight where such items are billed or credited as separate items to the customer.
2. The royalty or fee itself should be a given percentage of the net sales price of all licensed products made and used, sold, or otherwise disposed of by the licensee.
3. The contract should specify the time of payment. A typical arrangement might provide that payments would accrue at the time of sale or use, and payment itself would be required quarterly.
4. The contract should specify the currency in which the fees are to be paid so that the location of any foreign exchange risk is clear. In addition, the location of payment should be specified so that the burden of delay in converting receipts into disbursable funds is specified.
5. A report describing the number and type of products sold, the customer, and the date of sale should accompany each payment. This information is needed to allow verification of the accuracy of the amount remitted and to ensure that licensed products are sold only in those geographic or political areas covered by the license agreement.
6. The locus of tax liabilities must be specified clearly, including the liability for any type of tax not yet levied. The *Wall Street Journal* (October 28, 1975) described a situation in which ten Japanese utilities purchased enriched uranium ore in 1972 from the U.S. Atomic Energy Commission for $320 million. The uranium was to be stored on the AEC premises in Roane County, Tennessee, until needed in Japan in the 1980s. The Japanese entered into this advance purchase plan for the specific purpose of helping the U.S. balance of payments after the president of the United States had sought more Japanese purchases in the United States.

   The local municipality, discovering that the stored uranium was no longer U.S. government property, sent the Japanese utilities 1974 property tax bills totaling $3.8 million. The responsibility for additional taxes was not specified at the time of the contract. It takes little imagination to understand the difficulty the Japanese had in understanding why they should pay such a high price in U.S. taxes on a venture entered into for the express purpose of helping the United States!

7. Licensee personnel will probably visit the licensor's plant or office to acquire expertise, and licensor personnel will probably visit the licensee to monitor progress. The agreement should specify clearly who is to pay for these visits, as well as the amount of payment, expenses to be charged, and even the work pattern (days per week, hours per day, etc.) expected of such personnel.

In addition to these seven financial characteristics, the agreement should provide for such nonfinancial issues as limitations on use of the license in various geographic regions, sublicensing, expiration or termination of the agreement, arbitration or litigation procedures in the case of dispute, disposition of products and/or special tools at the end of the period of agreement, and surrender of trademark rights and blueprints. If the contract is written in two languages, one of the languages should be established as the controlling text.

Financial Management Implications

We noted earlier that payment of royalties and fees is especially suitable when unbundling of remuneration is desired. In joint ventures the resources contributed by one of the partners may include technology and know-how while the other partner may be the primary supplier of monetary capital. The supplier of technology can readily accept royalty or fee compensation for that input and then accept a smaller proportion of net income as return on its investment of monetary capital.

Not all companies desire unbundling. Some parent firms avoid sapping the competitiveness of affiliates with charges for services that could be regarded as remote. A Conference Board survey provided conflicting views about whether such charges should be levied.[4] Some firms reported that royalties were set high enough to cover any managerial or technical assistance. Others reported that affiliates should be able to stand on their own and pay royalties or fees on the same basis as any independent company.

Sometimes royalty and fee payments will be allowed by the host country, even when dividend payments are restricted. A company might organize the contractual part of its investment agreements so that if the free movement of funds via dividends is limited, options for positioning funds via royalties and fees remain open.

Income Tax Aspects

Royalty and management fees have certain tax advantages relative to dividends, especially when the host country income tax rate is above the parent rate. Royalties and fees are usually deductible locally. If the affiliate compensates the parent by dividends, local income taxes are paid before the dividend distribution and withholding taxes are paid on the dividend itself. The parent can take a tax credit for the local income and withholding taxes paid, but if the affiliate's combined tax rate is above that of the parent, part of the benefit may be lost. The entire benefit is gained when the payment is for royalties or fees.

This tax interaction is depicted in Exhibit 15.1. It is assumed that a foreign affiliate earns $5000 before payment of any return to the parent and before income taxes. The parent desires to receive $2000 before parent country taxes from its foreign affiliate. In the "bundled" column this amount is paid entirely as dividends, and in the "unbundled" column this amount is paid $1200 as royalties and fees and $800 as dividends. Host country income taxes are 50%, and parent country income taxes are 40%. For simplicity, the host country is assumed to impose no dividend withholding tax. The parent country "grosses up" in determining taxable income.

In the affiliate statement shown at the top of Exhibit 15.1, under the bundled assumption the affiliate pays no royalties and fees but pays income taxes of $2500, dividends of $2000, and reinvests the remaining $500. Under the unbundled assumption the affiliate pays $1200 of royalties and fees before determining taxable income. As a consequence, local taxes are lowered to $1900. After a dividend of $800, some $1100 is reinvested locally. From a local point of view alone, a tax savings is derived when the parent is compensated via royalties and fees rather than via dividends.

In the parent statement, $2000 of cash is received under both the bundled and unbundled assumptions. Because local income taxes are 50%, a sum equal to the cash dividend is added back to determine taxable income in the parent country. The parent tax liability is 40% of this—$1600 in the bundled case and $1120 in the unbundled case. However, the company may take credit for a proportion of income taxes already paid in the foreign country. In the bundled example this credit exceeds the tax liability and no income taxes are paid. As a consequence, some $400 of potentially valuable tax credit is wasted. In the unbundled example the parent applies a tax credit of $800 against the liability of $1120 and pays the difference, $320.

Exhibit 15.1 indicates two important effects. Without regard to fund positioning, the company is better off worldwide under the unbundled assumption, since worldwide taxes paid are less and as a consequence total reinvested earnings are greater. Under most circumstances the company will position more funds abroad under the unbundled assumption than under the bundled assumption.

EXHIBIT 15.1
Tax Effect, Bundled versus Unbundled Compensation to Parent Corporation

	Bundled	*Unbundled*
Affiliate Statement		
Net income before taxes and compensation to parent	$5000	$5000
Less royalties and fees	—	1200
Taxable income	$5000	$3800
Less local income taxes (50%)	2500	1900
Available for dividends	$2500	$1900
Cash dividends to parent	2000	800
Reinvested locally	$ 500	$1100
Parent Statement		
Royalties and fees received	$ —	$1200
Dividends received	2000	800
Total received from affiliate	$2000	$2000
Credit for foreign income taxes[a]	2000	800
Taxable income in parent country	$4000	$2800
Parent tax liability (40%)	$1600	$1120
Less credit for foreign taxes	2000	800
Income tax payable by parent	$ —	$ 320
Lost income tax credit	400	—
Total Taxes Paid		
Taxes paid to host government	$2500	$1900
Taxes paid to parent government	—	320
Total taxes paid	$2500	$2220
Total Funds Reinvested		
Reinvested in host country	$ 500	$1100
Reinvested in parent country	2000	1680
Total reinvested	$2500	$2780

[a]In the bundled case dividends of $2000 were 80% of available for dividends of $2500. Therefore tax credit is 80% of actual tax payment of $2500, or $2000. In the unbundled case dividends of $800 were 42.1% of available for dividends of $1900. Therefore tax credit is 42.1% of actual tax payment of $1900, or $800.

TRANSFER PRICING

A particularly sensitive problem for multinational firms is establishing a rational method for pricing the transfer of goods, services, and technology between related affiliates in different countries. Even purely domestic firms find it difficult to reach agreement on the best method for setting prices on transactions between affiliates. In the multinational case managers are forced to balance conflicting considerations. These include fund positioning, taxation, tariffs and quotas, managerial incentives, and joint venture partners.

Fund Positioning Effect

Transfer price setting is a technique by which funds may be positioned within a multinational enterprise. A parent wishing to remove funds from a particular foreign country can charge higher prices on goods sold to its affiliate in that country. A foreign affiliate can be financed by the reverse technique, a lowering of transfer prices. Payment by the affiliate for imports from its parent transfers funds out of the affiliate. A higher transfer (sales) price permits funds to be accumulated within the selling country.

Transfer pricing may also be used to transfer funds between sister affiliates. Multiple sourcing of component parts on a worldwide basis allows changes in suppliers from within the corporate family to function as a device to transfer funds.

The flow of funds effect can be illustrated with the data in Exhibit 15.2. This exhibit shows two different results in which a manufacturing affiliate incurs costs of $1000 for goods, which are then sold to a distribution affiliate. The distribution affiliate resells to an unrelated final customer for $2000. The gross profit for the consolidated company is $1000 under both combinations, and if each affiliate has the same income tax rate and if other expenses are constant, net income on a consolidated basis is $400.

Nevertheless, the low-markup policy, in which the manufacturing affiliate "charges" the distribution affiliate $1400 for the goods, results in a cash transfer of $1400 from the distribution country to the manufacturing country. The high-markup policy, where the goods are "sold" at $1700, causes an additional $300 of cash to move from distribution to manufacturing country. If it were desirable to transfer funds out of the distribution country, the high-markup policy would achieve this end.

Taxation Effect

A major consideration in setting a transfer price is the income tax effect. Worldwide corporate profits may be influenced by setting transfer prices to minimize taxable income in any country with a high income tax rate. Tax haven affiliates have been used as trade intermediaries to drain off the income from transactions between related affiliates.

The income tax effect is illustrated in Exhibit 15.3, which is identical to Exhibit 15.2 except that the manufacturing affiliate pays income taxes of 25% while the distribution affiliate pays income taxes of 50%. Under the low-markup policy the manufacturing affiliate pays $75 of taxes and the distribution affiliate pays $250, for a total tax bill of $325 and consolidated net income of $475.

EXHIBIT 15.2
Tax-Neutral Impact of Low versus High Transfer Price on Flow of Funds

Assumption: Both manufacturing affiliate and distribution affiliate pay income taxes of 50%.

	Manufacturing affiliate		*Distribution affiliate*	*Consolidated company*
Low-Markup Policy				
Sales	$1400	(sales) →	$2000	$2000
Less cost of goods sold	1000		1400	1000
Gross profit	$ 400		$ 600	$1000
Less operating expenses	100		100	200
Taxable income	$ 300		$ 500	$ 800
Less income taxes (50%)	150		250	400
Net income	$ 150		$ 250	$ 400
High-Markup Policy				
Sales	$1700	(sales) →	$2000	$2000
Less cost of goods sold	1000		1700	1000
Gross profit	$ 700		$ 300	$1000
Less operating expenses	100		100	200
Taxable income	$ 600		$ 200	$ 800
Less income taxes (50%)	300		100	400
Net income	$ 300		$ 100	$ 400

If the firm adopts the high-markup policy, so that the merchandise is transferred at an intracompany sales price of $1700, the same $800 of pretax consolidated income is allocated more heavily to the manufacturing affiliate and less heavily to the distribution affiliate. As a consequence, total taxes drop by $75 and consolidated net income rises to $550.

In the absence of government interference, the firm would prefer the high-markup policy. Needless to say, government tax authorities are aware of the potential income distortion from transfer price manipulation. A variety of regulations and court cases exist on the reasonableness of transfer prices, including fees and royalties as well as prices set for physical merchandise. If a government taxing authority does not accept a transfer price, taxable income will be deemed larger than was calculated by the firm, and taxes will be increased. An even greater danger, from the corporate point of view, is that two or more governments will try to protect their respective tax bases by contradictory policies that subject the business to double taxation on the same income.

EXHIBIT 15.3
Tax Effect of Low versus High Transfer Price on Net Income

Assumptions: Manufacturing affiliate pays income taxes at 25%. Distribution affiliate pays income taxes at 50%.

	Manufacturing affiliate		*Distribution affiliate*	*Consolidated company*
Low-Markup Policy				
Sales	$1400	(sales) →	$2000	$2000
Less cost of goods sold	1000		1400	1000
Gross profit	$ 400		$ 600	$1000
Less operating expenses	100		100	200
Taxable income	$ 300		$ 500	$ 800
Less income taxes (25%/50%)	75		250	325
Net income	$ 225		$ 250	$ 475
High-Markup Policy				
Sales	$1700	(sales) →	$2000	$2000
Less cost of goods sold	1000		1700	1000
Gross profit	$ 700		$ 300	$1000
Less operating expenses	100		100	200
Taxable income	$ 600		$ 200	$ 800
Less income taxes (25%/50%)	150		100	250
Net income	$ 450		$ 100	$ 550

Typical of laws circumscribing freedom to set transfer prices is Section 482 of the U.S. Internal Revenue Code. Under this authority the Internal Revenue Service (IRS) can reallocate gross income, deductions, credits, or allowances between related corporations in order to prevent tax evasion or to reflect more clearly a proper allocation of income. Under the IRS guidelines and subsequent judicial interpretation, the burden of proof is on the taxpayer to show that the IRS has been arbitrary or unreasonable in reallocating income. The "correct price" according to the guidelines is the one that reflects an "arm's length" transaction, i.e., a sale of the same goods or service to an unrelated customer.

IRS regulations provide three methods to establish arm's length prices: comparable uncontrolled prices, resale prices, and cost-plus. A comparable uncontrolled price is regarded as the best evidence of arm's length pricing; such prices arise when transactions in the same goods or services occur between the multinational firm and unrelated customers, or between two unrelated firms. The second-best approach to arm's length pricing starts with the final selling price to customers and subtracts an appropriate profit for the distribution affiliate to determine the allowable selling price for the manufacturing affiliate. The third method is to add an appropriate markup for profit to total costs, including overhead, of the manufacturing affiliate. The same three methods are recommended for use in European countries by the Organization for Economic Cooperation and Development (OECD) Committee on Fiscal Affairs.[5]

Although all governments have an interest in monitoring transfer pricing practices of multinational firms, not all governments use these powers to regulate transfer prices to the detriment of multinational firms. In particular, transfer pricing has some political advantages over other techniques of transferring funds. Although the recorded transfer price is known to the governments of both the exporting and importing countries, the underlying cost data are not available to the importing country. Thus the importing country finds it difficult to judge how reasonable the transfer price is, especially for nonstandard items such as manufactured components. Additionally, even if cost data could be obtained, some of the more sophisticated governments might continue to ignore the transfer pricing leak. They recognize that the foreign investors must be able to repatriate a reasonable profit by their own standards, even if this profit seems unreasonable locally. An unknown or unproven transfer price leak makes it more difficult for local critics to blame their government for allowing the country to be "milked" by foreign investors. On the other hand, if the host government has soured on foreign investment, transfer price leaks are less likely to be overlooked. Thus within the *potential* and *actual* constraints established by governments, opportunities may exist for multinational firms to alter transfer prices away from an arm's length market price.

Tariff and Quota Effect

In addition to the effects on income tax, transfer pricing may have an influence on the amount of import duties paid. If the distribution affiliate must pay ad valorem import duties, and if those duties are levied on the invoice (transfer) price, duties will rise under the high-markup policy. To illustrate, assume that a 10% ad valorem import duty is paid by the distribution affiliate in Exhibit 15.3. The total tax results are shown in Exhibit 15.4.

Under the low-markup policy import duties of $140 are paid. Because these are deductible, income taxes of the distribution affiliate are reduced to $180. Total taxes are $395. Under the high-markup policy, import duties of $170 are paid, reducing income taxes to $15 and causing total taxes to be $335. The high-markup policy remains preferable, but the difference between the two is eroded.

EXHIBIT 15.4
Interacting Tariff and Income Tax Effects on Transfer Prices

Assumptions: Distribution affiliate pays a 10% ad valorem import duty. Import duty is deducted before calculating income taxes.

	Manufacturing affiliate		*Distribution affiliate*	*Consolidated company*
Low-Markup Policy				
Sales	$1400	(sales) →	$2000	$2000
Less cost of goods sold	1000		1400	1000
Less import duty (10%)	—		140[a]	140
Less operating expenses	100		100	200
Taxable income	$ 300		$ 360	$ 660
Less income taxes (25%/50%)	75[a]		180[a]	255
Net income	$ 225		$ 180	$ 405
High-Markup Policy				
Sales	$1700	(sales) →	$2000	$2000
Less cost of goods sold	1000		1700	1000
Less import duty (10%)	—		170[b]	170
Less operating expenses	100		100	200
Taxable income	$ 600		$ 30	$ 630
Less income taxes (25%/50%)	150[b]		15[b]	165
Net income	$ 450		$ 15	$ 465

[a]Total tax payment: 140 + 75 + 180 = 395.
[b]Total tax payment: 170 + 150 + 15 = 335.

The incidence of import duties is usually opposite to the incidence of income taxes in transfer pricing, but income taxes are usually a heavier burden than import duties. Therefore transfer prices are more often viewed from an income tax perspective. In many instances, however, import duties are actually levied against internationally posted prices, if such exist, rather than against the stated invoice price. If so, duties will not be influenced by the transfer price policy. Income taxes will still be affected by both the residual location of operating profit and the deductibility of the assessed import duties.

Related to the tariff effect is the ability to lower transfer prices to offset the volume effect of foreign exchange quotas. Should a host government allocate a limited amount of foreign exchange for importing a particular type of good, a lower transfer price on the import allows the firm to bring in a greater quantity. If, for example, the imported item is a component for a locally manufactured product, a lower transfer price may allow production volume to be sustained or expanded, albeit at the expense of profits in the supply affiliate.

Managerial Incentives and Evaluation

When a firm is organized with decentralized profit centers, transfer pricing between centers can be a major determinant of managerial performance. This problem is not unique to multinational firms but has been a controversial issue in the "centralization versus decentralization" debate in domestic circles. In the domestic case, however, a modicum of coordination at the corporate level can alleviate some of the distortion that occurs when any profit center suboptimizes its profit for the corporate good. This statement might also be true in the multinational case, but coordination is often hindered by longer and less-efficient channels of communication and the need to consider the unique variables that influence international pricing. Even with the best of intent, a manager in one country finds it difficult to know what is best for the firm as a whole when buying at a negotiated price from an affiliate in another country. If corporate headquarters establishes transfer prices and sourcing alternatives, managerial disincentives arise if the prices seem arbitrary or unreasonable. Furthermore, as corporate headquarters makes more decisions, one of the main advantages of a decentralized profit center system disappears—local management loses the incentive to act for its own benefit.

The possible effect of changes in transfer prices on managerial incentives and evaluation is illustrated in Exhibit 15.5, which is almost identical to Exhibit 15.2. Income taxes have been kept at a constant 50% in both countries so that the income tax effect is neutralized. Consolidated income (before dividends) is $400 under either the high- or low-markup policy.

The effect of the two markup policies on standard income statement measures of efficiency can be seen in the ratios tabulated at the bottom of Exhibit 15.5. A shift from a low- to a high-markup policy causes the manufacturing affiliate to experience an increase from 40.0% to 70.0% in its gross markup and an increase from 10.7% to 17.6% in its net profit margin. Meanwhile, the distribution affiliate finds that its gross markup has dropped from 42.9% to 17.6%, while its net profit margin has declined from 12.5% to 5.0%. If management performance were judged on these traditional ratios, or if local bank credit depended on such ratios, local managers would prefer transfer pricing policies that would make their affiliate look good rather than those that would benefit the consolidated firm.

As we mentioned earlier, the positioning-of-funds effect operates in part through dividend policy. Using the example in Exhibit 15.5, we can now see how transfer prices might influence allowable dividend remittances

EXHIBIT 15.5
Tax-Neutral Impact of Low versus High Transfer Price on Income Statement Financial Ratios

Assumption: Both manufacturing affiliate and distribution affiliate pay income taxes at 50% of taxable income.

	LOW-MARKUP POLICY		*HIGH-MARKUP POLICY*		
	Manufacturing affiliate	*Distribution affiliate*	*Manufacturing affiliate*	*Distribution affiliate*	*Consolidated company*
Sales	$1400	$2000	$1700	$2000	$2000
Less cost of goods sold	1000	1400	1000	1700	1000
Gross profit	$ 400	$ 600	$ 700	$ 300	$1000
Less operating expenses	100	100	100	100	200
Taxable income	$ 300	$ 500	$ 600	$ 200	$ 800
Less income taxes (50%)	150	250	300	100	400
Net income	$ 150	$ 250	$ 300	$ 100	$ 400
Less dividends (given)	100	100	100	100	200
Addition to retained earnings	50	150	200	—	200
Gross markup (gross profit/cost of goods sold)	40.0%	42.9%	70.0%	17.6%	
Net profit margin (net income/sales)	10.7%	12.5%	17.6%	5.0%	
Dividend payout ratio (dividends/net income)	66.7%	40.0%	33.3%	100.0%	

in some countries. Assume, in Exhibit 15.5, that cash dividends remitted to the parent are in fact $100 for each affiliate, regardless of the markup policy. The measurement of the amount of dividends remitted as a percentage of net income could be either 66.7% or 33.3% for the manufacturing affiliate and either 40.0% or 100.0% for the distribution affiliate. Suppose that the various affiliates are operating in countries that define a "fair" dividend remittance as, say, 50% of net income. The high-markup policy would permit the manufacturing affiliate to declare a dividend of $100, because this amount would constitute only one-third of accounting earnings. The distribution affiliate, on the other hand, could sustain its $100 dividend only if a low-markup policy were adopted. Thus it can be seen that a possible side reason for using a particular type of markup policy would be the effect on allowable dividends if these were judged against the level of accounting net income.

EXHIBIT 15.6
Tax-Neutral Impact of Low versus High Transfer Price on Balance Sheet Ratios

Assumptions: Income statement for Exhibit 15.6 is for full year. Inventory and accounts receivable turn over once every 90 days; payables are paid in 60 days.

	LOW-MARKUP POLICY		*HIGH-MARKUP POLICY*		
	Manufacturing affiliate	*Distribution affiliate*	*Manufacturing affiliate*	*Distribution affiliate*	*Consolidated company*
Cash balances (given)	$ 100	$ 100	$ 100	$ 100	$ 200
Accounts receivable (¼ annual sales)	350	500	425	500	500
Inventory (¼ cost of goods sold)	250	350	250	425	500
Total current assets	$ 700	$ 950	$ 775	$1025	$1200
Less accounts payable (⅙ cost of goods sold)	167	233	167	283	167
Net working capital	$ 533	$ 717	$ 608	$ 742	$1033
Net plant and equipment (given)	500	500	500	500	1000
Net operating assets	$1033	$1217	$1108	$1242	$2033
Return on net operating assets (net income/net operating assets)	14.5%	20.5%	27.1%	8.1%	
Internally financed growth rate (addition to retained earnings/ net operating assets)	4.8%	12.3%	18.1%	0.0%	

The effect of transfer pricing on financial ratios is illustrated further in Exhibit 15.6. Assume that each affiliate carries a cash balance of $100; that accounts receivable and inventory turn over every 90 days and so are equivalent to one-fourth of annual sales and cost of goods sold, respectively; that accounts payable turn over in 60 days and are thus equal to one-sixth of cost of goods sold; and that net plant and equipment for each affiliate are $500.

Accounts receivable for the consolidated firm consist of the receivables of the distribution affiliate alone because the manufacturing affiliate's receivables are intracorporate and cancel out. Inventory for the consolidated company is carried at the manufacturing affiliate's cost and consists of twice the manufacturing affiliate's inventory—90 days of inventory at this cost held by the manufacturing affiliate and a second 90 days of inventory at this same cost held by the distribution affiliate.

The rate of return on net operating assets would be either 14.5% or 27.1% for the manufacturing affiliate and either 20.5% or 8.1% for the distribution affiliate. Measured profitability becomes primarily a transfer price question, with implications for both management control systems and for questions that might be raised by local politicians about the profitability of foreign-owned firms. Similarly, the rate of internally financed growth, as measured by the addition to retained earnings as a percentage of net operating assets, is significantly influenced by the choice of transfer prices.

Effect on Joint-Venture Partners

Joint ventures pose a special problem in transfer pricing, because serving the interest of local stockholders by maximizing local profit may be suboptimal from the overall corporate viewpoint. Often the conflicting interests are irreconcilable. When Ford Motor Company decided to rationalize production on a worldwide basis so that each division could specialize in certain products or components, it was forced to abandon its policy of working with joint ventures partly because of the transfer pricing problem. It had to purchase the large British minority interest in Ford, Ltd., in 1961, despite the well-publicized and ill-timed drain on the U.S. balance of payments. For identical reasons, General Motors has practically never worked with joint ventures until its recent arrangement with Toyota.

Transfer Pricing in Practice

Because successful pricing is a key element in achieving profits, transfer pricing strategies are inevitably corporate secrets. The small amount of information available, however, suggests that probably little uniformity exists. Most firms appear to maintain a "flexible" transfer pricing policy. In practice, to be "flexible" means to "comply" with tax and customs authorities' rulings on a case-by-case basis. So that transfer prices can meet the needs of managerial and profit center performance evaluations, a second set of books must be maintained.

Jane O. Burns has identified 14 variables potentially important in setting international transfer prices and obtained ranking of their importance in a survey of 62 U.S. multinational firms.[6] The 14 variables, in order of mean ranking, are shown in Exhibit 15.7.

Burns performed a factor analysis to identify underlying dimensions that account for the commonality of preferences for different variables. The resultant five most important factor groupings were the following:

EXHIBIT 15.7
Rank Order of Importance of 14 Variables in Transfer Pricing Decisions

Rank	*Variable*	*Mean ranking*[a]	*Standard deviation*
1	Market conditions in the foreign country	2.15	.872
2	Competition in the foreign country	2.26	.964
3	Reasonable profit for foreign affiliate	2.31	.975
4	U.S. federal income taxes	2.57	1.190
5	Economic conditions in the foreign country	2.61	1.037
6	Import restrictions	2.62	.986
7	Customs duties	2.70	.937
8	Price controls	2.80	.997
9	Taxation in the foreign country	2.84	1.143
10	Exchange controls	2.92	.954
11	U.S. export incentives	3.10	1.121
12	Floating exchange rates	3.16	.916
13	Management of cash flow	3.20	.928
14	Other U.S. federal taxes	3.64	.876

Source: Jane O. Burns, "Transfer Pricing Decisions in U.S. Multinational Corporations," *Journal of International Business Studies,* Fall 1980, p. 25.

[a]The mean for each variable is based on a scale of 1 = strongly agree through 5 = strongly disagree.

1. Internal foreign environment (competition in the foreign country and market conditions in the foreign country).
2. Influences on cash flows (U.S. export incentives, exchange controls, floating exchange rates, and management of cash flows).
3. Artificial barriers (customs duties, exchange controls, price controls, and import restrictions).
4. Taxes (U.S. federal income taxes, other U.S. federal taxes, taxation in the foreign country).
5. Economic structure (U.S. export incentives and economic conditions in the foreign country).[7]

In a study of the transfer pricing policies of 60 non-U.S. multinational firms and their U.S. affiliates, Jeffrey S. Arpan concluded that transfer prices were nearly always set by top-level parent company executives, regardless of nationality or degree of company decentralization for other decisions.[8] Nevertheless, distinct national differences were observed with respect to the weight accorded host country environmental variables and internal company parameters.

Canadian, French, Italian, and U.S. parent firms judged that the tax effect of transfer pricing was the most important consideration. British parent firms emphasized the strong financial appearance of their U.S. affiliates. Inflation was an important consideration by all parent firms except those in Scandinavia; these firms considered acceptability to the host government to be the most important determinant of their transfer pricing policies. German firms appeared to be least concerned about transfer pricing policies. Non-U.S. firms, in contrast to U.S. firms, did not consider the evaluation of managerial performance to be important because, contrary to the practice of many U.S. firms, they did not usually operate their foreign affiliates on a profit center basis.

BLOCKED FUNDS

When a government runs short of foreign exchange and cannot obtain additional funds through borrowing or attracting new foreign investment, it usually limits transfers of foreign exchange out of the country. This does not typically discriminate against foreign-owned firms because it applies to everyone. Depending on the degree of shortage, the host government might simply require approval of all transfers of funds abroad, thus reserving the right to set a priority on the use of scarce foreign exchange in favor of necessities rather than luxuries. In very severe cases the government might make its currency nonconvertible into other currencies, thereby fully blocking transfers of funds abroad. In between these positions are policies that restrict the size and timing of dividends, debt amortization, royalties, and service fees.

Multinational firms can react to the risk of blocked funds at three stages.

1. Prior to making an investment, they can analyze the impact of blocked funds on expected return on investment, the desired local financial structure, and optimal links with affiliates.
2. During investment they can attempt to move funds through a variety of positioning techniques.
3. Funds that cannot be moved must be reinvested so as to preserve their real value from deterioration from inflation and exchange depreciation.

Preinvestment Strategy

Management can consider blocked funds in their capital budgeting analysis, as was done in the example in Chapter 10. Temporary blockage of funds normally reduces the expected net present value and internal rate of return on a proposed investment. Whether the investment should nevertheless be undertaken depends on whether the expected rate of return, even with blocked funds, exceeds the required rate of return on investments of the same risk class. Preinvestment analysis also includes the potential to minimize the effect of blocked funds by means of heavy local borrowing, swap agreements, and other techniques to reduce local currency exposure and thus the need to repatriate funds. Sourcing and sales links with affiliates can be predetermined so as to maximize the potential for moving blocked funds.

Moving Blocked Funds

What can a multinational firm do to transfer funds out of countries having exchange or remittance restrictions? At least six general approaches have been used with varying degrees of success:

1. unbundling services,
2. use of fronting loans,
3. transfer pricing,
4. leading or lagging payments,
5. creating unrelated exports,
6. obtaining special dispensation.

Unbundling services Unbundling payments for services is the easiest and most acceptable method of transferring funds if restrictions are imposed on dividend remittances alone. However, many countries combine dividend restrictions with similar controls over other forms of remitting funds, such as debt repayment, interest payments, and fees.

Fronting loans A fronting loan is a parent-to-affiliate loan channeled through a financial intermediary, usually a large international bank. Fronting loans differ from "parallel" or "back-to-back" loans in that the latter involve offsetting loans between commercial businesses arranged outside the banking system. Fronting loans are sometimes referred to as "link financing."

In a direct intracompany loan the parent or an affiliate loans directly to the borrowing affiliate, and at a later date the borrowing affiliate repays the principal and interest. In a fronting loan, by contrast, the parent deposits funds in, say, a London bank, and that bank loans the same amount to the borrowing affiliate. From the bank's point of view the loan is risk-free, because the bank has 100% collateral in the form of the parent's deposit. In effect the bank "fronts" for the parent—hence the name. Interest paid by the borrowing affiliate to the bank is usually slightly higher than the rate paid by the bank to the parent, allowing the bank a margin for expenses and profit.

Use of fronting loans increases chances for repayment should political turmoil occur in the country where the borrowing affiliate operates. Government authorities are more likely to allow the local affiliate to repay a loan to a large international bank than to allow the same affiliate to repay

EXHIBIT 15.8
Tax Aspects of a Fronting Loan

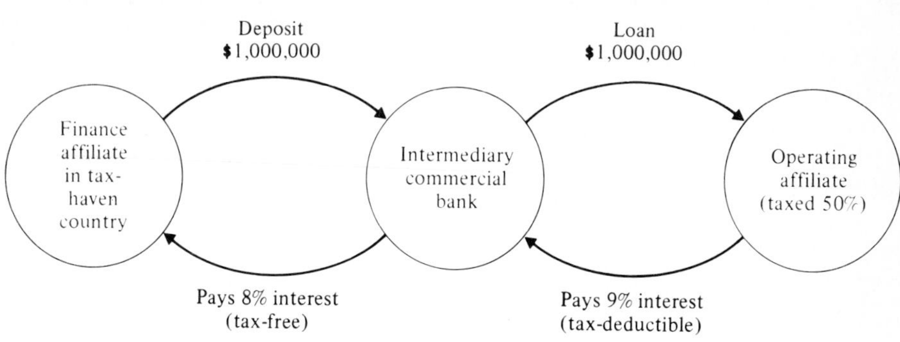

a loan to its parent. To stop payment to the international bank would hurt the international credit image of the country, whereas to stop payment to the parent corporation would have minimal impact on that image and might even provide some domestic political advantage.

A fronting loan may have a tax advantage. Assume, as depicted in Exhibit 15.8, a finance affiliate, wholly owned by the parent and located in a tax haven country, deposits $1,000,000 in an intermediary commercial bank at 8% interest, and the bank in turn lends $1,000,000 to an operating affiliate at 9%. The operating affiliate is located in a country where the income tax rate is 50%. Interest payments net of income tax effect will be as follows:

1. The operating affiliate pays $90,000 interest to the intermediary bank. Deduction of interest from taxable income results in a net aftertax cost of $45,000.
2. The intermediary bank receives $90,000, retains $10,000 for its services, and pays $80,000 interest on the deposit of the finance affiliate.
3. The finance affiliate receives $80,000 interest on deposit, tax free.

The net result is that $80,000 of cash is moved from the operating affiliate to the finance affiliate. Since the aftertax cost to the borrowing affiliate is only $45,000, the system has been able to move an additional $35,000 out of the country by virtue of the tax shield. If the finance affiliate had made a direct loan to the operating affiliate, the host government of the operating affiliate would be in a position to disallow the interest charge as a tax-deductible expense by ruling that it was a substantive dividend to the parent disguised as interest. Note that the fronting loan, as a device, provides no protection against changes in exchange rates.

Transfer pricing The potential fund positioning advantages of transfer pricing have been explained earlier in this chapter, but whether such an approach can succeed in moving blocked funds is debatable. The usual method of transfer pricing funds out of countries with stringent exchange controls is to manufacture parts or components locally for use elsewhere in the worldwide firm. Unique parts having no general market value except to the firm may be sold to an affiliate at marginal cost and incorporated into finished products sold elsewhere, with profit picked up by the affiliate making the final sale. Imported parts, components, or even equipment may be purchased from other affiliates at relatively high prices, moving funds out from the blocked funds country via higher import prices paid. The limit on this general approach is that officials of the host country have the power to insist on arm's length prices.

A slightly more sophisticated version of the transfer pricing approach for coping with blocked funds is for the affiliate in the country whose currency is blocked to export to affiliates and bill them in the local (blocked) currency. Since blocked currencies can usually be purchased very cheaply in exchange markets located *outside* the country whose currency is involved, the outside affiliate may absorb the profit from ultimate resale while avoiding the movement of hard currency funds to the exporting affiliate. Once again, this approach may be limited by a host government that prohibits exports billed in its own currency, although if the alternative is no export at all, the host government may relent. In addition, this approach does provide some support for the value of the blocked currency in external foreign exchange markets, since the importing affiliate does enter that market on the buy side.

Leads and lags Leads and lags were described in Chapter 7 as one way to react to expected foreign exchange rate changes. The approach is also useful in dealing with blocked funds, for by changing the time of payment to and from affiliates, at least part of the working capital can be shifted to affiliates outside the country with exchange restrictions. Such an approach may be a one-shot affair, however, for the local affiliate must continue to maintain a minimum level of its own working capital simply to remain in business.

Creating unrelated exports One approach to blocked funds that benefits both affiliate and host country is the creation of unrelated exports. Because the main reason for stringent exchange controls is usually a country's persistent inability to earn hard currencies, anything a multinational firm can do to create new exports from the host country helps the situation and provides a potential means to transfer funds out.

Some new exports can often be created from present productive capacity with little or no additional investment, especially if they are in product lines related to existing operations. Other new exports may require reinvestment or new funds, although if the funds reinvested consist of those already blocked, little is lost in the way of opportunity costs. A multinational firm already in Brazil, for example, might locate research and development laboratories there and pay for them with blocked cruzeiros. Key research personnel could be transferred to Brazil to supplement local talent, their salaries and expenses being picked up on the local payroll. A Brazilian architectural and engineering firm might be hired to provide services for the worldwide enterprise, being paid in cruzeiros to design plants in France or Florida.

Export equivalents can also be created with little investment in certain service activities. The Brazilian affiliate, for example, could host conventions or other business meetings in Rio de Janeiro for its multinational parent. Employees of the firm might be sent on company-sponsored vacations to Brazil, and employees of the parent flying anywhere in the world might be asked to use Varig, the Brazilian national airline, wherever possible, flying on tickets purchased in Brazil by the Brazilian affiliate and paid for with cruzeiros.

All such activities benefit Brazil because they provide export-oriented jobs, and they benefit the multinational firm because they provide a way to use effectively funds that would otherwise remain tied up in the Brazilian money market.

Another approach for a parent dealing with an affiliate in a blocked currency country is to arrange barter agreements. A country such as Brazil would probably not allow barter deals involving coffee or other commodities already sold on world markets for hard currencies, but it might permit a barter for exports of goods or services not normally exported. For example, Brazilian textiles might be bought from the Brazilian affiliate by the parent in exchange for imports into Brazil of the parent's products or equipment. The parent (not in the textile business) arranges for the sale of the textiles in the parent country. Whether or not such an approach is useful in any particular case depends on the implied transfer price (the barter terms, if no prices are stated). Barter agreements were common in the period immediately after the end of World War II. They were relatively uncommon (outside the Eastern Bloc countries) from the early 1950s to the early 1970s, but they appear to be coming back into use in the 1980s under the name "countertrade," as described in Chapter 14.

Special dispensation If all else fails and the multinational firm is investing in an industry that is important to the economic development of the host country, the firm may bargain for special dispensation to repatriate some portion of the funds that otherwise would be blocked. Firms in "desirable" industries such as data processing equipment, semiconductor manufacturing, instrumentation, pharmaceuticals, or other research and high-technology industries, may receive preference over firms in mature industries. The amount of preference received depends on bargaining among informed parties, the government and the business firm, either of which is free to make an agreement or not.

Self-fulfilling prophecies In seeking "escape routes" for blocked funds—or for that matter in trying to position funds through any of the techniques discussed in this chapter—the multinational firm may increase political risk and cause a change from partial blockage to full blockage. The possibility of such a self-fulfilling cycle exists any time a firm takes action that, no matter how legal, thwarts the intent of politically authored controls. In the statehouses of the world, as in the editorial offices of the local press and TV, multinational firms and their affiliates are always a convenient scapegoat.

Forced Reinvestment

If funds are indeed blocked from transfer into foreign exchange, they are by definition "reinvested." Under such a situation the firm must find local opportunities that will maximize rate of return for a given acceptable level of risk.

If blockage is expected to be temporary, the most obvious alternative is to invest in local money market instruments. Unfortunately, in many countries such instruments are not available in sufficient quantity or with adequate liquidity. In some cases government treasury bills, bank deposits, and other short-term instruments have yields that are kept artificially low relative to local rates of inflation or probable changes in exchange rates. Thus the firm often loses real value during the period of blockage.

Forced reinvestment may take the form of direct loans. The "back-to-back" or parallel loan discussed in Chapter 7 involves a situation in which an affiliate loans excess local currency to another firm for local use in return for an offsetting loan elsewhere in the world. If such offsetting loans are not possible, the blocked funds may perhaps be loaned to a local affiliate of a foreign firm, with interest charges to be paid in a foreign currency. The borrowing firm will find this arrangement desirable if by so doing it can avoid exchanging its own hard currency into the weaker blocked currency to make an investment.

Another use of blocked or restricted funds is to deposit them with the local office of a multinational bank as collateral for loans elsewhere in the world, as compensating balances against such loans, or as compensation for services performed for the parent or sister affiliates.

If short- or intermediate-term portfolio investments, such as bonds, bank time deposits, or direct loans to other companies, are not possible, direct investment in additional production facilities may be the only alternative. Often this investment is what the host country is seeking by its exchange controls, even if the fact of exchange controls is by itself counterproductive to the idea of additional foreign investment. Examples of forced direct reinvestment can be cited for Peru, where an airline invested in hotels and in maintenance facilities for other airlines; for Turkey, where a fish canning company constructed a plant to manufacture cans needed for packing the catch; and for Argentina, where an automobile company integrated vertically by acquiring an automobile transmission manufacturing plant previously owned by a supplier.

If investment opportunities in additional production facilities are not available, funds may simply be used to acquire other assets expected to increase in value with local inflation. Typical purchases might be land, office buildings, or commodities that are exported to global markets. Even inventory stockpiling might be a reasonable investment, given the low opportunity cost of the blocked funds.

MANAGING INTERNATIONAL CASH BALANCES

Cash balances, including marketable securities, are held partly in anticipation of day-to-day cash disbursements and partly as protection against unanticipated variations from budgeted cash flows. These two motives are commonly called the transaction motive and the precautionary motive. Cash may also be held for speculative purposes; however, this aspect is beyond our consideration in this chapter because it does not involve normal day-to-day operations.

Cash management in a multinational firm can benefit from centralized depositories, multilateral netting, mobilizing cash, and careful cash forecasting. These topics will be treated next.

Centralized Depositories

Operational benefits can be gained by centralizing cash management in any business with widely dispersed operating affiliates. Internationally the requisite procedure calls for each affiliate to hold only a minimum cash balance for transaction purposes. No cash for precautionary purposes is held locally—unless management of the central pool issues specific instructions to override the general rule. All excess funds are remitted to a central cash depository, where a single authority has responsibility for placing the funds in such currencies and money market instruments as will best serve the worldwide firm.

The central depository has advantages of size and information. It is located where information can be collected and decisions made about the relative strengths and weaknesses of various currencies. Interest rate information on alternative investments for each currency is also available, as is experience with the mechanical functioning of the various money markets. Although in theory such information might be available to the treasurer of each affiliate, in practice that individual can seldom specialize in money market management alone.

Funds held in the central pool can quickly be returned to a local affiliate that is short of cash. This return is achieved either by wire transfer or by creating a worldwide bank credit line. The bank would instruct its branch office in the particular country to advance emergency funds to the local affiliate.

Another reason for holding all precautionary balances in a central pool is that the total pool, if centralized, can be reduced in size without any loss in the level of protection. To illustrate, assume that precautionary balances are held separately in Italy, Germany, and France. In each country the budgeted cash balance is set at a level equal to three standard deviations above the expected cash need for the planning period. Cash needs are assumed to be normally distributed in each country, and the needs are independent from one country to another. Three standard deviations means there exists a 99.87% chance that cash needs can be met. The chance of being unable to meet cash needs is reduced to .13%. Cash needs, in dollar equivalents, are assumed to be as follows:

	Expected cash need (A)	*One standard deviation (B)*	*Cash balance budgeted for adequate protection (A + 3B)*
Italy	$10,000	$1,000	$13,000
Germany	6,000	2,000	12,000
France	12,000	3,000	21,000
	$28,000		$46,000

As shown above and diagrammed in Exhibit 15.9, the firm must maintain a total of $18,000 in potentially idle cash balances in the three European countries in order to have the requisite protection against uncertainties in its cash flow. The $18,000 plus the expected cash need of $28,000 results in a total budgeted cash balance of $46,000.

What would happen if the firm maintained all precautionary balances in a single account in one European financial center? Because variances are additive when probability distributions are independent, the equivalent standard deviation for the single account would be

$$\sqrt{(1{,}000)^2 + (2{,}000)^2 + (3{,}000)^2} = \$3{,}742.$$

A budgeted cash balance three standard deviations above the aggregate expected cash need would require 3 ($3,742) = $11,226 in potentially idle

EXHIBIT 15.9
Precautionary Balances (in thousands of dollars)

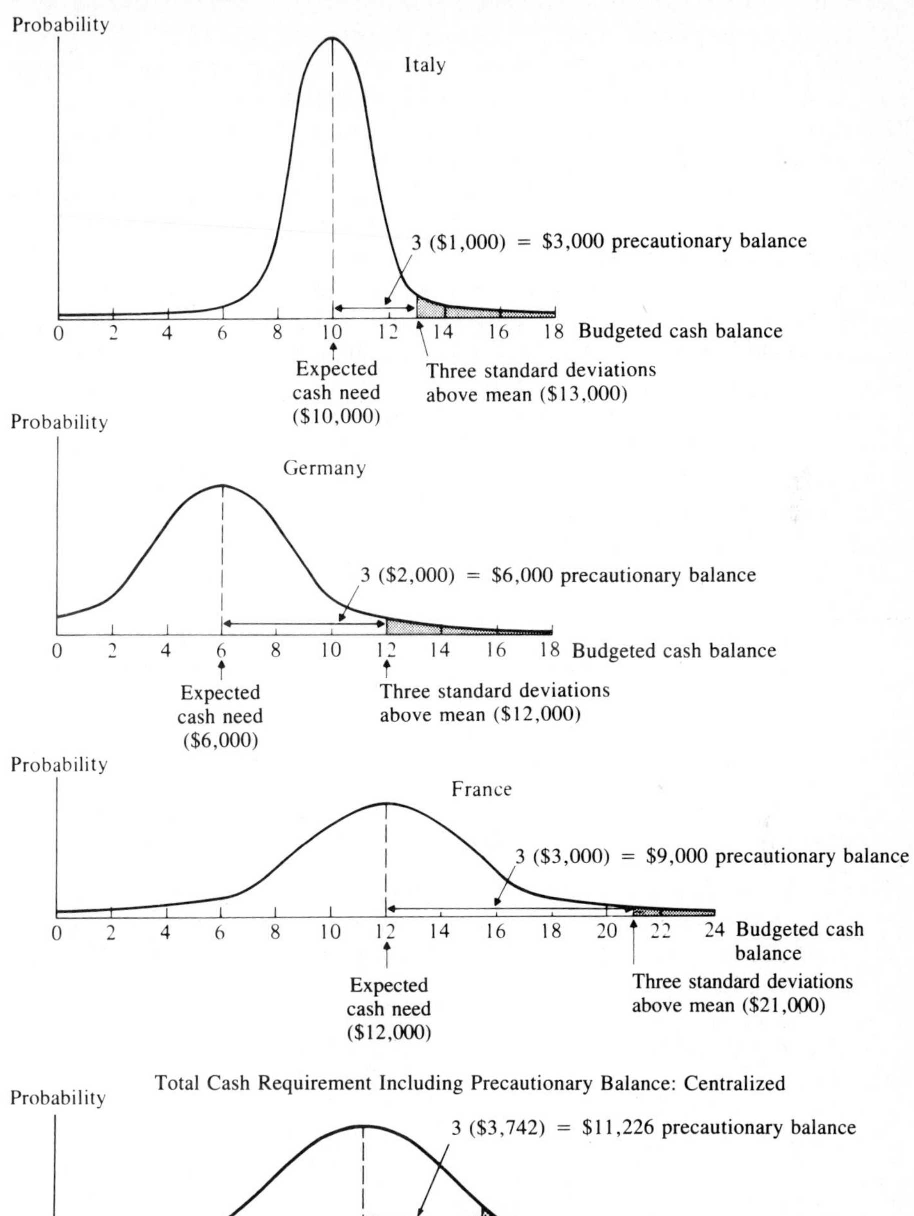

cash, or a total budgeted cash balance of \$11,226 + \$28,000 = \$39,226. Budgeted investment in cash balances is reduced by \$6,774.

Central money pools are usually maintained in major money centers such as London, New York, Zurich, and Brussels. Additional popular locations for money pools include the more common tax haven countries: Liechtenstein, Luxembourg, the Bahamas, Bermuda, Panama, and the Netherlands Antilles. Although these countries do not have strong diversified economies, they offer most of the other prerequisites for a corporate financial center: freely convertible currency, political and economic stability, access to international communications, and clearly defined legal procedures. Their additional advantage as a so-called tax haven is also desirable.

A second advantage of centralized cash management is that one affiliate will not borrow at high rates while another holds surplus funds idle or invests them at low rates. Managers of the central pool can locate the least expensive sources of funds, worldwide, as well as the most advantageous returns to be earned on excess funds. If additional cash is desired, the central pool manager can determine the location of such borrowing. A local affiliate manager would never borrow at a rate above the minimum available to the pool manager. If the firm has a worldwide cash surplus, the central pool manager can evaluate comparative rates of return in various markets, transaction costs, exchange risks, and tax effects.

Use of a centralized depository system does not necessarily imply use of a single bank, for the essence of the centralized depository is centralized information and decisions. Actual funds may be placed in as many banks as are desired.

Multilateral Netting—Reducing Misdirected Funds

Operationally financial managers of multinational companies have unique opportunities to minimize the opportunity cost to the company of misdirected and mislocated funds.[9] Misdirected funds are those that unnecessarily cross an international border or, more precisely, are unnecessarily changed from one currency to another. Such misdirection is expensive because of foreign exchange transaction costs and unnecessary float. Multilateral netting of payments is intended to reduce the cost of misdirected funds.

Mislocated funds are funds in the wrong currency. Mislocation is expensive because of the possibility of loss through deterioration of currency values and because interest rates earned in a given money market may not compensate for foreign exchange risk. Mislocated debt is corporate borrowing conducted in the wrong currency relative to exchange rate risk and interest rate costs. A central cash mobilization system is intended to reduce the cost of mislocated funds.

Multilateral netting of payments is useful primarily when a large number of separate foreign exchange transactions occur between affiliates in the normal course of business. Netting reduces the foreign exchange settlement costs of what would otherwise be a large number of crossing spot transactions. Multilateral netting is an extension of bilateral netting. If a Belgian affiliate owes an Italian affiliate $500, while the Italian affiliate simultaneously owes the Belgian affiliate $300, a bilateral settlement would call for a single payment of $200 from Belgium to Italy and the cancellation, via offset, of the remainder of the debt.

A matrix for a multilateral payments netting system is shown in Exhibit 15.10. Instead of paying every other affiliate, each member of the system notifies a central information office (usually the office of corporate treasurer) on designated dates of balances due to every other affiliate in the system. This information is arranged in a matrix, the net payment or receipt of each participant calculated, and specific transmittal instructions issued.

According to the data in Exhibit 15.10, without netting Belgium would make a minimum of three separate payments and would also receive three separate receipts. If Belgium paid on individual invoice rather than accumulated invoices for a single currency transaction, there would be a multitude of much smaller foreign exchange transactions whose total would equal the payment or receipt amounts of Exhibit 15.10. With netting Belgium is instructed to make just one or two payments, depending on how the net balances are settled. If all payments are made through a central pool and all funds disbursed from that pool, a total of four exchange transactions would be needed in the example—or three, if the

EXHIBIT 15.10
Multilateral International Payments Netting Matrix

	PAYING AFFILIATES				
Receiving affiliates	*United States*	*Belgium*	*France*	*Italy*	*Total receipts*
United States	—	300	400	500	1200
Belgium	400	—	200	300	900
France	500	300	—	100	900
Italy	600	500	200	—	1300
Total payments	1500	1100	800	900	4300

	Payment	*Receipt*	*Net payment*	*Net receipt*
United States	1500	1200	300	—
Belgium	1100	900	200	—
France	800	900	—	100
Italy	900	1300	—	400

U.S. dollar or one of the other currencies involved were the currency of settlement. Alternatively, instructions might be issued calling for direct remittance of the residual balances without use of a pool. In the example the United States might remit $300 to Italy, and Belgium might remit $100 to France and $100 to Italy.

Multilateral netting systems are usually maintained in a single currency of measurement. However, actual payment instructions can call for settlement in any currency. In the example the Belgian affiliate might remit $100 of Belgian francs to Sweden, it might remit $100 of kronor to Sweden, or it might settle in any other currency—including foreign currencies needed for future transactions of the Swedish affiliate.

A few countries limit or prohibit netting, and some permit netting on a "gross settlements" basis only. For a single settlement period all receipts may be combined into a single receipt, and all payments into a single payment. However, these two may not be netted. Thus two large payments, rather than a single smaller net payment, must pass through the local banking system.

Permission to net payments is granted by individual permit in some countries, such as France and Spain. Firms that manufacture locally are often given permission, while those that only sell are often denied. A survey of 194 multinational firms by Business International reported that 33% of the European and 28% of the U.S. firms used multilateral netting.[10] Furthermore, some individual firms reported savings of several million dollars.[11]

Multinational Mobilization—Reducing Mislocated Funds

A multinational cash mobilization system can be used to minimize mislocated funds by monitoring current and anticipated cash balances. Operation of a multinational cash mobilization system supplements use of a multilateral netting system in the effective operation of a centralized cash pool. Information collected by the mobilization system is also useful in the preparation of near-term cash budgets.

The basic nature of a multinational cash mobilization system will be explained with a simple four-country example based on Europe. Assume the European headquarters of a multinational firm operates a central cash pool in Belgium, and that the firm has operating affiliates in Britain, Sweden, Germany, and France. At the close of daily banking hours in each country, every affiliate reports its end-of-day cash balances in cleared funds to Brussels. This report is made after deposits and disbursements have cleared the local banking system. As is true for netting systems, the daily report will be in a designated reporting currency, with actual local currency cash balances translated at an exchange rate designated by the corporate treasurer's office. Assume the reporting currency is the U.S. dollar.

The daily cash report for each unit might appear as in Exhibit 15.11, although in fact such reports are usually transmitted in abbreviated form over the telephone or by telex. According to the reports shown in Exhibit 15.11, the British affiliate has an end-of-day cash balance in pounds sterling equivalent to $150,000. In other words, the British affiliate could have disbursed an additional $150,000 that day without creating a negative cash balance or exceeding intended overdraft privileges. The Swedish affiliate

EXHIBIT 15.11
European Cash Management Pool—Daily Cash Reports (in thousands of U.S. dollars)

DAILY CASH REPORT

Date: March 7, 19XX
Location: U.K.
End-of-day cash balance: +150

Five-day forecast:

	receipt	*disburse*	*net*
+1	300	400	−100
+2	400	350	+ 50
+3	300	250	+ 50
+4	250	650	−400
+5	200	250	− 50
Net for period			−450

DAILY CASH REPORT

Date: March 7, 19XX
Location: Sweden
End-of-day cash balance: −250

Five-day forecast:

	receipt	*disburse*	*net*
+1	100	200	−100
+2	100	150	− 50
+3	50	zero	+ 50
+4	200	75	+125
+5	200	200	zero
Net for period			+ 25

DAILY CASH REPORT

Date: March 7, 19XX
Location: Germany
End-of-day cash balance: +600

Five-day forecast:

	receipt	*disburse*	*net*
+1	400	100	+300
+2	350	100	+250
+3	300	150	+150
+4	300	400	−100
+5	200	100	+100
Net for period			+700

DAILY CASH REPORT

Date: March 7, 19XX
Location: France
End-of-day cash balance: +500

Five-day forecast:

	receipt	*disburse*	*net*
+1	100	400	−300
+2	300	100	+200
+3	500	200	+300
+4	100	100	zero
+5	150	225	− 50
Net for period			+150

reports a cash deficit at the end of the day of Swedish kronor equivalent to $250,000. Presumably local overdraft privileges will cover the deficit. Alternatively, the Swedish financial manager should have anticipated the shortage and requested an emergency transfer from the central pool before the Swedish banks closed. The German and French affiliates report local cash balances equal to $600,000 and $500,000.

The central pool manager compiles the reports at the end of each day in the form shown at the top of Exhibit 15.12. This daily cash ledger shows the end-of-day cash balance at each affiliate and the previously agreed-upon minimum balance that is to be maintained there for day-to-day operations. In this example, the British affiliate ended the day with a cash balance of $150,000, but it needed $200,000. At the end of the day it was $50,000 short of normal operating funds. Similarly, the Swedish affiliate was short, while the German and French affiliates had cash balances above their operating needs. For Europe as a whole, the company had a cash surplus of $225,000.

The essence of effective cash management is using information in the daily cash ledger to cover any deficits, decide upon any borrowing, or put any excess cash into money market instruments.

For example, if an imminent drop in value of the British pound were anticipated, the required minimum cash balance for the United Kingdom could be reduced from $200,000 to some lower level. If local overdrafts were possible, the required "minimum" might be a negative amount.

Daily cash reports from each operating division may contain one additional item of information, a forecast of cash receipts and disbursements for each of the following five days. This forecast, which moves forward day by day, serves at least three purposes. First, each division must revise its operating cash budget daily, and the actual cash result can be measured against the accuracy of the forecasts of each of the previous five days. Second, information that assists in the decision to transfer funds to or from the central pool is given. For example, although France currently has a cash surplus of $300,000 (Exhibit 15.12), the following day a deficit of $300,000 is expected (Exhibit 15.11). Depending on interest rates and the cost of exchange transactions, the central pool might instruct the French division to invest the surplus funds overnight in France against the following day's deficit, rather than to transmit them to the central pool and then cover the following day's deficit with a remittance from the central pool back to France. Third, an estimate of future net cash flows for the company is needed to determine the appropriate maturities for any investing or borrowing by the central pool. Should the Europe-wide net cash gain of $225,000 on March 7 (Exhibit 15.12) or any portion of it be put into longer maturities, or should it be put into the call money market because of cash needs anticipated during the next day or week? This point will be elaborated upon below.

EXHIBIT 15.12
European Cash Management Pool—Central Office Compilation

CASH LEDGER (CURRENT DAY)
(thousand-dollar equivalents of local curency)

Location	*End-of-day cash balance*	*Required minimum*	*Excess local cash balance*
The U.K.	+150	200	− 50
Sweden	−250	125	−375
Germany	+600	250	+350
France	+500	200	+300
Europe-wide cash gain (or loss)			+225

CASH TRANSFER INSTRUCTIONS
(thousands of U.S. dollars)

To the U.K.
( ) You send $________ to CENTRAL POOL.
( ) You send $________ to ________.
(X) You will receive $ 50 from CENTRAL POOL.
( ) You will receive $________ from ________.

To Sweden:
( ) You send $________ to CENTRAL POOL.
( ) You send $________ to ________.
(X) You will receive $ 75 from CENTRAL POOL.
(X) You will receive $ 300 from France.

To Germany:
(X) You send $ 350 to CENTRAL POOL.
( ) You send $________ to ________.
( ) You will receive $________ from CENTRAL POOL.
( ) You will receive $________ from ________.

To France:
( ) You send $________ to CENTRAL POOL.
(X) You send $ 300 to Sweden.
( ) You will receive $________ from CENTRAL POOL.
( ) You will receive $________ from ________.

Information received and tabulated in the cash ledger, top of Exhibit 15.12, is used for decisions about the instructions shown at the bottom of that exhibit. In this instance the United Kingdom is advised that it will be receiving $50,000 from the central pool. To avoid two exchange transactions, France is instructed to send $300,000 directly to Sweden, and Sweden is so advised. Sweden is also advised that an additional $75,000 will be remitted from the central pool. Germany is instructed to send its entire $350,000 to the central pool.

Note that many combinations are possible. All excesses could be sent to the pool and all deficits covered from the pool. In the above example the Swedish deficit was covered in part from the French surplus and in part from the pool. It could have been covered in part by a direct remittance from Germany, had that seemed appropriate to supplement the remittance from France. The daily cash report (Exhibit 15.11) shows that France is expected to have a $300,000 deficit the following day; French funds might instead have been left in that country overnight and the Swedish shortage covered by some other combination.

Cash Forecasting

Information from the individual country five-day forecasts is also compiled into a Europe-wide cash forecast, as shown in Exhibit 15.13. The sum of the columns shows for each day the Europe-wide cash gain or loss, and that figure will be used for planning maturities in the central money market pool, for decisions to approach the company's banks for more funds, or for decisions to repay bank loans. In this example the company will gain $425,000 over the week, but it will be short of cash on the first and fourth days.

The sum of the lines, shown on the right under "Five-day total," gives for each country its five-day cash result. This information will be used by management to decide whether or not daily excess funds should be sent to the pool or allowed to accumulate at the local level. It will also be used to decide where corporate bank borrowing should take place. Since, in the example, the United Kingdom is tending to run a consistent cash shortage, additional European borrowing might be done in London, unless interest rates in other countries are sufficiently lower than British rates to make borrowing in another currency more advantageous after calculating the cost of an exchange transaction and of covering in the forward market.

It must be emphasized that the presence of a cash surplus or cash deficit implies *nothing* about the efficiency of the division. Each operating division will have its own cyclical pattern over the week and over the month, depending on local payment customs. Cash shortages may reflect such cyclical patterns, or they may reflect investment in additional working capital or equipment needed to supply an expanding market.

EXHIBIT 15.13
European Cash Management Pool—Five-Day Cash Budget

Location	*Days from the present* +1	+2	+3	+4	+5	*Five-day total*
The U.K.	−100	+ 50	+ 50	−400	− 50	−450
Sweden	−100	− 50	+ 50	+125	zero	+ 25
Germany	+300	+250	+150	−100	+100	+700
France	−300	+200	+300	zero	− 50	+150
European cash gain by day, forecast	−200	+450	+550	−375	zero	+425

The cash management system shown in Exhibits 15.11 through 15.13 has necessarily been simplified in order to illustrate the basic relationships. A more realistic system might provide for multicurrency reporting, alternate-currency transfer instructions, and a longer cash budgeting forecast.

MANAGING RECEIVABLES

Multinational accounts receivable are created by two separate types of transactions: sales to related affiliates and sales to independent buyers having no ownership relationship with the selling firm. Because the economic consequences of an international receivable generated in a within-family transaction differ from those of a receivable generated in an independent sale, the two types must be considered separately.

Intracorporate Family Receivables

The location, currency, and amount of intracorporate receivables is a policy problem in allocation of resources on a global basis. Two techniques that are useful for this task are leads and lags and reinvoicing centers.

Leads and lags Suppose an Indian affiliate is expanding and needs to obtain equipment from a Swedish affiliate of the same firm. The traditional solution would be for the parent to transmit funds to India in return for additional equity in the Indian affiliate; these funds would then be used by the Indian affiliate to purchase the equipment from Sweden. Parent recovery in later years of a return on the funds advanced would depend on such exchange controls and rates of exchange as might exist at that time.

If the parent wishes to delay the date at which it increases its permanent equity investment in India—perhaps because of the possibility of devaluation, political upheaval, or the imposition of exchange controls—the parent might arrange for the Swedish affiliate to sell equipment to the Indian affiliate on longer-than-normal credit terms, with the parent supplying interim funds to the Swedish affiliate as necessary. Perhaps the equipment is shipped on open account with the understanding that payment need not be made for two years, even though normal sales terms from the Swedish affiliate are net 90 days. Swedish receivables and Indian payables rise, but the multinational firm as a whole is not affected. Since the Indian affiliate has an open and unpaid account payable, it is more likely that foreign exchange for payment of that debt will be available in India, even if that country finds itself in balance of payments difficulties, than it is likely that funds for dividend remittance to the parent on its equity investment will be available.

This technique may be restricted by the failure to have a formal loan agreement, especially if the sale had been from the parent rather than from an affiliate. The Indian government could consider payment of the account payable as a substantive dividend, possibly taxable in both India and Sweden.

The use of leads and lags in conjunction with intracorporate family receivables is feasible only with 100% ownership of the various affiliates, for the economic effect of extended payment terms alters the relative rate of return of the various units. This practice is unfair if each unit has minority stockholders separate from the corporate family, since they do not necessarily benefit from practices that benefit the multinational group of firms as a whole. Inequities may also arise between various profit centers in a group of wholly owned affiliates unless adjustments are made to reflect a particular center's sacrifice.

Reinvoicing centers A reinvoicing center is a separate corporate subsidiary that manages all transaction exposure from intracompany trade in one location. Manufacturing affiliates sell goods to distribution affiliates of the same firm only by selling to a reinvoicing center, which in turn resells to the distribution affiliate. Title passes to the reinvoicing center, but the physical movement of goods is direct from manufacturing plant to distribution affiliate. Thus the reinvoicing center handles paperwork but has no inventory.

Manufacturing units bill the reinvoicing center in their own currency and receive payment in their own currency. The reinvoicing center in turn bills distribution affiliates in their currency and collects that currency from them. Consequentially, all manufacturing units and all distribution affiliates deal only in their own currency, and all transaction exposure lies with the reinvoicing center.

Reinvoicing centers are often located in low-tax jurisdictions, such as Switzerland or the Netherlands Antilles. To avoid charges of profit shifting through transfer pricing, most reinvoicing centers "resell" at cost plus a small commission for their services. The resale price is frequently the manufacturer's price times the forward exchange rate for the date on which payment from the distribution affiliate is expected, although other combinations are possible. The commission covers the cost of the reinvoicing center, but does not shift profits away from operating affiliates.

The reinvoicing center should avoid doing business with suppliers or customers in the country of location so that it will be able to establish nonresident status. Although the exact definition of and benefits of nonresident status vary from country to country, in general a finance subsidiary not doing any local business may be free of some taxes, such as interest withholding taxes or capital formation taxes. Nonresident firms may have greater access to external foreign exchange markets than local operating firms; they may be freer to deal in external currency markets, including Euromarkets; and they may be allowed to own bank accounts in foreign countries when that is restricted for domestic firms. Nonresident firms are usually not restricted in either borrowing from or investing with foreign banks.

The primary advantage of a reinvoicing center is that management of all foreign exchange transaction exposure for intracompany sales is centered in one location. Reinvoicing center personnel can develop a specialized expertise in choosing which of many hedging techniques are best at any moment, and they are likely to obtain more competitive foreign exchange quotations from banks because they are dealing in larger transactions.

A second advantage is that by guaranteeing the exchange rate for future orders, the reinvoicing center can set firm local currency costs in advance. This enables distribution affiliates to make firm bids to unrelated final customers, and to protect against the exposure created by a backlog of unfilled orders. Backlog exposure does not appear on the corporate books because the sales are not yet recorded. Sales subsidiaries can focus on their marketing activities and their performance can be judged without distortion because of exchange rate changes.

A third advantage is the ability of the center to manage intra-affiliate cash flows, including leads and lags of payments, and multilateral netting. With a reinvoicing center all affiliates settle intracompany accounts in their local currencies. If cash flows are one way—that is, distribution affiliates only pay the center, which in turn only pays the manufacturing affiliate—netting is not needed. However, if affiliates manufacture and sell to each other, netting is a natural link with reinvoicing. With netting, the reinvoicing center need only hedge residual foreign exchange exposure.

The main disadvantage is one of cost relative to benefits received. One additional corporate unit must be created, and a separate set of books must be kept. The center will have an impact on the tax status and customs duties of all affiliates, as well as on the amount of foreign exchange business directed to local banks in each country. Establishment of a reinvoicing center is likely to bring increased scrutiny by tax authorities to be sure that it is not functioning as a tax haven. Consequently a variety of professional costs will be incurred for tax and legal advice, in addition to the costs of personnel operating the center.

Sales to Independent Customers

Management of accounts receivable from independent customers involves two types of decisions: In what currency should the transaction be denominated, and what should be the terms of payment? Domestic sales are almost always denominated in the local currency. At issue is whether export sales should be denominated in the currency of the exporter, the currency of the buyer, or a third-country currency. Competition or custom will often resolve the issue, but if negotiating room exists, the seller should prefer to price and to invoice in the strongest currency. Since the buyer would prefer to pay in the weakest currency, and since both parties are likely to be equally well informed about the risk involved, the usual result is a trade-off in which a price or a terms-of-payment concession is granted by the seller in order to obtain the sale in a hard currency. Alternatively, the buyer pays more or pays sooner if payment in a soft currency is desired.

Parties to the transaction are likely to deviate from this straightforward bargaining position only if they have different opinions about the relative strengths of the currencies involved or if their own financial situation is strong enough to absorb the weak currency position. For example, a seller is more willing to price and invoice in a weak currency if that seller already has debts in that currency, for the sales proceeds can be used to retire the debt without any obvious loss. From the point of view of opportunity cost, that seller nevertheless forgoes an exchange gain. The buyer may be willing to pay in a hard currency if the buyer intends to resell the merchandise in a hard currency.

The second factor is terms of payment. Considered by themselves, receivables from sales in weak currencies should be collected as soon as possible to minimize loss of exchange value between sales date and collection date. Accounts receivable resulting from sales in hard currencies may be allowed to remain outstanding longer. In fact, if the seller is expecting an imminent devaluation of its home currency, it might want to encourage slow payment of its hard currency receivables, especially if the home government requires immediate exchange of foreign currency receipts into the home currency. An alternative, if legal, would be for the seller to accept the proceeds abroad and keep them on deposit abroad rather than return them to the home country.

In some economies accounts receivable are used as a basis for short-term financing in preference to inventory financing. This situation occurs most often in inflationary economies and in economies in which the banking system is institutionally oriented toward discounting paper rather than financing merchandise.

In inflationary economies the demand for credit usually exceeds the supply. Often, however, a large business (be it multinational or a large local concern) has better access to the limited, cheaper credit that is available locally than do small domestic businesses such as local distributors, retail merchants, or smaller manufacturers. Assume, for example, that the cost of local credit to a large multinational manufacturer/seller is 30% per annum, while the cost of credit to a potential retailer/buyer in the same economy is 50% per annum. Both manufacturer and retailer will benefit by maximizing sales volume to the ultimate customer if the manufacturer finances the transactions as long as possible and adds the financing costs (at 30%) to the sales price. In other words, it is better for the seller to finance the buyer's inventory at 30% per annum in the form of long-term receivables than for the buyer to finance the inventory directly for 50% per annum.

Some banking systems, often for reasons of tradition, have a predilection toward self-liquidating, discountable bills. In many European countries it is easier to borrow from a bank on the security of bills (receivables in negotiable form) generated from sales than on the security of physical inventory. Napoleon is alleged to have had a philosophy that no good French merchant should be required to wait for funds if good merchandise has been sold to good people, provided a document exists showing sales of the items. The document must have the signature of the buyer and the endorsement of the seller and the rediscounting bank. Thus in France it is often possible to reduce net investment in receivables to zero by selling entirely on trade acceptances that can be discounted at the bank.

The European predilection for discountable bills has a very real rationale behind it. According to European commercial law, which is based on the "Code Napoléon," the claim certified by the signature of the buyer on the bill is separated from the claim based on the underlying transaction. For example, a bill is easily negotiable because objections about the quality of the merchandise by the buyer do not affect the claim of the bill holder. In addition, defaulted bills can be collected through a particularly speedy judicial process that is much faster than the collection of normal receivables. Thus there is nothing mystical about the preference of European countries for commercial bills, and retail buyers often finance their entire inventory with receivable financing from the manufacturer/seller.

In many countries government bodies facilitate inventory financing in the guise of receivable financing by extending export credit or by guaranteeing export credit from banks at advantageous interest rates. When the term of the special export financing can be extended to match the payment of the foreign purchaser, the foreign purchaser is in effect able to finance its inventory through the courtesy of the exporter's government.

In some environments credit terms extended by manufacturers to retailers are of such long maturities as to constitute "purchase" of the retailer, such "purchase" being necessary to build an operational distribution system between manufacturer and ultimate customer. In Japan, for example, customer payment terms of 120 days are fairly common, and a manufacturer's sales effort is not competitive unless sufficient financial aid is provided to retailers to make it possible or beneficial for them to buy the manufacturer's product. Financial aid is reported to take the form of "outright purchase of the retailer's capital stock, working capital loans, equipment purchase, subsidy or loan, and consideration of payment terms." Yet this is a normal way of doing business in the Japanese environment.

In summary, a multinational firm often manufactures or sells a product in a credit-short or inflationary economy, in a country where the banking system is oriented toward self-liquidating bills, or in locations where competition causes suppliers to finance their commercial customers. Longer collection periods have implications not only for the amount of financing that must be budgeted for a venture but also for the criteria by which the performance of local managers is evaluated.

INVENTORY MANAGEMENT

Operations in inflationary, devaluation-prone economies sometimes force management to modify its normal approach to inventory management. In some cases management may choose to maintain inventory and reorder levels far in excess of what would be called for in an economic order quantity model.

Under conditions where local currency devaluation is likely, management must decide whether to build up inventory of imported items in anticipation of the expected devaluation. After the devaluation imported inventory will cost more in local currency terms. One trade-off is a higher holding cost because of the bloated level of inventory and high local interest rates, which normally reflect the expected devaluation. A less obvious trade-off is the possibility that local government will enforce a price freeze following devaluation. This freeze would prevent the imported inventory from being sold for an appropriate markup above its now-higher replacement value. Still worse, the devaluation may not occur as anticipated, leaving management holding an excessive level of inventory until it can be worked down. Disposing of excessive inventory will be particularly painful if competitors have followed the same strategy of speculating on imported inventory.

Anticipating Price Freezes

To circumvent an anticipated price freeze, management can establish the local currency price of an imported item at a high level, with actual sales being made at a discount from this posted price. In the event of a devaluation sales continue at the posted prices but discounts are withdrawn. This technique circumvents the price freeze only if that freeze is expressed in terms of posted rather than effective price, and in any event it provides no protection against competitive price squeezes. An alternative is to sell at the posted price but increase selling, promotion, or other marketing mix activities, which can later be reduced.

If imported inventory is a commodity, another strategy is to purchase the commodity in the forward market. Then if local prices are frozen, the forward contract can be sold abroad for the same currency in which it is denominated. On the other hand, if local price controls are based on a fixed markup over cost, the forward contract can be exercised and the commodity imported at the now-higher local currency cost, which becomes the basis for the markup. If options on the commodity are available, the same benefit can be achieved. The certain cost of the option should be compared to the uncertain trading gain or loss on the forward contract.

Free-Trade Zones

A free-trade zone is a combination of the old idea of duty-free ports and new legislation that gives breaks on customs duties to manufacturers who structure their operations to benefit from the technique. The old duty-free ports were typically in the dock area of major seaports. Modern free-trade zones, by comparison, are often located away from a port area; for example, the Italian firm of Olivetti has such a zone in Harrisburg, Pennsylvania.

Free-trade zones increasingly are locations for assembly or manufacturing activity. Retailers use the zones to sort, label, or store imported clothing and appliances until the date of final sale, and manufacturers often complete work on partially assembled imports within the zone. When work is performed in a free-trade zone, import duties are usually assessed only on the lower import cost and not on the higher value created by work performed within the zone. Additionally, the time of payment of duties is usually delayed. An item imported into the United States in January for, say, three months of additional finishing and storage before an April sale will be charged duty in January. The same item left in a free-trade zone until April will be assessed the same amount of duty, but payment will not be made until April. Free financing of the duty charges for three months is obtained!

A free-trade zone can also be used to circumvent a price freeze because merchandise in the zone has not yet been formally imported. Often a price freeze will not apply to items not yet imported into the country. Alternatively, the importer retains an option to sell the merchandise elsewhere at world market prices without the loss of import duties and transactions costs that would have already been paid if the merchandise had been formally imported.

SUMMARY

Financial managers of multinational firms must control international liquid assets in order to maintain adequate liquidity in a variety of currencies while also minimizing political and foreign exchange risk. The first half of this chapter looked at ways that funds can be positioned in a multinational firm. The concept of unbundling remittances was described. Determinants of dividend policy were explained, and the use of royalties, fees, and home office overhead was discussed. Transfer pricing was considered in terms of possible conflicting goals of fund positioning, tax and tariff minimization, and fair treatment of managers and joint-venture partners. Techniques for moving blocked funds, such as fronting loans, leads and lags, unrelated exports, and forced reinvestment were discussed.

The second half of the chapter looked at uniquely international aspects of managing cash, accounts receivable, and inventories. Cash balances are held to provide planned disbursements and to protect the firm against unanticipated variations from budgeted cash flows in an array of currencies. Techniques of cash management include the use of centralized depositories, multilateral netting to reduce misdirected funds, multinational mobilization to ensure that funds are located where corporate interests are best served, and cash forecasting.

Accounts receivable management was discussed in terms of important differences between receivables from within the corporate family and those from independent customers. The use of reinvoicing centers was explained. Inventory management was viewed in terms of ways to protect inventory values in the face of adverse exchange rate changes and anticipated price freezes.

NOTES

1. Sidney M. Robbins and Robert B. Stobaugh, *Money in the Multinational Enterprise,* New York: Basic Books, 1973, p. 85.

2. *Ibid.,* p. 77.

3. The seven points listed are based in part on M. C. Holmes, "Check List for Foreign Licensing," *Business Lawyer,* November 1968, pp. 281–289. This article also includes suggestions on nonfinancial aspects of foreign licensing agreements.

4. James Green and Michael G. Duerr, *Intercompany Transactions in the Multinational Firm,* New York: The Conference Board, 1970, pp. 37–46.

5. "Transfer Pricing and Multinational Enterprises," Report of the Organization for Economic Cooperation and Development Committee on Fiscal Affairs, Paris: OECD, 1979.

6. Jane O. Burns, "Transfer Pricing Decisions in U.S. Multinational Corporations," *Journal of International Business Studies,* Fall 1980, pp. 23–39.

7. *Ibid.,* p. 26.

8. Jeffrey S. Arpan, "International Intracorporate Pricing: Non-American Systems and Views," *Journal of International Business Studies,* Spring 1972, p. 9.

9. These terms were derived from Karl Wünderlisch, "Centralized Cash Management Systems for the Multinational Enterprise," *Management International Review,* June 1973, p. 43.

10. Business International, *New Techniques in International Exposure and Cash Management, Volume 1: The State of the Art,* New York: Business International Corporation, 1977, p. 237.

11. Business International, *Solving International Financial and Currency Problems,* New York: Business International Corporation, 1976, p. 27.

BIBLIOGRAPHY

Arpan, Jeffrey S., *International Intracorporate Pricing,* New York: Praeger, 1972.

———, "International Intracorporate Pricing: Non-American Systems and Views," *Journal of International Business Studies,* Spring 1972, pp. 1–18.

Barrett, M. Edgar, "Case of the Tangled Transfer Price," *Harvard Business Review,* May/June 1977, pp. 20–36, 176–178.

Bergendahl, Goran, "Multi-Currency Netting in a Multi-National Firm," in Goran Bergendahl, ed., *International Financial Management,* Stockholm: Norstedts, 1982, pp. 149–173.

Bokos, William J., and Anne P. Clinkard, "Multilateral Netting," *Journal of Cash Management,* June/July 1983, pp. 24–34.

Booth, E. J. R., and O. W. Jensen, "Transfer Prices in Global Corporations under Internal and External Constraints," *Canadian Journal of Economics,* No. 10, 1977, pp. 434–446.

Burns, Jane O., "How IRS Applies the Intercompany Pricing Rules of Section 482: A Corporate Survey," *Journal of Taxation,* May 1980, pp. 308–314.

———, "Transfer Pricing Decisions in U.S. Multinational Corporations," *Journal of International Business Studies,* Fall 1980, pp. 23–39.

Burns, Jane O., and Ronald S. Ross, "Establishing International Transfer Pricing Standards for Tax Audits of Multinational Enterprises," *The International Journal of Accounting,* Fall 1981, pp. 161–179.

———, "Understanding the Effects of Section 482 on Intercompany Pricing," *U.S. Taxation of International Operations Service,* Englewood Cliffs, N.J.: Prentice-Hall, 1981.

Business International, *New Techniques in International Exposure and Cash Management, Volume 1: The State of the Art,* New York: Business International Corporation, 1977.

Cohen, Fred L., "Accelerating Foreign Remittances and Collection," *Cashflow,* May 1981, pp. 36–40.

Edmunds, J. C., "Working Capital Management in Multinational Companies," *Management International Review,* 1983/4.

Fielcke, Norman S., "Foreign Currency Positioning by U.S. Firms: Some New Evidence," *Review of Economics and Statistics,* February 1981, pp. 35–42.

Fowler, D. J., "Transfer Prices and Profit Maximization in Multinational Enterprise Operations," *Journal of International Business Studies,* Winter 1978, pp. 9–26.

———, "Comment on 'Transfer Prices and Profit Maximization in Multinational Enterprise Operations': Reply," *Journal of International Business Studies,* Spring/Summer 1982, pp. 121–124.

Gentry, James A., Dileep R. Mehta, S. K. Bhattacharya, Robert Cobbaut, and Jean-Louis Scaringella, "An International Study of Management Perceptions of the Working Capital Process," *Journal of International Business Studies,* Spring–Summer 1979, pp. 28–38.

Goeltz, Richard K., "Managing Liquid Funds Internationally," *Columbia Journal of World Business,* July–August 1972, pp. 59–65.

Granick, David, "National Differences in the Use of Internal Transfer Prices," *California Management Review,* Summer 1975, pp. 28–40.

Greene, James, and Michael G. Duerr, *Intercompany Transactions in the Multinational Firm,* New York: The Conference Board, 1970.

Greenhill, C. R., and E. O. Herbolzheimer, "International Transfer Pricing: The Restrictive Business Practices Approach," *Journal of World Trade Law,* May–June 1980, pp. 232–241.

Griffiths, Susan H., "Strategies to Upgrade Cash Management at Overseas Subsidiaries," *Cashflow,* March 1983, pp. 41–43.

Griffiths, Susan H., and Nigel J. Robertson, "Global Cash: International Cash Management Project Planning," *Journal of Cash Management,* May/June 1984, pp. 50–53.

Hollis, Martha, "A Multi-Currency Model for Short-Term Money Management," *Management International Review,* 1979/2, pp. 23–30.

Johnson, T. O., "International Cash Management: Slaying the Paper Tiger," *Banker,* October 1982, pp. 53–59.

Keegan, Warren J., "Multinational Pricing: How Far Is Arm's Length?" *Columbia Journal of World Business,* May–June 1969, pp. 57–66.

Kim, Seung H., and Stephen W. Miller, "Constituents of the International Transfer Pricing Decision," *Columbia Journal of World Business,* Spring 1979, pp. 69–77.

Kopits, George F., "Intra-Firm Royalties Crossing Frontiers and Transfer-Pricing Behaviour," *Economic Journal,* December 1976, pp. 791–805.

Kuhlmann, A. R., "Computers: The Answer for Global Cash Management," *Cashflow,* November–December 1980, pp. 48–50.

Lall, Sanjaya, "Transfer-Pricing by Multinational Manufacturing Firms," *Oxford Bulletin of Economics and Statistics,* August 1973, pp. 173–195.

Leff, Nathanial H., "Multinational Corporate Pricing Strategy in the Developing Countries," *Journal of International Business Studies,* Fall 1975, pp. 55–64.

Madura, Jeff, and E. Joe Nosari, "Global Money Management: One Approach," *Financial Executive,* June 1984, pp. 42–46.

Mees, Philip, "How the Computer Helps Handle the Cash," *Euromoney,* May 1981, pp. 143–148.

Merville, Larry J., and J. William Petty II, "Transfer Pricing for the Multinational Firms," *Accounting Review,* October 1978, pp. 935–951.

Ness, Walter L., Jr., "U.S. Corporate Income Taxation and the Dividend Remittance Policy of Multinational Corporations," *Journal of International Business Studies,* Spring 1975, pp. 67–77.

Nieckels, Lars, *Transfer Pricing in Multinational Firms,* Stockholm: Alquist and Wicksell, 1976.

Obersteiner, Erich, "Should the Foreign Affiliate Remit Dividends or Reinvest?" *Financial Management,* Spring 1973, pp. 88–93.

Parkinson, Kenneth L., "Dealing with the Problems of International Cash Management," *Journal of Cash Management,* February/March 1983, pp. 16–25.

Petty, J. William, II, and Ernest W. Walker, "Optimal Transfer Pricing for the Multinational Firm," *Financial Management,* Winter 1972, pp. 74–87.

Preston, Samuel, "New York CHIPS Goes over to Same-Day Settlement," *Euromoney,* March 1981, pp. 131–132.

Pugel, Thomas, and Judith L. Ugelow, "Transfer Pricing and Profit Maximization in Multinational Enterprise Operations," *Journal of International Business Studies,* Spring/Summer 1982, pp. 115–119.

Regensburg, H. Drumm, "Transfer Pricing in the International Firm," *Management International Review,* 1983/2.

Reinig, Thomas B., "How CBS Developed Its Own Foreign Cash Management Expertise," *Cashflow,* March 1983, pp. 44–45.

Rutenberg, David P., "Maneuvering Liquid Assets in a Multinational Company: Formulation and Deterministic Solution Procedures," *Management Science,* June 1970, pp. B-671–684.

Shapiro, Alan C., "Optimal Inventory and Credit-Granting Strategies under Inflation and Devaluation," *Journal of Financial and Quantitative Analysis,* January 1973, pp. 37–46.

———, "International Cash Management—The Determination of Multicurrency Cash Balances," *Journal of Financial and Quantitative Analysis,* December 1976, pp. 893–900.

———, "Payments Netting in International Cash Management," *Journal of International Business Studies,* Fall 1978, pp. 51–58.

Shoch, James R., III, "Management of U.S. Cash Flows for a Foreign-Based Multinational," *Journal of Cash Management,* May/June 1984, pp. 40–44.

Shulman, James, "When the Price Is Wrong by Design," *Columbia Journal of World Business,* May–June 1967, pp. 69–76.

Stone, Bernell K., "International versus Domestic Cash Management: The Sophistication Lag Fallacy," *Journal of Cash Management,* June/July 1983, pp. 6, 58.

Summa, Donald, "Remittances by U.S. Owned Foreign Corporations: Tax Considerations," *Columbia Journal of World Business,* Summer 1975, pp. 40–45.

Transfer Pricing and Multinational Enterprises, Report of the OECD Committee on Fiscal Affairs, Paris: Organization for Economic Co-Operation and Development, 1979.

Turner, Gale N., "The International Cash Management Environment," *Cashflow,* June 1981, pp. 30–31.

UNCTAD (United Nations Commission on Trade and Development), *Dominant Positions of Market Power of Transnational Corporations: Use of the Transfer Pricing Mechanisms,* Geneva: UNCTAD/ST/MD/6, 1977.

Wünderlisch, Karl, "Centralized Cash Management Systems for the Multinational Enterprise," *Management International Review,* June 1973, pp. 43–57.

Yunker, Penelope J., "A Survey of Subsidiary Autonomy, Performance Evaluation and Transfer Pricing in Multinational Corporations," *Columbia Journal of World Business,* Fall 1983, pp. 51–64.

Zenoff, David B., "Profitable, Fast-Growing, but Still the Stepchild," *Columbia Journal of World Business,* July–August 1967, pp. 51–56.

———, "Remitting Funds from Foreign Affiliates," *Financial Executive,* March 1968, pp. 46–63.

16

Performance Evaluation and Control

Three separate reporting systems are usually required in a multinational firm:

1. reporting for consolidated financial statements,
2. reporting for local statutory and tax reasons,
3. reporting for management decision making.

The third of these reporting systems relates to performance evaluation and control. A multinational firm must be able to relate actual results to predetermined and acceptable goals. It must be able to measure the performance of each of its affiliates on a consistent basis, and managers of affiliates must be given unambiguous objectives against which they will be judged. The criteria for internal measurement should be designed for that purpose, and not particularly be the by-product of reports prepared for financial accounting or for local statutory and tax purposes.

This chapter discusses complexities of international performance evaluation, commonly used criteria, how exchange rate changes can be treated within a budget control system, and how companies organize for international financial management.

COMPLEXITIES OF INTERNATIONAL PERFORMANCE EVALUATION

Financial evaluation of foreign affiliates is both unique and difficult. Evaluation by one foreign exchange translation method will present a different measure of success or of compliance with predetermined goals from that by some other method. Even though an internal system need not comply with such reporting rules as FAS #52 or FAS #8, evidence suggests that most firms start with the translation system used for financial reporting.

The results of any control system must also be judged against distortions of performance caused by widely differing national business environments. As we discussed in Chapter 8 on foreign investment decisions, many direct foreign investments are made to defend a firm's competitive position in oligopolistic markets. One should not evaluate such investments as if they were independent when, in fact, the motive is strategic interaction with the rest of the worldwide system. Benefits to the worldwide system can include such gains as profits to the parent or related affiliates from additional exports, royalties and management fees, advantages from participating in technological developments, preempting markets, enlarging economies of scale, and denying such benefits to competing firms.

Costs often not attributed to affiliates in a formal measurement system include implied costs to the parent of guaranteeing affiliate loans, or holding safety inventory in the home country to serve foreign affiliates.

Additional factors that distort an international measurement system arise because of decisions to benefit the world system at the expense of a specific local affiliate. For example, an affiliate in a low-interest country may finance another affiliate in a high-interest country. Although the system benefits, the first affiliate will have excess interest charges and the second will save on interest. Positioning of funds sometimes requires artificial transfer prices between related affiliates for tax, foreign exchange, or liquidity reasons. Management must devise a fair and consistent method of adjusting the basic reports to reflect the "self-sacrifice" of one affiliate for another.

Additional variables that may invalidate comparisons of reports from affiliates in separate countries include the following: nationally imposed barriers on fund remittances, differential rates of inflation, requirements for certain levels of legal reserves financed via earnings retention, customs that call for profit sharing with workers, differing standards between countries over primary corporate goals, and variations in the work ethic and/or labor productivity. By and large, these variables are not significant in differentiating among domestic affiliates, but a company that seeks to extend a domestic control system abroad must ponder the significance of the financial data obtained.

Thus control standards must take into account foreign exchange risk and the fact that traditional measures of performance may not be appropriate to reflect a foreign affiliate's contribution to the total firm.

PURPOSES OF MULTINATIONAL CONTROL SYSTEMS

In a survey of 125 multinational firms, William Persen and Van Lessig found that almost all firms expand and modify their domestic profitability measures when applying them to foreign affiliates.[1] In addition, some firms establish foreign affiliates for objectives not related to normal corporate profit-oriented goals. Such exceptions include ensuring sources of supply, maintaining a presence in a given market, and conforming with government regulations. Although these goals perhaps have some very long-run focus on profits, performance measurement in the short run is not meaningful.

Respondents identified four important purposes of an internal evaluation system.[2] In order of importance they are as follows:

1. *To ensure adequate profitability.* By choosing this criterion as the most important, respondents indicated that all other purposes are secondary to the basic corporate goal of profitability.
2. *To have an early warning system if something is wrong.* Although intuitively appealing, this goal is difficult to implement in practice because failure to meet targeted results may be due to valid and nonrecurring problems unique to international operations or to the fact that the original target was unrealistic.
3. *To have a basis for allocation of resources.* This goal arose primarily in the context of requests from foreign affiliates for new funds that total more than the parent has available. A fair and equitable means of rationing limited resources while serving overall corporate goals is needed.
4. *To evaluate individual managers.* Respondents indicated that managers are often evaluated by criteria in addition to profit contribution, such as their success in developing organizations or in expanding product lines.

CRITERIA FOR PERFORMANCE EVALUATION

Multinational firms almost invariably use more than one criterion when evaluating the results of their foreign affiliates. In addition, somewhat different criteria are used to evaluate affiliates than are used to evaluate the managers of those affiliates. The reason for multiple criteria springs from complications that are uniquely foreign: changing currency values, changing financial reporting rules (FAS #52 vs. FAS #8), different nominal and real interest rates, and organizational uncertainty about what these differences mean or who should be responsible for them. Two recent surveys have addressed the issue of performance evaluation of foreign affiliates.

Choi and Czechowicz Survey

In a research study conducted for Business International, Choi and Czechowicz found that multiple criteria are used to evaluate foreign performance.[3] Financial criteria dominate performance evaluation systems. Budget compared to actual is the single most important criterion both for 64 U.S. multinational firms and for 24 non-U.S. multinational firms. Return on investment is second in importance. Choi and Czechowicz's rankings of financial criteria are shown in Exhibit 16.1.

Performance of the affiliate as a unit and performance of the manager tended to be judged by similar criteria. Of interest in the survey is that U.S. multinationals rate cash flow to the parent as more important than cash flow to the affiliate, whereas non-U.S. multinationals reverse the order of ranking.

Choi and Czechowicz found strong evidence for the importance of nonfinancial criteria in the evaluation process. As shown in Exhibit 16.2, increasing share of the market is the single most important nonfinancial

EXHIBIT 16.1
Financial Criteria Used to Evaluate Performance of Overseas Unit and Subsidiary Manager

	US MNCs N = 64 AVG.[a]		*NON-US MNCs N = 24 AVG.*[a]		*TOTAL RESPONSES N = 88 AVG.*[a]	
Items	*Unit*	*Manager*	*Unit*	*Manager*	*Unit*	*Manager*
Return on investment	1.8	2.2	2.1	2.2	1.9	2.2
Return on equity	3.0	3.0	2.9	3.0	3.0	3.0
Return on assets	2.3	2.3	2.2	2.4	2.3	2.3
Return on sales	2.2	2.1	1.9	2.1	2.1	2.1
Contribution to earnings per share	2.8	3.2	3.5	3.4	3.0	3.2
Operating cash flow to subsidiary	2.5	2.7	2.2	2.5	2.4	2.7
Operating cash flow to parent	2.3	2.8	2.5	2.6	2.3	2.7
Residual income	3.4	3.3	3.4	3.2	3.4	3.3
Budget compared to actual sale	2.0	1.6	1.9	1.8	1.9	1.7
Budget compared to actual profit	1.5	1.4	1.4	1.3	1.5	1.3
Budget compared to actual return on investment	2.3	2.4	2.4	2.5	2.3	2.4
Budget compared to actual return on assets	2.6	2.7	2.7	2.2	2.7	2.5
Budget compared to actual return on equity	3.1	2.9	3.2	3.1	3.1	3.0

Source: F. D. S. Choi and I. J. Czechowicz, "Assessing Foreign Subsidiary Performance: A Multinational Comparison," *Management International Review,* 4-83, p. 16.

[a]1 = most important; 2 = important; 3 = less important; 4 = not used.

criterion for U.S. multinationals. Non-U.S. multinationals rank productivity improvement equal in importance to increasing market share.

Persen and Lessig Survey

The aforementioned Persen and Lessig survey ranked criteria for performance evaluation.[4] They also found that actual performance as compared to budget was the most important criterion. The remainder of their rankings differed, however, from Choi and Czechowicz. In descending order of importance, their ten most important criteria were:

1. *Operating budget comparisons.* This criterion was by far the most prevalent technique, although respondents conceded that interpretation of variances was difficult. Comparisons with budget were used to prevent surprises and to assess the degree to which targets were achieved.

EXHIBIT 16.2
Nonfinancial Criteria Used to Evaluate Performance of Overseas Unit and Subsidiary Manager

	US MNCs N = 64 AVG.[a]		*NON-US MNCs N = 24 AVG.*[a]		*TOTAL RESPONSES N = 88 AVG.*[a]	
Items	*Unit*	*Manager*	*Unit*	*Manager*	*Unit*	*Manager*
Increasing market share	1.8	1.5	1.7	1.6	1.8	1.5
Quality control	2.2	1.9	2.4	2.0	2.3	1.9
Cooperation with parent company and other affiliates	2.4	2.0	2.5	2.1	2.4	2.0
Relationship with host country government	2.1	1.8	2.4	1.9	2.1	1.9
Environment compliance	2.4	2.3	2.5	2.4	2.4	2.3
Employee development	2.4	2.0	2.4	2.2	2.4	2.0
Labor turnover	2.7	2.5	2.8	2.7	2.8	2.6
Research and development in foreign unit	3.1	3.2	2.8	2.7	3.0	3.1
Productivity improvement	2.2	2.1	1.7	1.6	2.0	2.0
Employee safety	2.4	2.2	2.2	2.3	2.4	2.2
Community service	2.9	2.8	2.8	2.5	2.9	2.7

Source: F. D. S. Choi and I. J. Czechowicz, "Assessing Foreign Subsidiary Performance: A Multinational Comparison," *Management International Review,* 4-83, p. 17.

[a]1 = very important; 2 = important; 3 = less important; 4 = not important.

2. *Contribution to earnings per share.* Some evidence was collected that this criterion was stressed more by large firms than smaller ones.
3. *Return on investment.* Survey results indicated some tendency for this criterion to be used more by large firms than smaller ones.
4. *Contribution to corporate cash flow.* Persen and Lessig note that the fairly high rating for this criterion is offset to some degree by the fact that most firms have not established standards to measure cash flow contributions. In part this lack of standards arises because of measurement difficulties introduced by centralized treasury control of cash.
5. *Return on sales.* This ratio is one component of the DuPont measuring system to be discussed below.
6. *Return on assets.* Conceptually this ratio is closely related to return on investment, the third most prevalent response.
7. *Asset/liability management.*
8. *Nonaccounting data.* Primary nonaccounting criteria are market share, quality control, and labor turnover.
9. *Long-term plan comparisons.* Since the first year of any long-term plan is the same as the current year's operating plan, this criterion is a longer-term extension of comparison to budget.
10. *Return on investment—inflation adjusted.* Persen and Lessig note that few firms actually have an inflation-adjusted procedure incorporated into their rate of return calculations, but many feel that they must move in this direction.

The list of ten most prevalent criteria did not include discounted cash flow or internal rate of return analysis, which appeared to be most relevant for the evaluation of new investments rather than ongoing business operations. Thus the study did not analyze the degree to which firms monitor their realized performance relative to their projections in the original capital budgeting analysis. This activity would seem to be a useful one, since it helps firms to learn by experience what kinds of forecasting biases are held by individual project analysts, managers, or other persons providing data for investment studies.

Performance Relative to a Budget

Not only is performance relative to a budget the most important criterion advanced in both surveys for measuring affiliate performance, but it is also implicit in the four major objectives of foreign affiliate evaluation discussed earlier. Budget analysis involves comparing actual sales revenue and operating expenses at the end of a time period with an earlier budget in which both sales and expenses were forecast. The essence of such a system is that any difference between actual and budget be explained in terms of price and/or volume variances. Variances are traced to the person or unit responsible. Variances are also part of the accumulated experience used to make a better budget in the ensuing time period.

The underlying principle of such a budget and variance analysis system is that operating management have control over those variables affecting the performance on which they are measured, and that they *not* be judged over variations in performance that they cannot influence.

THE IMPACT OF EXCHANGE RATE CHANGES ON PERFORMANCE EVALUATION

Foreign exchange rates enter a multinational control system at two points: in the drafting of an initial operating budget for a foreign affiliate at the beginning of a time period, and in the measurement or tracking of realized performance at the end of that time period.

Any foreign affiliate may have its operating budget developed in local currency units. However, control over a multinational network necessitates intercountry comparisons, which in turn means that the basic operating budget must also be expressed in parent currency terms. Hence a change in exchange rates will cause a variance between budget and performance. Such a variance is a price variance; however, it differs in implications from other price variances caused by unanticipated deviations in sales prices or factor costs. Design of the control system will determine where, within the corporate structure, responsibility for variances caused by exchange rate changes will lie.

Lessard-Lorange Model

A detailed explanation of the impact of exchange rates on a control system has been developed by Donald Lessard and Peter Lorange.[5] They point out that three possible rates might be used in either the budget process or the tracking process. Hence nine combinations are theoretically possible. Of these nine, five are reasonable while four are inherently illogical. The full range of combinations is shown in Exhibit 16.3.

At the time the actual budget is created (i.e., before the period of operations) two exchange rates can be used: (1) the spot rate at that time (the "initial" rate), or (2) a rate that is forecast to be in effect at the end of the budget period. This rate might well be the forward exchange rate since the forward rate may be the best unbiased predictor of future spot rates. A third possibility is to have a budget that is continually updated as exchange rates change. At the beginning of the time period this budget would be identical to a budget based on an initial rate; however, it would be revised with the passage of time, so that an end-of-period rate would be used in

EXHIBIT 16.3
Possible Combinations of Exchange Rates in the Control Process

Rate used for determining budget	*Rate used to track performance relative to budget:* Initial	Projected	Ending
Initial	A–1 Budget on initial Track on initial	A–2 Budget on initial Track on projected	A–3 Budget on initial Track on ending
Projected	P–1 Budget on projected Track on initial	P–2 Budget on projected Track on projected	P–3 Budget on projected Track on ending
Ending	E–1 Budget on ending Track on initial	E–2 Budget on ending Track on projected	E–3 Budget on ending Track on ending

Source: Donald R. Lessard and Peter Lorange, "Currency Changes and Management Control: Resolving the Centralization/Decentralization Dilemma," *Accounting Review,* July 1977, p. 630.

the last iteration. For tracking purposes performance may be measured at the end of the period by any of the same three rates.

Of the nine combinations shown in Exhibit 16.3, four appear illogical on their face and so have been shaded out. Combinations P–1, E–1, and E–2 involve exchange rate forecasts or updating of the budget based on exchange rates but ignore these data in the tracking step. Combination A–2 involves tracking at a rate projected at the time the budget is prepared but does not use this rate in preparation of the budget. The remaining five combinations are reasonable alternatives that involve variations in assigning the responsibility for minimizing exchange rate risk.

The three variations on the diagonal, A–1, P–2, and E–3, track at the same rate as used in the budget. Under these three combinations the operating manager has no responsibility for variations caused by changes in exchange rates. In the remaining two combinations, A–3 and P–3, some degree of exchange rate responsibility is given to the operating manager. The differences between these five combinations will be explained with a hypothetical example.

Assume that a foreign affiliate may invest in a project that will generate local currency (LC) incomes as follows:

Sales	LC100,000
Cost of sales	75,000
Operating expenses	10,000
Operating income	LC 15,000

For simplicity, assume no income taxes. Assume further that the contemplated venture necessitates a net investment in exposed assets of LC50,000; that the initial exchange rate at the time the budget is drawn is LC20 = $1; that there is an equal likelihood that the end-of-period exchange rate will be either LC20 = $1 or LC30 = $1; and that as a consequence the projected future exchange rate is the weighted average, or LC25 = $1. Lastly, assume that any change in the exchange rate will not have an effect on the local currency operating results.

From the format of Exhibit 16.3 the reasonable combinations of budget and performance measurement are as shown in Exhibit 16.4. Under the diagonal combinations of A–1, P–2, and E–3, budget and performance will be the same. Variance will be zero. As we indicated earlier, measurements of performance in these three combinations are free of any influence of exchange rate changes. The operating manager is not responsible for adjusting operations to incorporate beliefs about future exchange rates. The manager may still be charged with forwarding opinions and information to the corporate treasurer's office that will be useful in forecasting future exchange rates, but this responsibility is an advisory rather than an operating one.

Budget at initial; track at initial (A–1) If budget and tracking are at the initial rate (combination A–1), the project appears profitable both before and after the fact. The assumption in this instance is that exchange rates will not change, or perhaps that any attempt to predict future rates is useless. In either instance opinions about future exchange rates do not enter either budget or tracking process.

Budget at projected; track at projected (P–2) In combination P–2 a projection of future exchange rates is required. Budgeted profits are $100, rather than the $750 in combination A–1. The desirability of the project is influenced by the corporate treasurer's forecast of future exchange rates, and responsibility for judging the impact of exchange rate changes is placed on the corporate treasurer. The operating manager is free of such responsibility, and a change in exchange rates does not create a variance.

Budget at ending; track at ending (E–3) Combination E–3 involves revising the budget during the operating period as exchange rates change. Thus performance at the end of the time period will be measured in terms of the actual ending rate, and the budget will have been revised to incorporate that actual ending rate. In the example in Exhibit 16.4 this rate might be the possible ending rate of LC30 = $1 (shown in the exhibit), or it might be the equally possible ending rate of LC20 = $1. The latter combination is not shown, since in either instance variance of performance relative to budget will be zero. In combination E–3 the operating manager has no

EXHIBIT 16.4
Performance versus Budget under Alternate Control Systems (amounts in dollars)

	A–1				*A–3*		
	Budget at initial (LC20=$1)	*Track at initial (LC20=$1)*			*Budget at initial (LC20=$1)*	*Track at ending rate (50% chance LC20=$1)*	*(50% chance LC30=$1)*
Sales	5,000	5,000			5,000	5,000	3,333
Cost of sales	3,750	3,750			3,750	3,750	2,500
Operating expense	500	500			500	500	333
Loss on exposed assets[a]	0	0			0	0	833
Operating income (loss)	750	750			750	750	(333)
Variance from budget		0				0	−1,083

			P–2		*P–3*		
			Budget at projected (LC25=$1)	*Track at projected (LC25=$1)*	*Budget at projected (LC25=$1)*	*Track at ending rate (50% chance LC20=$1)*	*(50% chance LC30=$1)*
Sales			4,000	4,000	4,000	5,000	3,333
Cost of sales			3,000	3,000	3,000	3,750	2,500
Operating expense			400	400	400	500	333
Loss on exposed assets[a]			500	500	500	0	833
Operating income (loss)			100	100	100	750	(333)
Variance from budget				0		650	−433

			E–3		
			Budget at ending (LC30 = $1)	Track at ending (LC30 = $1)	See footnote b
Sales			3,333	3,333	
Cost of sales			2,500	2,500	
Operating expenses			333	333	
Loss on exposed assets[a]			833	833	
Operating income (loss)			(333)	(333)	
Variance from budget				0	

[a]Loss on exposed assets: beginning exposed assets = LC50,000 ÷ 20 = $2,500. If ending rate is LC25 = $1, ending exposed assets = LC50,000 ÷ 25 = $2,000; loss = $500. If ending rate is LC30 = $1, ending exposed assets = LC50,000 ÷ 30 = $1,667; loss = $833.

[b]Re combination E–3: if the ending rate were LC20 = $1, both budget and tracking would reflect this fact, with an ending variance of zero.

direct concern with changes in the exchange rate; and because the budget in E–3 is revised with the passage of time, it does not require a forecast at the time of preparation. Although the ending budget shows a 50% chance of loss of $333, derived in large part from a translation loss on exposed assets of $833, this information was not available and did not enter into plans at the beginning of the budget period.

Budget at initial; track at ending (A–3) The remaining two combinations, A–3 and P–3, place some degree of responsibility for foreign exchange risk on the operating manager. In combination A–3 performance is tracked at the ending rate and compared with a budget prepared at the initial rate. In the example used in the illustration, ending exchange rates have an equal probability of remaining at LC20 = $1 or of changing to LC30 = $1. If they remain the same, budgeted profit will remain the same ($750) and variance will be zero. However, if the local currency drops in value to LC30 = $1, a loss of $333 will result, with a variance from budget of minus $1083. Combination A–3 throws full responsibility for exchange rate risk on the operating manager, who may or may not have the ability to forecast future rates and the ability to adjust operations to achieve desired protection. Furthermore, such foreign exchange protection that is acquired is not coordinated with exchange protection decisions in the parent or other affiliates. At the extreme, one might imagine an operating manager in France buying pounds forward at the same time that the operating manager in the United Kingdom is buying francs forward. As each minimizes risk for the local affiliate, the firm as a whole pays for two transactions that net each other out and provide no additional corporatewide protection!

Budget at projected; track at ending (P–3) Combination P–3 judges the operating manager against a budget based on projected exchange rates. Variations in performance that result because actual exchange rates differ from projected rates are the responsibility of the operating manager. In Exhibit 16.4 operating income was either significantly above or below budget. A risk-averse operating manager might well make decisions to protect against this type of risk. Combination P–3 is perhaps useful if operating plans can be changed during the operating cycle in response to exchange rate shifts; in fact, it is designed to encourage such a response by the operating manager. However, if operating plans cannot be changed, minimization of the variance caused by actual rates deviating from projected may in fact be either difficult or expensive. Combination P–3 makes the manager responsible for "errors" in the original projection of future exchange rates, since an "error" in the original projection will influence the ending variance. Yet the manager is not responsible for the original projection against which results are judged.

Comparisons Of the various combinations, Lessard and Lorange support combination P–2, in which projected exchange rates are incorporated into both the budget and the tracking process. By using what they term "internal forward rates," Lessard and Lorange show that two major criteria for good management control systems are satisfied. Goal congruence exists because a corporatewide point of view will prevail in making decisions in which exchange rate changes might have an impact. Furthermore, operating managers are treated fairly in that they receive neither blame nor credit for variations in performance caused by exchange rate changes that are anticipated, since forward rates may be the best predictors of probable future spot rates.

In using the term "internal forward rates" to characterize combination P–2, Lessard and Lorange note that the corporate treasurer is acting in a manner analogous to an internal banker by "buying forward" receipts in foreign currencies at a guaranteed rate. The operating unit is "guaranteed" that its profits will be measured at the internal forward rate. In the meantime any actual forward protection can be coordinated on a companywide basis. Lessard and Lorange note that the use of internal forward rates necessitates exchange rate forecasting, a difficult task at best and one that may be fruitless in the light of evidence that some exchange markets are efficient and exchange rate changes random. Nevertheless, they observe that if future exchange rates are in fact random and unpredictable, even more importance attaches to the need to shield the operating manager from being judged by changes in operating performance caused by such variation.

Hyperinflation and Economic Exposure

The Lessard-Lorange model has recently been extended to incorporate distortions in performance evaluation caused by hyperinflation and economic exposure. Laurent Jacque and Peter Lorange have shown that use of the Lessard-Lorange model recommendations to evaluate affiliates located in countries experiencing hyperinflation and rapid exchange rate devaluation can yield distorted results.[6] Deviations from purchasing power parity can be expected under conditions of hyperinflation because countries vary in how they respond. Some countries prevent their exchange rate from adjusting freely, with a consequent currency overvaluation, while other countries allow free adjustment of their exchange rate. Jacque and Lorange suggest that management "environmentalize" their performance evaluation systems to take into account these different national reactions. Variances in an affiliate's operating results due to economic exposure, which is of course beyond their control, should be removed. A variance smoothing model is proposed as a means to accomplish this task.

Lessard and Sharp have also recognized the need to deal with realized variances in the operating budget of an affiliate caused by economic exposure.[7] Their analysis is valid for countries with or without hyperinflation, as long as they are experiencing exchange rate deviations from purchasing power parity. They suggest adjusting the budget performance standard based on realized exchange rates and a predetermined agreement on how operating performance is likely to be affected by changes in real effective exchange rates.

Exchange Rates in Performance Evaluation—Practice

Because the dominant method of performance evaluation is the degree of adherence to budgets, actual practice in relationship to the model set up by Lessard and Lorange is important. A survey by Business International found that 66% of the sample firms budgeted at projected and tracked at ending. This is combination P–3 in the Lessard-Lorange model. It makes the local manager responsible for deviations from the projected rate. Survey results are shown in Exhibit 16.5.

Opinions differ as to whether local affiliates should or should not be held responsible for variance caused by exchange rate changes, or whether the responsibility should somehow be a joint responsibility. Those who believe local management should not be held responsible argue that local managers have no control over exchange rate changes, or that over the longer run exchange rate fluctuations will offset each other and that real performance in the local market will, over time, produce adequate dollar results. Another reason advanced is that local managers lack ability or time to make sophisticated exchange rate forecasts.[8]

EXHIBIT 16.5
Percentage of Respondents Using Different Combinations of Exchange Rates in the Control Process

	RATE USED TO TRACK PERFORMANCE RELATIVE TO BUDGET		
Rate used for determining budget	*Initial*	*Projected*	*Ending*
Initial	2%	None	13%
Projected	None	11%	66%
Ending	None	None	2%

Source: Jean-Pierre Sapy-Mazella, Robert M. Woo, and James Czechowicz, *New Directions in Managing Currency Risk: Changing Corporate Strategies and Systems under FAS No. 52,* New York: Business International Corporation, 1982, p. 195.

Those who argue that the local manager should have full or partial responsibility for exchange rate–induced variance believe that this policy is essential to keep affiliate management aware of the need to think about possible exchange rate changes and that ultimately home currency profitability is the firm's goal. These firms usually expect the local manager to undertake whatever action seems appropriate to minimize exchange rate losses. Nevertheless, many of these firms treat exchange rate variance as a separate item in a variance report and remain very flexible about how much responsibility after the fact is charged to the local manager.

MAXIMIZING RETURN ON INVESTMENT

The third criterion for evaluating foreign affiliate performance that was identified earlier is return on investment, which is conceptually similar to the sixth criterion, return on assets, and is associated with the fifth criterion, return on sales. These criteria all evolve from a system developed by E. I. DuPont de Nemours and Company. The essence of this measure is illustrated in the right half of Exhibit 16.6, in which the goal of maximizing return on investment is shown to be the maximization of the product of profit margin and turnover. Operationally, a business unit is performing better if earnings can be maximized relative to sales, as well as if sales can be maximized relative to total assets.

Relevant adjustments to this concept to give it multinational validity involve deciding where and how foreign exchange management and other system-optimizing decisions should be made. The three key variables in the DuPont system are sales, earnings, and underlying investment. Sales for the foreign affiliate of a multinational company may differ from what that affiliate would sell if it were independent. For reasons of strategy or economies of scale, particular products might be either assigned or denied to the product line of any particular affiliate; export sales might be invoiced in any of a number of currencies in order to minimize exchange risk or position funds; and credit terms to customers might be dictated by firm decisions to lead or lag the flow of funds between countries. Lastly, sales to related affiliates may be influenced by transfer price decisions intended to benefit the system worldwide as well as by lead- or lag-induced changes in credit terms.

The relevant level of earnings is determined by subtracting various expenses from sales revenue. Perhaps the major international variation is whether foreign exchange losses will be subtracted from (or foreign exchange gains added to) the earnings otherwise calculated. If earnings are measured before subtracting foreign exchange losses, local operating managers are relieved of direct responsibility for minimizing such losses. Alternatively, such responsibility can be assigned to local management by

EXHIBIT 16.6
Systems Approach Using the DuPont Method of Financial Control, as Possibly Adapted to a Multinational Company

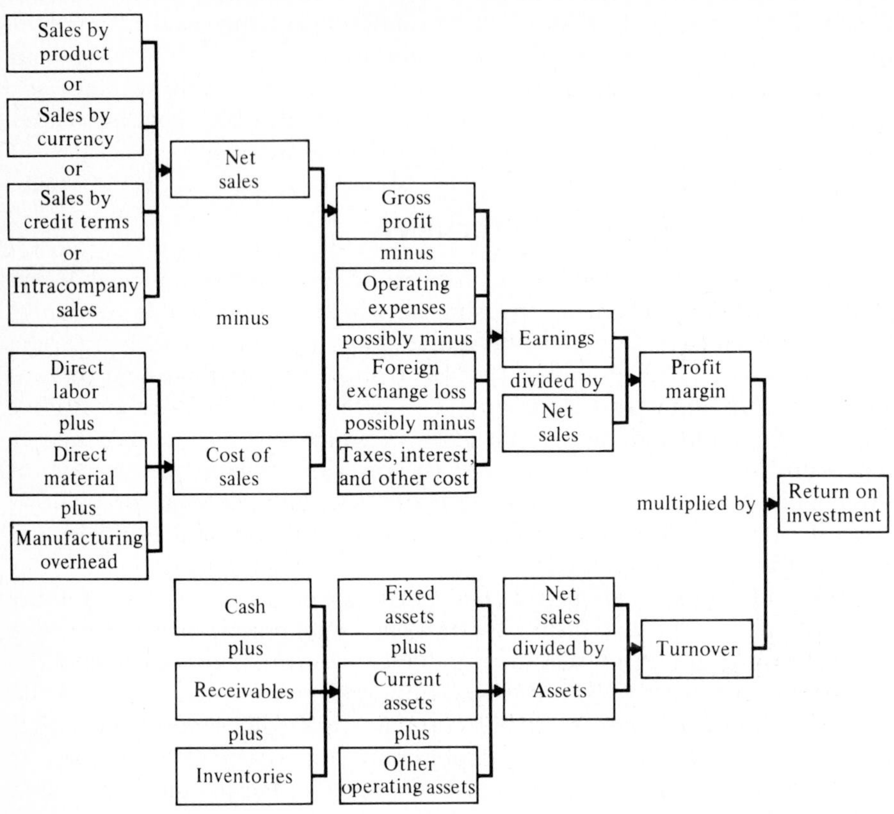

a variation in the calculation of earnings for control purposes. Taxes, interest, and other financial costs may, likewise, be included or excluded when calculating earnings for control purposes.

The third variable is assets, usually net assets after the deduction of depreciation but on occasion gross assets. As assets increase, with other variables held constant, turnover and return on investment fall. This feature is part of the multinational dilemma. Current asset magnitude in a particular foreign affiliate may be changed because of expected exchange rate changes. Fixed assets may be altered because of fear of future expropriation. In both instances the asset base will be distorted from what it would have been in a noninternational risk situation, with resultant variations in return on investment.

The DuPont system views the foreign affiliate as a component in a world system. If decisions are taken to minimize exchange or political risk or optimize total system results, adjustment procedures must be grafted onto the basic system. The ultimate objective is to have the foreign operations manager judged only on variables that that manager can control.

ORGANIZING FOR INTERNATIONAL FINANCIAL MANAGEMENT

How should the financial staff of a multinational firm organize itself to carry out tasks requiring specialized international expertise? Should international financial policy and/or decisions be made at corporate headquarters or at the local affiliate level, or perhaps at an intermediate regional headquarters? In short, who is responsible and where should that person be located?

In their pioneering survey of 187 U.S. multinational firms, Sidney Robbins and Robert Stobaugh identified three phases that multinational companies pass through as their foreign business becomes increasingly important.[9]

When a firm is just starting its overseas expansion, headquarters knows little about the unique financial problems of multinational business and does not believe any special attention is required. This phase, which Robbins and Stobaugh label "Ignoring the System's Potential," was found to occur primarily in "small" multinational enterprises. At this level international financial management at headquarters is characterized by a very small staff, or perhaps only a single person, with neither the time nor the experience to make decisions. This small central staff essentially monitors foreign affiliates, which in turn tend to operate very much on their own without parental supervision. At the local level managers strive to improve affiliate performance but not necessarily total system performance.

As the international business of multinational firms expands, Robbins and Stobaugh found, companies enter Phase 2, "Exploiting the System's Potential." Firms at this level tend to centralize most important international financial decisions in a central staff having the requisite expertise and desire to optimize the system. Evolution into Phase 2 occurs as parent management becomes aware that international financial decisions require a different expertise from domestic financial management. This awareness is brought on by experience, increased profit importance of foreign operations, and the need to consolidate foreign affiliates into parent financial statements.

Robbins and Stobaugh found that as a firm's foreign sales continue to expand, organization for financial management evolves into Phase 3, "Compromising with Complexity." At this point parent management finds itself facing a dilemma in which accumulated experience, the scale of foreign operations, and the relative importance of foreign operations all combine to suggest maintenance of tight central controls. However, the increased number of relationships among an increased number of affiliates makes centralized decision making too complex to be effective. This dilemma is resolved by having a relatively large central international finance staff, which delegates responsibility to the various affiliates in the form of specific guidelines prescribed in a "rule book" issued by headquarters. In effect, the central staff determines policy, issues appropriate directives, and then monitors the affiliates for their compliance with the directives. Actual decisions, however, are made at the local level. Robbins and Stobaugh observed that rule books or "bibles" are often in the form of several volumes of standardized procedures.

International Financial Specialist

What is current practice with regard to the use of international financial specialists within multinational companies? Two surveys of practice—one conducted by the Conference Board, which surveyed 252 U.S. multinational firms, and one by the Financial Executives Research Foundation, which surveyed 34 U.S. multinational firms and 53 of their foreign affiliates—concluded that the complexity and importance of the international finance function has created the need for a new type of executive who specializes in international finance.[10] The Conference Board study, for example, found that 137 companies of 252 responding have a specially designated executive, below the level of corporate treasurer or controller, concerned with financial management of international operations. In 113 of the 137 companies the position is full time, while in the other 24 companies an executive clearly designated as an international financial specialist devotes substantial but not full time to the task.[11] In a few of the companies international expertise on the part of *every* senior financial executive is deemed desirable, regardless of whether or not that person is at the moment involved with international operations.[12]

Exhibit 16.7 presents the statistical data behind the Conference Board's conclusions. As might be expected, bigger companies are more likely to have a separate international financial management function than are smaller ones. These data, of course, support the observations of Robbins and Stobaugh. Data in Exhibit 16.7 also show that large companies with foreign sales exceeding 10% of total sales are more likely to have an international financial executive than are similarly sized companies with a smaller proportion of foreign sales. The corresponding point of significance for smaller companies is 25% of sales being foreign.

EXHIBIT 16.7
Use of an International Finance Specialist

A. All Tabulated Companies

		COMPANIES WITH A SEPARATE INTERNATIONAL FINANCIAL EXECUTIVE		COMPANIES WITHOUT A SEPARATE INTERNATIONAL FINANCIAL EXECUTIVE	
Size of companies by sales	*Total in group*	*Number*	*Percentage of total in group*	*Number*	*Percentage of total in group*
Over $100 million	202	126	62	76	38
Under $100 million	50	11	22	39	78

B. Larger Companies (over $100 Million in Sales)

		COMPANIES WITH A SEPARATE INTERNATIONAL FINANCIAL EXECUTIVE		COMPANIES WITHOUT A SEPARATE INTERNATIONAL FINANCIAL EXECUTIVE	
Degree of international involvement	*Total in group*	*Number*	*Percentage of total in group*	*Number*	*Percentage of total in group*
More than 10% sales abroad	134	98	73	36	27
Less than 10% sales abroad	68	28	41	40	59

C. Smaller Companies (under $100 Million in Sales)

		COMPANIES WITH A SEPARATE INTERNATIONAL FINANCIAL EXECUTIVE		COMPANIES WITHOUT A SEPARATE INTERNATIONAL FINANCIAL EXECUTIVE	
Degree of international involvement	*Total in group*	*Number*	*Percentage of total in group*	*Number*	*Percentage of total in group*
More than 25% sales abroad	14	5	36	9	64
Less than 25% sales abroad	36	6	17	30	83

Source: Irene W. Meister, *Managing the International Financial Function,* New York: The Conference Board, 1970, p. 3.

Organizational Structure

The Conference Board study did not find that a single form of organization predominated, but prevailing practice could be grouped into three organizational archetypes:

1. centralized at corporate headquarters,
2. centralized at the headquarters of the international management unit,
3. split between corporate headquarters and some subordinate headquarters (i.e., central international unit, regional headquarters, product division headquarters, etc.).[13]

Centralization at corporate headquarters More than half the responding companies in the Conference Board survey centralized virtually all aspects of the international finance function at corporate headquarters, including responsibility for both financial policy and service activities. Functions covered included preparation of capital and operating budgets for international operations, protection against devaluation, financial analysis of foreign investment proposals, cash planning and administration, acquisition of funds, taxation, accounting, and financial controls for international operations.[14]

The main reasons cited for centralizing international financial functions at corporate headquarters were as follows:

1. To provide more sophisticated and specialized international financial services to the management of the international business.
2. To coordinate financial activities on a companywide basis.
3. To integrate international and domestic financial activities, including acquisition of funds on a corporate pool basis; global tax planning, capital budgeting, and working capital management; consolidation of foreign and domestic accounts; uniform reporting procedures; and comparative measurement of the performance of both foreign and domestic units.
4. To play a watchdog role in controlling international activities, rather than to provide them with better or more integrated service.[15]

The international financial executive at corporate headquarters typically reports to the treasurer, controller, or financial vice president. Exhibit 16.8 presents Conference Board data that summarize the reporting assignment of the international financial executive at the corporate level.

Duties of the international financial executive vary greatly among the firms surveyed. In some cases a senior financial executive is responsible for nearly all aspects of international finance except accounting. In other companies the international financial executive concentrates on treasury

EXHIBIT 16.8
Reporting Assignment of International Financial Executive within the Corporate Financial Unit

International financial executive reports to	*In companies with three top corporate executives, i.e., vice-president, finance (or equivalent), treasurer, and controller*	*In companies with two top corporate financial executives*[a]
Vice-president, finance (or equivalent), and chief financial officer	31%	—
Treasurer	38%	80%
Controller	31%	20%

[a]In companies with two top financial executives, the treasurer is most often the chief financial officer and frequently also a vice-president.

services, including acquisition of funds, credit and collection policies, management of working capital, protection of assets from devaluation, and review of investment proposals. In these companies budgeting and budgetary controls, profit planning and analysis, and accounting are handled in the corporate controller's office, in close cooperation with the international financial executive.[16]

Some companies in the survey did not designate a separate international financial executive but divided responsibilities between the functional departments of the treasurer and controller. In companies making this split, one group deemphasized international operations, whereas a second group required all senior staff executives to have both foreign and domestic responsibilities.[17]

Centralization at international headquarters According to the Conference Board survey, companies that centralize their international finance function at international rather than corporate headquarters fall into three groups.[18]

1. Foreign operations are organized under a legally and operationally independent international subsidiary. Examples are the Coca-Cola Company, GTE, IBM, and Chas. Pfizer & Company.
2. International divisions have historically operated as almost independent companies with their own strong finance departments. Examples are mainly among companies in capital-intensive industries.
3. International divisions have their own financial staffs, but financial variables are relatively unimportant in the determination of corporate

strategy. Examples are especially widespread among merchandising companies, but there appears to be a trend toward increasing emphasis on the financial variables in this group.

Function split between corporate and subordinate headquarters A large proportion of the companies in the survey split responsibilities for international financial management between the corporate level and subordinate headquarters (international division, regional headquarters, or product division). The corporate level typically determined policy and granted ultimate approval on major financial decisions, while day-to-day decisions to implement policy were conducted at the subordinate headquarters level. The study did not show any clear pattern, although the type of split depended on the form of organization by which the total international operations were conducted.

Corporate Responsibility for Key Financial Decisions

With whom does the responsibility for key financial decisions reside? For example, who determines and implements policies for foreign exchange management, political risk management, capital budgeting analysis, cost of capital and financial structure analysis, working capital management, evaluation of performance, and tax planning? The Conference Board survey casts light on who is responsible for some but not all of these decisions.

Foreign exchange management Responsibility for protecting firms from foreign exchange translation and transaction losses was found to rest in most instances with the financial executive concerned with the treasury function for international operations.[19] In particular, decisions on hedging in the forward market or on entering into currency swap arrangements were nearly always made by the chief financial officer or by a staff executive to whom responsibility had been specifically delegated. Companies operating through a separate international holding company usually assigned responsibility for foreign exchange management to this affiliate's chief financial officer. Responsibility for foreign exchange economic exposure was not investigated in the survey.

Capital budgeting, finance structure, and profit planning The scope and depth of corporate planning and analysis for international operations was found to depend on a number of factors, including the attitude of top management toward the necessity for an extensive analytical foundation and the ability of the financial staff to use imaginative analytical tools to help in the decision-making process.[20] The financial staff's role ranged from simply providing technical services to highly creative budgeting and preparation of detailed investment studies.

Companies that centralize most of the financial services for international operations at corporate headquarters usually assign budgeting to the corporate controller. Profit planning and analysis may be assigned to either the controller or the treasurer, as may studies that involve return on investment, analysis of the asset structure, and decisions on capital structure.

Acquisition of funds In most cases policy decisions on the acquisition of funds are made at the top corporate level, typically by the chief financial officer or an even higher level of authority. The Conference Board study indicated that this situation would be almost universally true for parent company borrowing in the international capital market or for parent company guarantees. About 85% of the respondents indicated that long- and medium-term borrowing by affiliates also had to be approved at the corporate level.[21] In the case of short-term borrowing, the assignment of responsibility centered on the following questions:

1. Who is responsible for setting up credit line limits and terms of credit for the foreign operating units to meet the budgetary requirements for short-term funds?
2. Who can authorize borrowing in excess of the amounts provided in the budget?
3. Who is responsible for the administration of controls over the use of credit to avoid overborrowing by the affiliates?

More than 60% of the sample group reported that establishment of credit lines was a corporate financial unit responsibility. The practice for excess borrowing and credit line controls varies greatly with individual companies.

Positioning of funds About 85% of the firms in the Conference Board survey indicated that the decision on whether to repatriate or reinvest funds was made at the corporate level.[23] About 70% named the corporate financial unit and 15% named the board of directors, a subcommittee of the board, or the chief executive officer. Only 13% delegated the decision to the chief international executive.

Of course, the local board of directors of each separately incorporated affiliate must make its own dividend decisions. In most cases this is a mere formality, but exceptions exist. For example, in the mid-1950s General Motors found it difficult to order its Australian manufacturing affiliate (100% owned by General Motors) to declare a large dividend because of the opposition of the subsidiary's Australian managing director. In cases in which the parent firm holds only a minority in a joint venture, the parent usually has little control over remittance policy.

Intersubsidiary financing Almost half the companies in the Conference Board study extended loans or credit between related affiliates.[24] In most cases the chief financial officer of the parent company or a treasurer, on the advice of the tax experts, approves overall guidelines on intersubsidiary financing.

SUMMARY

Multinational firms must design control systems that produce information in a form valid for internal evaluation and control of individual affiliates. In addition, managers of those units must be given clear directives and know that they will be judged accordingly.

The first section of this chapter discussed performance evaluation of foreign affiliates. Comparison of actual results with operating budgets is the dominant criterion for evaluation. Performance relative to budget in an international context involves decisions about which exchange rate to use in the budgeting process and which exchange rate to use in the assessment of results. Although a variety of combinations are possible, use of a projected exchange rate in budgeting and the end-of-period actual rate in assessment is most common.

The chapter concluded with a discussion of forms of organization for international financial management, with attention to the reasons why some corporations place major responsibility at corporate headquarters while others locate it in the foreign affiliates.

NOTES

1. William Persen and Van Lessig, *Evaluating the Financial Performance of Overseas Operations,* New York: Financial Executives Research Foundation of the Financial Executives Institute, 1979, pp. 11–12.

2. *Ibid.,* p. 16.

3. F. D. S. Choi and I. J. Czechowicz, "Assessing Foreign Subsidiary Performance: A Multinational Comparison," *Management International Review,* 4-83, 1983, pp. 14–25.

4. Persen and Lessig, *Overseas Operations,* pp. 64–68.

5. Donald R. Lessard and Peter Lorange, "Currency Changes and Management Control: Resolving the Centralization/Decentralization Dilemma," *Accounting Review,* July 1977, pp. 628–637.

6. Laurent L. Jacque and Peter Lorange, "The International Control Conundrum: The Case of Hyperinflationary Subsidiaries," *Journal of International Business Studies,* Fall 1984, pp. 185–201.

7. Donald R. Lessard and David Sharp, "Measuring the Performance of Operations Subject to Fluctuating Exchange Rates," *Midland Corporate Finance Journal,* Fall 1984, pp. 18–30.

8. Persen and Lessig, *Overseas Operations,* p. 95.

9. Sidney M. Robbins and Robert B. Stobaugh, "Evolution of the Finance Function," *Money in the Multinational Enterprise,* New York: Basic Books, 1973. This chapter was reprinted in substantially the same form as "Growth of the Financial Function," *Financial Executive,* July 1973, pp. 24–31.

10. Irene W. Meister, *Managing the International Financial Function,* New York: The Conference Board, 1970; and Edward C. Bursk, John Dearden, David Hawkins, and Victor Longstreet, *Financial Control of Multinational Operations,* New York: Financial Executive Research Foundation, 1971.

11. Meister, *Managing the International Financial Function,* p. 2.

12. *Ibid.,* p. 1.

13. *Ibid.,* p. 5.

14. *Ibid.,* p. 6.

15. *Ibid.,* p. 7.

16. *Ibid.,* p. 8–9.

17. *Ibid.,* p. 23.

18. *Ibid.,* p. 37.

19. *Ibid.,* p. 80.

20. *Ibid.,* p. 102–103.

21. *Ibid.,* p. 87.

22. *Ibid.,* p. 89.

23. *Ibid.,* p. 72.

24. *Ibid.,* p. 78.

BIBLIOGRAPHY

Aggarwal, Raj, and James C. Baker, "Using Foreign Subsidiary Accounting Data: A Dilemma for Multinational Corporations," *Columbia Journal of World Business,* Fall 1975, pp. 83–92.

AlHashim, Dhia, "Internal Performance Evaluation in American Multinational Enterprises," *Management International Review,* 1980/3, pp. 33–39.

Altman, Edward I., Tara K. N. Baidya, and Luis Manoel Ribeiro Dias, "Assessing Potential Financial Problems for Firms in Brazil," *Journal of International Business Studies,* Fall 1979, pp. 9–24.

Bursk, Edward C., John Dearden, David F. Hawkins, and Victor M. Longstreet, *Financial Control of Multinational Operations,* New York: Financial Executives Institute, 1971.

Choi, Frederick D. S., "Foreign Inflation and Management Decisions," *Management Accounting,* June 1977, pp. 21–27.

Choi, F. D. S., and I. J. Czechowicz, "Assessing Foreign Subsidiary Performance: A Multinational Comparison," *Management International Review,* 4-83, 1983, pp. 14–25.

Czechowicz, James, Frederick Choi, and Vinod Bavishi, *Assessing Foreign Subsidiary Performance, Systems and Practices of Leading Multinational Companies,* New York: Business International, 1982.

Douglas, Susan P., and C. Samuel Craig, "Examining Performance of U.S. Multinationals in Foreign Markets," *Journal of International Business Studies,* Winter 1983, pp. 51–62.

Farag, Shawki M., "The Problem of Performance Evaluation in International Accounting," *International Journal of Accounting,* Fall 1974, pp. 45–53.

Hosseini, Ahmad, and Raj Aggarwal, "Evaluating Foreign Affiliates: The Impact of Alternative Foreign Currency Translation Methods," *International Journal of Accounting,* Fall 1983, pp. 65–87.

Gernon, Helen, "The Effect of Translation on Multinational Corporations' Internal Performance Evaluation," *Journal of International Business Studies,* Spring/Summer 1983, pp. 103–112.

Imdieke, Leroy F., and Charles H. Smith, "International Financial Control Problems and the Accounting Control System," *Management International Review,* 4/5 1975, pp. 13–28.

Jacque, Laurent L., and Peter Lorange, "The International Control Conundrum: The Case of Hyperinflationary Subsidiaries," *Journal of International Business Studies,* Fall 1984, pp. 185–201.

Leksell, Laurent, "The Design and Function of the Financial Reporting System in Multinational Companies," in Lars Otterbeck, ed., *The Management of Headquarters-Subsidiary Relationships in Multinational Corporations,* New York: St. Martin's Press, 1981, pp. 205–232.

Lessard, Donald R., and Peter Lorange, "Currency Changes and Management Control: Resolving the Centralization/Decentralization Dilemma," *Accounting Review,* July 1977, pp. 628–637.

Lessard, Donald R., and David Sharp, "Measuring the Performance of Operations Subject to Fluctuating Exchange Rates," *Midland Corporate Finance Journal,* Fall 1984, pp. 18–30.

Morsicato, Helen Gernon, *Currency Translation and Performance Evaluation in Multinationals,* Ann Arbor, Mich.: UMI Research Press, 1982.

Morsicato, Helen Gernon, and Michael A. Diamond, "An Approach to 'Environmentalizing' Multinational Enterprise Performance Evaluation Systems," *International Journal of Accounting Education and Research,* Fall 1980, pp. 247–266.

Morsicato, Helen Gernon, and Lee H. Radebaugh, "Internal Performance Evaluation of Multinational Enterprise Operations," *International Journal of Accounting,* Fall 1979, pp. 77–94.

Persen, William, and Van Lessig, *Evaluating the Performance of Overseas Operations,* New York: Financial Executives Research Foundation, 1980.

Robbins, Sidney M., and Robert B. Stobaugh, "The Bent Measuring Stick for Foreign Subsidiaries," *Harvard Business Review,* September/October 1973, pp. 80–88.

Rodney, Earl, "Financial Controls for Multinational Operations," *Financial Executive,* May 1976, pp. 22–28.

Shapiro, Alan C., "The Evaluation and Control of Foreign Affiliates," *Midland Corporate Finance Journal,* Spring 1984, pp. 13–25.

Stewart, Bennett, "A Proposal for Measuring International Performance," *Midland Corporate Finance Journal,* Summer 1983, pp. 56–71.

17

Comparative Accounting and Financial Statement Analysis

Financial statements constitute the information base for a wide array of decisions. Comparing a firm's financial statements with those of its competitors helps managers evaluate their own performance or find how policies of their firms differ from those of other firms. Bankers and rating agencies use financial statements to assess relative strengths and weaknesses of applicants for credit. Security analysts, portfolio managers, and investors use them to help select among competing securities.

Financial statements are as useful as the underlying accounting data and degree of disclosure. Unfortunately, uniform worldwide standards of accounting, disclosure, and auditing do not exist. Each country has its own norms. Therefore, comparison of financial statements of firms based in different countries can be very misleading without a thorough understanding of comparative accounting.

Lack of uniform standards internationally complicates the task of managing multinational firms. Foreign affiliates must prepare several versions of their financial statements. One version must satisfy host country reporting and tax regulations. Another must satisfy the parent firm's financial and tax reporting requirements when the affiliate's statements are consolidated with those of the parent. Still a third version might be needed for managerial control and evaluation of performance.

Lack of uniform standards also creates information barriers for the investment community. Unfamiliar foreign accounting principles, lack of disclosure, and distrust of auditing standards can prevent investors from diversifying their portfolios internationally in an optimal manner. As was mentioned earlier in the book, barriers to the free flow of information can create market inefficiencies that inhibit firms seeking to lower their cost of capital by tapping international capital markets.

The purpose of this chapter is to highlight some of the principal international differences in accounting standards, disclosure practices, and auditing requirements. Even with such an understanding, however, it is easy to misinterpret the underlying economic situation being reported in financial statements. In particular, international comparisons using traditional ratio analysis can lead to unwarranted conclusions about risk, return, liquidity, and efficiency. One must also understand the economic, cultural, and political environment of the country in which the reporting firm is located. In the rest of this chapter we will classify and describe the main accounting, disclosure, and auditing differences. Then we will illustrate the use and misuse of international ratio analysis, using Japan and Korea as case examples.

CLASSIFICATION OF DIFFERENT ACCOUNTING SYSTEMS

Choi and Mueller have classified world accounting systems into four basic types, based on the philosophies behind each approach.[1] Their four frameworks are: (1) macroeconomic, (2) microeconomic, (3) independent discipline, and (4) uniform accounting system.

Macroeconomic Framework

A macroeconomic approach to accounting has been adopted by some countries, of which Sweden is perhaps the prototype. The underlying hypothesis is that the accounting system should facilitate government administrative direction of the economy, based on the following postulates:

- The firm is the essential unit in the economic fabric of a nation.
- The firm best accomplishes its goals through close coordination of its activities with the national economic policies of its environment.
- Public interest is best served if enterprise accounting interrelates with national economic policies.

On this basis the function of accounting is primarily to measure in monetary terms economic transactions and business events of business firms, so that economic planners are better equipped with the data needed to monitor and direct economic activities in desired directions.

Microeconomic Framework

A second set of countries, including the Netherlands, has adopted a microeconomic approach to accounting. Under this philosophy the major thrust of accounting thought evolves from traditional Western microeconomic theory.

Major postulates for a microeconomic-oriented accounting system are the following:

- Individual firms provide focal points for business activities.
- The main policy of a business firm is to ensure its continued existence.
- Optimization, in an economic sense, is a firm's best policy for survival.
- Accounting is a branch of business economics.

From these postulates springs the most important concept of microeconomic-oriented accounting: The accounting process must focus on maintaining constant, in real terms, the monetary capital of a business entity. Measurement of income centers on determining that increment in the value of the firm which, if it were removed, would nevertheless leave the firm with constant invested capital in real terms. Especially as developed in the Netherlands, the microeconomic approach to accounting has therefore focused quite heavily on adjusting for inflation.

Independent Discipline Approach

The third type of system is based on accounting as an independent discipline. The accounting systems of the United States, Canada, and the United Kingdom are of this type. This approach to accounting assumes that business is basically an art and that factors of judgment and estimation cannot be eliminated from business processes. Accounting is therefore a matter of independent judgment, and inductive reasoning from existing business practices is the foundation for creation of accounting concepts. From this pragmatic approach to accounting concepts and practices are developed "generally accepted accounting principles." Such principles are not clearly listed and defined; rather they are a set of conventions that have evolved through years of practice and through voluntary acceptance by the business community.

Under the independent discipline approach to accounting, accounts for a particular firm should be consistent from year to year, but no theoretical or practical reason exists for the reports of one firm to be maintained in a manner consistent with those of another, similar firm. One firm may transfer inventory costs on a LIFO (last-in, first-out) basis, while its competitor may use FIFO (first-in, first-out). An asset may be depreciated over ten years by one firm, while another business depreciates identical assets over some other lifetime. Each firm seeks to report its financial position and income in a manner that, in its subjective opinion, is an accurate portrayal of what has transpired.

Uniform Accounting Systems

Uniform accounting systems, involving identical terminology and account classifications for all firms, constitute the fourth approach. Some of its attractions are that it appears to make accounting more scientific, that it supplies a rational and consistent method for controlling the commercial sector of the economy, and that it affords a relatively simple way to achieve uniformity among firms. Training of personnel to operate the system is simplified since education consists primarily of "how-to-do-it" information. Accountants trained for or working for one firm can easily transfer to other firms. Uniform accounting also facilitates equitable collection of taxes and easier tabulation of national economic statistics.

Uniform accounting systems have several disadvantages, however. Such an approach is alleged to run counter to the actual nature of business because it seeks to treat alike what are in fact basic differences. Comparative analysis, although facilitated on a mechanical basis, may in fact suffer because the system provides less meaningful information for widespread public use. Uniform accounting is also alleged to conflict with modern concepts of managerially oriented accounting systems using statistical and economic concepts within a management information system. Uniformity, it is also charged, tends to restrict the development of new accounting theories and practices and to hinder the process of improving an existing system.

Uniform accounting systems in various forms have been adopted in France, Germany, and Argentina. In Sweden uniform systems are used in some economic sectors such as the metalworking industry but not in other sectors.

Accounting Measurement and Disclosure Framework

R. D. Nair has developed a two-way classification system, one based on similarity of measurement practices, and the other on similarity of disclosure practices.[2] He used factor analysis to group countries having similar accounting practices. The purpose is to provide empirical guidelines for determining when crossnational comparisons of financial accounting data might be appropriate.

Based on similarity of measurement practices, Nair found seven groupings which he describes as follows: "Group 1 can be characterized as a British Commonwealth group; Group 2 is composed largely of countries from Central America and Southern Europe; Group 3 is made up of countries from Central Europe and Scandinavia; Group 4 seems to represent what could be called a United States block; Group 5 consists entirely of South American countries; Group 6 has only two African countries while Group 7 is the single-country 'group' consisting of India."[3] Crossnational comparisons of firms between groups would be distorted by accounting noncomparability.

Based on similarity of disclosure practices, Nair found ten groupings. However, only two of the groups could be clearly characterized. One was a British Commonwealth group and the other a United States group.[4]

SPECIFIC DIFFERENCES IN ACCOUNTING PRINCIPLES

A helpful checklist of specific differences in accounting principles was developed recently by Bavishi, Choi, Shawky, and Sapy-Mazella in a study for Business International Corporation.[5] They analyzed financial statements over a three-year period (1978–1980) for 1,000 leading firms distributed among 20 industries, and based in 24 different countries. By comparing national treatment of 32 accounting variables they identified seven variables that are most frequently treated differently: (1) consolidation, (2) goodwill, (3) deferred taxes, (4) long-term leases, (5) discretionary reserves, (6) inflation adjustment, and (7) foreign exchange translation.

Consolidation of Accounts

The Business International study found that firms in 19 of the 24 countries surveyed consolidate both domestic and foreign subsidiaries more than 50% owned. The exceptions are Finland and Italy, where consolidation is a minority practice, India, and South Korea. German companies consolidate domestic but not foreign subsidiaries. Unconsolidated (minority owned) subsidiaries are carried at cost in Germany, Norway, and Sweden; and about half of the time in Australia, Denmark, and South Africa. Most other countries appear to use the equity method of carrying unconsolidated subsidiaries.

In the United States consolidation is generally required if the parent owns 50% or more of the affiliate, although exceptions exist when the affiliate is engaged in an entirely different line of business (e.g., when a manufacturing firm owns a finance company) or is in the process of liquidation or expropriation. Affiliates that are between 20% and 50% owned are usually carried on an "equity" basis, meaning that the parent carries them at the original cost of the investment plus the parent's share of all reinvested earnings since the time of purchase. If the affiliate has earnings in excess of cash dividends, the carrying value on the parent's books is gradually increased. Affiliates that are less than 20% owned are usually carried at cost. If a market value exists for their shares, this separate market value may be shown in a footnote.

Whenever a parent has a nonconsolidated foreign affiliate, an opportunity exists for manipulation of reported earnings. If the foreign affiliate is carried at cost alone, the parent does not recognize the affiliate's earnings until received as a dividend. In such instances, when domestic earnings need bolstering, the parent can funnel foreign profits into parent earnings via larger-than-usual dividend declarations from abroad. Similarly, earnings reported by the parent can be held down, if that is deemed desirable, by reducing the dividend flow from nonconsolidated affiliates.

Goodwill

Goodwill is not amortized in Germany and Malaysia, and is amortized by only a minority of companies in the United Kingdom, Switzerland, Ireland, Finland, Norway, Italy, and South Africa. Practice in the Netherlands is about evenly mixed, and no data were found for Brazil, Austria, or India. In the remaining countries goodwill is amortized.

Deferred Taxes

Accounting for deferred taxes when accounting income is not equal to taxable income is done in all countries except Belgium, Switzerland, Austria, Sweden, Finland, Norway, Italy, Spain, India, and South Korea.

Long-Term Leases

In contrast, long-term leases are capitalized on the balance sheet in only three countries, the United States, Canada, and Mexico. A minority of companies in Belgium also capitalize long-term leases.

Discretionary Reserves

Unlike U.S. practice, in which earnings are regarded as automatically reinvested unless distributed as dividends, in many countries practice is to dispose of all earnings in the form of specific appropriations to designated reserves, to cash dividends, as special bonuses to directors or officers, or to specific and permanent reinvestment. Unallocated retained earnings do not exist, except possibly for a small unallocated residual balance that is carried over to the following year.

General purpose, purely discretionary reserves are used to "smooth" income by charging a hypothetical nonrealized expense to the income statement in good years. This lowers income in the good year, but provides a "reserve" for arbitrarily increasing net income in an adverse year by reversing the charge. Obviously, use of such a reserve severely distorts any ratio based on net income or on the equity section of the statement. The authors report that they observed the use of reserves that impacted the income statement before calculation of net income in many countries. Countries where discretionary reserves were not allowed were the United States, Canada, Mexico, the United Kingdom, Ireland, Austria, Australia, South Korea, and South Africa.

In some countries allocations of the year's earnings must be approved by stockholders at an annual meeting, which takes place after publication of the annual report. Thus the annual report as such does not reveal the disposition of earnings. In these countries supplemental memoranda issued separately from the annual report are necessary to obtain a full perspective on disposition of earnings.

Inflation Adjustment

Historical cost is reported as the basic valuation approach in only five countries, the United States, Canada, Germany, Japan, and Australia, and as a minority practice in the Netherlands. Of these six countries, only firms in the United States provide supplementary inflation-adjusted financial statements on a consistent basis. Such supplementary statements are a minority practice in Canada, Australia, and the Netherlands. Additionally, statements from the United Kingdom and Ireland (neither of which adheres completely to a historic cost basis for its basic reports) include supplementary inflation-adjusted statements.

Foreign Exchange Translation

The Business International study, which was conducted in 1981, before the United States shifted to the current rate method of translating foreign financial statements, reported that only the United States and Canada used the monetary/nonmonetary method. The current-rate method was used by most countries in Europe and the Far East. United States, Canadian, and South Korean companies were the only ones that consistently took foreign exchange gains and losses into current income.

DISCLOSURE

The degree of disclosure in financial statements varies significantly by country. The main reason for such differences can be traced to differing assumptions about the purpose of published financial statements. In some countries, including the United States, the income statement is regarded as the financial statement of prime interest. Income statements usually reveal sales, various categories of expenses, and profits for an interval of time. Current trends within the United States are toward making income statements even more revealing. For example, major U.S. firms are required to disclose operating results by product or division lines. The balance sheet is relegated to secondary importance.

U.S. focus on the income statement derives from the fact that most large U.S. corporations are publicly owned, with stockholder wealth dependent primarily on stock market prices, which, in turn, are influenced to a large extent by reported and expected earnings per share. Because of U.S. tax laws and a general level of affluence in living standards, U.S. stockholders prefer increased wealth, as measured both by rising stock prices and/or increased dividends.

In most European and Latin American countries, the balance sheet is the most important statement, reflecting major concern in these countries over the ownership of wealth (as distinct from the creation of new income) and the strength of the firm relative to claims of creditors. Income statements provide a paucity of information from a public stockholder's point of view; and stockholders, in turn, are usually more concerned with dividends than with stock price appreciation. For example, European firms tend to hide earnings and to reveal less about how assets are valued than is common in the United States. Income statements often start with "gross trading profit" (i.e., gross profit) without any disclosure of sales or cost of goods sold. Trends in sales and in gross profit margins cannot be discerned, with the result that judgments about the competitive strength of a company are difficult to make.

Methods by which asset values and depreciation expenses are determined are often not explained. Indeed, notes to financial statements do not appear in the profusion to which the U.S. stockholder is accustomed. As a result, a comparison between firms of both asset position and depreciation impact on earnings is not possible. Furthermore, the degree of consolidation included in a published set of statements is often not revealed, with the result that the earnings of nonconsolidated subsidiaries are concealed. At times, nonrecurring income from the sale of assets is mixed with operating profit, further hindering the ability of an outsider to judge true earnings potential.

In some countries various forms of accelerated depreciation are permitted. However, in contrast with the United States, many foreign countries require "flow-through" accounting, with the result that the greater depreciation used for tax purposes must also be shown on public reports and so used to reduce reported earnings. By comparison, most U.S. firms use straight-line depreciation in reporting to their shareholders, even when using accelerated depreciation to reduce income taxes.

European secrecy is founded in part on tradition. However, the weight of custom is buttressed by the absence of significant legal requirements forcing disclosure of financial results for publicly owned firms; by lack of market pressures from creditors, such as banks and stockholders; and, at least until recently, by the lack of any great pressure for new public equity financing. Recently, the need to tap new sources of capital has forced some firms to reveal more information. An added reason often advanced for traditional European understatement of earnings is a fear by corporate officers and directors that, if higher earnings are reported, stockholders will demand higher dividends or trade unions seek pay increases. Tax avoidance is a third possibility, although in general tax collectors have access to greater internal data.

AUDITING

Because of the great diversity of accounting practices in various countries, the opinion of a competent, professional, and independent auditor is indispensable if dependence is to be placed on foreign financial statements. Most of the large public accounting firms have gone international with their clients, so that subsidiaries in Lima and Dusseldorf are audited by the same firm that audits parent books in New York or Chicago. Financial reports of local independent firms are often audited by a variety of parties with some official status, not all of whom have the professional qualifications of independence necessary to render a reliable opinion.

Variations in the auditor's function were explained in a comparison of legislation governing corporation audits in Latin countries with auditing practiced in what the author, a former vice-rector of the University of Buenos Aires, termed the "Anglo-Saxon" system.[6] The Latin countries all had statutes similar to the Italian Civil Code, which established that a *sindaco* should supervise the company's administration, take care that the requirements of the law and the bylaws were duly met, and check the company's accounts and records. However, in general the statutes prescribed no particular qualifications for becoming a *sindaco.* In English-speaking countries and in Scandinavian countries, on the other hand, financial reports were deemed to be a reporting to the owners as to how well management had fulfilled its trust. Because stockholders must base their evaluation of the efficiency of management on meaningful, full, and fair disclosure, it was the function of an independent auditor to determine that the financial statements accurately portrayed the data. However, auditing standards differ by country. For example, it has been reported that in Japan the "lowly" auditor would not dare cause loss of face on the part of the "senior" accounting manager by seeking to verify independently such accounts as accounts receivable and inventories.

Auditing procedures in various countries also differ in some respects. In many European and Latin American countries canceled checks become the property of the bank and are not returned with the bank statement. Therefore verification of disbursements is more difficult. European auditing standards do not normally require physical inventory taking or confirmation of accounts receivable. In some countries sampling and statistical approaches may be used to verify amounts, while in others detailed counts are required. In some countries auditors may have varying degrees of busi-

EXHIBIT 17.1

Mean Differences in Aggregate Financial Ratios, 1976–1978, for Japan, Korea, and the United States (unadjusted)

Enterprise category (number of firms)	*Current ratio*	*Quick ratio*	*Debt ratio*	*Interest earned*	*Inventory turnover*	*Collection period*	*Fixed assets turnover*	*Total assets turnover*	*Profit margin*	*Return on total assets*	*Return on net worth*
All Manufacturing											
Japan (976)	1.15	.80	.84	1.60	5.00	86	3.10	.93	.013	.012	.071
Korea (354)	1.13	.46	.78	1.80	6.60	33	2.80	1.20	.023	.028	.131
U.S. (902)	1.94	1.10	.47	6.50	6.80	43	3.90	1.40	.054	.074	.139
Chemicals											
Japan (129)	1.30	.99	.79	1.80	7.10	88	2.80	.90	.015	.014	.065
Korea (54)	1.40	.70	.59	2.40	7.10	33	1.60	.90	.044	.040	.100
U.S. (n.a.)	2.20	1.30	.45	6.50	6.50	50	2.80	1.10	.073	.081	.148
Textiles											
Japan (81)	1.00	.77	.81	1.10	6.20	66	3.50	.92	.003	.003	.017
Korea (34)	1.00	.37	.83	1.30	4.90	30	2.20	1.00	.010	.011	.064
U.S. (n.a.)	2.30	1.20	.48	4.30	6.50	48	5.80	1.80	.027	.049	.094
Transportation											
Japan (85)	1.20	.86	.83	1.90	3.90	116	4.50	.90	.017	.015	.092
Korea (14)	.95	.40	.91	1.90	18.60	18	1.10	.80	.026	.021	.221
U.S.	1.60	.74	.52	8.70	5.60	31	6.50	1.60	.049	.078	.161

Source: Adapted from Frederick D. S. Choi, Hisaaki Hino, Sang Kee Min, Sang Oh Nam, Junichi Ujiie, and Arthur I. Stonehill, "Analyzing Foreign Financial Statements: The Use and Misuse of International Ratio Analysis," *Journal of International Business Studies,* Spring/Summer 1983, p. 116.

Note: Data on Japan from the Bank of Japan, data on Korea from the Bank of Korea, and data on the United States from the U.S. Federal Trade Commission.

n.a. Not applicable.

ness relationships with the firms they audit. At the other extreme, an auditor in Denmark may not participate in any business enterprise because of the possible development of a conflict of interest.

USE AND MISUSE OF INTERNATIONAL RATIO ANALYSIS

Given the differences in accounting practices, a cross-country comparison of firms using traditional ratio analysis could easily lead to misleading conclusions.

Frederick Choi and five colleagues illustrated this point in a recent study that undertook a comparison of firms from Japan, Korea, and the United States using ratio analysis.[7] The Choi study first compared aggregate financial ratios for a large sample of manufacturing firms in the three countries, as shown in Exhibit 17.1. A close look at these ratios would suggest that Japanese and Korean firms are less profitable and efficient, and suffer higher financial risk, than their U.S. counterparts.

In order to remove the effects on aggregate ratios of size, industry, and other extraneous variables, a paired comparison was made between ten Japanese firms and ten U.S. counterparts. Likewise, eight Korean firms were compared to eight similar U.S. firms. With exception of the efficiency ratios, the same relative differences in ratios were observed as in Exhibit 17.1.

Since differences due to accounting principles might explain most of the observed ratio differences, the Choi study restated the ten Japanese and eight Korean statements to conform to U.S. generally accepted accounting principles (U.S. GAAP). Although accounting restatement made some difference, most of the same relative differences in ratios remained.

Despite the results of the ratio analysis, the Choi study concluded that it would be a misuse of ratio analysis to infer that Japanese and Korean firms are less profitable, less efficient, and riskier than their U.S. counterparts. One must delve more deeply into the underlying political, economic, and historical environment of Japan and Korea to explain each ratio.

Leverage

Two of the main measures of financial risk traditionally used in ratio analysis are the debt ratio (total debt at book value divided by total assets at book value) and times interest earned (EBIT divided by interest charges). The large sample of unadjusted ratios presented in Exhibit 17.1 shows Japanese debt ratios averaged 84%, Korean 78%, and U.S. only 47%. In the adjusted matched pairs comparison the Japanese firms averaged 64%, Korean firms 79%, and U.S. firms 49%. As shown in Exhibit 17.1, times interest earned for both Japanese and Korean firms was 1.60, compared with 6.50 for U.S. firms. Thus ratio analysis alone would suggest that Japanese and Korean firms are excessively leveraged by U.S. standards.

The financial risk of Japanese firms is not nearly as high as the ratios would indicate. As pointed out earlier in Chapters 1 and 12, enterprise groupings called *keiretsu* ensure that high levels of interdependence exist between banks and their related industrial borrowers. Consequently, a bank hesitates to impose financial penalties on delinquent borrowers, but would rather postpone interest and principal or even refinance the loan. If necessary, a bank will install one of its officials in the management of a borrowing firm in trouble. Other firms in the *keiretsu* group may prepay receivables owed to the troubled firm or slow down on their collections from it. In effect, the family holds together and the lending bank need not view itself as an outsider in the sense that a U.S. bank would. The bank's risk is reduced by assured backing from the central bank. It can also demand additional collateral from a firm if needed. In Japan, the cost of equity is substantially higher than the cost of debt because of a traditional system of issuing new shares at par, rather than higher market prices. Companies that have issued shares at market have had to return the premiums to shareholders in the form of higher dividend rates or stock dividends because of pressure from securities companies.

Not every feature of the Japanese system reduces financial risk. Lewis Freitas has identified some offsetting features.[8] Lifetime employment means that labor costs are fixed rather than variable as in the United States. Dividends are normally considered fixed on a per share basis, so that they in fact constitute a more or less obligatory cash outflow. Trade receivables are often discounted on a full recourse basis with local banks, at which time they are taken off the balance sheet. Were these receivables financed directly, additional debt would appear on the balance sheet. Additionally, because of close interties within groupings of firms, any given firm is likely to have fully guaranteed the debts of affiliates, unconsolidated subsidiaries, and possibly subcontractors whose relation to the firm is exclusive even though they are not legally defined affiliates.

The high leverage of Korean firms can also be explained by environmental factors. Korean firms face an extremely thin equity market that has only been in operation since 1973. In contrast, interest rates on borrowing from government-dominated commercial banks are subsidized, making the cost of bank debt cheap for major companies in comparison to the free market rates charged in Korea's unregulated curb market.

Additional help for Korean firms comes from the government directly, which grants tax and trade privileges and special financing to firms whose activities are deemed beneficial to the nation. The government can be counted upon to come to the help of these companies if they are in trouble, so a Korean firm with very large debt is viewed favorably, rather than unfavorably, because the debt is evidence of a close association with the government.

Liquidity

The average Japanese current ratio in Exhibit 17.1 was 1.15, and for Korea the ratio was 1.13. U.S. firms, by contrast, had an average ratio of 1.94. Patterns for the quick ratio were similar: 0.80, 0.46, and 1.10 respectively. In Japan, lenders prefer to make short-term loans because interest rates can be adjusted to market more frequently. Borrowers find short-term rates lower than long-term rates, and since the short-term debt is easy to renew, it becomes long-term in nature.

The Korean long-term market is not developed. Thus Korean firms find it necessary to rely on short-term debt, rolled over, to finance both working capital and long-term needs. Consequently, much of the short-term debt in the denominator of the current and quick ratio is in fact long-term in nature.

Efficiency

The greatest difference in efficiency ratios is between collection periods. The average collection period for Japan was 86 days, for Korea 33 days, and for the United States 43 days. In both Japan and Korea, a purchaser seldom pays cash on being invoiced, but instead takes another 20 to 30 days to pay. In Korea a note for an additional 60 to 120 days may be given, a practice which appears to spring from a need to accommodate the working capital shortage of important customers. The low Korean collection period is attributable to the fact that these notes are not included in the numerator of the ratio; if the Korean ratio is adjusted for notes receivable it averages between 105 and 110 days. In Japan the long collection period often stems from a desire to avoid putting a buyer in a financial bind, especially during a recession, so that its stable employment base will not be threatened. Such mutual support in difficult times helps assure future patronage.

The second efficiency ratio is fixed asset turnover. In Japan, sales were 3.10 times fixed assets, in Korea they were 2.80, and in the United States they were 3.90. The Japanese/U.S. difference is not significant. The reason for the lower turnover for Korean firms appears to rise from the fact that Korean development has been spurred by enormous investments in fixed plant and equipment. Much of this investment has been in heavy industries, such as chemicals, which need large fixed assets. The tendency to build well in advance of anticipated sales leads to a lower turnover. The ratio is further lowered because Korean price controls keep the numerator (sales) down for domestic goods as part of a policy of resisting inflation.

Profitability

Profitability was measured by both profit margins (return on sales) and return on total assets. Profit margins were 1.3% for Japan, 2.3% for Korea, and 5.4% for the United States. Since these were not offset by turnover ratio, return on total assets was 1.2% for Japan, 2.8% for Korea, and 7.4% for the United States. Return on net worth was 7.1%, 13.1%, and 13.9%, respectively, for the three countries. As can be seen, the ratios indicate that U.S. firms are significantly more profitable than their Japanese or Korean counterparts.

One reason appears to be that Japanese managers are not as concerned with short-run profits as their U.S. counterparts. Management jobs are more secure, and a greater proportion of shares is held by related banks, suppliers, and corporate customers. All of these parties are more interested in strong long-run basic business ties than in maximizing market price, especially in the short run. Additionally, price competition in export markets is very intense among Japanese companies, lowering margins and rates of return.

Profits are more important for Korean companies. However, export pricing policies and government controls keep prices and margins low.

SUMMARY

Financial statements provide the information for a wide variety of decisions. Comparability of statements internationally is hindered by lack of uniform accounting, disclosure, and auditing standards.

Accounting systems can be classified in several ways. One approach is to group them according to one of four underlying philosophical frameworks: (1) macroeconomic, (2) microeconomic, (3) independent discipline, and (4) uniform accounting system. Another approach is to group accounting systems based on similarity of measurement or disclosure practices.

Accounting principles vary worldwide in at least seven specific areas: (1) consolidation, (2) goodwill, (3) deferred taxes, (4) long-term leases, (5) discretionary reserves, (6) inflation adjustment, and (7) foreign exchange translation.

Disclosure practices vary significantly depending partly on the assumed purpose of published financial statements. U.S. firms focus on perfecting the income statement because of the belief that market value is influenced by reported earnings. Most European and Latin American firms concentrate on the balance sheet because of a concern over the ownership of wealth and the strength of a firm relative to claims of creditors.

Auditing standards vary widely with respect to the function and procedures of the audit and qualifications necessary to be an auditor.

International ratio analysis can lead to misleading conclusions. Ratios may be distorted by accounting differences. More importantly, ratio analysis needs to be interpreted in the context of a country's political, economic, and historical environment.

NOTES

1. Frederick D. S. Choi and G. G. Mueller, *International Accounting*, Englewood Cliffs, N.J.: Prentice-Hall, 1984, pp. 45–52.

2. R. D. Nair, "Empirical Guidelines for Comparing International Accounting Data," *Journal of International Business Studies,* Winter 1982, pp. 85–98. Data came from the 1979 Price Waterhouse & Co. survey of 267 accounting practices in 64 countries.

3. *Ibid.*, p. 93.

4. *Ibid.*, pp. 95–96.

5. Vinod B. Bavishi, Frederick D. S. Choi, Hany A. Shawky, and Jean-Pierre Sapy-Mazella, *Analyzing Financial Ratios of the World's 1000 Leading Industrial Corporations,* New York: Business International Corporation, 1981.

6. William Leslie Chapman, "Legislation on Corporation Audits in Many Countries Needs to Be Amended," VIII International Congress of Accountants, 1962; reprinted in Kenneth H. Berg, Gerhard G. Mueller, and Lauren M. Walker, eds., *Readings in International Accounting,* Boston: Houghton Mifflin, 1969, pp. 160–166.

7. Frederick D. S. Choi, Hisaaki Hino, Sang Kee Min, San Oh Nam, Junichi Ujiie, and Arthur I. Stonehill, "Analyzing Foreign Financial Statements: The Use and Misuse of International Ratio Analysis," *Journal of International Business Studies,* Spring/Summer 1983, pp. 113–131.

8. Lewis Freitas, "Views from Abroad: Japan," *Journal of Accounting, Auditing, and Finance,* Fall 1980, pp. 269–274.

BIBLIOGRAPHY

Alhashim, D. D., "International Dimensions in Accounting and Implications for Developing Nations," *Management International Review,* 1982/4, pp. 4–11.

Altman, Edward I., "Business Failure Models: An International Survey," New York: Salomon Brothers Center, Occasional Papers in Business and Finance, No. 5, 1982.

Arnold, Jerry, William W. Holder, and M. Herschel Mann, "International Reporting Aspects of Segment Disclosure," *International Journal of Accounting,* Fall 1980, pp. 125–135.

Arpan, Jeffrey, and Dhia D. Al Hashim, *International Dimensions of Accounting,* Boston: Kent Publishing Company, 1984.

Arpan, Jeffrey, and Lee H. Radebaugh, *International Accounting and Multinational Enterprises,* Boston: Warren, Gorham & Lamont, 1981.

Ballon, Robert J., Iwao Tomita, and Hajime Usami, *Financial Reporting in Japan,* Toyko: Kodansha International, Ltd., 1978.

Balhaoui, Ahmed, *International Accounting: Issues and Solutions,* Westport, Conn.: Greenwood Press, 1985.

Barrett, M. Edgar, "Financial Reporting Practices: Disclosure and Comprehensiveness in an International Setting," *Journal of Accounting Research,* Spring 1976, pp. 10–26.

Bavishi, Vinod B., Frederick D. S. Choi, Hany A. Shawky, and Jean-Pierre Sapy-Mazella, *Analyzing Financial Ratios of the World's 1,000 Leading Industrial Corporations,* New York: Business International Corporation, 1981.

Bavishi, Vinod B., and Harold E. Wyman, "Foreign Operations Disclosures by U.S.-Based Multinational Corporations: Are They Adequate?" *International Journal of Accounting,* Fall 1980, pp. 153–168.

Bindon, Kathleen, *Inventories and Foreign Currency Translation Requirements,* Ann Arbor, Mich.: UMI Research Press, 1983.

Castle, Eric F., "The Problems of Consolidation of Accounts of a Multinational Enterprise: Shell Group of Companies—Shell Transport and Trading Company, Limited, U.K.," *International Journal of Accounting,* Fall 1980, pp. 209–219.

Chang, Lucia S., Kenneth S. Most, and Carlos W. Brain, "The Utility of Annual Reports: An International Study," *Journal of International Business Studies,* Spring/Summer 1983, pp. 63–84.

Choi, Frederick D. S., "Financial Disclosure and Entry to the European Capital Market," *Journal of Accounting Research,* Autumn 1973, pp. 159–175.

———, "European Disclosure: The Competitive Disclosure Hypothesis," *Journal of International Business Studies,* Fall 1974, pp.15–24.

———, "Price-Level Adjustments and Foreign Currency Translation: Are They Compatible?" *International Journal of Accounting,* Fall 1975, pp. 121–143.

———, "Primary-Secondary Reporting: A Cross-Cultural Analysis," *International Journal of Accounting,* Fall 1980, pp. 84–104.

———, *Multinational Accounting: A Research Framework for the Eighties,* Ann Arbor, Mich.: UMI Research Press, 1981.

Choi, Frederick D. S., and Vinod B. Bavishi, "Diversity in Multinational Accounting," *Financial Executive,* August 1982, pp. 45–49.

Choi, Frederick D. S., Hisaaki Hino, Sang Kee Min, Sang Oh Nam, Junichi Ujiie, and Arthur I. Stonehill, "Analyzing Foreign Financial Statements: The Use and Misuse of International Ratio Analysis," *Journal of International Business Studies,* Spring/Summer 1983, pp. 113–131.

Choi, Frederick D. S., and Gerhard G. Mueller, *International Accounting,* Englewood Cliffs, N.J.: Prentice-Hall, 1984.

Choi, Frederick D. S., and Gerhard G. Mueller, eds., *Essentials of Multinational Accounting: An Anthology,* Ann Arbor, Mich: UMI Press, 1982.

Cunningham, Gary M., *An Accounting Research Framework for Multinational Companies,* Ann Arbor, Mich: UMI Research Press, 1978.

Da Costa, Richard C., James Fisher, and William M. Lawson, "Linkages in the International Business Community: Accounting Evidence," *Journal of International Business Studies,* Fall 1980, pp. 92–102.

Drury, D. H., "Effects of Accounting Practice Divergence: Canada and the United States," *Journal of International Business Studies,* Fall 1979, pp. 75–87.

Enthoven, Aldophe J. H., "International Management Accounting: Its Scope and Standards," *International Journal of Accounting,* Spring 1982, pp. 59–74.

Frank, Werner G., "An Empirical Analysis of International Accounting Principles," *Journal of Accounting Research,* Autumn 1979, pp. 593–605.

Freitas, Lewis P., "Views from Abroad: Japan," *Journal of Accounting, Auditing, and Finance,* Fall 1980, pp. 269–274.

Gray, Dahli, "Corporate Preferences for Foreign Currency Accounting Standards," *Journal of Accounting Research,* Autumn 1984, pp. 760–764.

Gray, Sidney J., L. B. McSweeney, and J. C. Shaw, *Information Disclosure and the Multinational Corporation,* New York: Wiley, 1984.

Hayes, Donald J., "The International Accounting Standards Committee—Recent Developments and Current Problems," *International Journal of Accounting,* Fall 1980, pp. 1–10.

Holzer, H. P., *et al., International Accounting,* New York: Harper and Row, 1984.

Holzer, H. P., and J. S. Chandler, "A Systems Approach to Accounting in Developing Countries," *Management International Review,* No. 4, 1981, pp. 23–32.

Jones, Edward H., "Decision-Making Based on Foreign Financial Statements," *Financial Executive,* February 1981, pp. 32–35.

Mueller, Gerhard G., and Lauren M. Walker, "The Coming of Age of Transnational Financial Reporting," *Journal of Accountancy,* July 1976, pp. 67–74.

Nair, R. D., "The Harmonization of International Accounting Standards, 1973–1979," *International Journal of Accounting,* Fall 1981, pp. 61–77.

———, "Empirical Guidelines for Comparing International Accounting Data," *Journal of International Business Studies,* Winter 1982, pp. 85–98.

Nair, R. D., and W. G. Frank, "The Impact of Disclosure and Measurement Practices on International Accounting Classifications," *Accounting Review,* July 1980, pp. 426–450.

Nobes, Christopher, *International Classification of Financial Reporting,* New York: St. Martin's Press, 1984.

Nobes, Christopher W., and R. H. Parker, eds., *Comparative International Accounting,* Homewood, Ill.: Irwin, 1981.

Pomeranz, Felix, "International Auditing Standards," *International Journal of Accounting,* Fall 1975, pp. 1–13.

Price Waterhouse International, Accounting Principles and Reporting Practices, 1979.

Radebaugh, Lee H., "Accounting for Price-Level and Exchange Rate Changes for U.S. International Firms: An Empirical Study," *Journal of International Studies,* Fall 1974, pp. 41–55.

Schoenfeld, Hanns-Martin W., "International Accounting: Development, Issues and Future Directions," *Journal of International Business Studies,* Fall 1981, pp. 83–100.

Stonehill, Arthur, Lee Remmers, Theo Beekhuisen, and Richard Wright, "Financial Goals and Debt Ratio Determinants, A Survey of Practice in Five Countries," *Financial Management,* Autumn 1975, pp. 24–41.

Watt, George C., Richard M. Hammer, and Marianne Burge, *Accounting for the Multinational Corporation,* Homewood, Ill.: Dow-Jones/Irwin, 1978.

Wright, Richard, and Sadahiko Suzuki, "Financial Structure and Bankruptcy Risk in Japanese Companies," *Journal of International Business Studies,* Spring 1985, pp. 97–110.

18

Tax Planning

For multinational operations tax planning has become an extremely complex but vitally important aspect of international business. To plan effectively, executives who have tax responsibility in a multinational business should have a background in public finance so that they can understand the principles of tax neutrality, equity, revenue, and morality. They should have experience in tax law in order to be able to follow the various tax rulings as they apply to international business practice, and they should also be able to read a number of foreign languages to keep abreast of foreign tax rulings. Naturally they should have accounting experience, since a large part of day-to-day tax administration involves decisions about whether specific transactions are tax-deductible or whether a particular transfer price can be defended as an "arm's length" transaction. Another job qualification is familiarity with the techniques of management science, because computerized tax-simulation models are now being used to find the optimal system for minimizing a corporation's global tax bill. These models take into account such factors as the legal structure of parent and subsidiaries (branch versus corporation), policies on the movement of funds among subsidiaries and parent, the various U.S. and foreign tax rates and tax-base definitions, tax treaties, and the risk of currency inconvertibility, or devaluation. Needless to say, the ideal international tax executive probably does not exist. Instead, tax planning is effected by group action, with each group member contributing expertise in one or more of the above areas.

With tax planning so complex, this chapter cannot aim to create tax experts. Rather it sets out to acquaint the reader with the overall international tax environment. At least a minimum of sophisticated knowledge of tax structures is needed by every international financial executive because many decisions require consideration of such factors. As we have shown earlier, taxes have a major impact on foreign investment decisions, financial structure, determination of the cost of capital, foreign exchange management, working capital management, and financial control. The sections that follow explain the most important aspects of the international tax environments and specific features that affect multinational operations.

NATIONAL TAX ENVIRONMENTS

Every country possesses its own bewildering array of taxes, making it imperative that the multinational corporation seek local tax counsel in each host country in which it operates. International accounting firms publish summaries, which are frequently updated. Two of the best of the accounting sources are Price Waterhouse, *Corporate Taxes: A Worldwide Summary*, and Ernst and Whinney, *Foreign and U.S. Corporate Income and Withholding Tax Rates.* Both are updated regularly.

Role of Corporate Income Taxes

The United States is almost unique in its heavy reliance on corporate and individual income taxes as a main source of federal tax revenue. Other countries rely proportionately more on indirect taxes, such as the value-added tax, turnover (sales) taxes, excise taxes, and border taxes. For example, Germany derives more than 40% of its federal tax revenues from the value-added tax, whereas the United States derives more than 65% of its federal tax revenue from income taxes and only about 10% from indirect taxes.

Nominally, domestic corporate income tax rates do not vary too widely among the main industrial countries. Some typical national tax rates on earnings of large corporations are as follows:

U.S.	46%	Japan	42%
France	50%	Canada	46%
U.K.	52%	Sweden	32%
Germany	56%		

Some countries differentiate between retained earnings and distributed earnings by charging a lower tax rate on distributed earnings. The dividend recipient pays some or all of the difference as personal income tax. The purpose of this provision is to eliminate part of the double taxation of dividends. For example, distributed earnings are taxed only at 36% in Germany and 30% in Japan.

A number of less industrialized countries have a relatively moderate corporate income tax rate as an incentive to encourage local private investment by both domestic and foreign firms. Some sample rates are these:

Argentina	33%	Philippines	35%
Indonesia	35%	Spain	35%
Korea	33%	Taiwan	35%

Certain countries assess extremely low corporate income tax rates either to stimulate local business enterprises or in some cases to attract tax haven affiliates of multinational firms. Examples of low-tax countries are these:

The Bahamas	0%
Cayman Islands	0%
Bermuda	0%
Hong Kong	16.5%
Switzerland	Less than 10% depending on profits and net worth

Corporate income taxes are also assessed at the local (state, provincial, canton, city, etc.) level in many countries. This action increases the overall effective tax rate, although local income taxes are usually deductible from taxable income at the national level. Examples of countries with relatively important local income taxes are these:

Germany	11–20%
Sweden	26–34%
Switzerland	5–35%
U.S.	5–10%

Some less developed countries give "tax holidays" to investing foreign firms as an incentive to invest. The "tax holiday" typically guarantees no income taxes for the first few years while the firm is being established. Another modus operandi is to allow accelerated depreciation, which in itself reduces the tax base toward zero.

Gradually corporate income tax rates in less developed countries have been increasing. Some critics have claimed that this increase is due to industrial countries such as the United States taxing foreign investment income but reducing the tax by the amount of foreign income taxes paid locally. Since foreign affiliates are probably indifferent as to whether taxes are paid to host or parent country authorities, there might be an incentive for the host country to raise its corporate income taxes to the point at which the foreign tax credit for foreign affiliates would just equal their parent country tax liabilities on income earned in the host country. Thus the corporate income tax rate of industrial countries supposedly acts as an umbrella for income tax rates in less developed countries. This criticism may have some validity in countries that rely heavily on foreign direct investment, particularly where the extractive industries predominate.

The various definitions of taxable corporate income create greater disparities than do differences in nominal corporate tax rates. A transaction that may be tax-deductible in one country, such as housing for corporate executives, may not be deductible in another. Brazil, Peru, and certain other countries plagued by inflation allow assets to be revalued in keeping with inflation, with correspondingly greater write-downs for tax purposes. Depreciation rates for tax purposes vary significantly among countries. Tax-free investment reserves are common in many countries. For example, in Sweden, Norway, Italy, and undoubtedly elsewhere, earnings can be set aside tax-free to be used at a later date for investment in underdeveloped parts of the countries, or in some cases to be spent in a countercyclical manner when the country is in recession.

Value-added Tax

One type of tax that has achieved great prominence is the value-added tax. It has been adopted as the main source of revenue from indirect taxation by all members of the EEC, most other countries in Western Europe, a number of Latin American countries, including Argentina, Brazil, Chile, Mexico, and Peru, as well as Korea and scattered other countries. During the past decade some members of the U.S. Congress, Treasury department, and a special presidential task force have all recommended that the United States adopt a version of the value-added tax.[1]

The value-added tax is a type of national sales tax collected at each stage of production or sale of consumption goods in proportion to the value added during that stage. In general, production goods, such as plant and equipment, have not been subject to the value-added tax. Certain basic necessities such as health-related activities and medicines, educational and religious activities, and the postal service are usually exempt or taxed at lower rates. Rates vary up to a high of 22% in Denmark. Some typical rates are France, 18.6%; West Germany, 13%; the United Kingdom, 15%; Norway, 20%; Sweden, 19%; Brazil 8–10%; Korea, 10%; and Mexico, 15%.

Exhibit 18.1 presents an example of how a wooden fence post would be assessed for value-added taxes in the course of its production and subsequent sale. A value-added tax of 10% is assumed. The original tree owner sells to the lumber mill, for $.20, that part of a tree that ultimately becomes the fence post. The grower has added $.20 in value up to this point by planting and raising the tree. While collecting $.20 from the lumber mill, the grower must set aside $.02 to pay the value-added tax to the government. The lumber mill processes the tree into fence posts and sells each post for $.40 to the lumber wholesaler. The lumber mill has added $.20 in value ($.40, less $.20) through its processing activities. Therefore the lumbermill owner must set aside $.02 to pay the mill's value-added tax to the government. In practice, the owner would probably calculate the mill's tax

EXHIBIT 18.1
Valued-Added Tax Applied to the Sale of a Wooden Fence Post

Stage of production	*Sales price*	*Value added*	*Value-added tax at 10%*	*Cumulative Value-added tax*
Tree owner	$.20	$.20	$.02	$.02
Lumber mill	$.40	$.20	$.02	$.04
Lumber wholesaler	$.50	$.10	$.01	$.05
Lumber retailer	$.80	$.30	$.03	$.08

liability as 10% of $.40, or $0.04, with a tax credit of $.02 for the value-added tax already paid by the tree owner. The lumber wholesaler and retailer also add value to the fence post through their selling and distribution activities. They are assessed $.01 and $.03 respectively, making the cumulative value-added tax collected by the government $.08, or 10% of the final sales price.

The value-added tax has several advantages, which led to its adoption in Europe.[2]

1. Under GATT rules, an indirect tax such as the value-added tax can be rebated on exports and levied on imports as a kind of border or excise tax. Thus the effective aftertax cost of goods that are exported is lower by the amount of the value-added tax than the cost of the same goods sold domestically. Whether exports become more profitable depends on how demand varies with the foreign import price, but at least there is more leeway to reduce prices competitively on exports than on domestic sales. GATT regulations do not allow direct taxes, such as the income tax on which the United States relies, to be rebated on export sales.

2. The value-added tax has been politically more acceptable in Western Europe than a number of alternative sources of tax revenue. For example, the value-added tax does not cause the same kind of economic distortions as some of the indirect taxes it replaces. In Germany the turnover tax required that a tax be assessed and collected every time a product changed hands. In the example in Exhibit 18.1 a 10% turnover tax would be collected from the tree owner. If the lumber mill was owned by someone else, that person, too, would pay a 10% turnover tax when selling the fence post to the wholesaler; etc. Since at no step is credit received for turnover taxes paid previously, the final tax bill includes taxes assessed on previously paid taxes. To avoid the compounding of taxes, many German firms had been forced to integrate vertically, even when this integration was undesirable from an economic or social point of view. Because it is not assessed on the basis of a change in ownership, the value-added tax avoids distortion due to compounding.

3. The value-added tax may have some advantages compared to the corporate income tax. Since the value-added tax is usually assessed on all consumption goods produced, it cannot be avoided by book write-offs, accelerated depreciation, loss carry-forwards, loose expense account practices, interest on debt, artificial transfer prices, etc. Profitable and unprofitable firms, no matter how much levered by debt, are taxed alike. Therefore it forces the unprofitable firm to improve or go out of business faster than it might otherwise, thus reallocating scarce economic resources in a more optimal manner from the national economic viewpoint.
4. The value-added tax has also been proposed as a substitute for property taxes, local sales taxes, payroll taxes, and miscellaneous indirect taxes. In each case there would be some political support for a value-added tax from groups believing that one of these other taxes is even more onerous.
5. The value-added tax is relatively easy to understand, calculate, and collect. There is even a strong self-enforcement feature. In most existing systems only value-added taxes that are invoiced are refundable. Therefore every purchaser has a strong incentive to see that sellers record the proper amount of value-added taxes that have been assessed up to that point.
6. A broad tax base is encouraged because firms not subject to the value-added tax do not typically receive refunds of value-added taxes previously paid by their suppliers, nor do firms subject to value-added tax receive refunds on purchases made from suppliers who are not subject to the value-added tax. In countries where the value-added tax is used, this feature has caused less pressure from industries wishing to be exempted from value-added tax.

Several disadvantages of the value-added tax have shown up in Europe and are being cited by factions opposing the introduction of a value-added tax in the United States.[3]

1. In nearly every country that has introduced the value-added tax, an increase in the rate of inflation has occurred. In Belgium, the price level rose at an annual rate of 7% in the first three months of 1971 after introduction of the value-added tax. The Dutch consumer price level increased by more than 8% after introduction of the value-added tax in 1969. The same trend was observed in the Scandinavian

countries and to a lesser extent in Germany. It is not altogether clear, however, that the observed inflation was a result of the value-added tax. In most of these countries other inflationary pressures were also at work. Moreover, if the value-added tax did not replace another tax of equal amount, inflation might have occurred no matter what kind of additional tax burden was introduced.

2. The value-added tax usually increases the total tax burden, even allowing for replacement of turnover, excise, and other indirect taxes. Of course, if more taxes need to be raised, it is not the fault of the value-added tax. Other taxes could have been increased instead.
3. The value-added tax is a regressive tax on consumption that merely replaces, or even supplements, other regressive taxes on consumption. It would be simpler and less confusing to call it a national sales tax, thus allowing the people to judge it by standards with which they are already familiar. Nevertheless, its regressive impact could be ameliorated by reducing other regressive taxes, redistributing income through other means, and levying reduced rates on certain necessities.
4. In the United States a national value-added tax could deflate the tax base of state governments that typically depend on sales taxes for their revenue. This deflation could be offset, however, through revenue sharing.

Other National Taxes

There are a variety of other national taxes, which vary in importance from country to country. The turnover tax and the tax on undistributed profits were mentioned before. Property and inheritance taxes are imposed in a variety of ways to achieve intended social redistribution of income and wealth as much as to raise revenue. Withholding taxes on dividend and interest payments to foreign investors are common in most countries but are usually modified by tax treaties. There are a number of red-tape charges for public services that are in reality user taxes. Sometimes foreign exchange purchases or sales are in effect hidden taxes inasmuch as the government earns revenue rather than just regulates imports and exports for balance of payments reasons.

Tax Morality and Diplomacy

The multinational firm faces not only a morass of foreign taxes but also an ethical question. In many countries taxpayers, corporate or individual, do not voluntarily comply with the tax laws. Smaller domestic firms and individuals are the chief violators. The multinational firm must decide whether to follow a practice of full disclosure to tax authorities or adopt the philosophy of "when in Rome, do as the Romans do." Given the local prominence of most foreign affiliates and the political sensitivity of their position, most multinational firms follow the full disclosure practice. Some firms, however, believe that their competitive position would be eroded if they did not avoid taxes to the same extent as their domestic competitors. There is obviously no prescriptive answer to the problem, since business ethics are partly a function of cultural patterns and historic development.

There is also a potential morality problem on the part of the host country. Some countries have imposed what seem to be arbitrary punitive tax penalties on multinational firms for presumed violations of local tax laws. Property or wealth tax assessments are sometimes perceived by the foreign firm to be excessively large when compared with those levied on locally owned firms.

PARENT COUNTRY TAXATION OF MULTINATIONAL OPERATIONS

Parent countries differ with respect to their treatment of foreign source income earned by their own multinational firms. Part of the difference stems from .varying interpretations of how to achieve tax neutrality. Other major differences include the treatment of the tax deferral privilege, the method of granting credit for foreign income taxes already paid to host countries, concessions gained in bilateral tax treaties, and the treatment of intercompany transactions. The way in which a parent country taxes foreign source income affects the way in which multinational firms organize their foreign operations. In particular, taxes have an important bearing on whether to operate overseas through foreign branches of the parent firm or locally incorporated foreign affiliates. It also affects the perceived desirability of utilizing foreign affiliates located in tax haven countries. A discussion of these issues follows. Technical details of U.S. taxation of foreign source income are further explained in the appendix to this chapter. The appendix consists partly of excerpts from Price Waterhouse, *U.S. Corporations Doing Business Abroad,* March 1976 edition and November 1976 supplement, which summarize the changes resulting from the Tax Reform Act of 1976.

Tax Neutrality

When a government decides to levy a tax, it must consider not only the potential revenue from the tax, or how efficiently it can be collected, but also the effect the proposed tax can have on private economic behavior.[4] For example, the U.S. government's policy on taxation of foreign investment income does not have as its sole objective the raising of revenue but has multiple objectives. These include the following objectives:

- □ the desire to neutralize tax incentives that might favor (or disfavor) U.S. private investment in developed countries,
- □ provision of an incentive for U.S. private investment in developing countries,
- □ improvement of the U.S. balance of payments by removing the advantages of artificial tax havens and encouraging repatriation of funds,
- □ raising of revenue.

The ideal tax should not only raise revenue efficiently but also have as few negative effects on economic behavior as possible. Some theorists argue that the ideal tax should be completely neutral in its effect on private decisions and completely equitable among taxpayers. However, other theorists claim that national policy objectives—such as balance of payments or investment in developing countries—should be encouraged through an active tax incentive policy rather than require taxes to be neutral and equitable. Most tax systems compromise between these two viewpoints.

In the case of U.S. taxation of foreign investment income, there is considerable theoretical debate about its impact on U.S. multinational firms. In particular, the concept of neutrality needs to be defined. One way to view neutrality is to require that the burden of taxation on each dollar of profit earned in U.S. operations by a U.S. multinational firm be equal to the burden of taxation on each dollar-equivalent of profit earned by the same firm in its foreign operations. This situation is called "domestic neutrality." A second way to view neutrality is to require that the tax burden on each foreign affiliate of a U.S. firm be equal to the tax burden on its competitors in the same country. This situation is called "foreign neutrality." The U.S. Treasury tends to favor the domestic neutrality viewpoint, whereas U.S. multinational firms tend to favor foreign neutrality.

In practice, it is difficult to measure domestic or foreign tax neutrality. How should different definitions of taxable income be taken into account? Should indirect taxes, such as turnover or value-added taxes, be considered part of the total tax burden? Since taxes purchase government services, how should the varying quantity and quality of these services be recognized?

The issue of tax equity is also difficult to define and measure. In theory, an equitable tax is one that imposes the same total tax burden on all taxpayers who are similarly situated and located in the same tax jurisdiction. In the case of foreign investment income, the U.S. Treasury argues that since the United States uses the nationality principle to claim tax jurisdiction, U.S.-owned foreign affiliates are in the same tax jurisdiction as U.S. domestic affiliates. Therefore, a dollar earned in foreign operations should be taxed at the same rate and paid at the same time as a dollar earned in domestic operations.

Tax Deferral

If the nationality principle of tax jurisdiction is upheld, it would end the tax-deferral privilege for many multinational firms. Foreign affiliates of multinational firms pay host country corporate income taxes, but many parent countries defer claiming additional income taxes on that foreign source income until it is remitted to the parent firm. For example, U.S. corporate income taxes on foreign source income of U.S.-owned affiliates incorporated abroad are deferred until the earnings are remitted to the United States. In the case of earnings of unincorporated foreign branches of U.S. firms, however, no deferral privilege exists. Foreign earnings are immediately subject to U.S. income taxes, but the parent also receives an immediate foreign tax credit for income taxes paid to the host country. Many of the industrialized countries treat the foreign source income deferral privilege in about the same manner as does the United States, but it is impossible to generalize about this point. In fact, some countries do not tax foreign source income at all.

Foreign Tax Credit

To prevent double taxation of the same income, most countries grant a foreign tax credit for income taxes paid to the host country. For example, if a Japanese affiliate of a U.S. firm earns the yen equivalent of $1,000,000 and pays $400,000 in income taxes (40% rate) to Japan, it can claim a credit against taxes due to the United States of $400,000 when it remits the earnings to the United States. Normally foreign tax credits are also available for withholding taxes paid to other countries on dividends, royalties, interest, and other income remitted to the parent. The value-added tax and other sales taxes are not eligible for a foreign tax credit but are typically deductible from pretax income as an expense.

Countries differ on how they calculate the foreign tax credit and what kinds of limitations they place on the total amount claimed. The U.S. method of calculating the foreign tax credit and limitations on its use is explained in the appendix of this chapter.

Tax Treaties

A network of bilateral tax treaties, many of which are modeled after one proposed by the Organization for Economic Cooperation and Development (OECD), provides another means of reducing double taxation. Tax treaties normally define how certain kinds of joint income should be allocated between national taxing jurisdictions. This issue is particularly important for firms that are primarily exporting to another country rather than doing business there through a "permanent establishment." The latter would be the case for manufacturing operations. A firm that only exports would not want any of its other worldwide income taxed by the importing country. Tax treaties define what is a "permanent establishment" and what constitutes a limited presence for tax purposes.

Tax treaties also typically result in reduced withholding tax rates between the two signatory countries. This practice is important to both multinational firms operating through foreign affiliates and individual portfolio investors receiving income from dividends, interest, or royalties.

Intercompany Transactions

The problem of intercompany transactions, particularly transfer pricing, has been discussed earlier in a broader framework than just its tax aspects. Nevertheless, the transfer price implications of Section 482 of the U.S. tax code, as well as similar provisions in other countries, are worthy of a more detailed analysis from the tax viewpoint. This subject is highly technical and one that often changes because of tax court rulings. Therefore we cannot do it justice in this book but suggest that the reader refer to articles cited in the bibliography.

ORGANIZING FOR FOREIGN OPERATIONS

A thorough knowledge of foreign tax environments and the manner in which the parent country taxes foreign source income is indispensable background for planning the way in which a multinational firm should organize its foreign operations.

Branch vs. Locally Incorporated Affiliate

A multinational firm normally has a choice of whether to organize a foreign affiliate as a branch of the parent or as a local corporation. Both tax and nontax consequences must be considered. Nontax factors include the locus of legal liability, public image in the host country, managerial incentive considerations, and local legal and political requirements. Although important, nontax considerations are really outside the scope of this chapter on tax planning.

One major tax consideration is whether the foreign affiliate is expected to run at a loss for several years after start-up. If so, it might be preferable to organize originally as a branch operation to permit these anticipated losses to be consolidated in the parent's income statement for tax purposes. For example, tax laws in the United States and many other countries do not permit a foreign corporation to be consolidated for tax purposes, even though it is consolidated for reporting purposes, but do permit consolidation of foreign branches for tax purposes.

A second tax consideration is the net tax burden after paying withholding taxes on dividends. Most countries charge a withholding tax on dividends paid to foreign residents in lieu of requiring them to file an income tax return. The actual amount of withholding tax varies from country to country but is usually modified by numerous bilateral tax treaties. For example, the rate charged by the United States varies anywhere from 30% for residents of countries with no tax treaty with the United States (such as Hong Kong), to zero for residents of the Netherlands Antilles. A non-U.S. multinational firm with a U.S.-incorporated affiliate would first pay the 46% corporate income tax on U.S. earnings and then an additional withholding tax on dividends remitted to the parent. If the U.S. affiliate is a branch, the withholding tax would be avoided. Thus a multinational firm would need to weigh the benefit of tax deferral of home country taxes on foreign source income, which could be achieved by incorporation of the foreign affiliate, against the possible extra tax burden paid to the host government in the form of withholding taxes on dividends.

A third tax consideration is important for firms engaged in natural resource exploration and development. Some countries allow exploration costs, and possibly part of development costs, to be written off as a current expense rather than require them to be capitalized and amortized over succeeding years. Therefore many of the multinational oil and mining firms choose to operate these activities overseas as branches rather than subsidiaries. U.S. firms have an additional incentive to use the branch form of organization overseas, because this practice permits their use of the special depletion allowances permitted under the U.S. tax laws.

Further complicating the choice of structure are the various special-purpose organization forms permitted or encouraged by some countries. These are normally motivated by a country's desire to increase their exports or to promote development of less developed countries. For example, a U.S. firm can reduce the effective tax on foreign income by establishing a so-called possessions corporation in a U.S. Possession such as Puerto Rico, Guam, or Samoa.

Tax Haven Affiliates

Many multinational firms of non-U.S. origin have foreign affiliates that act as tax havens for corporate funds awaiting reinvestment or repatriation. Since passage of the U.S. Revenue Act of 1962, tax haven affiliates are less advantageous than previously for U.S.-based multinational firms, although many still use modified versions.

Tax haven affiliates are partially a result of tax-deferral features on earned foreign income allowed by some of the parent countries to their multinational firms. Tax haven affiliates are typically established in a country that can meet the following requirements:

- It must have a low tax on foreign investment or sales income earned by resident corporations and a low dividend withholding tax on dividends paid to the parent firm.
- It must have a stable currency to permit easy conversion of funds into and out of the local currency.
- It must have the facilities to support financial services—e.g., good communications, professionally qualified office workers, and reputable banking services.
- It must have a stable government that encourages the establishment of foreign-owned financial and service facilities within its borders.

Switzerland is a typical location for a European tax haven affiliate by virtue of its excellent qualifications on all four points above. Curacao, Panama, Kuwait, Hong Kong, the Bahamas, and Liechtenstein have established themselves as alternative tax havens. In some cases the financial overhead facilities were not available but have been set up by multinational corporations seeking the ideal combination of location, communications, currency stability, and low taxes.

The typical tax haven affiliate owns the common stock of its related operating foreign affiliates. (There might be several tax haven affiliates spotted around the world.) The tax haven affiliate's equity is typically 100% owned by the parent firm. All transfers of funds might go through the tax haven affiliates, including dividends and equity financing. Thus the parent country's tax on foreign source income, which might normally be paid when a dividend is declared by a foreign affiliate, could continue to be deferred until the tax haven affiliate itself pays a dividend to the parent firm. This event can be postponed indefinitely if foreign operations continue to grow and require new internal financing from the tax haven affiliate. Thus multinational firms are able to operate a corporate pool of funds for foreign operations without having to repatriate foreign earnings through the parent country tax machine.

For U.S. multinational firms the tax-deferral privilege operating through a foreign affiliate was not originally a tax loophole. On the contrary, it was granted by the U.S. government to allow U.S. firms to expand overseas and place them on a par with foreign competitors, which also enjoy similar types of tax deferral and export subsidies of one type or another.

Unfortunately, some U.S. firms distorted the original intent of tax deferral into tax avoidance. Transfer prices on goods and services bought from or sold to related affiliates were artificially rigged to leave all the income from the transaction in the tax haven affiliate. This manipulation could be done by routing the legal title to the goods or services through the tax haven affiliate, even though physically the goods or services never entered the tax haven country. This maneuver left no residual tax base for either exporting or importing affiliates located outside the tax haven country. Needless to say, tax authorities of both exporting and importing countries were dismayed by the lack of taxable income in such transactions.

One purpose of the U.S. Internal Revenue Act of 1962 was to eliminate the tax advantages of these "paper" foreign corporations without destroying the tax-deferral privilege for those foreign manufacturing and sales affiliates that were established for business and economic motives rather than tax motives. Nevertheless, in some cases U.S. firms have found loopholes in the law, permitting them to continue to use their tax havens as originally intended. Others do not benefit from tax deferral but have found these affiliates useful as finance control centers for foreign operations.

SUMMARY

Tax planning for multinational operations is a complex technical subject that requires the inputs of experienced tax and legal counsel in both parent and host countries. Nevertheless, the financial manager of a multinational firm should be acquainted with the national tax environments in the host countries in which the firm operates. This environment includes the role of local income taxes, value-added taxes, and other indirect taxes, and the less tangible aspects of local tax morality.

The financial executive must also understand how the parent country taxes foreign source income in order to organize efficiently for foreign operations. Important considerations include how the parent's country views tax neutrality as well as how it treats tax deferral, foreign tax credits, and intercompany transactions. Bilateral tax treaties may also influence the way foreign operations are structured.

Finally, the financial manager must choose the specific organization form that would be optimal for each foreign location as well as for the group as a whole. This activity typically involves choosing the branch or corporate form of organization. It also might require use of one or more special-purpose corporations or tax haven affiliates.

NOTES

1. An excellent summary of the experience of various countries with value-added taxes, as well as information on each country's system, can be found in Price Waterhouse, *Value-Added Tax,* November 1979.

2. Dan Throop Smith, "Value-Added Tax: The Case For," *Harvard Business Review,* November/December 1970, pp. 77–85.

3. Stanley S. Surrey, "Value-Added Tax: The Case Against," *Harvard Business Review,* November/December 1970, pp. 86–94.

4. For a thorough analysis of tax theory applied to U.S. taxation of foreign investment, see Peggy B. Musgrave, *United States Taxation of Foreign Investment Income,* International Tax Program, Harvard Law School, 1969. Also see Lawrence B. Krause and Kenneth W. Dam, *Federal Tax Treatment of Foreign Income,* Brookings Institution, 1964. An excellent critique of the various proposals to tax-unremitted profits is presented in Robert Stobaugh (and four collaborators), *U.S. Taxation of United States Manufacturing Abroad: Likely Effects of Taxing Unremitted Profits,* Financial Executives Research Foundation, 1976.

Chapter 18: Appendix U.S. Taxation of Foreign Source Income

This appendix is designed to give the reader interested in the more technical aspects of the taxation of foreign source income a summary of certain key provisions of the U.S. tax code. The appendix is partly comprised of edited excerpts from Price Waterhouse, *U.S. Corporations Doing Business Abroad,* and Price Waterhouse, *Tax Reform Act of 1976.*[1] First, it covers how U.S. firms compute the foreign tax credit. Then it describes two special-purpose corporations available to U.S. firms, namely foreign sales corporations and possessions corporations. It concludes with a description of the unitary method of taxation.

FOREIGN TAX CREDIT

Computing the Direct Foreign Tax Credit

"Direct" tax is the term generally used to denote a foreign tax imposed directly on the U.S. taxpayer. Direct taxes would include the tax paid by the foreign branch of a domestic corporation on its earnings and foreign withholding taxes deducted from investment income of a U.S. individual or corporate shareholder or investor. Direct foreign tax credit is computed as shown in Example 1. It should be noted that the dividend included in U.S. income in Example 2 is $100, i.e., the gross dividend *before* deduction of the foreign withholding tax. This is called "grossing up."

Example 1—Branch		*Example 2—Corporation*	
		Dividend from foreign corporation	$100
Earnings of foreign branch	$100	Foreign withholding tax at 15%	15
Foreign income tax at 40%	40	Net amount received	85
Included in U.S. income	100	Included in U.S. income	100
U.S. tax thereon at 48%	48	U.S. tax thereon at 48%	48
Less foreign tax credit	40	Less foreign tax credit	15
Net U.S. tax payable	8	Net U.S. tax payable	33
Total taxes paid	$ 48	Total taxes paid	$ 48

Deemed Paid or Indirect Foreign Tax Credit

In certain circumstances a domestic corporation can claim a foreign tax credit for income taxes it has not *itself* paid to a foreign government but are treated as if or deemed paid by it. The taxes that thus become creditable are the foreign income taxes paid on its earnings by a foreign corporation, which has paid a dividend to a qualifying U.S. corporation. In order to qualify, the U.S. corporation must own at least 10% of the voting power of the distributing foreign corporation. Thus a U.S. parent company receiving a dividend from a foreign subsidiary can credit against its U.S. tax not only any dividend withholding tax (Example 2 above) but also a proportion of the foreign subsidiary's tax on earnings.

Furthermore, if the 10% owned (first-tier) foreign corporation itself owns 10% or more of another (second-tier) foreign corporation and the second-tier corporation owns 10% or more of a third-tier corporation, a portion of the second- and third-tier corporations' foreign income taxes will also be creditable to the U.S. taxpayer to the extent that earnings are distributed to the first- and second-tier corporation. However, there must be a minimum indirect ownership of 5% in the second- and third-tier corporations.

The amount of creditable foreign tax is measured by the proportion that dividends paid to the U.S. corporation bear to the foreign corporation's earnings and profits in the year in which the dividends are paid. If the dividends in any year exceed the earnings and profits of that year, the excess is thrown back to the prior year on a last-in, first-out basis. A dividend paid within 60 days after the end of the foreign corporation's fiscal year is normally treated, for U.S. foreign tax credit purposes, as paid out of that fiscal year's earnings. Thus in the case of a calendar year corporation, a dividend paid on February 28 would be treated as paid out of the earnings of the prior calendar year.

For purposes of the deemed paid credit, the earnings and profits of a foreign corporation must be computed in accordance with U.S. tax accounting principles. This computation will in many cases involve adjustments to a foreign corporation's earnings as recorded in its local books.

The following example illustrates the method of computing the indirect or deemed paid foreign tax credit:

Example 3—Deemed Paid Foreign Tax Credit

Earnings before tax of foreign corporation	$1,000
Foreign income tax at 30%	300
Earnings and profits after foreign income tax	700
Dividend paid to U.S. parent company	$ 700
Less foreign withholding tax at 15%	105
Net dividend received in U.S.	595

Foreign Creditable Taxes	
Direct credit for withholding tax	105
Deemed paid credit for subsidiary's tax:	
$\frac{\text{(dividend)}\quad 700}{\text{(earnings and profits)}\ 700} \times \text{(foreign tax)}\ 300$	300
Total creditable taxes	405

Included in U.S. Income	
Gross dividend received	700
Plus foreign deemed paid tax	300
U.S. gross dividend included	1,000
U.S. tax at 48%	480
Less foreign tax credit	405
U.S. tax payable	75

This example illustrated the following rules:

1. The formula for determining the amount of creditable deemed paid tax is

$$\frac{\text{dividend (including withholding tax)}}{\text{net earnings and profits of foreign corporations}} \times \text{foreign tax.}$$

2. Earnings and profits are net of foreign income taxes.
3. The foreign dividend to be included in U.S. income is the dividend received *plus* withholding tax *plus* deemed paid tax. The inclusion of the foreign deemed paid tax in income is known as the "gross-up."[2]

Limitation on Amount of Credit

If income is received from a foreign country that imposes higher taxes than those of the United States, the total creditable taxes could exceed the U.S. tax on that foreign income. The amount of credit a taxpayer can *use* in any year is therefore limited to the U.S. tax on that income. However, any "excess" foreign tax credits that cannot be used in a particular year can be carried back for two years and forward for five years and can be treated like foreign creditable taxes for those carry-over years.

The foreign tax creditable in any one year is limited according to the following formula:

$$\frac{\text{foreign taxable income}}{\text{total taxable income}} \times \text{U.S. tax (on total taxable income).}$$

This limitation is computed from all countries from which income is received. This "overall" method generally results in an averaging out of foreign taxes where income is received from both high-tax and low-tax foreign countries.[3]

FOREIGN SALES CORPORATION (FSC)

Over the years the United States has introduced into U.S. tax laws special incentives dealing with international operations. To benefit from these incentives, a firm may have to form separate corporations for qualifying and nonqualifying activities. The most important U.S. special corporation is a foreign sales corporation (FSC).

FSCs were introduced in the Tax Reform Act of 1984 as a device to provide tax-exempt income for U.S. persons or corporations having export-oriented activities. FSCs replaced domestic international sales corporations (DISCs), which had been created by the Revenue Act of 1971 for somewhat similar purposes.

FSCs vs. DISCs

Briefly, a DISC was a U.S. corporation formed to export U.S.-produced goods to either foreign affiliates or unrelated foreign buyers. A portion of the earnings and profits of a DISC were not taxed to the DISC, but instead were taxed to the DISC's shareholders when distributed or deemed distributed to them.

Almost from their beginning, DISCs were the subject of dispute between the United States and other signatories of the General Agreement on Tariffs and Trade (GATT). The Europeans contended that the DISC allowed an illegal export subsidy in violation of GATT regulations because it permitted indefinite deferral of direct taxes on income earned from U.S. exports. GATT permits indirect taxes such as value-added taxes to be rebated, but the provision on direct taxes such as income taxes is more complicated. Export income may be exempt from a member country's income taxes only if the economic processes by which that income arises occur outside the country. The United States did not concede that DISCs were in violation of GATT, but to avoid further disputes the United States replaced the DISC with the FSC.

A FSC differs from a DISC in that use of a FSC allows *permanent* exemption of certain income from U.S. taxes, whereas the DISC only allowed *deferral* of taxes. A FSC is a foreign corporation, whereas a DISC was a domestic U.S. corporation.

Tax Benefits of a FSC

"Exempt foreign trade income" of a FSC is not subject to U.S. income taxes. Exempt foreign trade income is income from foreign sources that is not effectively connected with the conduct of a trade or business within the

United States. Exempt foreign trade income is a portion of total foreign trade income.

A FSC's total foreign trade income is derived from gross receipts from the sale of export property; lease or rental of export property; incidental services provided with the sale or lease of export property; and fees for engineering, architectural, or managerial services. The exempt portion of the FSC's total foreign trade income depends upon the pricing rules used. "Export property" is manufactured, produced, grown, or extracted from the United States by an entity other than the FSC; and is sold, leased, or rented outside the United States.

If foreign trade income is based on arm's length pricing between unrelated parties, or between related parties under the rules of Section 482 of the Internal Revenue Code, then exempt foreign trade income is defined as 34% of the income from the transaction. If prices are set under special administrative rules established for FSCs, exempt foreign trade income is the fraction 17/23 of income from the transaction. That portion of total foreign trade income that is not exempt is regarded as effectively derived from the conduct of trade or business by a permanent business establishment in the United States, and is therefore subject to U.S. income taxes.

Exempt income of a FSC may be distributed to its U.S. shareholders on a tax-free basis. Dividends paid from nonexempt income of a FSC are fully taxable to the U.S. parent.

Creating a FSC

A corporation qualifies as a FSC if it maintains an adequate foreign presence, has foreign management, carries out some economic processes outside the United States that are related to its export income, and complies with appropriate transfer price legislation. These rules are to ensure that the FSC is a bona fide foreign corporation that earns its exempt income from economic activities conducted outside the United States.

Adequate foreign presence To establish an adequate foreign presence, a FSC must satisfy each of the following requirements:

1. The FSC must be a foreign corporation, incorporated under the laws of a foreign country or certain overseas possessions of the United States, such as Guam, American Samoa, the Commonwealth of the Northern Mariana Islands, and the Virgin Islands. Puerto Rico does not qualify because it is within the U.S. customs area. Most FSCs are owned by a single U.S. parent corporation. However, a FSC may have up to a maximum of 25 shareholders. This provision allows the benefits of FSCs to pass through directly to owners of closely held corporations.
2. A FSC may not issue preferred stock, although under some conditions separate classes of common stock are allowed. Congress was concerned

that different classes of stock might be used to direct some dividends to shareholders having taxable income and other dividends to shareholders having net operating losses.

3. The FSC must maintain a permanent establishment outside the United States, including an office, books, and records. The office must be in a fixed location, be equipped for the performance of the firm's business, and be regularly used for business activity of the FSC.
4. At least one member of the FSC's board of directors must be a nonresident of the United States.
5. The FSC must elect to be treated as a FSC, and the FSC may not be a member of an affiliated group of corporations that also includes a DISC as a member.

Foreign management The FSC must be managed outside the United States, as indicated by the following requirements:

1. All board of directors meetings and all shareholders meetings must be held outside the United States.
2. The principal bank account of the corporation must be maintained outside the United States.
3. All dividends, legal and accounting fees, and salaries of members of the board of directors must be disbursed from bank accounts outside the United States.

Foreign economic process Certain economic processes must take place outside the United States for each individual transaction for which tax exemption is sought:

1. The solicitation, negotiation, or making of the contract must take place outside the United States.
2. Foreign direct costs incurred by the FSC and attributable to each transaction must be paid by the FSC. Direct transaction costs are for processing customers' orders and arranging for delivery; billing customers and receiving payment; arranging and paying for transportation, advertising, and sales promotion; and assuming credit risk. The FSC must pay either 50% of each of the cost categories above, or 85% of the direct costs in any two categories.

Transfer pricing rules Taxable income of the FSC must be determined from transfer prices that are either based on arm's length pricing between unrelated parties or on use of Section 482 of the Internal Revenue Code for transactions between related parties. An alternative is for the FSC to price under certain "safe harbor" rules designated "administrative pricing rules."

POSSESSIONS CORPORATION

A business carried on to a substantial extent in a U.S. possession can be carried on by a separate U.S. corporation, which, if it meets the requirements for a possessions corporation, is not subject to U.S. tax on income earned outside the United States unless the income is *received* in the United States. Although technically a U.S. corporation, a possessions corporation is treated like a foreign corporation in nearly every respect. U.S. corporate shareholders of a possessions corporation may claim deemed paid foreign tax credit if they own 10% of its stock. Its dividends do not qualify for the dividends received deduction, and it may not be included in a consolidated U.S. return.

Requirements

To qualify as a possessions corporation, a corporation must satisfy the following requirements:

1. It is a domestic U.S. corporation.
2. At least 80% of its gross income is derived from within a U.S. possession.
3. At least 50% of its gross income is derived from the active conduct of a trade or business in a U.S. possession.

The requirements of 2 and 3 must be met for the three years preceding the end of the tax year or from date of incorporation for a new corporation.

Possessions of the United States include the Commonwealth of Puerto Rico, the Panama Canal Zone, Guam, American Samoa, and Wake and Midway Islands.

The U.S. Virgin Islands, although a U.S. possession, are especially excluded from possessions corporation benefits because of their peculiar tax situation. A U.S. corporation operating in the U.S. Virgin Islands pays its taxes, as computed under the U.S. Internal Revenue Code, to the Islands Treasury. However, under the Islands' incentive legislation, a qualifying corporation would receive a subsidy from the Islands of up to 75% of the tax paid. Thus, in effect, qualifying corporations would pay tax of about 12% (25% of 48%) on Virgin Islands income. In order to qualify, the corporation must meet the requirements similar to 2 and 3 above and must also satisfy the incentive legislation requirements.

Exclusion from Gross Income

A corporation meeting the above requirements excludes from U.S. gross income amounts earned outside the United States unless the income is received in the United States. Thus a possessions corporation should arrange to *receive* income initially outside the United States, although it may subsequently transfer it from a foreign bank account to a bank account in the United States.

Prior to 1976 a possessions corporation was exempt from U.S. tax until the income was paid as a dividend to the U.S. parent company.[4] Under the Tax Reform Act of 1976 U.S. corporations qualifying as possessions corporations are able to repatriate their income free of U.S. tax. The exemption is granted in an indirect way by subjecting the income to U.S. tax and allowing a credit equal to the U.S. tax.

Thus the possessions corporation's income is subject to U.S. tax, but a tax-sparing credit is allowed for U.S. tax at 46% on foreign source income attributable to the conduct of a trade or business in a U.S. possession and qualified possessions source investment income. The net result is that nonqualified income is subject to U.S. tax but possessions income is exempt from tax.

The income qualifying for this credit is as follows:

- Income from foreign sources that is attributable to the conduct of a trade or business in a possession.
- Qualified possessions source investment income that is defined as investment income (a) from sources within the possession in which the business is carried on, and (b) which the taxpayer establishes is attributable to the funds derived from the business or investment in such possession.

Other investment income is taxable in the United States on a current basis. However, investment income from any non-U.S. source earned before October 1, 1976, is treated as having its source in the possession in which the business is conducted.

No foreign tax credit is available to possessions corporations except to the extent that a foreign tax is imposed on income subject to U.S. tax but not eligible for the tax-sparing credit.

As regards the U.S. parent company of a possessions corporation, foreign taxes paid with respect to distributions from the possessions subsidiary are neither creditable nor deductible. An exception is provided for foreign taxes imposed on liquidations occurring before January 1, 1979, from earnings accumulated before January 1, 1976.

Dividends from possessions corporations are eligible for the 100% or 85% dividends received deduction, regardless of when the income was earned. Thus accumulated earnings from prior years can be repatriated by the possessions corporation to the U.S. parent with little or no U.S. tax.

An *election* is required to be filed to obtain the tax benefit of possessions corporation status. The election is for a ten-year period and may be revoked during that period only with the consent of the commissioner. An electing corporation is not includible in a consolidated return. Income accumulated by a possessions corporation is not subject to the accumulated earnings tax.

UNITARY METHOD OF TAXATION

The unitary method of computing taxes is used by some states within the United States to prevent multinational firms from using transfer prices or other arbitrary allocations to reduce the amount of income subject to state income taxes. The unitary method levies a state income tax on a proportion of the combined worldwide income of a multinational firm, rather than on local income alone.

Using the state of California as an example, the percentage of a multinational firm's worldwide income subject to California income tax is calculated by a formula that takes into account local and worldwide sales, property, and number of employees. Assume the following data and ratios:

1. California sales: $15 million
Worldwide sales: $150 million
Ratio of California to worldwide: 15/150 = 10%

2. California property: $20 million
Worldwide property: $100 million
Ratio of California to worldwide: 20/100 = 20%

3. California employees: 800
Worldwide employees: 10,000
Ratio of California to worldwide: 800/10,000 = 8%

The three percentages are added and divided by three, giving a ratio of 12.67%, which is then used as the proportion of consolidated worldwide income subject to California income tax.

Many foreign governments object that the unitary method violates international tax treaties negotiated with the United States. Under the U.S. doctrine of states' rights, however, states within the United States are sovereign in matters of taxation and are not bound by tax treaties signed by the federal government. The substantive objection of foreign firms is that under the unitary tax method individual states may tax a portion of their income earned in other countries. A further objection is that these firms must disclose their worldwide income, property, and employment. In some cases this information would not be disclosed either because it helps competitors or because the firm is privately held.

For example, a profitable non-U.S. multinational firm just starting a business in a state using the unitary method, and incurring the usual initial operating losses in that state, may find itself immediately liable for income taxes because of profits elsewhere. Foreign governments have argued that the unitary tax method is a strong incentive not to make a new investment in the "sinning" states. However, some states have seen this as an opportunity. For example, Oregon repealed its unitary approach and was quickly rewarded by three large new manufacturing investments from Japanese high technology multinational firms.

NOTES

1. Price Waterhouse and Company, *U.S. Corporations Doing Business Abroad* (updated periodically). The sections from Price Waterhouse are on pp. 653–656 (top) and 659–660. The remainder is from other sources.

2. Prior to 1976 these rates were modified when dividends were received from a less developed country corporation. The Tax Reform Act of 1976 removed this distinction.

3. The Tax Reform Act of 1976 eliminated a previous option to calculate the limitation on a "per country" basis rather than "overall" for all countries.

4. The rest of this section is quoted from Price Waterhouse, *Tax Reform Act of 1976*, November 1976, pp. 34–36.

BIBLIOGRAPHY

Benjamin, Robert Weld, "Tax Aspects of Operating a Possessions Corporation in Puerto Rico," *International Tax Journal,* Spring 1976, pp. 197–221.

Brecher, Stephen M., Donald W. Moore, Michael M. Hoyle, and Peter G. B. Trasker, *The Economic Impact of the Introduction of VAT,* Morristown, N.J.: Financial Executives Research Foundation, 1982.

Chown, John F., *Taxation and Multinational Enterprise,* London and New York: Longman, 1974.

———, "Tax Treatment of Foreign Exchange Fluctuations in the United States and United Kingdom," *Journal of International Law and Economics,* George Washington University, No. 2, 1982, pp. 201–237.

Christian, Ernest S., Jr., *State Taxation of Foreign Source Income,* New York: Financial Executives Research Foundation, 1981.

"DISC/FSC Legislation: The Case of the Phantom Profits," *Journal of Accountancy,* January 1985, pp. 83–97.

Feinschreiber, Robert, "The Foreign Tax Credit under Siege," *Financial Executive,* October 1979, pp. 56–62.

———, "Apportioning Interest Expense to the U.S. Branch of a Foreign Corporation," *International Tax Journal,* October 1980, pp. 51–75.

Feinschreiber, Robert, and Caryl Nackenson, "Obtaining Interest and Royalties from Foreign Subsidiaries: The Impact of *Xerox* v. *Maryland,*" *International Tax Journal,* October 1980, pp. 5–13.

Gelinas, A. J. A., "Tax Considerations for U.S. Corporations Using Finance Subsidiaries to Borrow Funds Abroad," *Journal of Corporate Taxation,* Autumn 1980, pp. 230–263.

Goldberg, Honey L., "Conventions for the Elimination of International Double Taxation: Toward a Developing Country Model," *Law and Policy in International Business,* No. 3, 1983, pp. 833–909.

Hartman, David G., "Tax Policy and Foreign Direct Investment in the United States," *National Tax Journal,* December 1984, pp. 475–487.

Heyde, Robert D., "Interplay of Capital Gains and Foreign Tax Credit," *Tax Executive,* July 1980, pp. 257–267.

Horst, Thomas, "American Taxation of Multinational Firms," *American Economic Review,* June 1977, pp. 376–389.

Johnson, Alan R., Lawrence Nirenstein, and Stephen E. Wells, "Reciprocal Enforcement of Tax Claims through Tax Treaties," *Tax Lawyer,* Winter 1980, pp. 469–487.

Kaplan, Wayne S., "Foreign Sales Corporations: Politics and Pragmatics," *Tax Executive,* April 1985, pp. 203–220.

LaMont, Howard, "Multinational Enterprise, Transfer Pricing, and the 482 Mess," *Columbia Journal of Transnational Law,* Vol. 14, No. 3, 1975, pp. 383–433.

Lee, Moon H., and Josef Zechner, "Debt, Taxes and International Equilibrium," *Journal of International Money and Finance,* No. 3, 1984, pp. 343–355.

Lent, George E., Milka Casanegra, and Michele Guerard, "The Value-Added Tax in Developing Countries," *IMF Staff Papers,* July 1973, pp. 318–378.

Levi, Maurice D., "Taxation and Abnormal International Capital Flows," *Journal of Political Economy,* June 1977, pp. 635–646.

Owens, Elizabeth A., *International Aspects of U.S. Income Taxation, Volume III,* Cambridge, Mass.: Harvard Law School International Tax Program, 1980.

Peat, Marwick, Mitchell & Co., *Foreign Sales Corporations,* New York: Peat, Marwick, Mitchell & Co., 1984.

Prest, A. R., *Value Added Taxation,* Washington, D.C.: American Enterprise Institute, 1980.

Price Waterhouse, *Corporate Taxes—A Worldwide Summary,* New York: Price Waterhouse, 1984.

———, *U.S. Corporations Doing Business Abroad,* New York: Price Waterhouse, December 1982.

Samuels, Leslie B., "Federal Income Tax Consequences of Back-to-Back Loans and Currency Exchanges," *Tax Lawyer,* Spring 1980, pp. 847–880.

Sato, Mitsuo, and Richard M. Bird, "International Aspects of the Taxation of Corporations and Shareholders," *IMF Staff Papers,* July 1975, pp. 384–455.

Schiff, Michael, *Business Experience with Value Added Taxation,* New York: Financial Executives Research Foundation, 1974.

Sharp, William M., Betty K. Steele, and Richard A. Jacobson, "Foreign Sales Corporations: Export Analysis and Planning," *Taxes, the Tax Magazine,* March 1985, pp. 163–200.

Wasserman, Michael G., "International Withholding on Corporate Capital Distributions," *International Tax Journal,* October 1980, pp. 27–50.

Williams, Thomas J., "The Credibility of Foreign Income Taxes: An Overview," *Taxes,* October 1980, pp. 699–709.

Problems for Part V

1. *Norwegian Ski Company*

   The Norwegian Ski Company of Oslo needs Kr1,000,000 for one year to finance a special project. The company can borrow Norwegian kroner in Oslo at 14%, or it can borrow Eurodollars in London at 8%. At present, Kr8.25 = $1.00. What kroner/dollar exchange rate one year hence would cause the firm to be indifferent as to its financing source?

2. *Faro de Catalon, S.A.*

   The treasurer of Faro de Catalon, S.A., just received "inside" information from a usually reliable source that the Catalonian escudo (E°) will be devalued 20% against the U.S. dollar within one week. Faro manufactures floodlights for the European market, with some components imported from Germany and some from the United States. Faro de Catalon is owned 100% by a U.S. parent, and its purchases are all from its U.S. parent or its sister affiliate in Germany.

   The assets and liabilities of Faro de Catalon, expressed in their escudo equivalents (in millions) but classified by actual currency of denomination, are shown below. (For example, Faro has dollar cash balances equivalent to E°100 million and Deutschemark cash balances equivalent to E°200 million, as well as E°600 million in actual escudos.)

	CURRENCY OF ACTUAL DENOMINATION			
	Escudos	*Marks*	*Dollars*	*Total*
Assets				
Cash	E° 600	E°200	E°100	E° 900
from German affiliate	1,600	200	—	1,800
from U.S. parent	1,000	—	300	1,300
from nonrelated customers	1,800	100	—	1,900
Inventory				2,300
Net fixed assets				5,000
Total				E°13,200

	CURRENCY OF ACTUAL DENOMINATION			
	Escudos	*Marks*	*Dollars*	*Total*
Liabilities and Net Worth				
Accounts payable				
to German affiliate	E° —	E°1,000	E° —	E° 1,000
to U.S. parent	—	—	800	800
to Catalonian vendors	1,300	—	—	1,300
Bank two-year term loans	2,000	—	2,000	4,000
Shareholders' equity				6,100
Total				E°13,200

Business firms in Catalon may buy foreign exchange from the central bank for any valid business purpose, but will not be allocated foreign exchange for obviously speculative purposes.

What steps might the treasurer take in anticipation of a devaluation of the escudo?

3. *Nipperkin Beverages*

Nipperkin Beverages has been exporting freeze-dried California wine to Australia for use by the many trekking and camping enthusiasts in that country. Sales are to a wholly owned distribution affiliate in Sydney. Because excess production capacity is available, Nipperkin considers the cost of an exported carton to be only its direct cost (i.e., no overhead) of $10 per carton. Cartons are currently sold to the affiliate at $15 per carton, and resold to the Australian public at $20 per carton. The price of $20 cannot be raised because at higher prices trekkers and campers will shift to freeze-dried beer from Bavaria.

Nipperkin is content to accumulate cash balances in Australia because of the possibility it might want to open a manufacturing plant there. The Australian dollar has been about as strong as the U.S. dollar, the Australian government appears stable, and local interest rates generally reflect free market forces.

Mr. Nip Perkin, owner of Nipperkin Beverages, was trained as an accountant and so believes that the goal of a firm is to maximize consolidated net earnings. Mr. Perkin asks if you think transfer prices should be raised 20%, left the same, or lowered 20%. Taxes are as follows:

Australian ad valorem import duty:	8%
Australian corporate income tax rate:	30%
U.S. corporate income tax rate:	50%

What do you recommend, and why? Do you have any qualifications?

4. *Namur Refrigerator Company*

Namur Refrigerator Company of Belgium manufactures electric refrigerators for sale to retail outlets in Belgium and, through a wholly owned distribution affiliate, to the Netherlands. Annual capacity of the Belgian factory is 4,000 refrigerators, but present production is only 3,000, of which 2,000 are sold in Belgium and 1,000 are exported to the Netherlands.

Within Belgium refrigerators are sold at a competitive price of BF12,000 each. Aftertax profit is BF1,200 per unit, calculated as follows:

Unit sales price		BF12,000
Direct labor	BF2,400	
Direct material	3,600	
Manufacturing overhead	2,000	
Total manufacturing costs		8,000
Factory margin		BF 4,000
Selling and administrative costs		1,600
Realized pretax profit per unit		BF 2,400
Belgian income tax @ 50%		1,200
Aftertax profit per unit		BF 1,200

Direct labor consists of hourly payroll costs for Belgian workers, and direct material is for components purchased in Belgium. Manufacturing overhead includes supervisory salaries and depreciation. Selling and administrative costs are for office salaries and rent.

Namur sells to its Netherlands affiliate at its manufacturing cost of BF8,000 plus a profit markup of BF800. Transportation and distribution costs add an additional BF800, and the refrigerators are resold to Dutch retailers at the guilder equivalent of BF12,000. This pricing decision was based on the following analysis of elasticity of demand in the Netherlands. (All prices are expressed in Belgian francs.)

Unit price	12,800	12,000	11,200	10,400	9,600
Import cost from Belgium	8,800	8,800	8,800	8,800	8,800
Transportation	800	800	800	800	800
Unit profit before tax	3,200	2,400	1,600	800	0
Less 50% Dutch tax	1,600	1,200	800	400	0
Unit profit after tax	1,600	1,200	800	400	0
Times sales volume	× 700	×1,000	×1,400	×2,000	×2,500
Total profit (000)	1,120	1,200	1,120	800	0

The unit price of BF12,000 in the Netherlands maximizes Dutch contribution to profits at BF1,200,000.

a. Is Namur's present pricing strategy correct?

b. Assuming that Namur wants to divide profits on export sales evenly between Belgium and the Netherlands so as to avoid difficulties with either tax authority, what final price and transfer price should the firm adopt for its sales to the Netherlands?

c. If the Netherlands income tax remains at 50%, but the Belgian tax is lowered to 30%, should a new transfer price be adopted? What policy issues are involved?

5. *Cinzano, S.A.* (This problem was supplied by Professor Russell Taussig of the University of Hawaii.)

Cinzano, S.A., a Liechtenstein corporation, prepares its financial statements in U.S. dollars. Cinzano invested Ps200,000,000 ($2,000,000) in Argentina on January 2, 1985, at a time when one Argentine peso was worth one U.S. cent. That was also the exchange rate when the 1985 budget was prepared. The projected December 31, 1985, exchange rate was 0.5 U.S. cents per peso, based on the firm's assessment of an equal probability that the exchange rate would be 0.2 cents or 0.8 cents per peso.

Cinzano's investment of Ps200,000,000 was for inventories of mosto and wines, and it anticipated the investment would remain at that peso balance for the near future. Cinzano assumes for planning that any change in the exchange rate will not have an effect on the local currency operating results. The actual exchange rate on December 31, 1985, was 0.2 U.S. cents per peso.

The budget for 1985 was:

Sales	Ps60,000,000
Operating expenses	40,000,000
Profit before tax	Ps20,000,000

Cinzano controls exchange risk from its home office in Geneva, and its chief financial officer recently read in an international business journal that about one firm in eight controls its overseas operations by budgeting and tracking at the initial exchange rate. Five percent of the firms surveyed by the authors budget and track at the ending exchange rate, while about one firm in eight budgets at the initial rate but tracks at the ending rate. Slightly more than one in eight budget and track at the projected rate.

a. Prepare a tabular presentation showing budget and actual under the four approaches. Which one is best in your opinion? Why?

b. How, if at all, would you change Cinzano's control system if the Argentine general manager were solely responsible for both transaction and translation gains and losses? Why?

6. *Frazier Products*

Frazier Products, a California corporation, has wholly owned subsidiaries in the Netherlands and Spain. Net income before income taxes, expressed in U.S. dollars, and corporate income tax rates for each country in which the firm operates are:

	Net income before taxes	*Income tax rate*
United States	$100,000	46%
Netherlands	60,000	56
Spain	40,000	30

Frazier Products currently retains all of its aftertax Netherlands income in the Netherlands, but declares and remits all of its aftertax Spanish income to California as a dividend. Consequently Frazier Products reports consolidated net income of $102,000 and has available cash from earnings for reinvestment within the United States of $75,600, calculated as follows:

		To net income	*To cash in the U.S.*
United States contribution ($100,000) (1 − 0.46):		$ 54,000	$54,000
Dutch contribution ($60,000) (1 − 0.56):		26,400	0
Spanish contribution			
Dividend from Spain	$28,000		
Add back 30% Spanish tax	+12,000		
Grossed-up income	$40,000		
U.S. tax charge @ 46%	18,400		
Credit for Spanish tax	12,000		
Additional U.S. tax	$ 6,400		
Dividend less tax:		21,600	21,600
Total consolidated contribution		$102,000	$75,600

Could Frazier Products increase its consolidated net income by any other policy, while retaining cash flow from foreign dividends of

$21,600, so that total earnings available for investment in the United States remain at least $75,600? Any funds not brought into the United States in any given year will be permanently reinvested in Europe.

7. *Bay Chemical Company*

An intentional loophole in French foreign exchange regulations in 1978 permitted prepayment of imports into France if financed with Eurocurrencies other than the French franc. Bay Chemical Company used this opportunity to combine in a single step the financing of Italian working capital and the reduction of translation exposure in Belgian francs.

Bay-U.S. had wholly owned affiliates in France and Italy, and the French affiliate in turn had a wholly owned affiliate in Belgium. Bay-Italy manufactured a chemical additive for export to Bay-France, which Bay-France in turn resold within France. Bay-Italy was financing its working capital via Italian bank overdrafts at 18% per annum. Bay-Italy wanted to refinance its working capital and hoped to raise the needed funds at less than the 18% cost within Italy. It could borrow in other countries at rates significantly lower than were available in Italy, but repayment would be delayed at least five years because of Italian exchange controls.

Bay-Belgium, the wholly owned affiliate of Bay-France, had a net exposed position of BF12,500,000. At that time the current spot rate was BF6.25 = FF1.00, and Euro-Belgian francs could be borrowed in Paris at 7% per annum. During the course of the following year, Bay-France planned to import additives from Bay-Italy at an anticipated cost (in French francs) of FF2,000,000. On instructions from the U.S. parent, the following events took place:

- Bay-France borrowed BF12,500,000 in the Eurocurrency market for one year at 7% per annum.
- Bay-France then prepaid Bay-Italy for one year's imports, paying BF12,500,000, the Belgian franc equivalent of FF2,000,000.
- Bay-Italy exchanged the Belgian francs at once for Italian lire and repaid its Italian overdrafts. During the course of the ensuing year, Bay-Italy shipped additives to Bay-France in accordance with the terms of sale.
- During the year, Bay-France received additives from Italy with a book cost of FF2,000,000 and resold them at a 25% gross markup for FF2,500,000. Bay-France's customers paid in French francs.
- At the end of the year, Bay-France repaid the Euro-Belgian franc loan plus interest. At year end the spot rate was BF5.50 = FF1.00.

Record each of the above steps as it might appear in journal form in the books of Bay-France.

a. What was the effect of each of the above steps on the translation exposure of Bay-U.S.?

b. What was the effect of each of the above steps on the transaction exposure of Bay-U.S., and/or any of its affiliates?

c. How much gross profit did Bay-France make on the sale of Italian additives?

d. What year-end exchange rate would cause Bay-France to just break even?

8. *Albion Merchandising Company*

Albion Merchandising Company earned net income before income taxes of $6,000,000 in 1984. All this income was earned in the United States, and Albion Merchandising paid U.S. income taxes of $2,760,000 on 1984 income.

In 1985 Albion Merchandising established a foreign affiliate, which reported net income abroad for 1985 of $1,200,000 before foreign income taxes of $480,000. Albion Merchandising remitted the remainder of its foreign income (i.e., after foreign income taxes) back to the U.S. parent as a dividend.

Albion Merchandising's 1985 income and tax situation from domestic U.S. operations were exactly as they had been in 1984. Albion Merchandising was eligible for a foreign tax credit on dividends from abroad.

a. What is Albion Merchandising's total tax payment to the U.S. government for 1985?

b. What is the net cash flow to Albion Merchandising from its foreign operations in 1985?

Author Index

Subject Index